MW01165524

Treat this book with care and respect.

*It should become part of your personal
and professional library. It will
serve you well at any number
of points during your
professional career.*

Administrative

Office Management

B. Lewis Keeling
Senior Associate Professor, Business Studies
Bucks County Community College
Newtown, Pennsylvania

Norman F. Kallaus, Ph.D.
Chairman, Business Education
College of Business Administration
The University of Iowa
Iowa City, Iowa

John J. W. Neuner, Ph.D., C.P.A.
Professor Emeritus, Baruch College of the
  City University of New York
Visiting Professor, Iona College,
  School of Business Administration
Formerly a partner of John B. Thurston & Company,
  Management Consultants

Published by

G52 **SOUTH-WESTERN PUBLISHING CO.**

CINCINNATI   WEST CHICAGO, ILL.   DALLAS   PELHAM MANOR, N.Y.   PALO ALTO, CALIF.

ISBN: 0-538-07520-1

Library of Congress Catalog Card Number: 76-4227

Cover illustration: the Westinghouse ASD Group by Westinghouse
Architectural Systems Division

2 3 4 5 6 7 K 4 3 2 1 0 9 8
Printed in the United States of America

PREFACE

Since the first edition of this book over 35 years ago, tremendous advances have occurred in office technology, giving a new thrust to administrative office management. The computer, word processing, telecommunications, reprographics, and micrographics — to mention but a few significant advances — have revolutionized many phases of office work. With these innovations have come new specialists, new systems and procedures, and new problems. Alongside the technological strides have come a new set of pressing human problems as well as corresponding advances in understanding human behavior. The usual office operation places people together — working together, planning together, and oftentimes disagreeing together — making the study of human behavior, including group interaction, basic to an understanding of the office management process. We believe that the solutions to many problems arising in today's offices lie in an intelligent application of technology and in a sincere effort to meet the varying needs of today's office workers. Thus, in this revision emphasis is placed upon the office manager's need to understand the role of technology and to refine his or her ability to work through and with people in order to manage the information function.

Along with the discovery of new products and new systems and procedures in the office have come new problems resulting from the increased governmental control over business through taxation and regulatory agencies. This phase of our everyday life, which has been affected increasingly by the entangling web of income tax laws, social security legislation, unemployment compensation laws, occupational safety and health legislation, affirmative action programs, and laws relating to retirement and benefit plans, has demanded that more and more forms be completed and that a myriad of reports be filed by business organizations. The record-keeping demands imposed by the federal, state, and local governments place an increasingly heavier workload upon business offices, all without contributing to the firm's profit objective. Faster and more efficient methods and equipment must be employed so that more information can be processed without increasing labor costs. This Seventh Edition is designed to enable the office manager to find even better methods of doing a larger volume of office work at the same or less cost than before.

To manage effectively the collection, processing, storage, retrieval, and distribution of information is the responsibility of office administrators. In addition to the basic office functions over which they have traditionally exercised control, today's office managers are assigned new information responsibilities that necessitate new systems to meet these needs. The result has been a revolution of workers and machines in the office as well as the development of new approaches in coordinating these two key work components.

To meet the challenging and changing business scene described above, students of office management must study and understand — not merely be introduced to — management philosophies and principles of modern administrative practices. They must appreciate the role of human resources as the basic ingredient in the office function. Since the office manager is a manager of people, successful office practices and policies must be studied. It is the purpose of this book to contribute to the knowledge of students in these areas of study. Such knowledge will provide the basis and framework for intelligent and timely decision making as participating members of the management team.

No textbook, especially one that has enjoyed so many years of successful use, is the product of the authors alone. Hundreds of business firms and managers, teachers, students, and the editorial staff have contributed their ideas, experiences, and suggestions to make this one of the outstanding textbooks in its field, translated into several languages, with special printings for governmental agencies both here and abroad.

B.L.K.
N.F.K.
J.J.W.N.

CONTENTS

Part 3   Leadership and Human Relations in Office Administration

Part 4   Controlling Administrative Office Operations

Part 1

Administrative Office Management in Modern Business

Through the years emphasis in the office has changed. The administrative office manager is no longer the "keeper of the books" but rather a manager of information. This theme — *information management* — is created in the opening part of this textbook and maintained as the predominant focus of attention throughout the book.

In the opening chapter this new role of the office manager is discussed along with the various schools of management thought that have evolved over the years. As one specialized area of management, the office has shifted from many narrow traditional concepts and practices to a more expansive set of responsibilities for managing all phases of the information-production process so that managerial decisions can be made more quickly, more accurately, and more economically.

As the second chapter explains, automation has been introduced into the office to provide more efficient methods of processing information. At the same time it has created new problems for the information manager as new systems have been developed for meeting management's insatiable appetite for information. As a result of automated office operations, which include such sophisticated tools as the computer, administrative office managers have available an arsenal of machines, equipment, and new operating procedures, and thus possess a far greater capability for managing the information processes of their organizations.

As the specialist in information management, the office manager must work with all other managers in the firm to develop and coordinate the human and technological resources needed in today's complex organization. What is involved in this management process constitutes the heart of this textbook.

Chapter 1

THE INFORMATION MANAGEMENT CONCEPT

To many people, even today, an office is a place where correspondence, preparation of forms and reports, record keeping, and filing are handled by typists, secretaries, bookkeepers, file clerks, machine operators, supervisors, and managers. In such a setting the emphasis is often placed upon the physical product — the letters, memorandums, and reports being written; the statements and invoices being prepared; the notes taken and minutes recorded; and the file cabinets filled with carbon copies and duplicated materials. This type of office prevails in practice, but to the student of administrative office management this a superficial picture of the office.

In contrast to the older view of the office, a vastly different office world is slowly but surely emerging. It is a setting more comprehensive in nature, relying on electronic machine systems and exerting far greater impact on the organization it serves. In this new office, emphasis is not upon the *record* or *form* produced but upon the *information* it contains. Emphasis is not upon the *machine* but upon the *system* within which both the machine and the worker function.

Administrative office management, which may be looked upon as synonymous with information management, has become a dynamic field of work comprising administrative systems, data processing, reprographics, word processing, records management, telecommunications, and micrographics. The changes that have come about with the new view of the office world have brought greater specialization for most office workers and the need for administrative office managers with broader knowledge and understandings.

In small or large, new or old offices the specific duties and responsibilities of administrative managers may differ. Basically, however, their duties and responsibilities are similar in function. The functions and the principles of effective information management presented in this book are just as applicable to small as to large offices and to old as well as to new offices.

THE FUNCTION OF MANAGEMENT

Any form of group endeavor, whether it is a social club, a governmental unit, or a business enterprise, requires leadership and direction at various levels to realize its objectives. In a business firm the person who leads and directs, who is in charge, is known as the *manager* or the chief administrator. Typically, the manager is responsible for planning, organizing, and controlling all resources and for leading or directing people into a functioning, productive, unified organization. Essentially management is a process involving all the activities related to decision making, coordination of group effort, and leadership. Management's function, then, is to blend effectively manpower, materials, money, methods, machines, and morale to set and to achieve the goals of the firm. Therefore, the function of management includes dealing with economic factors, human and material resources, and, especially important, with directing people.

Management activities are performed at several levels in any organization, from the office of president to a supervisor. Titles held by managers vary considerably, depending upon the nature of the work managed and the kinds of responsibilities assigned to the position. Usually managerial levels are divided as shown in Figure 1-1.

THE ADMINISTRATIVE OFFICE MANAGEMENT FUNCTION

What has been said about management in general applies also to management of the office function. The administrative office manager, therefore, is responsible for planning, organizing, and controlling all of the office activities in the firm and for leading or directing people to attain the objectives of the firm or company.

Traditionally the office management function was limited mainly to the basic clerical services and personnel. With the passing of time and the development of new and more efficient methods of information handling came the demand for more information and for more decisions made at greatly accelerated rates. Management began to place greater reliance upon the office force as the new technology with its greater power of communication and computation gave the office force greater information-processing power. The "one-department office" concept gave way to the broader, company-wide administrative management concept in which the administrative office function becomes centralized in one administrative head.

During the early 1960s, the office function became the *information-management* function. This concept gave to

Managerial Levels	Managerial Titles	Typical Responsibilities
Top Management	Board of Directors President Vice-President	Developing long-range plans and policies; selecting and evaluating key executives.
Middle Management	Controller Sales Manager Treasurer Production Manager Administrative Office Manager	Assisting top management in planning; developing intermediate-range plans; establishing departmental policies; initiating and reviewing operating systems.
Supervisory Management or Operating Management	Office Supervisor Accounting Supervisor Word Processing Supervisor	Making detailed plans; supervising day-to-day operations; assigning tasks to personnel.

Fig. 1-1
Managerial Levels, Titles, and Responsibilities

the office a company-wide responsibility for the collection, processing, storage, retrieval, and distribution of information. As will be described in Chapter 2, these activities represent a system of related procedures for handling the information cycle; and when properly organized, they constitute an area of study. As a result, information, or more properly the information system, has become an academic discipline out of which have emerged new applications of information technology. Traditional office work, such as oral and written communications, computing and reporting, record keeping, accounting, and filing, still remains but in a modified form.

The scope and responsibilities of administrative office management are presented in this book through an identification and analysis of each of the managerial functions as applied to office activities. The logical sequence — planning, organizing, leading and controlling — of these functions and activities is outlined in Figure 1-2.

Managerial Functions	Office Activities
Planning:	Coordinating the various information-processing services, such as communications, records management, mailing, and reprographics; procuring a suitable office site; equipping the work areas with modern, functional, and efficient office furniture, machines, and equipment; staffing the office with qualified employees so that the work will flow smoothly and quickly.
Organizing:	Applying basic principles of office organization in planning the working relationships among employees, equipped with the best physical facilities, to achieve the maximum productivity.
Leading:	Directing and supervising effectively the office activities; adopting and implementing workable personnel policies that will maintain a desirable level of morale; training, orienting, promoting, and compensating office personnel; providing for static-free communication lines back and forth between employees and employer.
Controlling:	Developing, installing, and improving administrative office systems and procedures to be followed in completing each major phase of office work; supervising the procurement, preparation, and use of office forms and other supplies; measuring the work done and setting standards for its accomplishment; reducing the costs of office services; preparing budgets, reports, and office manuals as means whereby costs are reduced and controlled.

Fig. 1-2
Managerial Functions and Office Activities

The Role of the Administrative Office Manager

As a principal party in the collection, processing, storage, retrieval, and distribution of information, the administrative office manager plays an important role in the decision-making process. The manager's task becomes one of providing the decision maker, at the least possible cost, with information that is accurate, accessible, and sufficiently current to be useful.

No two office managers have the same job responsibilities. In one firm the office manager may be an accountant, with the added supervision of correspondence, mailing, filing, and general administrative services. In another firm the office manager may assume the chief responsibility of the personnel manager or the credit manager with miscellaneous supervisory activities. In another company the office manager may be the office services executive who supervises and is responsible for rendering services to all office divisions. These services may include mailing, records management, word processing, messenger service, telecommunications, and office maintenance.

Though no two managers have the same responsibilities, most do perform some common activities. In an analytical study of the role of the office manager, Schmidt and Lappe found that of all the office managers surveyed, the three activities performed most often are personnel hiring and relations, job analysis, and written communications (letters and reports).[1] Similar findings were revealed a few years earlier in a study undertaken by Smith and Warner. In their study they discovered that the office manager spends the major portion of his or her time in written and oral communications, with about twice as much time in oral as in written communications. Smith and Warner also found that most of the office manager's time is spent in personnel relations — hiring, training, and promoting employees — and in systems analysis work.[2]

The differences in responsibilities assigned the office manager are due to several factors, among which the size of the organization is most important. Many large banks, for example, employ 3,000 or more workers in their offices, and some insurance companies employ 10,000 or more. Naturally, in such organizations where the processing of information comprises the main output, the volume of the service activities is so great that their supervision and direction under an office manager are necessary. On the other hand, in smaller organizations where the office force is not so great and where the factory staff is the primary source of business activity, the office service activities may come under the supervision and direction of the accountant, the controller, the treasurer, the credit manager, or the personnel manager.

Today, with their varying job responsibilities, office managers may associate themselves with one or more professional organizations, such as the Data Processing Management Association, the Association of Records Managers and Administrators, the Society for Management Information Systems, the

---

[1]Gene W. Schmidt and William C. Lappe, "Analysis of Role of Office Manager," *The Delta Pi Epsilon Journal*, Vol. 16, No. 1 (November, 1973), p. 27.

[2]Harold T. Smith and S. ElVon Warner, *Administrative Office Management Preparation* (Provo: Brigham Young University, 1971), Epitome.

International Word Processing Association, the Society for Advancement of Management, and the Administrative Management Society. For example, more than 15,000 persons whose work is related to administrative office management comprise the membership of the Administrative Management Society. This organization, consisting of more than 170 chapters in the United States, Canada, West Indies, and 31 other countries, is concerned with identifying, developing, and communicating progressive business management knowledge and techniques. As the first means of recognizing managers as "professionals," the Administrative Management Society inaugurated its Certified Administrative Manager (C.A.M.) program in 1970. Candidacy is open to all management personnel, and to achieve the C.A.M. designation and to gain membership in the Academy of Certified Administrative Managers, an individual must meet the following five program standards: (1) pass the five-part C.A.M. examination covering personnel management, financial management, control and economics, administrative services, and systems and information management; (2) have two years of experience at the administrative management level; (3) submit character references to certify high standards of personal and professional conduct; (4) provide evidence of leadership ability; and (5) show evidence of communication ability. The emergence of this certification program is further evidence of the broadening scope and responsibilities of the manager in today's modern office.

The Management of Tomorrow's Information

Today a new dimension has been added to the management function;
management is now considered the process of converting information into action. At all managerial levels there is a growing interest in improving the rationality of decisions and to do so the decisions must be made upon the basis of reliable information. Several factors at work in the economy in the early 1970s and projections of their activity into the latter part of the twentieth century account for much of this newly added dimension.

According to the Bureau of Labor Statistics, by 1985 the population of the United States will number about 236 million, an increase of more than 12 percent from the 1972 level.[3] During the 1980s the labor force is projected to grow by about 1.1 percent each year to reach 114 million in 1990, even though the rate of growth will have dropped sharply from earlier periods. By 1985 the unemployment rate is expected to level off at 4 percent. During the period 1972 to 1985, gross national product is expected to increase about 4 percent each year, while personal income is projected to increase at 10.4 percent a year until 1980, when the annual rate of increase will fall to 8.3 percent until 1985. A significant increase in expenditures by the federal and state and local governments is also predicted.

As a result of the growth in population and labor force and of the rise in business and personal incomes, a significant demand for goods and services will emerge. With the increased expenditures at all levels of government, the

[3]"The United States Economy in 1985, Population and Labor Force Projection," *Monthly Labor Review* (December, 1975), pp. 3–42. See also "Revised Projections of the U.S. Economy to 1980 and 1985," *Monthly Labor Review* (March, 1976), pp. 9–21; and "New Labor Force Projections to 1990," *Monthly Labor Review* (December, 1976), p. 3.

projections anticipate tomorrow's need for more communications, more paper work, more power and energy consumption, and more taxes and regulations; in short, there will be the need for more relevant data — *information*. With the scope of decision making no longer local but increasingly international in nature, decisions will become far more complex. In the decision-making process, too many facts and data can be provided, however; and with too much data, confusion and disorder result. Tomorrow's need is not so much for information as such, but *what to do* with the information. Someone must be able to produce only that useful information which relates to a specific problem or function. Thus, the role of the information manager in future systems will be a crucial one as those systems increasingly incorporate the use of highly sophisticated minicomputers in complicated hookups for the distribution of information and intelligence.

Looking ahead to the nature of management in the 1980s, some foresee an organization headed by a president and executive services, which give personal services support to the president, assisted by three vice-presidents, one of whom is the vice-president of information services.[4] This vice-president is responsible for organizing the computer centers, information flow, office management, medical programs, training, public relations, and research and development. This new breed of management specialist, the information manager, and a new information function are slowly emerging in many large companies. In addition to having expertise in manag-

ing administrative services, the information manager must have some of the training and experience required of a systems analyst, a records management specialist, a data processing manager, and a communication specialist. To fill such a position the manager must possess technical familiarity with machine systems and concepts, conceptual skills for visualizing better ways to manage, and supervisory skills for handling the combined technicians and clerical staff making up the information team. Such a management position requires broad experience and education to understand and to manage the information-handling function in the business.

The administrative office manager has always been a manager of facts and information, an informing manager. He or she has had the responsibility for developing and maintaining good systems, efficient personnel, and reliable equipment. With the advent of the new information technology of equipment, programming, and systems, the office manager's sphere of responsibility has extended throughout the company; for it can be said that information is information wherever it is found.

A management information system concept has developed, linking together all information functions of the firm into a company-wide information network. Such a network is illustrated in Figure 1-3 in which the coordinating function (the information center) represents the central intelligence center or data base for the organization. A network of this type can theoretically provide a single point of inquiry for access to all records and information anywhere in the company. It links together information sources on customers, sources of supply, and product information as well as market and financial information.

---

[4]Richard Allen Stull, "A View of Management to 1980," *Business Horizons* (June, 1974), pp. 10–11.

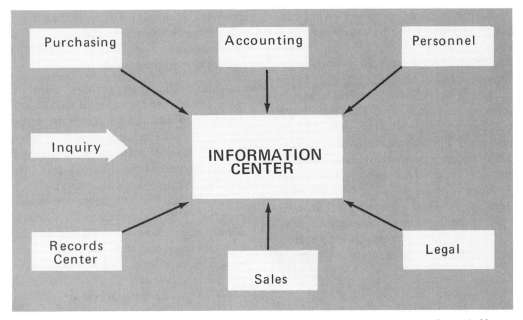

Source: Robert A. Shiff, "Information — Not Just Pieces of Paper," *Information and Records Management* (October–November, 1966), p. 21.

Fig. 1-3
A Company-Wide Information Network

Such information is ingested from the external environment as well as transmitted within the internal environment. At the present time this information function is being organized into a central information system by many large firms as well as governmental agencies. Since such a system is complex, involving new positions, new equipment, and often reorganization, it is normally planned in stages to cover several years.

SCHOOLS OF MANAGEMENT THOUGHT

Administrative office managers have followed several approaches through the years in the management of the information function. Basically the efficient office reflects a perceptive manager — one who by training, experience, and intu-

ition has sensed the need for improvement and has taken steps to effect necessary changes. Intuitive managers are still very much in demand at all managerial levels, since they are able to direct people effectively toward the firm's objectives. Unfortunately, many people — perhaps most people — are not gifted with powerful intuition. Such a group turns to education to learn about the technical, administrative, and human skills required to manage the firm.

Over the years the various functions in the management process have been identified and attempts have been made to classify the approaches used by management theorists and practitioners. In this discussion the divergent streams of management thought are divided into three schools — classical, behavioral, and management science. Each school of thought emphasizes a somewhat different approach to management and draws separate conclusions as to the most significant factors in the management process. These differing conclusions have become basic to the management process and over the years have been looked upon as principles of management. Although students of administrative office management may not find the specific answers they desire in the literature of these schools, they will discover established principles that will serve as guideposts for any action they take and as aids in better understanding the information-management concept.

The Classical School

The Industrial Revolution of the eighteenth and early nineteenth centuries made possible the mass production of goods and created the modern industrial organization. The new companies with their great potential for production were little understood and the need for knowledge about the management of such firms soon became apparent. Hence it is not surprising that the early approaches to the study of management concerned themselves with the major characteristic of the newly formed businesses — production. The early theorists emphasized the essential nature of management and its relationship to the production process. Those "traditionalists" who today follow this approach believe that managers should concentrate their attention and energies on increasing the efficiency of the production process.

Intertwined in the development of classical management theory were two views toward the management of work and of organizations — scientific man-

agement and total entity management. These views and a few of their representative advocates are briefly discussed in the following paragraphs.

Scientific Management. Scientific management was developed to solve two major problems: to increase the output of the average worker and to improve the efficiency of management. Scientific management has been called doing that which is most logical; that is, using common sense in the decision-making process. What is required in scientific management, however, is a higher order of common sense involving careful definition of problems and development of plausible solutions.

The *scientific method of problem solving*, which characterizes scientific management, involves the use of logical, systematic steps to develop effective solutions to problems. The method is commonly used to solve problems in engineering and in the physical sciences, such as chemistry and physics. Many phases of information processing utilize the scientific management approach to problem solving. This is especially true of systems analysis, which is discussed in Part 4, Chapter 17, of this text.

In the scientific method for solving office problems, logical steps are carefully formulated and followed:

1. The problem must first be recognized and carefully defined.
2. Information relating to the problem must then be collected, classified, and analyzed.
3. A tentative solution to the problem (sometimes called a hypothesis) is then developed and tested to determine its usefulness and validity.
4. On the basis of the test, modifications may be made in light of new findings or changed conditions, after which the solution is put into practice.

5. A follow-up is made in order to check upon the effectiveness of the solution in meeting the objectives toward which the solution was applied.

Frederick W. Taylor. A pioneer in the study of the production function, Taylor is looked upon as the father of scientific management. Using his engineering background, in the 1880s Taylor studied work standards and the relationship of output to wages. His emphasis was on management at the shop level rather than on general management, and he was concerned mainly with the efficiency of workers and managers in actual production.

Taylor considered each worker a separate economic man who was motivated by financial needs. He believed that workers tended to restrict their output because of their fear of displacement. To minimize this fear, Taylor suggested that workers be educated to understand that their economic salvation lay in producing more at a lower cost. The effectiveness of his argument could be proved to workers by placing them on a piecework system, and thus by producing more, they would earn more. Underlying Taylor's entire approach to scientific management was the conviction that there is *one best way* of doing everything, whether it be using a shovel or filing a piece of paper.

Taylor's contributions brought about increased efficiency and the development of a variety of methods and procedures for implementing the concept of management.[5] Taylor saw several new functions emerge for managers: the replacement of rule-of-thumb methods with scientific determination of each

element of a person's job; the scientific selection and training of workers; the need for cooperation between management and labor to accomplish work in accordance with the scientific method; and a more equal division of responsibility between managers and workers, with managers planning and organizing the work.

Frank and Lillian Gilbreth. In the early 1900s the husband and wife team of Frank and Lillian Gilbreth furthered the development of scientific management thought by inventing devices and using techniques to aid workers in developing their fullest potential through training, tools, environment, and work methods. Among their accomplishments were: the first use of motion pictures to study and improve motion sequences; development of the process chart and the flow diagram to record process and flow patterns; exploration into the area of fatigue and its effect on health and productivity; and their insistence that the principles of management and motion study be applied to self-management.

William H. Leffingwell. Leffingwell, looked upon as the father of office management, was the pioneer first credited with applying the principles of scientific management to office work. His book, *Scientific Office Management*, published in 1917, was the forerunner of all modern studies in office management. The Five Principles of Effective Work, illustrated in Figure 1-4 on page 12, were developed by Leffingwell. Since these principles can be related to the proper management of all work, they may be easily applied to the office. For example, any office manager must plan what work must be done and how, when, and where it must be done, and

---

[5]Frederick W. Taylor, *The Principles of Scientific Management* (New York: Harper & Bros., 1911).

1	**Plan**	
		1. What work is to be done
		2. How it is to be done
	To plan rightly, you must know —	3. When it is to be done
		4. Where it is to be done
		5. How fast it can be done
2	**Schedule**	
		1. Definite
	The work must be scheduled. A	2. In harmony with other schedules
	schedule, to be effective, must	3. Difficult to accomplish, but
	be —	4. Possible to accomplish
		5. Rigidly kept
3	**Execute**	
		1. Skillfully
		2. Accurately
	It must then be executed —	3. Rapidly
		4. Without unnecessary effort
		5. Without unnecessary delay
4	**Measure**	
		1. As to your potentiality
		2. As to your past records
	The work accomplished must be	3. As to the past records of others
	measured —	4. As to quantity
		5. As to quality
5	**Reward**	
		1. Good working conditions
	If your work is accomplished	2. Health
	effectively, you should be re-	3. Happiness
	warded with —	4. Self-development
		5. Money

Fig. 1-4
Leffingwell's Five Principles of Effective Work

by whom it must be done (Principle 1). By recognizing the total office plan of organization and product development, the manager can coordinate the efforts of all workers, machines, and information to formulate a proper work schedule to agree with the plan (Principle 2). Furthermore, proper operating systems and procedures, record-keeping practices, methods for executing the plan as well as measurements, standards, and layouts for getting the work done effectively must be developed (Principles 3 and 4). Perhaps of most importance, the office manager must select, train, motivate, compensate, and promote the employees to keep their interests and those of the firm at an optimum level (Principle 5).

Total Entity Management. In their writings, which emphasize an overall approach to the administrative problems of management, the followers of the total entity management school of thought searched for effective means of directing the entire business firm.

Henri Fayol. In 1949, Fayol's book *General and Industrial Management*[6] was published in the United States. In this work Fayol presented his concept of the universal nature of management, developed the first comprehensive theory of management, and stressed the need for teaching management in schools and colleges. Fayol was the first to state a series of management principles which would provide guideposts for successful management coordination. He felt that his success as a manager of a large French coal mining firm was not due to any personal characteristics of his leadership but was the result of having applied a set of general administrative principles that could be identified and taught to others. Fayol looked upon the elements of management as its functions — planning, organizing, commanding, coordinating, and controlling. In his writings he stressed over and over that these elements applied not only to business but universally to political, religious, philanthropic, military, and other undertakings. His thesis was that since all enterprises require management, the formulation of a theory of management is necessary to provide for the effective teaching of management.

Mary Parker Follett. The work of Follett, a political philosopher and social critic, spanned the gap between Taylor's scientific management and the new social psychology of the 1920s that promoted better human relations in industry, a first concern of modern management.[7] Noting that people had not yet learned to live together, she called for a revolutionary new concept of association. This concept was found in her one principle which stated that group organization was to be the new method in politics, the basis for the future industrial system, and the foundation of international order. Many of the fairly recent departures in management thought were anticipated by Follett: the need to depersonalize authority in recognition of the "law of the situation"; the application of behavioral science to problems of organization; the constructive uses of conflict; the psychology of power; the nature of horizontal communications and of multiple management; and, above all, the social responsibilities of management.

The early traditionalists emphasized the structure and the formal relationships in business firms. By calling upon others to develop knowledge about the actual work situation, they did not ignore the human element. They developed an extensive body of knowledge and schemes of logically related concepts, many of which form the basis for the organization of this book and more specifically the discussion of principles of planning and organizing in Part 2.

The Behavioral School

Scientific management is still used as the basis for solving business problems, but coupled with it is a growing concern for the human element in management. Today there is a clear-cut

[6]Henri Fayol, *General and Industrial Management* (New York: Pitman Publishing Corporation, 1949, translated from the French and originally published in 1916).

[7]Mary Parker Follett, *Dynamic Administration*, edited by Henry C. Metcalf and L. Urwick (New York: Harper & Row, 1941).

recognition that workers are interested in more than money. They have social and psychological needs of great importance to them as well as to the person who is their manager.

Becoming interested in the human element within the organization, managers began to conceive two approaches which would increase emphasis upon the members of the organization. The *human relations approach*, in the final determination of success and failure, calls attention to the importance of the individual within the system. The *behavioral science approach*, cutting across the fields of psychology, sociology, and anthropology, emphasizes interpersonal relations and democratic actions on the part of workers.

Human Relations Approach. In the 1920s and 1930s there emerged the idea that people were important considerations in management, since through people, objectives were established and achieved. The human relations approach was stimulated by a group of researchers from Harvard University who conducted studies in 1927 through 1932 among a group of women workers at the Hawthorne plant of Western Electric in Chicago.[8] The research team, headed by Elton Mayo, was formed to study the effects of the physical environment, such as changes in the levels of illumination in the working area upon the productivity of the workers. The results were confusing at first. When the lighting was increased, output rose; but, on the other hand, when the lighting was decreased, work output still continued to rise. After

other such puzzling results, an analysis of the study showed that the workers were highly motivated, not by the degree of illumination provided but, rather, by their feelings of importance. It mattered to them that they were really making a contribution.

The group also examined other effects. They varied the working conditions such as rest periods, hot lunches, and working hours; used interviews to determine attitudes; and analyzed the social organization among workers. During the studies it was found that changes in the work environment had little long-term effect upon worker productivity. The explanation offered was that the workers were made to feel more than just cogs in machines and that management realized their importance. Since management had asked for their opinions on working conditions, the workers felt that their relationships with management were no longer impersonal. The workers felt they had achieved status and some degree of respect. The Hawthorne experiment proved that the road to more effective worker effort lay in recognizing the emotional as well as the physical well-being of the employees, explaining to them the reasons for management decisions, and making them aware that management appreciated the importance of their work.

The Hawthorne study placed new emphasis upon the social and psychological factors in the study of work. As a result of this concern with human relations, a new direction — the behavioral science approach — was given to the study of management.

Behavioral Science Approach. Early theories of behavior tended to explain all behavior on the basis of a single need, such as Freud's theory of libidinal drive and Jung's concept of the

---

[8]See Elton Mayo, *The Human Problems of an Industrial Civilization* (Cambridge: Harvard University Press, 1933), and F. J. Roethlisberger and William J. Dickson, *Management and the Worker* (Cambridge: Harvard University Press, 1939).

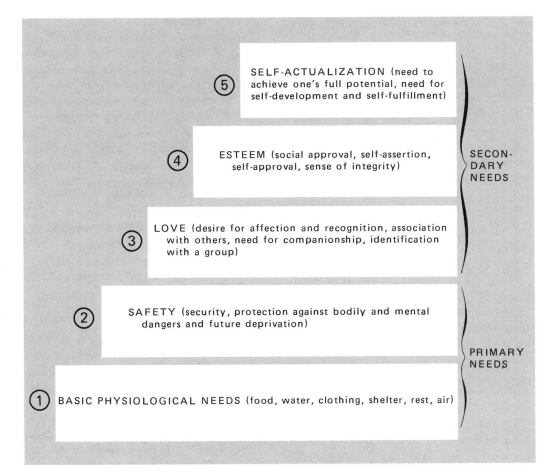

Fig. 1-5
Maslow's Hierarchy of Needs

need or drive to assert one's ego. Modern behaviorists typically list several needs ranging from three (physical, social, and egoistic) to 15 in number. Since one cannot see human needs but must infer their pattern from a study of human behavior, it is expected that there will be different theories about human needs and various systems for their classification.

Maslow's Hierarchy of Needs. One classification of human needs comes from Abraham Maslow, a psychologist who developed a theory of human motivation.[9] The hierarchy of needs, according to Maslow, is shown in Figure 1-5. As the lower needs become satisfied, they are no longer motivating factors, and the higher needs become dominant. A need at one level does not have to be completely satisfied before the next need emerges, however. Very few people ever fully realize the fulfillment of the higher level needs; very few become self-actualized.

***

[9]Abraham Maslow, *Motivation and Personality* (New York: Harper Bros., 1954).

The administrative office manager must recognize that the need pattern of each worker is different and should not assume that a single approach can be used to motivate all workers toward the accomplishment of the organizational objectives. Further, office managers should become aware that well-satisfied needs do not motivate. After obtaining a reasonable gratification of lower prerequisite needs, the worker will be stimulated to direct his or her action toward satisfying a higher level need.

McGregor's Views of Worker Behavior. The nature of people, with all their apparent contradictory feelings and emotions, has long puzzled philosophers. Some see people as having a capacity for tenderness, sympathy, and love — with little need for external regulation. Others see people as having tendencies toward cruelty, hate, and destruction, with the need for close control and regimentation for the good of society. Such a dual nature of people was introduced into management theory by Douglas McGregor. From observing traditional managers, McGregor inferred that their practices and approaches for managing workers and their work were based on the assumptions labeled Theory X in Figure 1-6. An opposite set of assumptions, labeled Theory Y, was presented by McGregor as a more realistic assessment of managing workers and their work.[10]

The early view of managing workers and of working, Theory X, is based on limited experience and little or no scientific study. According to this theory, the subordinate is characterized by irrespon-

sibility, selfishness, and apathy. Thus, managers who evaluate worker behavior from this point of view conclude that restrictive controls are necessary. Theory Y, on the other hand, outlines some critical features of managing workers and human motivation that spring from controlled experiments by highly trained researchers. In essence, this theory points to the fact that workers have wants or needs that are never completely fulfilled. The assumptions of Theory Y represent the behaviorist's faith in the capacity and potential of workers and this, in turn, would lead managers to create conditions under which all workers would have the opportunity to self-actualize.

The perceptive office manager is one who recognizes not only that workers become ill if they are denied a proper diet but also that they become equally ineffective if they are denied the means for satisfying their psychological needs. Since office managers work closely with subordinates, it is vital for them to understand the behavioral patterns both of themselves and of their workers. Thus, conditions can be created that will enable employees to fulfill their needs and that will enhance productivity as well as the organizational climate.

Herzberg's Theory of Job Motivation. According to the theory formulated by Frederick Herzberg and his associates as a result of their research conducted at the Psychological Service of Pittsburgh,[11] people work in an

[10]Douglas McGregor, *The Human Side of Enterprise* (New York: McGraw-Hill, Inc., 1960), pp. 33–57.

[11]Frederick Herzberg, Bernard Mausner, and Barbara B. Snyderman, *The Motivation to Work* (2d ed.; New York: John Wiley & Sons, 1959). See also Frederick Herzberg, *Work and the Nature of Man* (Cleveland: World Publishing Company, 1966).

Theory X
The Traditional View of Worker Behavior

1. The average man dislikes work inherently.
2. The average man will avoid work if he can.
3. Most people must be coerced, controlled, or threatened with punishment to get them to work toward the achievement of organizational goals.
4. The average man prefers to be directed, to avoid responsibility.
5. The average man has relatively little ambition and wants security above all.

Theory Y
The Current View of Worker Behavior

1. The average man does not inherently dislike work but, depending on conditions, may find work to be satisfying or punishing.
2. Man will exercise self-direction and self-control to achieve organizational objectives under certain conditions.
3. Man will seek to attain his firm's objectives if there are sufficient rewards provided.
4. Under proper conditions the average man will seek responsibility.
5. The capacity to use imagination and originality is widely found in the population.
6. In our modern society most people do not utilize all their mental potentialities.

Fig. 1-6
Traditional and Current Behavioral Theories

environment wherein two kinds of factors — hygienic and motivator — are present. Those experiences that create positive attitudes toward the work arise from the job itself and function as *motivators*. Examples of motivators are those incidents associated with feelings of self-improvement, achievement, and the desire for and the acceptance of greater responsibility. The other set of factors — *hygienic* — is related to productivity on the job but peripheral to the job itself. Examples of hygienic factors are pay, working conditions (such as heating, lighting, and ventilation), company policy, and quality of supervision. When the hygienic factors are felt to be inadequate by the workers, the factors

function as dissatisfiers. But when the hygienic factors are present, they do not necessarily motivate employees to greater productivity; instead, they make it possible for the motivators to function.

The positive feelings that may be aroused as a result of the peripheral work conditions, such as a word of encouragement from the office supervisor or a pay increase, are relatively brief in duration. When employees are highly motivated and find their jobs interesting and challenging, they are able to tolerate considerable dissatisfaction with the hygienic factors. Although the hygienic factors cannot be ignored or slighted, a full measure of all hygienic factors does not make jobs interesting nor bring about the attainment of the firm's goals. The task of the office manager is to increase the presence of such motivator factors as achievement, recognition, the work itself, responsibility, and advancement — topics that are discussed in detail in Part 3.

The Management Science School

The *management science approach* to decision making, also known as the quantitative or mathematical approach, embodies the use of engineering and mathematical skills to solve complex decision-making problems. Simply stated, decision making is nothing more than making a conscious choice between two or more alternative courses of action. While this definition is readily understandable, the selection of such courses of action — that is, how a decision is made — is more complex. Managers of the old school made decisions on the basis of common sense or intuition, using a kind of educated guess. The *sound* decision, however, is made upon the basis of reliable information. To make such a decision, the series of events shown in Figure 1-7 occur.

Management science came to the forefront during World War II when the logistics of global war called for precise methods of gathering reliable information as part of the decision-making process. Following the war, management science, augmented by technological advances in computerization, has been applied to problems of peacetime production. Managers in today's competitive world face many decisions that deal with an uncertain, unpredictable future. In recent years attention has been focused on the use of reason or logic in the decision-making process in which as much objective fact (and as little subjective feeling) as possible is used. Technology has enabled managers to collect volumes of data to perform precise calculations and analyses as substitutions for judgment. Examples of such scientific methods for making decisions include sampling, factor analysis (used, for example, to determine whether advertising in newspapers, television, or radio has the greatest effect upon sales), linear programming, queuing or waiting-line theory (studying, for example, the behavior of waiting lines at a supermarket checkout counter), and

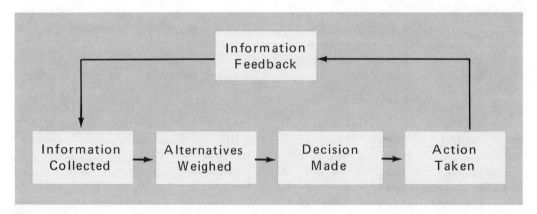

Fig. 1-7
Information and Decision Making

game theory (such as studying the interactions of competitors in a manufacturing industry). Many of these techniques of decision making employ the use of higher level mathematics, and many depend for their increased use upon the rapid calculating ability and accuracy of the computer. The student of administrative office management is encouraged to understand these scientific approaches to decision making, since these tools and techniques are becoming increasingly recognized and utilized by practicing managers. Several of the quantitative tools of analysis are described and applied to problems of office management decision making throughout this textbook.

QUESTIONS FOR REVIEW

1. What are the six "M's" that must be organized and coordinated through the management process in order to insure business success?

2. How may administrative office management be defined?

3. With the emergence of the information-management function in the 1960s, what changes occurred in the traditional office function?

4. What is meant by the statement that no two office managers have the same job responsibilities?

5. What are the requirements for achieving the C.A.M. designation?

6. What job qualifications will be needed by tomorrow's information manager?

7. Describe the major characteristics of a management information system.

8. What are the distinguishing features of the classical school of management thought?

9. List the steps in the scientific method of problem solving.

10. (a) Why is Leffingwell looked upon as the father of office management?
    (b) What are Leffingwell's five principles of effective work?

11. What were the major contributions made by Mayo and his research team to the development of the behavioral school of management thought?

12. What are the implications of Maslow's theory of human motivation for today's administrative office manager?

13. Contrast the underlying assumptions of McGregor's Theories X and Y of worker behavior.

14. What contributions has the management science school of thought made to office management?

QUESTIONS FOR DISCUSSION

1. Since the dawn of management, the concept of total information has been an ever-present dream. Today, however, instead of being a means for better decisions, information has become an end product, with the computer turning out more information than a manager can use. Comment upon the validity of these statements.

2. Do most managers have great informational needs or, rather, do they have need of new methods to understand and process the information already available to them?

3. Several schools of thought prevail in administrative management circles today. If you were supervising clerical operations in a modern office, which philosophy would you want to prevail? Why?

4. The findings of many industrial researchers and the conclusions reached by much of the business press reflect increasing signs of middle-management malaise — a decline in morale, outright disaffection, and mounting frustration. What reasons can you advance for this changing attitude on the part of middle managers?

5. An office worker in an insurance company was asked to describe the requisite characteristics of a good office manager. The worker's answer indicated, among other things, that such an executive must be a self-starter, a highly motivated individual with the ability to see what is needed and the capacity to make plans and then to follow through. If the right person is in the job, he or she will take orders from the situation. Do these statements apply equally well to all office executives, including the office manager? If the right office manager is in the job, how is he or she able to take orders from the situation?

6. Forecast how the office manager of the 1980s will differ from his or her counterpart of the 1970s.

7. Would it be pointless to advocate an approach to management based entirely upon science? Would it be equally pointless to advocate an approach resting solely upon art? Explain.

8. Richard Conarroe, in his management book *Bravely, Bravely in Business*, has observed that self-interest is the single most pervasive force in business. By this statement Conarroe means that when someone is asked to do something, the person is asking himself or herself, "What's in it for me?" When something happens or changes in a company, each person involved is asking himself or herself, "How does this affect me?" Do you agree with these observations regarding the pervasiveness of self-interest? Explain.

PRACTICAL OFFICE MANAGEMENT CASES

Case 1-1   **Feeling the Backlash of Tokenism**

After graduating from the Peace Valley Junior College at age 20, Marie Fisher was employed as executive secretary by Alpha

Testing Service, publishers of office employment tests. She worked five years in the secretary post and then was promoted to administrative assistant to the vice-president of office services, Glen Hall. After serving as administrative assistant for six years, Fisher is presently earning $15,500 annually.

Three weeks ago Hall announced his resignation and has just left to accept a newly created personnel post with a bank in Amsterdam, Holland. Alpha executives have been searching for a replacement for Hall and are struggling with the decision whether to promote from within or to recruit fresh executive talent from outside the firm. Within the company the only qualified candidate for the vice-presidency is Fisher, according to the evaluations made by the firm's president, Richard Skinner.

After today's meeting with his executive officers, Skinner has jotted down the following bits of information about Fisher:

> — 31 years old; married; no children; underwent hysterectomy two years ago; no plans for adopting children.
> — very attractive appearance; a winning personality; exceptional work habits; truly dedicated to her job; in many respects sharper than Hall.
> — husband is a professor of music (tenured) at Avery University, a nearby four-year university; appears happy on the job; no plans for relocating in the near future.
> — with Hall, under a company membership, has regularly attended monthly chapter meetings of the Administrative Management Society.
> — served on the board of directors and as vice-president, educational services, of the local chapter of Administrative Management Society.
> — during past two years has attended seminars dealing with word processing, communications, and effective management of time.
> — often called upon to speak to high school and junior college groups about the role of women in management; has written two articles urging passage of the Equal Rights Amendment.
> — has studied upper-level management courses in the evening program at Avery under the company's tuition reimbursement plan.
> — actively working with National Organization for Women (NOW).

Since Hall's announcement of his resignation, Fisher has been thinking about the open position and her chances of being promoted to vice-president. Recently Fisher has been asking herself these questions:

> — If I were to be promoted, would it be anything more than tokenism? Would top management be promoting me because of my qualifications to handle the job or solely because I am female? Would this promotion be a dead end for me?
> — From the ads in the daily newspaper, I note that the starting salary for the open position is $20,000. If I were promoted from within, could I expect to receive $20,000?
> — I know I am the only one from within the company being considered for the post. I also know they are seriously considering two males,

both of whom have been interviewed recently. Must I, because I am female, have to prove that I am twice as good as any male from the out-side?

— How would I overcome the possible resentment on the part of my subordinate male managers? How would I overcome the resistance of those females who might dislike working for me?

Assuming the role of company president, how would you answer the following questions?

1. Do you agree with Fisher that she must be twice as good as a rival male in order to obtain the vice-presidential position?
2. How do you account for the fact that women such as Fisher, who aspire to managerial positions, must overcome what appear to be insurmountable obstacles?
3. What advantages would there be for the company in promoting Fisher to the position? in selecting an outsider to serve as vice-president?
4. If Fisher were to be promoted, how would you convince her that the advancement should not be looked upon as tokenism?

Case 1-2   Reorganizing the Information Function

The California Savings and Loan Association was founded 35 years ago in Beverly Hills. Since that time it has grown in size to include 25 branch offices in each of the principal Los Angeles sub-urbs. The principal function of the Association is to serve as a banking facility for California residents. Presently it has demand deposits of $105 million on hand and approximately $87.5 million on loan.

To handle the growing volume of paperwork accompanying the savings and loan functions, the main office employs the personnel shown in Figure A on the next page.

Each of the branch offices is organized in an identical fashion with these personnel: an office manager who also serves as the branch loan manager, an assistant loan officer, a secretary, and two tellers. All systems and procedures, forms, and reports are devel-oped centrally in the main office, although equipment and supplies are usually purchased from local office supplies stores in the imme-diate area of the branch office. No standard practices have been de-veloped for the purchase of equipment, for the hiring or work per-formance of employees, or for office services, such as duplicating, transcribing, calculating, and correspondence.

The Savings and Loan vice-presidents, as chief operating of-ficers of the Association, have recently become aware of the great diversity of operating practices in the branch offices. After personal visits to each of these offices and a conference with the manager of

President's Office:	President Administrative Assistant Secretary
Vice-Presidents' Offices:	Vice-President (Savings) and Secretary Vice-President (Loans) and Secretary Vice-President (Trusts) and Secretary
General Office Personnel:	1 branch office coordinator 10 tellers 12 bookkeepers 8 accountants 14 clerk-typists 3 file clerks
Data Processing Department:	Manager, Data Processing Services 5 junior programmers 3 senior programmers 3 systems analysts 8 machine operators (keypunch, tab machines, computer console)

Fig. A
Main Office Personnel

data processing and the branch office coordinator, they discovered that each of the information-handling activities lacked coordination and was in need of thorough study both from the standpoint of the branch offices and the Association.

Accordingly, J. B. Kingsley, the president, was advised to authorize such a study. From his office came the memorandum, shown in Figure B on the next page, addressed to the vice-president (Savings), the senior officer under the president.

Prepare a report for the president which contains your recommendations. The report should give attention to the following:

1. Define the information function for the firm.
2. What personnel would be required to handle a full-scale systems study of the paperwork and information functions? Elaborate.
3. What organizational and personnel changes would you recommend? Why?
4. Identify each of the key information-processing activities and show how each should be organized.
5. Clearly show your recommendations relative to both the main office operation and the branch office operations.

CALIFORNIA
SAVINGS & LOAN ASSOCIATION

To: R. T. Baker
From: J. B. Kingsley   Date September 17, 19--

It has come to my attention that the future success of our organization may well be hampered by the present status of our administrative office management setup. I believe, therefore, that a company-wide study should be initiated immediately in which all aspects of the information function be examined in depth.

You are hereby authorized to proceed as follows:

    1. Select in-house or outside consulting help in order to provide an intensive review of our information activities.

    2. Be alert and imaginative so that a total system or unified organization will result.

    3. Since the data processing installation (a large-scale computer) is of recent origin, assume it is functioning satisfactorily and has the capability to handle our present and future needs. However, consult the data processing manager freely as a resource person.

Send me your recommendations as soon as possible.

Fig. B
Authorization Memorandum

Chapter 2

AUTOMATION AND THE INFORMATION FUNCTION

Business firms that have been most successful in automating the operations in their offices have focused from the beginning on using the computer to generate more timely and accurate information for planning, organizing, and controlling their activities. These firms thoroughly investigated the economic feasibility of converting from manual to automated operations and carefully planned every step along the way. Computer technology provides the manager with a degree of statistical control over company operations that was impossible to achieve not long ago. Now the quantity of information generated and stored is accelerating daily, and information can be summoned forth and turned on, like electricity, in a matter of seconds. Better control over company operations is possible, but only if the users of information communicate within an effective relationship with those who produce the information.

In this chapter the nature of automated operations in the office is discussed and their impact on the information function is analyzed.

THE NATURE OF AUTOMATION IN THE OFFICE

In the office *automation* refers to those self-regulating processes in which work is completed mostly by machines and with a minimum of human effort. Automation as a modern philosophy of problem-solving takes form in the office through the techniques of automated data processing.

Automated data processing (ADP) can be looked upon as a self-regulating process in which information is handled with a minimum of human effort and intervention. In an automated data processing system, data are recorded in such a form that further use can be made of the data without need for any subsequent manual recording. Automated data processing is not truly automatic, however, because it demands outside direction and frequent interruption of the processes. People are still the directing force; but once the step-by-step instructions have been carefully constructed, or *programmed*, the machines can do the work more quickly, more economically, and more accurately than manual methods. The punched-card system and the electronic computer system of automated data processing are briefly discussed in the following paragraphs. These systems are further discussed in Chapters 20 and 21.

The Punched-Card System of Processing Data

The *punched-card* or *unit record system* of processing data is based upon a code, or machine language, by means of which data are represented by holes punched in cards. In the punched-card data processing system alphabetic and numeric data contained in typewritten or handwritten form on original source documents are known as *input*. The punched cards upon which the data have been recorded are called *input media*. By means of sensing devices, machines can read and process electrically the data represented by the punched holes. The punched-card machines can be used to sort, collate, reproduce, and print the data as desired and to perform all types of arithmetic calculations. The processed data become the *output*, and the business forms upon which the processed data appears, such as summaries, tabulations, and reports, are called *output media*.

The Electronic Computer System of Processing Data

The computer system is a group of interconnected machines that process data with incredible speed, a speed that makes the electronic computer system superhuman. *Electronic data processing* refers to the use of electrical impulses, traveling at the speed of light, which record, compute, and transmit alphabetic and numeric data. Both the data to be processed and the instructions to process the data are stored in the memory cells of the computer or other input media. Although there are many brands and models of equipment varying in design, construction, and capability, all aim toward the same objective — to handle information more quickly, more accurately, and more economically.

Like the punched-card system, the electronic computer system depends upon a code, or a machine language. Alphabetic and numeric data appearing on source documents in typewritten or handwritten form must be recorded in code form on punched cards, paper tape, magnetic tape, or some other input medium. The coded data and instructions for their processing are "fed" into the computer where they are stored in the form of electrical impulses. Computations are performed, comparisons are made, and summaries are prepared according to the instructions. Processed data are then written out of the computer in the form of punched cards, punched paper tape, magnetic tape, or printed business documents and reports.

With today's electronic data processing systems, firms are able to concentrate control over their information management activities through a central headquarters. They are also able to extend the influence of automation to their systems and procedures — from inventory and payroll to production, sales, and personnel. In so doing, businesses attempt to visualize all the elements of the corporate function in their relationships with one another and with the overall objectives of the firm. From this "total systems" concept, companies learn that much more can be accomplished by computers than by clerical and accounting jobs. Their capabilities can be tapped to perform the traditional applications (payroll processing, inventory control, accounts payable, and accounts receivable) as well as operations research applications such as spotting deviations from planned programs (exception reporting), adjusting planning schedules, forecasting business trends, simulating market conditions, and solving production problems. (Operations research and two of its techniques of managerial control — linear programming and waiting-line analysis — are discussed in Chapter 25.) Since the office manager is a manager of information and since each of these applications revolves around the processing of data, an active role must be taken in studying and improving the management information systems.

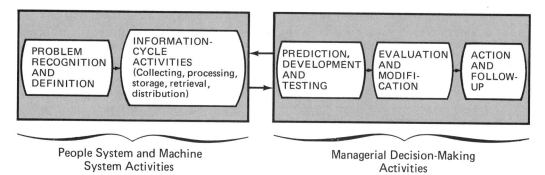

People System and Machine
System Activities

Managerial Decision-Making
Activities

Fig. 2-1
Phases of a Management Information System

MANAGEMENT INFORMATION SYSTEMS

A *management information system (MIS)*, usually operated as a computer-based system, has as its purpose the supplying of timely information to managers for use in drawing conclusions, making predictions, recommending courses of action, and, in some cases, even taking action. A management information system encompasses all the subsystems within and external to an organization by which data are collected, recorded, and processed for operational purposes. The data may be obtained by telecommunications, by personal contact with other people, by studying and analyzing systems and procedures, as well as from data processing units. The system exists to provide information to support managers in directing the enterprise in the accomplishment of its objectives. Supplementing this purpose are the processing of the data and the keeping of historical records.

Role of People in Information Systems

All the activities in the information cycle (collecting, processing, storage, retrieval, and distribution) are not per-

formed entirely by automated machines and equipment, for an information system is composed of people as well as of machines. In the scientific method of problem solving, described in Chapter 1, people play an active part in each of the steps that lead to decision making in a management information system. Each of the following logically organized activities, charted in Figure 2-1, relies upon people action:

1. The problem is recognized and clearly defined for the organization for which decisions are to be made and for which information is to be collected.[1]
2. Data relating to the organization's problem are collected, processed, stored, retrieved, and distributed.
3. Based upon the relevant data obtained in Step 2, predictions are made in the form of hypotheses. These tentative solutions are further developed and tested.

---

[1]See Richard Mason, "Management Information Systems, What they Are, What They Ought to Be," *Dimensions of American Business* (New York: McGraw-Hill Book Co., 1975), p. 147. In this article the author shows how management information systems progress from data bank approaches to predictive information systems to decision-making information systems to action-taking information systems.

4. The predictions are evaluated by managers with regard to the objectives or goals of the organization. Modifications may be made in the hypothesis to fit the real-world situation, and finally a course of action is selected to be taken.
5. Action is taken and follow-ups and periodic reviews are provided to make sure that the solution to the problem continues to meet the objectives toward which the solution was applied. Changes in technology or availability of labor may change the efficiency or profitability of the contemplated course of action. The development of word processing equipment is an example of how technology has changed office management and altered the procedures by which communication problems are solved.

Criteria for Evaluating Management Information Systems

The overall effectiveness of a management information system may be evaluated by examining five criteria — relevance, economic feasibility, accuracy, flexibility, and timeliness.

Relevance. The system and the information supplied by it must be *relevant* to purposeful needs of the business. Lying behind the current explosion of paperwork is the presence of electronic devices of a bewildering array and variety, all dedicated — paradoxically — not just to production, but to reproduction, duplication, and permanent storage of vast quantities of irrelevant data, which companies seem determined to retain.[2] Thus, the objective of the system and its byproducts must be

clearly stated at the outset; and it must be determined who will use the information, how they will relate to the system, and in what fashion the system will satisfy the stated aims. Today the task is to discover more effective ways of using present systems, as well as developing new systems. The objective of the system must center about the information, not the data, and about the understanding of relationships drawn from the information, not the mere retention of permanent records.

Economic Feasibility. The system must be *economically feasible*, and its cost must be compatible with the benefits sought and the results to be achieved. Huge sums of money are being spent on information systems; and information, like any asset, must be managed with skill and efficiency to yield the greatest return on investment.

Accuracy. The information system must provide adequate controls to assure *accuracy*. A firm may currently have a computerized system that is not being utilized and also have a duplicate manual system which, although recognized as inefficient by its users, is necessary in order for the managers to perform their functions. Such a situation represents one of the worst kinds of cost ineffectiveness and is not uncommon.[3] The development of this situation can be prevented by carefully considering the requirements for systems control at the time of designing the system.

Flexibility. The system must provide a high degree of *flexibility* to handle normal growth for the future and to

---

[2]Quoted from *The Office* in "Are We Drowning in Data?" *Management Review* (September, 1970), p. 48.

[3]Burton J. Cohen, *Cost-Effective Information Systems* (New York: American Management Association, 1971), p. 15.

handle the inevitable changes in the planning process or in the company's operations. To aid in providing flexibility, general and operating managers must play a more prominent role in the designing of the system to make sure that it is tailored to the company from the top down.[4]

Timeliness. The system must provide for *timeliness* through its response time. The increasing complexity of business and the speed up in decision making made possible by electronic devices demand that the output of meaningful information be accelerated. The quantity of data is not enough; the data must be accurate, logical, and timely. The quality of the output information depends upon the quality of the input data. No information system, especially a computerized system, can convert faulty source data into logical results.

PLANNING FOR AUTOMATED OFFICE OPERATIONS

Today electronic computers are in use by business firms representing every major industry. Computer installations have proved especially feasible in banks and insurance companies whose routine, repetitive operations are readily adaptable to programming. Computers are being used for accounting operations, inventory control, and the planning and control of production. According to a report in *Administrative Management*, developments in computer usage among the 500 leading companies

in the United States indicate these trends:

1. Elevating the data-processing managers to the vice-presidential level, selecting them for their business judgment first and their computer knowledge second.
2. Expanding the accounting-type applications to many additional areas, such as project control, time reporting of manpower, and also to computer costing systems.
3. Extending the use of the computer beyond the handling of accounting problems to areas such as management control, selection of vendors, and simulation of a business environment to aid in decision making.[5]

Small companies, too, can reap the benefits of electronic data processing. Three alternatives are open to these small companies: (1) utilizing the services of a commercial data processing service center; (2) renting or sharing time on another firm's computer during its idle hours; or (3) leasing or buying a minicomputer. The *minicomputer* is a table-top machine that has many of the logic and arithmetic capabilities of the larger computers. The minicomputer is used to perform tasks such as billing, accounts receivable, and accounts payable, which are too complex for the desk calculator and too simple for the large computer. According to a survey of the small business computer industry undertaken by *Modern Office Procedures*, about 60 percent of the new users of small computers purchase rather than lease their computers.[6] The purchase

---

[4]William M. Zani, "Blueprint for MIS," *Harvard Business Review* (November-December, 1970), p. 96. This very fine article presents a general scheme for relating systems to the jobs they are really supposed to do.

[5]Frederik H. Lutter, "EDP Perspective: Danger or Opportunity," *Administrative Management* (January, 1970), p. 16.

[6]Charles N. Ritley, "Datanomics: Proving the Theory," *Modern Office Procedures* (May, 1975), pp. 71–82.

price ranges from under $5,000 to over $100,000, with the majority of the surveyed users within the "under $60,000" category. Monthly lease charges range from less than $500 to over $4,000, with over 80 percent of the users paying less than $3,000 each month.

The advantages and disadvantages of each of these approaches used by small firms in automating their information management function are discussed in Chapters 20 and 21.

The Feasibility of Installing a Computer

A *feasibility study* is undertaken to determine whether specific operations can be improved and if the installation of machines and equipment and the adoption of revised systems and procedures are economically justified for these improvements. The two basic questions to be answered in a computer feasibility study are: (1) Is a computer necessary? and (2) If so, which one is best?

Compiling all the data on present and proposed systems and procedures, meeting with committees and subcommittees, working with the representatives of several computer manufacturers and studying their proposals, preparing all the specifications for the computer installation, and orienting employees to the new roles they will play may conservatively require two years or more. All of these activities are time-consuming and costly, especially for those, such as the office manager, who are directly involved in the feasibility study. Often, however, the office manager has found that the investment in the feasibility study returns a dividend whether or not it is decided to install the computer. Some firms find that, as they commence

to analyze their existing paperwork operations and then determine the costs of the labor and equipment presently used, improvements in systems and procedures are originated that more than pay for the study itself. Also, the feasibility study group usually develops into an excellent medium for communications across functional boundaries, and its members gain greater insight into the functional interrelationships within the company. Finally, those workers who institute and participate in the study are positively motivated as a result of the contributions they make.

Guidelines for a Computer Feasibility Study

Generally the installation of a computer is technically and economically feasible when office operations meet the following conditions:

1. Greater speed and accuracy are required in processing data and in preparing management reports.
2. Complexities of present data processing systems and procedures cannot be simplified without electronic assistance. If a company is spending an inordinate amount for the rental of office machines or if the present office machines system is working at or near capacity, the firm might operate more economically with a small computer system.
3. Investment in computer equipment is substantially offset by both quantitative and qualitative benefits. Offsetting factors include better customer service, lower costs to consumer, and improved control over internal operations, such as keeping inventory at desired levels.

To determine whether the office operations meet the requirements discussed and whether a computer installation represents the best solution to a company's information-management problems, the office manager or the person in charge of planning the feasibility study needs certain guidelines, such as those listed below:[7]

1. *Select a qualified person to undertake the feasibility study.* Does the person have a thorough knowledge of company policies, accounting systems, and records retention? Does he or she possess the ability and interest to work with endless details and the persistence to see the job through? Has the person the ability to organize, direct, and supervise others? Has the person the ability to visualize the requirements of the installation and understand what costs are involved in operating the system? The person who is selected to coordinate the feasibility study preferably will be the one who eventually manages the installation.

2. *Assign the person initial responsibility for the feasibility study and provide him or her with adequate authority to complete the job.* Is the person able to select, within reason, the resources needed to complete the study? Does he or she possess sufficient authority to perform the assigned duties without being hampered by company policies or secondary responsibilities?

3. *Obtain the full cooperation of top management.* Is top management backing the feasibility study from the beginning so that the project is not doomed to failure before it starts? Does top management understand that the company organization may possibly have to undergo major changes, such as the elimination of a major unit, before the system can attain its full potential?

4. *Obtain the full cooperation of middle management and operating personnel.* Have the appropriate employees been assigned full-time responsibilities for certain phases of the study? Are personnel at the operating level involved in the initiation and planning of the computer project so that their support is obtained in carrying out the installation of the computer?

5. *Evaluate the need for outside help.* If there are no systems and procedures personnel in the company, is advice being solicited from the computer manufacturers' staffs or from private consultants?

6. *Determine the benefits to be realized from a computer system.* To what extent will clerical costs be reduced? Will the system accumulate data quickly and accurately enough to provide management with an up-to-date picture of internal operations at any time? Will the processing of payroll and other personnel data be completed more efficiently, accurately, and economically? Will the system provide for closer control over inventory as the result of being better able to estimate future needs? Will customers be provided better service as the result of a speedup in processing their orders?

7. *Consider all relevant factors in each computer proposal before making the final decision.* Does this computer offer the greatest anticipated return in clerical savings? What are the personnel requirements? How do the overall installation and operating costs, quality and speed of maintenance, and reputation of the manufacturer compare? Is the system compatible with existing systems? Can the system be expanded by adding on peripheral equipment as the

---

[7]For a step-by-step procedure to be followed by small companies considering the feasibility of installing an in-house computer, see Myles A. Vogel, "How to Do Your Own Computer Feasibility Study," *Modern Office Procedures* (February, 1975), pp. 50, 52. Also see Vincent V. Amato, "Computer Feasibility Studies: The Do-It-Yourself Approach," *Management Review* (February, 1970), pp. 2–9.

company's needs change? Is it more economical to lease or to purchase the equipment?[8]

Insuring the Success of Automated Operations

After the feasibility study has been completed, the computer proposal approved and accepted, and the tentative installation date obtained from the computer manufacturer, much additional planning is needed to insure the success of the installation. The necessary tools for planning and controlling each long-range computer project must be provided so that management can determine how much is being spent on computer efforts and whether a particular application has been successful. Application of the computer to each project should be analyzed from the standpoint of costs and expected results. The estimated costs of each project must be provided for in the budget so that the actual costs and the progress to date can be compared with the planned costs and progress. With the high-speed processing and output of the computer lurks the potential danger that huge quantities of meaningless data may be generated. As a result, management becomes flooded with too many facts. Therefore, adequate control systems, designed with the goals and values of the firm in mind, must be established to keep irrelevant and unproductive activities from creeping into the computer operations.

All major changes in work flow, areas of responsibility, and manpower requirements must be planned well in advance in order to minimize the ad-

verse effects upon the employees affected. As part of the changeover to computer operations, some of the jobs will be performed at isolated machine stations where the noise level is high and where constant attention to speed and accuracy is required for repetitive work. A "man-to-machine" relationship comes to be substituted for the "person-to-person" relationship to which employees have been accustomed. Since any change in the work environment gives rise to upset and restiveness among employees, the office manager should keep abreast of all proposed changes to anticipate their effects upon employee attitudes. Efficiency will be attained only when people and machines are included in a carefully worked-out plan that takes into account the interests, frustrations, capabilities, emotional drives, and career aspirations of the people involved. As part of the feasibility study, it was stressed that the full cooperation of the operating personnel should be obtained at the very beginning of the computer study. By serving on committees involved in studying the effect of changes upon present systems and procedures, supervisors and key workers come to realize that they are involved in the decisions being made. As a result, they can accomplish a great deal in working with their subordinates by "selling" a successful future for automated operations.

Following the announcement of the decision to install a computer, one of the most marked changes in employee attitudes comes about — the fear of layoff. To deal with this fear, the administrative office manager should utilize all available media — house organs, bulletin boards, departmental conferences, and personnel meetings — to inform the workers of the planned changes several

---

[8]See Chapter 5 for a discussion of leasing or buying office equipment.

months before the installation date. These measures have proven very effective in maintaining employee morale and displaying to the workers that management is interested in their welfare.

Maintaining Effective Interaction Between Producers and Users of Computer Services

Following the installation and operation of the computer, problems may result from a poor relationship between the data processing systems staff and those who use the computer services. For example, in many organizations, users do not trust the data offered them by the systems staff. Tensions and frustrations often mount on the part of data processing technicians who know best how to operate the computer but who are not always fully aware of the environment in which the outputs are to be used. Then, too, the data processing staff often participate as outsiders in decision-making processes that produce outcomes over which they had little influence. Rather than place the blame upon technical people for "cold systems" — called so because they are made up of machines and not people — some feel that the fault lies with middle and upper management. It is management "who turned over all aspects of the system to technically trained people and gave those people, mostly youngsters just out of college, no training in the people side of the system."[9]

A study undertaken by McKinsey and Company showed that the more successful computer users were those firms with top managers who showed a strong constructive interest in the operation and development of computer projects. A study conducted a few years later at Ohio State University concluded that among the firms surveyed in Ohio and Indiana there is a significant relationship between the amount of interaction by top management and systems management and the perceived profitability of computer operations.[10] To ensure more effective interrelationships between the data processing systems staff and the users of the computer services, members of the systems staff should be assigned as liaisons with each major computer user group in the firm. Thus, the staff actively becomes involved in what the group does and is able to learn the goals, needs, and operating constraints of the user group. Executives who use the computer services should be helped to understand what the computer can do — its capabilities and limitations — rather than become involved in the technical aspects of its operation. The aim here is to encourage users to plan realistically regarding the applications of computer resources rather than attempt to become technicians involved in computer operations. All data processing projects should be subjected to periodic reviews by a joint team of technicians and managers to emphasize both the impact of new applications on the operations of the firm as well as to pinpoint the cost savings effected. Finally, so that those people who design the systems and write the computer programs can learn the "business" of the firm, management should provide training courses including not only technical training but also courses with titles

[9]Leslie Matthies and Ellen Matthies, "The People's Side of the Management System," *The Office* (April, 1975), p. 60.

[10]Clifford Elliott, "What Managers Can Do to Break the EDP Barrier," *Administrative Management* (January, 1974), p. 50.

such as "The Work that Our Departments Do," "Respect the Contribution of Each Worker," "How to Make the System Respond to People's Needs," and "Designing Significant Reports for Managers."[11]

THE EFFECTS OF AUTOMATION IN THE OFFICE

With the increasing number of automated applications to the management of information, consideration must be given to the effects of automation upon the labor force and office jobs, the education and training of office workers, middle management, and company operations. In their long-range planning, managers must be aware of the human as well as the economic consequences of automation. In purely economic terms, automation will be successful and will work most effectively, according to former Secretary of Labor Wirtz, if "we take care of the human implications and the human concerns which automation creates."[12]

Effects upon the Labor Force and Office Jobs

Society has been characterized by a certain amount of unemployment as the result of every major technological advance since the Industrial Revolution. Many of the jobs people had been accustomed to performing fell by the wayside as the result of technological advances. In each instance, however, society adjusted itself and moved forward. Just as a new technology eliminates jobs, it also creates new jobs and expands the level

and variety of human wants. For example, consider the telephone industry, which began using automatic dial equipment in the 1920s. Today almost all local calls and about 75 percent of the long-distance calls are completed without operator assistance. Yet the number of employees in the Bell System has increased several-fold. "If the current volume of calls were handled as they were before automation, it would require all the workers in the country."[13]

As indicated in Chapter 1, it is expected that the labor force will climb to 114 million by 1990. It is also projected that in 1985 the white-collar work force (professional and technical workers, managers and administrators, clerical workers, and sales workers) will constitute about 53 percent of all workers.[14] Many employees will be working on machines and systems yet to be produced and will be relying on skills yet to be developed.

Women in the Labor Force. A large part of the projected increase in the labor force will consist of women workers whose participation in the labor force has increased consistently for nearly three decades and which has more than counterbalanced a decline over the same period in the participation by men. In 1970, women represented 40 percent of all workers in nonagricultural industries. Expansion of the coverage and liberalization in the requirements of retirement, pensions, and disability programs in both the private and public

---

[11]Matthies and Matthies, *loc. cit.*

[12]*Modern Office Procedures* (April, 1965), p. 16.

[13]Frank G. Goble, *Toward 100% Employment*, An AMA Survey Report (New York: AMACOM, A Division of American Management Associations, 1973), p. 23.

[14]"The United States Economy in 1985, Projected Changes in Occupations," *Monthly Labor Review* (December, 1973), p. 19.

sectors have enabled older men to retire earlier, while younger men have generally been remaining in school longer before they permanently enter the job market.[15] Changing attitudes toward the role of women outside the home, the trend toward smaller family size, expanding opportunities in trade and service jobs, the increase in the number of households headed by women, and the lowering of discriminatory employment barriers by legislation have been important causal factors in the increased entry of women into the labor force.[16] Many of these women, possibly one fourth, participate on a periodic rather than a permanent basis, and thus it is expected that a large reservoir of part-time workers will continue to be available.

Despite the influx of women into the labor force, their position still does not equal that of men. Their earnings continue to fall behind men's, averaging only about 58 percent of male income. Women are still in a relatively small number of occupations, mostly in the traditional "women's occupations," such as secretary, clerical worker, nurse, and teacher. Those who make it into other occupations usually find themselves in low-level jobs with limited futures. Although working women today are found predominantly in white-collar occupations, only a very small percentage of them hold prestigious white-collar positions. According to the 1970 census, 15 percent of all working women were in professional and technical fields, 50 percent were in clerical jobs, and less than 5 percent were managers and administrators. This represents only a slight increase over 1950.[17]

Professional and Technical Workers. As a result of the growth in the demand for goods and services, stemming from population growth and rising business and personal incomes, it is forecast that the rate of growth for professional and technical workers will be faster than that for all other work groups. Other factors accounting for this rate of growth include a continuing concentration of population in metropolitan areas and a continuing growth of research in natural and social sciences. The demand for professionals to develop and use computer resources is also expected to grow rapidly.

Managers and Administrators. Among managers and administrators, the changes in the size of business and organization have caused the number of salaried managers to rise, while the numbers of self-employed have declined. The requirements for salaried managers is expected to continue to grow rapidly as industry and government increasingly depend on them. Technically trained managers will be needed to administer the research and development programs and to make decisions on the installation and use of automated machinery and automated data processing systems. Today about 60 percent of the work force is engaged in tasks not directly related to the production of goods. For every unskilled worker, there are five managers and

---

[15]Joseph L. Gastwirth, "On the Decline of Male Labor Force Participation," *Monthly Labor Review* (October, 1972), pp. 44–46. See also Karen Schwab, "Early Labor Force Withdrawal of Men: Participants and Nonparticipants Aged 58–63," *Social Security Bulletin* (August, 1974), pp. 24–33.

[16]Government regulations affecting the selection, training, compensation, and promotion of office workers are discussed in Chapter 11.

---

[17]Carolyn J. Jacobson, "Women Workers: Profile of a Growing Force," *AFL-CIO American Federationist* (July, 1974), pp. 9–15.

professionals; however, many so-called professionals are still engaged in routine work that is essentially clerical.[18]

Clerical Workers. Since, as indicated in Chapter 1, the meaning of the office function has expanded to include all information-processing activities in a firm, many new jobs will be added to the job titles usually found in the office. For example, increased use of the computer and its related equipment has created many new positions, all of which are office positions. In its annual survey of salaries, the Administrative Management Society now includes 20 clerical and data processing job titles below the rank of administrative manager:[19]

Mail Clerk — File Clerk	Secretary B
General Clerk B	Secretary A
General Clerk A	Correspondence Secretary
Accounting Clerk B	Keypunch Operator B
Accounting Clerk A	Keypunch Operator A
Bookkeeping Machine Operator	Tabulating Machine Operator
Offset Duplicating Machine Operator	Computer Operator B
Telephone Switchboard Operator	Computer Operator A
Typist-Clerk	Programmer
Stenographer	Systems Analyst

In its area wage program the Bureau of Labor Statistics has added three EDP occupations (computer operator, computer programmer, and systems analyst)

to the office and plant jobs regularly surveyed.[20] The survey, completed in June, 1973, included 125,000 men and women in these three occupations in all metropolitan areas of the United States. The total employees of these three occupations numbered only slightly more than the 119,000 keypunch operators within the scope of the survey. In the employment of EDP workers among nonmanufacturing establishments, the insurance carrier industry (which is within the finance, insurance, and real estate group) was the largest employer; banking ranked second. These two industries employed almost one of every four EDP workers surveyed.[21]

Clerical workers became the largest single occupational group in 1970. Two of the fastest growing occupations have been secretaries and typists, which increased over 80 percent in 1960 through 1970. This rise was partly due to the high concentration of these workers in finance, trade, and other rapidly growing service-producing industries. Also, since these jobs involve a high degree of personal contact, they were relatively unaffected by office automation.[22]

Generalizations about the impact of computer technology on clerical jobs are difficult to make. While the extension of computer usage spurred increases in some clerical occupations between 1960 and 1970, the demand for others decreased; still others, such as secretaries, were relatively unaffected. The fast growth of computer technology did produce substantial employment

---

[18]"Trends and Forecasts: Managers: More Movement at the Top," *Administrative Management* (January, 1974), p. 24.

[19]*Office Salaries Directory for United States and Canada, 1977–1978* (Willow Grove: Administrative Management Society, 1977).

[20]Donald J. Blackmore, "A Salary Profile of Electronic Data Processing Occupations," *Monthly Labor Review* (March, 1975), p. 51.

[21]*Ibid.*, p. 52.

[22]"Changes in the Occupational Structure of U.S. Jobs," *Monthly Labor Review* (March, 1975), p. 30.

gains for two groups of office machine workers — keypunch and computer and peripheral equipment operators, whose numbers rose over 75 percent during the 1960s. In contrast, shipping and receiving and stock clerks grew only moderately, as some inventory procedures were automated. Telephone operators also increased slowly as automated dialing equipment handled the work formerly done by operators.[23]

Among other large clerical occupations, cashiers and bookkeepers each expanded over 60 percent during the 1960s. The significant employment rise for cashiers accompanied the fast growth in the number of self-service stores, especially in the suburbs. Bookkeepers increased rapidly as record keeping also expanded.[24]

Throughout the latter part of the 1970s and the mid-1980s, it is forecast that employment in clerical jobs will grow faster than the total employment rate. According to the biennial *Occupational Outlook Handbook*, job openings will be ample through the mid-1980s for clerical workers, stenographers and secretaries, typists, computer console and auxiliary equipment operators, programmers, systems analysts, bank clerks and tellers, insurance actuaries, accountants, marketing researchers, and personnel workers.[25] These projections are based on continued technological innovation in computer applications and in the design of office equipment and communication devices, and, of course, on the key factor of overall economic growth. It is expected that the growth rate in the employment of some clerical

jobs will be retarded, while for other jobs, the rate will rise rapidly. For example, the use of computers to handle routine, repetitive work is expected to reduce the need for clerks in filing, payroll computation, inventory control, and customer billing. On the other hand, the number of clerks needed to prepare input materials for the computer is projected to increase greatly.

It is a foregone conclusion that in the future business information will be generated and processed to an even greater extent than ever before. Therefore, the information processors in our society, whether they are typist-clerks or programmers, will continue to grow in number and importance.

Effects upon Education and Training of Office Workers

There is no way to measure with any degree of accuracy the net effect that automation will have upon the education and training needs of office workers over the next decade. However, as a result of the changing occupational structure of the work force and the differing rate of growth among industries, the demand for workers with specific occupational skills and educational backgrounds will be significantly affected. Clearly there will be a rising demand for workers with a high level of education and training, while there will be a lessening of opportunities for the less skilled and less educated. By 1985, over three out of four persons in the civilian labor force will be high school graduates, and nearly one worker in five will have completed four years of college or more.[26]

---

[23]*Ibid.*, p. 31.
[24]*Ibid.*
[25]"Washington Report, The Labor Department's Employment Forecast," *The Office* (June, 1974), p. 58.

[26]Denis F. Johnston, "Education of Workers: Projections to 1990," *Monthly Labor Review* (November, 1972), pp. 22–31.

Due to the increase in college enrollments over the past decade, an overabundance of workers with a college degree has forced many of them into the clerical ranks. The expansion of professional, technical, and clerical jobs absorbed only 15 percent of the new educated workers in the early 1970s; the remaining 85 percent accepted jobs previously performed by individuals with fewer credentials.[27] The economy has not been changing rapidly enough to require or to absorb the spectacular increase in the educational level of the work force.

Although through the mid-1980s the fastest growth in job openings will occur in professional and technical fields, the majority of the 60 million job openings expected to become available by 1985 will not require four years of college. The *Occupational Outlook Handbook* points out that "because many occupations are becoming increasingly complex . . . occupational training such as that obtained through apprenticeship, junior and community colleges, and post high school vocational courses is becoming more and more important to young people preparing for successful careers."[28]

Along with the growth of education, the formal education requirements for jobs have risen. Today many managers use the academic credential as a screening device for employment and hope that the diploma requirement will provide a productive, disciplined work force. Based on studies on productivity, absenteeism, and turnover, however,

there is little evidence of a positive relationship between workers' education credentials and their job performance.[29] Over the years society has criticized the educational system for not doing its job, but too often the response has been to raise the educational requirements in the hope that the next higher level will solve the problem. As a result, the employment opportunities for noncollege jobseekers are further limited, problems of underemployment are created, and job dissatisfaction occurs among workers whose formal education exceeds the actual requirements of the jobs.

To meet the personnel needs of companies having or contemplating automated operations, there must be adequate liaison between school systems, industry, and government with respect to future job requirements. Management has a role to play in presenting the current needs of office education at each level of the school system so that the goals of office education are well defined and related to the total educational program. For the great diversity of office occupations, training is needed at various educational levels. The office manager can aid by establishing clear-cut standards for office operations so that business teachers and counsellors as well as personnel and training directors have a better picture of job classifications and job requirements that will help them in training and advising students and employees more specifically for office employment. The changes that come about in the type, pattern, and requirements of certain office occupations

---

[27]*Work in America*, Report of a Special Task Force to the Secretary of Health, Education, and Welfare (Cambridge: MIT Press, 1973), p. 135.

[28]"Washington Report, The Labor Department's Employment Forecast," *The Office* (June, 1974), p. 58.

[29]"An Overview on the Human Side of Enterprise," *A Look at Business in 1990*, A Summary of the White House Conference on the Industrial World Ahead (Washington: U.S. Government Printing Office, 1972), p. 191.

should be reflected in the educational offerings of schools and in the training manuals of business firms. To accomplish this goal, there must be a continuous examination of office education subject matter and the methods of instruction. More and more the office manager is coming to realize that education and training are a life-long program. Training is continuously needed in basic skills such as English, arithmetic, and human relations — the ability to follow instructions, to respond to supervision, and to maintain the proper attitude toward the work to be done as well as toward the employer.

As mentioned earlier in this chapter, the employees should be informed of management's plans and of the anticipated effect that automation will have on the number and types of jobs available in the company. For those workers presently employed who can be retrained to develop the new skills required, retraining programs should be provided. The person in charge of training may be helped by the computer manufacturer who in many cases will provide retraining programs on the company premises. Then, too, more and more public and private educational facilities have expanded their facilities to include adult education retraining programs and upgrading programs for employees. Employees not possessing the necessary qualifications for retraining may be reassigned to other departments or aided in relocating elsewhere in the community.

Effects upon Middle Management

Middle management in one company may cover jobs far different from and at different levels than those in another company. For the purpose of this discussion, *middle management* is defined to include all managers below the highest level of policy making, as shown in Figure 1-1, page 4. Thus, in most business firms the administrative office manager falls into the category of middle management.

With the advent of automation, predictions were made that the job of middle management would become obsolete and that the numbers of middle managers would be severely reduced. Experience, however, proved these predictions to be in error; in the early 1950s a tremendous expansion of middle management positions began. As pointed out by Peter F. Drucker, "In every developed country middle-management jobs, in business as well as in government, have grown about three times as fast as total employment in the past 20 years; and their growth has been parallel to the growth of computer usage."[30]

Since the early 1960s, except for periods of economic recession in 1970 through 1971 and 1974 through 1975, there has been a steady growth in the demand for competent middle managers. With the growth of electronic data processing applications, there has developed an increased need for managers to work with data processing systems personnel to make the types of operating decisions that involve advanced financial analysis, simulation, and improved management information systems necessary for efficient organizations.

There are two major reasons why middle-management jobs have not been dramatically decreased as the result of the computer. First, the managerial decisions made at this level involve far too

---

[30]Peter F. Drucker, *Management: Tasks, Responsibilities, and Practices* (New York: Harper & Row, Publishers, 1974), p. 331.

many intangibles and too much abstract thinking to subject the problems to mechanical analyses. On the other hand, managers are aided by the computer in making far more intelligent decisions. Much of the former uncertainty surrounding their jobs can be removed, and they will thus be better able to rely upon analyses than intuitive judgment. Many problems heretofore insolvable due to the time-consuming chore of dealing with a huge quantity of variable data can be converted into well-structured problems for the computer. In a matter of seconds or minutes, the manager is supplied with information that formerly may have required hours, months, or perhaps years for its availability. Rather than reduce the degree of judgment required of middle managers, the increased emphasis upon computer operations should result in a middle management position that is more highly structured. While some jobs requiring little skill and judgment may move down the management ladder, other jobs requiring the compilation and interpretation of computer data will move upward.

Second, the availability of automatic equipment that can do a job more quickly than it can be done by manual methods does not necessarily mean that the equipment will be automatically installed and used. If a company must spend perhaps $140,000 each year to cover the rental fee or the depreciation charges on a computer installation, the equipment should be able to accomplish, as a minimum, the work of seven $20,000-a-year managers. Automatic machines perform at their optimum level when performing routine, repetitive operations — tasks entirely unlike the unstructured problems facing managers. Thus, from the viewpoint of re-

turn on investment, the cost of applying computers to solving many managerial problems is prohibitive. The administrative manager must develop cost consciousness in the area of electronic data processing. The absence of effective managerial direction over the EDP function has brought much waste and inefficiency into computer operations. A.T. Kearney & Company, management consultants, conducted a study of 89 companies and their 155 computer installations and found that: (1) only 48 percent of the available machine time is used productively, (2) computers are operated only 64 percent of the available time, (3) 25 percent of manned hours are wasted in idleness, reruns, machine maintenance, and down time, and (4) 42 percent of the companies surveyed do not maintain accurate records of computer performance.[31] Undoubtedly a great deal of the poor computer productivity, as evidenced in the findings above, is traceable to poor management practices. There is need for managers who deal with data processing functions to understand systems concepts and to be able to view their companies as a total system and to understand its relationship as a subsystem of a larger social and economic environment. As pointed out earlier, managers should understand the basic concepts of computer technology and be aware of the capabilities and limitations of computers. To extend their decision-making abilities, middle managers should familiarize themselves with the wide range of quantitative methods of management

---

[31]"EDP Productivity at 50%? Three Shifts an Answer, Training Is Another," *Administrative Management* (June, 1971), pp. 66–67. Also see "Computers Make Management Efficient — But Who Makes Computers Efficient?" *Management News* (December, 1970), p. 7.

science.[32] Managers need not know how to perform the mathematical calculations, but they should be able to determine the input requirements of data and be able to evaluate the output in terms of its validity and relevance to the problems at hand. Finally, today's middle managers must be skilled in the art of communications and human relations, for without these skills managers are unable to utilize the human resources that have been freed by computer technology. It is useless to free workers from their routine and repetitive tasks unless they can be motivated to become creative in the solution of problems.

Effects upon Company Operations

During the 1940s and 1950s many large firms expanded throughout the world, and expansion required them to decentralize operations. With the introduction of automation, however, many companies began to recentralize their operations by using a central computerized information system at the home office to collect, process, and transmit information throughout the world. Westinghouse with its Pittsburgh-based telecomputer center (merging the telephone system with the computer) is in continual communication with more than 300 locations, field offices, warehouses, and distributors, thus permitting rapid reporting and control over inventory, order processing, marketing, sales, and production activities. Ac-

counting functions, too, are greatly accelerated as information is handled by machine. Similar accounting applications in government, such as the processing of social security data, are now centralized.

In medium-size and small firms a reverse trend, that of decentralizing operations, has appeared. For example, systems planners expect a large number of specialized and localized *data bases* (large libraries of filed data) to be functioning for doctors, lawyers, credit agencies, employment agencies, merchants, and banks. To provide for more efficient utilization of expensive automated equipment, it is anticipated that the use of computer centers will increase in the future. A *computer center* brings together all electronic data processing within a centralized department, possibly under a vice-president of information services, whose responsibility is to see that the proper reports and information get to the right place at the right time. It is expected that a number of firms will establish *regional information centers* to handle the accounting work for their divisions and plants, with the actual decisions being made on a decentralized basis. This should provide more information intelligence upon which division and plant managers may base their decisions.[33]

All these developments bring about a rethinking of the entire business structure and the concept of management. As a result of scientific advances and technological change, management is now able to regroup all the elements of control under a single roof. The centralization of information processing, the

---

[32]The tools of managerial control used in applying the basic concepts of scientific management and behavioral science to the solution of office problems are discussed in later chapters. See Chapter 4, page 74; Chapter 10, page 268; Chapter 12, page 330; Chapter 23, pages 659–672; and Chapter 25, pages 722–723.

[33]Richard Allen Stull, "A View of Management to 1980," *Business Horizons* (June, 1974), pp. 10–11.

establishment of total systems and procedures, and the ability to project more accurately the company's goals, costs, and budgets all serve to justify the need for a full understanding of the managerial functions — planning, organizing, leading, and controlling. Automation in the office will never eliminate the need for people. They will be relieved of the repetitive monotonous functions of recording, transcribing, computing, and summarizing, howover. People will still be required to generate data at the source, to prepare the input media for the machines, to program and control the machines, and most importantly to interpret the output of the machines. The need will be for office managers who have expanded responsibilities for managing information and who can supply this information to the various decision centers of the company.

QUESTIONS FOR REVIEW

1. From the viewpoint of office operations, what is automation?
2. Compare these terms:
   a. Automated data processing.
   b. Punched-card data processing.
   c. Electronic data processing.
3. Describe the basic flow of data into, through, and out of a punched-card data processing system.
4. For what purpose is a management information system developed?
5. How may the effectiveness of a management information system be evaluated?
6. In what ways can a small firm benefit from electronic data processing in automating its information management function without purchasing a large-scale computer?
7. Why does a business firm undertake a computer feasibility study?
8. Under what conditions is the installation of a computer generally feasible from a technical and economic viewpoint?
9. What steps can the administrative office manager take to minimize the employees' fears of layoff when they first learn about the decision to install a computer?
10. What approaches should be followed in developing more effective interaction between the users of information and the data processing systems staff which produces the information?
11. What factors have been responsible for an increased number of women in the labor force?
12. What are the fastest growing occupations in the clerical work force? What factors account for this growth?
13. When the educational requirements for jobs are raised, what are the effects upon noncollege jobseekers? upon college jobseekers?

14. How may the middle management level of a business firm be adequately defined?

15. What are the major reasons that middle-management jobs have not decreased as a result of computerized office operations?

QUESTIONS FOR DISCUSSION

1. Many computer scientists believe the full impact of the computer will be felt only when the computer becomes a mental and intellectual extension of the person who uses it. Such thinkers prophesy the day when there will be a real symbiosis (living together in close, intimate association) between the user and the computer in the solution of problems. Do you think that this viewpoint applies to the use of computers in the office? Why?

2. Two statements made with reference to the concept of systems are: (a) A business system is a social system, and (b) The machine is not a system. Explain the significance and interrelationships of these two statements.

3. As the computer assumes more and more importance in the decision-making process, what effect do you foresee upon middle managers and their planning functions?

4. Computers today link large corporate headquarters with their many branch offices to provide "instant information" on such vital matters as sales, inventories, and production data. To the administrative office manager this information made possible by the computer actually improves the centralized control over all key business functions. Discuss.

5. In most management conferences where executives discuss the impact of computers, problems of machine usage, including programming, are assumed to be manageable. On the other hand, the more difficult and frustrating and less manageable factor is called the "people problem" — getting people to work well with machines and with new machine-based systems. In what ways can the administrative office manager assist top management to improve this people-problem situation?

6. One of the major users of paperwork and information handling is the banking system. To alleviate some of the mounting problems of dealing with the billions of checks written each day, systems analysts predict a "checkless society" in our future. Discuss the impact of this development on the general nature of such a society, the changes it would precipitate in the operation of bank offices, and the far-reaching influences of such a development on other sectors of the business society.

7. Even though the number of women in the work force has increased tremendously in recent years, the working woman, as well as the

woman who is looking for a job, continues to find herself up against barriers when applying for a management position. What do you see as the major barriers that face the working woman or the female job-seeker?

8. The director of systems development for a large computer manufacturer has stated that the shortage of computer programmers is becoming so acute in this era of mounting computer sales that it is preventing many users from employing their computers to maximum advantage. What educational qualifications and type of background would you look for in the employment of a computer programmer?

9. Electronic computers make sweeping changes in the way that business data are handled and in the amount of information made available to top management. Do you believe that the selection of a computer is the top responsibility of the president of a company? Explain carefully.

PRACTICAL OFFICE MANAGEMENT CASES

Case 2-1   Processing Customer Complaints[34]

You are the administrative manager of a growing manufacturing company which has sharply increased its sales volume over the last year. It has come to your attention that there have been an increasing number of customer complaints in recent months regarding poor service. An example of a typical complaint is indicated in the following letter from the Johnson Machine Works, a small customer:

Gentlemen:

On January 3, I received a shipment of 100 (one hundred) #10 widgets from your company. I refused to accept the shipment since my order had been for 10 (ten) #100 widgets. I telephoned Jack Deegan, your sales representative, and he assured me the error would be corrected. On January 5, I received a computer-prepared bill for 100 #10 widgets which represented the erroneous shipment. I ignored the bill based on my conversation (and assumption) that corrective action would be taken by Mr. Deegan.

In subsequent weeks, the situation was further confused by the following events:

(1) In a second telephone conversation with Mr. Deegan on January 26, I asked why I still had not received my correct shipment and indicated there was an urgent need for parts ordered. He indicated that verification had been requested from the Shipping Department and he did not know

---

[34]*AMS News* (Willow Grove: Administrative Management Society), January, 1971, p. 3.

why I hadn't received the corrected order. He then promised to expedite matters by cancelling my old order and resubmitting the order which would be handled by the newly automated Order Department.

(2) On January 29, I received a past-due notice for the 100 #10 widgets. I telephoned Mrs. Jones of your Billing Department and she said all billing adjustments had to originate with Mr. James at the warehouse who is responsible for key-punching adjustments.

(3) I subsequently called Mr. James and found that in order to correct my account I would have to call Mr. Smith in the Shipping Department.

(4) I next contacted Mr. Smith and was informed he was on vacation.

(5) On February 5, I received my correct order of 10 #100 widgets.

(6) On February 11, I received a bill for the 10 #100 widgets, and a past notice of payment due for the 100 #10 widgets with a threat of legal action.

(End of Letter)

Upon investigation, you learned that all parties had followed prescribed procedures — which consisted mainly of preparing the proper forms for keypunching and verification. The punched cards prepared by keypunching were then used to enter updated information into the computerized order, inventory, and accounting system.

You determined that the growing number of complaints could not be attributed to clerical or procedural errors and that under normal work loads the present system of handling customer complaints was adequate. You also decided that the increasing difficulties in processing complaints efficiently was directly related to the rapidly growing sales volume, and the greatly increased number of unique or "exception" complaints resulting from that volume.

What would be your recommendations to correct this situation?

Case 2-2   Planning a Feasibility Study

The following information relates to the administration of Palmer Plastics, Inc., a rapidly expanding manufacturer of novelty plastic toys and plastic kitchen and hardware utensils.

The growth of Palmer Plastics, Inc., parallels the rising expansion of the economy in general during the past 20 years. Starting as a partnership of two brothers in a converted brickyard in Pueblo, Colorado, it quickly prospered, expanding from a management team of two executives, an office staff of five, and a factory work force of 40 supervisors and laborers to a management team of 32, an office force of 15 supervisors and 78 general and special clerks, and a plant production force of 520. During this period of growth, annual gross sales have leaped from $400,500 to over $3,560,000, and expectations are for even greater growth in the future.

The novelty of the products and their durable composition have skyrocketed Palmer Plastics into the national spotlight. Advertising in national magazines and television and emphasizing the regional uses of the products (such as "Shoreline Toys" for the coastal and Great Lakes market and agricultural specialties for the rural home-maker) have gained a wide sales margin for the manufacturer over old-line, more conservative competitors. Even as the home office was growing, sales offices (comprising a sales supervisor, several sales representatives, and a small clerical staff) were opened in Denver, San Francisco, Omaha, Houston, Birmingham, Chicago, Cincinnati, Newark, and Worcester, Massachusetts.

During the short, fast-moving history of Palmer Plastics, total emphasis was placed on selling and promotion and perfecting the production function. The latest equipment, newest methods, and most highly trained engineering talent were procured. Extensive on-the-job training programs were held to assure that all production workers and their supervisors were properly meshing and working together as a team. Top management paid only passing attention to the office function, whose work force had grown much faster than the production force. Frequent suggestions, however, came from the more efficient sales offices for improving paperwork systems. These suggestions were acknowledged but never acted upon. No automated data processing equipment was used.

Presently the firm is divided into five divisions as shown in Figure A. Second largest in number of employees (behind the manufacturing division) is the general administrative division.

Each of these divisions has experienced growing pains: excessive worker turnover, many new staff members, increasing paperwork, difficulty in meeting deadlines, and a feeling of desperation in keeping up with the work. Coordination among divisions (such as the relationship between sales, purchasing, inventory, and accounting functions) has not been achieved; and the forms, methods, and systems in use are geared to manual processing of information, the use of typewritten forms, out-of-date machines, and hand posting of accounts and inventory records. Briefly, the firm has geared its productive operation in the plant to the age of automation while its office operation remains in the "horse and buggy" age.

During the past two months several serious breakdowns in administration have occurred: (1) inability to update the inventory records resulted in a serious failure to order several of the key chemical components required to fabricate toys for the lucrative Christmas market; (2) due to a widespread epidemic of the Asian flu, over 60 percent of the office and payroll staffs were away from work on the average of ten days, thus resulting in long delays in paying the workers; and (3) the billing operation was found to be over two weeks late in processing all accounts, which resulted in delayed sales income for the firm.

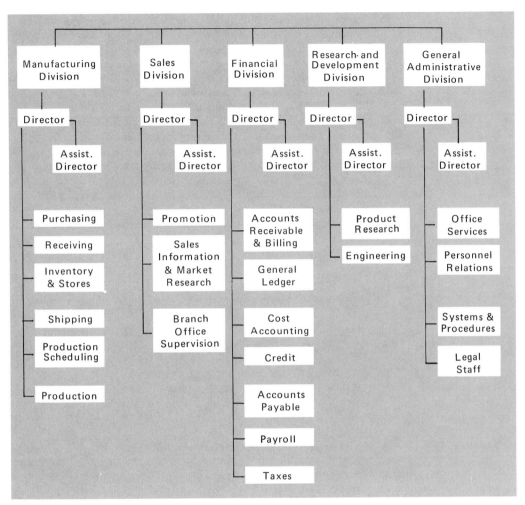

Fig. A
Divisional Structure of Palmer Plastics, Inc.

As a result of these crucial problems, the vice-president, Harriet Douglas, and the directors and assistant directors of each of the divisions held a series of meetings to evaluate or assess the cause of the problems. From these meetings and without further consultation came the following series of observations and proposals to the top management of Palmer Plastics, Inc.:

1. The information system of the firm is slow, unwieldy, and unfitted to meet modern processing needs.
2. A need exists for the immediate introduction of a medium-size electronic computer.

3. A separate and new data processing department is required. Due to the fact that the director of the financial division, a certified public accountant, has had three years of punched-card processing experience and is responsible for all accounting work (an important use of data processing services), it is recommended that this person head the new data processing department.

4. The directors of the divisions, all highly trained in their fields and all college graduates, shall conduct their own feasibility study to be headed by the director of the financial division.

5. A service center (a data processing firm specializing in the processing of other firms' data) can satisfactorily handle all overload processing until a new data processing installation is installed. Such an agency should be contacted immediately to serve as an interim processing agent.

6. A functioning computer installation can be expected within 10 to 12 months.

Evaluate the feasibility approach recommended for Palmer Plastics. In this evaluation determine:

1. What type of information should have been presented and to whom?

2. Which are the faulty assumptions made by the divisional directors? Suggest substitute assumptions that spring from a more effective use of the scientific method.

3. Specifically, outline the most comprehensive method of solving the problem of considering the need for the mechanical processing of information. What part should the firm's top management play in such an approach? What part should their departmental managers and supervisors play?

4. If you were the president of Palmer Plastics, what type of feasibility study would you insist on before committing the firm's resources to the procurement of an expensive computer?

Part 2

Planning and Organizing Administrative Office Operations

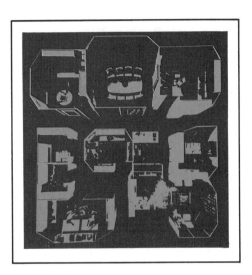

To achieve the objectives of the firm, planning is performed at all levels of management. *Planning* is the management function of analyzing relevant information from the past and the present and assessing probable developments of the future so that a course of action — the *plan* — may be determined that will enable the firm to meet its stated goals.

Organizing is the management function by which the work, the work place, and the workers are brought together to form a controllable (manageable) unit — the *organization* — to accomplish specific objectives. Organizing occurs at all levels of office operations — from the clerical employees who organize their work around their skills and tasks to the executives who supervise the activities of complex units.

In the second part of the textbook the functions of planning and organizing office operations are examined by first reviewing several basic principles of management, each of which serves as a guide to the office manager in working with and through people to get the job done. Next, the nature of the work place is investigated as attention is focused upon the management of office space and the physical and psychological factors of office environment. Finally, the work itself is planned and organized through a discussion of office services such as written communications, telecommunications, information and records management, and graphic information systems.

Chapter 3   # PRINCIPLES OF PLANNING AND ORGANIZING OFFICE OPERATIONS

Over the years thoughtful leaders from many fields of study have expressed in statement form certain generally accepted and fundamental truths called *principles*. Thus, there are principles of conduct, principles of marketing, and principles of management, to name a few. Principles change, new behavioral principles are identified, traditional principles are attacked, and principles are discarded when they no longer serve their purpose. Office managers need a keen understanding of the basic principles and concepts pertinent to their field of specialty. Since principles are the backbone of decision making, the essence of intelligent planning, and the basis for evaluating situations, an understanding of the principles of management is essential to the planning and organizing of administrative office operations.

The best approach to the development of a healthy office organization hinges upon a careful planning of the nature of the work to be done and the particular needs of the people involved. In their summary of studies undertaken by students of management and organization, Morse and Lorsch found that firms with highly predictable tasks perform better when their organizations are planned along the highly formalized procedures and management hierarchies of the classical approach.[1] Firms characterized by having highly uncertain tasks requiring extensive problem solving are less formalized and emphasize self-control and member participation in the decision-making processes. Studies indicate that there is no one best organizational approach and that organizations must be designed and developed so that the characteristics of the organization *fit* the nature of the task to be done.[2]

GUIDING PRINCIPLES OF MANAGEMENT

Effective management results in a smoothly functioning office organization that obtains the maximum of results with a minimum of effort. Organization is a means to an end, not an end itself. A prerequisite to organizational health is a sound structure, but the structure is not health itself. Peter F. Drucker has stated, "The test of a healthy business is not the beauty, clarity, or perfection of its organization

---

[1]John J. Morse and Jay W. Lorsch, "Beyond Theory Y," *Harvard Business Review* (May-June, 1970), pp. 61–68. In this article the authors go beyond Theory Y and introduce a Contingency Theory which emphasizes that the appropriate pattern of organization is *contingent* on the relationship between task, organization, and people.

[2]*Ibid.*, p. 62.

structure. It is the performance of people."[3] The following principles underlie efficient management and healthy organization, and the effectiveness of these principles is measured by the performance of people in achieving results — the ultimate test of good management.

Principle of Objectives

The objectives of a business or a group of functions within the business must be clearly defined and understood.

An *objective* is an end or a goal to be achieved. Although objectives are usually specific and realistic, they may be broad and range from general, overall statements of an organization to specific, narrow statements about an individual's activities.[4] Objectives, usually established as part of the planning process for one-year and five-year periods, are revised at regular intervals in order to adjust for any major changes. In many progressive companies today, top management has the responsibility for setting quantifiable and attainable objectives and then directing the organization toward the accomplishment of those objectives. This contemporary management approach — management by objectives — is discussed in Chapters 12 and 24.

There should be a *policy* — a broad guidepost to action — developed to define and reflect each of the firm's objectives. The objective of a firm may be to maximize profits by increasing sales, and this objective in turn determines the

nature of the sales function. Similarly the objective of the production function is to create a volume of goods to meet the increased sales and to do this at the lowest possible cost. The objective of the administrative office management function is to coordinate the information-processing activities of production and sales so that the unit cost of the product or service may be reduced and productivity of the organization increased. Here, administrative office management is a facilitating function subordinate to the other functions.

Principle of Responsibility

Responsibility for organization exists with managers at all levels, beginning with top management and extending to the first-line supervisor.

The overall responsibility for a sound organization structure belongs to top management, those who are responsible for policy making. The chief executive officer of the firm must determine the major functions and responsibilities of individuals who report directly to that level in the organization. The company's long-range plans and objectives are formulated at this level, and proper planning and organization by top management are essential to their being accomplished.

In the same manner as top management accepts its responsibility for organization, each succeeding level of management from middle management down to first-line supervision must complement this responsibility. Each level, therefore, should first approach its organizational responsibility by:

1. Identifying its major objectives and purposes.
2. Determining the activities necessary to carry out those objectives.

[3]Peter F. Drucker, *Management: Tasks, Responsibilities, Practices* (New York: Harper & Row, Publishers, 1974), p. 602.

[4]M. Valliant Higginson, *Management Policies I, Their Development As Corporate Guides*, AMA Research Study 76 (New York: American Management Association, 1966), p. 17.

3. Determining the most logical pattern of organization to carry out its activities and meet the needs of its workers.
4. Fixing responsibility for the accomplishment of these objectives.
5. Establishing proper communications and relationships to unify all efforts and develop team spirit.

This same process is used at every level of management throughout the company. The only difference lies within the scope of responsibility and authority of the job and the direction of detail, as graphically illustrated in Figure 3-1. This figure shows that as one

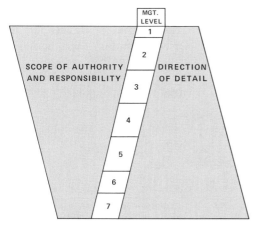

Fig. 3-1

The Change in Scope of Authority and Responsibility And the Change in Direction of Detail As One Moves Up and Down Management Levels

moves down the levels in the organization, there is less responsibility and authority but more direction of detail. As one moves up, the reverse is true.

Principle of Unity of Functions

All business organizations are composed of various functions that are interrelated and which must work together to achieve the major objectives of the business.

A business organization may be likened to a system, and each of the major functions of business (production, distribution, finance, and personnel) may be regarded as a subsystem. The four subsystems are interrelated, and the effectiveness of any one functional subsystem is dependent upon the operations of the other three. Like the circulatory system of the human body with its subsystems of arteries, veins, and capillaries, the needs, requirements, and objectives of each functional system and its subsystems must be clearly defined initially. Each of the component parts must be considered in relation to the other parts of the system, expanding or contracting those activities as needed in terms of operations that will satisfy the overall objectives of the firm.

The principle of unity of functions requires that: (1) the various functions be in proper balance as determined by the relative importance of their contributions to the achievement of the company's objectives; (2) there be a certain amount of stability should changes in personnel occur; (3) there be flexibility to meet seasonal or territorial fluctuations; and (4) there be a possibility for growth and expansion to take care of future changes. As a result of planning and building the organization around the main functions of the business, the need for people is decided. The organization must be designed to best serve the purposes of the firm; then workers are selected who are best qualified for the positions created.

A survey undertaken by the Dartnell Institute of Business Research showed that the seven major functions performed by office administration executives are office management, credit and collection, purchasing, data processing, building supervision, employment, and accounting.[5] Successful administrative office managers accept the premise that their information-processing work supports and coordinates every activity related to the organization. An office manager's activities are so closely interrelated that none of them can be considered without considering the others. For example, the providing of word processing services must be related to the needs of the word originators, to records management, to mailing, and to supervision; and the activities of personnel relate to each of those just mentioned. In addition to this, the people in charge of the other functional units, such as production or distribution, must work with the administrative manager because in one way or another their activities are interrelated. Similarly, as the office organization is expanded and assistants or departmental heads are added, all must work together under the direction of the administrative manager as a coordinated team. This integration must be constantly kept in mind because it increases the efficiency of the information processing function by reducing the cost of the work.

Drucker states, "The simplest organization structure that will do the job is the best one."[6] The organization structure of office operations is made good by the problems it does *not* create. The simpler the structure, the more easily the organization will be understood by all office workers, the clearer the interrelationships among the workers will become, and the less there will be to go wrong. To create an office organization with the greatest possible simplicity, one must structure and position within the simplest possible design those key activities needed to produce key results. "Above all, the architect of the organization needs to keep in mind the purpose of the structure he is designing."[7]

The development of an office organization based upon simplicity and clear-cut interrelationships aids in overcoming the phenomenon known as *Parkinson's Law*, which unfortunately does occur at times in all types of organizations. C. Northcote Parkinson, who formulated this "law," observed that: (a) work expands to fill the time available for its completion without much regard for the volume or usefulness of the tasks to be carried out, (b) work expands to fit the organization that is developed to perform that work, and (c) there is a tendency for each unit within an organization to try to build up its importance by expanding the number of personnel.[8]

Principle of Assignment of Responsibilities

Effective organization is made up of people who perform the work assigned.

After the specific activities necessary to accomplish the planned goals have been determined and those activities have been grouped into a logical structure, the duties and responsibilities must be assigned to specific positions and people. Where similar but not identical assignments are given to several individuals, the similarities should be explained and the differences pointed out to prevent misunderstanding. Lines of

[5]"Who Runs the Office?" *The Office*, Vol. 70, No. 3. (September, 1969), p. 26.
[6]Drucker, *op. cit*, p. 601.
[7]*Ibid.*, p. 602.
[8]C. Northcote Parkinson, *Parkinson's Law* (Boston: Houghton-Mifflin Company, 1957).

authority must be established. The organization should encourage its people to exercise the maximum initiative within the limits of their delegated authority. Thus, ideas can be originated at lower levels of the organization and flow by upward communications to the higher levels of management.

Provision must be made for incentives (financial and nonfinancial) to do the work effectively, and each individual must know the interrelationship of the work within a function and among various functions. Good office organization cannot exist without 100 percent participation. To bring about good organization, one should accept the fact that human resources are the keynote — the personnel available or that can be made available to the firm.

Principle of Delegating Authority Commensurate with Responsibility

Individuals in the organization must be given authority commensurate with their assigned responsibility so that they can be held accountable for the performance of their duties.

Authority is the right to command or the right to act and the power to make decisions. *Responsibility* is the obligation and accountability for properly performing work that is assigned. There must be a clear-cut flow of authority and responsibility from the top to the bottom of the organization to carry out all functions, to effectively exercise managerial control, and to insure no duplication and overlapping of assignments.

In addition to maintaining parity between authority and responsibility when they are delegating, managers must determine how much of each should be delegated to subordinates. When managers delegate only a limited amount of rights and obligations, the authority is said to be *centralized*. If, on the other hand, a large amount of each is delegated to lower levels, the authority is *decentralized*. Decentralized authority is consistent with the recommendations made by today's behaviorists who stress that a greater share in the management decision-making process should be given to subordinates in the organization.

A study of the organization and administrative practices within 75 manufacturing concerns, ranging in size from 40 to 600 workers, found that a leading cause for complaint by various members of management was the failure to delegate authority.[9] The delegation of authority is perhaps one of the most difficult jobs the supervisor has to learn. As pointed out in Chapter 12, some supervisors never learn to delegate but instead insist on handling the many details themselves. Other supervisors pay lip service to the principle of delegation but actually operate their departments like autocrats. Some managers give their assistants many responsibilities but little or no authority. If, however, office supervisors are to manage their departments successfully, they must delegate authority properly. As a minimum they should delegate enough authority to get the work done, to allow their key workers to take initiative, and to keep work flowing in their absence. Of course, the people to whom responsibility and authority are delegated must accept the rights and obligations and be competent in those areas for which they are being held accountable.

---

[9]Rollin H. Simonds, "Are Organizational Principles a Thing of the Past?" *Personnel* (January-February, 1970), p. 17.

Principle of Unity of Command

For individuals to know clearly to whom they report, each employee should receive orders from and be responsible to only one supervisor.

On many occasions office workers receive orders from more than one supervisor. Such workers often fail to function efficiently because they do not know from whom they should receive their orders or which work should be done first. In some instances two supervisors may be in charge of one department and if the lines of authority are not properly drawn, one supervisor will not know where his or her command stops and the other's begins. Confusion results, and morale and organization discipline may be eventually destroyed when an office employee is accountable to several supervisors, each of whom may have varying standards for judging the completed job. By reporting to only one supervisor, the essence of the principle of unity of command, workers should know exactly what is expected of them and also the supervisors should know exactly who reports to them.

Each office employee should be directly responsible to the individual who has been designated as the authority on a specific job or assignment. Perhaps in one firm the administrative office manager may report to the controller because of conditions existing in that company; in another firm where the office services are strictly sales oriented, the office manager may report to the vice-president of sales. Who is to report to whom depends upon the organizational structure, objectives, and conditions within each company. In fact, with today's emphasis on task forces and project teams, middle managers or staff

personnel may find themselves reporting to half a dozen bosses.[10]

Principle of Span of Control

For effective supervision and leadership, the number of subordinates under the immediate supervision of the supervisor should be limited.

Span of control, also known as *span of management*, refers to the number of employees who are directly supervised by one person. There is no predetermined formula that rigidly defines the span of control, since each situation must be carefully evaluated after an analysis of all factors involved. Among these factors are: (1) the capacity and skill of the office supervisor and the subordinates, (2) the type of direction and control exercised over subordinates together with the latitude extended to them in decision making, (3) the stable or dynamic nature of the operation, (4) the technical nature of the work, (5) the amount of time that the executive spends on other than supervisory work, (6) the type of organization, and (7) the number of interpersonal relationships inherent in each given situation.

Considerable controversy exists among traditional managers and the behaviorists over what constitutes the specific limits of a span of control. When the span is limited, a greater opportunity for closer supervision and regimentation is provided. The number of levels or layers in the organization usually becomes greater and thus creates a "tall"

---

[10]See "Today's New Managers Are Changemakers," condensed from *Business Week* in *Management Review* (November, 1969), pp. 29–35.

pyramidal organization structure. As the span is lengthened, the degree of freedom for the individual subordinate becomes greater and the organization is characterized by fewer levels. Some management authorities have looked upon 12 to 15 subordinates as the maximum span at the lower levels in the organization. Early writers on management theory stated emphatically that the span of control at the top level should not be more than five to six subordinates whose work interlocks. Later studies, however, show that many companies do not adhere to the recommendation of having five, or, at the most, six subordinates report to each superior.[11] With the advent of the computer and management information systems, wherein subordinates are often performing similar kinds of work, it is possible by means of routine control procedures to increase further the number of persons supervised. For example, a Dartnell Institute of Business Research survey notes that the typical office services manager supervises 42 employees and has two assistants.[12] In their study of determining the requirements for the position of administrative office manager, Smith and Warner found that 83 percent of the managers supervise directly 10 or fewer employees and indirectly 75 or fewer. It was also noted that females tend to supervise directly a larger number of employees than males.[13] Schmidt and

Lappe found in their analysis of the role of the office manager that 55 percent of the managers had fewer than 10 employees under their direct supervision; 30 percent exercised direct control over 11 to 20 employees; and 15 percent had more than 25 employees under their direct supervision.[14]

There is a tendency to look upon the most satisfactory span of control as one that avoids an overly tall pyramidal structure and does not overtax the executive's mental and physical capacities. To encourage independence and self-control among workers, the overly long chain of command is flattened by decreasing the number of supervisory levels.

FORMS OF ORGANIZATION

Organization is usually effected on a functional basis; that is, according to the basic functions of business — production, distribution, finance, and personnel. Within each of these basic groupings, the functions may be further subdivided. Four forms of organization may be set up to plan the work, to fix responsibility, to supervise the work, and to measure its results. They are: (1) line, (2) functional, (3) line and staff, and (4) committee.

Line Organization

The earliest and simplest form of organizational structure is the *line*

[11]Ernest Dale, *Planning and Developing the Company Organization Structure*, Research Report No. 20 (New York: American Management Associations, 1952), p. 56. See also Ernest Dale, *Organization* (New York: American Management Associations, 1967), pp. 94–96, for a more recent survey of the behavioral work on organizations.

[12]"Who Runs the Office?" *loc. cit.*

[13]Harold T. Smith and S. ElVon Warner, *Administrative Office Management Preparation* (Provo: Brigham Young University, 1971), p. 9.

[14]Gene W. Schmidt and William C. Lappe, "Analysis of Role of Office Manager," *The Delta Pi Epsilon Journal*, Vol. 16, No. 1 (November, 1973), p. 26.

organization, also known as the *scalar* or *military* type. In some offices a rather strict form of discipline and organization may be carried on, with the work subdivided and delegated on a military line. Authority is passed down from top management to middle managers in charge of particular activities and from them down to supervisors who are directly in charge of workers at the operative level. As shown in Figure 3-2, authority flows in an unbroken line from the president to the worker.

The line organization is simple and easily understood by workers, for there is a clear-cut identification of duties and division of authority and responsibility. The performance of duties is directly traceable to a worker and the immediate superior in command. The line organization is characterized by a minimum of red tape in decision making, thus enabling action to be taken quickly. On the other hand, each supervisor is responsible for a wide variety of duties, and may not be expert in all these areas. Thus, there is a lack of specialization at the supervisory level. At each succeeding level of organization, the wide and varied duties performed tend to overload

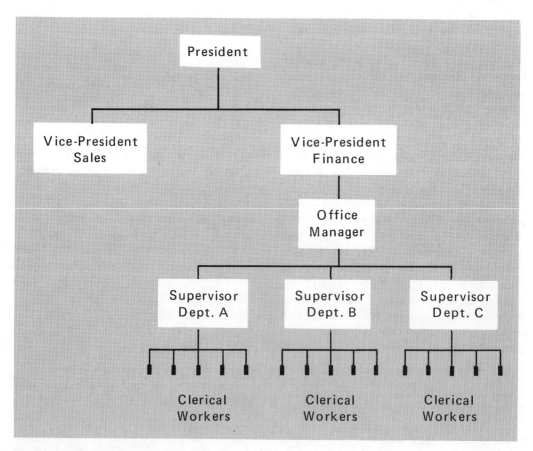

Fig. 3-2
Line Organization

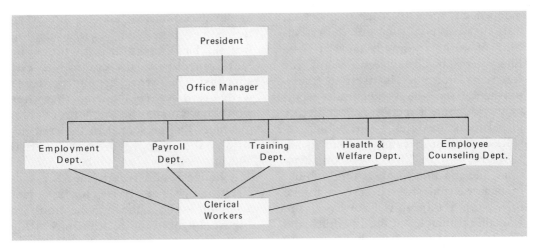

Fig. 3-3
Functional Organization Applied to the Office

middle managers and supervisors. As a result, they are unable to tend to all matters requiring their personal attention. Usually there is little coordination among departments as each department is concerned chiefly with its own work.

The line form of organization is found in governmental agencies, in military organizations, and in some business firms. There are relatively few business offices that follow a "pure" line organization, but within large firms some phases of work may be developed on a line organization plan.

Functional Organization

The concept of *functional organization* was originally developed by Frederick W. Taylor to provide for specialized skills at the supervisory level in the plant.[15] To handle the mental and clerical aspects of production, a clerical force consisting of a time and cost clerk, an instruction card clerk, an order of work and route clerk, and a shop disciplinarian was provided. The objective of functional organization was to provide for specialists at the supervisory level who would carry out each of the diverse duties of the supervisor's position in the line organization. If applied to the office, the functional form might appear as shown in Figure 3-3. All matters pertaining to employment would be handled by the employment department; all payroll work, by the payroll department; all training and orientation, by the training department; all health, welfare, and morale problems, by the health and welfare department; and all employee counseling, by the counseling department.

In the functional form of organization, each supervisor grows in an individual specialty and devotes time to only one phase of work. Such specialization provides for increased efficiency, since the workers are given expert and skilled supervisory attention. However, with the development of so many kinds of

[15]Taylor's contributions to the classical school of management thought are described in Chapter 1. From 1880 through 1890, Taylor formulated fundamental principles, called duties of management, that challenged the traditional methods of management. See Frederick W. Taylor, *Scientific Management* (New York: Harper & Bros., 1947).

independent specialists, the overspecialization causes confusion due to overlapping of authority and a lack of fixed lines of responsibility. As a result, the functional form lends itself to "buck passing." Since the workers must report to two or more supervisors, conflicting instructions are often given, which results in friction. Because of all its disadvantages, a "pure" functional organization, like the line form, is rarely found in business today. As described in the following paragraphs, however, the workable principles of the line form and the functional form have been brought together in the commonly used line-and-staff form of organization.

Line-and-Staff Organization

In a *line-and-staff organization*, near the top management level of a business firm, policies and practices are carried out on a line plan. Further down the line of authority and responsibility, the work is carried out on a functional basis, department by department. The staff feature emerges when a group of experts assist management as advisers to all the various departments. In many concerns the office manager becomes a functional officer covering certain business activities but acts as a staff officer to many other functional departments by advising on matters such as records management, word processing, and other office services that may be performed in other departments.

As shown in the partial line-and-staff organization chart in Figure 3-4 on the next page, there is a clear-cut flow of authority and responsibility from the top to the bottom of the organization. Operating efficiency through specialization is achieved since middle managers, such as the assistant controller, directly control the employees under them and

are held responsible for specific activities. Supervisors, such as the head of office services, report through the assistant controller to the controller. The supervisors, however, are not burdened with all the varied duties that they would have under the line form of organization. The personnel in the staff positions shown in Figure 3-4 (internal auditing, systems and methods, personnel, budgets, and reports) serve as advisers and provide services for line managers throughout the organization. (In Figure 3-4 only the relationship of the staff positions to the controller is illustrated.)

An *assistant-to*, serving as a personal assistant to his or her chief, is often found in many firms. The assistant-to the president, as shown in Figure 3-4, is a form of staff authority, while the assistant manager, such as the assistant controller, is part of the line. The duties of the assistant-to vary widely from one firm to another and may vary from time to time within the same company. Usually the assistant-to has no specific function to perform and the duties vary with the assignment at hand. No line authority is associated specifically with the position since authority is granted only for the completion of each individual assignment. The assistant-to does not act in his or her own behalf, but as a personal representative of his or her superior.

Traditionally staff officers do not give orders directly to line workers nor do they ordinarily have the authority to put their recommendations into action. The authority and responsibility for executing operations rest with the line officers. Today, however, as a result of the increased complexity of business operations and the development of new concepts in technology and the behavioral

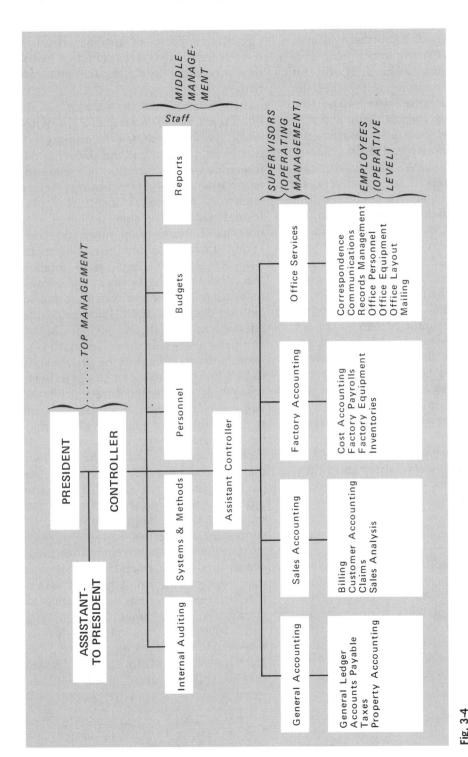

Fig. 3-4
Partial Line-and-Staff Organization

sciences, the traditional distinction between line and staff has become blurred in many firms. Danger arises when specialists are added to the staff without any clear understanding of how their activities interact with those of the line personnel. Disagreements arise and friction occurs when staff departments usurp line authority and exert this authority over individuals and departments in line positions. Line managers, in turn, hesitate to accept accountability and abdicate their authority. It should be remembered, however, that the line is a user of the services rendered by staff personnel, whose job is to make the line operations more productive at less cost. Questioning whether the line and staff is an outmoded concept, James L. Hayes, the president of the American Management Associations, has stated: "Elimination of the distinction between line and staff in no way lessens the importance of the traditional staff person — on the contrary, it gives real meaning and recognition to the quality of his work."[16]

Alternatives to the duality of the line-and-staff concept, which inherently creates problems of interpersonal relationships, are presented in the following section.

Committee Organization

With the growth of larger and more complex enterprises the need for interaction and coordination among personnel at all levels has increased. As a result, "group executives" or "plural executives," whose authority is not always clearly defined, have emerged.[17] Such a committee form of organization is usually employed in conjunction with, or as a modification of, the line-and-staff plan.

Experience has shown that people often react more favorably to a group decision than to the dictatorial authority of one person. Through the participative interaction of the members of the group, committee management brings better teamwork and makes supervisory personnel think of the company more as a unit than in terms of their own individual departments. Committee management helps develop broader views to improve the conduct of the business, to coordinate the programs and activities, and to develop decisions and discuss problems affecting more than one segment of the company's organization. In many instances the judgment of the group tends to be better than that of a single individual. As a result of pooling the knowledge and experience of all members on the committee, any plans developed may be executed more easily since all members participated in the development of the plans. Because of having participated in the decision-making process, committee members are further motivated to see the plan through to its successful completion.

On the other hand, committee management is slower in reaching decisions than one person, but it has the advantage of eliminating snap judgments. In committee management the majority rules, and thus no one individual is fully responsible for the decisions made. This leads to the disadvantages of divided responsibility, and oftentimes, a

---

[16]James L. Hayes, "Line and Staff: An Outmoded Concept?" *Management News* (October, 1973), p. 4.

[17]Ambrose Klotz, "Line and Staff Today: We Need to Redefine Their Roles," *Administrative Management* (March, 1968), p. 22.

compromise decision that may not be of the best quality. Also, the use of committees requires many group meetings that can consume much valuable time in doing little more than displaying ignorance and exchanging prejudices. Successful committee organization results when companies do not put before the committee those problems that should be handled by individual executives.

Sometimes the committee organization is expanded by the addition of a second echelon known as a *management council*, which enables as many of the supervisory personnel as possible to participate. The management council can be effective in handling specific problems pertaining to individual departments and in helping to sponsor new ideas and theories for consideration by top management. Other types of committee management found are: (1) the various executive and operational *work groups* that are formed to obtain coordination among the primary functions of the firm, (2) *task forces* consisting of representatives of several functions to handle interfunctional problems, (3) *staff groups* whose primary purpose is to integrate a basic management activity such as planning within the firm, and (4) *program* or *project management* wherein each individual project is established as a distinct organizational element with a manager who integrates the functional groups into one operating unit to handle the various phases of the project.

Informal Organization

A wonderful plan of organization can be wrecked by a poor office administrator, and a poor organization plan may be made effective by a top-rate office manager. The manager must keep in mind the value to be gained from cultivating those working relationships among people in the firm which do not appear on the organization chart — those relationships that make up the *informal* or *unwritten organization*. No organization chart can portray the infinite person-to-person relationships that make up an informal organization, and no company can exist without the interaction of people at all levels. The administrator must become acquainted with and work through those individuals who have the ability to help or to impede work even though their names or positions do not appear on the company's organization chart. Often an informal channel is more effective and efficient than the formal line in passing information, obtaining feedback, solving problems, and revising procedures.

Because the informal organization is an ever-shifting and undefined structure, it is vulnerable to expediency, manipulation, and opportunity.[18] Among the abuses of informal organization are those vertical abuses that occur when the appropriate lines of authority and communication, up and down the organizational chain, are ignored or distorted. For example, vertical abuse occurs when a top-ranking executive, such as the vice-president of finance, makes direct contact with and gives orders to someone far down the line of authority, such as a programmer, by skipping the intervening layer of supervision, the manager of the data processing division. With the manager possibly not having knowledge of the contact and the

---

[18]Raymond F. Valentine, "The Pitfalls of Informal Organization," *Introduction to Business, A Contemporary Reader*, edited by Joel J. Lerner (Englewood Cliffs: Prentice-Hall, 1969), p. 88.

assignment of work given to the programmer, the responsibility of the manager deteriorates. Other abuses occur when two or more workers informally agree not to comply with an official pronouncement on policy or procedure. Substantial harm can result, and company policy tends to be seriously distorted or mishandled.

THE ORGANIZATION CHART

Organization charts, such as those illustrated in this chapter, present graphically the line of authority, the span of control, and the responsibility for work in each function or department with as much detail as possible. Oftentimes several charts may be necessary to give a complete and intelligent guide to company organization. Organization charts are an important tool of management in indicating the flow of work and the responsibility for its achievement. Merely because a chart is in existence, however, is no assurance that there is good organization. Since they show only the present structure, with little regard for tomorrow or the day after, many charts quickly become obsolete. Traditional organization charts are also criticized because they show only the formal relationships within a firm and ignore the informal organizational interrelationships.[19]

Figure 3-5 on the next page presents ten suggestions for preparing organiza-

tion charts.[20] These suggestions are not hard-and-fast rules, and they should be modified when the occasion demands. Often the organization chart is presented in the *organization manual*, which explains in narrative form the organization, duties, and responsibilities of the departments and their respective divisions.

CENTRALIZED vs. DECENTRALIZED ORGANIZATION

Theoretically, centralizing the office work is desirable because it fixes responsibility under a capable manager, avoids duplication, and permits better supervision with a more even distribution of the individual work load. The nature of office work often does not permit such an acceptable theory, however, for office work does not permit such a clearly defined function as production or distribution. Office work is made up of many diverse services such as communications, correspondence, records management, reproduction, mailing, and accounting. Furthermore, many firms have plants and branch offices located throughout the country and abroad.

The operations of branch offices vary with different firms. In many firms the branch office is merely a branch sales office under the direction of a branch sales manager who has as much clerical and accounting assistance as necessary. Under this arrangement the office manager in the home office provides little in the way of guidance and control, except perhaps to issue manuals or instruction sheets for certain clerical procedures. The rest of the work is

---

[19]William L. Brockhaus, "Planning for Change with Organization Charts," *Business Horizons* (April, 1974), pp. 47–51. The development of pro forma organization charts as a means of meeting the criticisms of traditional organizational charting is presented in this article, which describes how organization charts may be used to their maximum as instruments of company change and policy.

---

[20]Henry L. Sisk, *Management and Organization* (3d ed; Concinnati: South-Western Publishing Co., 1977), p. 265.

1. Identify the chart fully showing the name of the company, date of preparation, and title of person or name of department responsible for preparation. If the chart is for one division of the company only, include such information as part of the title.

2. Use rectangular boxes to show either an organizational unit or a person. Plural executives and other committees occupy one box.

3. The vertical placement of the boxes shows relative positions in the organizational hierarchy; however, due to space limitations, line units are frequently shown one level below staff units. (See Figure 3-4.)

4. Any given horizontal row of boxes should be of the same size and should include only those positions having the same organizational rank.

5. Vertical and horizontal solid lines are used to show the flow of the line of authority.

6. If necessary, use dotted or broken lines to show the flow of functional authority.

7. Lines of authority enter at the top center of a box and leave at the bottom center; they do not run through the box. Exception: the line of authority to a staff assistant or an assistant-to may enter the side of the box. (See Figure 3-4.)

8. The title of each position should be placed in the box. The title should be descriptive and show function. For example, vice-president is not sufficient as it does not show function. The functional area, e.g., manufacturing, should be included even though it is not a part of the official title. Titles should be consistent; if necessary, revise titles so they are both consistent and descriptive.

9. Include the name of the person currently holding the position unless personnel turnover is so great that revision of the chart becomes unduly burdensome.

10. Keep the chart as simple as possible; include a legend if necessary to explain any special notations. When preparing a separate chart for an organizational unit, include the superior to whom the unit reports.

Fig. 3-5
Suggestions for Preparing an Organization Chart

ordinarily directed by the branch sales manager. Some branches are established on a somewhat autonomous basis with each branch acting like a separate unit. In such a branch the office manager is faced with the same duties and responsibilities as any other office manager. In some firms there is a greater volume of office work than in others. For example, in life insurance companies, banks, and brokerage firms, the amount of information processing looms greater than in a manufacturing or a retail organization. With all the foregoing variables in mind, the question of centralized versus decentralized authority tends to become an individual problem for each firm.

One-Location Operations

Where all office work is confined to one location or building, it is possible to centralize the bulk of the clerical work under a capable, experienced, and well-trained manager who has assistants supervising the various office services. In such cases it is possible to maintain a word processing center, which uses the latest and most efficient dictating and transcribing equipment. Also, centralized filing, mailing, and reproduction departments may be established. These services can then be provided more expertly, at less cost, and with better supervision. There may still be some decentralized office work performed by executive secretaries and others who maintain personal or confidential files.

An example of centralization found in some offices is the *satellite administrative services center* or *substation*. The substation is a compact work station that handles much paperwork and many clerical activities that are usually scattered throughout a number of offices. One of the major objectives of such a substation is the handling of a growing work load with the same number of office workers. With the right person in charge, the center provides an organization with higher quality and lower cost services than conventional centralized services.[21] The administrative services substation, under centralized direction and control, links together the work stations in close proximity to the needs of the users of office services. A typical satellite services substation provides such administrative services as stationery and supplies, quick reproduction of copies,

word processing, filing, records management, mail and communications, library, and information retrieval. A newly established substation may be organized to supply a minimum number of local administrative services such as mail, stationery supplies, and fast copies in a defined area that serves operations in close proximity. As the substation proves successful in meeting the needs of the users, additional services may be provided in a sort of a building-block plan. Ideally all the substations are linked with other substations, with the central services unit, and with the computer information center.

Multilocation Operations

When a firm maintains plants and offices in several locations, many of the office services are often decentralized to permit more efficient operations. As a result, a certain amount of duplication of supervision and investment in equipment occurs, and the position of the office manager may become less responsible. However, when the office services are decentralized because of multilocation operations, the accounting work is often removed from the office manager's authority and centralized in one location such as the home office. This has been made possible by better telecommunications systems, as discussed in Chapter 8. Centralizing the accounting function is not only less costly but also more efficient. The work is done more accurately; and by means of more timely reports, management can make better use of the accounting and statistical information.

---

[21]"Satellite Administrative Service Centers," *Administrative Management*(February, 1969), pp. 26–28.

1. Define the two functions of management, planning and organizing.

2. For what reasons are policies developed by a business firm?

3. What steps should be taken by each level of management as it approaches its organizational responsibility?

4. Explain how a business organization may be compared with a system of the human body.

5. What conditions must be met in the organization for the principle of unity of functions to operate effectively?

6. Which one of the functions of business — production, distribution, finance, and personnel — represents the keynote to good office organization? Why?

7. (a) Distinguish between authority and responsibility.
(b) What is the relationship of accountability to responsibility?

8. Why should an office worker receive orders from and be responsible to only one supervisor?

9. What factors should be taken into consideration when determining the office manager's limits of span of control?

10. What are the advantages and the disadvantages of the line form of organization?

11. Explain why the functional form of organization lends itself to "buck passing."

12. (a) Describe briefly the line-and-staff form of organization.
(b) In this form of organization is the position of office manager ordinarily classified as line or staff?

13. What are the differences between the position of an assistant-to and that of an assistant manager?

14. What advantages and disadvantages are associated with committee management?

15. (a) What is informal organization?
(b) What are some of the abuses to which informal organization is exposed?

16. How does the organization chart serve as an important tool of management to the administrative office manager?

17. Describe how office services are provided in a satellite administrative services center.

1. Does Parkinson's law have greater application in office work than in factory operations? Why?

2. What effect does each of the following have on the organizational planning for office work?
a. Geographic decentralization of the office services.
b. Automated office systems and procedures.

3. Lt. Col. L. F. Urwick, founder of a management counsulting firm, has observed that in business no one is ever quite certain of the status of the assistant-to and this very uncertainty breeds resentment. What can management do to overcome this uncertainty and provide for efficient operations in the staff position of assistant-to?

4. Explain the significance of the following statement when applied to office administration: "Too much harmony in business operations is not always evidence of efficient business operations."

5. How do policies of "promoting from within" and "the use and training of understudies" affect office organization and administration?

6. Why are levels of management important in planning an organization? What effect do levels of management have on the functional phase of office organization?

7. It has been observed that the fundamental problem with organizations today is the absence of the employees' all-important feelings of belonging to a worthwhile enterprise where they can grow and contribute, where they can feel they are part of a cause to which they can dedicate their talents and energies. What is your reaction to this concept of motivation? How do you account for this feeling on the part of many of today's workers?

8. Ken Koerber, supervisor of the records management center, has tried on several occasions during the past three months to make improvements in the filing methods. Whenever he suggests changes to his superior, his recommendations are ignored or Koerber is stymied by the remark, "It has always been done this way, and your suggestions have been tried before without success." Koerber feels this is not a satisfactory answer and would like to bypass his superior and go to a higher level of authority for approval of his ideas. Discuss how you feel Koerber's problem should be resolved.

9. "The delegation of decision making, which is sometimes known as decentralization, is a current fad. Many believe that all problems would apparently dissolve if only the boss would delegate and decentralize." What are your reactions to these comments made by the chairman of the board of a large insurance company?

10. Sarah Taylor, administrative manager of office services for an electronics company, finds herself involved in many operational details even though she does everything that is necessary for delegating responsibility. In spite of defining authority, delegating to competent people, spelling out the delegation, keeping control, and coaching, she is still burdened with a mass of detailed work. What reasons can you advance for Taylor's overinvolvement in details in her daily work?

11. Juarez, Inc., has recently undertaken some organizational changes. A junior board of directors, consisting of the middle managers of the various operating departments, was established. Membership on the junior board is carefully determined by the executive committee of the regular board of directors. Membership of the junior board is on

a rotating basis, and each member serves a one-year term. The junior board is made up of 15 members who meet every two weeks, at which time the following problems are considered:

a. Mechanization and automation of various operations.
b. Salary schedules and employee benefits.
c. Sales and marketing ideas.
d. Quality and service control of sales.
e. Business expansion, working conditions, and employee grievances.

Discuss the advantages and disadvantages of such an organizational plan and the relationship between the participative and the conceptual action of authority, responsibility, and accountability.

PRACTICAL OFFICE MANAGEMENT CASES

Case 3-1   Reorganizing the Administrative Services Function

The Glen Cove Electronics Company started as a small postwar organization interested in the improvement of telecommunications devices. Over the past 30 years the firm has expanded steadily and recently has received several large orders from the government for satellite components. The office expansion that has taken place has been under three vice-presidents, each of whom is in charge of one of the functions of manufacturing, marketing, and finance. No one person in the company has been assigned the responsibility for administrative services.

The functional vice-presidents maintain their own filing, stenographic, mailing, and duplicating departments. Supervisors are in charge of the functional activities under the headings of manufacturing, marketing, and finance. Part of the organization chart indicates that there are supervisors in charge of purchasing, receiving, storing, accounts payable, factory payroll, cost accounting, and shipping. Under the heading of marketing there are supervisors in charge of sales, advertising, credit, and accounts receivable. Under the direction of the vice-president in charge of finance are financial accounting, taxes, governmental reports, and office payroll.

Many of the supervisors of these activities have been shifted into supervisory positions with little knowledge of systems or methods. The supervisors are hard pressed to get out the work because of inefficiency, lack of knowledge, and needless duplication of records and work. Office equipment had been ordered from time to time and placed where it was thought it would be used later.

The president of the company, J. W. Winston, has recently been overwhelmed by the difficulty in obtaining information. Whenever information is wanted, several different sources must be contacted, and much time is wasted in locating the information. Winston is also beginning to notice idle equipment in the offices and delay in the preparation of certain operating reports.

Winston has recently had a conference with the three vice-presidents in charge of manufacturing, marketing, and finance and has indicated dissatisfaction. The three executives feel they cannot change any of their work routines or give up any of their present personnel.

Winston feels that something must be done in the interest of a more efficient organization and lower costs. You have been called upon to find out how it might be possible to reorganize the office services so that a better utilization of present personnel and equipment might achieve the objectives of greater and faster output and reduced costs. You are asked to prepare a report, including a chart showing the reorganization of the work in this concern, and to indicate the changes in the organization that you would make. (Since many of the details of this concern are not given, it will be necessary to assume conditions prevalent in most manufacturing concerns having an office staff of 60 persons.)

Case 3-2   Preparing an Organization Chart of the Administrative Office Management Function

You have just accepted the position of administrative office manager of the Holt Manufacturing Company, which has 120 office employees. The company has planned to centralize as many of the office services as possible and develop a staff department whose sole job will be to study and improve office systems and procedures. In addition, it is your plan to organize the work so that it will be properly supervised and controlled. As administrative office manager in charge of all office services, you report to the treasurer of the company, who in turn reports directly to the president.

The proposed plan of supervision includes the following personnel: (The estimated number of employees needed in each department, including the supervisor or the officer of that department, is given in parentheses.)

     a. Jean Sardi, assistant administrative office manager, handles office space, office equipment, and reports. (19)

     b. Roberta Willard, chief accountant, in charge of general accounting, budgeting, and data processing. (15)

     c. Richard Jarvis, assistant personnel manager, handles the factory personnel problems. Jarvis reports to the personnel director, Wilma O'Keeffe who, in her staff position, reports directly to the president. (12)

     d. Melina Sotakos, assistant to the president, handles all legal affairs. (4)

     e. Charles Greene, in charge of office systems and procedures, a staff position. (4)

f. Robert Ahlert, in charge of internal auditing, a staff position. Ahlert has the title of auditor. (5)

g. Anita Montez, supervisor, directs the word processing center. (15)

h. Carl Mann, supervisor, directs the filing and mailing departments. (25)

i. George Russell, supervisor, is responsible for office communications, supplies, and reproduction services. (20)

On the basis of the above information, you are asked to prepare a partial organization chart showing the line-and-staff arrangements.

1. In this chart below each person's title, place the name of the person responsible for the direction or supervision of the work. Under each supervisor's name indicate some of the activities that will be directed by that person.

2. Prepare a brief explanation of the line-and-staff authority as outlined on your chart.

3. Estimate the weekly cost of office salaries of all employees except the president, assistant-to the president, and the treasurer. Assume an average salary of $160 a week for the 110 clerical office workers; for the 10 supervisors and officers, assume a salary commensurate with the responsibilities of their positions. (Current salaries for office personnel may be obtained from sources such as: "Middle Management Salary Survey" and "Office Salaries Directory for United States and Canada" prepared by the Administrative Management Society; "Annual National Survey of Professional, Administrative, Technical, and Clerical Compensation" prepared by the Bureau of Labor Statistics; and research studies undertaken by *Administrative Management* and *Nation's Business*.)

4. Assume that office salaries represent five percent of gross sales. What would you estimate to be the minimum weekly sales volume required to justify the cost of this office work?

Chapter 4   **SPACE MANAGEMENT
IN THE OFFICE**

In all cities the search for more office space for housing a growing clerical work force continues unabated. Skyrocketing costs of such space, increased costs of labor for maintenance and cleaning, and the effort to solve production and status problems of employees through a better working environment are all factors that provide motivation for giving more attention to managing office space.

The space available for performing office work constitutes the "geography" of the office. Until recently the term "office layout" was usually used to categorize discussions as to how office space can be effectively utilized. Newer concepts with respect to space allocation for office work have led to substituting the term "space management" for "office layout." To understand newer concepts of space management, it is essential to recall that the function of the office is to process information. In the office, information flows in a manner like the flow of materials in a factory. In each there are routes or aisles of transport, in each the transportation time must be held to a minimum, and in each a strong need exists to keep the number of work stations for the loading and unloading of information (or materials) to a minimum without sacrificing the accessibility of the service or the product. Regardless of the type of product (a factory product, a paper product, or simply oral communication), how space is planned and utilized affects the efficiency and productivity of the workers.

One should also consider as valid the traditional concept of the office as a service center of the firm. Robert Propst, president of Herman Miller Research Corporation and a qualified critic of the office function, suggests that the traditional purpose of the office was "to provide an environment that was conducive to work on the part of the individual."[1] That office, he believes, should grow with and be an extension of the individual and the work he or she performs.

The need to control space carefully is critical if a new office building is being planned, an old building is being renovated, or the layout of a present building is being analyzed with a view toward reshuffling people, furniture, and equipment. The planning of a new office building or the renovation of an old building requires careful study to obtain the most efficient use of space. In this chapter the objectives and principles of space management are discussed, and applications of good layout are examined and illustrated.

OBJECTIVES OF SPACE MANAGEMENT IN THE OFFICE

Space management in the office involves the physical features of the office, especially those relating to the design of the building (such as window locations, elevators, and the plumbing, heating, and electrical systems); the needs of the organization including departmental

---

[1]*Business Equipment Manufacturers Association News*, November 3, 1969, p. 11.

locations, special facilities such as reference services, the computer installation, and executive office requirements; the work being performed; the nature of and the number of employees presently working as well as the number contemplated in the future; and the equipment and the furniture required to complete the work assigned.

Space management in the office has these specific objectives:

1. To provide sufficient office space and to maximize its use.
2. To assure employees as well as customers and the general public of comfort and convenience.
3. To develop work flows that are effective and low in cost.
4. To design work stations that are conducive to good working methods and that are in keeping with the work-flow system.
5. To coordinate the utilization of space with all related environmental factors (such as heat, light, color, and noise control).
6. To permit flexibility in layout for rearrangement of work stations and for expansion or contraction of space needs.
7. To consider carefully the interpersonal communication needs of the office staff in providing an environment free of communication barriers.
8. To review periodically all aspects of the space management program and make improvements when necessary.

The principles of space management were developed with these objectives in mind. The remaining sections of this chapter use these objectives as a frame of reference.

THE PHYSICAL OFFICE: GEOGRAPHY OF THE SYSTEM

Planning and organizing an efficient, economical space management program require careful and continuous study. If one considers simply the growth in the annual average white-collar employment (a gain of 489,000 from 1974 to 1975[2]) and the provision of space for this huge work force, the enormity of the space management problem is clear. In fact, in most corporations the increase in office personnel still ranges from 4 to 7 percent annually.[3]

When occupying a new building or renovating an existing building, management finds it advisable to consult reliable space planners and interior designers. Such specialists make recommendations based upon a complete assessment of economic, efficiency, and esthetic or appearance factors. Within the firm a team approach is normally required to help plan and approve the new office design. Working with the architect are the systems analysts, industrial engineers, department heads, industrial psychologists, and industrial relations personnel. The administrative office manager should, of course, play a significant role in planning and outlining the work-flow needs of the office.

In planning a new office building, generally the essential physical features, such as supporting pillars, elevators, rest rooms, lockers, and cafeteria, can be located where they are most desirable. More frequently, however, the firm is moving into a new location in an existing building where these physical features must be accepted as they are. Planning the arrangement of departments and equipment and work flows, therefore, must be carried on around the present location of these fixed factors. Such

---

[2]*Monthly Labor Review* (September, 1976), p. 73.

[3]Hans J. Lorenzen, "The Office Landscape: A Management Tool," *Journal of Systems Management* (October, 1969), p. 14.

an approach also typifies the firm that is making changes in its space management plan in its present location.

One technique of planning long-range projects, such as a new office layout, uses the Gantt Project Planning Chart. The underlying principle of a Gantt chart is that the work planned and the work done are shown in the same space in their relation to each other and to time. This chart, developed by Henry Laurence Gantt early in this century, has been viewed as one of the most widely recognized planning methods.[4] In the basic Gantt chart shown in Figure 4-1, project activities are listed along the left margin from top to bottom in sequence of the planned activity. To the right of the title are frames indicating the time required to complete the project. Horizontal bars drawn next to each activity, and under the appropriate time frame, make it easy to visualize the planned starting date, duration, and planned completion date. Across from the first activity, the top bar indicates planned performance time; the second bar shows actual performance time. A vertical data line signifies that the project has been updated.

Other long-range planning techniques, such as the Critical Path Method (CPM) and Program Evaluation and Review Technique (PERT), are discussed in Chapter 23.

ORGANIZATIONAL NEEDS IN SPACE MANAGEMENT

The organization of an office usually influences its layout. In many large firms, such as pharmaceuticals, industrial chemicals, and agricultural chemicals, the plant and office locations are separated. Many of these firms, too, have branch offices that are decentralized geographically. Probably the most common type of organization, especially for small offices, is a departmental plan arranged according to the functions of purchasing, marketing, accounting, credit, and administrative services.

Analyzing Space Needs

In analyzing and planning the best utilization of office space, the following factors must be considered: the interrelationships existing among departments, the number of persons located in each department, the type and flow of information-processing work, and the need for private offices. One basic principle must be observed — the space plan must follow work flows or work functions rather than preferences of personnel or purely esthetic considerations.

In analyzing the personnel and space needs at regularly scheduled intervals, a form such as that shown in Figure 4-2 may be used. The number of personnel needed in each of the various kinds of office space is estimated, along with the square footage for each of the special work centers and storage areas. Space guidelines, such as those presented later in this chapter, are used to assign a predetermined number of square feet to each of the various kinds of office

---

[4]Gantt, along with Frederick W. Taylor (see Chapter 1, page 11), pioneered in the field of scientific management. In 1877 Gantt joined Taylor in his experiments to raise productivity and decrease costs at the Midvale Steel Works in Philadelphia. Gantt felt that a scientific determination of the best and fastest method for each piece of work was still required but no longer would this be the ultimate aim of scientific management. More and more Gantt became convinced that what counted were employee morale and motivation. In his system of management was the idea that, "each man has assigned to him the part he can do best, and . . . he does it with pride and joy to the best of his ability."

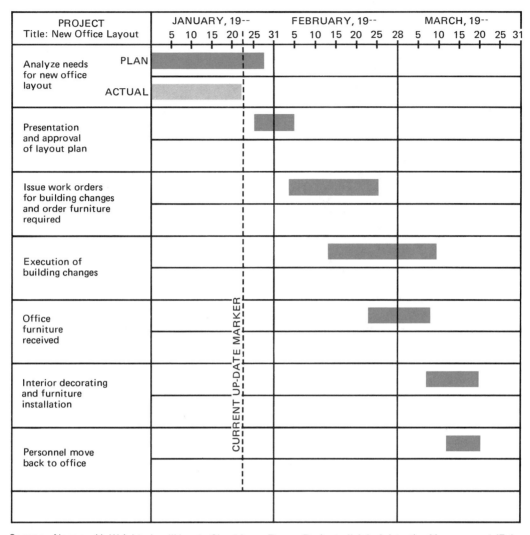

Source: Norman H. Wright, Jr., "How to Chart Long-Range Projects," *Administrative Management* (February, 1975), p. 46.

Fig. 4-1
Gantt Chart Planning Method for a New Office Layout

work needed. With the addition of a fixed percentage of aisle space, the total square feet needed for the department or cost center may be obtained. After the head of each department has undertaken annually such an analysis, possibly as part of the budget preparation, a summary of all analyses can be prepared to guide the firm in estimating its total future space needs.

Work Flow

In an office, *work flow* is the movement of information between superiors and subordinates or laterally among

ANALYSIS OF
PERSONNEL AND SPACE NEEDS

Department or Cost Center _____

Date _____

	Number of Personnel Needed						
	1978	1979	1980	1981	1985	1990	Remarks
Office Space :							
Officers, managers, department heads							
Private offices							
Open offices							
Administrative/executive secretaries							
Other_____							

	Square Feet Needed						
Special Work Centers :							
Conference room							
Training room							
Reference services							
Reception center							
Data processing center							
Switchboard							
Mail room							
Word processing center							
Other_____							
Storage Areas :							
Open-shelf filing							
5-drawer file cabinets							
Store rooms (supplies, etc.)							
Vault							
Storage (inactive files)							
Other_____							

Fig. 4-2
Form Used in Analyzing Personnel and Space Needs

workers at the same level. An optimum layout is not derived simply from a quick overview of an office operation; rather it emerges slowly from an intensive analysis of information flows. Involved is a study of the division of labor, the nature and frequency of information-processing documents, and the distribution of documents within and, where applicable, outside the firm. The frequency and quantity of documents processed, the number of work stations involved, and the total cycle time of each process should be measured.

Many offices function around a key (or source) document that contains the basic information, and most of the other records are offshoots of the key document. In an insurance company this document is an application for insurance; in an employment office, an application for work; and in a wholesale house, a customer's order. In studying information flows, it is necessary to trace the movement of each key document or set of documents from the time it enters the office until the time it is completely processed. From this study the work flow (with connecting functions along the way) can be plotted, and in this way the entire office function can be patterned. Since this processing takes place primarily among people, major emphasis should be given to the layout of each work station in the total work flow. However, computers and other data processing machines assist the workers to an increasing degree in the exchange of information. The interaction of all such components must be considered in an effort to create a true information processing center.

Perhaps the most common method of analyzing information and communication flows is to examine the organization chart. In the chart illustrated in Figure 4-3 on page 78, the organization is depicted as a matrix. The most frequent communications, shown by the thick lines, are often the informal channels, as discussed in Chapter 3. These communications channels are not shown formally on the organization chart but must be disclosed through systems studies of information flow. In space-planning programs interviews are usually conducted by asking the question "Who communicates with whom?" Figure 4-3 shows a top executive (such as a president), a subordinate line with three vice-presidents, followed by six equal-level positions of, perhaps, department supervisors. Information flows into and out of each box. Such hidden processes of information exchange must be identified before a sound space management program can be completed.[5]

When office work flow is analyzed for efficiency, it will be found that the flow is most effective when it is continuous — that is, when intermittent storage stops are eliminated. Therefore, processing time at each work station must be identified and verified, transport time between work stations eliminated or reduced, and storage time decreased, if not omitted. A more extensive discussion of work flow and work efficiency is found in Chapter 17.

Space Planning by Function

Although computers and other automated processing methods have caused changes in organizational patterns, the basic organizational unit of specialized functions continues to be the department. The conventional departmental layout is characterized by isolated groups and wall barriers that uniformly

---

[5]Lorenzen, *op. cit.*, p. 15.

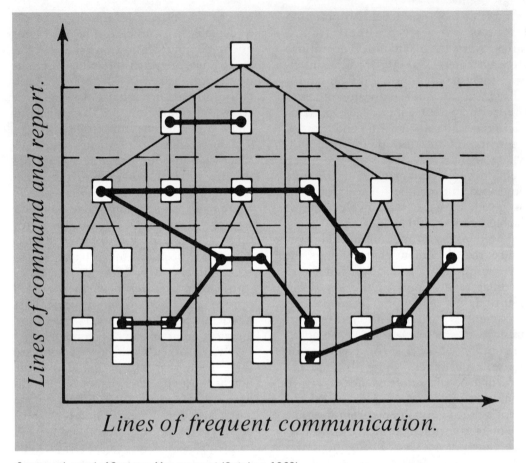

Source: *Journal of Systems Management* (October, 1969).

Fig. 4-3
Main Communication Flows in the Organization

enclose areas. Critics of this layout style suggest that it prevents or hinders interaction and communication and denies the existence of interdepartmental work flow. To overcome the criticisms of the conventional layout plan, a relatively new concept — the office landscape — has emerged. Each of these styles of layout is described in the following paragraphs.

The Department. Departments should be arranged so that the work flow proceeds in an uninterrupted man-

ner and passes through as few hands as possible. The planning of space will necessarily require a study of the office systems and procedures, the arrangement of furniture and equipment, and, of course, the personnel.

Certain principles should be followed in providing a layout for departments. Departments with constant or frequent contact with the public should be located near the reception area or have direct access to the corridors in order to minimize the traffic through

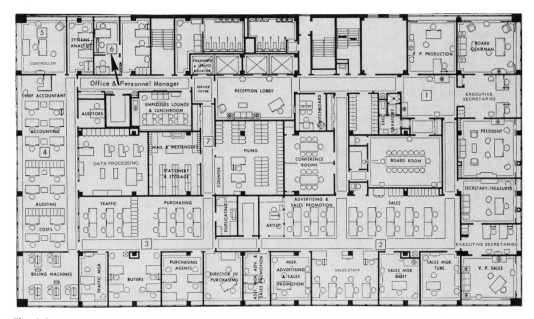

Fig. 4-4
How Departments are Located in a Conventional Office Layout

open working areas. For example, the personnel and the purchasing departments have frequent contact with outside business representatives and should be located near the reception area. Operating departments, such as sales, should be near the executive and administrative area, whereas the controller's department may be remote from the executive area.

The following description and Figure 4-4 indicate how departments are located in one conventional office layout:[6]

1. Executive Suite. This area is isolated at one end of the offices for maximum privacy. Note that it is self-contained, has its own access corridor, and is grouped around its own foyer.

2. Sales Department. Also relatively self-contained, it is close to the conference rooms for sales meetings, has adequate windows for highly paid personnel, and has its own access corridor close to the executive suite.

3. Purchasing Department. This has fairly close contact with sales at the executive level. Due to considerable outside traffic, it has its own corridor to the reception area. This department uses duplicating facilities heavily. The traffic department reports to the director of purchasing.

4. Accounting Department. Note that this area is provided with maximum window space for employees doing close and tedious work. Adjacent to the data processing center, the accounting department uses at least half of the center's services. There is space for its own filing cabinets, frequently and exclusively referred to, and it is relatively isolated for minimum distraction. Located at the extreme end of

---

[6]Taken with permission of *Management Magazines, Inc.*, from *Integrated Office* (Fall, 1953), p. 16.

the office, it has the least contact with other departments.

5. Controller. An important executive, the controller is given a corner office. Typically, this executive is in charge of the accounting and data processing operations and supervises the office and personnel managers. While the controller has relatively close contact with the "policy-making" personnel in the executive suite, it is more important to be near the departments reporting directly to him or her.

6. Office and Personnel Department. In addition to being in charge of "housekeeping," this department originates forms and interviews and manages personnel. Since it has heavy traffic from the outside, it is close to the reception area. Since mail deliveries, job applicants, and personnel with individual problems channel through the department, it is located near the service areas.

The Office Landscape. The office landscape concept of space planning began in Germany, where it is called *Bürolandschaft*. The *office landscape*, also referred to as the *open plan* or *free flow*, brings together all the functional, behavioral, and technical factors to determine the layout of individual work centers, work groups, and departments. This layout, illustrated in Figure 4-5, is characterized by open space, free of the conventional walls and corridors. Work stations are located by rearranging movable elements such as desks, chairs, screens, book shelves, files, and planters without changing fixed installations (light fixtures, air-conditioning outlets, partitions, or floor coverings). Each individual grouping of work stations is arranged, without regard to windows or other conventional constraints, in a nonuniform fashion dictated by natural lines of work flow and communications.

Since the office landscape is largely an open-plan model, there are normally no private offices. Privacy is provided by using movable, sound-absorbing screens and plants. The status of workers is determined more by their work assignments than by their locations. Upperechelon executives may have a larger amount of space, a different color of desk top, and possibly a circular table; but, beyond this, there are few visible signs of rank.

The open plan provides flexibility for layouts that shift as the work shifts. For example, when a project group is formed to tackle a specific problem, the team can be brought together in an open but clustered layout. When their work is completed, the team can disband, and the enclosing cluster of partitions, screens, and plants may be easily rearranged when a new team with new problems emerges. Within each cluster, the communication barriers are removed and environmental problems such as heating, air conditioning, and lighting are minimized.

In the open plan the amount of usable space, expressed as a percentage of the gross space available, is greater than in the conventional grid layout of row after row. In landscaped offices the utilizable space may run as high as 80 and 90 percent. For example, in Montgomery Ward's landscaped offices in Chicago, of the 606,500 square feet of gross floor space available, 87 percent, or 526,000 square feet, is available as net usable space.[7] In the landscaped office of the Administrative Services Building of Purdue University, the ratio of net assignable space to gross space is 79

---

[7]"The Design Is Total at This 'Office of the Year,'" *Administrative Management* (February, 1975), p. 22.

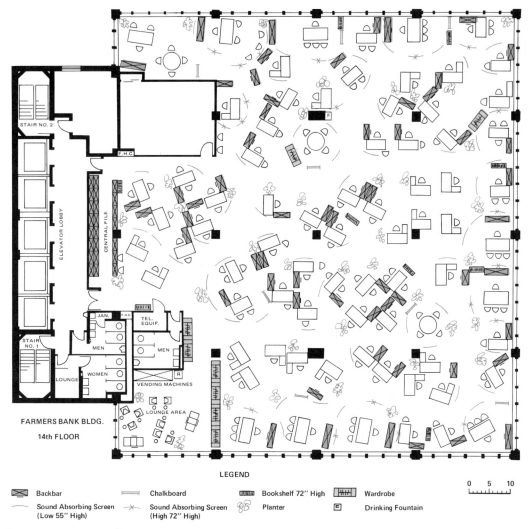

LEGEND

Backbar		Chalkboard		Bookshelf 72" High		Wardrobe
Sound Absorbing Screen (Low 55" High)		Sound Absorbing Screen (High 72" High)		Planter		Drinking Fountain

0   5   10

Source: Freon Products Division, E. I. du Pont de Nemours & Co.

Fig. 4-5

Office Landscape Space Plan of Working Groups Arranged According to Their Communication and Information-Flow Requirements

percent, or about 15 to 20 percent higher than in conventional buildings. The university considers this increased utilization of space the equivalent of a $1 million savings in construction costs.[8]

To determine how much savings accrue from open planning, the costs should be compared on a per-work-station basis with those of the conventional office plan. In spite of the increased costs of carpeting, acoustics control, and other environmental controls that accompany office landscaping, the users of open planning indicate that savings are

[8]"Landscaped Administration Building Wins 1st Award," *Administrative Management* (April, 1971), p. 23.

forthcoming. For example, John Hancock of Boston, in landscaping their home office of two million square feet, calculated a space savings of eight percent per person, which amounts to a total savings of $300,000. At du Pont, in Wilmington, Delaware, the landscaped offices were completely rearranged in one weekend for 36 cents a square foot, in comparison with $4.50 per square foot under a conventional layout. At the Port of New York Authority, landscaping enabled the planners to provide landscaped work stations costing $360 each in contrast to private offices costing $1,000 per work station.[9]

SPACE PLANNING IN FUNCTIONAL WORK CENTERS

Over the years the traditional image of the office has centered around the desk. This common piece of furniture has served as work surface, storage center, and conference and counseling aid. Recently, however, space specialists have intensively studied the work in offices and have developed new concepts and theories that weaken the hallowed images of the desk-centered office. With marked changes in office equipment through improved computing facilities, microfilm viewing, high-speed copying machines, and new communication services providing audible, graphic, digital, and written information, space-planning and work-flow patterns have changed to make the best possible use of all available facilities. This section discusses new space concepts that are built around the idea of work centers in the office.

---

[9]"Landscape: Revolution or Evolution?" *Modern Office Procedures* (October, 1970), p. 82.

Work Center Concept

The office is, more than anything else, a thinking place. Personnel must be placed at strategic locations for thinking — that is, for dealing with information from its collection through its transmission stages. In another sense the office may be considered as a place where work situations or tasks are generated. Related to these views is the recognition that most, if not all, office work centers around communication. In fact, behavioral scientists stress that better morale and more productivity can be expected if space planning makes adequate allowance for easy conversational exchange.

The basic unit of office space planning is the individual work station or work center where each employee performs the bulk of assigned responsibilities. When all the work stations are combined, whether departmentally or in some other functional sense, the total work place or group work center is the result. Consideration of both the individual and the group work center concepts is necessary to achieve the optimum use of office space.

Individual Work Center. With most office employment certain basic furniture and equipment at each work station are assigned. Such items as a desk or table for work surface and work storage, counters and shelves, files, machines, and seating facilities are normally required for each worker. With the exception of the one-person office, each work station must be designed so that it merges with the other work stations in the total working environment.

Group Work Center. No one work station exists by or for itself; rather it serves as one part of a larger group working toward a group goal. All the work centers, therefore, must be space-planned and coordinated to fit into a total work environment. An example of such an environment is illustrated in Figure 4-6.

A department is the typical working environment for groups of workers. For example, everyone specializing in hiring, testing, evaluating, and training workers is housed in a personnel department or division. Each of the multiwork tasks and the work centers at which these tasks are completed must be planned and spaced so that they relate to the needs of the total personnel function of the department.

The administrative office manager's responsibilities include coordinating all work centers into an arrangement that facilitates the combined teamwork of all the individual members. In deciding how best to utilize the available space, the office manager has available several options. Of primary concern to the manager are the questions of whether to design private or large general office areas, or both, and how to provide for the

The Deltona Corporation

Fig. 4-6

The Records Storage and Retrieval Center — a group work center wherein the coordinated efforts of all workers are directed toward attainment of the firm's information-processing needs.

special work centers commonly found in most organizations.

Private vs. General Offices

Over the years the private office has been widely regarded as one very important status symbol of executive success. Today, however, the rising costs of office space and the increasing popularity of office landscaping cause the office manager to study several factors before deciding whether to design private offices or general, open offices for workers.

Management must weigh the relative advantages and disadvantages of using private offices. The reasons usually given for providing private offices are: (1) they create prestige in the eyes of employees and visitors for top management, department heads, and high-level staff people; (2) the nature of the work being done, such as research, planning, and financial report preparation, is confidential; and (3) the work, such as computer programming, requires a high degree of concentration. On the other hand, the private office makes efficient use of about 50 percent of the space allocated to it and thus is an expensive method of providing utilities, such as heating, lighting, and air conditioning. The private office is relatively inflexible, for its permanent partitions are expensive and difficult to remove; it provides barriers to supervision of employees as the supervisor is separated from the employees; and it sets up arbitrary barriers to oral communications in the office.

Movable partitions and screens can be used to provide a certain amount of privacy in work without the disadvantages of the private office. The use of partitioning meets the needs of those

workers who require work privacy and provides needed flexibility for rearranging work stations as work patterns change.

In some office buildings the number of private offices is decreased in favor of large general offices controlled by bays. A *bay* is the unit of floor space used for control purposes. Its size varies from 300 to 450 square feet. The bays may be separated by lines drawn on the floor or by supports from ceiling to floor, or they may be shown only on the blueprints. Types of work as well as types of office equipment are often segregated in offices by means of bays. Along with the use of bays in large areas, conference rooms may be provided for the use of those executives who occasionally need privacy. However, many top-level executives will always continue to need and prefer private offices.

Special Work Centers

Many large firms have developed work centers somewhat different from the typical ones found in all businesses. Three special work centers commonly found are: the reception center, the reference services center (sometimes called the library), and the data processing center.[10]

The Reception Center. The reception center serves not only to promote efficiency in office operations but also as a promotional medium of the firm. Thus, this area should be well arranged and kept orderly, for visitors get their first impression of the business

---

[10]For a review of other special work centers, such as the files department, vaults, interviewing rooms, and conference rooms, the reader should consult *Office Standards and Planning*, Art Metal, Inc., Jamestown, NY 14701.

when they step into its reception center. The center—the introductory chapter to the biography of the firm—should express honesty, reliability, and efficiency.

The reception center should be located in an area where visitors cannot see the main office in order to prevent interruption of work, as the attention of the workers is often distracted by the flow of callers. In planning a reception center, at least ten square feet should be allocated for each visitor; therefore, the size is determined by the maximum number of visitors expected at any one time.

Reading material should be supplied to the visitors, who may have to wait until those upon whom they call are ready to receive them. As it may be assumed that many of the callers are interested in some product or service of the company, often some literature or a display of these subjects is provided. If reading material or displays are provided, the lighting should be sufficient for comfortable reading.

The Reference Services Center. To encourage their employees to be well informed on both general and special topics, many companies have established libraries or reference services centers. In planning the space for reference services, some firms design the area to serve a dual function — to serve as a reference area and to utilize the book shelves as room dividers.

Businesses also maintain special libraries as a service-rendering unit that makes available whatever knowledge and experience it can accumulate to further the activities of the organization. As such, the special library is really an information bureau, with a limited number of reference books, technical handbooks, and other publications in the special field of the company.

Before deciding whether a company reference services center is feasible, these questions should be answered:

1. How much of the research done by executives and scientists in the company is unnecessary because someone else has already done it?
2. When a person is assigned to a market research, public relations, or other project, how much time should be spent on preparatory research?
3. How often are junior executives and secretaries sent out to "look something up" in a local library? How long does it take?
4. What is the cost of distributing multiple copies of business periodicals and little-used reports?
5. How much time and money do executives devote to telephoning around the country seeking information before making important decisions?[11]

A firm may obtain assistance in setting up its reference services center by contacting The Special Libraries Association, which will provide a library consultant free of charge (except for travel expenses), if the visit does not require more than one day's time. The consultant will survey the company's existing facilities and offer recommendations on costs, techniques, space and equipment requirements, and staff requirements. The Association also makes available a listing of professional consultants who are experienced in the firm's subject field so that the firm can select its own consultant, determine the length of the consultation period, and agree upon the fee.[12]

---

[11]Peter R. Weill, "Are You Ready for a Company Library?" *Administrative Management* (August, 1963), p. 44.

[12]Firms considering the formation of a special library should contact The Special Libraries Association, 235 Park Avenue South, New York, NY 10003.

The Data Processing Center.

Many administrative office managers are faced with the problem of designing and constructing facilities to handle the space needs of the data processing staff. The computer and its related peripheral equipment require a well-controlled environment if they are to operate at optimum efficiency. A computer center is illustrated in Figure 4-7. Because of the cost and complexity of large-scale computers, their installation requires extensive planning. Although the location and size of the computer center will be greatly influenced by the particular computer system being installed, consider-ation must also be given the following factors: the flow of work within the firm; the location of key auxiliary areas such as the mail room, the supply room, and the maintenance area; the availability of air conditioning, electricity, fire protection, and other necessary services; and plans for future expansion.

If the computer center is to be located in a multistory building, the floor above the computer center should be watertight so as to prevent possible water damage to the equipment. Ordinarily basements are avoided as a site for the computer center because of their dampness and the possibility of flooding

The Deltona Corporation

Fig. 4-7
A Computer Center

as the result of the weather or faulty plumbing. Noncombustible, fire-resistant walls, floors, and ceilings should be used in the construction of the computer center to completely cut it off from others parts of the building. The flooring should be sturdy, for medium and large-scale computer systems produce a loading of 100 to 250 pounds per square foot.

One of the most important elements to be considered in the computer center is the temperature and humidity control. Extremely high temperatures can cause malfunctioning within the component parts of the computer system, and low temperatures may cause condensation on the electronic parts. For most computer systems the ideal temperature is between 65° and 75° F. Too much humidity in the center can impair the operation of magnetic tapes and disks, paper tapes, and card readers, while too little humidity can cause electrostatic charges to build up on cards and tapes, thus causing them to stick and bring about errors. The recommended relative humidity in a computer center is between 40 and 60 percent. Although most computers and magnetic tape units have built-in dust filters, care should be taken to protect the computer from dust, smoke, and other particles that affect the computer system adversely.

In planning the site for the computer center another very important factor to be considered is the electrical installation. The wiring arrangements should be gauged to the system being installed and should follow the manufacturer's specifications. Unless careful provisions are made for the proper wiring needs, it may be necessary to undertake expensive rewiring of the area or to make wiring changes within the equipment. If terminals for minicomputers are placed in other departments for direct entering of source data, provisions for special wiring at these locations must also be considered.

Computer systems are extremely delicate, and down time can be very costly. Therefore, prior to the layout of the computer center, extensive preinstallation planning must be undertaken with the data processing manager. In planning and executing the computer installation, the administrative office manager is well advised to make full use also of the expert assistance of the computer manufacturer and its sales representatives and outside consultants if necessary.

PRINCIPLES OF SPACE MANAGEMENT

In this chapter attention is devoted to layout as a key factor in achieving office efficiency. As such, layout may be considered a component part of office systems and procedures. Other components of office systems are work methods and routines, personnel, as well as furniture and equipment.

Space Guidelines for Efficient Work

The following space guidelines will aid the administrative office manager in achieving work efficiency. A more intensive study of systems and procedures is contained in Chapter 17.

1. To reduce communication and transportation lines to a minimum, a straight-line flow of information (forms, records, reports, etc.) rather than a crisscrossing of lines is recommended.

2. Large open spaces are better than small room spaces cut out of the same area. Supervision and control can be more easily maintained, communication between individual employees is more direct, and better light and ventilation are possible.

3. Movable partitions, screens, and planters should be used rather than fixed walls as alternatives to private offices.

4. Space should be conserved as much as possible without cramping individuals in work centers. Large sums of money can be saved by making better use of space, especially that space above the surfaces of desks and tables.

5. Those offices requiring considerable contact with the public (such as the purchasing, sales, and personnel departments) should be located in a place accessible to the public. Those offices requiring confidential work or privacy (such as accounting, computer programming, and research and development) should be removed from the easy accessibility of the public.

6. Space allocation should be based on major work flows which function around source documents such as the purchase order, the time card, and the sales invoice. This implies that departments having a great deal of cross-communication with other departments should be located adjacent to each other. Examples of this relationship are the personnel and payroll departments. Employees who have the most communication with other departments should be located nearest the exits.

7. Future work requirements should be forecast in relation to the projected sales volume. One guideline to use in such forecasts is the average rate of increase in volume of office work over several typical growth years.

The factors of lighting, ventilation, noise levels, and interior decoration,

which also must be considered in planning a layout because of their effects on worker efficiency, are discussed at length in Chapter 6.

Space Guidelines for Personnel

The number of employees to be housed in a given area both at present and in the future has an effect on the amount of space to be used. Because there are so many variables in allocating space in an office, it becomes difficult to set standards of space requirements. Single-occupancy private offices may vary from 200 to 600 square feet, whereas those in open office spaces may require only 75 to 100 square feet each. In addition, allowance must be made for space allotted to reception centers, display rooms, filing rooms, and employee lounges. It becomes difficult to compute the average amount of space required for each employee. The best that can be achieved in setting space standards is to group employees and set minimum and maximum guidelines for each group, as shown below:

1. Private offices vary from 600 square feet for senior executives to 200 for senior assistants, and 75 to 100 square feet for cubicles in an open office space.

2. In traditional space-managed plans, general offices have 80 to 100 square feet per work station in smaller departments, or in units where there are high-level nonexecutive personnel, or where the visitor traffic is heavy. In large clerical work areas, the allowance may be reduced to 40 to 80 square feet per work station.

3. In office landscaping the goal is to plan offices with undivided areas of at

least 100 by 100 feet, for 80 to 100 employees. There should be as few interior walls as possible.

4. Aisles and corridors will probably require about 10 to 15 percent of the total area of private and general offices.

5. Conference and board rooms require 25 square feet for each person for rooms housing up to 30 persons and 8 square feet per person for areas housing 30 to 200 persons.

6. Central files require about 6 square feet per letter-size ($8\frac{1}{2} \times 11''$) cabinet and about 7 square feet for the legal-size ($8\frac{1}{2} \times 13''$) cabinet.

7. Coat room allowances are $1\frac{1}{2}$ square feet per person for two rows of racks with an aisle between.

8. Telephone switchboard requires 50 square feet for basic equipment per operator position.

Space Guidelines for Furniture and Equipment

The placement of furniture and equipment requires an inventory of the quantity, description, and size of each piece of furniture and equipment. In locating each item on the floor plan, the guidelines in Figure 4-8, shown on pages 90-92, may be used.

THE OFFICE SPACE STUDY

The importance of making office plans and revising the layout is recognized not only by administrative office managers but also by the manufacturers of office supplies and equipment. There are several methods by which a space study may be undertaken. All of these are usually based upon a floor plan, drawn according to the customary (English) or the metric scale, of the office space available. Over the next 10 to 15 years manufacturers of office furniture, equipment, and supplies as well as office managers will be greatly concerned with converting from the customary or English system to the metric system of measurement.

The Metric System in Space Planning

The *International Metric System* — technically the Système International d'Unités, or SI — is the measurement language of almost every country in the world. Conceived in France during the French Revolution, the metric system grew out of dissatisfaction with the lack of uniformity in the European measurement system. The metric system consists of seven base units of measure, as shown in Figure 4-9.

The name of each metric unit consists of the base unit and a prefix. *Kilo* means 1,000; thus one kilogram equals 1,000 grams. *Centi* means one-hundredth. Thus, one centimeter is one-hundredth of a meter and one centigram is one-hundredth of a gram.

The decimal base of the metric system is one of its most important features, for units of any given measurement are always related by multiples of ten. There are 10 millimeters in a centimeter, 100 centimeters in a meter, and 1,000 meters in a kilometer. The decimal base makes conversion from one unit of length to another very simple. To multiply or divide, one simply moves the decimal point to the right or to the left. For example, to calculate the number of meters in 75 kilometers, multiply by 1,000 by moving the decimal point three places to the right — 75,000

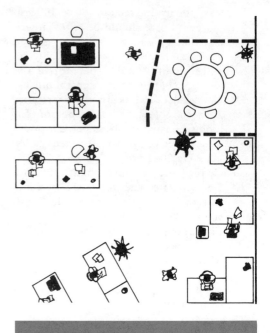

1. The width of major traffic aisles may vary from 5 to 8 feet. Less traveled aisles should be 3½ to 5½ feet wide.

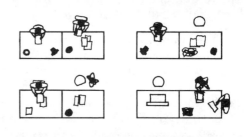

2. Aisle space between desks should not be less than 36 inches.

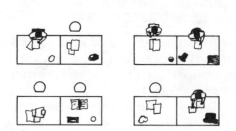

3. Space between desks facing in the same direction — that is, the space occupied by chairs — should not be less than 28 inches, preferably 36 inches.

Fig. 4-8
Space Guidelines for Furniture and Equipment (page 1)

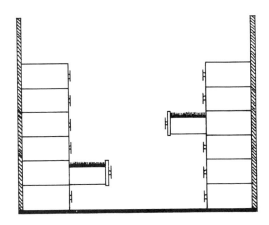

4. If active files open up front to front —
that is, to an aisle — the width of the
aisle, when the file drawers are open,
should not be less than 30 to 40
inches.

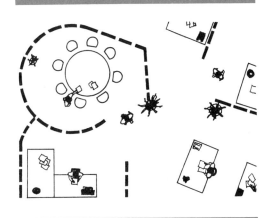

5. In open planning, the plants should
grow to between 3½ and 5 feet, unless
they are to be used as visual barriers,
when 7-foot plants with more fullness
and breadth are recommended.

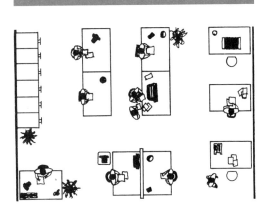

6. Desks should generally face the same
direction, unless the employees are
clustered together in work centers.

Fig. 4-8
Space Guidelines for Furniture and Equipment (page 2)

7. No more than two desks should be placed side by side so that each desk will be on an aisle, thus permitting easy flow of traffic.

8. Desks should be arranged to give a straight flow of work — that is, so that a person will receive work from the desk beside or in back of him or her.

9. File cabinets should be placed against walls or railings if possible.

10. Those who do the closest work should have the best light. No workers should face the light, and the window light should be at the left of an individual.

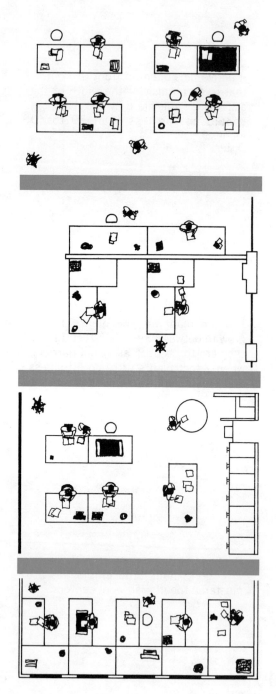

Fig. 4-8
Space Guidelines for Furniture and Equipment (page 3)

Name of Metric Unit	Metric Symbol	Used to Measure
Meter	m	Length
Kilogram	kg	Mass (weight)
Kelvin	K	Temperature (commonly called the degree Celsius, °C, formerly centigrade)
Second	s	Time
Ampere	A	Electrical current
Candela	cd	Luminous intensity
Mole	mol	Amount of substance

Fig. 4-9
Base Units of Metric System

meters. To calculate the number of kilometers in 4,397 meters, divide by 1,000 by moving the decimal point three places to the left — 4.397 kilometers. Multiples and equivalent tables for the meter are summarized in Figure 4-10, shown at the top of page 94.

The United States is the only industrial nation in the world not on the metric system or involved in an official changeover. However, many United States multinational corporations — firms producing in foreign nations and in the United States — have been using both metric and the United States standards for years. This "dual dimensioning" assures that all layouts, blueprints, machines, and parts are calibrated in both metric and United States standards. Legislation has been passed, which calls for the United States to make a planned conversion to metric measurement within an unspecified time. Under the Metric Conversion Act of 1975 a Metric Conversion Board will synchronize the voluntary conversion by business, industry, and also by educational institutions.

In converting to metric measurement the dimensions of office supplies, furniture, equipment, and machines, as well as the length and width of office space, currently given in the customary or English system, office managers will find the conversion tables in Figure 4-10 of great help.[13]

Preparing Office Layout Models

Four methods of preparing a model of the office layout are described in the following paragraphs:

1. The first method, shown in Figure 4-11 on page 95, makes use of colored paper cutouts of all types of equipment such as desks, chairs, files, and safes. Each piece of furniture and equipment is drawn to the same scale as the floor plan to maintain proper relationships when the cutouts are pasted into position. This is the simplest and least

---

[13]For very precise measurements, exact conversion factors may be found in "Units of Measurement, Conversion Factors and Special Tables," reprinted from "Units of Weight and Measure, International (Metric) and U.S. Customary," NBS Miscellaneous Publication 286, May, 1967 (Washington: United States Department of Commerce, October, 1972).

Base Unit Meter (m)

Common Multiples

deka (da) = 10
1 dekameter (dam) = 10 meters

hecto (h) = 100
1 hectometer (hm) = 100 meters

kilo (k) = 1000
1 kilometer (km) = 1000 meters

Common Submultiples

deci (d) = 0.1 or 1/10
1 decimeter (dm) = 0.1 or 1/10 meter

centi (c) = 0.01 or 1/100
1 centimeter (cm) = 0.01 or 1/100 meter

milli (m) = 0.001 or 1/1000
1 millimeter (mm) = 0.001 or 1/1000 meter

English-Metric Equivalents

Approximate Values

1 inch	=	25.4 mm
1 inch	=	2.54 cm
1 foot	=	0.305 m
1 yard	=	0.91 m
1 square inch	=	6.5 cm²
1 square foot	=	0.09 m²
1 square yard	=	0.8 m²
1 cubic inch	=	16.4 cm³
1 cubic foot	=	0.03 m³
1 cubic yard	=	0.8 m³

Metric-English Equivalents

Approximate Values

1 mm	=	0.04 inch
1 cm	=	0.4 inch
1 m	=	39.37 inches
1 cm²	=	0.16 square inch
1 m²	=	10.8 square feet
1 m²	=	1.2 square yards
1 cm³	=	0.06 cubic inch
1 m³	=	35.3 cubic feet
1 m³	=	1.3 cubic yards

Fig. 4-10
Units of Measurement — Conversion Factors

expensive method of illustrating a proposed layout.

2. The second method, illustrated in Figure 4-12 on page 96, makes use of a plastic template. The cutout areas indicate the size and shape of the various types of equipment and the special symbols that are used to prepare flowcharts of the work within the office. Plastic templates are available from most manufacturers and distributors of office furniture and equipment.

3. A third method uses a floor grid drawn to scale, as shown in Figure 4-13 on page 97. The top surface of this board may be made of cork so that the scale models of desks, chairs, tables, screens, plants, and office equipment may be pinned down when set up. Once the plan has been laid out, it is possible to use it for the basis of discussion among executives and workers. Photographs may be made as a guide for installation.

4. A fourth method (the simulated office space model) relies upon the actual construction of full-size replicas of selected office areas.[14] In such complete mock-up offices, executives and office workers can sit in their actual offices and know beforehand what their work stations will be like. They can examine and test all the various components as provided by different manufacturers. Colors and textures can be evaluated and examined together in the same proportions and arrangements in which they will be ultimately used. This method, the most expensive of all, is feasible only when large sums of money are to be spent on large quantities of space.

[14]For additional information on the use of full-size replicas in planning the offices of Bristol-Myers and General Motors headquarters in New York, see "Complete Mock-Up Offices Used to Plan Real Ones," *Administrative Management* (April, 1969), pp. 30–31.

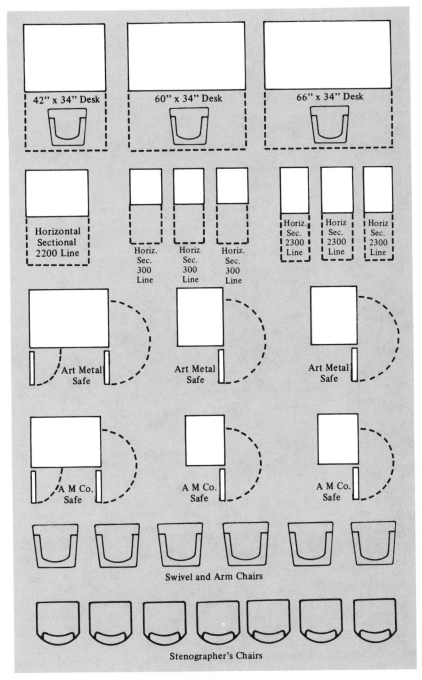

Art Metal, Inc.

Fig. 4-11
Colored Paper Cutouts Drawn to Scale for Use in Preparing Office Layouts

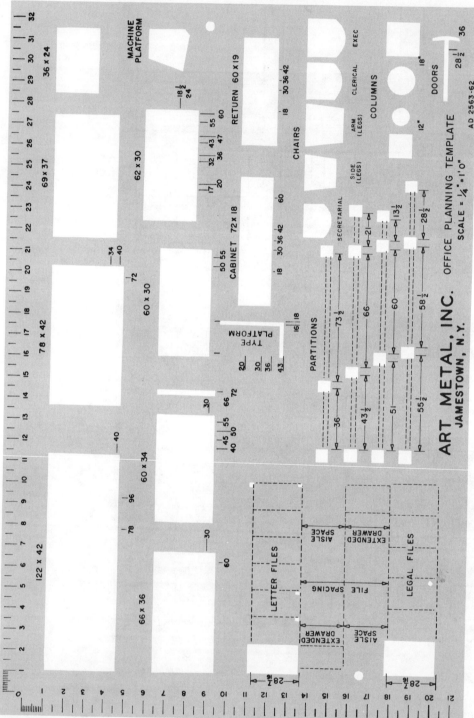

Art Metal, Inc.

Fig. 4-12
Plastic Template

"Visual" Industrial Products, Inc.

Fig. 4-13
Layout Board with Scale Models of Furniture,
Machines, and Equipment

QUESTIONS FOR REVIEW

1. What is the significant difference in meaning between the terms "office layout" and "space management"?

2. What factors are involved in managing office space?

3. How is the Gantt Project Planning Chart used in planning an office layout?

4. How does work flow influence the planning of office space?

5. Of what significance to space planning is a study of a company's informal channels of communications?

6. What are the main features of departmentalized office layouts?

7. Define the concept of space planning known as office landscape.

8. How does the office landscape provide for privacy?

9. What features of landscaped offices bring about the greatest savings in space planning?

10. What is the work center concept?

11. List the advantages and disadvantages of providing private offices.

12. The first glimpse that the visitor has of an organization is its reception center. How important is this area, and how may its space be properly planned?

13. Discuss the uses of a company reference services center that are not provided by an up-to-date metropolitan or university library.

14. To plan properly the space allocated to the data processing center, many environmental factors must be considered. Cite those factors that you consider most important and be prepared to defend your choices.

15. Which offices within a typical manufacturing firm should be located near the public entrance? away from the public entrance? Why?

16. What space guidelines are available to aid the office manager in locating desks?

17. What is the name of the metric unit that measures length? mass? temperature?

18. Of what significance is the decimal base to the metric system?

19. A standard-size office desk is 60 ″ × 34″. Convert the measurements of this desk to centimeters.

20. Describe the four methods of undertaking an office space study.

QUESTIONS FOR DISCUSSION

1. Assume you have been appointed by the Administrative Management Society to develop a set of criteria for making annual awards to the best "space-managed" offices in America. What would your set of criteria include?

2. Wolfgang Schnelle, head of the Quickborner Team, a West German consulting firm that pioneered in office landscaping studies, has stated:

   The more routine the work, the more it is written. The less routine, the more it is spoken.

   Paper flow is not a concept of great concern in office landscape. The concern is that people, staff groups, can verbalize their needs.[15]

   What is the relevance of these statements to the underlying concepts of office landscaping?

---

[15]Walter A. Kleinschrod, "The Case of 'Office Landscape,'" *Administrative Management* (October, 1966), p. 19.

3. In the law offices of Olsen, Peterson, and Pugh there are 32 lawyers, a certified public accountant, 10 legal secretaries, and 14 clerical employees. The firm is now planning its new quarters, which will be ready late next year. The partners realize they have a lot to learn in their planning. What suggestions can you offer them in the area of initial planning to make sure that a satisfactory space plan is devised for the office?

4. Wilkins, Inc., is moving to a new building in which the office area is 28′ × 14′. This space will be occupied by Tom Lyons, the office manager; his assistant; a secretary; a typist; and a community college student who works part-time. In this area there will be need for desks and chairs for all employees, chairs for visitors, two file cabinets, bookcases, a cabinet and rack for literature, and a coat rack. Lyons would like to have partitions or screens around his area because he does a great deal of dictating and confidential interviewing. However, Lyons does not want it to appear that he is appropriating the only two windows in the office, both of which are on one 14-foot wall.

   What suggestions can you offer Lyons as he begins to plan his space requirements? Should Lyons be concerned that others will feel he is unjustifiably entitled to all window space? Sketch a space plan for the new area, in which you indicate the size of desk you recommend for each employee.

5. The data processing center of Farley's Men's Wear is converting from punched-card machines to a small-scale computer installation. Much of the same space (50′ × 42′) will be utilized for the computer as was utilized for the punched-card machines, though parallel runs (using both computer and punched-card systems) will be in effect for one month while the new system is being "debugged." Reba Ferguson, the data processing supervisor, must come to some space management decisions as soon as she considers this information:

   a. The staff of three keypunch operators will be retained. Three keypunch machines and one verifier machine also will be retained.

   b. All other staff will be retrained and retained. They consist of five machine operators, two of whom will be retained for computer operator positions.

   c. One programmer and a senior systems analyst will be employed.

   d. Appropriate space must be provided in the present quarters for the new equipment (a computer, the console, two tape drive units, the keypunch and verifier machines, one input-output card unit, one card-to-tape converter, and one printing unit), as well as for the supervisory personnel, the programming and systems personnel, and the machine operators.

   Develop a plan of suggested space allocations, along with a list of unanswerable questions at this point in time. How can the space plan incorporate all machines required during the parallel runs?

6. Well-planned layouts anticipate future work requirements, and thus an office work area is often initially designed for multiple functions.

For example, when the secretarial area (18′ × 18′) in Figure A was initially planned for the Crawford Company, it was felt that at a later date the space might be converted either to an executive office or possibly a clerical work area.

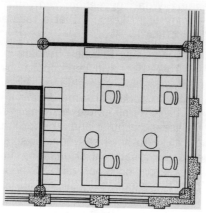

Source: Jeffrey E. Clark, "Office Space Programming," *The Office* (June, 1971), p. 34.

Fig. A.

Secretarial Work Area

Assume that the needs of the Crawford Company have changed and prepare a revised layout of Figure A for an executive office containing one desk, two visitors' chairs, a credenza, and a conference table with four chairs. Next, prepare a revised layout of Figure A for a clerical work area housing nine clerical desks and chairs.

7. Doctors Skaggs and Sigman, specialists in internal medicine, have moved to a new second-floor location in a surburban office building. One of their last unsolved space problems is the reception center (shown in Figure B on the next page) where a limited amount of space is available in which to accommodate a growing number of medical patients. The size of the reception space (22′9″ × 11′) is small, and it is an inner office. Due to the construction of the building and the permanence of the wall partitions, no changes in basic building construction can be made. However, railings, movable partitions, and screens may be employed in the space plan in an effort to provide maximum seating and comfort, and space for the usual furniture and accessories for a waiting-reception room. Only one receptionist, who is also the administrative assistant, will be stationed in this area.

As administrative assistant to the two physicians, design a new space plan for this area in which space is utilized efficiently for the maximum number of patients as well as for your work station. In your plan consideration should be given to types of furniture, furniture groupings, and environmental factors such as color, lighting, and ventilation.

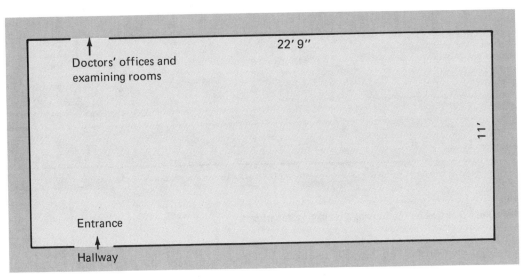

Fig. B
Doctor's Office Reception Center

8. Those who have researched the topic of metrication (conversion from the customary to the metric system of measurement) have found that metrication is just as controversial today as it ever was. What arguments can you advance for the customary system of measurement? for the metric system?

Case 4-1   Designing the Office for a Purchasing Department[16]

The Lansing Purchasing Department is moving to a new office, which, as shown in Figure C at the top of page 102, measures 55′ × 15′. In the space assigned, work stations must be provided for a purchasing agent, an assistant purchasing agent, a buyer, a mail-and-file clerk, an invoice clerk, a bid clerk, and two typists. Later, another typist may be added.

Sketch a layout of the new office in which the following working relationships and location of physical factors are shown:

1. One typist, who doubles as a receptionist, should be positioned near the reception area.
2. The second typist and the one to be hired should be located at the rear of the office, yet near the private offices and records.

---

[16]Adapted with permission from Marybelle C. Pratt, "A Good Buy in Office Space," *Modern Office Procedures* (August, 1966), p. 32.

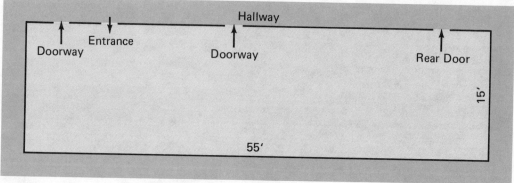

Fig. C
New Office Quarters for the Lansing Purchasing Department

3. The bid clerk and the invoice clerk should be near the private offices of the assistant purchasing agent and the buyer and the reception room. Space should be provided at each work station for cabinets or files beside the desks for records storage.
4. The work area for the mail-and-file clerk should be set up near the rear of the office close to the back door to simplify the moving of incoming and outgoing mail. Nearby the clerk's desk will be the current files and the mail table. Other machines and extra files, marked for expansion and storage, can be placed in this area.
5. All three private offices should be grouped together for good communications. Locating them near the reception room shortens the trips that visitors have to make and keeps visitors out of the rest of the office. All three offices should have desks with side returns with cabinets or have credenzas behind the desks to hold the many reference books that purchasing officials must use.
6. Place the conference room near the reception room and the private offices to shorten trips and to offer convenience for everyone. Use three tables, which can be pushed together into one long table for large conferences or which can be used separately when just a few people have to confer.
7. The conference room should be entered through the reception room door. The purchasing agent may enter the conference room from his or her office. The hallway entrance makes it easy to bring in displays, charts, easels, and other conference material.
8. A vault, measuring $4' \times 7'$, is to be installed at the far end of the office, near the rear door.

Case 4-2   Revising a Proposed Layout for an Overseas Office

Blodgett, Inc., a multinational corporation engaged in processing petrochemicals, has its manufacturing plant and headquarters office in New Orleans. Overseas plants and sales offices are located in Rotterdam, Lyons, Munich, and Zurich. A new plant and sales office are now being constructed in the suburbs of Linz, Austria.

Marc Randall, manager of administrative services, has the responsibility for coordinating all phases of space management, forms design and control, and office systems analysis in the home office and all overseas offices. Although the company has just announced its long-range plan for conversion to the metric system, Randall has been faced with the problems of dual dimensioning of layouts and measurements of forms and office supplies for the past several years. An example of the kind of dual dimensioning problem faced by Randall has just arrived in this morning's mail.

Colette Horvath, the newly selected manager of the sales office in Linz, has airmailed a layout of the new office to Randall. This layout, illustrated in Figure D, has been designed by Horvath for a staff of 12 persons. The office expects, however, to employ 14

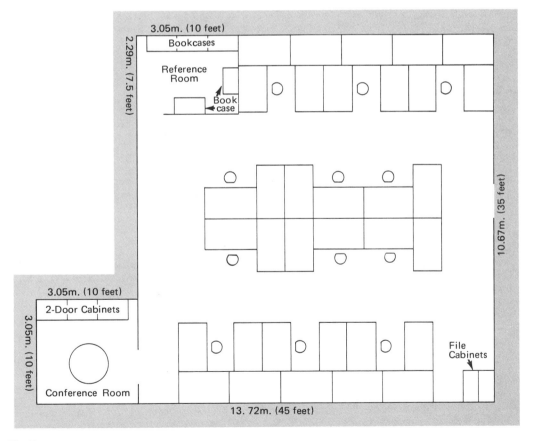

Fig. D
Proposed Layout for the Linz Sales Office

workers when the plant opens and to provide work stations for three more persons three months later. In her accompanying letter, Horvath has asked Randall for his ideas on rearranging the present 12 work stations to provide for the additional five. Horvath does not want the 17 workers to be overcrowded.

In earlier correspondence with Horvath, Randall indicated that Horvath should purchase office furniture with dimensions similar to the following:

Furniture	Sizes in Centimeters (and inches)
L-shaped modular units consisting of single-pedestal desk (right-hand or left-hand)	152.4 × 76.2 × 76.2 (60 × 30 × 30)
and	
desk	152.4 × 76.2 × 76.2 (60 × 30 × 30)
Round table	106.7 × 76.2 (42 × 30)
Cabinet, 2-door	91.4 × 45.7 × 182.9 (36 × 18 × 72)
File cabinet, large	38.1 × 68.6 × 144.8 (15 × 27 × 57)
Book case	91.4 × 38.1 × 106.7 (36 × 15 × 42)

Randall has recommended that Horvath observe the following guidelines regarding minimum space allocations:

Space between desks facing in the same direction:
    72 to 90 cm (28.4 to 35.4 inches)
Space for the two main aisles:
    1.22 to 1.83 m (4 to 6 feet)

Based upon the information Randall has given Horvath and upon the layout submitted by Horvath, prepare a revised layout of the Linz office showing how the 17 work stations may be provided without overcrowding. Because of the permanent partitioning enclosing the conference room and the reference room, the arrangements of these two rooms must remain as shown in Figure D.

Chapter 5

THE OFFICE ENVIRONMENT: FURNITURE AND EQUIPMENT

One convenient way of describing the office environment is in terms of its physical and mental factors. In addition to furniture and equipment, or furnishings, the physical environment of the office includes its size or dimensions, types of surfaces (color of walls, type of floor, window coverings), the nature of the lighting provided, noise control and acoustical materials, air conditioning and ventilation, and background music. Each of these factors has physical characteristics that strongly affect the mental condition of the workers — their morale and overall attitude toward work and toward each other.

Management considerations regarding the selection, procurement, maintenance, replacement, and control of office furniture and equipment are important and complex responsibilities of the office manager. These will be discussed in this chapter. The psycho-physiological impact of the other factors that make up the physical office environment will be treated in Chapter 6.

SELECTION

No one can know everything about the physical environment in which he or she works. Yet, the office manager, as the custodian of the information center of the firm, is usually expected to have available a large body of information about the office furniture and equipment required for the firm. In addition, the of-

fice manager is expected to know what office furnishings are available for consideration by the firm. To provide such information, the office manager should have available, or should know where to obtain, information about each of the following items:

1. Principal types of furniture and equipment and reputable suppliers of each.
2. Reliable statistics for comparing the effectiveness of competing brands of equipment and furniture.
3. Current prices on all items and preferably catalogs representing each major supplier's merchandise.
4. Criteria for deciding on the need for such equipment and for selecting the equipment.
5. Knowledge about the impact of the equipment on the information system, particularly the training or retraining needed, new suppliers, and operating costs.
6. Possibilities for standardizing equipment throughout the firm.
7. Procurement alternatives (such as renting, leasing, or purchasing) and quantity purchasing options.
8. Maintenance, repair, and replacement considerations.

In a world in which technology is providing an almost endless array of new products and machines, office managers must be constantly alert to make sure that they have the best equipped office environment possible. They should have a good understanding of the principal uses or applications of the various office furniture and equipment and be able to assist not only their own staffs but also the staffs of other departments in their firms in choosing the most appropriate office furnishings.

Office Furniture

Modern office furniture manufacturers continue to expand both the types and the various styles of their products. Generally all such manufacturers include filing cabinets, desks, tables, and chairs as well as other related items in executive, managerial, and clerical lines. Since filing equipment is discussed in Chapter 9, only the common types of furniture will be discussed in detail in this chapter.

The cost of office furniture is a significant part of the overall cost of the space in which office work is accomplished. As a rule, furniture is purchased rather than leased or rented, for it is intended to last for a long period of time. Thus, the office manager should give serious attention to the selection and use of office furniture. If properly selected, office furniture can assist the office manager to increase employee productivity, to lower production costs, and to retain efficient people.

Office Desks. The desk is a universal symbol of office work. Whenever a desk is found, paperwork is performed. The desk fulfills many purposes in the office. Primarily it provides a suitable surface for processing information that is usually in written form. The desk is considered to be the central part of the work station, frequently as a place on which (or along which) data processing or word processing machines are positioned. In all cases, too, the desk furnishes a storage place for supplies needed and data collected.

The cost factor is important in the selection of office desks. In most cases, even when a company owns its office building, estimates are made of rentals that should be charged against each department and division. Each component unit space and each department and division, in turn, is charged rental space. The annual cost of desk space in offices in large cities may be as much as $10 a square foot. A desk 60 inches by 34 inches occupies a space of over 14 square feet. This space, at $10 a square foot, would rent for more than $140 a year. The rental for the chair space, which would approximate 60 inches by 30 inches, or 12½ square feet, would be $125, making a total of more than $265 for the desk and chair. However, a desk 48 inches by 30 inches would probably be satisfactory for many office workers. This desk and a smaller chair would occupy only 20 square feet of space, making the space rental amount $200 a year, or about $65 less than that charged in the case of the larger desk and chair.

Types of Desks. Desks may be broadly classified into two types: (1) according to size and shape, or style, and (2) according to use or function. Desks classified as to style and function may take any one of the descriptions given in Figures 5-1 and 5-2.

Modular Furniture. Layouts using modular furniture combine separate furniture units that are designed according to the *unitized* or *modular construction principle*. This principle is based upon an approach to building office work stations composed of components (such as storage or cabinet units, work surfaces, and dividers or partitions), each of which has a specific function. Functionally designed modular

1. Flat-top, single—pedestal, 40 to 60 inches wide, suitable for sales representatives or clerks whose work does not require the use of large-size records. The term *pedestal* refers to the drawers contained on one side of the desk (single-pedestal) or on both sides of the desk (double-pedestal).

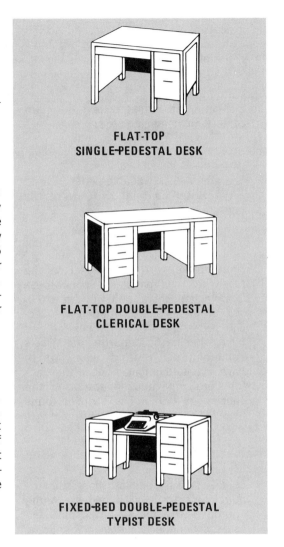

FLAT-TOP SINGLE-PEDESTAL DESK

2. Flat-top, double—pedestal, 50 inches wide, suitable for workers using many papers; 50 to 55 inches wide, suitable for workers requiring the use of many papers and their storage; 55 to 75 inches wide, suitable for supervisors or clerks using large records or books. Probably the 60 by 30 inch double-pedestal desk is the most popular size for general office work.

FLAT-TOP DOUBLE-PEDESTAL CLERICAL DESK

3. Fixed bed, single-or double—pedestal, suitable for stenographers and clerks. The fixed-bed desk is full height except for that portion immediately in front of the occupant, which is constructed at the conventional height, with an adjustable base for raising or lowering the typewriter or office machine.

FIXED-BED DOUBLE-PEDESTAL TYPIST DESK

Fig. 5-1
Styles of Desks

furniture, as illustrated in Figure 5-3, is based upon motion and time studies of the work to be done, such as that undertaken by the Gilbreths.[1]

Most manufacturers have designed modular office furniture to meet more accurately the description of the working tools or the work center of the office

---

[1]Frank and Lillian Gilbreth, whose contributions to the scientific management school of thought are listed in Chapter 1, sought to obtain the one best way to work. In their micromotion studies, work was divided into the most fundamental or basic motions known as *therbligs*. (The term therblig is derived from the name Gilbreth, spelled

backwards). The motions were studied separately and in relation to one another, and from these studied motions, when timed, methods of least waste and least motion were developed. The measurement of work and the development of work standards are treated in detail in Chapter 23.

1. Executive desks, with top, 66 to 78 inches wide, extending over a double-pedestal.

2. Clerical desks, double-pedestal, for employees not needing a typewriter.

3. Secretarial desks, double-pedestal, with a typewriter contained in one of the pedestals.

4. Typist desks, with a fixed bed for the typewriter. The modular L-shaped desk is a single-pedestal unit with an extension on either side containing the second pedestal. In order processing and billing and traffic departments, typists commonly use fanfold desks, which have a metal compartment in the back for storing the unused portion of the continuous forms. The strip of forms feeds easily from the compartment into the typewriter.

5. Special desks, such as those for key-punch operators, with pedestal units equipped with file trays for punched cards. Other specially designed units include those that accommodate copying machines and reproduction supplies.

6. Machine desks, specially designed for use with calculating machines of various types. A recessed section is provided at either end of the desk so that the machine sits lower than the standard desk height.

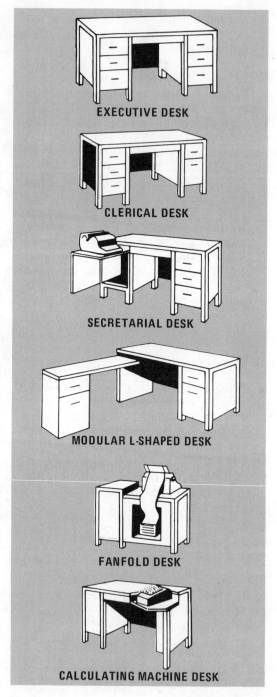

EXECUTIVE DESK

CLERICAL DESK

SECRETARIAL DESK

MODULAR L-SHAPED DESK

FANFOLD DESK

CALCULATING MACHINE DESK

Fig. 5-2
Functions of Desks

Steelcase Incorporated

Fig. 5-3
A modular furniture layout in which shelves and files are designed to hang up out
of the way on the wall panels, but to support any workload.

employees. This has been accomplished
as shown in Figures 5-3, 5-4, and 5-5 by
reducing the floor space required for
desk working area by approximately 20
percent; providing interlocking, interchangeable units for greater ease and
speed of output; and fully utilizing the
work area by building the desk complete with bookcase, file, and dwarfed
partitions.

The main advantages attributed to
modular furniture layouts include the
conservation of floor space and more
productive work motions. The most
common modular unit is the L-return, a
flat surface, with or without storage
room below, which is attached at right
angles to the desk. This type of modular
furniture arrangement, when compared
with the conventional rectangular desk
arrangement shown in Figure 5-4,
achieves not only a saving in space but
also greater work efficiency. (The conventional desk arrangement shown in
the top of Figure 5-4 occupies 7,920
square inches. The modular furniture
arrangement shown in the bottom occupies 6,468 square inches. Techniplan is
a trade name for the manufacturer's
modular arrangement of work stations.)

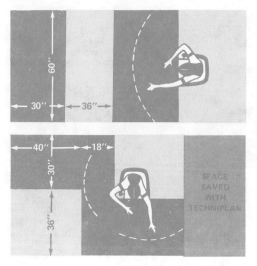

Globe-Wernicke Company

Fig. 5-4
Space Saved Using Modular vs.
Conventional Furniture Layouts

A careful study of the diagrams in Figure 5-5 shows the relative space advantages offered by modular furniture arrangements over conventional furniture groupings. Note how the various furniture arrangements provide for flexibility in the use of this type of furniture. Many other groupings are possible, subject to both the imagination of the administrative office manager and the limitations of space.

Tables. Tables serve as desks or desk-substitutes, as a place for sorting when considerable flat work surface is necessary, as a work surface for conferences and meetings, and as a place for storage. For many office jobs the use of a table is preferred to a desk of any kind and is, in addition, more economical. Such a table should be provided with one or two small drawers, which will be sufficient for most purposes for the clerk using it.

In many firms where executives and others meet and work together in groups, a large conference table is usually provided. While some conference tables found in board rooms of large corporations are custom designed to harmonize with the office decor, a wide variety of styles (from the traditional rectangular shapes to the more modern boat-shaped, oval, curved, and round styles) is available from office furniture distributors in all large cities.

Many other types of tables are also available. These include machine stands (for typewriters, calculators, and other machines), reception area tables, and panel-end (enclosed end) tables for conferences or as companions to desks.

Chairs. The total work center for the typical office worker utilizes a desk and a chair, both of which contribute to the worker's physical comfort. In turn, physical comfort is closely related to the worker's mental condition upon which performance ultimately rests.

It is important that office workers be comfortable to prevent strained posture when sitting for hours while performing their work. The office manager can detect many signs of fatigue by taking a close look at the workers' postures. It will be found many workers sit with their feet entwined around the chair legs or humped over their work, because the chair or the desk or both are not the right height. Such incorrect sitting positions may not be due to careless posture, but often result from defective seating.

All office chairs, other than side chairs, should be adjustable as to height and should revolve. The back support should be vertically adjustable and horizontally adjustable forward and back. If the back support is provided with a spring tension, the tension should be adjustable. If workers have to bring their work to their eyes, they need arm rests on their chairs. If workers have to

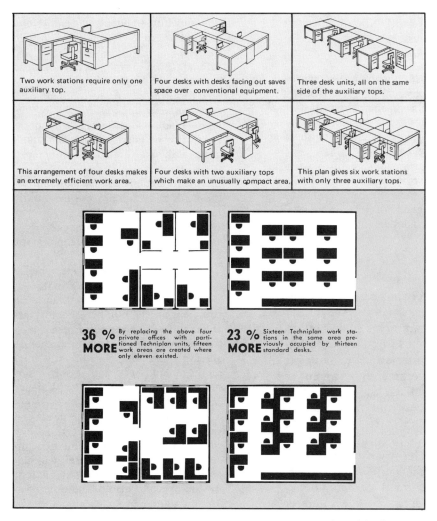

Two work stations require only one auxiliary top.

Four desks with desks facing out saves space over conventional equipment.

Three desk units, all on the same side of the auxiliary tops.

This arrangement of four desks makes an extremely efficient work area.

Four desks with two auxiliary tops which make an unusually compact area.

This plan gives six work stations with only three auxiliary tops.

36% MORE By replacing the above four private offices with partitioned Techniplan units, fifteen work areas are created where only eleven existed.

23% MORE Sixteen Techniplan work stations in the same area previously occupied by thirteen standard desks.

Globe-Wernicke Company

Fig. 5-5
Space-Saving Possibilities of Modular Furniture Layouts

bring their eyes and arms to the work, they do not need arms on the chairs. Studies have proven that proper posture while working in the office not only reduces fatigue but also improves the health of workers by making them less susceptible to colds and headaches. This, in turn, benefits the firm as a result of less absenteeism, fewer errors, and a larger volume of production.

Most office chairs are designed to fit as closely as possible the contours of the body. Saddle seats are one example of the contour designs normally used in the construction of wooden chairs. Correctly contoured seats, especially those covered with foam latex, add to the worker's comfort. Many workers also like wooden seats supplemented with felt pads.

The main types of office chairs are classified as follows:

1. Executive chairs, completely adjustable to the physical characteristics of the executive, or in swivel and tilt-back styles.
2. Stenographer posture chairs, with or without swivel base.
3. Clerical posture chairs, with or without swivel base, with or without arms.
4. Side chairs, straight back and four legged, designed for use by visitors since these chairs are not suitable for all-day sitting.

Other Furniture and Accessories. The preceding discussion has indicated that desks, tables, and chairs are the key furniture items in any office. While this continues to be true, the forward-looking administrative manager will modify the working environment as conditions (particularly the layout), the financial resources, and the tastes of management dictate. It has become common to find extra furnishings such as sofas, end tables with harmonizing table lamps, coffee tables, art objects, credenzas, refreshment centers, bookcases, planters, screens, office valets or coat racks, and magazine racks in the office. These accessories provide an environment that is more conducive to relaxed work, concentration, and enjoyment of the hours spent on the job.

Principles of Furniture Selection. While it is obvious that office furniture should be selected on the basis of its contribution to the performance of office work, more specific selection criteria are required. The following principles should be considered in the selection of all office furniture:

1. The furniture should be attractive and modern in style and harmonize with the decor of the office — a feature that affects the volume, accuracy, and morale of the workers.
2. The furniture should be of good quality, solid construction, and suitable design to facilitate the work to be done. Furniture of good quality is usually more attractive and more economical to maintain.
3. The furniture should be suitable for the work to be done. Since each office has individual requirements, use by similar offices is not necessarily a strong reason for adoption of the furniture.
4. The furniture should be adaptable to multipurpose use wherever possible.
5. The quantity of furniture should be sufficient for the number of employees and the types of tasks performed.
6. Specialized items of furniture, such as sorting racks and portable furniture pieces, should be installed only if savings in clerical costs and convenience can be justified.
7. The furniture should fit the needs and preferences of the workers. They should be consulted regarding new furniture purchases, and where their suggestions cannot be followed, reasons for the decision made should be communicated to them.
8. The alternatives of metal or plastic versus wood furniture should be carefully weighed. For superior durability under hard wear, metal office furniture should be considered. Normally metal furniture is more flexible, is constructed with interchangeable units or parts, and is used most widely in areas such as the general office where many units are required. On the other hand, wood furniture is also long lasting and has the added values of warm tone, rich appearance, and prestige that enhance the attitude of the office worker toward the job. Wood furniture is often found in executive offices.

9. The furniture should contribute to comfortable working conditions. This principle involves the nature of the work to be performed and the economy of physical effort as well as the speed of various operations.

Office Equipment

In addition to the furniture required for the office, a great array of office equipment is available. The term office equipment, as used here, refers primarily to office machines and devices that are found in the office.[2]

Essentially an office machine is an information machine. Whether it is a typewriter, an electronic calculator, a photocopier, or a computer, each of these machines deals with information. Then, too, office equipment is the intermediary between people and their work. It enables employees to accomplish more work in fewer hours with greater accuracy and with better quality. Furthermore, some equipment, such as the teletypewriter, helps employees to transmit the results of their work to others over long distances and to receive rapid feedback. Not only the types and brands of equipment but also the number of their possible uses continue to grow at an accelerated rate.

A modern approach to equipment selection starts with a feasibility study, as discussed in Chapter 2, in which the entire information processing system is

identified and the role of the equipment in such a system is clarified. Such a study requires concentrated and prolonged thought with well-documented answers to the key questions involved.

To assist the administrative office manager in making equipment-selection decisions, the following criteria should prove helpful:

1. Equipment should be chosen for any job or task for which it is more efficient than the worker. Where job monotony due to unchallenging, repetitive work tasks is found, a machine should be considered as part of enriching the job as well as increasing production.
2. High-volume, rather than low-frequency or one-time only, applications point to the need for machines. From such high-volume applications come better service, more prompt report preparation, and other positive results.
3. Where equipment can provide higher quality of output, it should be utilized. For example, compare typewritten versus handwritten reports.
4. The need for accuracy should be determined, and where internal machine checks and controls can provide such accuracy, a machine should be selected.
5. Equipment should be installed whenever it will reduce the actual cost of performing office work. The costs of service contracts, of operation, and of layout alterations required must be considered in calculating the total cost of the equipment installation.
6. To handle urgent work, high-speed requirements, or peak loads in the office work schedule, appropriate equipment should be considered.
7. Not only the capabilities but also the limitations of equipment should be carefully considered. Such limitations include the digital capacity of

---

[2]For discussions concerning specific types of office equipment, see Chapter 7 (Written Communications in the Office), Chapter 8 (Telecommunications in the Office), Chapter 9 (Information and Records Management), Chapter 10 (Graphic Information Services), and Chapter 19 (Mechanization of Basic Accounting Systems). Office equipment used in automated business information systems (such as computers and punched-card equipment) is discussed in Chapters 20 and 21.

numbers handled, size of forms and records, cycling speeds, numbers of copies required, complexity of mathematic processes, number of storage registers, longevity of expected performance, and trade-in value.

8. Both operating and supervisory personnel involved with the equipment should be consulted for their machine preferences. In addition, the impact of training or retraining required for proper machine operation should be considered.

9. The availability of ready, reliable maintenance service should receive top priority in equipment selection. If equipment is not working properly or not working at all, this constitutes an added cost of office operations.

10. Assuming that usage of the equipment allows, effort should be made to procure equipment that has these features: simplicity (for ease of operation, of learning, and of maintenance); flexibility (for use in many situations); portability (for easier use in several office departments); and adaptability (for immediate integration into a present office system).

11. Before purchase, lease, or rental, equipment should be "test run" in the office situation where it is considered for installation. In some cases a one- or two-week trial period is recommended for small machines. For the larger, more expensive machines in the computer family, longer parallel runs, as explained in Chapter 2, are carried out.

12. Standardization of office equipment is desirable. By standardizing on sizes, styles, and brands, it is possible:
    a. To obtain lower prices through larger purchases.
    b. To lower the maintenance costs by servicing fewer brands of machines.
    c. To develop, if necessary, the company's own service department more easily and economically.
    d. To economize by having one group of employees who can operate any of the machines.
    e. To train operators more simply and easily.
    f. To purchase and use office forms to fit the brands of machines.
    g. To simplify the computation of depreciation and trade-in value of the equipment, which is important from the standpoint of both income taxes and disposition of equipment by trade-in.

PROCUREMENT

The selection of office furniture and equipment is an important and complex responsibility of the office manager. Office furniture, which is intended to last for a long time, is usually purchased rather than leased or rented. However, the same is not necessarily true of office equipment, which is subject to much wear and tear as well as to increasing technological improvements. The remainder of this chapter will be devoted to the other closely related managerial considerations of procuring, maintaining, replacing, and developing centralized procedures for assuring the proper control and utilization of equipment.

Although office equipment may be purchased outright, in 1970 most companies with assets of less than $500,000 procured one half of all their new equipment by leasing. Over the past several years leasing has gained immense popularity. According to the American Association of Equipment Lessors, the volume of goods under lease increased from $20 billion in 1969 to $40 billion in 1974.[3]

---

[3]Donald B. Romans, "Why Leasing Is Becoming So Popular," *Nation's Business* (June, 1975), p. 74.

An *equipment lease* is a contract that enables an equipment user (lessee) to secure use of a tangible asset by making periodic payments to the owner (lessor) of the asset over a specified time period. Under a lease, which usually extends over a longer period of time than a rental, there is no intent — stated or implied — for the user to obtain equity or to purchase the equipment. During the life of the lease the lessor retains ownership of the asset and the claim to any residual value in the equipment at the end of the lease period.

Almost all types of office machines and equipment — small office appliances, electronic data processing equipment, and reprographic equipment — can be leased.[4] Many companies rent or lease their data processing equipment, such as card-punch machines, input/output terminals, optical scanning equipment, and computers. With the increased experience and knowledge being gained in the field of data processing, however, managers have been inquiring more and more into the practicability of buying rather than leasing small, low-priced computers. In a survey by *The Office* of some 250 firms, of the companies that use small computers, 44 percent of the machines were purchased; 39 percent were leased; and 17 percent were rented.[5] One year later *Modern Office Procedures* surveyed a representative cross-section of small computer users, who indicated that 61.9 percent had purchased and 38.1 percent

had leased their computers.[6] It is also interesting to note that those who leased their small computers were spending, on the average, $1,790 per month; those who had purchased their small computers spent, on the average, $56,489.[7]

Many of the advantages claimed to be gained from leasing, as cited in a later section, are being reappraised by computer users in relation to lease payments that have already surpassed the original purchase price of the equipment. In some firms increased applications of their present installations have caused the additional lease payments to become a greater cost factor than the original estimates.

Equipment can be leased from a variety of sources: directly from the manufacturer or through the manufacturer's distributor; from a local office equipment dealer; from an independent leasing company that leases various brands of office machines and equipment; and from many banking organizations, insurance companies, pension funds, finance companies, and other financial institutions that provide some form of equipment leasing service.

Kinds of Lease Agreements

Since leases can be tailored to meet the special needs of the parties involved, there is an almost limitless variety of actual lease contracts. For purposes of this discussion, the various kinds of lease agreements will be grouped into four categories: (1) short-term, (2) long-term with renewal option, (3) long-term with purchase option, and (4) sale-leaseback.

---

[4]For an in-depth, four-year study of the opinions and experiences of some 300 lessors and lessees, see "Leasing in Industry" by Henry G. Hamel, a 1970 report available from the National Industrial Conference Board, 845 Third Avenue, New York, NY 10022.

[5]"Experience of Users with Business (Mini) Computers," *The Office* (June, 1974), p. 18.

---

[6]Charles N. Ritley, "Datanomics: Proving the Theory," *Modern Office Procedures* (May, 1975), p. 75.

[7]*Ibid.*

Each of these plans is briefly described in the following paragraphs.

Short-Term Lease. The short-term lease, which is almost a straight rental, is used to obtain extra equipment, such as typewriters and calculating machines, for peak workload jobs, such as year-end inventory. The major advantage of this leasing plan is that the needed equipment is made available immediately with the need for little cash outlay. For example, an electric typewriter may be leased for about $30 a month.

Long-Term Lease with Renewal Option. Under this plan the lease usually runs between 75 and 80 percent of the useful life of the equipment. On the average the leases run from three to five years. At the end of the lease period, the lease can be renewed at a reduced rate. During the period of useful life, the payments equal the original price of the equipment plus financing charges.

Long-Term Lease with Purchase Option. This plan is similar to the long-term lease discussed above, except that during the lease period the user is building up equity to take ownership of the equipment at the end of the period. The user gains the flexibility of being able to upgrade the equipment, without any penalty, during the lease period. Since the equipment has a tangible value that can be used as a trade-in on new equipment when a new lease is signed, the threat of obsolescence is eliminated.

Under income tax regulations this form of lease may be interpreted as a conditional or installment sale and thus the company is denied tax deductions for the lease payments. Since there are no precise guidelines as to when a fi-nancial lease qualifies for favorable tax treatment, the parties to the lease agreement should seek a private Internal Revenue Service ruling in advance if they are setting up a lease with terms that are dependent upon favorable tax treatment.[8]

Sale-Leaseback. Under the sale-leaseback plan, the company purchases its equipment, sells it to a lessor, and then leases it back. Thus, the company receives almost 100 percent value of its fixed assets in the form of immediate cash. This plan may prove very useful when working capital is needed quickly.

Advantages of Leasing

The advantages that accrue from leasing include:

1. Working capital is freed for day-to-day cash flow. In some leases no down payment or deposit is required. In other leases a down payment equal to the first year's leasing cost may be needed to acquire the equipment. Such minimum stipulations free a firm's capital for other revenue-producing investments or for expansion.
2. Budgetary control is facilitated since the amount of regular lease payments is easily determinable. A hedge against inflation is also provided since the

---

[8]For a discussion of apparent Internal Revenue Service criteria for financial lease agreements that qualify for favorable tax treatment, as deduced by practitioners, see Steven J. Weiss and Vincent John McGugan, "The Equipment Leasing Industry and the Emerging Role of Banking Organizations," *New England Economic Review* (Boston: Federal Reserve Bank of Boston, November/December, 1973), p. 7. Also see J. T. Conner and G. R. Yocum, "Banks as Lessors — the Tax and Accounting Aspects." *Magazine of Bank Administration* (April, 1973), p. 30, and Ralph E. Davis, "The Bank Customers' Lease or Buy Decision," *Bankers Magazine* (Summer, 1966), pp. 88–89, and Hamel, *op. cit.*, p. 37.

same dollar lease payments are spread over a period of years. Thus, in times of spiraling inflation, a constant sum of money paid out five years into the future on a five-year lease will be paid in inflated dollars, which have less purchasing power than the same amount spent in the current year.

3. Some leases offer the lessee an opportunity to contract out specialized services such as maintenance and record keeping, which are associated with the use of certain kinds of equipment. For example, under some leases the lessor services and maintains the equipment for the user and provides insurance coverage. The lease also relieves the necessity of disposing of the equipment when it is no longer needed.

4. Flexibility, unavailable in other methods of financing, is provided the lessee. New firms often need equipment immediately but are initially unable to budget substantial funds for lease payments. Under long-term leases, payment schedules can easily be worked out to mesh with the lessee's seasonal pattern of cash flow. For example, a deferred-payment lease offers flexibility in payment methods. By means of deferring its payments, a company is able to generate income before the first lease payment comes due.

5. Leasing offers the equipment user an additional source of financing. Lease financing may be available to companies when other sources of financing cannot be obtained on reasonable terms. For example, leasing offers one of the few ways that small companies without access to credit can obtain new equipment, especially during periods of costly money. Specialized forms of financial leasing, such as leveraged leases, offer users of high-cost equipment a means of realizing significant savings. In a *leveraged lease* the lessor (usually a bank or syndicate of banks) puts up 20 to 40 percent of the cost of the equipment and borrows the

remainder of the money from insurance companies, pension funds, or other institutional investors through the sale of debt secured by the equipment and the lease payments. The savings result when the lessor, who puts up only a fraction of the money, claims tax benefits on the entire cost of the equipment. Thus, the lease rate charged by the lessor can be reduced.[9] The leveraged lease is popular because the effective interest cost to the lessee is typically half the prime rate. Thus firms can finance capital equipment over a 15-year period at 4 percent interest.[10]

6. For companies that use highly specialized equipment, protection may be obtained against obsolescence risk. In many cases the equipment can be replaced during the life of the lease, and thus throughout the lease period, the company can take advantage of the latest advances in technology.

7. Tax benefits may be realized since the lease payments may be treated as business expenses fully deductible for income tax purposes. As noted earlier, however, under some lease contracts an option to buy during or at the end of the lease period may be looked upon by the Internal Revenue Service as an installment or conditional sales contract, and thus the lease payments may not be tax deductible. Generally, if a lessee anticipates sufficient taxable income, borrowing to purchase equipment offers greater tax benefits and is less expensive than leasing, especially under accelerated depreciation rules now in effect.[11] Even so, deductible

---

[9]"Rent-A-Anything; More Companies Lease a Variety of Equipment Instead of Purchasing It," *The Wall Street Journal*, October 1, 1973, pp. 1 and 3.

[10]Peter S. Redfield, "Leveraged Leasing May Help to Solve Capital Shortage," *Administrative Management* (May, 1975), p. 80.

[11]Weiss and McGugan, *op. cit.*, p. 8.

lease payments under short-term leases or leases with variable payment schedules may be attractive to lessees under certain circumstances.[12] Further, a small company can often take advantage of the investment tax credit. The tax credit can be assigned to the leasing company, which is legally the owner of the equipment, and the small firm's leasing rate, in turn, can be lowered. Such an arrangement allows many small companies to benefit from tax credits that would not be available under other finance plans.[13]

8. Rapidly expanding companies and those opening branch offices are aided by the package plans of some lessors, under which equipment can be added as the needs of the company grow.

Deciding to Lease or Buy Equipment

If after a feasibility study, a need for equipment is determined, the following factors should be carefully analyzed and investigated before making the decision to lease or to buy:

1. *Relative net cost of purchase and lease.* If the equipment is to be used for more than one shift a day, it may, in terms of direct cost, be economical for many firms to purchase the equipment. However, each firm should conduct its own capital budgeting study, as in the case of any other capital investment, perhaps by using valuation methods such as return on investment, payback

period, lease-buy break-even point, discounted cash flow, and present value.[14]

2. *Threat of obsolescence.* Companies that are concerned that their installations may soon become obsolete as the result of technological advances often decide to lease although it may be less expensive to buy.

3. *Useful life of the equipment.* Although an analysis of useful life is very difficult, a realistic appraisal must be made of how long the equipment will serve the company's needs. For example, in some firms long-range planners are at work developing great changes for the future that may radically affect the role of the present data processing installation. To forecast the future, the data processing staff must analyze the firm's plans and trends for sales, production, and purchases in order to determine the need for new or expanded automated processes.

4. *Amount of base fee.* Often a firm pays a base fee that entitles the company to operate the equipment, such as a computer, a certain number of hours each month. Regular overtime usage requires the payment of additional rent, which is directly determinable with the installation of time recorders on the equipment. All terms governing the basic rental period should be spelled out in advance. For example, if the equipment breaks down for a few hours, is the company charged for

---

[12]Richard R. MacNabb, "Leasing of Industrial Equipment," *Leasing of Industrial Equipment,* Machinery for Allied Products Institute and Council for Technological Advancement (Washington: U.S. Government Printing Office, 1965), pp. 3–4.

[13]For the extent to which a business is eligible for the investment tax credit, see James B. Bower and Harold Q. Langenderfer, *Income Tax Procedure,* current edition (Cincinnati: South-Western Publishing Co.).

[14]For an illustrative example of determining the lease-buy break-even point, see Frank B. Gardner, "EDP Equipment: Rent or Buy?" *Management Bulletin No. 10,* Vol. 4 (Willow Grove, Pa.: Administrative Management Society), pp. 2–10. See H. N. Broom and Justin G. Longenecker, *Small Business Management* (4th ed.; Cincinnati: South-Western Publishing Co., 1975), for a discussion on traditional measures of investment valuation and theoretically correct methods of valuation. Also see Robert M. Soldofsky and Garnet D. Olive, *Financial Management* (Cincinnati: South-Western Publishing Co., 1974) for a well-developed presentation of capital budgeting theories and practices.

these hours or does the manufacturer assume the loss?

5. *Maintenance services.* The contract to buy or to lease should clearly indicate the type of maintenance services — preventive and repair — that will be provided by the manufacturer or the vendor. The availability of skilled help, when needed, should be determined.

6. *Residual value of equipment.* In making cost comparisons between leasing and buying, the residual or trade-in value of equipment at the end of its useful life is often overlooked. With a growing market for used equipment, the firm may realize a substantial trade-in value for that equipment which has a system life shorter than its productive life.[15]

7. *Interest costs.* When placing the costs of leasing and buying on a comparative basis, the firm should consider the rate of interest it pays for borrowed money or the rate it expects to earn on an investment of the funds.

Aid in making a wise decision on whether to purchase or to lease equipment may be obtained from the firm's own financial specialists and auditors, independent consultants, and the various lessors, such as equipment manufacturers, many of whom will prepare a detailed analysis of purchase and lease factors.

MAINTENANCE

As indicated above, maintenance is an important factor to be considered by the office manager when purchasing or leasing equipment. Many office machines must be operated almost contin-

uously each work day. With automatic machines and equipment handling the bulk of information processing, the servicing of these machines becomes a major consideration. When machines and equipment get out of order, office workers are unable to perform their work until repairs have been made, unless there is some unused standby equipment.

Depending somewhat upon the complexity of the equipment and the number of machines being used, service and maintenance of office equipment may be handled by one or more of the following methods:

1. Service contract with the manufacturer of the equipment or with an independent service firm.
2. Service by the company's internal service department.
3. Use of a manufacturer's or independent service representative on a per-call basis with no contract.

Service Contract

Service contracts, also known as maintenance agreements, maintenance guarantees, and business equipment efficiency agreements, provide for periodic cleaning and lubrication, inspection, and replacement of worn-out or defective machine parts. By purchasing a service contract, a firm may be able to save money in the area of "hidden costs." For example, each time a service representative on a per-call basis renders service, an invoice must be processed and a check written to cover the fee charged. This office operation may cost, on the average, from $7.50 to $10. If, however, a service contract has been purchased, only one annual billing would have been made, and thus the need for processing only one invoice and writing

---

[15]See "Secondhand Systems, Market for Used Computers Is Multiplying; Customers Buy Older Models at a Discount," *The Wall Street Journal*, February 7, 1974, p. 34.

only one check. A second hidden cost lies in the amount of machine downtime, a cost that can never be measured exactly. Involved are not only the idle time of the machine operator but also the possible delay in operations being performed by a higher salaried supervisor. Preventive maintenance, which forms a part of the manufacturer's service contract, may reduce or eliminate the number of breakdowns.

Under the service agreement of one manufacturer of office machines and equipment, typewriters are inspected once a year, while input-processing (dictation) equipment is cleaned and lubricated only during service calls. The annual service agreement rate for electric typewriters ranges from $49.50 to $62, depending upon the model. Rates for input-processing (dictation) equipment range from $35 to $45 each year. Parts are checked for wear and are replaced without charge on an exchange basis (except motors, batteries, and platens). Quantity discounts are granted, and a zone charge is added to the maintenance charge for each unit of equipment located more than 15 miles from the manufacturer's nearest point of service. For equipment not under a service agreement or for calls made beyond the one annual inspection, the cost of each service call is $23 per hour.

In the servicing of typewriters, some firms, especially those in small outlying communities, enter into an agreement with a local typewriter service firm. For a fixed fee, the firm inspects, cleans, and repairs each typewriter in the office at regular intervals.

Internal Service Department

To maintain its own service personnel, a company must be fairly large. Involved in the installation of a service department are the relatively high salary rates of trained service personnel, the hidden costs of their employee benefits, the cost of retraining the personnel as new machine models appear on the market, and the cost of the space allotted to the servicing area.

Since typewriters are very important both from the viewpoint of the number involved and the amount of the investment, their care and maintenance are important. Many offices issue instruction sheets to all typists on how to care for their machines so that they will operate efficiently and require a minimum of servicing and repairs. If there are a large number of typewriters in use, it may be desirable to have several employees devote their time to servicing and repairing typewriters.

Per-Call Basis

Some firms feel that it is more economical to pay for each individual service call as the service is needed. For example, one Pittsburgh firm, with 600 typewriters in its general office, reports that until several years ago, the annual cost of the service contract for the typewriters was $25,000. The maintenance policy was changed to a per-call basis, which resulted in annual expenditures of less than $5,000.[16] In the case of particularly troublesome and highly automated equipment, however, repeat calls are often necessary. When a fixed-fee manufacturer's service contract is used, such calls are the manufacturer's problem.

REPLACEMENT

Equipment for office work may frequently become obsolete because of

---

[16]"Test Reports on Typewriters, 1975," Buyers Laboratory, Inc., p. 4.

newer and better models placed on the market. Therefore, it becomes necessary for office managers to select the best machine available at the time of purchase and to use this machine until its efficiency lessens, at which time the old machine may be replaced with a newer model without too great a loss. This loss can be absorbed by the business if a sound trade-in policy has been established at the time of purchase.

Office furniture, fixtures, and machines may be depreciated over a period of 10 years under any of the commonly used methods of determining depreciation such as straight-line, units-of-production, declining-balance, and sum-of-the-years-digits.[17] For example, assume that a company purchases a new office machine for $5,000. The estimated residual value (also known as the scrap, salvage, or trade-in value) is $300 and the estimated life of the asset is 10 years. Using the straight-line method of determining depreciation, the annual depreciation expense is computed as shown below:

$$\frac{\$5,000 \text{ (purchase price)} - \$300 \text{ (residual value)}}{10 \text{ years (estimated life)}}$$

= $470 (annual depreciation).

Due to the factor of obsolescence, however, some special-purpose machines, such as data handling and information processing equipment, may be depreciated at an accelerated rate or over a fewer number of years. Returning to the example above, assume that the firm elects to speed up the amount of depre-

ciation in the early years of the machine's life by using the declining-balance method of determining depreciation. It is decided to apply double the straight-line depreciation rate (computed without regard to the residual value) to the cost of the asset less its accumulated depreciation. At the end of the first year the amount of depreciation is calculated as follows:

$5,000 (purchase price) × 20% (2 × 10%, the straight-line rate) = $1,000.

At the end of the second year the amount of depreciation is computed as follows:

$5,000 (purchase price) − $1,000 (accumulated depreciation) × 20% (2 × 10%, the straight-line rate) = $800.

Although in the example above the estimated residual value is not considered in determining the depreciation rate nor in computing the periodic depreciation, the asset should not be depreciated below the residual value.

Depreciating office machines and equipment at an accelerated rate reduces the income tax expense in the earlier years of the asset's life. Thus, the amount of funds available to pay for the asset or for other investment-producing purposes is increased. Of course, assuming that the cost of repairs tends to increase with the age of an asset, the reduced amounts of depreciation in later years are offset to some extent by increased maintenance expenses.

If, in the example above, the firm had elected to depreciate the office machine over a period of five years, each year $940 (20 percent of the cost less residual value) would be written off as depreciation expense. Such an accelerated policy permits the trading in of the machines at least every five years and thus

---

[17]For a complete discussion of the various depreciation methods, see C. Rollin Niswonger and Philip E. Fess, *Accounting Principles* (12th ed.; Cincinnati: South-Western Publishing Co., 1977), Ch. 9.

enables the firm to take advantage of technological improvements.

With a planned replacement program for its machines and equipment, a firm is able to predict each year, with a high degree of accuracy, the exact cost of its equipment needs. The cutoff point of operating efficiency and economy can be established for each piece of equipment; the number of new items to be purchased can be forecast, and the amount for maintenance during the coming year can be budgeted. A planned replacement program also enables the firm to establish better control over its maintenance costs, especially those that tend to rise during the latter years of machine usage. By closely controlling the replacement schedule of office machines, the firm can avoid those additional expenses that arise during the period when the equipment is old and requires extensive reconditioning, replacement of parts, and special cleanings. An intangible advantage in the area of prestige and morale also characterizes the company having a planned replacement program. By means of such a program, the company is able to present to its customers, visitors, and employees a modern image of a businesslike, well-equipped, up-to-date office.

CENTRALIZED CONTROL

The procurement, maintenance, and replacement of equipment should be centrally controlled, particularly in the large office where specialization of function is found and where enormous sums are invested in machines and equipment. Usually this function is the responsibility of the manager of administrative services. Such a program of control consists of the following list of activities:

1. Maintaining an up-to-date file of information on office equipment and equipment trends.
2. Setting up a central records control system for the plant assets to show the following kinds of information:
   a. The equipment owned/leased/rented by the firm.
   b. Where the equipment is used.
   c. What the equipment is used for.
   d. Company and manufacturer serial numbers.
   e. Complete description of type of equipment.
   f. Date of purchase.
   g. Cost.
   h. Service history.
   i. Maintenance costs.
   j. Current depreciation expense and accumulated depreciation.
   k. Book value (purchase price less accumulated depreciation).
3. Establishing machine and equipment standards.
4. Controlling the selection and purchase of machines in line with use to be made of the machines.
5. Developing effective procedures for maintenance and replacement of the machines.
6. Maintaining a periodic review of all equipment and machine installations.
7. Functioning as a central clearinghouse for all equipment needs within the firm and as the contact point for all vendors outside the firm.

The small office, too, has need for equipment controls. Although it is unlikely that much specialization of function will be found in the small office, the control of equipment should be assigned to a competent individual who can give it the attention it deserves.

1. To be both up-to-date and able to provide the most service to their firms relative to the physical environment of the office, what types and sources of information should administrative office managers have available?

2. In the selection of office desks and chairs of what significance is the cost of the square footage occupied by the desks and chairs?

3. Describe a modular furniture layout and indicate its major advantages.

4. What is the basis for the design of modular furniture layouts?

5. What are the characteristics of a good posture chair? Why is the selection of a good chair just as important as the selection of a suitable desk?

6. You have been asked to provide a comprehensive set of criteria for selecting office furniture. What should be included in your set?

7. From the standpoint of machine usage, what factors must be taken into consideration before an office machine is properly selected?

8. What are the advantages of standardizing the sizes, styles, and brands of office machines and equipment? In what respects do these advantages of standardization apply to office furniture?

9. What are the characteristics of an equipment lease?

10. Explain the operation of a long-term lease with purchase option. From the lessee's point of view, what are the advantages and disadvantages of such a lease plan?

11. What are the benefits that may be realized by the firm that leases rather than buys its office equipment?

12. After a feasibility study has been conducted, what factors should be carefully studied before making the final decision to lease or buy the needed equipment?

13. What is meant by a "service contract" for office machines and equipment?

14. Why might a firm select a depreciation method by means of which the office equipment is depreciated more quickly over its early years of life than during its later years?

15. Office managers should develop a definite trade-in program for their office machines and equipment. Indicate the advantages of such a trade-in program.

1. Speaking at a seminar on office space planning sponsored by the American Management Association, Lewis W. Shirey of GF Business Equipment, Inc., stated: "Through leasing a company can afford better furniture — furniture that more adequately suits the job

function, enhances the company's image, and has a more pronounced effect upon employee morale."[18] The average cost of a furniture leasing program was based on $35 per $1,000 a month. It was
felt that leasing is suitable for new companies without extensive
capital and for those firms unable to obtain financing. However, the
total cost of a leasing program is greater than the actual cost of
furniture if purchased. What are some of the other drawbacks to the
leasing of office furniture?

2. A leading management consulting firm, with 65 branch offices in the
United States, has recently centralized the purchasing of all office
equipment through its headquarters office in New York City. Each
branch office selects its equipment from a manual published by the
company. If, for example, one office wishes to purchase a calculator, the branch manager investigates the equipment available in the
company's manual and requisitions the purchase of the calculator
through the central purchasing unit in New York City. What advantages can you cite for this type of centralized procurement of equipment? What disadvantages can be anticipated?

3. The increasing popularity of leasing office furniture and equipment
marks a shift in the attitude of business firms toward the practice of
leasing. "For years, the ownership ethic among businessmen was so
strong that, except in the railroad industry where rolling stock has
been leased for years, leasing was a thing that nice companies just
didn't do," observed Peter K. Nevitt, president of First Chicago
Leasing Corp., an affiliate of the First National Bank of Chicago.[19]
How do you account for this shift in the attitude of companies
toward leasing?

4. When purchasing metal desks, most office managers closely check
the top, usually made of laminated plastic or linoleum, to make sure
that the top best fits their needs. What do you see as the advantages
of a laminated top? of a linoleum top?

5. Sources for the purchase of office furniture include manufacturers,
dealers, and designers and architects. What advantages and disadvantages might you anticipate as you consider each of these sources
of supply?

6. After a feasibility study, the Yerkes Paper Company has determined
the need for $10,430 of small computing equipment, which it can
either purchase or lease. Over a five-year period, the lease payments
for the equipment would cost $19,980. The lease payments include
insurance and all maintenance costs. At the end of five years, the
estimated trade-in value of the equipment, if purchased, would be
$2,500. If the equipment were purchased, the annual insurance
costs would be $150 and the estimated maintenance expense would

[18]"Furniture Leasing," *The Office* (June, 1975), p. 164.
[19]"Rent-A-Anything; More Companies Lease a Variety of Equipment Instead of
Purchasing It," *The Wall Street Journal*, October 1, 1973, p. 1.

total $300 each year. Assuming that the interest on the investment in the equipment over a five-year period is $4,900, discuss the advisability of leasing or buying the equipment.

7. As part of its program of standardizing office furniture and equipment, the Ruston Products Company is replacing 300 secretarial and clerical posture chairs at a cost of $26,000. Janet Huckabay, office manager of Ruston, is finding selection of office furniture and equipment increasingly difficult. Seven competing firms have offered Huckabay chairs which not only look alike and operate the same but also cost nearly the same. Huckabay wants her selection of a supplier to be a wise one. Discuss the procedure you would follow if you were Huckabay.

8. As office manager for the Quinn Oil Company, you have the responsibility for trading in the old office furniture and selecting new items. You have met with several vendors of office furniture, and you have learned that the trade-in allowance on the old furniture is practically the same with each source of supply. Thus, the trade-in allowance is not to be considered in your selection of vendor. Your survey of the offices indicates the following needs:
   a. Two private office areas, in each of which a double-pedestal executive desk, an armchair, a credenza, and two visitors chairs are to be provided.
   b. Three executive secretaries, whose desks are located nearby the private office areas, are to be provided with secretarial desks and chairs.
   c. Four stenographers, whose entire workday is spent in transcribing, are to be given desks and chairs.
   d. Five clerks, engaged in various accounting tasks other than typing, are to be provided with single-pedestal desks and chairs.
   e. Three accountants must have new work centers, each consisting of a single-pedestal desk with attached top return, a chair, and a credenza.

Prepare a report in which you discuss the style, type, and size of desk, chair, and credenza that should be selected for the employees and for the two private office areas. Consult office furniture and equipment catalogs to determine the approximate cost of each piece of furniture.

PRACTICAL OFFICE MANAGEMENT CASES

Case 5-1   Purchasing New Office Furniture and Reducing the Rental Costs

In the Farber Company the supervisor in each of the nine departments is responsible for preparing a year-end report in which the department's actual operating costs are presented for the present year and compared with those estimated for the year. One element of cost charged each department is rent for the space occupied by desks and chairs. Currently, the company charges each department rent on the basis of $8.50 per square foot occupied by desks and chairs.

In the Order Processing Department the estimated rent for the current year, totaling $5,210.50, was determined as follows:

Quantity of Desks and Chairs and Dimensions	Square Footage Occupied @ $8.50/sq. ft.	Rental Cost
15 single-pedestal clerical desks (48" × 30")	150	$1,275.00
10 double-pedestal clerical desks (60" × 36")	150	1,275.00
25 flexback posture chairs (30 inches of space is allocated between desks)		
15 desks @ 30" × 48"	150	1,275.00
10 desks @ 30" × 60"	125	1,062.50
1 executive desk (72" × 36")	18	153.00
1 executive swivel chair (40 inches of space is allocated) 40" × 72"	20	170.00
Totals	613	$5,210.50

Garven Williams, the administrative services manager, learned a few weeks ago that, as a result of renewing its lease, the company will be charging each department $8.75 per square foot occupied by desks and chairs, effective January 1 of the next year. This increase in rental cost has been communicated to each department head.

Angela Accardi, supervisor of the Order Processing Department, has been studying her furniture needs for the next year in relation to the company's furniture replacement program and the increased rental costs that will be charged her department. In a feasibility study recently conducted, Accardi talked with her workers about smaller desk sizes in relation to their work patterns, body motions, and the flow of paperwork. The firm's replacement program indicates that all 25 of the clerical desks and posture chairs will be replaced at the beginning of the new year; the executive desk and swivel chair will be retained for another two years.

Realizing the benefits to be gained from standardizing the size, style, and brand of desks and chairs, Accardi has decided upon 15 new single-pedestal desks that measure 45" × 24" and 10 new double-pedestal desks that measure 55" × 24". The present space allocation of 30 inches between desks for each posture chair will remain unchanged; the dimensions of the new chairs are the same as those being replaced. Accardi has selected a vendor who will supply, as a package deal, the 25 desks and 25 chairs for $3,920.

Prepare a cost estimate report for Accardi for the new year in which you show:

1. The estimated rental cost for the department at the increased rental charge.
2. The annual savings to be realized by the department as a result of selecting desks of smaller size.
3. The number of years required to recover the cost of the new desks and chairs, assuming that all space saved as a result of the smaller desk size is freed to a nearby department.

Case 5-2   Selecting Service Contracts for Office Machines

The Arcadia Manufacturing Company is located in a small suburban community about 50 miles from Harrisburg, Pennsylvania. The company is engaged in the production of small parts and subassemblies for electrical appliances such as toasters, mixers, blenders, and deep fryers. Its products have received increasing acceptance among the appliance manufacturers for whom they are fabricated, and the result has been a continuing increase in production, personnel, accounting, and related activities.

One of the areas of deep concern to the president, Kenneth Milani, is that the administrative staff is growing at a rate almost twice that of the factory work force. With this growth in administration has come a repeated emphasis on keeping office costs in line and on trying to find the best means of providing all the available mechanization possible to supplement the clerical work force. At the same time the office machines must be kept up-to-date and in good operating condition.

Presently the company is wrestling with a problem concerning the servicing of its basic office machines and is delaying temporarily a decision to automate some of the common office systems such as inventory and purchasing. A recent count of the office machines shows that there are 40 electric typewriters, ten of which are less than one year old; 20 are two to three years old, and the remaining ten are four or more years old. In addition to the typewriters, there are three ten-key adding machines, each six months old, principally used for payroll and production work, and two accounting machines, each two years old.

A decision must be made soon as to the best method of servicing these machines. These options seem possible:

1. A local independent repairer is willing to service all machines at these costs:
   Electric typewriters: $45 per machine, plus parts, each year
   Ten-key adding machines: $35 per machine, plus parts, each year
   Accounting machines: $120 per machine, plus parts, each year

The service agreement on each type of machine includes a quarterly inspection (that is, one inspection per machine every three months) at which time the machines are cleaned and adjusted.

2. Two of the machine manufacturers' distributors are located in Harrisburg, about one hour's traveling distance away. The manufacturer's service agreement for the electric typewriters is $55 per machine annually, including a zone charge since the Arcadia Company is located beyond the radius point of the manufacturer's service office. This amount includes one annual inspection, emergency service calls during regular working hours, and all parts except motors, batteries, and platens.

The accounting machine manufacturer provides a similar service at a per-machine cost of $150 per year after the first year's use. This amount covers the replacement of all defective parts, except platens. Machines are examined every six months under this firm's agreement.

A unique situation presents itself regarding the ten-key adding machines, which are import models with no branch service office in Pennsylvania. Although these machines are relatively new and have performed very satisfactorily, attention must be given to their service. When contacted about the possibilities for servicing the machines, the manufacturer's representative recommended a local repairer be contacted in case of machine malfunction. Otherwise, the machine would have to be returned to the nearest service representative on the East Coast, some 200 miles away. The warranty on the ten-key machine covers a one-year period during which all defective parts will be replaced free of charge, provided the defective machine is shipped direct to the East Coast office.

Prepare a report in which you outline clearly for Milani, the president of Arcadia, the best course of action, giving reasons to substantiate your recommendations for:

1. The type of service you recommend for the typewriters.
2. The type of service that would be preferable for the accounting machines.
3. How the servicing of the adding machines should be handled.

Chapter 6

THE PSYCHO-PHYSIOLOGICAL OFFICE ENVIRONMENT

Human beings, ecologists maintain, are greatly influenced by their environment. This is true whether they are functioning in the classroom, on the factory assembly line, or in the office. Recognizing this fact, psychologists and industrial engineers have studied the relationships of workers with their tools and machines to determine how these items affect the workers' attitudes and performances. The result is a new field of knowledge called *ergonomics* (from the Greek *ergos*, or work, and *nomos*, or natural laws) that brings together the physiological factors that make an effective work environment and the psychological factors that explain how workers react to that environment.[1]

The office environment involves the proper utilization of space and the effective arrangement of furniture and equipment (discussed in Chapters 4 and 5, respectively) along with other *physiological* factors such as lighting and noise control, the effective use of color, and office surface coverings. As ergonomics studies have shown, each of these factors also has *psychological* implications

due to the effect upon the behavior, attitudes, and morale of the office workers, and ultimately their productivity. The purpose of this chapter is to analyze the office environment from an ergonomic viewpoint as well as from the viewpoint of conserving energy in the office.

THE OFFICE ENVIRONMENT AND WORKER BEHAVIOR

To understand the productivity of office workers, one must examine their motivations and satisfactions as well as their frustrations and conflicts — in short, their overall job behavior. Psychologists continue to study this complex behavior phenomenon to ensure that both management and workers perform at maximum efficiency.

A major part of the difficulty in understanding human behavior stems from the fact that it is largely intangible and emotional and therefore is subject to varying interpretations. While the study of human behavior constitutes the specialized field of study of psychologists, any well-adjusted worker as well as any effective manager must possess a good working knowledge of the common-sense principles of practical psychology. He or she must be able to adjust to other people's personalities, recognize and solve personal problems, and motivate and challenge subordinates.

The office environment plays a large role in the human behavior of the office

---

[1]Ergonomic studies are cited in psychological, engineering, architectural, and business journals, among others. To bring these multidisciplinary references together, *Modern Office Procedures* has published excellent reviews of ergonomic studies including "Ergonomics: A Breakout on a New Discipline" (September, 1973), pp. 49–50; Fred W. Back, "A Systems Approach to Ergonomics," (October, 1974), pp. 54–56; and Archie Kaplan, "Sensory Experiences in the Office," (October, 1974), pp. 62–64.

staff. Although illustrations of this point are almost limitless, the following examples typify how *physiological* factors have a great impact on the *psychological* condition of the workers:

1. The executive private office "guarded" by a private secretary. The president of a highly regarded research corporation contends that such an arrangement inhibits person-to-person communication, isolates the manager and worker from each other, and gives the secretary a sentry role to play. Such an executive is removed from the main current of thought and action.
2. The across-the-desk "confrontation" of manager and worker. Psychologists often regard this physical arrangement as pitting the manager against the worker. When superiors confine themselves to the "boss" side of their desks, they take the role of information senders; and the workers become information receivers. Managers thus occupy a dominant position, one in which feedback and the easy flow of information are prevented. Such a situation psychologically inhibits the natural responses of workers and affects their work and working relationships.
3. The uniform, impersonal, institutional work stations for each executive and each worker. If the office contains row after row of desks, chairs, files, and tables, and if the office is depersonalized and institutional rather than personal, even "homey" in character, lacking interest, comfort and convenience, then the environment detracts from, rather than encourages, the development of good worker spirit and productivity.
4. A lack of definition of the unique personalities and job responsibilities of each employee. The employee's physical environment should promote concentration as well as easy communication, depending upon the particular job to be performed. A receptionist may

well be provided with a highly interesting setting with bright colors, modern functional furniture, background music, and unusual displays of the firm's services or products. The receptionist's personality, too, should be in harmony with this public relations-information function.[2]

It makes good psychological sense, too, to let employees assist in the planning of their physiological environment. Whether it be the layout and work design, color selections, or other environmental conditions, having a voice in the office environment will give the office staff a greater feeling of belonging and of participating in the planning of their work. Figure 6-1 illustrates the interaction of the combined psycho-physiological factors and their influence on worker productivity.

THE SURFACE ENVIRONMENT

The *office surface environment* comprises the walls, ceilings, and floors as well as other basic building features such as windows and pillars. Other objects whose surfaces affect the environment are the furniture and equipment that make up the office facility. Each of these physical items has a pronounced effect on the psychological reaction of office workers to their jobs.

Effective Use of Color

In planning the physical factors of the office, color must be considered first, because color has an effect on the lighting conditions as well as on the

[2]Robert L. Propst, "The Psychology of Sensory Values" (From a speech given before the Business Equipment Manufacturers Association, New York, October, 1969).

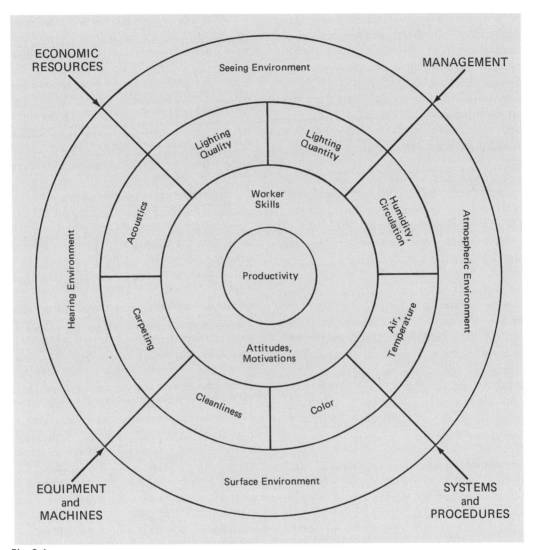

Fig. 6-1
Interaction of the Psychological and Physiological Factors in the Office Environment

feelings of workers. In fact, color sets the mood for relaxation or concentration in an environment.

Color is functional — it "works" for the office in various ways, depending upon the assignments of the employees. Thus, color formulas differ for the receptionist and the accountant, or for the conference room and the drafting department. Light colors are essential in offices where close work on white paper is done. Gray colors have the effect of putting workers to sleep. Strong colors like red or orange often have such a stimulating effect as to cause headaches. If the walls, woodwork, and other fixtures in the office are the same color, a sleep-producing effect is created. If the office has windows, warm colors such as yellow, peach, pink, brown, and tan can be used for eastern or northern exposures. For southern exposures, cool colors such as green, yellow-green, blue-green, and blue can be used. Although deeper colors can be used opposite windows, they should not be used on the window side because the contrast between the window and the dark colors is too great for visual comfort.

Color Dynamics.[3] The use of color influences the company's image as well as the health, morale, and efficiency of the employees. Therefore, color plays a dynamic role in planning the decor of the office.

Image. The image of a business firm is created substantially by the impression customers receive, either consciously or subconsciously, from the appearance of its offices. Attractive, cheerful, and efficient-looking offices tend to inspire feelings of confidence and trust; a drab, uninviting, or poorly painted office can induce a feeling of doubt or mistrust.

Health. Both the physical and mental health of office workers are directly affected by color. For example, the color of walls, furniture, and paper forms often causes eyestrain due to insufficient lighting or an improper reflection factor. This may cause employees to suffer headaches, sluggish or tired feelings, and other unhealthy effects that reduce the volume and accuracy of their work.

Morale. The attitudes of workers toward the other employees and their work are also affected by the use of color. For example, color influences the emotions and moods and ultimately the thinking and concentration powers of office workers. The so-called "warm" colors create cheerful feelings while colors that are "cool" effect an atmosphere of quiet restfulness.

Efficiency. As numerous studies show, color has a strong impact on the personal efficiency of workers. Industrial engineers report that production increases from 15 to 30 percent when colors are selected scientifically. One firm estimated that absenteeism was reduced 20 percent as a result of an improved color plan. A study made by the Public Buildings Administration and the U.S. Public Health Service measured the working efficiency of a group of employees using business machines. In the study three conditions were checked: (1) the original room, which had poor light and dark colors on machinery and floors; (2) the same situation with new flourescent lighting installed; and (3) the same room but with new lighting plus light gray floors and equipment and pale green walls. The results of the study were reported as follows:

From condition one to three, worker efficiency on one task improved 37.4 percent. However, a conservative figure of 5.5 percent was set for the general increase in productivity for the entire department. In cash value this was equivalent to a saving on gross payroll of $139.25 for each employee per year.[4]

[3]The term *Color Dynamics* refers to a painting system from Pittsburgh Paints, manufactured by PPG Industries. More information on the use of color to combine function and proper color use in decorating offices can be obtained from the Public Relations Department, PPG Industries, Inc., One Gateway Center, Pittsburgh, PA 15222.

[4]Faber Birren, "Impact of Color on Employee Morale and Productivity," *New Concepts in Office Design* (Elmhurst: Business Press, 1968), p. 93.

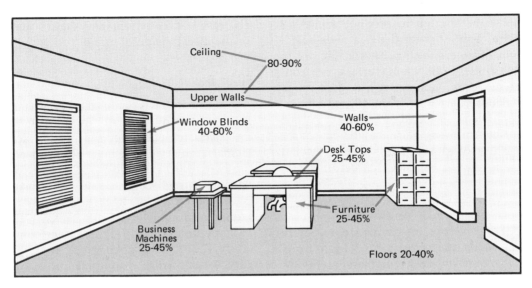

Fig. 6-2
Recommended Reflectances for Office Surfaces

Color, however, does not function alone. Rather, it is the combined effect of color and light, the visual work factors, that must be considered. For example, color and light influence office dimensions. Long, narrow offices can be made to seem wider by using darker, advancing colors on the end walls and lighter, retreating colors on long side walls. The impression of monotonous proportion can be avoided in square rooms by painting one wall, preferably the window or opposite wall, a color or value different than the others. For example, high ceilings seem perceptibly lower when painted darker than the walls.

Reflection Factors of Color. An understanding of the reflection factors of office surfaces and certain colors is of prime importance in controlling the brightness ratios. A *reflection factor*, sometimes called a *reflection ratio* or a *coefficient of reflection*, is the ratio of the total light reflected from a surface to the

total light striking that surface. To ensure the proper surface colors in the office, reflectance values of colors used should be restricted to those ranges shown in Figure 6-2.[5] Representatives of paint firms as well as specialists in office interior decorating can furnish valuable advice on office color selection at little or no cost.

Wall and Ceiling Colors. Many attractive and psychologically pleasant wall and ceiling colors are available. Such colors should be chosen with this general principle in mind: office walls and ceilings should be light enough to reflect light rather than absorb it, but

---

[5]*American National Standard Practice for Office Lighting*, RP-1, American National Standards Institute (New York: The Illuminating Engineering Society, June 21, 1973), p. 13. This reference is an excellent source of information on various aspects of lighting, including lighting criteria, lighting systems, the thermal environment, and the lighting standards recommended for specific office areas.

not light enough to produce annoying glare. Table 6-1 furnishes a wide selection of colors with reflection factors to meet all of the main surface environment needs. Generally, a middle range reflection factor between 40 and 60 percent has been found to be best for office walls. Annoying glare may be caused by the use of glossy paint. Therefore, flat paint should be used for ceilings and side walls.

Furniture and Equipment Colors. Glare on furniture is often caused by the reflection of light from glass tops on desks or from metal or other highly polished surfaces. For this reason dark shiny tops are not recommended for desks at which a great deal of continuous close work is performed. Instead, light-colored furniture with a nongloss or satin finish is the best choice from the point of view of reflection. Contrasting changes in light and dark color surfaces must also be controlled. Having a computer terminal operator look at dark machine dials or an equally dark terminal screen and then quickly shift his or her glance to white forms will unnecessarily tax the operator's eyes. Thus, equipment manufacturers offer surfaces that provide a soft

contrast between light and dark colors in the direct vision of office workers.

Floor Coverings

With emphasis given to all phases of the surface environment in the office, the psychological effect and the physiological comfort of adequate floor coverings come into play. Several classes of floor coverings are available. The most traditional type of flooring, wood, is available in many styles and lends itself to many decorating designs. Other commonly used floor coverings, such as vinyl asbestos tile, are durable and available in many colorful designs. Hard-surfaced coverings, such as marble, brick, and flagstone, are used to withstand heavy traffic in areas such as reception centers. However, many firms show a marked preference for carpeting all areas of the office, including the computer room, where elevated floors are required for access to the computer's electrical installations.

Carpeting creates a quiet, relaxed atmosphere in which to work. Through the use of carpeting, a feeling of luxury which enhances worker satisfaction is created. Since carpeting is a much more comfortable floor covering on which to

REFLECTION FACTORS OF COLORS

Color	Reflection Factor Percent	Color	Reflection Factor Percent
White	82	Golden yellow	51
Gray-white	76	Medium gray	46
Light cream	74	Dark orange	37
Very light green	70	Copper-yellow	27
Lemon-yellow	67	Medium red	21
Medium pink	60	Cadet blue	15
Very light blue	60	Dark red	12
Light gray	56	Dark green	10

walk, employee fatigue is reduced. It is also safer to walk on carpeting than on high-gloss, slippery tile or concrete. Carpeting's acoustical qualities as well as its ease of maintenance also offer advantages over other floor coverings.

A careful study should be made of the office functions (executive office or general office) and their traffic volume. In addition, these performance factors of carpeting should be considered: (1) ease of maintenance, considering fiber, weight, and soil resistance; (2) acoustical qualities (discussed in the section, "The Hearing Environment"); (3) control of static electricity; and (4) resistance to excessive wear. A reputable dealer or a commercial consultant can help managers to select the best type of carpeting to meet the needs of each office.[6]

THE SEEING ENVIRONMENT

Information processing in the office requires an adequate lighting system that must be evaluated in terms of its effect on people and their performance. Lighting, therefore, should not be taken for granted; inadequate and improper lighting contributes to eyestrain, which, in turn, may be the cause of many disorders such as muscular tension, fatigue, an increased blinking rate, and worker irritability. Unfavorable lighting conditions may also cause poor workmanship, mistakes, and decreased production as the result of inability to see the work clearly.

The main objective for the seeing environment is to provide efficient and comfortable lighting as an aid to office operations and to help provide a safe place to work. In particular, lighting affects the ability to see visual tasks with speed and accuracy; visual comfort; and the visual environment or the pleasantness of the space in which people live and work.[7] The use of natural lighting (daylight) and artificial lighting should be considered.

Natural Lighting in the Office

Although natural light can be put to use in many ways in the office, it must be controlled to some extent. Direct sunlight would, for example, produce glare, discomfort, and eyestrain; and on cloudy days, no sunlight would be available. But natural light can be "captured" as it comes in through the wraparound "curtain" of windows common to contemporary architecture. Unfortunately, the cheerfulness of natural light is often lost by heavy draperies, venetian blinds, or partitions that obscure portions of the light. Proper use of casements and window screens that diffuse the light, deflect glare, and protect the view of nature is recommended.

Quantity of Lighting

Research on the seeing needs at work has established a unit for measuring illumination, the *foot candle* (F-C), which is the amount of light produced by a standard candle at a distance of one foot. Generally the higher the foot-candle level of illumination attained, the better are the health, morale, and efficiency of the employees. Good lighting (including an absence of glare and sharp shadows) increases production because

---

[6]An excellent source of information on carpet and its selection and care, is the *Carpet Specifier's Handbook* that may be purchased from The Carpet and Rug Institute, Box 2048, Dalton, GA 30720.

[7]*American National Standard Practice for Office Lighting, op. cit.*, p. 5.

it enables employees to see more clearly and more quickly and to work more safely. Most utility companies will measure the level of illumination with a light meter and will make recommendations for changes in lighting where needed.

In making decisions on the needed quantity of illumination, the office manager should have a knowledge of the visual tasks expected of the workers. Some tasks, such as drafting, require close detail work and high foot-candle levels; others, such as conferring and interviewing, involve less concentrated reading and, therefore, considerably less quantities of light. Table 6-2 provides recommended minimum illumination levels for various types of office work.

Quality of Lighting

While the quantity of lighting can be easily measured, its quality is more difficult to ensure. There should be no compromise with lighting quality, however, for it affects visual comfort, the atmospheric climate, and the effectiveness of workers in the office.

A first consideration in achieving quality of lighting is the *brightness ratio*, that is, the ratio of *foot-lamberts* between two surfaces such as a visual task and its surroundings. (A foot-lambert is a unit of brightness approximating one foot-candle emitted or reflected.) If the brightness of a visual task is 60 foot-lamberts and that of a dark desk top against which it is viewed is 5 foot-lamberts, the brightness ratio is 12 to 1. This amount of brightness may cause visual discomfort. Normally the brightness ratio should not exceed 3 to 1.

Reflection and direct rays of sunlight and artificial light are not the only causes of eye discomfort. There are other causes that are all too common in offices today. A lighting fixture, or

---

RECOMMENDED ILLUMINATION LEVELS

Types of Office Area or Office Work	Minimum F-C on Task
Cartography, designing, detailed drafting	200
Accounting, auditing, tabulating, bookkeeping, business machines operation, reading poor reproductions, rough layout drafting	150
Regular office work, reading good reproductions, reading or transcribing handwriting in hard pencil or on poor paper. Active filing, index references, mail sorting, critical visual tasks in conference rooms	100
Reading or transcribing handwriting in ink or medium pencil on good quality paper, intermittent filing	70
Reading high contrast or well-printed material, tasks and areas not involving critical or prolonged seeing such as conferring, interviewing, inactive files, and washrooms	30
Corridors, elevators, escalators, stairways	20*

Table 6-2

Source: Adapted from *American National Standard Practice for Office Lighting*, RP-1, The Illuminating Engineering Society (1973 ed.), p. 7

*Or not less than 1/5 the level in adjacent areas.

luminaire, that is insufficiently shaded or shielded when in the visual field causes eye fatigue. If more than one fixture is in the visual field, the luminaires should be shaded or lowered to emit no more than 400 foot-lamberts. Other factors, such as the finishes of room surfaces and office equipment, can also strongly influence the visual comfort level. The reflectance of room surfaces has a considerable effect upon the utilization of light. Ceilings, walls, and floor coverings act as secondary light sources; and if proper color reflectances are used, increased utilization of light and reduced shadows can be achieved.

Office Lighting Systems

Besides natural lighting, which is usually not sufficient in quantity to meet all office lighting needs, two types of artificial lighting are available: incandescent light and fluorescent light.

Incandescent light is produced in filament lamps or bulbs. Such bulbs have a high power-factor rating, use much current, emit noticeable heat, and produce a steady light that strengthens yellow, orange, and red colors. In fact, incandescent light utilizes less than 10 percent of the input energy to produce light; the balance of the energy produces heat. Incandescent light fixtures and lamps are less expensive than fluorescent fixtures and tubes, but they are less efficient because of the difficulty in providing recommended levels of illumination.

Fluorescent light is produced by the action of ultraviolet waves on coated phosphors on the inside of tubular bulbs. Fluorescent lamps do not emit nearly so much radiant heat as incandescent lamps and consume about one third of the wattage for an equal amount

of light emitted. Their chief advantages are: low cost of operation, low radiant heat emission, resemblance to natural daylight in color, and ability to increase levels of illumination without rewiring the building. The use of a *luminous* ceiling, shown in Figure 6-3, provides an efficient system for general offices by diffusing the lighting evenly and indirectly over the entire work area.

The distribution of light is controlled by the type of luminaire chosen. Lighting systems should be designed so that the lighting equipment is spaced according to its light distribution and the characteristics of the room. Most lighting manufacturers publish spacing-to-mounting height ratios that should not be exceeded, and data are also available for predicting daylight distribution and sky conditions to be expected from various types of window arrangements.

Improving Lighting Systems

Any good lighting system is work- and worker-dependent; that is, the system must be designed considering the workers' unique assignments, their moods and periods of concentration as well as their overall visual comfort.[8] Such a complex task requires the technical skills of a lighting engineer and the work knowledge of the administrative office manager. Working as a team they must determine how to coordinate

---

[8]Information on improving lighting systems can be obtained from local light companies as well as from the Illuminating Engineering Society, 345 East 47th Street, New York, NY 10017. Two other valuable references on improving lighting are James F. Finn, "New Ways to Improve Office Lighting," *Administrative Management* (September, 1973), pp. 26–28; and Archie Kaplan, "Energy and Ergonomics: Task Lighting," *Modern Office Procedures* (September, 1974), pp. 73, 75.

*Designed for United Financial Center, Los Angeles,
by Welton Becker & Associates, Architects*

Fig. 6-3
Office Area Using Luminous Ceiling Lighting System

tasks and comfort needs of the workers, brightness requirements (such as spacing of luminaires), wiring and switch requirements, methods of light diffusion (such as glass partitions and doors), types of light fixtures that are efficient yet economical and convenient to maintain, and the relative advantages and disadvantages of incandescent versus fluorescent lighting.

The wise and efficient use of human energy, office space, lighting systems, and electrical energy must all be combined into a set of working guidelines for improving the seeing environment as shown below:

1. Emphasize seeing, rather than lighting alone, and the impact that good visibility has on employee mood and efficiency.

2. Consider the recommended illumination levels outlined in Table 6-2.

3. Provide maximum illumination for each task considered individually for each worker, and avoid the monotony

of standard illumination for the entire office area.

4. Make use of the visual comfort probability (VCP) guidelines for comparing and selecting suitable luminaires. A VCP rating of 70 is recommended for room areas such as offices and indicates the percentage of people who would consider the lighting system acceptable (in terms of discomfort from glare) when seated in the least desirable position in the room.[9]

5. Measure lighting conditions with a light meter, available from the local light company.

6. Minimize (and eliminate if possible) all glare and shadows.

7. Shade office windows so that sun rays are not permitted to shine directly on work surfaces.

8. Clean frequently all reflectors, lamps, windows, shades, or blinds. (Accumulated dust on lighting units can reduce the available light by an estimated 25 to 40 percent.)

9. Consult a qualified illuminating engineer for technical assistance in designing an office lighting system.

10. Provide supplemental task or work station lighting, such as desk lamps, to meet special seeing requirements by increasing the foot-candles of work areas.

THE HEARING ENVIRONMENT

Sound in the office environment can be good or bad. When sound is soothing to workers or helping office production, like background music and necessary conversation, it is good; when sound is irritating and distracting, like street noises and vibrating machines, it is bad. Unwanted sound is called *noise*, a factor that must be carefully controlled in the efficient office.

To understand noise control one must first understand some of the basic features of sound. Sound intensity is measured in *decibels*, with one decibel (db.) representing the lowest sound detectable by the human ear in quiet surroundings. From this point a decibel scale can be drawn at intervals of one or more decibels to represent increases in sound intensity detectable by the human ear. Since the decibel scale is logarithmic and not arithmetic, a small increase in the decibel level represents a large increase in sound intensity. Thus, 50 db. is twice as loud as 40 db., and 60 db. four times louder.[10] Figure 6-4 illustrates a scale in which common sounds and noises are ranked.

In determining a reasonably comfortable hearing environment, several elements must be considered. One is the pitch or frequency of the sound. Generally the more vibrations or cycles per second, the higher the pitch. Since high sounds are likely to be annoying, a pitch about the level of an alto voice is most pleasant. The duration of the sound as well as the number of times it occurs each day also affect the office worker. For example, a 90-db. sound occurring 30 times a day for a few minutes could be acceptable over an 8-hour day; but a higher intensity sound measured at 115 db. and occurring seven times a day could be tolerated for about only 15 minutes' duration. Studies by the federal government have shown that the age and the sex of workers as well as the

---

[9]James F. Finn, "New Ways to Improve Office Lighting," *Administrative Management* (September, 1973), p. 26.

[10]Jerome Gates, "Finding a Cure For the Noisy Office," *Office Products News* (May 16, 1975), p. 31.

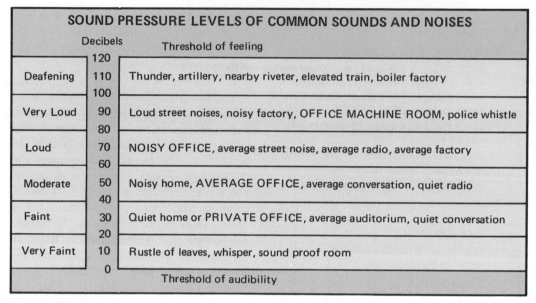

Source: "Stop, Look, and Listen to Your Office Environment," *Modern Office Procedures* (March, 1970), p. 18.

Fig. 6-4
Sound Pressure Levels of Common Sounds and Noises

distance traveled by the sound also affect the hearing environment.[11]

Recommended maximum levels of noise for efficient office work are as follows: (1) for the private office, 40-50 db.; (2) for the general office, 60 db.; (3) for the accounting office, 65 db.; and (4) for data centers, 80 db. Permitting the noise levels to extend beyond these maximum levels will result in physical and psychological problems for workers.

---

[11]The U.S. Department of Health, Education, and Welfare (HEW) publishes valuable materials on noise control. One such reference is *Occupational Exposure to Noise*, HSM 73-11001, 1972, available from the Superintendent of Documents, U.S. Government Printing Office, Washington, DC 20402. Related materials from private industry are also valuable, such as *Sound Control Construction: Principles and Performance*, 2d ed., 1972 available from United States Gypsum, 101 South Wacker Drive, Chicago, IL 60606.

Sources of Noise

In the modern city where most offices are located, noise may well be the most common negative feature of the environment. Automobiles, motorcycles, and trucks alone account for a sizable portion of this condition. These external elements of noise are carried into the office itself where the two key ingredients of office work — machines and personnel — are found. These two latter factors constitute the principal sources of all internal office noise.

It is not uncommon in even the smallest offices to find several electric typewriters, at least one copier, and one duplicating machine as well as air conditioning and heating equipment. Larger offices will have additional equipment like data processing machines, especially keypunch and printing machines, and teletypewriters and a telephone system connecting each work station with the internal and external environments. When these machines are in operation — many of them at the same time — for a large part of the work day, the cumulative noise level is very high. In fact, the sound from four or five typewriters alone has been measured at 80 db., not much less than the 90 db. produced by the nerve-racking noise of a pneumatic drill in the street.

While the machine is often considered the chief culprit of office noise, office personnel also contribute their share. Conversation, conferences and telephone calls, and interpersonal work assignments all cause vocal noise; and the distribution of processed data causes transportation noise as workers move from one location to another.

Effects of Office Noise

Noise in the office is more than unpleasant; in the short run it diminishes the worker's efficiency and hence increases office costs. In the long run noise may even have serious effects on the worker's health.

Office machine noise is a serious problem because it lowers employee morale and efficiency. Noise interferes with communication and makes concentration exceedingly difficult if not impossible, and in turn makes people irritable, fatigued, and less productive. High levels of noise may impair hearing and narrow the arteries, thereby raising the blood pressure and lessening the supply of blood to the heart. Over a prolonged period, excessive noise can cause hearing and sleep loss and even emotional damage.

Through the years, government and industry studies agree on the serious implications of uncontrolled noise. By

measuring caloric energy expended, one study showed that typists used 19 percent more energy in a noisy environment than the same group in a quiet office. Individuals subjected to bursts of 90-db. sounds experienced a significant decrease in their decision-making performance; and experiments in Germany have shown that, at 70 db., the human body's nervous system develops stress.

On the other hand, when noise levels are carefully reduced, positive effects upon workers and their work are found. One study showed that sound conditioning increased the overall efficiency of office employees 8.8 percent, decreased typists' errors 29 percent, and decreased machine operators' errors 52 percent. The turnover rate also decreased 47 percent. These results indicate that a quiet environment improves productivity.

Controlling Office Noise

Increased pressures at the local, state, and national levels to improve the living environment have had far-reaching implications on the control of noise. One important federal law passed in 1970, the Occupational Safety and Health Act (OSHA), restricts permissible noise levels at a place of work to 90 db. for eight hours, or 95 db. for four hours. Usually this maximum level is applied to industrial settings, such as construction sites, rather than to offices and is seriously questioned by managers who feel that the level should be lowered to 85 db. (the threshold of hearing damage if the noise level is sustained). When considerable concentration is required even this noise level should be reduced by 50 percent.

Two main efforts characterize an effective noise control program: (1) eliminating the source of the noise, and (2) reducing the effect of the noise through the use of sound-absorbing materials. For the latter approach, a noise reduction coefficient (NRC) has been developed that measures the amount of noise absorbed or removed from the area. For example, an acoustical screen with an NRC rating of 85 absorbs 85 percent of the noise striking it. The highest attainable NRC rating is 95.[12]

At the root of any noise control program is this basic fact: hard surfaces reflect sounds while soft surfaces absorb them. Each of the following effective noise-reduction practices illustrates this essential point.

Layout and Location. Exterior noises can in some cases be eliminated or reduced in intensity if the office is relocated. For example, there is considerably less noise on the tenth floor of a large building than on the first floor. Keeping doors and windows closed, if possible, also helps reduce unwanted sound. "Noisy" departments, such as those having many machines, can be segregated into a remote, corner location, thus isolating the noise from the departments requiring a more quiet working environment. Acoustical screens, which absorb some of the noise, may also be used in areas where it is too noisy for workers to function efficiently.

Personnel. To reduce the noise created by office workers, efficient layout is recommended to decrease the amount of required walking. For example, placing side by side two office workers required to do considerable

work together can reduce telephone calls and cut down on frequent moving about. Conferences can be scheduled for private offices, and workers can be instructed to converse in low tones and to restrict informal personal interaction to break periods.

When working conditions will not permit a noticeable reduction in noise, some firms assign deaf workers to tasks that necessarily retain a high level of noise over an extended period. Other firms with jobs that have intermittently high noise levels select workers under 25 years of age, as studies show that this age group tires less quickly than older workers and can adapt more easily to changing conditions.

Surface Coverings. When a large office has hard walls, floor, and ceiling coverings, the room is acoustically "live" and sounds reflect back and forth. Workers are thus immersed in the noise and feel that it comes from everywhere. If, however, the office is heavily treated with sound-absorbing materials, the reflected sound is reduced; and what sound remains seems to come directly from the source, say a machine, and seems to be less annoying. If the office environment is too quiet, the workers become conscious of their own bodily processes, and the slightest movements and insignificant sounds become disturbing. Usually such workers prefer some "masking sound" — a kind of "acoustical perfume" — to cover up the little sounds that might otherwise become distracting. The term *white noise* is used to describe such a source of sound. White noise provides a uniform sound distribution representing all frequencies in equal amounts throughout the work environment. The hum of electrical equipment and luminaires is

---

[12]Jerritt A. Ritter, "Screening Out Noise," *Management World* (December, 1973), pp. 9–10.

typical of this type of sound.[13] Music, too, is used to "mask" or hide unwanted noises and can have a positive psychological effect on office workers. The nature of music in the office and its effect upon workers is discussed in "The Atmospheric Environment."

Floor Coverings. Since hard floor coverings or hard surfaces reflect rather than absorb sound, uncovered concrete floors in the office are to be avoided at any cost. Resilient coverings such as rubber, asphalt, and cork tile, however, have considerable absorption qualities. High-pile carpeting is the preferred floor covering for reducing office noise from footsteps, the movement of chairs and desks, and the dropping of objects. Carpeting also aids in muffling other sound waves directed to the office area.[14]

Wall Coverings. Any room contains considerable absorptive material — in the walls, furniture, ceilings, and floors, as well as in the people and their clothing. To achieve a reduction in the office decibel level, the absorption materials must be increased considerably. Fabrics in upholstered office furniture and draperies have noise-reducing qualities and are used both for window and wall treatments and inner office partitions. Draperies should be spaced about three or four inches away from the windows to obtain the best sound absorption. Modern office designers frequently utilize carpeting on walls and pillars as well as on floors for its decorative effect and to further absorb sound.

Ceiling Coverings. Wall and ceiling surfaces in modern offices are often finished in plaster applied on concrete or hollow tile. Every sound produced in such offices is intensified and permeates the entire room, unless some absorptive material is placed on the office surfaces. The material most frequently used as a ceiling covering to reduce noise is acoustical tile. Dozens of styles and types of acoustical tile are available, with one firm producing more than 70 types for office use.

Machines and Equipment. Typical of a modern information center is SNOCOM, a centralized data base that maintains police records for five cities in southwest Snohomish County in Washington. In an average month over 2,200 calls for assistance go out from two dispatch consoles. At the same time, more than 7,000 telephone calls and nearly 8,000 inquiries into the computers and 50,000 radio transmissions are handled monthly. In such an active information-processing environment, office noise reaches alarming proportions, necessitating a program for proper noise control.

Besides placing all noisy machines in one soundproof location — which is not always possible and still does not improve conditions for the machine operators — the following noise-reduction

---

[13]White noise represents a highly technical subject in acoustical engineering. For more information on this topic, consult Lyle F. Yerges, *Sound, Noise, and Vibration Control* (New York: Van Nostrand-Reinhold Company, 1969) and the *Encyclopedia of Science and Technology* (New York: McGraw-Hill Book Co., 1974), p. 136.

[14]Information on flooring is available from two associations: Asphalt Tile Institute, 101 Park Avenue, New York, NY 10017, and the Vinyl and Rubber Flooring Division, the Rubber Manufacturers' Association, 444 Madison Avenue, New York, NY 10022. Some manufacturers, such as Armstrong Cork Company, will give free advice relating to the installation of flooring.

possibilities, should be considered by the office manager:

1. Enclosures such as partitions or acoustical screens control noise at individual work stations and isolate noisy machines. In an area where utmost quiet and privacy are desired, the tall screen with good sound-absorbing properties is recommended.

2. Ear plugs, properly fitted, may reduce loudness as much as 80 percent at certain noise levels. However, many people do not like the idea of wearing earplugs, stating that they can get accustomed to noise.

3. Bells on telephones and typewriters can be muted; noiseless typewriters may be considered if nonelectric machines are to be used.

4. Rubber-tired casters and bumpers on movable equipment should be required. All such equipment should be kept properly oiled and adjusted.

5. Well-built file cabinets with easy-moving suspension drawers should be selected by the manager.

6. Noisy machines should be encased in sound-engineered acoustical cabinets. (Figure 6-5 shows a table-model acoustical enclosure used with data processing machines.)

In the final analysis, however, the administrative office manager should apply common sense in the noise control program. One can test a single piece of equipment or evaluate the office as a whole by determining whether a normal telephone conversation can be conducted next to the operating equipment without raising the voice or shouting. If not, a noise problem exists.[15]

---

[15]Jerome Gates, "Finding a Cure For the Noisy Office," *Office Products News* (May 16, 1975), p. 31.

THE ATMOSPHERIC ENVIRONMENT

Air-conditioned surroundings are assumed by most people to be a basic atmospheric requirement for the comfortable office. There are, however, additional factors, such as air temperature and circulation, and the general condition of cleanliness that affect the physical atmosphere of the office. Similarly, the overall psychological office climate is also affected by these factors and by the music-while-you-work concept. Each of these atmospheric elements is discussed in this section.

Music in the Office

Music in the office is designed to reduce fatigue due to strain, monotony, or just plain tiredness from long periods of work. Music *in itself* does not increase efficiency, reduce errors, or keep employees from leaving their jobs. Music helps relieve the boredom and mental strains that lead to poor productivity and dissatisfaction. The amount of benefit to be received from music in the office is related to the type of work being performed. The more tedious, monotonous, or repetitive the work, the greater the soothing effect that background music may have on mental fatigue.

A number of firms, such as Muzak, that specialize in furnishing music to offices and factories have made careful studies of what kind of music to use and when to use it. One large supplier of music to offices has found that music for offices must be more subdued than music for factories. Distracting influences in the music, such as vocals, loud brasses, or changes in tempo, are usually avoided; strings and woodwinds in

Gates Acoustinet, Inc.

Fig. 6-5
Acoustical Cabinets for Muffling Machine Noise

orchestras predominate. A good music program incorporates all types — classical, semiclassical, show tunes, and popular music. The music should be so unobtrusive that it can be absorbed without mental distraction. Furthermore, the music should not be continuous. It should be turned on and off for brief periods, totaling about one to two and one-half hours a day.

An Administrative Management Society (AMS) survey of 336 member companies of varying types and sizes in the United States and Canada showed that 254 of these firms provide music for their employees. Of the 254 firms 70 percent use piped-in music; 63.8 percent use wire and 36.2 percent use radio; 75 percent have the music professionally programmed, while only 25 percent prepare the programs themselves.[16] Most respondents felt that music can improve employee morale, relieve job monotony, and help to level out disturbing noise peaks. Although the majority of respondents felt that music helps "cool down" temperamental workers, that same majority stated that music does not help to reduce turnover or help in recruiting.

---

[16]"Piped-In Music Is Money to Employers," *Administrative Management* (March, 1971), p. 66.

Although case studies of manufacturers of music systems indicate that music in the workplace results in significant increases in productivity, there is a lack of scientific research on the subject. Nevertheless, consistent reports from highly reputable firms such as Lever Brothers and Eastern Airlines show highly favorable employee reactions to the use of music. Only a small percentage (below 10 percent) of workers dislike music, but the work force in any office should be polled regarding their music preferences.[17]

Air Conditioning in the Office

To many people air conditioning means cooling the office to a temperature that is comfortable for work. Temperature, however, represents only one of several atmospheric elements that are controlled by air-conditioning equipment. When the total air environment is conditioned, it is scientifically treated so that its temperature, circulation, humidity, and cleanliness are all accurately and constantly controlled.

Air conditioning in an office contributes to mental activity and boosts efficiency; its "liveness" gives employees vigor. Bad, dry, and dusty air reduces the efficiency and hampers the production of employees. This is especially true in work, such as office tasks, that is largely mental in nature. A lack of air conditioning means lowered vitality, headaches, and "four o'clock fatigue."

The United States General Services Administration has conducted an extensive study of the impact of air conditioning on office workers. Two large offices — one air-conditioned, the other not — were studied for five months to compare employee performance. In the air-conditioned office it was found that productivity increased 9.5 percent; absenteeism decreased 2.5 percent; and clerical errors were down slightly, .9 percent.[18]

Temperature. Extended and scientific research by the American Society of Heating, Refrigerating, and Air-Conditioning Engineers and the United States Public Health Service has determined the most healthful and comfortable air conditions for normal people, at both sedentary and active occupations, in offices, shops, and homes. Although there is no temperature level that will please everybody, the most comfortable and healthful temperature for work is below 70°. This is true, however, only when proper humidity or moisture is maintained. The normal body temperature of the human being remains constant, winter or summer, so long as health prevails.

Thermal (heat) comfort, therefore, is the result of a proper balance in temperature, relative humidity, and air motion. The thermal environment may be created by using the outside temperature in combination with the number of lighting fixtures and their relationship to room surfaces, the number of workers in the office, the number of large office machines, the height of the ceiling, and the material used in constructing the

---

[17]*Ibid.*

[18]"Does Your Office Need Air Conditioning?" *Modern Office Procedures* (March, 1961), p. 26. This article describes several other surveys in which the findings show increases in efficiency of 24 to 51 percent and decreases in absenteeism of 25 to 30 percent after the installation of air conditioning. Similar information on a word processing center is summarized in the article by Molly Ersay, "Creating an Efficient and Attractive Place to Work," *Modern Office Procedures* (March, 1975), p. 54.

building. The development of *space conditioning*, or *heating with light*, which combines air conditioning and heat, captures this heat and puts it to use. Cool air is brought into the office to cool the lighting fixtures and prolong their life; at the same time the fixtures warm the air. During the summer the warm air is blown out of the building, thus helping to reduce the air-conditioning load; in the winter the air is recirculated to help heat the office.

Some lighting systems often provide enough heat to warm offices without the need for additional heat, and in some instances the heat from the air is drawn off into storage tanks for later use when the lights are off. In other systems the lighting fixtures are tied in with thermostats that turn on the lights during the night to help heat the offices.[19] An increasing number of newly constructed office buildings make use of this "heating with light" method.

Air Circulation. Even though a reasonable room temperature is maintained, the air must be circulated to prevent each person from becoming encased in air that approaches skin temperature and the saturation point. Ideally, ten cubic feet per minute of outside air should be provided each person; and the air flow should be gentle and not drafty, preferably not exceeding 25 feet a minute. Circulating air has a cooling effect, even though its temperature

may be high, because it accelerates the evaporation of body moisture.

Several effective methods of keeping air in motion are commonly found. The older, least expensive equipment, the fan, is used satisfactorily in small offices and often as supplementary equipment in large offices. It may be placed anywhere within the office for circulating the same air. The newer type, often called a "vent fan," is placed in a window opening, facing the outdoors. Pushing out stale air and odors and admitting new air, the vent fan provides a complete change of air every few minutes. However, the vent fan is not coordinated with temperature and moisture control. Air may also be kept in motion through blowers, which are used in the larger office buildings, schools, and public buildings. Each blower consists of a motor-driven fan, enclosed in a chamber, with large tubes leading away from it. These tubes are distributed throughout the building, with openings in different rooms. The fan pushes air through the tubes. This air escapes through the openings in the rooms, forcing the other air to move.

Humidity. Air-conditioning equipment adds or removes moisture from the air. It humidifies the air during the winter and dehumidifies it during the summer. The removal of moisture from the air is accomplished by condensation. The temperature of the air is lowered below its dew point, thereby causing the excess water to condense and fall into the tank of the conditioning machine.

If the relative humidity of the atmosphere is high, it makes one feel colder on a cold day and hotter on a hot day. One is more comfortable in a room with a temperature of 65 to 70° if the air is reasonably moist than in a room where

---

[19]For additional information on the thermal environment and on the conservation of light heat energy, see the *American National Standard Practice for Office Lighting*, RP-1 (New York: The Illuminating Engineering Society, June 21, 1973), pp. 18–20. In this reference the thermal energy available from light sources is discussed along with systems for heat transfer through air, water, and ceiling heat systems. Additional information is available from the local light company.

the air is dry and the temperature several degrees higher. Studies show that the relative humidity can drop to as low as 25 percent without affecting human comfort, but sensitive equipment may malfunction due to static buildup at lower humidity levels.[20] Generally, the relative humidity should be approximately 50 percent for comfort and health.

Cleanliness of the Office. The total conditioning of office space calls for maintaining an environment that is free of dirt, dust, odors, and other unpleasant or harmful conditions. First of all, clean conditions are more healthful for workers and promote a good environment in which to work. Complex equipment, too, requires dustless surroundings to function in an optimum manner. From the management standpoint, a clean, sparkling office environment connotes a feeling of efficiency and of regard for both customers and employees.

The complete air-conditioning system provides a well-controlled, clean environment. Ultraviolet lamps that destroy a large percentage of airborne bacteria in large work locations are available, often reducing the incidence of common colds. Mechanical air filters, too, are used to strain foreign particles out of the air through cloth, felt, cellulose, glass fibers, or other air filtering materials.

EVALUATING THE TOTAL ENVIRONMENT

The administrative office manager is advised to develop a program of periodic evaluation and renewal of the total office environment. Included in such a program would be the factors listed below:

1. *Maintaining the surface environment*: scrubbing, polishing, mopping, waxing, buffing, and sweeping the floors; vacuuming the carpet; cleaning the stairs and elevators; policing the lobby and corridors; and washing and repainting walls and ceilings as needed.
2. *Lighting:* cleaning and replacing fixtures and bulbs.
3. *Windows:* washing inside and out; cleaning and maintaining window shades and draperies.
4. *Restrooms:* cleaning and servicing.
5. *Outdoor factors:* maintaining the lawn; driveway cleaning; landscaping.
6. *Miscellaneous factors:* general utility work including moving and rearranging equipment; refurbishing equipment; exterminating insects.
7. *Maintenance cost controls:* keeping records of maintenance time expended and labor costs per 1,000 square feet of office space cleaned. (In relatively clean air-conditioned offices consider eliminating daily or nightly cleaning and switching to dry-mopping and dusting every other day. As much as one third of the cleaning costs can be saved with this plan.)

CONSERVING ENERGY IN THE OFFICE

The United States, which uses more energy per capita than any other nation, faces a serious energy shortage. Although it has only about 6 percent of the world's population, its people consume about 35 percent of all the energy, mostly petroleum, used in the world. As the largest user of energy in the United States — about two thirds of the nation's energy supply — American

---

[20]Ersay, *op. cit.*, p. 54.

business has an opportunity and need to achieve significant energy savings without reducing production. As a national average, the electricity consumption for a commercial building occupying one million square feet breaks down in this way: general lighting, 54 percent; advertising and display, 7 percent; elevators, 11 percent; fans and air-handling equipment, 10 percent; pump and motors, 3 percent; and office equipment, 13 percent.[21]

Administrative office managers share the responsibility with other managers to study their overall energy needs and to develop energy conservation programs within their firms. An increasing amount of assistance from governmental agencies and private industrial and professional associations is available to aid in meeting this goal.[22]

The Energy Management Program

Energy management is the application of the same basic techniques to the use of energy resources that one would apply to administration, finance, marketing, or production in any well-run business. Successful approaches to energy management typically include the prac-

tices described briefly in the following paragraphs.

Appointing an Energy Coordinator. To spearhead the company program, an energy coordinator or special power consultant group should be selected. Working through the plant manager, the energy coordinator designates managers who, in turn, are held accountable for energy resource management in each department.

Conducting an Energy Audit. In an energy audit the manager surveys the energy required to complete each process, the actual energy used, and the variance between projected and actual use. The goal is to reduce the variance. With the audit a manager knows what is being spent for energy and for what purpose, and thus is able to develop sound conservation measures. Without the audit, the manager encounters difficulty in finding out what can be done to conserve energy. Energy suppliers, such as the local light or power company and machine contractors, are available to review a firm's energy requirements.

Setting Energy Conservation Goals. Exactly how large the goal of energy conservation should be or how it should be expressed will depend upon the individual situation. But whatever the goal, it should be specific and measurable (for example, reducing the electricity consumed by 15 percent), and conscientiously applied. Employees should be made aware of the need to save energy and reduce energy costs in their personal lives as well as on the job. Examples of such savings, as they relate to office building construction and to lighting, heating, and cooling systems

[21]U.S. Department of Commerce, Office of Energy Programs, *Energy Management: Trade Associations and the Economics of Energy* (Washington: U.S. Government Printing Office, undated), p. 15.

[22]Information on energy management and energy cost reduction is available from both the Domestic and International Business Administration and the Office of Energy Programs, U.S. Department of Commerce, Washington, DC 20230; from professional groups like the National Mineral Wool Insulation Association, 211 East 51st Street, New York, NY 10022; and from the Electric Energy Association, 90 Park Avenue, New York, NY 10016. Also, the local light company will furnish practical guidelines for saving energy.

in the office are described in the following section.

Energy Conservation Methods

Until recently energy appeared to be in plentiful supply and relatively inexpensive, accounting for an average of less than five percent of each dollar of operating costs of a business. As a result, many business executives did not have a strong incentive to conserve energy. But as prices rose sharply and the availability of energy supplies became more unpredictable, the impact of the energy problem on all phases of the economy — the office included — caused growing concern to management. How to cut energy usage and reduce energy costs have become high-priority management problems.

Management control of energy use must be assigned the same importance as other key functions, and efficiency measures designed to reduce energy waste must be instigated. Energy savings in the 10 to 15 percent range have been reported in trade publications and other sources from the use of such conservation methods as described in this section.[23]

Building Construction. An estimated 20 to 30 percent of a building's heat supply can be lost because of poor insulation in a poorly constructed build-

ing.[24] The installation of proper insulation and weather stripping to confine heat and cooling can save much energy. Also, moving people from floor to floor in high-rise buildings expends great amounts of energy. Energy can be conserved through horizontal expansion of office buildings along with decreasing the use of floor-to-ceiling windows and incorporating awnings to reduce the influx of heat.

Conserving Light. A number of lighting engineers contend that there is 10 to 20 percent too much lighting in modern office buildings — that many times it is so intense that the main function of the air conditioning is to remove the heat that the light causes. In many commercial buildings the recommended lighting has gone as high as 124 F-C although the recommended level is 70 (as compared to a minimum in Great Britain of 10 F-C).[25] This excessive lighting not only consumes scarce energy but also adds to the rising cost of office services.

Office lighting costs can be effectively reduced by as much as 15 percent by following these simple conservation measures:

1. Provide planned operation and maintenance procedures, keeping lighting equipment clean and in good working condition.
2. Turn off lights when not needed for work tasks. Where safety and security

---

[23]For good sources of information on energy conservation, consult the Office of Energy Programs (OEP), U.S. Department of Commerce, Washington, DC 20230. The material in this section was adapted from OEP publications as well as from energy conservation bulletins of the Iowa-Illinois Gas and Electric Company, Davenport, IA 52801.

[24]Dwayne Meisner, "The Whole Office Catalog," *Administrative Management* (February, 1974), p. 29.
[25]Walter Kleinschrod, "Editorial: The Energy Crisis Could Change the Way We Run Our Offices," *Administrative Management* (September, 1973), p. 25.

are not a factor, there is no need for lighting. In some locations, such as inactive storage areas, every other light can be turned off without impairing the illumination.

3. Minimize outside flood lighting and use of electric signs. Time clock controls can be used to turn off lights that should go on at dusk and off at dawn.

4. Control window brightness and utilize daylight as practicable. Where feasible, individual switches for each fixture can be provided to allow workers at each station to select desired lighting levels. Also, solid-state dimmers can help to obtain desired lighting levels.

5. Use light colors on ceilings, walls, floors, and furnishings. Light colors can increase the amount of light available by as much as 30 F-C, thereby decreasing the amount of artificial light required.

6. Use efficient light sources and luminaires. Since incandescent lamps are about 30 percent as efficient as fluorescent lamps in terms of light output per electrical energy, greater use of the more efficient fluorescent lamps (for indoors) and metal Halide lamps (for outdoors) should be considered.

7. Design the lighting system for the tasks to be performed. Where tasks are fixed and known, the lighting should be designed accordingly (such as fixtures attached to the furniture close to the task), but less lighting should be provided in surrounding nonworking areas. By furnishing task-oriented lighting rather than general high illumination levels throughout the office, use of electrical energy can be reduced by 20 to 50 percent.

Conserving Heat. Energy used for heating buildings comprises about 18 percent of the total energy consumed on a national basis. In an energy management program the heat conservation

objective, therefore, should be to reduce the relative requirements for existing or newly installed essential space heating. Many of the following conservation suggestions can be implemented at little or no cost:

1. Maintain an efficient heating plant. To reduce energy waste in heating, the furnace or boiler should be in good condition with appropriate air supplied for combustion. Air filters should be cleaned or changed, and vents, flues, and burners kept clean.

2. Set thermostats lower. If the office temperature is maintained at 70° to 80° F. (or about 21° to 26° Celsius), consider lowering the settings to 68° F. (20° Celsius) during the workday and suggest that office personnel wear warmer clothing. Generally for each degree above 68° F. of a thermostatic setting, it will cost three percent more for heating. The smaller the difference between the indoor and outdoor temperature, the higher the savings in energy and in heating costs. Over-night and weekend settings should be lowered to 60° to 62°.

3. Control heating by the thermometer, not by the calendar.

4. Reduce temperatures in public spaces, corridors, hallways, lobbies, and other nonwork areas. People usually move through these spaces, but seldom sit for hours at a time; and hence a lower temperature is recommended for saving energy.

5. Close off rooms not used and turn off the heat to those rooms.

6. Reduce to a minimum the openings to the office. Windows and doors represent a huge heating load. Windows should be checked for air leakage; and where a constant stream of people enter and leave the building, double sets of doors or revolving doors should be used.

7. Let the sun help maintain room temperatures. The "greenhouse" effect

translates into energy savings because less heat is required from the heating plant, but the shades and draperies should be drawn at night to conserve or confine the heat.

8. Concentrate evening work or meetings in a single heating zone. Then, it becomes possible to reduce the heating in the remainder of the building.

9. Wear warmer clothing. Generally bare arms and ankles tend to make a person feel cooler in heated spaces while long sleeves, sweaters, and heavier and longer socks will allow a worker to remain comfortable at the lower room temperatures.

Conserving Cool Temperatures.
The amount of energy consumed to provide summer cooling can be reduced by improving the energy performance of cooling systems, by reducing the loads

imposed on these systems, and by periodically reassessing the levels of cooling needs. Involved are adequate equipment maintenance and the use of equipment only when it is needed by people or by essential work processes. The use of window shades, too, can aid the cool-conservation program; shades are used as window and door insulation. It is essential not to overcool. Studies of summer cooling have shown that, with suitable clothing, temperatures approaching 80° F. (or 26° Celsius) and relative humidity levels approaching 60 percent may be acceptable. At such levels, an estimated 15 percent reduction in energy can be achieved compared with 75° F. (or 22° Celsius) and 50 percent relative humidity. Lightweight clothing, too, can help workers adjust to the higher temperature settings necessary to reduce costs.

QUESTIONS FOR REVIEW

1. Define the term "ergonomics." What is its relationship to productivity in the office?

2. What key factors account for the difficulty in understanding human behavior?

3. In what way does color influence the firm's image and the health, morale, and efficiency of its employees?

4. Color dynamics is a more important psychological problem than most office managers realize. Explain the physical and psychological effects of the following: (a) warm colors, (b) strong colors, and (c) same color for the entire office area and fixtures.

5. What is meant by the reflection factor of colors? How does this factor affect the problem of color dynamics?

6. Identify the various alternatives for floor coverings in the modern office, and compare the relative values of each to the improvement of the office environment.

7. What is a foot-candle? What are the recommended illumination levels for various office jobs?

8. How can the quality of lighting be measured?

9. Compare the relative advantages of fluorescent and incandescent lighting. Which type of lighting is recommended for general office use?

10. What is a decibel? Discuss the relative sound levels of common office noises and how noise can be controlled in an office.

11. What psychological and physiological effects are found in workers subjected to undue noise?

12. How does a noise-reduction coefficient (NRC) differ from a decibel rating?

13. Why do administrative office managers use music in the office environment? Is there conclusive evidence that music improves office productivity?

14. What are the atmospheric factors which comprise the total air-conditioned environment?

15. Outline the principal phases of an energy management program.

16. In the typical firm, what energy conservation methods are available for reducing lighting, heating, and cooling costs?

QUESTIONS FOR DISCUSSION

1. In an interview a design consultant remarked, "Offices that lack human qualities dull the senses, slow the mind, reduce the ability to discriminate, and increase the chance of error." The consultant also said that when the individuality of workers is not recognized in the planning and design of offices, the workers become bored and, as a result, less efficient and productive. Discuss several techniques that may be employed to overcome the feeling of boredom on the part of employees, thus making the offices more human.

2. A problem common to many offices is suddenly presented in your office: the older workers complain of feeling cold during much of the winter season while the younger workers complain of feeling too warm. How can the interests of both groups be considered in resolving this "conflict of interests"?

3. Personal conversations among the general office staff and transportation of paperwork have become excessive, in the view of Stan Policano, office manager. In observing work flows, he notes that the

physical layout appears to need revision, and the physical environmental factors require study. Outline the sequential steps you would recommend Policano follow in order to study, revise, and test an improved office design. Your principal objective, Policano stresses, is controlling the hearing environment and reducing internal noises.

4. You and the other 20 members of your office staff have become accustomed to inexpensive energy supplies required to operate your headquarters office. As a result, heating, lighting, and cooling costs have never been questioned. Suddenly, however, you have been given an ultimatum to reduce by 15 percent the costs of all forms of energy used in your office. Discuss how you would plan, organize, and implement an energy management program, indicating from whom you would seek advice and how you would handle the principal human reactions to energy reductions.

5. Jennifer Palmer, a highly regarded ergonomic specialist, has agreed to speak to your administrative office management staff on the practical benefits of ergonomic planning to office productivity. As office supervisor for your firm, you need to compile a list of factual cost-benefit questions that you want covered in Palmer's talk. What would your list include?

6. One of your most efficient keypunch operators, Elton Smith, complains about the increasing problems he is having with noise from his own machine and that of the other six keypunch machines positioned near him. The keypunch section is isolated in one corner of a large general office with appropriate acoustical screening, but Smith himself is not isolated from the noise. His performance, normally the highest in the section, has dropped off sharply in recent weeks; and he has expressed to you, his supervisor, on several occasions his growing concern about the noise problem. However, he insists on staying on the job until he reaches 62 years of age, five years from now. What steps can be taken to remedy this situation and permit Smith to regain his former operating efficiency?

7. The McKenna Manufacturing Company is planning to move its plant and offices to a city in the Tennessee Valley district where there are cheaper power and a good trainable labor supply. The city selected has a population of 20,000. Very little manufacturing has been done heretofore in this city. The firm will require space for 1,400 factory workers and 400 office employees. The temperature in this city varies from 5° F. in the winter to 108° F. in the summer. In addition to providing space for the needs of the plant and the office, the site selected has sufficient area for ample parking.

   As the office administrator of this firm, you are asked to recommend the physical factors that should be considered and the facilities to be installed; you want the employees to work in a healthful environment which promotes good morale and encourages employees to a high productivity.

8. Because the office employees of Tresnak Mills have complained about the quality and quantity of lighting in their various offices, a

survey was made to determine the suitability of the present lighting system. The survey involved the use of a light meter and a team of one office supervisor and one representative of the light company who found these conditions:

a. In the general office where 20 accountants and marketing personnel work constantly at their desks, there are 500-watt filament lamps, indirect luminaires, spaced 10 feet apart, providing 25 F-C. (Indirect luminaires direct 90-100 percent of the light to the ceiling and upper side walls from which it is reflected to all parts of the room.)

b. In the word processing department where there are ten correspondence secretaries, the indirect luminaires contribute 100 F-C.

c. In the records center where there are three file clerks and one files supervisor, the light offered is 50 F-C.

d. In the drafting room which faces north, there are 120 F-C of light.

e. In the three private offices occupied by top management, the use of task-oriented lighting provides 70 F-C.

f. All hallways and lobbies provide 70 F-C of light.

Analyze the lighting conditions in these areas. Suggest improvements that you would make and give the reasons for your suggestions on the lighting conditions.

PRACTICAL OFFICE MANAGEMENT CASES

Case 6-1   Renovating the Office Environment

The Vernon Corn Products Corporation, located in a midwestern city of 120,000, is engaged in the processing of corn and cane for shipment throughout the country. Its principal products are syrups, molasses, and cooking supplies to complement the waffle and pancake products produced in another subsidiary. The firm was started by a conservative midwestern family more than 90 years ago and has steadily grown from a work force of five (the Vernon family alone) with annual sales of $750 to its present size of 1,150 with annual sales totaling approximately $25 million. The firm is still a close corporation, headed by a member of the founding family, Marcia Vernon. As president, she seems to reflect the industrious, conservative point of view of the founder.

The office occupies the entire three-story brick building located due south and within 100 feet of the two huge processing plants. This building was constructed 35 years ago. Nearby is a trunkline of the railroad used in shipping packaged products as well as carload lots to large institutional users of the firm's products. Due to its north-central geographic location and also due to the fact that the prevailing summer breezes usually blow from the south, the office area retains a moderately cool summer temperature and has not been air-conditioned. In fact, no basic structural changes have been made in the building since it was built, although the building has been maintained in a spotless condition and painted regularly every four years.

The building is laid out according to the following plan:

First floor: mail room and reprographic services (near the elevator); records center; purchasing department; sales and advertising departments; engineering department; shipping services.
Second floor: financial offices; accounting department; data processing.
Third floor: general office services; executive offices.

Traditionally the general office function has been the responsibility of the accounting department, which has been highly cost conscious. As early as 1915, a cost accounting system was installed to control the plant's processing operation; and in the office a detailed cost accounting system was put into operation in 1938. As a result it is generally believed that costs have been contained and that the major effort toward maximizing profits for the firm has been satisfied.

The office services group is responsible for general office work for the entire firm. Although the department executives and their assistants have secretarial help for departmental work, the bulk of the office work, such as correspondence, reproduction work, and typing of reports and forms, is handled by the word processing center on the third floor. Other responsibilities of the office services group are centralized filing, ordering office supplies, designing and procuring office forms, and other related clerical services. Included in the general office services group are the office manager; an administrative secretary, Don Binnall; the word processing center consisting of 15 correspondence secretaries supervised by a veteran employee, Gertrude Erickson; and a general clerical pool of 12 who are responsible for filing and other clerical tasks, headed by Prudence Robillard.

Recently Juanita Perez, a young, ambitious senior accountant, has been transferred from the accounting department to replace Roger LeBlanc, the office manager, who has retired after 32 years in his position. Perez is approximately the same age as Vernon and was chosen for the position because of her fine performance in the accounting department, her overall knowledge of the firm, and her educational background in general management, data processing, and information systems. It appeared to Vernon, to whom Perez reports, that Perez could integrate the many information-processing activities of the firm into a workable system. She is already knowl-edgeable concerning the firm's combined punched-card and small-scale computer system on the second floor, a unit that has recently expanded so that its six keypunch operators have been forced to take temporary quarters in one section of the general office services area.

Within three months after assuming her new position, Perez conducted an intensive office audit to determine the scope and con-dition of her area of responsibility. In this audit Perez discovered the following significant facts:

1. A "total systems" approach should be considered in which data process-ing systems are developed for each of the departments in the firm.
2. While the entire office environment needs modernization to reflect a more progressive image for the firm, immediate attention should be cen-tered on the general office area and executive suites. Specifically:

   a. The entire building should be air-conditioned. Although meteoro-logical records indicate that, on the average, only 20 days each sum-mer have temperatures above 90° F., an offsetting feature is the fact that 80 of the 90 days during the summer season have relative humid-ity levels above 75 percent. In addition, the workers in the office have complained repeatedly about the open windows in the summer which let in sickening odors from the corn processing operation as well as dust and soot from the close proximity of plant and railroad. For these reasons several of the newly employed workers have been leav-ing work at 3 o'clock due to nausea and complications. Clothing bills (for laundry and dry cleaning) and building maintenance costs are considered to be extraordinarily high. Circulating fans are available for moving the air, but succeed only in drawing the plant odors and dust through the office.
   b. With 30 typewriters plus additional machines, such as a stencil-dupli-cating machine, three ten-key adding machines, and the six keypunch machines in the general office area, a high noise factor has developed. Space is not a problem, so it would appear that some segregation and acoustical treatment would be possible. The original vinyl asbestos tile floors and plastered walls and ceilings are found throughout the entire office building.
   c. An open landscape plan for the open general office area should be considered.
   d. Transportation of finished correspondence and typed reports to the first and second floors entails noise and disruption of work on the third floor.
   e. Traditionally the office staff has shown intense loyalty to Vernon, but the new additions to the office staff are more concerned with comfort and convenience and recognize that their general office skills have a ready market in other expanding businesses and industries in the same city.
   f. Perez's absentee records indicate that during the three months' tenure in her position, 82 percent of the general office clerical staff have taken both of the sick days permitted each month. Four of the

workers under the age of 25 have indicated a desire for other employment unless working conditions become more competitive with other modern firms.

g. Several talks with the veteran office workers, Don Binnall and Gertrude Erickson, indicate that both feel that conditions are satisfactory; but they do indicate some anxiety with a change in leadership, from the standpoint of both Perez and Vernon, who assumed the presidency nine months ago after a transfer from another family interest in a neighboring state.

3. The executive suite consists of Vernon's office; an office for her secretary, Jules Cunningham; and a two-room suite for the executive vice-president (and nephew of Vernon), Donald Hanekamp, and his secretary. This suite is small, plain, and furnished with the same steel furniture found in the general office area. Vernon's overall conservatism, it was assumed, accounted for this situation, although all the equipment and furniture except the data processing machines were inherited from her father who preceded her as president.

4. Perez has contacted three firms dealing with office environments who have submitted bids for renovating the general office, for air-conditioning the entire building, and for ideas on conducting the office operation without interruption during the renovation process. Recently Perez has discovered that Vernon, who is quiet, though pleasant, is herself a certified public accountant as well as a chemical engineer, a fact that causes Perez to hesitate to submit the results of her audit or any of her recommendations to Vernon.

After considering the above situation carefully, analyze the problems involved and answer the following:

1. What key behavioral problems are involved in this situation, and what are their likely effects on office productivity? What can be done about them without a general overall revamping of the office environment?

2. What inferences can Perez draw from Vernon's background that will assist in the improvement of the general office and executive suite environments?

3. What should Perez do to correct the situation? If your answer to this question is to submit an audit report with recommendations, what main points should this report include?

4. On a person-to-person basis, what can be done to improve the rapport between Perez and Vernon?

Case 6-2   Planning and Organizing an Energy Conservation Program

Lidia Diaz, manager of the Phoenix branch office of La Plata Records, occupies a unique position in her firm. Since Phoenix is in the heart of a nationally recognized vacation area, the top managers of the firm frequently visit the office while on vacation. Further, as the largest of the branch offices in a very progressive city, the Phoenix office is expected to operate as a model of efficiency for each of the other eight offices scattered across the country.

Recently Diaz was informed by her superiors that an energy management program must be developed by the Phoenix office, and if successful, similar programs would be inaugurated across the country. As a result, Diaz is vitally concerned that her own office staff approach the energy management problem with care, considering both the budget and worker needs.

Intuition tells Diaz that there are many opportunities for conserving energy in the two-story, 100-by-150-foot office. She feels that installing permanent outside shades around the entire building on both floors would reduce by one third the heat from the hot Arizona sun which shines 90 percent of the time. However, because the second-floor recording studios for guest artists face northwest and provide a view of the scenic Camelback Mountain, some alternative to shades must be found for this 100-foot span. It appears that one half of the second floor where the executive offices are located might be converted from the present "total-ceiling" lighting to task-oriented lighting. Usually electric typewriters are left running when not in use and lights are not switched off in unused storage areas. Corridor lighting accounts for one tenth of all light used and can be reduced by two thirds. The savings from these changes, Diaz speculates, might run as high as 15 percent.

Heating is not a problem in the warm Phoenix climate, and the offices are adequately air-conditioned. It is even possible that the cooling equipment is overworked because of the heat generated from an overlighted first floor lighting system and the overcrowded conditions. Regardless of the natural light available, a custodian turns on all lights at 7 a.m. and off at 7 p.m. after completing the cleaning duties, even though the official work hours are 8 a.m. to 5 p.m.

Some of Diaz' suggestions sound feasible and others like "pennypinching." In talking with you about a conservation program, she makes these general comments:

> Look, the accounting department will give me all the detailed cost data I need on the energy we use. Don't worry about that. What I want you to do — as quickly as you can — is to consider how we can save energy in the future and how we can estimate the savings from such a program. We must be thorough and be able to defend what changes we make, as our ideas will be used by other offices later. But we can't ignore the employees, for they have much at stake. After all, they spend at least eight hours a day here and must be happy and comfortable on the job. Tell me how we can get a handle on the problem, and get as many suggestions as possible from reliable people in the firm.

At the same time Diaz hands you a cost summary showing that last year air-conditioning costs were $4,900; other electrical energy costs about $3,100 (roughly 9 percent of which is allocated to office machines); and gas heating costs (for hot water and furnace heat) approximately $1,000. The annual payroll of 41 clerical employees totals $465,000.

As assistant to Diaz, do the following:

a. Consider how you would organize a company-wide energy management program and determine the major users and specific uses of energy.
b. Making assumptions about energy uses for five departments, project present uses into the future with energy cost data from the utility company. Suggest possible energy savings with sample data your research provides.
c. Consider employee suggestions and attitudes toward energy conservation and how productivity might be directly or indirectly affected by changing working conditions.
d. In a report to Diaz outline your ideas about the feasibility of energy savings and their effects on both the budget and employee productivity. Recommend a plan for organizing the energy management program as well as stressing the importance of saving energy as a part of a national conservation effort, notwithstanding changeover costs.

Chapter 7

WRITTEN COMMUNICATIONS IN THE OFFICE

Communication is the lifeblood of the modern organization. It blends together skills and understandings, language and logic, and the human attitudes that enable managers, employees, and customers to exchange information and to make decisions. Without communication the primary managerial functions of planning, organizing, leading, and controlling would be impossible; with communication, the company's goals — and the procedures for implementing them — can be attained.

In an age when there is growing interdependence between people and organizations, the volume of written communications increases at an alarming rate, resulting in huge administrative costs. Similarly, the media — whether mail or some mechanical means — used to move these communications to the user also continue to expand and cause major problems for the administrative office manager. Both of these areas of concern and the systems designed to produce effective written communications are discussed in this chapter.

THE WRITTEN COMMUNICATION SYSTEM

The two broad categories of communications found in the office are *oral communications* (speaking and listening) and *visual communications* (reading and writing). While all of these communica-

tion activities are common to offices, studies at The University of Iowa have shown that an oral-to-visual communication ratio as high as 50-to-1 exists for blue-collar workers, while for white-collar workers at all levels a 3-to-1 ratio is found. A related study at Ohio State University found that white-collar workers spent 9 percent of their work day in writing, 16 percent in reading, 30 percent in talking, and 45 percent in listening.[1]

Stemming from a natural human need to communicate, oral communications, as a rule, are informal and unstructured in the office. Written communications, on the other hand, occur less frequently but make up the greater part of the formal communication system and hence constitute the chief point of emphasis in an office communication system. The term *written communications* refers to the various media (such as letters, memorandums, reports, and procedures as well as machine-generated communications) by which information is transmitted from a sender to a receiver (see Figure 7-1, next page). Such media must be planned and organized into a productive operation to provide efficient service inside and outside the

---

[1]Ernest G. Bormann, William S. Howell, Ralph G. Nichols, and George L. Shapiro, *Interpersonal Communication in the Modern Organization*, © 1969, p. 170. Reprinted by permission of Prentice-Hall, Inc., Englewood Cliffs, New Jersey.

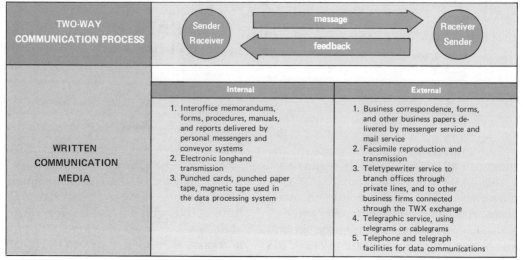

TWO-WAY COMMUNICATION PROCESS	Sender Receiver	message → ← feedback	Receiver Sender
WRITTEN COMMUNICATION MEDIA	**Internal**		**External**
	1. Interoffice memorandums, forms, procedures, manuals, and reports delivered by personal messengers and conveyor systems 2. Electronic longhand transmission 3. Punched cards, punched paper tape, magnetic tape used in the data processing system		1. Business correspondence, forms, and other business papers delivered by messenger service and mail service 2. Facsimile reproduction and transmission 3. Teletypewriter service to branch offices through private lines, and to other business firms connected through the TWX exchange 4. Telegraphic service, using telegrams or cablegrams 5. Telephone and telegraph facilities for data communications

Fig. 7-1
The Written Communication System Within the Office

company. The total set of components — involving information, media, personnel, equipment, and procedures — makes up the *written communication system*.

In setting up an effective written communication system, the following conditions are essential:

1. Information must be transmitted quickly enough to be current.
2. Information must be accessible — that is, easily retrieved for use.
3. Information must be provided on an economical basis, bearing in mind the volume of messages sent and the urgency with which each must be sent.
4. Information should be accurate and be received in a usable condition.

To meet these systems requirements, the administrative office manager must be familiar with the various forms of communication, must be able to identify those messages that must be written, and must understand the company's information and equipment needs to handle the distribution of messages efficiently.

WRITTEN COMMUNICATION MEDIA

As Figure 7-1 indicates, both internal and external communication media are available to the personnel of an organization. Because these media are so well known, they may be taken for granted and, consequently, their true effectiveness may never be realized. In this section the most common written communication media are briefly reviewed to emphasize their main characteristics and overall purposes.

Internal Written Communications

Written communications that remain within the firm usually fall into six categories: (1) interoffice or interdepartmental memorandums; (2) paper forms; (3) reports and related working papers; (4) written procedures, sometimes called standard practice instructions; (5) manuals; and (6) those media used in electronic longhand and data processing systems. The management of forms is discussed in Chapter 18 and data processing media in Chapters 20 and 21; the other media are treated in this chapter.

Interoffice Memorandums. Informality, brevity, and low cost are basic requirements of interoffice communications. Interoffice memorandums are used within a company to record short messages, often in handwritten form, and to speed them to their destination with a minimum of time and clerical effort. One such memorandum format uses a preassembled three-copy form that permits an office worker to handwrite a short message on the top half of the form, send the original and second copies to the addressee, and retain the third copy for file. If the occasion demands, the addressee may then write an answer on the lower half of the original memorandum form, retain one copy for file, and return the original copy to the sender.

Reports. More formal and longer than memorandums, reports are used to convey information to management for decision making. Common report topics include sales reviews, financial analyses, and summaries of planning, organizing, and forecasting activities. Many large concerns, including the federal government, have developed reports management programs that are designed to eliminate unnecessary reports, reduce the number and cost of report copies, and simplify and standardize report formats.[2]

Written Procedures. In large organizations where considerable detail and many people must be combined to accomplish work, written procedures are developed. These procedures are formal instructions explaining how to complete a task or solve a problem, thus helping to ensure uniform, efficient work at a lower cost. The development and analysis of office procedures are discussed in detail in Part 4.

Office Manuals. Office manuals are formal communications of management control developed to acquaint employees with the rules and regulations of the company. In addition, they are used to assign responsibility for performing certain duties and to establish procedures for performing those duties. With such information in printed form, worker time is saved and the need for constant repetition of instruction is eliminated.

Manuals should be written in a simple, direct, readable style; prepared as economically as possible; and distributed to all employees requiring the information included. Such manuals should be evaluated and revised regularly to ensure that they are both usable and used.

Four types of manuals are commonly found: (1) *policy manuals*, for communicating decisions, resolutions, and pronouncements of the board of directors who establish company policies; (2) *organization manuals*, for explaining the organization and the duties and responsibilities of the various departments; (3) *administrative practice manuals*, which

---

[2]Reports management is one of the main elements in the paperwork management program of the General Services Administration, U.S. Government. For more information on this topic, see Wilmer O. Maedke, Mary F. Robek, and Gerald F.

Brown, *Information and Records Management* (Beverly Hills: Benziger, Bruce & Glencoe Press, 1974), Chapter 10; and August F. Reussow, "A Sound Reports Program," *Records Management Quarterly* (October, 1974), pp. 20–24.

contain the procedures and standard methods for performing the company's work; and (4) *departmental practice manuals*, such as the two closely related manuals on communication that are described below.

Correspondence Manual.

The correspondence manual is designed to standardize the policies, procedures, and methods of creating correspondence in a company. Typical contents of such a manual include the organization and composition of letters to create good will, quality control of company correspondence, word selection, sentence and paragraph construction, mechanical problems of correspondence, and supervision of correspondence.

Communications Manual.

The communications manual guides employees in selecting suitable communication services at the least cost to the company. In the manual various telecommunication media, such as the telephone and telegraph, are illustrated, along with the functions and comparative costs of each.

External Written Communications

In addition to the internal communications found within business firms, Figure 7-1 points out a set of external written communications that are transmitted from one firm to another as well as to other receivers outside the firm. Typical of this class of communications are the telecommunication messages produced by modern technology (such as facsimile reproduction, teletypewriter, telegraph, and data communications) and the traditional written media, such as business correspondence, forms, and other papers that remain in widespread

use. (A discussion of telecommunication media appears in Chapter 8.)

In this chapter the business letter is highlighted because of its universal use and its values to management. Even though it cannot interrupt an important conference with a loud ring, the business letter continues to be one of the best devices for getting management attention. As an office record, "A letter may be put aside briefly, then carefully read when the active pressures of the business day have subsided. Equally important, a carefully written letter is concise, and doesn't waste the time of the reader with comment." [3] Even in the age of automation when telephone and computer communications receive increasing attention, the popularity of the business letter remains. Estimates show that in the United States alone, more than 2.5 million letters are written every hour of the day, resulting in as much as $20 million being spent daily on letter production alone. Communication by mail is indeed a multibillion dollar operation. [4]

The composition of an original letter is expensive and may in many cases be unnecessary, especially where standardized messages (form letters and form paragraphs) would suffice. Under many circumstances, well-designed standardized communications are just as effective and considerably less expensive. [5] When properly applied, the

---

[3] Frank K. Griesinger, "Wiring the Written Word," *Administrative Management* (September, 1974), p. 24.

[4] Quoted from Lou Kriloff, president of the Letterpower Institute, in *The ABCA Bulletin* (September, 1974), p. 21. (The *Bulletin* is a regular publication of The American Business Communication Association.)

[5] A full discussion of these letter alternatives is found in Maedke, Robek, and Brown, *op. cit.*, pp. 203–206, as well as in these publications of the

1. Write for your reader, keeping in mind the purpose of the message.	7. Maintain a friendly, positive, sincere tone.
2. Organize the facts in a logical order.	8. Give careful attention to appearance (neatness, placement, and appropriate form).
3. Keep sentences as brief as possible but vary length to maintain interest.	9. Proofread carefully to avoid mechanical errors (spelling, punctuation, capitalization, and incomplete sentences).
4. Maintain good transition and flow within paragraphs.	10. Read carefully before signing. Remember that the message represents you and your organization or company.
5. Use simple, familiar words.	
6. Use action verbs.	

Fig. 7-2
Guidelines for Creating Effective Written Communications

guidelines shown in Figure 7-2 will greatly assist in the production of effective written communications.

SYSTEMS FOR PRODUCING AND TRANSMITTING WRITTEN COMMUNICATIONS

To provide written communications in the right form, at the right time, at the right place, and at the least possible cost, systems must be designed for producing and transmitting written communications to the ultimate user. Included in this systems responsibility is a good understanding of the dictation-transcription function as well as the various resources (human and machine) available for transmitting information over distances.

Almost universally, correspondence, formal reports, and procedures appear in typewritten form. Such text is produced

from handwritten notes, dictation notes taken by a shorthand-writing or machine-writing stenographer, messages dictated directly to a typist, or recorded information dictated to a voice-recording machine. While each of these message-producing systems is still commonly used, increasing reliance is being placed upon machine dictation to produce written communications.

Dictation-Transcription Systems

Many executives prefer giving shorthand dictation to a secretary or using machine dictation because it is faster than longhand; and, when properly dictated, the communications may be more efficiently transcribed. Equally important is the fact that by using a dictating machine, an executive can dictate at any time or place without the need to wait for the secretary to be released from other duties. The secretary, too, is free to schedule time independently of the dictator.

Although there may seem to be a bewildering number of machine models

---

Records Management Division, National Archives and Records Services of the General Service Administration: *Form Letters*, *Guide Letters*, and *Plain Letters*, all published in 1955.

and brands, dictating equipment falls into three broad categories: *discrete media* (stand-alone or individual) *machines*, both portable and desk-top models; *discrete media central recorder systems* that are connected by private wire or PBX (private branch exchange telephone); and *endless loop systems*, either individual or centralized. For recording purposes both the stand-alone units and the central recorder systems utilize belts, cassettes, magnetic disks, tape spools, and cartridges; dictation-only, transcription-only, and combination dictation-transcription machines are also available. Portable units, such as shown in Figure 7-3, have greatly increased in popularity largely due to their light weight, low cost, and compatibility with transcribing machines. In addition, portable units permit dictation away from the office when there are no telephones handy.

Endless loop systems eliminate the handling of the recording media. The endless loop is a continuous tape that is permanently encased in a "tank." After the tape is recorded, it drops into a tran-scribing channel, the dictated material is transcribed, and then the tank cycles back to the dictation channel, thus allowing for the continual flow of dictation. Such a system can accommodate up to six dictation stations, utilizing one station at a time.

Under the decentralized dictation plans found in small offices, each department retains a staff of transcribers for that department, with one transcriber being assigned to serve one or more dictators. In larger companies, greater efficiency is obtained by centralizing the dictation-transcription function using one of two systems: either a central recorder system, such as shown in Figure 7-3 which is interconnected through a telephone system with automatic changing of the 24 fifteen-minute cassettes; or an endless loop system that may employ the telephone and can accept incoming dictation for 24 hours a day.

Typewriters

The typewriter is synonymous with office work; and its product, the tran-

Portable Unit

Photos courtesy of Phillips Business Systems, Inc.

Fig. 7-3

Central Recorder System

Dictation-Transcription Machines

script or the typed form, constitutes the most common form of output in the office. There are three categories of typewriters: (1) *manual* (nonelectric) *typewriters*, such as the portable, which may be used by individuals who must travel, and the office standard that may be used where typewriting volume is not great or where cost is a major consideration; (2) *electric typewriters*, intended for large-volume typewriting, which are capable of increased output and higher quality copy, and require less human energy than manual machines; and (3) *automatic typewriters* that are driven by paper tape or some magnetic medium (tape or card), and are designed for large-volume typing of form letters and documents.

A wide variety of special typewriter features are available to the buyer who has determined the transcription requirements of his or her office. Some of these features are: repeat functions on some keys, such as underlining; interchangeable type styles as provided by manufacturers of machines with the ball typing element (see Figure 7-4); two-color ribbon selection; interchangeable carriages and varied carriage sizes; special correction features that eliminate erasing; and optional symbols on special keys.

Communication Transmission Systems

Carrying the written communication to the ultimate user is the function of the transmission system. Where speed and urgency, multiple copymaking, and considerable distance are important considerations, transmission equipment

Fig. 7-4
A Modern Typewriter with Interchangeable Type Elements

plays a key role in the distribution of information. Most of the machines responsible for such transmission function are very closely related to telecommunications and are treated in Chapter 8. Within the local office areas, however, less speed and shorter distances are involved in transporting information. In such cases personal messenger and conveyor systems are useful. The volume of information to be moved helps to determine whether the use of personal messengers, conveyor systems, an electronic longhand device, or a combination of these methods, best fits the needs of the organization.

Personal Messenger Systems. Although numerous mechanical devices have largely supplanted the use of office messenger service, such service is still maintained in some offices to save the time of executives in interoffice communication. Maintaining such service depends upon the number of delivery locations and the distances between them, the time provided for delivery, the bulk and weight of the papers to be delivered, and finally the cost of the service.

Many concerns find a messenger system is more expensive than mechanical means of communication. However, the difference in cost can be charged to the expense of training workers for the more responsible positions to which messengers are commonly promoted as they become more familiar with the methods of the business. Some small concerns, however, such as printing and photoengraving establishments, find messenger service the best method of picking up copy and delivering the finished product.

Office Conveyor Systems. Whenever large amounts of paper are circulated on a continuing basis and such pa-

perwork can be distributed to fixed locations, *conveyor systems* should be considered. Such systems help to maintain an efficient flow of work by preventing the buildup of papers. Office conveyor systems minimize the movement of office personnel and, therefore, increase worker productivity by decreasing wasted hours spent away from the work station. Conveyors, often called "automatic office boys," are available in several types, of which the most popular types are the *multichannel conveyor* and the *pneumatic tube*. Brief descriptions of these two systems follow.

Multichannel Conveyors. Multichannel conveyors are used to transport papers horizontally between work stations. The papers travel continuously, as sheets, file folders, or small batches, in an upright position between two stationary vertical guides that are moved by a motor-driven belt beneath them. The conveyor is fast (200 to 300 feet per minute), quiet, clean, safe, and less obtrusive than most other types of conveyors; and most important, it keeps people at their desks. The major disadvantage of the multichannel conveyor is that it cannot climb vertically from one floor to another. However, vertical lift conveyors are available for moving trays of paper between floors.

Pneumatic Tube Systems. Pneumatic tube systems typically work in this way: papers to be distributed by each department are sent to a control station in a container large enough to hold many ordinary-size business papers. At the station they are hand sorted, placed in a tube container, and carried by a conveyor belt to the appropriate dispatch chutes for quick routing to the delivery points. The result is a more efficient use of employees' time than would be required to transport papers from one department to another.

Large companies use these "air chute" systems where speed and accuracy of transmission are more important than cost or where the volume of documents transmitted is so large that the cost of maintaining a large staff of messengers would exceed the cost of the tube system. The pneumatic tube system entails high costs of installation, unless the equipment is installed during the erection of the building.

Electronic Longhand Transmission. Electronic longhand transmission sends longhand messages electronically in one's own handwriting whereby the messages are received almost simultaneously with the writing. The system is used almost exclusively for communications within the firm — between departments, warehouse and office, branch and main offices. One excellent application of the electronic longhand machine is made in the telephone order-processing procedure. A sending machine, such as that shown in Figure 7-5, is installed on the desk of the telephone order clerk

and a second machine, the receiving unit, is placed in the shipping or packing department. As an order is received on the telephone, the clerk can write simultaneously on both machines. Thus, before the customer has completed the call, the processing of the order can be under way in the shipping department.

MANAGEMENT OF WRITTEN COMMUNICATIONS

In any system there exists a tendency to move toward a state of disorder if no controls are placed on the system. As one of the major obstacles in most offices has been the absence of managerial control over written communications, this point is especially important for written communication systems. Poor writing habits are not easily overcome, particularly when they are accepted by the general office staff. When important bottlenecks occur, the following writing problems — all having to do with ineffective or nonexistent controls — appear:

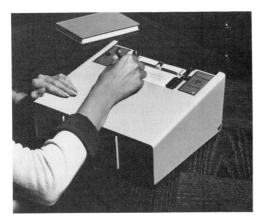

Telautograph Corporation

Sending Unit   Receiving Unit

Fig. 7-5
Electronic Longhand Sending and Receiving Units

1. *Poor writing quality.* While most people can write well enough to be understood, one source suggests that "the real art in writing is to be able to write so that one cannot be misunderstood."[6] Writing weaknesses abound, especially those relating to sentence and paragraph structure, organization of the message, and a knowledge of sound writing psychology.

2. *Use of gobbledygook.* The excessive use of technical terms or gobbledygook often results in the reader failing to understand the message the sender meant to convey. It is preferable for management to emphasize sending clear, straightforward messages and to omit all gobbledygook.

3. *Excessively long response time.* Responses to written communications received in the office should be quick, for delays can lose customers and slow down operating effectiveness. By utilizing faster production methods — such as machine dictation of letters and standardized, preprinted (form) letters — most messages can go out within hours rather than days or weeks. The use of automatic equipment, as discussed in this chapter, will also speed up the production and distribution of letters.

4. *Lack of sound communication management.* Without controls over the communication function, the problems outlined in this section occur again and again. However, with a realistic management program that includes setting policies and standards for all communication media, the company can effectively meet its objectives of conveying information between the firm and its customers or, internally, between management and the employees or departments. To achieve these goals means identifying and maintaining the quality of written communications, improving the systems for producing documents, and reducing correspondence costs.

Organizing the Correspondence Function

Two main processes are essential to the development of effective business correspondence: *word origination*, the process of composing or constructing messages; and *transcription*, the procedures involved in transforming dictated or handwritten rough-draft copy into finished form.

A number of studies have shown that the dictation method of word origination improves productivity. Some executives even maintain that machine dictation allows a person to compose letters at four times the speed of handwriting and about twice the speed of dictation to a stenographer.[7] Thus, with the ready availability of dictating machines and stenographers, it would seem that most executives would dictate most of their correspondence. However, such is not the case; the "yellow-pad" method of handwriting correspondence persists even though it is a slower means of creating text copy and in many cases more expensive than other methods. Thus, more emphasis on effective use of dictating machines seems necessary.

Word Origination by Dicating Machines. Because business executives require training in the use of dictating machines, the following procedures for effective dictation habits should be adhered to:

---

[6]*Correspondence Management* (Washington: General Services Administration (GSA), National Archives and Records Service, Office of Records Management, 1973), p. 1.

[7]Robert A. Johnston, "Closing the Communications Gap," *Office Products News* (January 17, 1975), p. 31.

1. Collect all relevant information necessary to organize, compose, and dictate the message.
2. Prepare the information in a form that facilitates the dictation process.
3. Control the dictation by providing for proper sequence of the thoughts to be communicated, by eliminating distracting mannerisms, and by effectively using the voice.
4. Maintain quiet physical surroundings.

One large firm utilizes the following approach for training its dictators:

1. The dictator is asked to write out and then read the material to a machine or a secretary, avoiding the temptation to read too fast or to slur word connectives and word endings.
2. Once this is mastered, the writer is taught to dictate from an extensive, written outline of the key thoughts in each paragraph.
3. This is followed by dictation from a very concise outline in which emphasis is placed on good organization and which reduces the amount of writing to a minimum.
4. As the dictator improves in technique and experience, he or she gradually becomes able to dictate from a mental outline alone.[8]

Many large firms — especially insurance companies and banks where much correspondence originates — train their executives and correspondents in the best methods of writing business letters and provide for a systematic review of the quality of the letters written. Among the methods used are: (1) periodic conferences with the correspondents, correspondence supervisors, and the transcription supervisor, (2) the development and use of a correspondence manual to guide the executives and employees in improving their work and standardizing their output, and (3) an analysis of each dictator's work by means of a transcription report, such as that shown in Figure 7-6, page 172. Dictating machine manufacturers also provide software packages — films, tapes, and workbooks — that assist word originators to learn good dictation techniques and letter-writing skills.

Organizing Transcription. Organizing the transcription of the written communication in the small and medium-size office starts with the selection of an experienced, well-trained person who can obtain the cooperation of both the dictators and the transcribing personnel. This person may have a full-time supervising job that involves training transcribers, setting standards, and measuring the output of each employee, as well as analyzing the quality of output. Large firms have, to an increasing degree, embraced the word processing concept discussed later in this chapter.

Reducing Correspondence Costs

The cost factors that make up letter writing vary from day to day, from office to office, and even from department to department in the same firm. Nevertheless, many executives and supervisors do not realize what factors must be considered in correspondence costs and therefore are unable to analyze and to control them. The basic factors that must be considered by firms when analyzing their correspondence costs are:

1. *Preparation and dictation*, which cover the time required for jotting down notes, consulting records, and

---

[8]Glenn R. Coleman, Jr., "Du Pont's Engineering Has a Practical Program for Dictation Training," *AMS Professional Management Bulletin: Administrative Services* (December, 1969), p. 18.

TRANSCRIPTION REPORT

To _____ Date _____

Difficulty was encountered in transcribing for the following reason:
_____ Dictated before disk or belt was in motion.
_____ Dictated beyond end of disk or belt.
_____ Dictated too fast. _____ Too slow. _____ Too loud.
_____ Enunciation not clear.
_____ Failed to spell proper names or unusual words.
　　　　Examples: _____
　　　　_____
_____ Failed to indicate corrections.
_____ Failed to indicate length of letter or memo.
_____ Failed to distinguish between numbers or letters of like sound.
_____ Failed to indicate that paragraph(s) or tabulation was to be inserted.
_____ Failed to indicate extra copies on indicator slip, requested copies at end or in middle of memo or letter.
_____ Failed to give proper instructions on how to set up.
_____ Failed to indicate beginning or end of quotation, indentation, or tabulation.
_____ Failed to enclose correspondence.
_____ Failed to indicate number of disk or belt when dictation is continued on two or more disks/belts.
Any questions on this report should be discussed with the Correspondence Supervisor.

　　　　　　　　　　　　　　　　　　　_____
　　　　　　　　　　　　　　　　　　　Operator's Name/Number

INSTRUCTIONS TO OPERATOR: Prepare this report in duplicate. Return one copy to dictator with the transcribing folder and one copy to Correspondence Supervisor.

Fig. 7-6
A Transcription Report

conferring with others, as well as actual dictation. For the average-length letter of 175 words, it is estimated that ten minutes are required for preparation, and five to ten minutes for actual dictation.

2. *Shorthand and typing*, which cover the work of the stenographer or the machine transcriber. The actual typing takes seven or eight minutes.

3. *Reviewing and signing the letter* takes the dictator two more minutes.

In addition to these basic costs, there are the costs of stationery and sup-

plies, mailing, filing, and the general office overhead (such as depreciation and utilities expenses).

In 1977 the Dartnell Corporation estimated the cost of dictating, typing, mailing, and filing an average business letter in the United States to be $4.47, based upon an executive dictator's weekly salary of $360 and a secretary's weekly salary of $168.[9] To produce

_____
[9]"Target Survey" (Chicago: The Dartnell Corporation, 1977), p. 2. In this report the estimated cost of an average Canadian letter was $4.15.

these letters, salary represents the largest cost factor ($1.05 for the 7 minutes of executive dictation time, and $1.26 for the estimated 18 minutes of secretarial transcription time). Thus, labor cost becomes the factor where the greatest savings should be sought. In Table 7-1 this savings in time can be noted as the method of originating correspondence moves from stenographic dictation to form letters where no dictation is required. For an executive dictator earning $25,000 a year (or 20 cents a minute), such dictation costs range from $4.00 to $0.

In controlling correspondence costs, the objectives are to reduce the time necessary to produce each letter without impairing its effectiveness. The following list of suggestions for reducing correspondence costs, should be carefully investigated by the office manager:

1. *Learn to write short letters and interoffice communications* since they are more effective and save time not only for the dictator and the transcriber, but also for the reader.
2. *Teach executives how to prepare for dictation.* All dictation should be done at one time, as early in the day as possible. All necessary information should be on hand so that uninterrupted dictation may be completed. Time wasted here is a dual loss — the cost of the executive's time and that of the transcriber.
3. *Eliminate unnecessary dictation* by having the transcriber compose the replies to routine correspondence. By having the executive place on the letter to be answered a notation indicating the nature of the reply, much executive time can be saved.
4. *Use form letters where applicable.* Form letters play an important part in reducing the cost of office correspondence if they are carefully prepared and intelligently used. (See the cost comparison shown in Table 7-1).
5. *Use printed or mimeographed postal cards or form letters* as acknowledgements of incoming letters when no special answer is required.
6. *Eliminate all overtime and peak loads* by scheduling letter writing in accordance with its importance and urgency. All mail should be answered the same day as received, if possible, but this should not be overdone, resulting in overtime costs.
7. *Conduct letter clinics.* Having a communications consultant or a letter adviser in the organization examine all

TIME FACTORS IN CREATING A TYPICAL 175-WORD LETTER

Action	Minutes Required		
	Steno Dictation	Machine Dictation	Form Letters
Planning what to say ...	10	10	0
Dictating	10	5	0
Looking up a letter	0	0	1
Transcribing—typing....	7	8	1.5
Reviewing—signing......	2	2	.5
Total minutes...........	29	25	3

Table 7-1

carbon copies of letters and prepare suggestions for reducing their length and improving their tone will do much to improve and to expedite the letter-writing function.

8. *Use simplified letter styles* to reduce typing time. One such letter style developed by the Administrative Management Society is characterized by: (a) extreme block form with date at top at the left-hand margin, (b) name and address in block form for use with a window envelope, (c) formal salutation replaced with a letter-subject line, (d) complimentary close omitted, and (e) letter language simplified. Advocates of this letter style have found that about 10 percent of the typing time can be saved on a 96-word letter.

9. *Answer letters by telephone whenever possible*, especially when no written record of the reply need be kept.

10. *Record answers to incoming queries on the bottom of the incoming documents* and make copies of these documents to send out as answers. The originals are then filed.

WORD PROCESSING

Operating an office is becoming increasingly expensive. As one executive states, "A large part of this expense problem is due to the fact that 25 years ago the average office worker was typing 55 to 60 words a minute and making $45 a week. Today the same worker is still typing at that rate and making $150 to $175 a week."[10] Thus, over the years in spite of the technological developments in the office, such as the perfection of the electric typewriter, the output

per worker has remained fairly constant. However, the cost of this output has continued to spiral. To combat this problem, word processing has been developed to bring the efficiency and economy of factory production methods to the office. What this new concept of word processing involves and how it can be applied in the office are discussed in this section.

The Word Processing System

The term *data processing* has become a household word during the past several decades, and its efficiency in transforming numeric data into useful information is widely accepted. However, data processing systems do not solve the typical office problem of the large-volume, inefficient processing of words.

A *word processing system* transforms the words originated by a person into the final product — the printed communication — and forwards it to its destination. As shown in Figure 7-7 the system embodies a series of operations that combines the three basic elements — input, processing, and output — as well as the means of delivering the words to their point of use.

With the introduction of the Magnetic Tape/Selectric Typewriter (MT/ST) and some innovative systems ideas from Germany in the late 1960s, powerful new word processing equipment with multiple capabilities was provided. For example, the MT/ST and newer generations of equipment can produce regular typewritten copy, store the typewritten copy on magnetic tape, and "play back" an exact duplicate of the original copy. Also, such a machine can be used to revise or correct copy by

---

[10]John R. Hansen, "Short Memos or Long-Winded Reports — Automated WP Can Hold Down the Cost," *Infosystems* (October, 1975), p. 29.

typing over the word or sentence to be changed. What this machine and a succession of more sophisticated equipment have proved conclusively is that many of the word processing functions can be performed by machines with many cost-saving benefits.

In the traditional "one-to-one" manager-secretary arrangement, letter production has a personal touch. A secretary in this setting is usually hired as a generalist to perform many clerical tasks besides typing letters. Such a variety of work makes it difficult to establish controls over the secretarial work, and the lack of controls leads to lowered productivity and higher office costs. The results of a study of 53 secretaries in a large company show a breakdown of tasks (see Table 7-2) in which only about 20 percent of the secretarial time is spent in typing-related tasks.

As an alternative to the general secretary, firms employing word processing systems divide the written communication responsibilities of the office staff into two groups: (1) correspondence secretaries and (2) administrative

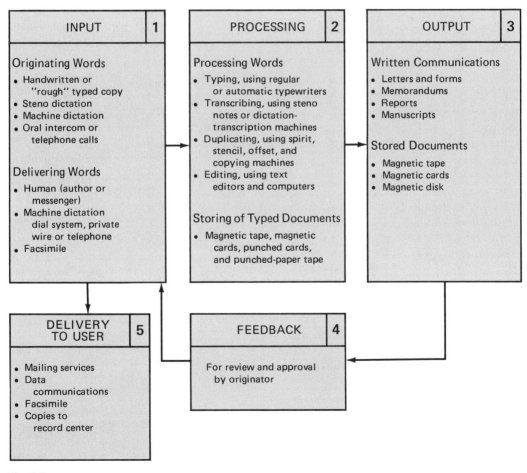

Fig. 7-7
A Word Processing System

BREAKDOWN OF SECRETARIAL TASKS

Task	Percent of Time
Taking dictation	2
Typing and proofreading	19
Filing	5
Using the telephone	8
Mailing services	5
Errands (getting coffee, extra copies, etc.)	12
General clerical work	31
Personal time	4
Waiting for work	14

Table 7-2

Source: Walter A. Kleinschrod, *Word Processing* (New York: AMACOM, a division of American Management Associations, 1974), p. 6.

secretaries. *Correspondence secretaries* (sometimes called word processing operators) are keyboard specialists capable of far greater output per hour than the traditional general secretary whose typing work is continually interrupted by other required tasks. Correspondence secretaries usually perform the heavy-volume typing work in centralized departments under production supervisors who assign work based upon the task requirements and the skills available. In contrast, *administrative secretaries* are freed from large-volume typing responsibilities and therefore are better able to handle the remaining clerical services — answering the telephone, filing correspondence, and handling various mailing responsibilities. Administrative secretaries work in small administrative-support centers and report to several executives for their day-to-day work assignments.

Objectives of Word Processing Systems

The cost-conscious executive expects topnotch efficiency and high quality in the production of written commu-nications. This includes a faster turnaround time (the time that elapses from word origination until the finished document is returned for approval) and an increasingly lower unit cost of production than are normally possible from the traditional executive-secretarial team.[11]

Advocates of word processing point to the following benefits that may be anticipated from this type of written communication program:

1. Better supervision of the work, as the word processing operator is supervised by a specialist in secretarial work rather than by an executive with more general management responsibilities.

---

[11]A leading spokesperson for word processing is Walter A. Kleinschrod, editorial director of Geyer-McAllister Publications, Inc., New York, the editor of *Administrative Management* and *Word Processing World*, and publisher-editor of the newsletter *Word Processing Report*. Kleinschrod has also authored *Management's Guide to Word Processing* (Chicago: The Dartnell Corporation, 1975), which deals with both the theory and practice of word processing and the systems requirements for designing, maintaining, and evaluating word processing centers in both large and small organizations.

2. More opportunities for measurement of the typewritten output, from simple tallying of documents to line counts per day, week, or month. Thus, an incentive system based upon work quantity and quality can be set up.

3. Higher quality productivity by reducing the retyping of copy and achieving error-free "hard copy" (completed paper documents); elimination of the retyping operations for many form letters or repetitive typing operations; great reduction in the proofreading required; and much faster revision in the contents of documents.

4. More consistent service for management (such as faster turnaround time, lower per-unit communication costs, and better use of equipment and personnel by leveling the peaks and valleys in the work). Companies that have successfully converted to word processing find that unit costs can be reduced from 10 to 95 percent depending on the number of "rewrites" required, since all the words stored (on magnetic tape, for example) do not require retyping. In addition, as much as 30 percent can be shaved off unit costs because of increased productivity with two to six times more work being produced by the same operator.[12]

5. Closer ties between the magnetic-recording media of word processing systems and the company's data processing system.

6. Greater career opportunities in both the word processing and administrative-support areas, with more management positions opening up for the secretaries.

Along with these claims of efficiency and cost savings come some negative views of word processing. These include the loss of executive status by middle managers who must give up their own secretaries, and a secretary's corresponding loss of esteem by changing from a high-status private secretary to a production-line word processing operator. With the emphasis on equipment in word processing, a danger exists that the human element may be pushed aside — that the operators might become merely cogs in the system. When such is the case, as a University of Minnesota study has disclosed, there is undue pressure on operators to produce more work in less time and, as a result, boredom from performing too much repetitive work sets in. To overcome these problems, it has been suggested that the workload be reviewed each month to establish reasonable standards, that holders of both repetitive and special jobs be rotated to provide more variety in their work, and that job descriptions be clearly written to spell out future advancement levels.[13]

How to motivate the word processing operators and enrich their jobs calls for an understanding of the social, psychological, and physical needs of workers as discussed in Chapter 1. In addition, it requires that word processing managers carefully select and train their workers and remain sensitive to the dehumanizing problems found in an "assembly-line" form of office system.

Organizing Word Processing

Typing operations account for almost three fourths of all written communications. When an administrative office manager senses the need for bringing greater productivity to these

---

[12]Benjamin W. Tartaglia, "The Economics of Word Processing," *Journal of Systems Management* (November, 1973), p. 10.

[13]"As We See It," *The Office* (February, 1974), p. 156.

operations, a word processing feasibility study should be conducted.

Feasibility Study. In the feasibility study, the practicality of converting to word processing can be assessed by determining answers to these questions about work assignments:

1. How is secretarial work distributed?
2. What secretarial tasks (typing and non-typing) are performed in each of the departments?
3. How much time is taken and required by each task, and how important is each in relation to the time being consumed?
4. Are secretaries with special skills and abilities called upon to perform duties requiring lesser skills?
5. What word-origination activities occur in each department, in what volume, and requiring what amount of time?
6. What is the estimated wait time for communications to be processed and returned to the word originator?
7. How much of the work can be adequately measured?

The feasibility study often reveals many unrelated and unnecessary time-consuming tasks, wasted motions, and duplication of work, all resulting in low performance and poor work quality. This points to a need for new efforts in managing word processing functions.

Organizational Patterns for Word Processing. Word processing, like other organizational functions, involves certain trade-offs. The more centralized, routinized, and highly specialized the word processing function becomes to handle large-volume typing operations, the more the personal touch is sacrificed. Similarly, the less centralized and less specialized it becomes, the more difficult it is to control the work assigned. In facing the issue of how

much centralization of work to provide, two organizational patterns — differing only in degree — emerge.

The Word Processing Center. A production operation as pictured in Figure 7-8 brings together in a central location under a company-wide supervisor all of the written communication responsibilities. This organizational plan, usually found in large firms, requires large volumes of work, major investments in new equipment, considerable training of staff and supervisors, as well as qualitative and quantitative controls over the work. In effect, it represents automating the production of written communications.

The Typing Cluster. Small organizations may not be able to afford a word processing center. In its place they frequently compromise with a middle-of-the-road plan in which the main typing work is performed by a cluster of typing specialists working directly with the word originators. These typists work with three or four administrative secretaries who specialize in nontyping duties. With this arrangement the personal touch between the managers and the secretarial staff is maintained while at the same time, several advantages of centralization (especially work measurement and typing competence) are effectively retained.

Converting to Word Processing

Changing from a traditional executive-secretary team to a word processing system can be traumatic for the office personnel. Experience shows that the "people" problems during the conversion stand out in importance, for many employees believe that having a private secretary is one of the prestige factors of

Montgomery Ward

Fig. 7-8
A Word Processing Center

high-level administration; and when a secretary is moved away or transferred, the administrator may feel demoted or insulted. The secretary, too, may be "tied" to an executive and an executive title and may feel demoted by being moved to a word processing center.

Orientation lectures are useful to explain the benefits of word processing. Office machine representatives can provide educational materials to explain their systems; and organizations, such as the International Word Processing Association, sponsor publications and programs to help in the conversion process and to provide ongoing technical assistance to the word processing staff.

An effective plan for converting to word processing must have the support of top management and should include (1) choosing an appropriate form of organization; (2) orienting the word origi-

nators to the values of the system; (3) selecting personnel, equipment, and physical facilities; and (4) establishing operating procedures.[14] While all of these activities are important to the success of word processing, only the most basic procedures relating to personnel, equipment, and production are covered in this text.

Word Processing Personnel. The typical positions and lines of promotion found in a centralized word processing system are chartered in Figure 7-9. This chart also serves as a useful guide in establishing job levels in a word processing system that is not fully centralized.

---

[14]Eileen F. Tunison, "People + Equipment + Procedures = Word Processing," *Office Products News* (June 20, 1975), p. 15.

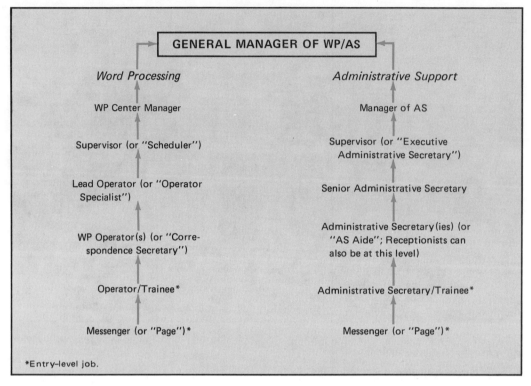

Source: Walter A. Kleinschrod, *Word Processing* (New York: AMACOM, a division of American Management Associations, 1974), p. 9.

Fig. 7-9

The Organization of Word Processing (WP) and Administrative Support (AS) Personnel in a Word Processing Center

The general manager of word processing and administrative support (WP/AS) holds the key position in the center. Such a person must understand the organization and the communication needs of all departments. Further qualifications for such a position include the administrative abilities needed to develop a strong communication program and to understand and motivate people, as well as an expertise in the use of methods, procedures, and equipment.

Reporting to the manager of the word processing center are those individuals assigned to word processing activities, which are mainly large-scale or "power" typing. Under the manager of

administrative support are those staff members who are largely responsible for nontyping duties. The WP staff requires qualifications considerably different from their counterparts in the AS group. Effective WP operators must enjoy production typing, possess at least an average typing skill, and be able to adapt to the magnetic tape, card, or core equipment being used. An excellent spelling skill is also important. In contrast, the AS staff requires general clerical skills with lower typing qualifications.

Word Processing Equipment.
While desks, files, storage cabinets, and other furniture and appliances are

required for word processing, two categories of hardware — *dictation equipment* and *automated typing equipment* — constitute the basic word processing machines. Dictation equipment was discussed earlier in this chapter since it is used in traditional correspondence production as well as in word processing systems. Automated typing equipment, on the other hand, is mainly associated with word processing and is discussed briefly in this section.

Three office keyboards — the typewriter, the teletypewriter, and the keypunch — have brought revolutionary progress to the office. In the age of word processing, a fourth type of keyboard — the automated typing machine — is available to do the work of its predecessors as well as perform two new functions, word storage and text editing. Automated typing machines are classified as stand-alones and interactive systems.

Stand-Alone Typing Machines. The *stand-alones* or individual units may be simply typewriters or paper-tape units used for repetitive typing and paragraph selection. Modern stand-alones also perform the text editing functions of deleting, adding, and retyping of corrected (edited) copy. Generally these machines offer low-cost, large-volume typing and provide letter-perfect correspondence. More complex stand-alones, such as the cathode-ray tube (CRT) machine, allow an operator to retrieve and display stored copy on a screen so that any changes may be recorded and visually examined before the corrected text is stored. Automated equipment is discussed in more detail in Chapter 21.

Interactive Systems. *Interactive systems* involve terminals linked to computers and their printout machines as the output equipment in word processing. These systems permit a number of operator stations to share the power of a computer and provide output to a variety of printers. Some minicomputer systems, for example, allow 10 to 12 input stations to be linked together; larger systems may band together up to 100 stations.[15]

Production Standards and Controls. Most word processing centers develop standards of work performance by borrowing from other firms and adapting these standards to their own situations. (The method-time-measurement technique for developing standards, discussed in Chapter 23, is one example.) Other companies develop their own standards by utilizing counts of daily, weekly, and monthly work units produced, usually counting the number of lines of copy produced.[16] Also, comparative per-page costs for typing and proofreading various types of publications by alternate methods are prepared for use in analyzing paperwork costs.

MANAGEMENT OF MAILING SERVICES

It is easy to forget that the written communications prepared in the office have little value until they are transmitted to their point of use. Many of these communications dealing with order processing, cash flows, and information exchange depend on fast, accurate, and dependable service, such as that provided

---

[15]Amy D. Wohl, "Selecting Word Processing Equipment," *Management World* (November, 1975), pp. 3–4.
[16]Walter A. Kleinschrod, *Word Processing* (New York: AMACOM, a division of American Management Associations, 1974), p. 15.

by the telecommunication systems cited in Chapter 8. However, even in the age of "instant-message" sending, the distribution of the bulk of the written communications is most dependent upon well-managed mailing services. Each year more than 100 billion letters and packages are handled by the U.S. Postal Service, with large firms themselves receiving from 50,000 to 100,000 mail items daily. This points out the size of the mailing operation and the need for developing accurate, speedy, and economical mailing services.

Business mail may be classified as *internal* (interdepartmental or intradepartmental mail, which is distributed by messengers and conveyors); and *external* (incoming and outgoing mail). Since mailing services exist for all departments of a business, the mail department or mailing center has become a key part of the company's communication system. Good mailing services ensure the quickest, most economical, and most direct flow of mail from the sender to the receiver, reduce delays in completing work, and create a positive image with customers. The mail department, therefore, enhances all business relationships.

Planning and Organizing Mailing Services

When setting up a new or revised service function, management typically considers whether to centralize or to decentralize the function. While there are strengths and weaknesses in each of these organizational patterns, the general trend has been and continues to be a centralized organizational plan for mailing services. The centralized organizational plan may take two forms. In some

offices both internal and external mail are handled through a centralized mailing department. In other offices incoming mail is handled centrally by one person or department, and outgoing mail is processed by the department in which it originates. In the small office one person may handle both incoming and outgoing mail.

Proper planning and organizing bring about savings in time and costs, not only in the mailing center but in other departments as well. This latter economy is achieved when higher paid clerks, stenographers, and secretaries are released from the time-consuming necessity of interrupting their regular duties to attend to matters that can be handled more efficiently by the mailing department. The mailing center personnel can also bring increased specialization to their work, a fact that becomes increasingly essential as more and more mailing services become mechanized. With the centralization of mailing services, operations for handling both incoming and outgoing mail are more easily systematized and supervised, and labor-saving devices can be applied to the mailing function. The fact that the mailing department is centralized, in turn, makes it more accessible — and usually more valuable — to the departments it serves. Overall improvements in control then tend to follow.

Establishing an Effective Mailing System

The main elements of a well-designed mailing system, shown in Figure 7-10, include *staff, equipment,* and *operating procedures* for both incoming and outgoing mail. How to combine each of these components into an

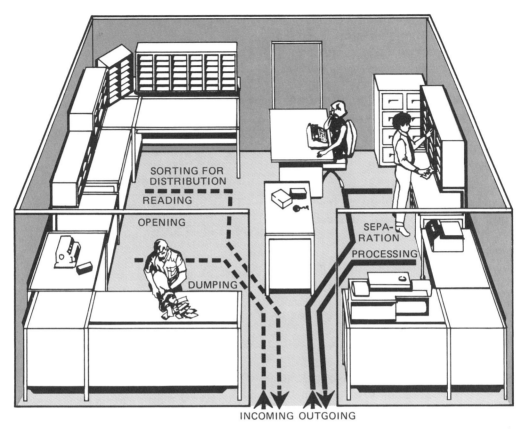

SORTING FOR
DISTRIBUTION
READING
OPENING
DUMPING

SEPA-
RATION
PROCESSING

INCOMING OUTGOING

Pitney-Bowes, Inc.

Fig. 7-10
Major Work Flows in a Modern Mailing Center

effective mailing system is discussed in this section.

Providing Trained Personnel. In the small organization a part-time office employee may combine the duties of mail clerk with those of messenger, file clerk, or another related job. On the other hand, the large organization will appoint one person as mailing center supervisor and provide the person with sufficient additional help to handle the operation satisfactorily.

The supervison of the mailing function requires an experienced person who understands the company organization, the mailing routines, and the regulations of the U.S. Postal Service.[17] Such a person must also be able to recruit, train, and command respect of the subordinates. The following duties are usually assigned to the mailing center supervisor and staff: handling incoming and outgoing mail, developing

---

[17]To help in the updating and training of mail center personnel, the U.S. Postal Service has set up a Postal Customer Council with chapters in more than 700 locations throughout the nation. This free service includes a subscription to the informative publication, "Memo to Mailers." More information about a nearby Council and its services is available from the local post office.

schedules for pickup and delivery of mail, providing internal messenger service and service to all departments on postage and mailing services, selecting and training personnel for the mailing center, and obtaining equipment. Related nonmailing duties, especially those pertaining to duplicating and collating tasks, may also be assigned to the mailing center staff from time to time.

Procuring Efficient Mailing Equipment. When considering which equipment will be used in the mailing center, what is most critically needed is a systems point of view — that is, seeing the center as a smoothly running combination of various mailing functions. Thus, the equipment needed must be selected in relation to its contribution to the overall efficiency of the operation and to the time it saves employees. A good measure of the need or worth of a machine is whether the value of the employee's time saved is greater than the depreciation and cost of the machine used. If the time saved is worth more than the cost of the machine, considering depreciation, then the use of the machine is worthwhile.

Equipment used to handle incoming mail includes letter openers, time and date-stamping machines, mail sorting racks and devices, and sorting tables. Equipment for handling outgoing mail includes addressing machines, folding and inserting machines, and metering and weighing machines. Other equipment for tying and transporting the mail may also be obtained as needs dictate. Some of the most common types of equipment used in the mailing center are described in the following paragraphs.

Postage Meter Equipment. Postage meter equipment generally consists of two parts: an office mailing machine and a detachable postage meter. The meter is licensed for use by the U.S. Postal Service. The meter, which prints the amount of postage and accounts for government revenue under official lock and key, is leased from the manufacturer who is held responsible to the post office for its proper operation and replacement when necessary. To purchase postage, the meter is taken to the nearest post office where it is "set" for one convenient lump sum. The postage is paid in advance just as when buying ordinary stamps.

Among the advantages attributed to postage meter equipment are: speed in sealing, stamping, and stacking the mail in one operation; elimination of waste and misuse of postage; and better control over postage costs. Also, by means of the postage meter, the firm's trademark, slogan, or advertising message can be imprinted on the mailing piece at the same time the postage impression is made.

Addressing Machines. Repetitive addressing of packages and envelopes is greatly simplified by the use of addressing machines. These machines imprint a complete name and address on a label or envelope faster than a typist can type a single line. Models are available that imprint account numbers, district or territory codes, and sales representatives' code numbers. These machines range from hand-operated, portable models to large, electronic models. The computer, too, may be used for printing out addresses in label form that can be attached to the mail and documents. Optical scanning addressers are also used to prepare labels. By optically scanning programmed instructions on a punched card, these addressing machines perform specific functions such as print/skip, sort, count, and stop. In selecting such machines the size of the mailing list, the frequency of mailing, and the size and variety of forms used should be considered.

Folding and Inserting Machines. For volume mailings, such as promotional mail, routine billings, or bulletins, folding and inserting machines are necessary. Some of these machines fold, insert, and seal units of three or more mail items at one time at a rate of 5,000 units per hour. To handle the mailing of bank statements, one large bank required 992 worker hours before the use of a folding-inserting machine; with its use, the time was reduced to 227 worker hours.

Mailing Scale. Probably the simplest but most essential item of equipment is the mailing scale. Studies have shown widespread problems with overpayment of postage because of an inaccurate scale or the underestimating or overestimating of postage required when no scale is available. The accurate weighing of mail eliminates these problems as well as the delays of mail returned because of insufficient postage.

Developing Effective Operating Procedures. The staff of the mailing center should have a well-developed plan of control over the incoming and outgoing mails as well as over the general operations of the center. Particularly important are the following operating procedures.

For incoming mail:

1. Insure early delivery of mail to the firm by the post office or early mail pickup at the post office by company vehicles.

2. Sort personal letters and company correspondence, and then time-stamp the first-class company mail for prompt delivery to addressees. (Large firms assign the sorting of mail to persons who are thoroughly acquainted with the company, its products, and the work of the operating departments to insure accuracy of distribution.)

3. Design and use a register for recording the receipt of all important mail, such as classified or secret documents, and registered or certified mail.

4. Establish efficient schedules for the delivery of mail to all departments. One schedule guideline is that mail be processed and delivered within one hour after it is received or one hour after the beginning of the workday.

For outgoing mail:

1. Understand and apply the postal regulations and observe carefully the dispatch time schedule of the post office, airlines, and the United Parcel Service.

2. Maintain a prompt, regularly scheduled pickup service so that mail received in the mailing center during working hours can be dispatched the same day. To achieve these scheduling requirements the mailing center supervisor should consider establishing staggered or split work shifts.

3. Control postage to prevent "shrinking" resulting from such factors as accidental loss, mutilation, pilferage, or improper rating of the mails.

4. Develop an efficient routine for processing the outgoing mail. In some concerns the outgoing mail is handled departmentally, in which case each department seals, stamps, and mails its own correspondence. Firms having a centralized mailing unit may deliver

mail to the mailing center with the letters folded and inserted in envelopes, leaving only the sealing and stamping to be done by the center personnel; while others deliver the addressed envelopes with enclosures, giving the mailing center the additional duties of folding and inserting.

For general operations:

1. Combine the activities of the mailing department with other service departments such as filing, messenger service, or duplicating. Some of the employees of these departments can be assigned to the mailing department during rush periods.

2. Use adequate equipment, such as collators, tying machines, sorting racks, and date-time recorders, to expedite the work, even though this equipment will not be in continuous use throughout the day.

3. When considering the purchase of new equipment, question whether time will be saved by the machine and, if so, how important the time saved is in relation to the cost of the equipment.

4. Assure proper conformance to the center's standard operating procedures by periodic evaluation of the mailing center operations.

5. Discourage the handling of personal mail except under extraordinary circumstances. The time spent on handling personal mail places an extra burden on mailing center personnel who will have, accordingly, fewer minutes to give to company business.

Reducing Mailing Costs

With the tremendous volume and cost of distributing business mail it is surprising how little attention is given by the business firm to its mailing function. The increasing impact of inflation, however, demands that administrative office managers find more effective methods of controlling mailing costs. Two of the most basic requirements for achieving such control are a thorough knowledge of the postal regulations and a company-wide education program that stresses unnecessary mailing costs which result from needless communications. Some mailing practices and rules of business procedures which relate to these two ideas and can result in savings are listed below:

1. Use the telephone for in-town communication, unless a hard copy is needed. Letters afford one-way communication; the telephone, two-way communication. For out-of-town communication, WATS-line service, discussed in Chapter 8, may be less expensive than letter writing.

2. Periodically purge and update mailing lists. Not only are obsolete names and addresses inaccurate but they also increase the cost of the material being mailed as well as the cost of its handling.

3. Combine mailings if possible. For example, why send two letters when one will do? Usually it pays to bulk rather than send each piece separately.

4. Reduce the weight of mailed items. This can be accomplished by condensing letter length, reducing attachments and enclosures, using both sides of the paper on which the communication is typed, and reducing the weight and size of the stationery in order to place the mailing in another weight class.

5. Use the first-class postage for all letters (except bulk mailings) within the continental United States. For speedy delivery of overseas mail, airmail postage is recommended.

6. Deposit first-class, long-distance mail in the post office by 11 a.m. each business day. If both the sender's and addressee's cities are served by commercial airlines, the mail will usually be delivered the next day.

7. Justify the use of special-delivery service. Prompter delivery to the addressee should be the determining factor.

8. Insure packages accurately. Consider that reimbursement for their loss is determined according to their actual value, not their declared value. United Parcel Service rates should also be investigated, for their basic charge includes insurance coverage.

9. Use registered mail only when the item has insurable value. Otherwise use the less expensive certified mail, which provides a receipt to the sender but does not insure the value of the item mailed.

10. Answer all letters promptly. This practice avoids the necessity for sending follow-up letters that add to the volume and cost of mail handled.

11. Use business reply envelopes with a central permit number whenever possible instead of enclosing stamped return envelopes. When the business reply envelope is returned by the addressee, the post office of the sender collects the regular postage plus a small fee for the reply privilege.

12. Print in advance the envelopes for branch mail, thus saving the cost of typing addresses each day. Further economies will result from holding all but the most urgent branch mail and enclosing it in one envelope at the close of the day.

13. Use window envelopes to eliminate the typing of the recipient's name and address and the problem of matching the addressed envelope with the appropriate letter; also use duplex or combination envelopes for sending first- or third-class mail as an enclosure with second-, third-, and fourth-class parcels.

14. When the rapid transmission of messages is required, consider the use of Western Union's Mailgram in which a letter is typed on a cathode ray tube device and transmitted at high speeds over telephone lines to a computer for processing and local delivery. When this service is used, savings can be realized through reduced clerical labor time involved in handling and distributing copies of correspondence as well as through the elimination of postage and related costs.

15. Periodically check the postal scales against the post office scales to ensure accuracy and dependability.

QUESTIONS FOR REVIEW

1. In what ways do managers rely on the communication process to fulfill their overall responsibilities?

2. How do visual communications compare with oral communications in terms of frequency and importance in the office?

3. What types of written communication media are often used in both external and internal office communications?

4. Of what value are office manuals as a tool of managerial control over the communication function?

5. Identify the main principles or guidelines required to create effective written communications.

6. Describe the operation of an "endless loop" dictation-transcription system.

7. In the age of automation, what circumstances still justify the use of personal messenger systems in offices?

8. Cite several of the key reasons for written communication problems in the office. What effective controls may be applied to eliminate these problems?

9. Why is the time factor stressed as the most important component of correspondence cost to be reduced?

10. What basic elements make up a word processing system? What function does each element perform?

11. What are some of the advantages and disadvantages of the word processing/administrative support form of work specialization in the office?

12. What steps should an administrative office manager take to determine whether a firm can justify a word processing center?

13. In what ways can the work produced in a word processing center be measured in order that production standards may be set up?

14. In what ways has the mailing center become mechanized? In your answer, point out areas in which mechanical limitations exist and thus require the retention of human skills.

15. What arguments can be given *against* a central mail facility?

QUESTIONS FOR DISCUSSION

1. Many business-writing problems are deeply rooted in the past communication habits of the writers. Explain how these writing habits might be changed in a company-wide program of communications improvement.

2. What is meant by a "letter clinic"? Should a letter clinic be conducted by the firm's executives or by some outside specialist?

3. If it is true that the greater the salary of an executive, the higher the cost of the letter, it would follow that the highest paid executives should spend a minimum of time writing letters. Is this true? Explain.

4. Assume you have been asked to prepare an outline for your superior regarding the relative merits of machine dictation as compared with

shorthand dictation. What specific advantages and disadvantages does each dictation method offer?

5. At a recent meeting of the Administrative Management Society, a communication specialist made this basic point: "The communication process is not measurable, and, therefore, cannot be controlled." Discuss.

6. The newly employed supervisor of Valentine Products' mailing center has been studying the center's mailing operations and has observed the following:

   a. Only rarely is outgoing mail sorted; the feeling seems to be that this is the function of the post office.
   b. Repeated requests from other departments come to the mailing center regarding mailing rules and economies. Each caller is referred to the U.S. Postal Service for answers.
   c. Even though some of the firm's products are perishable and others breakable, no standardized labels have been established by the mailing center to ensure that all such packages receive the special handling they require.
   d. The firm's main office is in an industrial park area four miles from the city's post office. By utilizing the post office delivery trucks, first-class mail is delivered daily at 9:45 a.m. and 2:45 p.m.
   e. The mailing center supervisor has been told by one of the workers that the volume of mail serviced by the mailing unit has increased a good deal in the past five years. In fact, a bimonthly mailing to 30,000 selected households throughout the country alone taxes the staff of three full-time persons since all assembling of enclosures and other postal tasks must be done manually, with the exception of affixing postage, which is done by meter machine.

   The mailing center supervisor knows that the mailing unit is not following good mailing center practices. What are the implications of each of the present practices, and what recommendations can you give to the new supervisor for improving each of them?

7. As administrative office manager for Barta's Engineering Consultants, you sense that the cost and efficiency of the typing and transcription work are excessively high — perhaps as much as 30 to 40 percent above the costs of doing similar work in nearby firms. From your analysis of typing work patterns and costs during the past six months you have concluded that most of the problems can be attributed to: (1) improper employee selection due to the shortage of qualified clerical help; (2) the absence of any valid preemployment tests for measuring the skills, aptitudes, and interests of job applicants; (3) the fact that beginning typists are poorly trained and have little knowledge of business systems, work costs, English fundamentals, and spelling; (4) inadequate supervision, including a certain amount of laxness in discipline; and (5) no records of the production rates of the clerical staff.

How can each of the problems cited above be resolved, given your goals of improving the quality and quantity of the work and at the same time reducing the work costs?

PRACTICAL OFFICE MANAGEMENT CASES

Case 7-1   **Determining the Feasibility of a Word Processing Center**

Range Rider Products is engaged in the manufacture of specially tooled leather goods. The company employs 20 stenographers in the three departments of its plant offices. You have been recently employed as office manager, with a base salary of $15,000 and the promise of a $2,000 bonus after the first year if you can reduce the costs of office work at least $10,000 a year.

You feel that one of the first possibilities for reducing costs is to centralize and mechanize the dictation and transcription work. In order to estimate the savings that might be effected, you have made a survey of the cost of the work as it is presently done and what it would cost if it were mechanized. The survey of the stenographic and transcription work for a period of one month (four weeks) is shown in Table A. The work is done on a decentralized basis.

After some preliminary thinking, you feel it would be advisable to transfer the present transcription work to a word processing center that would be responsible for the bulk of the firm's typing tasks. In the center there would be several general-copy typists, transcribing machine operators, and general clerical workers (nontypists). Assume that the following weekly salary rates are in effect:

SURVEY OF STENOGRAPHIC AND TRANSCRIPTION WORK

Kind of Work	Time Spent in		
	Department I (Minutes)	Department II (Minutes)	Department III (Minutes)
Dictation	10,400	6,000	8,800
Transcription	26,000	16,000	24,000
Clerical work (filing) ..	16,000	23,000	10,800
General typing	20,800	20,000	1,800
No work	1,500	160	250
Totals	74,700	65,160	45,650

Table A

Department I (8 stenographers) transcribed 33,000 lines of dictation.
Department II (7 stenographers) transcribed 20,000 lines of dictation.
Department III (5 stenographers) transcribed 28,500 lines of dictation.

stenographers, $150; typists, $140; general clerical workers, $125; and transcribing machine operators (who can transcribe on the average 5,000 lines of dictation per week), $145. All employees work an estimated 154 hours each month (four weeks).

The word processing center would serve 15 executives. A remote-control telephonic dictation system with 12 dictating stations would be required, since three of the executives would double up with the others. The equipment would be depreciated over a period of six years. The total installation cost for the recording stations and transcribing machines is estimated at $9,000, with an annual service maintenance cost of $500. It is estimated that the annual cost of supplies will be $400.

On the basis of this information, you are asked to prepare a report for the administrative office manager that will prove conclusively the savings that can be effected by mechanizing and centralizing the dictation and transcription work. This report should include:

1. Time spent in dictation under the present method.
2. Time spent in transcription under the present method and the number of transcribing machine operators that are needed.
3. Time spent in general typing under the present method and the number of general-copy typists that are needed.
4. Time spent in clerical work under the present method and the number of general clerical workers that are needed.
5. The savings that would be realized (a) during the present year and (b) during the next five years.
6. The effect upon the conditional bonus arrangement with the office manager.

Case 7-2 Evaluating and Reorganizing the Mailing Center

Resource Conservators, Ltd., of Toledo, Ohio, and Toronto, Ontario, has just appointed you as administrative office manager in the Toledo office. The company maintains ten branches located in key cities throughout the United States and Canada. In the Toledo office there are these departments: sales, accounting, purchasing, data processing, word processing, records management, manufacturing, engineering, shipping-receiving, and the executive offices.

In evaluating the present office systems and procedures, you find that the problems of handling the mail as described below seem to require top priority.

Incoming Mail. The mail is picked up at the main post office at 8:30 a.m. and 12:30 p.m. by Frank Strauss, one of the sales correspondents, since his trip from home in the morning and his return from lunch take him past the post office. The mail is very heavy, often numbering 4,000 pieces a day. For example, this morning's mail brought the following 1,741 pieces:

- 100 communications from the branch offices
- 50 order cancellations
- 10 letters from sales representatives requesting price reductions
- 300 checks and money orders in payment on account
- 30 applications for jobs
- 50 credit references
- 1 letter from the Internal Revenue Service
- 160 invoices for goods purchased
- 200 advertising circulars
- 470 orders from customers
- 80 C.O.D. requests
- 40 complaints for orders not yet delivered
- 20 complaints of errors in invoices
- 200 inquiries for price lists and catalogs
- 30 letters stating inability to ship goods ordered

When the mail reaches the office, Strauss, the switchboard operator, and a file clerk sort the mail into two stacks — addressed to persons and addressed to the firm. The mail addressed to persons is sorted and delivered unopened. The mail addressed to the firm is open by a hand-operated opener at the rate of 100 pieces a minute. Whenever there is an enclosure in a letter, it is clipped to the covering letter. After all the letters have been opened, their contents are sorted into wire baskets, each of which is labeled for one department. When the sorting has been completed, the mail is distributed, which is usually not before 10:30 a.m. or 2:30 p.m.

Outgoing Mail. The daily outgoing mail averages between 1,100 and 1,200 pieces, not including the printed advertising circulars. The circulars, numbering from 20,000 to 30,000 pieces, are sent out regularly on January 2, April 1, July 1, and October 1. The daily outgoing mail typically consists of the following:

- 400 sales invoices
- 200 letters enclosing price lists and catalogs
- 100 letters to the branch offices
- 400 letters acknowledging orders, answering complaints, etc.

Stamped window envelopes are used for the sales invoices and stamped envelopes for the letters, except those addressed to the branch offices. The latter are sent in specially printed envelopes that require the individual affixing of stamps. There have been numerous instances of mail returned for insufficient postage, a situation which has been creating delays and ill will.

Each department sends its sealed, stamped letters to Frank Strauss' office by 4:00 p.m. All outgoing mail is taken to the post office by Strauss at 4:30 p.m.

After carefully considering the facts presented, prepare a report in which you:

a. Criticize the present methods of handling the incoming and outgoing mail.
b. Present your suggested methods of reorganizing the mailing work, including comments on personnel, equipment, and mailing routines. Give your reasons for recommended changes in the routine and estimate the cost of the equipment that should be purchased. (Prices may be obtained from equipment catalogs.) Assume that two mail clerks will be employed at $120 a week and that a supervisor earning $180 a week will devote half of his or her time to the mailing work. Set up a schedule for handling the mail under the reorganized plan.

Chapter 8

TELECOMMUNICATIONS IN THE OFFICE

Since its invention by Alexander Graham Bell in 1876, the telephone has become the one most valuable communication instrument throughout the world. Its name (coming from two Greek words — *tele*, far, and *phone*, sound) explains the basic purpose of the telephone — transmitting sounds over distances too far for the human voice to carry. In all aspects of modern life the telephone helps to draw people together to solve problems and to carry out their responsibilities in organizations.

During the past two decades the telephone industry has successfully added written communications to its growing list of customer services. Written communications can be transmitted over long distances by wire and wireless methods, and as the computer has been drawn into the communication network, transmission of computerized data from one or several locations to all corners of the globe is possible. This capability of "instant" message sending permits management to maintain minute-by-minute contacts among widely scattered branch offices as well as between companies and the public. It also speeds up the exchange of written information and facilitates decision making.

To describe the new systems for transmitting sound and writing over long distances, a new word — *telecommunications* — has been coined. In the broad sense, it involves voice communication, the sending of written communications by wire, computer-linked data communications, and other rapidly expanding services of the communication carriers (the telephone and telegraph companies). Each of these aspects of telecommunication systems — in addition to the management needs of these systems — is discussed in this chapter.

TELECOMMUNICATION SYSTEMS

The modern economy within which business operates grows more dynamic and complex. As competition among businesses and the number of firms going bankrupt continue to increase, management has to utilize every feasible resource to improve the profit picture. Successful large businesses expand from local to national concerns — and, in many cases multinationally — because of consumer familiarity with and acceptance of their products and services and because of their ability to compete. Much of this growth depends upon communication facilities that enable business firms to respond quickly to the demands of markets and consumers wherever they are located.

To survive, let alone prosper, both large and small companies are recognizing the need for good communication. Large firms, such as Mobil Oil and the Olin Corporation, require an extensive specialized staff to organize their communication functions. For example, the Olin Corporation maintains a headquarters staff of twenty for administering their voice and wire-message networks, with home-office specialists supervising international and domestic communications. Staff consultants and communication analysts also are needed to coordinate their work with the data processing department. A telephone switchboard system is required, too.

Smaller companies utilize voice communications to an increasing degree for speeding up the flow of information. With such simple devices as the telephone and teletypewriter, orders can be received and processed, raw materials and supplies purchased, personnel recruited, and financial data prepared. By linking the telephone to the computing facilities of a commercial service bureau, the small business manager has the same type of computing and communication power as the larger firm.

The design of a telecommunication system depends on many considerations — the type of information to be transmitted, the way it is to be used, the location of users, the environment in which the users operate, and even the human sense organs. For example, the human ears, unlike the eyes, can receive information from all directions. Moreover, the ears cannot be closed in the same way the eyes are closed, making the ears well suited to certain types of messages, such as warning and emergency signals.[1] Representatives of equipment vendors and communication carriers, such as the Bell System and Western Union, as well as private consultants specializing in communication systems, are available to help in the development and installation of an effective telecommunication system.

Telecommunication systems solve the problems of time and distance in the sending and receiving of messages. Usually, these systems are classified as (1) voice communication systems, (2) systems for transmitting written communications by wire, and (3) data communication systems. These systems, which transmit messages by wire, are described in the following sections.[2]

VOICE COMMUNICATION SYSTEMS

From a sender's standpoint in a sender-receiver relationship, *voice* (or oral) *communications* are originated and conveyed to listeners who receive and respond to the messages. When such communications are considered from the receiver's point of view, they are called *aural* (referring to hearing) *communications*. Generally, voice communications are most suitable when the following conditions are found:

1. The message to be transmitted is short, simple, and uncomplicated. Such a message does not require further study.
2. Speed of transmission is important. Sending messages by mail, for example, can be slow and subject to unpredictable delays.
3. There is no need for later reference to the message. However, by means of

---

[1]For an interesting comparison of the complementary roles played by the eyes and ears in communication, see Alphonse Chapanis, *Man-Machine Engineering* (Belmont: Wadsworth Publishing Company, 1965), p. 33.

[2]Communication by microwave is an alternative to wire communications. In a microwave radio-relay system, signals in the super-high frequency range are sent between towers located approximately 30 miles apart, where the signals are amplified and retransmitted until they reach their destination. One important advantage of microwave systems is their wide bandwidth, which makes possible the crowding of more separate channels (and hence more message-sending potential) into the allocated space without interfering with each other. Communication satellites use similar methods for transmitting information from one earth location to another.

voice-recording equipment, vocal messages can be retained for later reference much the same as the written messages.

4. Visual channels of communication are overloaded. A telephone call, for example, may get more immediate attention from an office executive than a special-delivery letter waiting in the in basket on the executive's desk.

5. The environment is not suitable for receiving visual messages, as in a dim or dark location, or when office workers have to move around frequently in the work environment.

In considering the needs of an effective voice communication system, the office manager should evaluate carefully the conditions listed above and the effect that each has on disseminating information. Where one or more of these conditions is present, one of the following voice communication systems should be considered: (1) the telephone, (2) intercommunication systems, (3) paging systems, or (4) audiovisual communication systems.

The Telephone

The ring of the telephone is the most common machine sound in the office; it calls attention to a waiting business message. Not long ago telephones were used primarily for exchanging conversations between two points and required only telephone sets, lines, and usually a central-office switchboard. With the growing and expanding communication needs of business, however, a much more elaborate communication network has emerged. Instead of a few telephones placed in strategic locations throughout a company, today's office has adopted systems that can handle not only voice, but also video, graphics, and data communications, with each providing additional functions to the original telephone concept. However, the basic nature and purpose of the telephone remain the same.

Several types of telephone calls can be made. One type of call refers to the *distance* involved. Local, long-distance, and overseas calls fall into this category, with 95 percent of all calls made in the United States being local calls. Another classification refers to the *nature* of long-distance calls made. This group includes station-to-station and person-to-person calls, collect calls, third-person calls (when the operator is asked to charge the cost of the call to a telephone number different from that of the one being used), credit-card calls, and code-billing calls (similar to credit-card calls except that the customer dials an assigned code over the direct-dial network that is used to bill the customer for the call made). In addition, a wide variety of communication services is available and is described later in this chapter.

Types of Telephone Systems. Except for very small offices, the telephone systems in most firms require the use of a switchboard to handle several incoming or outgoing calls simultaneously. The volume of the simultaneous calls determines the kind and size of system needed. Three types of telephone systems in use are: PBX, PABX, and Centrex.

PBX. PBX, or *private branch exchange*, is a manually operated switchboard or console in offices where there are frequent interoffice and outside calls. This system enables a person in one department to call a person in another department without having to place the number through the central telephone exchange. The switchboard may be operated by one or more persons, depending upon the number of extensions and the volume of calls. Where volume is heavy, a dial PBX is recommended in which the attendant uses a pushbutton console to answer and connect incoming calls.

PABX. PABX, or *private automatic branch exchange*, is more or less restricted to large business concerns. It is a telephone switching system that enables the subscriber to obtain an outside line automatically — usually by dialing one digit. In the simpler PBX devices such a line must be obtained through an operator. Current PABX devices are constructed with selected switching mechanisms that can, for example, hold incoming calls until the extension is free and then be put through automati-

cally, thus saving operator time. (See Figure 8-1.) More sophisticated PABX equipment can perform automatic route selection to determine the least expensive route (foreign exchange, Wide Area Telecommunication Service, or direct-distance dialing), thereby eliminating the need for a switchboard attendant. With such equipment, telephone communications are handled automatically, and, thus, clerical costs are reduced.

Centrex. Centrex, or *central exchange*, provides the same features as dial PBX but performs certain additional functions. A principal reason for its increasing popularity is Direct Inward Dialing (DID) or Centrex I, which permits incoming calls from almost anywhere in the country to be dialed directly to any Centrex station without the

Fig. 8-1
A PABX Console with Switching Gear for Routing Incoming Calls

need of an operator. Centrex II offers additional features at increased cost. Included in the Centrex II package are consultation hold, add-on conference calls, station transfer, and night answers from any station. A third version of Centrex utilizes an electronic switching system equipped to provide even more automatic functions.[3]

Automatic Telephone Systems. The ease and simplicity with which the telephone can be used often lead to a waste of worker time and money. The cost-reduction measures outlined later in this chapter as well as several types of automatic telephone equipment discussed in this section largely eliminate the need for operating personnel and help keep costs within reasonable bounds.

Automatic Dialing Systems. In planning the installation of a telephone system, the administrative manager should investigate automatic dialing equipment which will guarantee accuracy in dialing, free the switchboard operator for other duties, and overcome the need for remembering frequently used numbers. Two automatic dialing systems are the *Card Dialer* and the *Touch-a-matic*.

The Card Dialer consists of a six-button key set and an automatic dial unit with storage pockets accommodating about 40 dialing cards. Up to 14 digits can be punched into each card to identify the number called. To place a call, the appropriate card is inserted into a slot of the instrument, the receiver is lifted, and the start bar is pushed. The

Card Dialer, illustrated in Figure 8-2, is available on standard dial telephones as well as on the Touch-Tone telephones (with 10 decimal-digit keys for the rapid registration of numbers).

Courtesy of
Northwestern Bell Telephone Co.

Fig. 8-2
The Card Dialer

The *Touch-a-matic* is an automatic dialing system that stores up to 31 telephone numbers in a solid-state memory device for local and long-distance calling. The unit also "remembers" the last telephone number dialed by hand; and in the case of a busy line, the number can be "redialed" automatically by pressing the "last number dialed" button. Figure 8-3 illustrates this unit.

Automatic Call Distribution Systems. Companies with a large volume of incoming calls should investigate the *automatic call distributor*, which allows calls to be routed to answering points as attendants become free to handle them. As calls come in to the order department, reception areas, and other departments usually dealing

---

[3]For more information on Centrex, see Frank K. Griesinger, "Is CENTREX Right For You?" *Administrative Management* (August, 1973), pp. 22–23, 78, 80–81.

Courtesy of
Northwestern Bell Telephone Co.

Fig. 8-3
The Touch-a-matic Telephone

with the public, the calls are "held" until a station becomes free. A "held" call may also include a recorded response advising the caller that all lines are temporarily busy and asking the caller to remain on the line. Stored calls are released in the order received as the stations called become available. A related automatic system — *automatic identification of outward dialing* — records call data on paper or magnetic tape from which a computer printout is produced. The printout is then used for analyzing the messages and allocating toll charges to the appropriate departments.

Intercommunication Systems

Since nearly two thirds of the telephone traffic in most companies is internal calls, a large share of telephone expense is created inside the firm. Fortunately, many employees making internal calls do not need an outside line, and hence an alternative type of communication line should be considered. Such an alternate is the *intercom-*

munication (or intercom) *system* that is used within the company as a privately owned, small-scale telephone system tying together all departments.

Intercommunication systems incorporate two types of stations: master and substation. An operator at a master station can call any other master station or substation in the system; in contrast, substation operators can call master stations only. These systems can operate compatibly with telephone systems, although, as a rule, most intercoms do not need a central switchboard, which makes their installation and maintenance simpler. Some systems have headsets and switching systems like private telephones; others utilize speakers that enable employees to talk to one another without tying up expensive PABX equipment and the telephone lines. Since intercommunication systems are bought outright, there is no per-call charge.

Intercommunication systems utilize equipment that is available in many forms. Included are desk units, paging horns, central switchboards, and stations ranging in number from two units to many dozens of "interconnects." With this wide array of equipment, managers have at their fingertips many of the new services listed below:

1. Hands-free operations that let operators talk while working with their hands, searching through files, or moving about without using a handset.
2. Handset systems that give privacy to workers. These units can be installed on desks, walls, or in drawers to avoid distractions or being overheard by a caller from another station. If a station user does not want to be interrupted by a caller, the caller can be sent an "absent" signal.

3. Override and executive priority features that allow a designated station to cancel or interrupt ongoing conversations in order to transmit messages of urgency or extreme importance. The secretarial transfer mode routes calls to a secretary's desk when the executive does not want to be interrupted.
4. One- or two-way conversation arrangements between executives and their staffs, or simultaneous conference calls to a number of stations.
5. Tie-in between the intercom system and the word processing center, enabling all word originators to dial a number on the intercom set, dictate their correspondence, and have it typed without leaving their desks.

Since intercommunication machines connect two or more departments within a firm, an interdepartmental systems study must be conducted to determine the most effective equipment installation required. For example, after one large insurance firm installed a new central filing system, it became clear that new communication services would be required since telephone requests for files would be delayed due to other uses of the telephone system. As a result, a private intercom system was installed, and files were requested without disturbing the regular telephone conversations.

Paging Systems

In many large organizations such as department stores, manufacturing plants, banks, and insurance companies, executives sometimes move about the offices regularly. When urgent matters arise, to locate executives by telephoning the various departments may waste valuable minutes. To avoid this, paging systems that operate through the telephone switchboard have been developed. Each important executive is given

a number. The switchboard operator, who also operates the central station of the paging system, "plugs in" or makes the electrical connection for the number of the executive being called. Throughout the office or plant, a signal corresponding to the executive's number will sound. When this signal is heard, the executive picks up the nearest telephone, calls the switchboard operator, and receives the message. In another type of paging system, the switchboard operator or the receptionist speaks into a microphone and summons the attention of the paged person through loudspeakers distributed throughout the area. This system is one-way only but covers large areas. More than one paging location can be provided and music or other signals can be transmitted through the loudspeakers.

For maintaining voice contact with people who are often away from their offices, pocket-size paging systems are used to receive voice messages up to several miles away from the central transmitter. No wires or external antenna are needed. When communication is desired with an executive anywhere within the transmitting area, the clerk signals the executive by radio, after which the person paged can either communicate by radio or go to the nearest telephone to receive the message.

Audiovisual Communication Systems

Both voice and pictures can be transmitted simultaneously via the more advanced equipment provided by the communication industry. Two of the media for sending and receiving audiovisual messages are discussed here.

The *Picturephone*, developed by the Bell Laboratories in 1927, adds the visual dimension of a television screen to the regular telephone, thus enabling the user to see as well as to talk with the person called. Because of its relatively great expense, the Picturephone has been adopted by only a few major corporations for internal use to take the place of more expensive personal conferences and to transmit all types of written information including drawings, charts, and computer printouts.

A related audiovisual medium — television — has many business applications and is widely used for certain information-processing functions. For as little as $2,000 a closed-circuit television system can be installed to provide two-way sound arrangements along with a related picture message.

Banks, in particular, make use of closed-circuit TV. In one installation, the closed-circuit system makes signature verification between the bookkeeping department and the bank's drive-in windows fast and easy. The teller simply phones the bookkeeping office and asks for a certain signature to be placed on the monitor. The bookkeeper does so, and the teller needs only to glance at the monitor for a large, sharp picture of the signature. Mechanized files make the signature card almost instantly available, thus keeping transaction time to a minimum. The system is also used to alert tellers on new stop-payments, holds, and lost checkbooks.[4]

---

[4]Two other television systems, still considered experimental, offer great potential for the office. One is EVR (Electronic Video Recording), a system for storing images and sound on a cartridge for playback through a standard TV set. A similar system — Homefax — was developed by RCA and works through the TV receiver to produce printed copy in the home or office. An electrostatic printer, much like an office copier, is activated by the signals received through the TV antenna, turning out one printed page every ten seconds.

SYSTEMS FOR TRANSMITTING WRITTEN COMMUNICATIONS BY WIRE

Voice communications and the various mailing services discussed earlier have several limitations in transmitting information. Voice communications provide sound only; and the typical mail service transmits only letters, forms, or reports at a relatively slow pace, and often delays or loses them in transit. Wire communications, however, do not possess these limitations.

In many instances management requires a communication system that is capable of sending at high rates of speed information in written form to distant locations. Thus, communication systems other than the telephone and the mails are essential. Three of these systems that utilize wire transmission methods — facsimile, the teletypewriter, and the telegraph — are considered in this section.

Facsimile Services

With the facsimile method an exact duplicate of any record (written, drawn, or typed) is transmitted between two distant points. This method differs from electronic longhand transmission (described in Chapter 7), which is designed only for the internal transmission of written materials. By means of a sensing device, the facsimile sending unit "sees" the original copy, converts it to audio signals, and sends it over telephone lines to a receiving unit that recreates the original document from the electrical signals. In minutes the recipient has an exact copy of the original document.

The facsimile service of "sending records by phone" has been widely accepted by business management for it offers the fastest means of sending visual communications over long distances. Letter-size documents can be transmitted over normal telephone lines in just four minutes with the facsimile unit shown in Figure 10-12, page 275. A Chicago bank, for example, speeds stop-payment notices on checks by transmitting the notice from its bookkeeping office to its main banking office blocks away; and a large midwestern electronics firm uses a facsimile network to transmit graphic information (drawings, charts, and advertising copy) to various decision centers around the country. No special training is required to operate the facsimile machines and in many instances the cost of transmitting the documents is significantly lower than by voice or mail communications.

Teletypewriter Services

The *teletypewriter*, illustrated in Figure 8-4, is a machine used for transmitting written conversations just as the telephone is a means of transmitting oral conversations. The teletypewriter,

Western Union

Fig. 8-4
The Teletypewriter

similar to a typewriter, transmits electrical impulses over telephone lines. A simultaneous reproduction of the message is typewritten on machines in neighboring or distant offices. Through the use of punched tape, there has been a great expansion in the use of teletypewriters as terminal equipment for sending messages to and receiving messages from the computer.

Two illustrations of the many applications of the teletypewriter are given. In a shoe manufacturing company, orders are teletyped on specially designed forms from the sales offices directly to the plants. One teletyping of an order at the sales office produces sufficient copies locally for the use of the sales office. At the same time the necessary copies are produced at the plant, thus enabling it to plan for immediate production. As a result of this installation, the firm was able to eliminate several days in the time required to produce and ship an order. Another firm has its receiving machine equipped with a duplicating typewriter ribbon and special duplication stencil paper, so that as the information is received, a stencil is prepared. The stencil is then used to make copies without the delay of retyping. Both of these applications represent the first step in an automated data processing system, as explained later in Part 4.

Telegraphic Services

For decades Western Union telegrams served as models of fast, accurate, and dependable message delivery. With the development of complex communication networks, new types of telegraphic services have now become available. For example, Western Union has developed the Mailgram, discussed in Chapter 7 for faster delivery of messages than is possible by the U.S. Postal Service. In addition Western Union has created a teleprinter service, *Telex*, which is an international network of Western Union Teleprinter subscribers, linked to dial-up exchanges located in almost every large city. After data have been punched into a tape and verified for accuracy, the teleprinter operator dials the number of one of the 50,000 teletypewriter machines in the United States; and within eight seconds, the called machine responds and receives the message on a receiving teleprinter unattended by an operator. The per-minute cost of this service ranges from 20 to 60 cents. For example, a one-minute Telex transmission between Boston and Pittsburgh (482 miles apart by air) costs less than 25 cents as compared to a direct dialed long-distance call costing more than $1 for three minutes. Western Union also furnishes a similar TWX (teleprinter exchange) service with direct connections provided between subscribers.[5]

DATA COMMUNICATION SYSTEMS

In Chapter 7, dealing with the preparation and sending of written messages, communications took on a meaning that referred to messages which are interpreted, understood, and acted upon by people. In this chapter, a different type of communications — *data commu-*

nications — is discussed. This concept of communications has a technical meaning that refers to the accurate movement of information at electronic speeds over long distances from one machine to another. Since data communication usually involves the direct use of the computer, the combination of data processing and telecommunication equipment, personnel, and procedures constitutes the *data communication system*, one of the most important subdivisions of an information system.

Figure 8-5 shows the makeup of an information system and the important part that communication plays in it. In this figure the lower half of the diagram contains elements that are directly related to the movement of information: terminals for sending and receiving information, lines for carrying information,

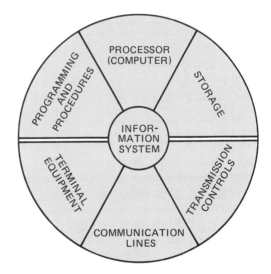

Source: Adapted from *System/360, Introduction to Teleprocessing*, (Poughkeepsie: IBM Corporation, DPD Educational Development — Publication Services, 1970), p. 62.

Fig. 8-5
Data Communication Elements in an Information System

---

[5]A thorough discussion of the various methods of sending written communications is found in Frank K. Griesinger, "Wiring The Written Word," *Administrative Management* (September, 1974), pp. 24–27, 30, 32, 34, 90. Of special interest to office managers are the various types of TWX and Mailgram services provided jointly by Western Union and the U.S. Postal Service. When the term *teletype* is used, usually it refers to different forms of teletypewriter equipment, although the name is the registered trademark of the Teletype Corporation.

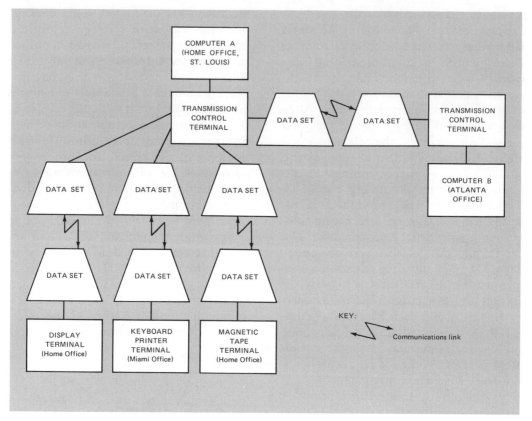

Fig. 8-6
A Data Communication System

and controls for meeting accuracy and other transmission requirements.[6] The upper half of the figure deals with the "backup" support required to move information: programs and procedures which furnish the processing instructions necessary for the computer, and the storage component for retaining the information until it is sent via communication lines to the destination.

Data communications is a highly complex, technical field embracing the areas of computers, engineering communications, and electronics. To understand it thoroughly one must possess a technical background beyond that necessary for managing the modern office. However, the administrative office manager must be responsible for understanding the functions of the data communication system outlined in Figure 8-6 rather than the technical characteristics of the system. As such, the following basic nontechnical concepts making up the data communication process must be considered:

[6]For an excellent orientation to data communication concepts see *Data Communications in Business: An Introduction*, (New York: American Telephone & Telegraph Company, 1965). For an intermediate-level treatment see K. J. Asten, *Data Communication for Business Information Systems* (New York: The Macmillan Co., 1973).

1. A *transmitter* and *receiver* of information. Usually this means some type of input-output terminal such as a typewriter, teletypewriter, or cathode-ray tube device as shown in Figure 8-7, page 206. The computer may also serve as a receiver of information from a terminal.

2. A *converter* on both the transmitting and the receiving ends. This device converts the numeric signals of the terminals and computers into analog signals that can be transmitted over the dial-up (telephone) network. The term *data set* is used to describe such a converter device.

3. A *communication network* (sometimes called channels, links, or lines) for carrying information from one location to another. Examples of such channels are communication satellites, microwave, and coaxial cables as well as the regular telephone lines.

4. *Transmission speeds*, or the rates at which the channel can accommodate data transmission. Voice communication lines operate at medium speeds (over 300 bits, or binary digits, per second) while wideband or high-speed lines used in data communications operate at rates of 18,000 bits per second or higher and are capable of transmitting data directly from one computer to another at much higher speeds. A more complete discussion of the binary number system common to computer processing is included in Chapter 21.

5. *Error detection* to determine that the data received are identical to the data transmitted. Since the telephone lines do not provide automatic checking facilities, the burden of error detection and correction falls upon the computer and terminal equipment at either end of the communication channel. This detection-correction procedure is handled through a combination of programming techniques.

6. *Terminal control*, especially the controls needed to ensure that the computer input/output equipment identifies and distinguishes between the data and the control information — such as the programs — that must be transmitted over the same communication channels. Other controls involve deciding which terminals are to send and receive data.

7. *Communication tariffs*, or the monthly charges that the user must pay to the common carrier for the use of the communication lines. These tariffs are regulated by federal and state agencies.

By understanding how each of these concepts functions, the office executive will come to appreciate the practicalities and limitations of the data communication system for the office. In addition, such an executive will be better prepared to work with representatives of the common carriers and other organizations engaged in marketing communication services and equipment.

Objectives of Data Communication Systems

Data communication systems are "information movers" that extend the services of data processing equipment to remote locations for the inquiry, processing, or reception of information. Because of their linkup with the computer, data communication systems possess vast computing power; and with their interconnection with the communication lines of the telephone industry, they can overcome the "distance" and "time" barriers. In effect, the Atlanta branch office in Figure 8-6 can receive and transmit information to the St. Louis home office with the same efficiency as the Miami branch office; each branch

Courtesy of IBM

A Typewriter Terminal

Courtesy of IBM

Cathode-Ray Tube Display Terminal

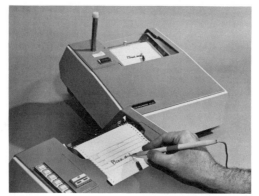

Infolink Corporation

Electrowriter Facsimile Terminal

Texas Instruments Inc.

Portable Data Terminal

Fig. 8-7
Terminal Equipment

becomes equidistant from the home office so far as the exchange of information is concerned. Data communication systems thus permit management to achieve the following important objectives:

1. *Time reduction*, such as reducing delays in preparing payrolls and delivery of orders as well as the time for preparing invoices and statements; decreasing delays in updating inventory and other accounting records.

2. *Operating efficiency*, such as providing an integrated information system serving all departments of a company; linking together all distant branches of a company or governmental agency (a national law-enforcement communication system is one example); making more selective and current information available to management.

3. *Cost saving*, such as reducing costs of order handling, inventory, data processing, and record keeping; better estimation of inventories needed, thereby reducing inventory size without delaying shipments of orders.

4. *Improved customer service*, such as better estimating of delivery of orders and shortening the time required to determine stock available in order to quote delivery dates to customers.

Organizing a Data Communication System

Of the two methods used to move information (the physical method, as in the case of the mail and personal messenger systems; and the electrical method, such as the telephone), only the electrical transmission method employed by data communication offers the potential to meet the need to send volumes of information at great speeds to distant places. Such a system usually develops as a result of an overtaxed computer center that has had its efficiency curtailed by bottlenecks in the communication process.

To help in the organization of such a system, management can draw from many reliable sources. Numerous private consultants in data communication are listed in large-city telephone directories, and major vendors of communication equipment provide systems consultant help. These consultants represent the best information sources for small firms that do not have internal computing equipment. Large firms with data processing departments will have the necessary in-house help from their systems staff to begin the planning process for organizing a data communication system, but normally outside consultant help is required during the latter phases of the systems study.

The task of organizing a data communication system should be approached by the use of the scientific method, discussed in Chapter 1, which follows certain logical steps, such as those listed below:

1. Define the problems facing the business regarding its information transfer. Typical problems are late arrival of information, obsolete and inaccurate data, and mutilation of records.

2. Gather and analyze the facts relating to the problem. Special attention should be given to these features of any information system: the type of information distribution (one source to one receiver or one source to many receivers); information volume, such as the average daily volume of messages presently in the system, the average number of

characters in each message, the average daily total transmission time; the form of the information (hard copy, magnetic tape, or visual display); and the accuracy of the information.

For example, the accuracy of numeric information requires more rigid standards for sending the astronauts into space than the accuracy of alphabetic information (such as misspelled words in a business letter). Typically the most common human errors are made in keypunching and in telephone dial-up.

3. Consider the urgency of the information. Considerable ranges in urgency exist in systems. For instance, there is less urgency in sending out accounting statements than that required for making air reservations for an imminent flight.

4. Determine the cost of the system. In one sense, cost determines whether the system can be obtained; in another, it may be influenced greatly by the absence or presence of the other factors, suggesting the interdependence that exists among these planning considerations. Cost should not be evaluated in terms of dollars alone, but rather in light of the values and benefits accruing to the organization for the amount invested. Also, improved customer service and the effect that good communications play on competition should be considered.

Thus, the proposal for organizing a data communication system should indicate how well the planned system will meet the information needs of the company, how much the system will cost, and what benefits it will provide. Also, priority should be given to the personnel and basic equipment requirements of such a system. Each of these factors is discussed briefly.

Data Communication Personnel. As noted in Figure 8-5, the data communication system represents a merger of the computer and communication technologies. From the computer field, operators are required to direct the use of the computer and its related peripheral equipment, including the storage devices. In addition, there is a need for analysts and programmers to design and ensure that the systems objectives are met.

As a rule, data communication systems are added to existing large-scale data processing systems and utilize the personnel of the original data processing center. In addition, data communication systems, due to their added complexity, require several new types of personnel — *data communication managers*, who have full responsibility for the telecommunication system; *data communication analysts*, who work with the data processing analysts to consolidate the processing and communication of data; and *data-entry workers*, such as key-entry supervisors and key-entry operators whose work is basically related to the use of terminals and related data-entry equipment.[7]

To recruit and train data communication personnel, several methods are employed. Some firms contact the various sources of experienced workers (discussed in Chapter 11) while others maintain policies of promoting from within the data center. In general, large firms conduct periodic on-site training programs to keep the skills of their personnel at a high level. Smaller firms

---

[7] "1975 Salary Survey," *Infosystems* (June, 1975), pp. 34–43.

handle their training needs by hiring consultants and the services of such professional associations as the Data Processing Management Association and the Association for Systems Management. The more technical subjects dealing with communication engineering are usually covered in seminars provided by the communication carriers.

Data Communication Equipment. Some of the basic operational questions that face those who decide to install a data communication link to their data processing system are these: What are the various ways of transmitting data over long distances at fast rates of speed? In what form can the data be sent and received? And what are the equipment requirements for data communications? Machines and other devices must be provided to collect, transmit, switch, translate, and receive data. Due to the technical nature of this equipment, only a brief discussion of the most common type — the terminal — is given here, for it is widely used by office personnel with little need for operator training.[8]

A *terminal* refers to any input-output device attached to a computer system whose primary purpose is to transmit and receive data from one location to another. The most prevalent types of terminals, some of which are shown in Figure 8-7, are *alphabetic keyboards* (typewriters and teletypewriters) and *printers* that may include external data storage media such as paper tape, cassettes, cartridges, or diskette devices; *display terminals* with keyboards and a television-like screen for projecting the

information image; and *banking terminals* that accept coded identification cards and/or keyed input to permit a variety of banking transactions, including dispensing and accepting cash, to be carried out automatically. Also included may be *point-of-sale terminals* by means of which sales and inventory information-processing activities are automated, and *industrial data collection terminals* operated by factory workers to collect production control, inventory, and timekeeping information.[9]

Terminals vary in function and power but all share in the process of person-to-machine interaction. Through the use of a cathode-ray tube display terminal with a typewriter keyboard, an executive can enter into the input device requests for up-to-the-minute information on sales, inventory, and costs, bypassing the time-consuming channels of a data processing center and personal trips to the center. In return, the manager can receive immediate feedback on the screen from the computer file (or on a typewriter terminal or in some other medium such as the punched card). With the interactive hard-copy terminal, the executive simply depresses the "print" button for a hard copy of the record displayed.

Most data can be transmitted over standard telephone lines. In order to transmit the information, two broad types of transmission systems are used: the *point-to-point communication system* by which data are transmitted at varying speeds over private, leased, or regular telephone lines between two or more terminals; and the *computer-based*

---

[8]In addition to terminal equipment, data transmission equipment constitutes the other main category of data communication equipment.

[9]For a comprehensive discussion of trends in the use of terminals in telecommunications, see Roy M. Salzman, "The Computer Terminal Industry: A Forecast," *Datamation* (November, 1975), pp. 47–50.

networks that permit a large number of people located throughout a wide area to communicate via telephone lines with each other and a central computer. Typical of the latter type of system is the large firm in which the computer links the headquarters office, the plant, and the regional and warehouse facilities with all orders and other messages sent by telephone to the computer center at the headquarters office. Such close linkage within a large firm brings about better control, faster processing of orders, tighter inventory systems, and other benefits. Other uses of terminal equipment and applications of data communication systems are discussed in Part 4 of this text.

TELECOMMUNICATION SERVICES

Since the early days of wire communication when simple long-distance and local telephone calls and standard telegrams were transmitted, a wide range of communication services has been created to meet the insatiable information needs of business and society. Five services that are important to the office function are: leased lines, Data-phone, Wide Area Telecommunication Service (WATS), Touch-Tone Data Service, and Wideband (or Broadband) Data Service.

Leased Lines

A *leased line* is a teletype or telephone line made available to the subscriber on a full-time basis between specific points. *Telpak* is the name given to the American Telephone and Telegraph service in which telephone lines are leased as a group between two points. Such services are useful for large-vol-ume, point-to-point transmission of data, voice, teletypewriter, and facsimile messages for a flat rate. Telpak rates, which are based on the message-sending capacity of the communication line and the distance spanned as well as terminal charges, are substantially lower than those for an equivalent number of single telephone channels. Both the Bell System and Western Union provide leased-line services at identical rates.

Data-phone Service

Data-phone is a registered trademark name for the data set and the service of the American Telephone and Telegraph Company. This service provides for the use of data sets and the same dial telephone network that is used for local or long-distance voice communications. Its main use, however, is to transmit data rather than voice communications. To place a data call, the user lifts the telephone receiver connected to the Data-phone, receives the dial tone, and then dials the number associated with the data set at the destination. At the receiving end, the call is answered manually by an attendant. As soon as the operators confirm that the business machine terminals are ready to transmit and receive data, the telephones at both terminals are switched from a "talk" mode to the "data" mode, which enables the machines to receive and transmit data. Data-phones are also available for automatically answering calls.

With data sets, companies are able to improve their information-processing operations, provide faster delivery of products and services, and reduce costs by using data transmission facilities as an immediate, direct link to their customers or to branches scattered throughout the country. For example, one firm saves its customers about $30,000 each year by enabling them to reduce their inventories and the clerical details related to the purchasing procedure. This firm uses card-reader devices and Data-phone sets for machine-to-machine transmission of sales orders by telephone. In the operation of the automated ordering system, each customer is supplied with cards that contain a picture of the item described and priced in the catalog. When the customers wish to order, they select the appropriate card for the item needed, dial the telephone number of the supplying company, insert the card into the connecting card reader, and register the desired quantity. The card reader feeds these data to the Data-phone, which converts the data to tones suitable for transmission over the regular telephone network. In the offices of the supplier, a data-set receiver converts the incoming tones into impulses that are fed into a keypunch, which produces punched cards that duplicate the transmitted data. In the data processing department, the cards are rapidly processed into orders, shipping lists, and acknowledgments.

Wide Area Telecommunication Service (WATS)

WATS (formerly called Wide Area Telephone Service) is a long-distance telephone service through which an unlimited number of voice or data communication calls may be made for a flat monthly charge. Many users find that WATS is an economical and efficient service because of the volume and length of their messages as well as the widely scattered distribution of company locations. Both in-state and out-of-state rates are available.

Two forms of WATS service are available: inward or outward full-time service, and measured time inward or outward service. *Outward WATS* is designed for only outgoing calls in which the user dials a call in the same way as an ordinary long-distance call. *Inward WATS* is restricted to incoming calls and is offered at the same rates and covers the same geographic zones as outward WATS. All outlying locations dial in to a central number, which is the billing location for all charges.

WATS lines are available for rent on a full-time basis (24 hours a day, seven days a week); or they may be rented in measured form in which a "package" of talking time — usually 600 minutes — is provided at a fixed monthly charge. Additional talking time is billed as overtime in tenths of minutes. This service can provide substantial savings if there is a large volume of necessary long-distance calls. When properly used, WATS lines can reduce toll costs by as much as 70 percent, depending on the amount of conversation and the distance of the call.[10] To be sure that adequate controls are placed on this service — especially the tendency to make unauthorized personal calls — users should consult the local telephone company for suggestions in the proper use of WATS.

---

[10]Frank K. Griesinger, "The Whys and Wherefores of WATS," *Administrative Management* (October, 1973), p. 26. For additional references on this important communication service, consult Frank K. Griesinger, "'Save a WATS,' or Short-cuts to Good Use of a Long Distance Phone Service," *Administrative Management* (December, 1973), pp. 26–28, 91; and Lowell M. Mason, "WATS is Key to DATA Service," *Administrative Management* (August, 1975), pp. 62–63. The last reference describes an interesting DATA (Direct Access Terminal Assistance) information service tying together 1,000 district representatives of an insurance society with their home office.

Touch-Tone Data Service

The Touch-Tone telephone (discussed earlier in this chapter as an automatic telephone instrument) provides an easier and faster means of placing regular telephone calls than the rotary dial telephone. Its keyboard design approximates the layout of the keypunch keyboard and can be used by operators to place calls without looking at the keyboard. In addition to its regular use for transmitting vocal messages, the Touch-Tone telephone may be used to send digital data signals after the connection with a distant terminal device has been established. (The regular rotary dialing telephone does not have this capability.) Because of this extra function, a Touch-Tone telephone can serve as a communication terminal to send data to a computer, a teletypewriter, or a keypunch machine, giving both small and large offices the capability of linking up with a computer system.

Wideband Data Service

Wideband Data Service automatically links two subscribers over transmission channels that are selected as best meeting their communication needs. This type of service provides for varying types of transmission. The equipment transmits the voice alone or digital data contained in punched cards, punched paper tape, magnetic tape, or computer storage devices. By means of a pushbutton voice-data instrument, the user selects a broad bandwidth that will furnish the most economical data transmission. Thus, the user can select one width for transmitting punched-card data and another width for use by computers in their communications with one another. These machines, with their greater ca-

pabilities, transmit at rates that cannot be satisfactorily handled over the narrow telegraph channels or voice bands. Transmission speeds in the bandwidths vary from the teleprinter speeds to more than 4,800 words a minute by means of tape devices. Wider bands that would enable computers to communicate at rates of more than 50,000 bits per second are now available.

MANAGING TELECOMMUNICATION SYSTEMS

There should be no need to remind managers that the principles of organization outlined in Chapter 3 should be applied to *all* systems under their jurisdiction. Yet in the case of telecommunication systems — especially those dealing with the telephone — the system is too often taken for granted, its operating costs ignored, and its overall efficiency assumed. The effective office manager will not fall into these traps; rather he or she will carefully plan the telecommunication services, establish controls over their operation, and take special efforts to reverse the trend for communication costs to increase as time and company growth go on. Each of these topics is discussed in this section, along with a futuristic concept — the management decision center — that may emerge as the pushbutton decision center for the company.

Planning Telecommunication Services

"Planning First — Hardware Last" is a slogan long advocated by systems consultants. Because of the great cost and because of the importance of modern telecommunication systems, large firms should first consider setting up a centralized telecommunication department to plan their total communication needs before any new equipment or services are secured. Large companies like Nabisco, Inc., and Mobil Oil have organized corporation-wide programs for coordinating their voice and data communication needs for all departments. A person qualified in the total area of communication systems and services should be chosen to supervise the department and charged with the responsibility for providing effective and economical communications. Smaller firms may hire consultants to evaluate their communication systems and to offer suggestions for improvement.

Since modern telecommunication systems normally involve all departments, a total-systems approach is necessary in order to study the communication needs of the entire firm. One effective technique for beginning such a study is to organize an ongoing committee of personnel representing all departments, who know firsthand the communication needs of their units. Too many firms are satisfied with what has been used in the past and make little effort to study new media or methods. Most manufacturers of communication equipment will provide, without obligation, consultants to survey the needs of the company. In fact, the willingness of a sales representative-analyst to perform this service may be used as a guide to the dependability and reliability of the company represented.

Prior to 1969, telecommunication services and equipment were purchased or leased from the common carriers. However, with the landmark Carterfone decision of June, 1968, it became legal for other firms to provide equipment and services to telecommunication users.[11] These firms — called *interconnect companies* — offer a variety of voice and data communication equipment that can be connected to the lines of the common carriers. With more firms in the market, more intensive planning and analysis of the telecommunication needs of the firm are required. The increase of firms also means a more competitive environment in which more negotiating and "shopping around" are necessary but in which potentially better equipment prices are possible.

Establishing Telecommunication Controls

The procedures for planning and organizing data communications — discussed earlier in this chapter — may be applied to the overall telecommunication system. Basically, this means defining the information requirements of each department — *who* makes *what number* of calls of *what type* to *what destination(s)* under *what circumstances*? A

---

[11]The Carterfone is a device that is connected to a two-way radio base station for use when both radio and telephone calls are made with the base station. The Carterfone automatically switches on the radio transmitter when the telephone caller is speaking and returns the radio to a receiving condition when the caller stops speaking. Prior to 1969, the common carriers applied a tariff on the use of the Carterfone by their customers. With the Carterfone decision (the case involved the Carter Electronics Corporation, manufacturers of the Carterfone, versus the American Telephone and Telegraph Company and other telephone companies) the Federal Communications Commission (FCC) ruled that it is unreasonable to continue the application of such tariffs in that such a practice prohibits the use of interconnecting (switching) devices that do not adversely affect the telephone system. In effect, this ruling permits firms other than the common carriers to provide without tariff interconnecting equipment for use with the telephone equipment.

firm may simplify the collection of such information regarding its telephone requirements by using a form such as that shown in Figure 8-8 for both inside and outside calls. By compiling data from each of the extension telephones, the analyst is able to determine what features of the telephone system are needed and those that are largely provided for personal convenience.

Some companies periodically monitor their telephone usage by the hour to determine which departments make the most outside calls. As a result of such studies, frequently it is found that extra features such as add-on conference calls, multibutton call directors, and user transfer of calls are rarely used. A

record of the volume of messages also helps to determine if dial-up facilities would be more economical than private-line service.

When selecting new equipment, detailed proposals should be sought from vendors in which information on the equipment and needed supplies, the availability and cost of maintenance service, and guarantees in writing about the reliability of the equipment are provided. With new equipment, personnel skills of many kinds are required and should receive top priority in the equipment decision. Many times equipment vendors as well as the local telephone company will conduct a free traffic study showing both the amount and type of

EXTENSION **478**

INTERNAL CALLS				OUTSIDE CALLS				COMMENTS
WITHIN MY UNIT		WITH OTHER UNITS				Conf. Calls	Help for Info.	
Made A	Rec'd. B	Made C	Rec'd. D	Made E	Rec'd. F	G	H	
THL THL THL II	HIL HIL III	THH	THH I	HIL HIL THH HIL HIL	THH THH III	—	—	

DATE *12/4/—*

Source: Adapted from Joseph F. Lawless, "How to Analyze Your Telephone Requirements," *The Office* (November, 1974), p. 82.

Fig. 8-8
A Telephone Usage Report Form

message sending for guidance in determining how many operators are required at each hour of the day. In addition, they can offer helpful suggestions in selecting and training telephone and teletype operators, as well as aid executives in determining when to use the telephone, the facsimile process, or some alternate communication system.

Reducing Telecommunication Costs

Three of the most important kinds of telecommunication expenses in which possibilities exist for cost reduction are: telephone costs, other wire communication costs, and data communication costs.

Telephone Costs. The ease with which the telephone is used in the office often leads to a waste of time and money. With modern equipment and services like the WATS line, personal convenience is often substituted for the actual communication needs of the company. Calls are often made when the mails could be used; and person-to-person calls are chosen when direct-distance dialing without the aid of an operator would suffice.

Some cost-reduction suggestions regarding the use of the telephone are listed below:

1. Use an intercommunication system, Private Automatic Branch Exchange (PABX), or Centrex system wherever it will relieve the work of the regular office telephones. Thus, the company switchboard is bypassed, and the telephone of the person called rings directly, saving considerable work time.

2. Use a paging system where its cost of operation is proven more economical than other systems in use.

3. Make comparative cost studies of mail, telephone, and other telecommunication media and provide instructions in their use. Some firms post charts showing the comparative communication costs for each type of message to the principal cities of the United States.

4. Use monthly budget figures and allocation of communication expenses for control purposes. When division and department heads are required to budget all items of communication equipment and its use and to account for expenditures against this budget, they will be more cooperative in eliminating waste. The monthly summary of telephone expenses should cover the actual dollars allocated to each department for equipment cost, the volume of local messages assigned to each department, all long-distance calls charged to the department, other charges or credits assigned to the department, allocation of telegraph costs to departments using these facilities, and an accurate allocation of each department's use of special services such as WATS and Telpak.

5. Study intercommunication costs in terms of the time of the employees — payroll cost — that is saved by the use of mechanical methods. Payroll cost is still the major item to be controlled for an efficiently operating office.

6. Analyze carefully each month's telephone bill with equipment itemizations provided by the local telephone company. Direct charges for such fees as message-unit and toll charges for long-distance, third-party, and credit-card calls should be indicated.

7. Request from the telephone company an itemization of the telephone service and equipment charges. With

such information in hand, alternatives to telephone service and equipment can be planned and the most economical services chosen.

8. Study how intensively the equipment is being used (the telephone company will conduct such a survey) and remove least effective equipment.

9. Wherever possible, keep a daily log of all toll calls made. Messages should be classified by the name of the caller, the destination, and the purpose of the call. The log may then be compared against the monthly invoices to ensure accuracy of the call record. If many calls are being made to one area, the installation of a WATS line may be justified.

10. Switchboard operators should fill out call slips by means of which all calls are charged directly to the cost center (usually a department) involved. Where no switchboards are used, only authorized personnel should place toll calls using telephone credit cards charged to their cost center.

11. Discourage unusually long calls. Some companies limit toll calls to 6 minutes each. Rates for time beyond the first minute give a discount for overtime of 29 percent on a coast-to-coast call, or 27 percent on calls covering 100 miles. The shorter the call, the lower the cost.

12. Save as much as 35 percent by dialing station-to-station. An additional 20 percent can also be saved by calling after 5 p.m., when a night rate exists.

13. Use direct-distance dialing rather than credit cards. The credit card gives a record of calls made but adds as much as 290 percent for operator handling on calls of 100 miles or less.

14. Analyze calls for essential messages. One company secured a computer printout of all WATS calls grouped by phone number and found that 34 percent were personal. To correct this problem, restrict outgoing lines to employees whose duties require long-distance calls. Periodically employees should be urged to keep personal calls at an absolute minimum.

The manner in which the telephone is used indirectly affects the cost of the service. A company gets the most from its telephone dollars when its switchboard operators are experienced, well-trained, and relieved from other office duties to give undivided attention to placing and receiving calls. All personnel should be instructed to answer and place their own telephone calls rather than through third parties — usually secretaries — which saves time. Handy up-to-date directories expedite the handling of incoming and outgoing calls. Often these directories include instruction sheets for improving the use of the telephone, stressing courteous, efficient telephone techniques.[12] When used properly, the telephone helps to create and maintain a good public image and is a good public relations tool.

An appropriate means of consolidating information on the use of the telephone and other telecommunication media is the communications manual, discussed in Chapter 7. Such a manual serves as an effective tool of managerial control, for it provides company

[12]For additional hints on reducing telephone and intercommunication costs, see Frank K. Griesinger, "Reading Between the Lines of a Phone System Proposal," *Administrative Management* (March, 1975), pp. 30–31, 68, 70; Frank K. Griesinger, "Softening the Blow of the Big Phone Rate Hike," *Administrative Management* (July, 1975), pp. 20–22; and Frank K. Griesinger, "Shortening Those Long Distance Calls," *Administrative Management* (September, 1975), pp. 54, 56, 58.

guidelines on all phases of telecommunication equipment and services available within the firm and helps employees to make wise choices in the use of alternate telecommunication methods. Thus, the manual serves as a yardstick by which the telecommunication system can be measured.

Other Wire Communication Costs.

Administrative office managers rely heavily upon sending hard copies of written and graphic messages; for this reason they purchase great numbers of facsimile and teletype equipment. With new high-speed machines on the market (some facsimile equipment transmits at speeds of less than one minute for an average document), transmission is five times faster than on earlier equipment but more expensive.[13] Office managers face a trade-off decision between the higher transmission rate and the higher costs of new equipment, which may be as much as seven times the monthly rental of the older units. The number of documents transmitted daily as well as the total lines sent should be carefully studied. From 11 p.m. to 8 a.m., many of the telephone companies provide facsimile-transmission rates for as little as 35 cents a minute compared with the daytime direct-dial rate of $1.45. Thus, when messages can be delayed a few hours, a later time for message sending is preferred. An additional cost-saver is the arrangement provided by facsimile service companies for accepting messages from subscribers to be transmitted over the company's leased lines at a rate lower than that paid by individual subscribers.

[13]Richard E. Hanson, "Higher Speeds Reduce the Cost of Fax," *Administrative Management* (August, 1974), pp. 24–27.

Data Communication Costs.

Data communication systems utilize both computer and telephone equipment. Thus, their cost levels are dependent upon many of the telecommunication controls discussed in this section. Suggestions on reducing data communication costs, particularly those relating to such computer-communication concepts as time sharing and multiprogramming are considered in Part 4.

The Management Decision Center

Since telecommunication systems have become a "fact" of life, managers of large organizations have at hand the potential for pushbutton control of the decision-making process. Machines are available for storing, retrieving, processing, and collecting data and for displaying alphabetic and numeric data in tables, diagrams, and plots. With display terminal keyboards readily available, executives can inquire of the computer data bank and receive immediate answers to questions on sales and other revenue and expense items.

The equipment for performing these information systems tasks is often brought together in the quiet of a management decision center where concentration and executive discussion can take place. Such control centers or decision rooms have appeared in some of the largest firms, and parallel the centralized command posts of the armed forces where decision strategies and tactical planning are developed and executed. Actually, this decision center is really a communication center with human control over sound, light, tape recorder, film projector, microphone, and telephone-to-computer communications.

Once management sets the decision rules and has collected the data for making the decision, then that unique human quality, judgment, enters the picture and "tells" the manager what decision to make. All that the combined power of the equipment, the data files, and the system can do is to get the information to the mind of the manager. All things considered, the human being still remains the ultimate information processor.

1. What are the main differences between telecommunications and communication by telephone?

2. Identify the conditions that should be considered before designing a voice communication system.

3. What improvements in telephone equipment have expanded the use of this medium in today's business office? How do these improvements aid in expediting office work?

4. What are the major features of the Direct Inward Dialing system of Centrex?

5. What features of intercommunication systems enable the office manager to communicate more effectively?

6. Cite several advantages of using facsimile services over voice communications to handle routine message sending.

7. The teletypewriter has in recent years grown more popular as a medium of office communications. Explain the reasons for this increased use.

8. What is meant by the term "data communication systems"? Explain the more common types of data communication systems in use today.

9. How do you account for the increased use of data communication systems in modern office procedures?

10. Prior to developing a data communication system within the firm, what factors should be carefully analyzed and studied?

11. What is a terminal? Briefly describe the most common types of terminals used in data communication systems.

12. Explain the nature and purpose of the most common telecommunication services.

13. What steps should be taken by an office manager to ensure adequate controls over telecommunication operating procedures and costs?

14. Cite six specific ways in which telephone costs may be reduced and controlled.

QUESTIONS
FOR
DISCUSSION

1. Why should the small-office manager be interested in data communications since the small office cannot afford such costly systems?

2. Identify five common messages (both voice and written) that are sent in the modern office. Show what methods you would recommend for transmitting these messages in the most effective manner. In each case defend your choice.

3. Intuition tells you that many of the employees in your office are tying up the telephone lines with unauthorized personal calls for many hours each week. How can you obtain information on this problem without undue prying? Once you have reliable information, how can the problem be resolved?

4. Nancy West supervises the communication section in the home office of the Rocky Mountain Insurance Company located in Colorado Springs. With a growing amount of interoffice mail to be distributed to the eight home-office departments as well as to the 15 regional offices throughout the country — and with the high cost of postage and the unpredictable delays in mail delivery — West has decided to make a careful study of the entire interoffice message distribution system. She discusses her feelings about the needs of such a system and asks you, her assistant, to undertake a study in which you do the following:

   a. Develop a list of major criteria by which she could make decisions about the best means of communicating within the home office and also with the branch offices.

   b. Study all feasible methods of communicating with the branch offices. Since West has indicated some good experience with, and preference for, facsimile services, investigate this service very carefully and point out its limitations and strengths.

   c. In a short report outline your main recommendations to West. Make reasonable assumptions about the cost of communication services and the branch-office message volume. Current office management periodicals can provide cost-estimate information.

**PRACTICAL
OFFICE
MANAGEMENT
CASES**

Case 8-1   **Reorganizing a Data Communication System**

The Rinko Shoe Company has its main office in St. Louis, Missouri, with branch offices and warehouses in Buffalo, New York; Trenton, New Jersey; and Harrisburg, Pennsylvania. The office manager, Vince Canelli, has been faced with mounting telephone costs resulting from the increased sales volume. He feels that the present system of having one switchboard to handle all incoming and outgoing calls in the main office with similar arrangements in the branch offices is not up-to-date and efficient. In addition to voice communications within the firm as well as from the outside, thought must be given to the movement of alphanumeric information from each branch office to the headquarters in St. Louis and vice versa. Presently each of the branch offices processes its records on a decentralized basis. The large-volume operations connected with sales, purchase order processing, the maintenance of inventory, customer billing, and creditor payments are handled locally in each branch.

Recognizing the improvement in data communication and computing facilities, the firm is contemplating the recentralization of its accounting function in the main office in order to reduce a certain amount of duplication in office work, but more importantly, to provide management with up-to-the-minute operating data from which decisions can more easily be made. As a result of the proposed move toward centralization, it is expected that the present medium-scale computer system can accommodate the extra load by operating on three eight-hour shifts and by reducing some of the unnecessary administrative reports presently being prepared.

On the basis of the information given above, suggest how the company can develop a data communication network that will handle effectively the following:

1. Daily interoffice telephone calls for the office staff of 120 employees in the ten departments in the St. Louis main office.
2. Long-distance telephone calls from St. Louis to each of the branch offices, normally occurring many times each day (although no accurate record has been kept).
3. Interbranch calls which occur from five to ten times daily for each branch.

Case 8-2 Controlling the Operations of a Telephone System

Maude Welte, a newcomer to the political world, has recently been elected mayor of a large southeastern city that has the highest unemployment rate in the country. Largely because of her strong stand on cutting costs in all departments — especially the sprawling administrative "empires" created by her predecessors — Welte was "swept" into office and raised hopes that at last someone could control the municipal budget and hold taxes in line.

In discussing operating costs with the budget director, John Dana, Welte became aware of the unwieldy telecommunication network used by the city and three specific problems that needed immediate attention: (1) Supervision is lacking with regard to the switchboard, its two operators, and the 200 telephones in City Hall.

The public has been critical of the lack of courtesy and personal attention given their calls; business suppliers of goods and services to the city offices have reported similar experiences. (An automatic switching device transfers after-hours calls to the adjacent City Police Office.) (2) No record is kept of long-distance calls. While it is assumed that the City Hall staff will concentrate its calls within the city, Dana suspects that many toll calls are being placed each day to the state capitol where municipal interests are represented in the state legislature. The three new departments making up the Division of Environmental Control alone have counterparts in the state government for which continuous communication seems necessary. (3) Alternate methods of communication have never been identified. In fact, it has been assumed that telephone costs are extremely low when compared with personal visits. Thus, an uncontrolled number of calls have been made, increasing the total annual telephone bill for City Hall from $34,000 to $45,000 in the last two years.

Welte concurs with Dana that, from a political as well as an economic standpoint, the telecommunication system needs an overhaul and asks that such a study be made. Dana, in turn, delegates the responsibility for the study to you, his staff assistant, with these general comments:

> Let's give our new mayor a complete report on what it's costing to use our telephones at City Hall. We'll need to know (1) how many long-distance calls are made for what length of time each day and to what locations; (2) how much it costs for long-distance calls for various lengths of time within the state; (3) whether a WATS line would be practical (and if so, what type of service); and (4) how satisfactory a Centrex system might be.

> Also, the qualifications and training of all telephone users (and that includes everybody from general clerks to the mayor herself) need to be studied. What information does a good telephone user need? What skills are preferred for good telephone technique? How can the use of the equipment be controlled, especially for personal and unusually long calls?

From the information that Dana has provided, you are asked to prepare a report for him covering the questions he posed in his talk with you. Be sure to include estimates of the amount of money that can be saved during the next fiscal year using sample data (such as call data for low, medium, and high rates of usage) along with estimated costs for each usage rate utilizing both telephone and WATS-line call rates. If 15 percent of all telephones are used to make toll calls and 35 percent are used for intraoffice calls exclusively, make reasonable assumptions about the overall system required to minimize telephone costs without curtailing service. The business office of the telephone company will provide data on costs and service to help in the solution of this case.

Chapter 9

INFORMATION AND RECORDS MANAGEMENT

One of the most important tools used by managers is information. With information they solve problems and make decisions involving not only the day-to-day operations of the business but also long-term policies that affect its very survival. Thus, modern managers have a great need for the right information, in the right order, in the right place, at the right time, and at the lowest possible cost.

In order to "capture" information for use by management, countless types of records are created by the office staff. In fact, with the development of information machines like the computer, the task of records creation has been so greatly facilitated that a danger of over-recording exists. As an example, it has been estimated that American business creates records at the rate of 125 million cubic feet a year; and the federal government alone contributes an additional 4.5 million cubic feet to this mountain of paper.[1] In both sectors many unnecessary records are doubtlessly created.

In the wake of this paperwork explosion, management faces several pressing problems directly affecting its ability to use information — that of determining what records are necessary to the operation of the organization; and that of taking effective measures to control the total records system. To cope with these important problems, information and records management programs have been developed as a vital function in administrative office management.

THE RECORDS CONTROL CYCLE

To feed management's insatiable appetite for information, many different kinds of records are produced. Some records contain information that is recurring in nature while others are needed but once; some are used internally and others externally. *Transaction records*, such as purchase and sales orders, statements, and paychecks, are used to record business operations and account for approximately 85 to 90 percent of any company's records. *Reference records*, on the other hand, are used as administrative documents and represent the remaining 10 to 15 percent of a firm's records.[2] Reports, procedures, correspondence, and financial planning materials fall into this category of reference records.

Each of these records is a tangible paper document. But a new dimension in record keeping entered the business world when the punched-card and computer systems were applied to information storage and retrieval. While data on

---

[1]Harold Roger Hart, "Records Management and the Paper Crunch," *Records Management Quarterly* (January, 1974), p. 5.

[2]Mina M. Johnson and Norman F. Kallaus, *Records Management* (2d ed., Cincinnati: South-Western Publishing Co., 1974), p. 252.

paper may serve as input to and output from the computer, intangible information in magnetized form on tapes, disks, drums, and cores within the computer system has greatly expanded the modern information system and given new responsibilities to the administrative office manager. The demand for paper records to be used in manual records systems continues to expand and is explained in part by the tremendous paper-producing capabilities of the computer itself.

Whether business information is stored on paper or in magnetic files within a computer system, both types of records follow the same life cycle: (1) creation, (2) storage, (3) retrieval when necessary, and (4) return to storage or final destruction. These phases in the life of a record constitute the *records control cycle*.

RECORDS MANAGEMENT AND CONTROL

Records management is an organizational function responsible for the development of systematic controls over records creation, storage and retrieval, as well as retention and disposition. Such a broad, many-sided function cannot be considered to be synonymous with the filing or storage operation, which represents one small phase in the life span of a record. However, this misconception sometimes occurs. The objectives of a well-developed records management program as found in large-scale industry are charted in Figure 9-1, shown on the next page. This concept of the program is organized around the creation-through-disposition life cycle of the record, with appropriate adminis-

trative procedures being set up to handle each stage in the cycle.[3]

Objectives of Records Management

Records management, like any other management function, should be goal-oriented and service-minded. This means that objectives must be set up as standards against which the performance of the program can be measured. As an outgrowth of this general service objective, other more specific program objectives emerge. They are:

1. To provide accurate, timely information whenever and wherever it is needed in the firm.
2. To develop and maintain an efficient system for creating, storing, retrieving, retaining, and disposing of the firm's information.
3. To protect the firm's information requirements, and to design and control effective standards and periodic evaluation methods relating to the management of the records, equipment, and procedures.
4. To assist in the education of company personnel in the most effective methods of controlling and processing the company records.

Figure 9-1 clearly outlines each of the control phases in the records management program and the most important objectives of each phase. A careful

---

[3]The General Services Administration (GSA) of the federal government has developed a continuing education program in records management that emphasizes the management of correspondence, reports, forms, directives, and mail as well as records maintenance, disposition, and program evaluation. Handbooks on each of these topics are available from the Superintendent of Documents, U.S. Government Printing Office, Washington, DC 20408.

RECORDS MANAGEMENT PROGRAM

RECORDS CREATION Objectives	RECORDS STORAGE AND RETRIEVAL Objectives	RECORDS RETENTION Objectives	RECORDS DISPOSITION Objectives
1. Eliminating needless forms, correspondence, and reports from present files.	1. Providing classification and coding systems for records storage.	1. Developing a classification system for retaining records.	1. Setting up an inactive records center (or storing records in a commercial center).
2. Controlling the creation of records.	2. Selecting proper equipment and supplies for the storage and retrieval systems.	2. Surveying departments to determine records status.	2. Reducing records to microform wherever possible.
3. Employing efficient standards for designing records.	3. Developing and maintaining well-controlled file storage and protection system.	3. Setting up a retention schedule.	3. Transferring inactive records from active storage to archives.
4. Applying cost standards and controls to records creation.	4. Selecting and training files personnel.	4. Periodically purging files of inactive records.	4. Developing a control procedure for inactive storage and for the destruction of records.
	5. Reviewing and updating storage and retrieval systems when needed.		

Fig. 9-1
Objectives of a Records Management Program

study of these objectives is necessary in order to understand the real mission and the overall control cycle of records management as the information watchdog in the modern organization.

Organization of Records Management

Historically the responsibility for the office function, including control over its records, has been assigned to the controller, the treasurer, or the firm's secretary, each of whom has major information-processing duties. As the office function expanded into a separate information management area, it was natural for it to include the management of information and records.

The setting for records management as shown in Figure 9-2 places the function in a natural environment of related activities. In organizations that give full recognition to information management at the top management level, a new position, vice-president of information

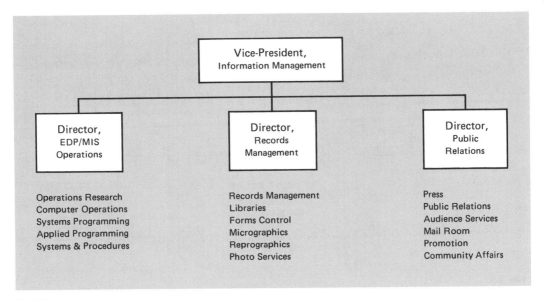

Fig. 9-2
Information and Records Management Organization Chart

management, has been created.[4] The vice-president has jurisdiction over such related areas as electronic data processing (EDP) and management information systems (MIS) operations; a public relations function specializing in the distribution of information; and finally, the records management area. In this setting the records manager is responsible for achieving the objectives of a full-fledged records management program as well as other technical services, such as micrographics and reprographics, all of which involve records or documents.

In the small firm this degree of specialization will not be found, but the same general administrative functions remain. For example, a personnel director may be required to handle administrative services, such as systems analysis

and data processing. In another firm, the office services manager may handle personnel selection, placement, training, and general office management functions including records and forms control, while the systems and data processing services may be the responsibility of another person. Most important is that related work be grouped together and assigned to those individuals who by aptitude, interest, and training are most highly qualified for such assignments.

Administration of Records Management

The administration of records management means setting appropriate objectives (as outlined in Figure 9-1) and then planning and organizing the program to achieve them. The strong role that administration plays in records management was highlighted in a national study of 244 members of the

---

[4]James O. Leonard and G. Theodore Nygreen, "Information Management: The Systems Approach to Information and Records Management," *Information and Records Management* (November, 1974), p. 10.

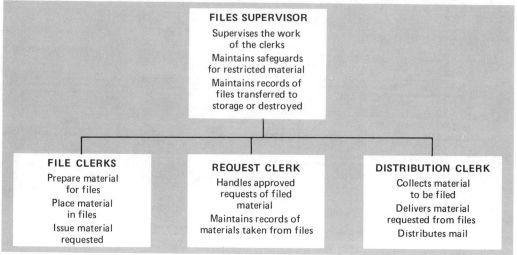

Fig. 9-3
Hierarchy in a Files Section

Association of Records Managers and Administrators. In this study Wilmer O. Maedke found that the most frequently reported responsibility of records managers was program organization and administration, with 68 percent of the respondents reporting this responsibility.[5]

As an information administrator, the records manager is vitally concerned with what information the organization needs to accomplish its objectives; where this information can be found; how it can best be stored, processed, and retrieved; and finally, how the program can be administered in a minimal time and at least cost.

Records Management Personnel. Because the records management program encompasses the entire organization, an executive familiar with the information needs of the entire firm, its objectives, and its structure should be

chosen as records manager. This type of position requires a generalist familiar with principles of management, economics, and accounting, as well as a specialist in information storage, retrieval, and files management. Although records managers need not be data processing specialists, they should understand the concepts and applications of information-processing equipment.

Reporting to the records manager most typically are the filing personnel shown in Figure 9-3. The files supervisor would normally report to the records manager or someone at an equivalent level. In many firms new records management positions are being created as the records system becomes more highly automated. Such positions as tape librarian, program library records clerk, and documentation clerk are becoming common in larger offices such as banks, insurance companies, and utilities.

Costs of Records Management.
In manufacturing operations, cost accounting has long been utilized to

---

[5]Wilmer O. Maedke, "The Records Management Profession: A Profile Survey," *Records Management Quarterly* (July, 1968), p. 35.

determine direct and indirect costs of all work units produced. In the office, on the other hand, few controls have been applied to paperwork costs. But with costs continually rising and with administrative work taking more and more of the profit dollar, office managers are stepping up their efforts toward controlling office costs. Figure 9-4 identifies the paperwork costs in administrative work that must be controlled.

Calculating precisely the cost of records management becomes a complicated task because of the variability of cost factors such as salaries, office rent, and the estimated life of the equipment. However, certain basic factors can be determined. For example, in one firm each file clerk is responsible for 15 four-drawer file cabinets, and for every 10 file clerks there is one supervisor. A file clerk is paid $6,000 a year, on the average, and a supervisor, $8,250. The purchase price of each four-drawer file cabinet is $140. Using these figures and other costs obtained from the firm's records, the annual cost of maintaining one four-drawer file cabinet may be calculated as follows:

File clerk's salary	$400
Supervisor's salary	55
Cost of cabinet, depreciated over 10-year period and ignoring trade-in value	14
Floor space, 6 square feet, @ $10 per square foot	60
Supplies, $12 per cabinet	12
Transfer file and supplies	40
Total annual cost of maintaining one four-drawer file cabinet	$581

While each of the other cost factors offers good opportunities for saving paperwork dollars, the records manager must give primary attention to reducing the costs of personnel, which typically represent from 70 to 80 percent of filing costs. Salaries, for example, may be controlled through better selection and training of workers and through improved work methods and performance

Cost Factors	Specific Paperwork Costs
1. Personnel	a. Clerical and supervisory salaries b. Fringe benefits of workers
2. Furniture and equipment	a. Depreciation of assets b. Rental and lease charges c. Maintenance and upkeep expenses
3. Space (for active and inactive records)	a. Owned space b. Rented or leased space c. Taxes d. Utility expenses (telephone, light, heat, and janitor service)
4. Supplies	a. Stationery and forms b. Folders, cartons, and labels c. Printing d. Postage

Fig. 9-4
Paperwork Costs of Administrative Operations

standards for the processing, storage, and retrieval of records. In addition, the records manager must develop a cost consciousness among all, workers and effect a better utilization of time, equipment, and supplies. Specific systems and measurement concepts that will help achieve control over records are discussed in Part 4.

Reducing the Costs of Records Management. Waging war against rising office costs is a never-ending process that requires the office manager to study constantly the filing systems in use to make sure they meet all the information needs of the company. The following suggestions may help the office manager reduce costs and at the same time improve operating efficiency:

1. Centralize those files used by all departments. In the data processing department, a data librarian should be appointed to keep track of each data item by means of visible files and control boards.

2. Provide a layout for the filing department that will insure a smooth and efficient flow of work to and from the files.

3. Use work-facilitating equipment such as file racks, sorting racks, file guides, and colored folder labels.

4. Schedule the collection and distribution of the materials to be filed or to be delivered from the files.

5. Develop a sound method of transferring inactive records from the files and a workable schedule for records retention and destruction.

6. Use special file cabinets, such as map files and voucher files, for papers or records that do not fit into regular letter-size or legal-size file drawers. Punched cards should be filed vertically to protect them against bending and folding so they will run smoothly through the high-speed processing equipment. Magnetic tapes and disks must be protected from dust, heat, and humidity. Since dust and dirt deposits can cause loss or garbling of the data stored, the media should be filed in tight-fitting cases and stored in special cabinets that hold the reels vertically. To prevent damage to magnetic disks, they should be stored in cabinets that lock the disk packs in place so they will not slide around.

7. Consider the microfilming of records in lieu of storing records in transfer cases. By comparing the annual cost of storing the same number of documents in transfer cases with the cost of microfilming, a break-even point can be quickly established. (See Chapter 10.)

8. Develop a filing manual for use in training employees and for controlling the filing work.

9. Carefully estimate and check on the volume of work that should be done in the filing department. Use workers from the mail department or other departments during rush periods in the filing department.

10. Purchase durable equipment and supplies. It is estimated that the average file drawer is opened and closed 100,000 times during its useful life. Cheap cabinets are wasteful because their poor construction prevents rapid filing. Supplies of poor quality interfere with efficient filing because they must be constantly replaced.

11. Use the expert services of the manufacturers of filing supplies and equipment, provided there is a qualified

person in the firm to aid in the selection of the equipment and to supervise its operation after it has been installed. Otherwise, the installation may result in a waste of money for the firm.

12. Consider hiring a records control specialist who will analyze the files to see that outdated papers are disposed of, important ones retained, and papers that are neither useful nor important are kept in some location where they can be stored cheaply.

These preceding suggestions should prove an excellent outline for the records supervisor in reviewing the work and for the administrative office manager in evaluating the records management function.

Evaluation of Records Management. The administrator of the records management program must regularly ask this question: How well is the program meeting its objectives? The answer to this question will be found through a planned program of evaluation. One rule of thumb recommends that an audit be conducted at least every two years to answer the types of questions shown in Figure 9-5. As soon as weaknesses have been identified by the audit, corrective measures such as improved forms control and better filing procedures can be applied.

Through the years other guidelines have been created by records managers for evaluating the efficiency of the records program. Expressed as efficiency ratios, the most useful of these guidelines are:

1. *The reference ratio*:

$$\frac{\text{number of records requested}}{\text{number of records filed}}$$

To illustrate, a records management audit shows 600 documents requested out of a total file of 12,000. The reference ratio is .05, or 5 percent. A reference activity of 5 percent or less is normally considered low and points to the need for transferring records from active storage to archives or possibly even destroying them.

2. *The accuracy ratio*:

$$\frac{\text{number of records found}}{\text{number of records requested}}$$

For example, 9,250 records out of a possible 9,500 requested are located. This means that there is 97.37 percent accuracy for the filing system and that the files are in excellent operating condition. Industry practices show that if this ratio falls below 97 percent, the files should be studied carefully, especially for these suspicious problems: (1) too many private files (as in executives' desks); (2) improper indexing and coding; (3) poor charge-out procedures; and (4) insufficient cross-indexing and referencing.

3. *Personnel ratios*. A federal government formula recommends one employee for each 5,200 cubic feet of record receipts for each year, one person for performing references on each 7,000 cubic feet of records stored per year, and one employee for each 4,700 cubic feet of records destroyed.[6] It is also suggested that 60 percent of the total personnel time should be allotted to the physical inventory of records.[7]

---

[6]William Benedon, *Records Management* (Englewood Cliffs: Prentice-Hall, 1969), p. 111.
[7]*Ibid.*, p. 15.

Audit Factor	Specific Questions
1. Scope of the records system	a. How is the program organized? b. How many files are in use?
2. Type of filing and retrieval systems	a. What filing systems are used? b. What types of controls are used (charge-outs, cross-references, etc.)? c. How are private, confidential, and departmental files controlled?
3. Records personnel	a. Who does the filing and finding? b. How are they supervised? c. What kind of performance standards are in effect?
4. Records users	a. Who uses the files? b. What access do users have to the files?
5. Records control procedures	a. Are filing policies and procedures set up? b. Is a records manual available and in use? c. Are records retention and disposition systems in effect?

Fig. 9-5
A Records Audit Checklist

4. *Physical layout ratio.* The records center should maintain a ratio of three cubic feet of records for every square foot of floor space (including aisles and access space). Thus, about 300 cubic feet of records should be stored in a 10-by-10 foot room.[8]

5. *Operating cost ratio.* Reasonable costs per cubic foot of stored inactive records should range between $.80 and $1.25 (a ratio determined by dividing the total operating costs of the center by the volume of records stored.)[9] For example, 100,000 cubic feet of records costing $100,000 to store would represent $1 per cubic foot of record cost, well within this operating cost ratio.

With these evaluation techniques it is possible to compile periodic reports on the volume of records received and destroyed; how much records space is available and how much it costs; what patterns of reference activity are found; how much filled and unfilled file housing is available; and other information such as the number of files destroyed. Data of this type will be useful for further improvement of the records management program.

Records Management Manual. The complete records management program includes a manual that formalizes the records control organization and all of its operating procedures. Such a manual helps to fix responsibility for carrying out the program and identifies and assigns all the duties for operating the program. It is also helpful for training new employees and for systematizing and explaining to all office workers the approved methods for creating, using, and disposing of records.

---

[8]"Filing Systems: Guidelines for Today and Tomorrow," *Modern Office Procedures* (March, 1975), p. 47.

[9]Benedon, *op. cit.*, pp. 117–118.

Wilson Jones Company   *Fimaco, Inc.*

Fig. 9-6
Special Filing Equipment for Data Processing Records

In the large organization a comprehensive records management manual may contain: (1) objectives, scope, and responsibilities of the program; (2) assignment of personnel duties for the program; and (3) functional areas, such as files management, forms and reports control, micrographics and reprographics, active and inactive records control, and records retention and disposition.[10] In the small office these same control principles can be compiled in an operations notebook for use by the files personnel and the office manager.

Management of Automated Records

In this computer age much information is recorded in magnetized form on

tapes, disks, and drums. What is produced might, therefore, be called an "invisible" record, although it is still a record and still requires a schedule of retention and other record controls. However, many records produced by a computer system are later printed out in hard-copy form on paper and, therefore, may be stored and retrieved like other paper records. Special equipment is required to store both the magnetic tapes and the computer printouts, but this equipment is nontechnical in nature and can be readily procured by the records manager. Figure 9-6 pictures such equipment.

On the other hand, the management of automated records is not a simple matter. It demands a sound understanding of the unique qualities of coded records as well as some of the common features that such records share with regular paper documents. To protect and to control the data on automated

[10]For a comprehensive discussion of the development of a records manual, see Wilmer O. Maedke, Mary F. Robek, and Gerald F. Brown, *Information and Records Management* (Beverly Hills: Glencoe Press, 1974), pp. 275–289.

records, usually two magnetic tapes — the original and a copy — are required and both are filed manually by a control name or number. Accuracy of the records is provided in several ways: (1) by internal computer checks; (2) by means of carefully tested computer programs; and (3) by verifying the accuracy and completeness of the data before they enter the computer system. Moreover, printouts of the contents of magnetic tapes or disks are also useful to prove the accuracy of the stored records. A printout thus enables an accountant to trace hard-copy reports back through the computer system to the source documents to determine the reliability of the accounting records.

As time goes on, more and more records will be kept in "invisible" form, thus requiring close cooperation among the records manager, the systems personnel, the data processing manager, and the operating departments. Close contact, too, should be maintained with legal counsel regarding federal and state retention requirements as well as interpretations relative to automated records.

Another type of record, the microform, must also be considered. This whole family of records, ranging from manual microfilm records to computer output microfilm (which merges the computer and the microfilm concepts) increases in importance and use from year to year. Microrecords and related micrographic topics are treated in Chapter 10.

RECORDS CREATION

Everyone in a company, from a file clerk to the corporate president, uses records and plays some part in their creation. If there is no control program, records continue to multiply and soon clog the firm's communication channels. For this reason the records management program begins with records creation.

Control over records creation rests initially upon this basic principle: *the record that is not created will not have to be controlled.* Records creation is, therefore, a preventive maintenance program that builds its case around honest answers to these questions:

1. Who may create the interdepartmental records?

    Generally, all employees may create records, but only those responsible for interdepartmental information flows (such as departmental supervisors and managers) should have the authority to create records.

2. When and where are records created?

    Employees in all offices may create records when a need arises. Frequently no effort is made to determine how badly the record is needed or if an identical or similar record exists.

3. How are records created?

    Records are created by hand or machine (typewriters, duplicating machines, and the many types of data processing machines).

4. Why are records created?

    Records transmit and store needed information. Sometimes, however, the need is more imagined than real.

5. How can records creation be adequately controlled?

    The creation can be controlled through a user's justification of all key records. Before a new form is designed, for example, its need must be justified by the user (see Chapter 18). Similarly, before any letter is written or before the number of carbon copies is determined, a careful study of the information needs of the department must be made. This study is usually subject to some centralized control.

INFORMATION AND RECORDS STORAGE

With the current attention being given to computers and magnetic storage devices, it might seem that the era of the file cabinet has ended. This, however, is not the case. In small and large offices alike, the manual filing system continues to furnish the maximum storage service in the records system.

Experience shows clearly that an office filing system cannot manage itself, regardless of how well it is organized. On the contrary, its management requires that careful consideration be given to many important administrative factors, such as the following: (1) setting up effective filing systems, (2) organizing the files, (3) procuring filing equipment and supplies, and (4) evaluating the effectiveness of the filing or storage equipment.

Filing Systems

Quick access to all types of stored records — whether they are on paper or film or magnetized bits on tape — is assured with an effective filing system. The term *filing system* refers to the procedures and methods used to classify, arrange or sort, and store records for fast accessibility when needed. There are two such systems, *alphabetic* and *numeric*, each of which can be subdivided in this manner:

1. Alphabetic Systems
   a. Correspondence filing (by name)
   b. Geographic filing
   c. Subject filing
2. Numeric Systems
   a. Numeric filing
   b. Chronologic filing

Most firms will use both of these systems, each having a particular prefer-

ence for a type of record-keeping function. For example, a credit office may maintain accounts receivable files in name (customer) order; a purchasing department, its purchase orders in order sequence (numeric); a personnel department, its personnel requisitions in files by type of position (subject); or a traffic department, the incoming receipt of goods in files by delivery dates or perhaps by a time-of-day scheduling chart (chronologic).

Files Organization

Record-keeping requirements differ from office to office, depending on the size of the office staff, the nature of the business operation, and such factors as competition and governmental regulation and control. Two types of files organization are commonly found in offices: decentralized filing and centralized filing. Recently a variation of the centralized filing plan, called network filing, has appeared. The advantages of each of these forms of files organization should be well understood by administrative office managers, as the filing system represents their primary sphere of responsibility.

Decentralized Filing. Under a *decentralized filing* plan, each office division maintains its own filing system and equipment; and the work is performed by one or more employees who may have other types of office work to do. Such an arrangement often results in needless duplication of equipment; less efficient personnel to do the filing work, since such employees may also perform other office duties; and possibly a confused filing system, since in one department the filing methods may be entirely different from, if not inconsistent with, those of some other department.

The main arguments for decentralized filing are:

1. The confidential nature of the material filed suggests that it be kept from the majority of the employees.
2. Unnecessary delay in getting papers from the centralized department is avoided.
3. The papers filed will not be required by any other department.

Centralized Filing. The basic rationale for *centralized filing* is that records of general value throughout the firm should be shared and then stored and controlled by a centralized department. Such a centralized location and control provides these benefits:

1. The retention and disposition of all records, as well as the control over their creation, are facilitated, and a total records management program is thereby enhanced.
2. Responsibility for the files is placed in the hands of specialists, and greater overall personnel efficiency becomes possible.
3. Needless duplication of equipment, supplies, and records is eliminated and fewer dollars are wasted from poor procurement practices and uncontrolled use of equipment and supplies.
4. All related records are kept together, which ends much of the confusion of lost records. More uniform filing methods are followed, thus resulting in greater accuracy and quicker retrieval.

As the firm expands in size and the volume of information to be processed and stored increases, there is a tendency to centralize the records management and filing work. However, even where a centralized filing system is found, some of the work may be decentralized.

Network Filing. A "compromise" form of files organization appears in many large offices. This plan, called *network filing*, permits departmental files to be located within each department with centralized control residing in a records management department. In such a control center a "locator index" is maintained for the records that are filed in each department and is used to trace documents to their storage location where the classifying, indexing, coding, and actual filing work are done. The index also serves as a central data bank by furnishing information on all major records stored in the organization.

The administrative office manager must weigh carefully the advantages and the disadvantages of the several filing plans. No doubt a compromise will have to be reached, but only on the matter of the confidential nature of the filed material. The records to be filed departmentally should be kept to a minimum and, if possible, filed only temporarily in departmental files.

Filing Equipment and Supplies

The old axiom "Before you invest, investigate" clearly applies to the procurement of filing equipment and supplies. When these items are to be purchased, the office manager faces an overwhelming number of sources of supply and of alternate brands and models.

In the selection of filing equipment, the manager should first consider the intended use of the equipment and then the savings possible through standardization of equipment and supplies. Other factors the manager should study before an investment is made in filing equipment are: (1) the types and sizes of records, (2) managerial preferences for requesting information, (3) the appearance, design, space-saving features, and durability of the equipment; and (4) its capability for saving worker time.

Records vary widely in size from small cards to large drawings and blueprints. As a result, many different kinds and sizes of files will be required. Filing equipment may be classified as: (1) vertical, (2) horizontal, (3) visible card, (4) rotary card, and (5) mobile (see Figure 9-7).

Vertical Files. In vertical files, papers are filed on edge in a compact, accessible manner. The file cabinet with one to six drawers is the most common vertical file in which cards as well as larger documents, such as letters and memorandums, are stored. In standard letter-size cabinets the file width averages 15 inches; for legal-size cabinets, 18 inches. The file depth for both ranges from 24 to 28½ inches. These dimensions involve important space costs, with approximately 6 square feet as a general space requirement for each vertical file cabinet. Figure 9-8 illustrates how a better utilization of floor space can be achieved by *increasing* the number of file drawers and at the same time *decreasing* the amount of floor space needed for a given number of files. Also, less stooping and walking are required of files personnel, and as a result, the filing work is accomplished more quickly and easily.

In *open-shelf filing*, folders are arranged on shelves to permit unlimited visibility, a high degree of compactness, and quicker access to the records than is true of cabinet files. To eliminate dust and fire hazards, manufacturers provide doors that can be opened to form working shelves. Open-shelf files may run to the ceiling, necessitating the use of ladders; however for rapid file retrieval, shelves for active records should be accessible without a stool or ladder.

Open-shelf filing is far more compact and generally less expensive than cabinet filing. Studies conducted by the Department of the Navy have found that open-shelf equipment costs 50 percent less than cabinet files, and its space requirements cost 20 percent less than cabinet files. On the other hand, open-shelf supplies cost about 100 percent more for folders and 70 percent more for guides.[11] (Supplies costs, however, are relatively minor when compared with the costs of equipment and space.)

Other vertical files include the *roll-out* or lateral file in which the drawers roll out sideways, thus exposing all the stored records in half the aisle space required by drawer files; and the *rock-a-file*, in which drawers rock sideways, also requiring less floor space.

Horizontal Files. Horizontal filing equipment is used for storing papers or records, such as maps and drawings, in a flat position. Often, horizontal filing equipment of counter-high design is purchased so that, at no extra expense, the files may also serve as a counter-high working area.

Visible Card Files. Visible card files permit complete visibility of the key reference data (names, account numbers, and telephone numbers, for example) recorded on the edge of each card. The speed with which the cards can be located and entries made justifies the use and cost of this type of equipment. Visible files are available in the form of trays that lie flat horizontally in a cabinet, on revolving racks, or in loose-leaf book binders. Signaling devices such as metal tabs, plastic strips,

---

[11]William Benedon, *Records Management* (Englewood Cliffs: Prentice-Hall, 1969), p. 246.

Open-Shelf Vertical File

Horizontal File

*Remington Rand Office Systems Division,
Sperry Rand Corporation*

Visible Card File

*Remington Rand Office Systems Division,
Sperry Rand Corporation*

Motorized Card File

Acme Visible Records, Inc.

Rotary Card File

Watson Manufacturing Company

Mobile File

**Fig. 9-7
Types of Filing Equipment**

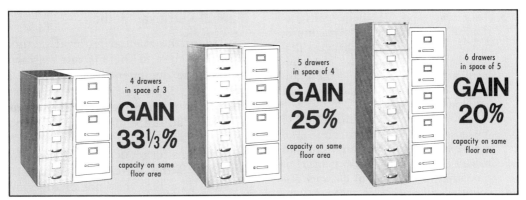

Fig. 9-8
Space-Saving Filing Equipment

or color indicators may be used with the cards to indicate such conditions as past-due accounts, accounts exceeding the credit limit, type of merchandise purchased, and classification of the accounts.

Rotary Card Files. In rotary card files the records rotate in a circular fashion from a common hub, and documents may be removed or added by rotating the file to the desired location. Larger rotary files are motorized, permitting an operator to have push-button control over a cabinet of record card trays to bring the desired tray to the work at desk or counter height.

Mobile Files. Equipment for mobile filing is designed for very large, active record systems. The mobile file station shown in Figure 9-7 provides a desk-chair work station for the files operator with access to all divisions of a file by moving back and forth on a fixed work-station track. In another type of mobile file the clerk sits in the center of a doughnut-shaped desk and locates the records desired by rotating the desk. Such equipment applies the basic engineering principle that it is more efficient and less fatiguing to have the work

brought to the worker than to have the worker go to the work.

Evaluation of Filing Equipment

A worker's efficiency depends to a great extent upon the tools and equipment available for use. Because of this fact, an objective appraisal of the filing equipment being used should be made as one means of measuring the efficiency of a filing department. To make such an evaluation the entire filing system must be studied. All components of this system interact with the filing equipment when the system is operating. The records manager of one large firm recommends that any thorough evaluation of filing equipment should cover these systems components:

1. *Time*, which includes motion and time analysis to compare the relative merits of open-shelf filing with conventional drawer filing.
2. *Methods*, such as the effects of equipment on work styles; how the equipment helps the workers to meet their objectives; how much equipment shortens the transportation of records; and how much new training is required to use new equipment.

3. *Equipment*, especially the proper functioning of equipment and machines; machine flexibility to fit changing procedures; the compatibility of equipment and office decor; and the availability of service on machines and equipment.
4. *Money*, that is, the economies related to the cost and operation of the equipment; how much worker time and money are saved; what use is made of time saved; what types of quantity discounts can be achieved through standardization of equipment; and the wise use of both vertical and horizontal space.
5. *Materials*, such as buying sturdy, reusable guides and folders; color coding for faster filing; and employing file labeling systems to promote faster retrieval of materials.
6. *Miscellaneous factors*, such as keeping up-to-date information on the filing equipment market; periodic training of the files personnel; and maintaining a well-planned layout for the files equipment.[12]

INFORMATION AND RECORDS RETRIEVAL

Retrieval, simply stated, refers to the process of locating stored information, a critically important phase of records control. The specific procedures for retrieving documents and information vary to a great extent from office to office, depending upon whether a small-office manual system (largely worker controlled) is involved or whether large-scale computer storage, which is typically dominated by machines, is utilized. However, in either case the steps followed for retrieving records are those shown in Figure 9-9.

[12]R. B. Austin, "Evaluating Filing Equipment and Supplies," *Information and Records Management* (March, 1974), pp. 22, 24.

Manual Retrieval Method

Under the manual retrieval method a worker goes to the file and extracts from it the document desired. Such a system is simple in theory but is often difficult to put into practice. For example, when an office manager asks a secretary to "Get that report from the file on our plans for reducing labor costs for next year," the search may be unsuccessful. The files may not divulge any such report with the key words "reducing labor costs for next year" used by the office manager. More than anything else, the difficulty in this case involves a problem in communication. The secretary must search for the record under the labels given by the requester; and if unsuccessful, the secretary must find acceptable synonyms and use them in the search until the record is found.

Frequently, manual index files are set up to help locate filed information when users ask for a record on a basis different from that by which the document is filed. In a personnel department, for example, a record might be filed under an employee's social security number. When employees' records are requested by name, however, there is need for a duplicate index file of employees' names which are cross-referenced to their social security numbers.

Machine Retrieval Methods

In a machine retrieval system, people usually do the planning and organizing of the retrieval system, and the machines execute the search operations. Office executives, faced with a growing need to reduce information-processing time, retrieval time, and space costs, have turned to machine retrieval to solve many information problems.

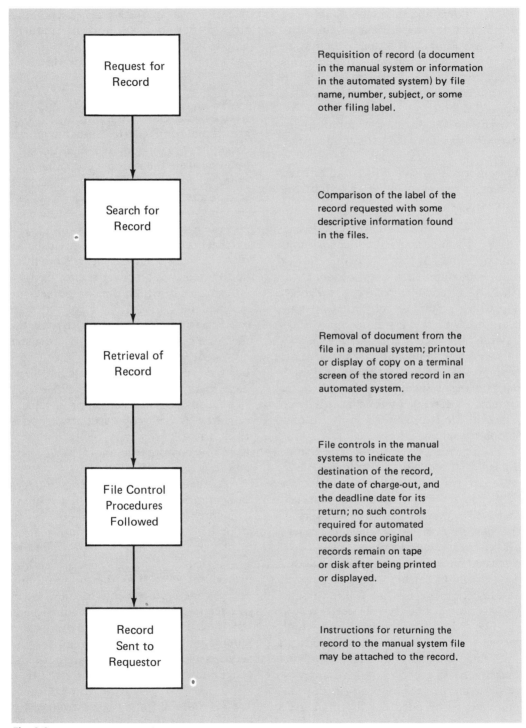

Request for Record	Requisition of record (a document in the manual system or information in the automated system) by file name, number, subject, or some other filing label.
Search for Record	Comparison of the label of the record requested with some descriptive information found in the files.
Retrieval of Record	Removal of document from the file in a manual system; printout or display of copy on a terminal screen of the stored record in an automated system.
File Control Procedures Followed	File controls in the manual systems to indicate the destination of the record, the date of charge-out, and the deadline date for its return; no such controls required for automated records since original records remain on tape or disk after being printed or displayed.
Record Sent to Requestor	Instructions for returning the record to the manual system file may be attached to the record.

Fig. 9-9
Steps for Retrieval of Record

To understand the machine retrieval of information, one must first remember that in an automated system data may be stored in coded form in punched cards for use in punched-card machines, in computers, and in the tape and disk storage devices of computer systems. Even though such data are stored in "invisible" form, they are usually identified as specific records in machine storage. The information stored in an automated system is retrieved as described in the following paragraphs.

Retrieval by Punched-Card Machines. Each punched card usually contains information about only one unit or item appearing on a source document (the so-called *unit-record principle*). Thus, great numbers of cards must be punched, and the result is bulky files. Payroll time cards, product sales cards, and accounts receivable cards are typical examples of such files, many of which become input records to the computer system. Retrieving punched cards from a payroll file is illustrated in the following paragraph.

In a payroll system codes may be assigned to the records as follows: A "1" code for full-time salaried workers, a "2" code for full-time hourly workers, and a "3" code for part-time workers. If the payroll manager wishes to retrieve all full-time salaried workers' cards from a master file, a card sorter could be used for retrieval by setting a selection switch at "1" (the code for the full-time salaried workers). The deck of cards would then be fed through the machine which leaves the cards with the "1" code in one stack and the other cards in a second stack. These cards would then be ready to be run through a printing machine to be decoded for the manager's use. If only a few cards are needed from a large card file, a clerk can retrieve them by hand in a short time. The re-

trieval of an aperture card, a combination punched card and microform, which is discussed in Chapter 10, follows these same retrieval procedures.

Retrieval by Computer. The computer system stores information internally and externally. Internally, data are stored on magnetic drums, magnetic cores, and magnetic disks. Externally, but connected with the computer, are other means of storage, such as magnetic-tape devices, paper-tape devices, and punched-card machines. While the computer can store information internally or externally, it must also have the capability of finding what has been stored. To do this requires a proper search (retrieval) program in which the computer is instructed how to search a collection of machine-readable records. Since the machine can recognize in a record a specific code, word, or phrase, it can seek out the pertinent records and list them, copy them, compile them, or cause them to be displayed on a screen or physically retrieved as hard-copy records. In addition, the records may be transmitted from one computer to another and printed out at a remote location.

As mentioned in Chapter 8, modern data communication facilities include typewriter-keyboard terminals by which an individual may retrieve information from a computer file. To do so requires a knowledge of the appropriate coding procedures as well as the programming and storage requirements for the system in question. Here retrieval is immediate, but the cost of getting data into computer storage is high and requires the services of skilled systems analysts and programmers.

Advanced Retrieval Systems. Innovations for improving the manner by which information is retrieved from files continue to appear, coming particularly from specialists in the library and computer sciences. One of these developments maintains that records can be indexed and summarized on the basis of certain words which they contain. Furthermore, if such key words are truly representative and descriptive of the record's contents, they can serve as the vehicle for the storage and location of information. While the idea is old (filing by book title and report title has long used this technique), what is new is that descriptive words can be used to extract specific information from a larger body of printed matter.

The Keyword in Context (KWIC) indexing system shown in Figure 9-10 is an example of the new retrieval systems. Key phrases, subtitles, or headings are underlined and each document is given a code number. These data are keypunched into a card and processed by a computer to obtain a printed list of phrases aligned in alphabetical order. Retrieval can be quickly effected by using the number assigned to the record that is also listed.

RECORDS RETENTION

A records retention program is the records manager's prescription for combatting the serious "disease" of paper hoarding. Specifically, *records retention*

involves the survey of all existing records, the development of schedules for retaining records, and the systematic transfer from active files to inactive storage or disposal of those records no longer needed.

The Records Survey

Before any problem can be solved, its overall dimension must be known. Similarly, before firm control can be maintained over a records system, the office or records manager must be well acquainted with all the records of the firm, especially those important documents operating in interdepartmental channels. To maintain control the records manager should survey all key records, either by sending a questionnaire to all departments and asking for copies of their records or, preferably, by personally visiting each department. An on-the-spot visit has several advantages over the questionnaire method. It makes direct personal contact between the records manager's office and the user's department; also, it enables the surveyor to get important information about records as well as to collect samples of filled-in forms and other records for the central file. With this information on hand, the manager can then construct the records retention schedule.

SAL OF COAL OR DOMESTIC IRON ORE DISPO	0272	00 00
TIMBER COAL OR DOMESTIC IRON ORE GAIN OR LOSS IN CASE OF	0631	00 00
IMPERFECT OR IRREGULAR ORGANIZATION	6012	03 02
ELECTION IRREVOCABLE	1361	02 00
RUSTEE OR BENEFICIARIES IRREVOCABLE TRUST & IN HAND OF T	1015	03 01
MUTUAL DITCH OR IRRIGATION COMPANIES	0501	12 01

Source: *Records Management Handbook: Information Retrieval — Managing Information Retrieval* (General Services Administration, 1972), p. 36.

Fig. 9-10
An Index of Keyword Titles

The Records Retention Schedule

A definite policy should be developed and followed in keeping material in the files, in microfilming papers, in placing materials in the vaults of a records center, and in destroying records. In large offices the approval of records retention schedules often involves top management and the accounting and the law departments in conjunction with the heads of the departments who hold the records. In small and medium-size offices, top management ordinarily has the responsibility for approving the records retention schedules.

Before a records retention schedule can be developed, companies should classify their records in one of four ways: *vital, important, useful,* or *unnecessary.* Records considered vital or important are retained indefinitely; those considered useful may be retained for several years; and unnecessary records are destroyed. Such decisions depend in part on the federal, state, and local laws that set up minimal retention periods for records.[13]

Records must be available at all times for inspection by Internal Revenue Service agents, and they must be retained as long as the contents may become material in the administration of the law. This is usually a period of at least four years after the date the tax to which they relate becomes due or the date that the tax is paid, whichever is later. However, the loss or destruction of older records is not recognized as a valid excuse for failure to produce them. The statutes of limitation in the various states also affect the decision of how long records and correspondence should

be kept. A suggested schedule for the retention of business records is presented in Figure 9-11, pages 244 and 245.

RECORDS DISPOSITION

The final phase in the records control cycle, *disposition*, involves two types of records: those inactive records that may not be destroyed and are transferred to lower cost storage; and other records, no longer needed, that are destroyed. Procedures for records transfer and records destruction are discussed in this section.

Transferring Inactive Records

The decision to transfer records to inactive storage should involve records center personnel and the members of each department responsible for such records. Several transfer practices are available, depending upon the nature of the records operation.

One such transfer practice, called the *periodic method*, requires file materials to be examined at fixed intervals of six months or one year; and all materials considered to be inactive are then placed in inexpensive record boxes and sent to inactive storage. However, periodic inspection is a laborious job and may interfere with more pressing work, and for this reason inspection may receive a low priority.

In the *duplicate equipment method*, one variation of the periodic method, last year's materials are kept in inactive file cabinets located next to the present active files. At the end of the year, the contents of last year's files are placed in transfer cases, and the present fiscal year's file becomes the "back" file. Although this method is fairly expensive in terms of equipment needed, it is very efficient.

---

[13]For the provisions of federal laws and regulations relating to the retention of records by the public, see *Guide to Records Retention Requirements* (Washington: U.S. Government Printing Office, 1975).

Under the *continuous* or *perpetual* method, records are transferred to inactive files as they reach a certain age or when it seems likely they will no longer be used. Such a method works well with case files in law offices, customer files in real estate offices, or job files in construction firm offices where the termination of a job usually means very infrequent reference to the files. For other types of offices, the continuous method may be considered rather inefficient.

Storing Inactive Records

In the small firm transferred materials should be kept in that part of the general office area that is least desirable for general use. (Storerooms or unattractive, inaccessible portions of a main office are examples.) Housing for inactive files should be of inexpensive but durable construction, usually fiberboard, and

kept in an orderly manner so that desired information may be located without too much delay. Figure 9-12 presents 10 points for the office manager or files supervisor to keep in mind at the time of transferring the files.

In larger offices a *records center* or archives is often set up to store the inactive records of all departments. With these facilities available, records personnel periodically transfer the contents of the file cabinets to inactive storage cases on steel racks that extend to the ceiling in the records center. One standard-size steel rack occupies 17.5 square feet, holds the contents of ten 4-drawer file cabinets, and costs $80. The comparative annual savings (excluding personnel costs) under this transfer approach is calculated as shown in Table 9-1.

Rather than set up their own archival units, some firms prefer to use commercial records centers that offer a wide range of services at a low per-record

---

ANNUAL SAVINGS WITH A RECORDS CENTER

Filing Costs for Four-Drawer File Cabinets in Active Storage		Filing Costs after Records Are Transferred to Inactive Storage	
1 file cabinet @ $140, depreciated over a 10-year period and ignoring trade-in value	$14.00	1/10 steel rack @ $80, depreciated over a 10-year period and ignoring trade-in value	$ .80
Floor space, 6 square feet @ $10 per square foot	60.00	6 cardboard containers @ $.50	3.00
Overhead and maintenance, 6 square feet @ $3 per square foot	18.00	Floor space, 1/10 of 17.5 square feet @ $2 per square foot	3.50
		Overhead and maintenance, 1/10 of 17.5 square feet at $2 per square foot	3.50
Total Costs	$92.00	Total Costs	$10.80

Annual Savings: $92.00 − $10.80 = $81.20

Table 9-1

RECORD	RETAIN (YEARS)
ACCOUNTING AND FISCAL	
Accounts Payable Invoices	6
Accounts Payable Ledger	P
Accounts Receivable Ledger	P
Authorizations for Accounting	SUP
Balance Sheets	P
Bank Deposit Books and Slips	3
Bank Statements and Reconciliations	4
Bonds and Records	P
Budgets and Cost Files	3
Capital Asset Record	3 AD
Cash Books and Receipt Registers	P
Checks, Cancelled; Payroll	2
Checks, Cancelled; Voucher	3
Checks, Dividend	6
Check Registers	P
Cost Accounting Records	5
Drafts Paid	3
Earnings Register	3
Entertainment Gifts and Gratuities	3
Estimates, Projections	7
Expense Reports, Employee	7
Financial Statements, Certified	P
Financial Statements, Periodic	P
Fixed Asset Control Register	3
General Journal	20
General Ledger	20
Labor Cost Records	3
Note Ledgers	P
Payroll Register	7
Petty Cash Records	4
Profit and Loss Statements	P
Property Asset Summary	10
Salesman Commission Reports	3
Tabulating Cards and Magnetic Tape	1
Trial Balances, Monthly	5
Work Papers, Rough	2
ADMINISTRATIVE	
Audit Reports, Internal	6
Audit Reports, Public and Government	15
Audit Work Papers, Internal	6
Classified Documents: Control, Inventories, Reports	5
Correspondence, Executive	P

RECORD	RETAIN (YEARS)
Permits to Do Business	P
Records of Mergers, Consolidations, Acquisitions, Dissolutions, and Reorganizations	P
Reports to Securities and Exchange Commission	P
Securities: Documents of Issuance, Listing, and Registration	P
Stock Certificates, Cancelled	15
Stock, Stock Transfer, and Stockholders Records	P
Stockholder Minute Books	P
LEGAL	
Claims and Litigation of Torts and Breach of Contract	P
Copyrights	P
Law Records: Federal, State, Local	SUP
Patents and Related Data Trademarks	P
MANUFACTURING	
Bills of Material	3
Drafting Records	P
Drawings and Tracings, Original	P
Inspection Records	2
Laboratory Test Reports	P
Memos, Production	P
Product Development: Design, Engineering, Research, Tooling, and Specifications	UC
Production Reports	P
Quality Control Reports	3
Reliability Records	P
Stores Issue Records	3
Tool Control	3
Work Orders: Cost, $1,000 or Less	3
Work Orders: Cost, More than $1,000	6
Work Status Reports	UC
OFFICE SUPPLIES AND SERVICES	
Inventories	2
Office Equipment Records	6
Requests for Services	1
Requisitions for Supplies	1

RECORD	RETAIN (YEARS)
Purchase Orders	3 AE
Purchase Requisitions	3
Quotations	1
PRODUCTS, SERVICES, AND MARKETING	
Correspondence	3
Credit Ratings and Classifications	10
Development Studies	P
Presentations and Proposals	P
Price Lists, Catalogs	SUP
Prospect Lists	SUP
Surveys	P
PUBLIC RELATIONS AND ADVERTISING	
Advertising Activity Reports	5
Community Affairs Records	P
Contracts, Advertising	3 AT
Employee Activities and Presentations	P
Exhibits, Releases, Handouts	4
Internal Publications (1 Record Copy)	P
Layouts	1
Manuscripts	1
Photos	1
Public Information Activity	7
Research Presentations	P
Tear Sheets	2
SALES	
Contract Progress Reports	3 AE
Contracts with Customers	3 AT
Contracts with Representatives, Agents, Distributors, Etc.	3
Mailing and Prospect Lists	SUP
Market Research Studies and Analysis	OBS
Order Register	OBS
Orders Filled	OBS
Sales Correspondence	3
Sales Invoices	3
Shipping Notices and Reports	3
SECURITY	
Classified Material Violations	P
Courier Authorizations (After Trip)	1 Mo.

Records Retention Schedule

Item	Retention
Correspondence, General	7
Directives from Officers	P
Forms Control (1 Record Copy)	P
Systems and Procedures Records (1 Record Copy)	P
Work Papers, Management Projects	P

COMMUNICATIONS

Item	Retention
Bulletins, Communications	P
Messenger Records	1
Postal Records: Registered and Insured Mail Logs, Meter Records, and Stamp Requisitions	1
Telecommunications Copies	2
Telephone Directories	SUP
Telephone Records: Installation, Location, Rental Charges, Moves	P

CONTRACT ADMINISTRATION

Item	Retention
Contracts Negotiated, plus Bailments, Changes, Specifications, Procedures, and Correspondence	P
Customer Reports	P
Reports: Materials Relating to Distribution, Revision, Form, and Format	P
Work Papers	OBS

CORPORATE

Item	Retention
Annual Reports	P
Authority to Issue Securities	P
Authorizations and Appropriations for Expenditures	3 AE
Bonds, Surety	P
Capital Stock Ledger	20 AT
Charters, Constitution, Bylaws, and Amendments	P
Contracts	P
Election Records, Corporate	P
General Cashbooks, Treasurers' and Auditors'	P
Incorporation Records and Certificates	P
Insurance Policies	3 AE
Licenses: Federal, State, Local	UT
Minutes, Resolutions: Meetings of Board of Directors, Stockholders, and Directors' Committees	P

PERSONNEL

Item	Retention
Accident Reports, Injury Claims, Settlements	30 AS
Applications, Changes, Terminations	P
Attendance Records	7
Disability and Sick Benefits Records	6
Employee Activity Files	2
Employee Contracts	6
Fidelity Bonds	3 AT
File: Individual Employee	5 AT
Garnishments	5 AS
Health and Safety Bulletins	P
Injury Frequency Charts	P
Insurance Records: Group, Employee	11 AT
Job Descriptions	3 or SUP
Medical Folders, Employee	5 AT
Rating Cards	3 or SUP
Time Cards	3
Training Manuals	P
Union (Collective Bargaining) Agreements	3

PLANT AND PROPERTY

Item	Retention
Depreciation Schedules	P
Inventory Records	P
Maintenance and Repair, Buildings	10
Maintenance and Repair, Machinery	5
Plant Account Cards, Equipment Records, Historical Folders	P
Property Deeds	P
Purchase or Lease Records	P
Space Allocation Records	2 AT

PRINTING AND DUPLICATING

Item	Retention
Copies Produced: Charts, Technical Publications	1 or OBS
Film Reports	5
Negatives	5
Photographs	1 or OBS
Production Records	1

PROCUREMENT AND PURCHASING

Item	Retention
Acknowledgements	UC
Bids, Awards	3 AT
Contracts	3 AT
Exception Notices	6
Price Lists	OBS

Item	Retention
Employee Case Files	5
Employee Clearance Lists	SUP
Fire Prevention Program	P
Investigation Reports	10
Protection: Guards Badge Lists, Protective Devices	5
Subcontractor Clearances	2 AT
Vistor Clearance	2

TAXATION

Item	Retention
Annuity or Deferred Payment Plan	P
Depreciation Schedules	P
Dividend Register	P
Employee Withholding Statements	4
Excise Exemption Certificates	4
Excise Reports	4
Inventory Reports	P
Tax Bills and Statements	P
Tax Returns and Working Papers	P

TRAFFIC AND TRANSPORTATION

Item	Retention
Aircraft Operating and Maintenance	P
Bills of Lading, Waybills	3
Delivery Reports	3
Employee Travel	1
Export Declarations	4
Freight Bills	6
Freight Bills	6
Freight Claims	6
Household Moves	SUP
Rates and Tariffs	3
Receiving Documents	1
Routing Records	6
Shipping and Related Documents	2
Vehicle Operation and Maintenance	

LEGEND FOR RETENTION PERIOD

AD — After Disposal
AE — After Expiration
AS — After Settlement
AT — After Termination
OBS — Until Obsolete
P — Permanently
SUP — Until Superseded
UC — Until Completion of Job or Contract
UT — Until Termination

Source: Reprinted from the May, 1975 issue of *Modern Office Procedures* and copyrighted 1975 by Industrial Publishing Company, Division Pittway Corporation.

Fig. 9-11
Records Retention Schedule

1. Determine and tabulate by number of inches the amount of material that can be destroyed.
2. Remove this material from the old files or transfer cases.
3. Rearrange the transfer files in such a way as to provide empty drawer space within the immediate proximity of the next year's files.
4. Prepare a list of the names for which folders or folder labels must be prepared. Analyze the files to be sure you include folders for new customers, and break down bulky folders with chronological folders.
5. Indicate on the label list which names are most active so that special name guides and chronological folders in the proper size breakdown may be obtained.

6. Determine the number of folders needed, for both individual and chronological.
7. Place the order for labels, folders, and other supplies 60 to 90 days before they are to be used.
8. Type the labels from rolls or pads and keep in alphabetical order.
9. Apply the labels to the folders and place in cartons in front of the miscellaneous folders in the same order as they will be placed in the active file.
10. On transfer day merely remove what has been current material to its new location and place the newly prepared material in the space provided for the current files.

Fig. 9-12
A Procedure for Transferring Inactive Records

storage cost. In addition to the centralized storage advantages provided by company records centers, commercial records centers offer specialized services such as regular records destruction, inventory control, reference activity reports, file purges, copying and microfilm services, and access to records by telephone. In fact, experience shows that over 95 percent of all references to records in commercial centers are handled over the telephone.

Protecting Vital Records

The information stored in a firm's files has a value like any other asset and as such should be carefully protected. When accurate data about a company's customers, creditors, inventory, and sources of supply are lost through fire, theft, or some natural hazard, discontin-

uance of the business is always possible. Too often management comes to this realization after the disaster has struck and the records are no longer available.

As a protection against disaster, business executives insure their property, including business records, against risk of loss. However, information is a unique asset and difficult, if not impossible, to replace; and no protection is available for the loss of information contained in records. Therefore, extraordinary measures, some of which are outlined below, must be taken to protect these vital records:

1. *Special fire-resistive housing* includes files, vaults, and safes both on and off the premises. Magnetic tape is highly flammable, requiring unique safes that keep interior temperatures below 150° F.

2. *Dispersion* entails transporting vital records to locations away from the business. Small firms can combine their resources with those of other firms and establish cooperative storage centers or utilize commercial centers (such as the records centers operated throughout the country by Bekins Van & Storage Company and Leahy and Company). Large firms can exchange records among their branch offices to assure adequate protection.

3. *Duplication* pertains to reproducing vital documents so that copies may be stored in locations remote from the original records. Microforms and magnetic tape records are especially easy to reproduce.

4. *Standard fire discipline* permits no smoking around computer installations, keeps combustible materials cleared from storage areas, and assures that vault doors are closed when not in use. In addition, adequate alarms, proper sprinkler systems, and fire extinguishers should be installed.

Each year those stored records that are no longer required should be destroyed. Departmental managers must be notified what materials are to be destroyed in accordance with the records retention schedule. To avoid errors in destroying still useful records, an authorization form signed by the departmental manager should be used and retained in the records center (or, in the files of the smaller office) as evidence of the final disposition of the records. Within the office, paper shredders are often used to destroy records. Documents may also be sent to local paper companies to be recycled if the information on the records is not confidential in nature.

QUESTIONS FOR REVIEW

1. In what ways does information serve as an invaluable tool for modern management?

2. Briefly describe the common types of records found in most offices as well as the principal uses of each type of record.

3. Identify the typical steps in the records control cycle.

4. What are the principal areas of responsibility of an information manager at the vice-president's level?

5. What is the relationship between information management and records management?

6. Describe the areas of competence typically required of a records manager. In particular note the data processing needs of the records manager.

7. Compare the various types of administrative costs as well as the relative weight of each in determining the cost of maintaining files.

8. Cite several methods and techniques that are available to an office manager for reducing records costs.

9. What evaluation measures are available for assessing the efficiency of the records system? of the records personnel? of the utilization of space?

10. In what respects do automated records differ from regular paper records?

11. How can control be extended over the creation of records?

12. Show clearly how most firms utilize both alphabetic and numeric filing systems.

13. Compare the advantages and disadvantages of decentralized filing, centralized filing, and network filing.

14. Before making an investment in filing equipment, what key factors should be studied?

15. How does the cost of open-shelf filing compare with the cost of cabinet-type filing?

16. What systems components should be included in a thorough evaluation of filing equipment?

17. How does the process of retrieving a record from a file cabinet compare with the retrieval of information from a computer system?

18. Why is the records survey considered to be such a fundamental part of the records management program?

19. List the various classifications of records for retention purposes as well as the disposition of records that fall into each category.

20. Distinguish between the periodic and the continuous methods of records transfer.

21. What are the principal advantages of a commercial records center as contrasted to a company records center?

22. Besides storing records in fire-resistive files, what other methods are available for protecting records?

QUESTIONS FOR DISCUSSION

1. The statement has been made that a records manager controls the decision-making process. Would you expect top management to agree with this statement? Give reasons for your answer.

2. On a records management conference program was a panel of four experts: two from cost-conscious insurance companies, and two from a federal government agency. During the program the spokesperson for the governmental point of view made the statement that "Records management is records management, wherever it is found," a point with which the insurance panelists took exception. What are the implications of this statement to both government and private sectors?

3. A highly successful law firm of five young attorneys specializing in criminal law is located in your city. To handle their administrative work is a small staff which includes a receptionist, five typists, two

legal secretaries, and one general office clerk who handles all the filing work, along with other duties. As time goes on, office space becomes more cramped; active and inactive files are not separated, thus presenting retrieval problems. The office has become an actual eyesore to its high-level clients; it is even embarrassing to the attorneys themselves. Gerald Waller, the senior attorney responsible for the operation of the office, hears of your records management interest and training and asks you to "take a look at our office and come up with some practical recommendations for improvement." How would you proceed? What questions would you ask, and what would you include in your report to Waller?

4. The reference and accuracy ratios appeal to you as simple techniques for evaluating your filing system. What kind of procedures must you set up in order to use these ratios in your filing department? Considering overall costs, would the use of these ratios "pay for themselves" in terms of the benefits they provide?

5. As office manager of Asaki Products, you are aware of the need for a records manager to provide firmer control over your records, both manual and automated, than your present files supervisor can provide. No one on your staff has the capabilities to assume such a managerial position except perhaps Kenya Nishi, a bright young college-educated administrative assistant, who declines your invitation to apply for the position. Therefore, a decision is made to search for a qualified person to fill the new records management position, a task requiring answers to these questions: (a) What specific job qualifications need to be identified and included in a job description? (b) Who should be involved in the interviewing and selection process? (c) Where would you seek good applicants for this position? Discuss how you would handle the search for this new manager, including possible counsel from present department managers.

6. In a large metropolitan hospital Sharon Wiseman, the hospital administrator, is searching for better methods of handling the expanding volume of records. She has compiled the following list of her most urgent problems:

   a. 150 X-rays are developed and processed daily (none of which are destroyed).

   b. 300 outpatients' and 2,500 inpatients' records must be handled daily with Medicare forms adding to the problem by 10 percent each year.

   c. 15,400 health insurance forms were processed during the past six months.

   d. No central depository of records is available.

   e. Physicians are growing more impatient with the slow retrieval of medical records from the files but are resisting the use of microfilmed records.

   f. The hospital administrator is in charge of all records, assisted on a full-time basis by three file clerks.

   Assuming the accuracy of these facts and the existence of other equally pressing problems, recommend to Wiseman a comprehensive plan for improving her records management practices, including records retention and protection programs.

7. As a new records manager, you have recommended to the departmental managers in your firm that a centralized master file be set up for all key departmental records in a centralized location. Access to any record would be almost immediate — by telephone, by computer terminal, or by personal messenger. The departmental managers appreciate your expertise but will not relinquish physical control over their records. Assuming the overall justification of your recommendation, what kind of strategy would you develop to persuade these executives to reconsider your recommendation? What compromise solution might be arranged?

8. The Blakely Corporation, a medical supplies wholesaling firm, has always considered its records to be adequately protected in locked, steel file cabinets. Recently, however, their office manager questioned the adequacy of such protective measures after witnessing the devasting fire that destroyed a neighboring office and all its records — especially its accounts receivable. Rumor has it that that firm may not recover from this loss; and, as a result, the Blakely management has decided to investigate a more foolproof protection system. Explore a comprehensive plan for records protection, considering both on-site and off-site possibilities, their costs and their benefits.

9. Now that warehouse records storage is available for inactive records in your firm, you as manager of records administration must decide on appropriate transfer methods for these large-volume records that cannot be destroyed: (a) voucher checks; (b) cost accounting records; (c) general correspondence; (d) job applications; and (e) depreciation schedules. Consider the most critical phases of this problem, especially those relating to the transfer policies and procedures that must be developed and approved to ensure an efficient transfer plan.

PRACTICAL OFFICE MANAGEMENT CASES

Case 9-1 Taking a Records Inventory

Arlo's Environetics specializes in the production of pollution-control devices. Its office staff of 300 has quadrupled in the five years since the firm began operations. With greatly expanding markets for its products, Arlo's has concentrated on the production and distribution of its products and has allowed the office to run itself to the point where an uncontrolled records problem has developed. No one is officially responsible for either the storage or the retrieval of records, and everyone assumes that Harold Martino, the hard-working office manager, should control all the paperwork even though he does not have the time nor the training to do so.

Realizing that the records explosion problems and management's increased information needs are curtailing factory operations, the office manager asks you to study the overall records problems in the firm. Some of his principal concerns are stated as follows:

1. There are four times as many office employees as when the firm started, but no additional file clerks have been added. The three clerks just can't keep up with the work.
2. No one in the office knows what key interdepartmental records exist. A set of each of the main records should be on file together with information about their use.
3. Nothing has been done to understand the problems associated with the data processing department's records. In fact, control over costs, equipment and supplies, and just everything has been ignored. Filing space is running out and records protection is now under question. The whole operation needs to be studied.

Prepare a report for the office manager recommending solutions to these problems. Since a records inventory has highest priority for him, give it your first attention and include a copy of a form that could be used to survey the records as well as to control the records inventory.

Case 9-2 Reorganizing the Records Systems

Soon after you accepted the position of office manager of Novak Industries six months ago, these serious records problems came to your attention: Obsolete wooden file cabinets, some dating back to the 1940s, are in use and are difficult to operate; most of the 30 obsolete, four-drawer file cabinets are crammed with records (correspondence, accounting documents, and invoices) from 1960 to the present; no retention or transfer systems are in effect; no filing manual exists; and there are no efficient storage or retrieval procedures in operation. Furthermore, no office personnel have been specifically assigned to the records function. Three general clerks do the filing, although all 40 of the office employees have full access to the files. Each general clerk is paid a weekly salary of $140. Present company expansion and a corresponding increase in paperwork have placed a severe strain on the old-fashioned records system. Further growth of the firm and a larger office work force are anticipated, and a reorganization of the entire records system is needed soon.

One office employee, Connie Knowling, has helped you study the records system. Because she likes records work, is a good, careful worker, knows the firm and its records problems, and has the cooperation of the office staff, you have appointed her as records supervisor at a weekly salary of $200. In this position she is responsible for coordinating all records activities, procuring equipment and supplies, providing whatever systems changes and controls she deems necessary, and devoting about 25 percent of her time to filing operations. Knowling has been given one full-time files assistant at a salary of $150 a week, with the possibility of adding a part-time worker from another department if the workload requires. The salary of the part-time worker would be one half of the annual salary paid the files assistant. With these appointments, centralized control would be placed over all records.

Knowling's first recommendations for managing the records involve the purchase of modern steel five-drawer units that would eventually replace the old file cabinets. She has suggested the use of the duplicate method of transferring records from active to inactive storage. During the first year of operation those records that are more than one year old would continue to be retained in the present four-drawer files, which would be called the "back" or inactive files. Next to these inactive files would be the active files housed in the new file units.

At the end of the first year, the contents of the "back" files would be purged and about 50 percent of the filed materials would be placed in newly purchased transfer cases in a storage room. The old file cabinets, having no salvage value, would be destroyed. The new units purchased at the beginning of the current year, containing the current year's materials, would then become the "back" files. New file units would have to be purchased to serve as the active files for the second and succeeding years. At the end of the second year, when the "back" files are purged, their contents would be stored in transfer cases. A similar procedure would be followed at the end of each year. It is estimated that 50 percent of the "back" files will be purged at the end of each year before the records are placed in the transfer cases.

For the past two months Knowling has studied the records storage patterns of the firm. Approximately 4,000 incoming letters and 3,000 carbon copies of outgoing correspondence and billing statements require filing each week. Each 26-inch drawer in the standard-size file cabinet holds approximately 5,000 papers. To handle the storage requirements of the proposed system, Knowling has consulted sales representatives of filing equipment firms who have provided the following quotations for equipment and supplies:

Five-drawer filing units, letter size, 26-inch cabinet drawers	$200.00 each
2 File shelves (attachable to either side of a file drawer to facilitate the filing operation)....................................	12.50 each
2 Filing stools..	20.00 each

Flip-top corrugated fiberboard letter-size files (regular
file-drawer size).. 2.30 each

1 Combination sorting tray-tote cart.................................. 40.00 each

The supplies required for the first year for the active files and the second year for the "back" files are:

Alphabetic file guides, pressboard (20 to each file
drawer).. $35.00 per   100

File folders (75 to each file drawer) .... 50.00 per 1,000

100 out guides (manila).. 15.00 per   100

2,000 cross-reference sheets (required each year) ...... 22.50 per 1,000

In the transfer files, only file folders will be used in each file drawer.

In addition to submitting these quotations, the equipment representatives mentioned the need to consider depreciation on the equipment items in the records center. For the sake of simplicity, they recommended the use of the straight-line method of calculating depreciation (explained in Chapter 5) in which file cabinet units and the other filing equipment would be depreciated over a 10-year period, with no residual value remaining.

Before a formal proposal for setting up a new records center can be approved by the president of the company, it is necessary to obtain an objective analysis of costs. You are asked to prepare a report that shows the cost of equipping and operating the records center during the next five years as well as the anticipated benefits to be obtained, making reasonable assumptions where necessary. In your report cover each of the following items:

1. Present and proposed payroll costs in the records center. Assume that salaries in the records center increase by about eight percent each year. Further, assume that the services of the part-time worker are required at the beginning of the second year.
2. Anticipated annual savings in payroll costs over the five-year period.
3. Costs of operating the records center, including depreciation expense, for each of the five years. Assume that the paper workload increases by five percent each year after the first year.
4. Total savings to be realized over the five-year period as a result of centralizing the records function and installing the new office equipment.

Chapter 10

GRAPHIC INFORMATION SERVICES

The same technology that spawned the computer and extended the information processing power of the office has been applied to the field of graphic information services. The result is an area of administrative office management that offers more effective ways of satisfying the information needs of modern organizations. Two of the principal graphic services — *micrographics*, the study of miniaturized (micro) records, and *reprographics*, the field of records reproduction — are discussed in this chapter.

MICROGRAPHIC SERVICES

Microfilm was regarded as little more than a novelty until the 1930s when it began to be used commercially. Its use was "spurred on by the invention of a machine in which a conveyor belt was synchronized with a motion picture camera to make a permanent, miniature record of bank checks."[1] Soon many businesses recognized the value of microfilmed records largely as a means of saving space.

The information explosion has expanded the emphasis upon microfilming as solely a means of saving space. Office managers, faced with serious problems such as space, storage, and information retrieval, turned to computer specialists for answers. As a result, microfilm has become a broad information systems tool that involves software and equipment for indexing, storing, and retrieving information; for reducing paper-management costs; and for improving administrative operations. To reflect this expanded view of microfilm, the term *micrographics* was created to represent the total process of reproducing regular-size records in microimage format (or of reproducing microimages in larger size). Also involved are related services for producing and using microfilm in both manual and computer systems as well as in telecommunications. The physical form of such records may appear as hard copy on film or paper or as soft copy, projected on a viewing screen or video terminal as discussed in Chapter 8.[2]

Why Microforms are Used

Generally companies convert records to microform for these reasons: to protect vital records; to conserve space; to speed up the storage and retrieval of information; to integrate microrecords with the management information system, including the computer; and to facilitate the reproduction and transmission of records.[3] While microforms have the capabilities to meet these needs, several limitations of miniature records

---

[1]Dale Gaddy, *A Microform Handbook* (Silver Spring: National Microfilm Association, 1974), p. 5.

[2]"Infosystems: Micrographics Report," *Infosystems* (April, 1975), p. 33.

[3]Joseph L. Kish, Jr. and James Morris, *Microfilm in Business* (New York: Ronald Press Company, 1966), p. 3.

must be considered, the greatest of which is the need for reader equipment to enlarge the size of the photographed record for the user. Other limitations include the bulk and lack of portability of the equipment involved when a user must transport both readers and microforms. Also, records subject to constant change are usually not filmed, for the updating of filmed records is a costly process and more easily carried out on the original paper documents.

Records in Microform

Whereas microrecords were originally stored on rolls of film, now there are many different microforms available. Usually microforms are divided into two broad classes: *unitized* microforms, such as a payroll file that is prepared as one complete set of data without reference or attachment to any unrelated material; and *nonunitized* microforms that may frequently contain unrelated units of information from many departments of a firm on the same continuous length of film. Each of these microforms is illustrated in Figure 10-1, along with national survey data describing the relative frequency of their use. Utilities and insurance companies use micrographics more than other industries, a fact that is explained by the tremendous number of records created in these service industries.[4]

Microfilm. Microfilm is usually produced on rolls 16mm or 35mm in width and 100 feet in length. This size of roll holds approximately 3,000 documents which are 8½″ × 11½″, or about 40,000 bank checks. The width of the film selected depends on the size of the

original material to be photographed, the desired reduction ratio for the microimage, and the use of microfilm in the intended application. The *reduction ratio* expresses the number of times the size of a record is reduced photographically. If, for example, a page from a book is reduced at a ratio of 24 to 1 (expressed as 24X) — a medium reduction — the microimage is 1/24 the width of the original page or 1/576 (1/24 squared) of the overall size.

Roll film is often used to store inactive records, while the cartridge or cassette form is used where automatic data retrieval is required. Film is easily stored, and when in negative form it can be employed to reproduce a positive microfilm roll. The negative may then be sent to an off-site facility for vital records protection. Unlike other microforms, roll microfilm makes browsing and updating difficult. To add related documents requires splicing into the original roll, which is a slow and costly process.

Fiche. Fiche (pronounced "fēsh"), the French word for "card," is a microform that appears on a transparent sheet of microfilm. *Microfiche* is arranged in a grid pattern; its most common size is the standard 4 by 6 inches (which adheres to the National Micrographics Association standard of 105mm by 108mm, 24X reduction, with 98 frames, or 7 rows of 14 images each). *Ultrafiche*, which is similar to microfiche, permits ultra (very) high reduction ratios, often as high as 2400X. Bank systems use ultrafiche to record customer transactions; and other large organizations, such as General Motors and Sears Roebuck, use ultrafiche systems for storing catalog data. Copies of each fiche can be easily retrieved and inexpensively reproduced

---

[4]"Microfilm — It's Bigger Than You Think," *Infosystems* (April, 1974), pp. 24–27.

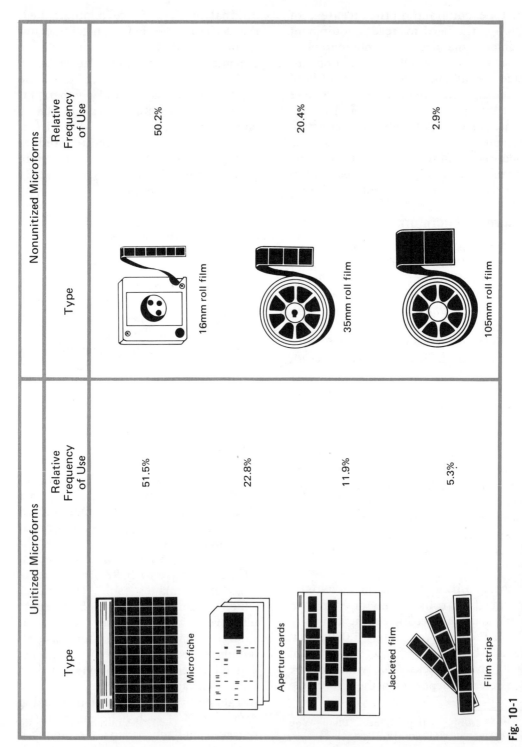

Fig. 10-1
Common Microforms and Their Relative Frequency of Use

for distribution throughout the world. Updating is simplified by replacing an obsolete fiche with a current one.

Aperture Cards. This microform is a standard 80-column punched card with a precut hole over which a portion of 35mm microfilm is mounted. The card is typically used for the storage of large, bulky engineering documents and drawings. Besides its space-saving quality, it has the added advantage of permitting keypunching into the card for faster storage and retrieval. Retrieval and refiling of the card may be done manually or by a sorting machine simply by reading the printed or punched data at the top of the card. The file is updated by removing the old card and substituting a new one.

Jacketed Film. This type of microrecord is essentially an individual storage medium in which two pieces of clear plastic are fused together to form channels. Strips of microfilm may be inserted into these channels, and any strip or portion of a strip may be easily removed. The ease of updating this microform is an advantage in maintaining personnel and medical records, general correspondence, and customer and policyholder files.

Micrographic Systems

Micrographic services should be considered as an important subdivision of the total information system. Thus, a micrographic system is a complex "mixture" of hardware, software, and personnel necessary to carry out all the micrographic responsibilities of the company. In large firms these tasks are delegated to a specialized in-house unit; for smaller firms, service bureaus can be used for this specialized activity.

Hardware. Basic to any micrographic application are four types of hardware: cameras to photograph the records; processing equipment to convert the images made on film into negatives or master microforms; duplication equipment to reproduce copies of microforms; and readers or reader-printers, to enlarge the microrecords for human use.[5]

Readers. *Readers*, or viewers, project magnified images of the microrecords onto a viewing screen and are essential to any micrographic system. Readers vary in size from portable hand-held or lap viewers to larger equipment designed for a table work station. The selection of a reader depends upon the type of microform used; thus, there are microfiche readers, roll film readers, aperture card readers, and others that will accept almost all microforms. Reader-printers combine the reading function and the production of hard-copy printouts of microform images. For example, should the viewer desire a hard-copy after viewing an image on the reader-printer, he or she simply presses a button and a copy is released from the machine. Most reader-printers produce 8½-by-11-inch printouts, but some may have the capability of enlarging copy up to 18 by 24 inches. Figure 10-2 illustrates several common readers and a reader-printer.

Storage Equipment. The various types of microforms can be stored in a

---

[5]The photographic equipment used for microfilming is highly technical in nature and beyond the scope of this discussion. Readers interested in a more comprehensive description of such equipment should contact the National Micrographics Association (formerly the National Microfilm Association), 8728 Colesville Road, Silver Spring, MD 20910.

Bell & Howell

Microfiche Reader

Bell & Howell

Microfilm Reader-Printer

Bell & Howell

Microfiche Briefcase Reader

Fig. 10-2
Microform Readers and Reader-Printer

haphazard fashion (in desk drawers and on desk tops) or in a systematic manner (utilizing efficient storage equipment and methods) much the same as any other records. For the nonautomated system, a variety of storage equipment is available, as Figure 10-3 illustrates. Desk-top files for quickly accessing microfiche as well as specialized, larger units for storing each of the various microforms are found. Combination cabinet units for storing microfiche, aperture cards, and film jackets are also available and provide quick retrieval of the microform and handy access to the viewer. Film reels are often stored on shelves that offer a compact method for saving space and yet permit fast retrieval of the stored records. Often standard 4-by-6-inch index card boxes are used to store microfiche with alphabetic or numeric tab cards to separate the contents. Usually aperture cards are filed in standard punched-card storage cabinets.

Storage Environment. Records on film are highly sensitive to temperature and humidity conditions. Generally the average air-conditioned office is well suited for preserving such records. Where controlled atmospheric conditions are not found — as in some company archives — over long periods of time the microrecords may crack, mold, or attract dust or dirt that can scratch the surface of the image and thus

Business Efficiency Aids, Inc.

Desk-top Fiche Storage

Business Efficiency Aids, Inc.

Combination Unit

Fig. 10-3
Equipment for Storing Microforms

Managerial Needs	Technical Needs	User Needs
Understanding micrographics	Photographing and processing film	Understanding procedures for storing, retrieving, maintaining, preserving, and destroying records
Designing an effective system of micrographic services	Procuring and maintaining equipment	Using simple equipment (readers, printers, and retrieval or display units) to retrieve information
Managing and controlling all microrecords	Providing continuous service to management	
Anticipating company information needs		

Fig. 10-4
Personnel Requirements for the Micrographic Function

destroy all or part of the stored information. Other hazards, such as fire and theft, require the same environmental controls as given to paper records (see Chapter 9).

Software. To operate the various micrographic services, an effective set of rules, instructions, and procedures or *software* is needed. Software involves indexing techniques and procedures for photographing and processing the records as well as control procedures for storage and retrieval. Some of the software items are entirely manual in nature, while others, such as those required for photographing records in computer output microfilm, operate according to programmed instructions. Generally the same types of control must be employed for storing and retrieving microrecords as those mentioned in Chapter 9. However, the specific details of the equipment, supplies, and procedures are custom designed for each micrographic system.

Personnel. The administration of a micrographic services program requires certain managerial and technical knowledge and skills. Assuming that the micrographic function is operated internally without outside help, the various needs of all personnel involved, as outlined in Figure 10-4, must be satisfied. Due to the simple nature of the equipment, users in most firms can be taught the fundamentals of machine and software operation in a short time. Managerial and technical needs, on the other hand, cannot be so quickly satisfied.

Management of Micrographic Services[6]

Microfilm programs initially were not planned in the typical organization;

[6]The discussion in this section focuses upon internally managed programs in large firms. Many small firms will require an outside agency to handle micrographic services. For a comprehensive treatment of micrographic service bureaus, see David Tierney, "Advantages to Management of Service Bureau Microfilming," *The Office* (March, 1975), pp. 92–93.

they just grew, starting with the filming of cancelled checks and accounts payable files onto roll film to save space and equipment. When new microforms like the aperture card and microfiche appeared on the market, they were usually added, but were not coordinated between the various applications and departments. Often the result became a set of fragmented, nonstandardized, inefficient, and poorly directed programs. Thus, duplication of equipment is found, a lack of standardization in indexing prevails, and little interchangeability of equipment among departments is possible.

To avoid these problems, a micrographic management program is needed. Its purpose is to establish controls over the development, implementation, and maintenance of all micrographic services and to procure and use the most efficient hardware and software for the entire firm. Such a program pulls together into one integrated system all micrographic applications in the firm and permits maximum benefits for the costs incurred.[7]

Planning and Organizing Micrographic Services. The objectives of micrographics involve entire systems; for this reason administrative office managers must look throughout the record system for signposts that indicate the existence of potential applications of micrographic systems in their firms. Eight conditions that, when found,

point to the probable need for micrographic services are outlined below:

1. Large-scale posting operations.
2. High rate of lookups to voluminous files.
3. Need to maintain a record at several locations.
4. Need to capture information on documents in transit.
5. Need to provide an audit trail or method of tracing each microform back to its original source document.
6. Need for an inviolate file (that is, no charge-outs permitted).
7. Need to maintain a large data bank beyond computer capacity.
8. Periodic duplication of a constantly updated file.[8]

Before embarking on such a program, however, a feasibility study should be conducted. To assist in collecting and organizing the voluminous amount of study data, micrographic systems analysts recommend the use of a systems grid (Figure 10-5). As input, answers to questions, such as those following must be obtained: How many people or departments will be involved in the creation of records? What types of equipment, materials, and supplies will be used? And what facilities are necessary to implement the records system? In a similar way questions must be asked about the volume of paper used, the format of each record, turnaround time for the information, how the information will be used, and how the information flows from its origin to its destination.[9] From this information the benefits of a micrographic services program may be anticipated and compared with the

---

[7] For an excellent discussion of micrographic management, see Joseph L. Kish, Jr., "Microfilm is Coming of Age," *Business Graphics* (April, 1975), pp. 6–7. Other good references include William Benedon, *Records Management* (Englewood Cliffs: Prentice-Hall, 1969), pp. 161–178; and selected issues of *Microfilm Techniques* and *Information and Records Management* periodicals.

[8] Alan G. Negus and Edward J. Malkiewich, "The Use of Microfilm as a Creative Systems Tool," *Information and Records Management* (September, 1972), p. 42.

[9] *Ibid.*, p. 43.

expected costs. If such benefits exceed costs, a decision should be made to develop the program.

Converting to Micrographic Services. During the process of converting to micrographic records, the records manager should continue to maintain the hard-copy file until the records retention committee decides that the original documents are no longer necessary. In a manual information system, many active records will still be maintained in their original form. If, on the other hand, the information system is highly automated and the active records can be easily retrieved from the microfile itself, the paper records may be destroyed. However, a duplicate backup file of microrecords should be created for security purposes.

Establishing Operating Procedures. After the conversion to microfilm, procedures for operating the micrographic services program must be

	People	Equipment	Materials	Facilities
Input	1. Document Preparation Clerks 2. System Coordinator 3. Delivery & Mail Service 4. Camera Operator	1. Cameras 2. Work Tables 3. Flood Lights 4. Meters	1. Source Documents 2. Unprocessed Film	1. Preparation Area 2. Filming Area 3. Temporary Storing Area
Process				
Output				

Fig. 10-5
A Systems Grid Form for Collecting Micrographic Feasibility Data

established. The office manager should conduct orientation sessions explaining in detail how the new procedures are to be followed, why they are necessary, and where assistance can be found if needed. These procedures include:

1. *Acquiring equipment.* Of most importance will be the reader, for this machine is usually the only major equipment item that is directly used by each department. Other equipment, such as cameras, processors, and duplicators, will be selected by the micrographic department or the records manager, who may be assisted by outside microfilm specialists.

2. *Analyzing records to be filmed.* Old, brittle paper, torn pages, and turned down or crumpled sheets must be mended, and staples and other fasteners removed. If the data on the record are not legible, the record should not be filmed. Great variation in document size requires a slower and more expensive camera and will add to filming costs.

3. *Describing records to be filmed.* Physical characteristics, such as the name and size of the record, as well as the type and color of paper stock on which it is printed; volume of records to be filed; whether the records are one- or two-sided; and a statement of their condition should be recorded.

4. *Preparing records to be filmed.* The responsibilities of the film requestor (such as removing staples and arranging records in filing sequence) should be listed.

5. *Estimating personnel and equipment required.* It is recommended that the following kinds of information be determined: (a) total number of drawers in job; (b) estimated drawers to be filmed per camera per day; (c) number

of cameras required; (d) total working days required to complete jobs; (e) average number of persons regularly assigned; and (f) film readers required for reference purposes after job is completed.[10]

6. *Filming and processing records.* Specifications such as record size and format of desired output, number and type of duplicate microforms to be made, what coding system to use, desired reduction ratio, and any specific quality control tests to be run should be confirmed.

7. *Inspecting records.* The inspection and inspection procedures should be identified.

8. *Packaging records.* How the processed film is to be indexed, where and when delivery is to be made, and where duplicate records are to be sent should be determined.

9. *Storage procedures.* Each storage procedure should specify the current retention period for each microrecord as well as how the records are filed (alphabetically, numerically, or chronologically). Too, it is important that the frequency of reference to records be known. A formal procedure for requesting microrecords should be developed to serve as evidence not only of records charged out but also of records activity.

10. *Disposing of original records.* Location of original records should be designated, as well as when, how, and by whom original records are to be destroyed.[11]

---

[10]William Benedon, *Records Management* (Englewood Cliffs: Prentice-Hall, 1969), p. 172.

[11]Adapted from Joseph L. Kish, Jr., "A Checklist Approach to Microfilm Proposals," *Business Graphics* (February, 1975), p. 27.

Indexing Systems. Access to any frame on film is fairly easy, if the user knows the location of the frame. To find a microimage requires some form of identification or index on the film by which the frame can be located. Three primary indexing methods, shown in Figure 10-6, are in popular use.

Flash Target Indexing. Flash target indexing is used on roll or cartridge microfilm. With this indexing technique each 100-foot roll or cartridge is divided into five 20-foot lengths by means of a clear "flash" area numbered consecutively from 1 through 5. The alphabetical or numerical filing key for each record noted is on each sheet from which labels for each microfilm carton or cartridge can be prepared.

Code Line Indexing. Code line indexing employs a visual code along with special readers equipped to use this method. When the records are photographed, a special camera with high-density lights forms code lines between each microimage. Later when the roll or cartridge film is viewed in a reader, these code lines appear as solid dark lines that move up and down in accordance with the scale installed along each vertical side of the viewing screen. A user scans the film at high speed, watching the code lines until the position of the lines along the scale indicates a position that is within 10 frames of the desired record. The advance to the desired frame can then be quickly accomplished.

Image Control Indexing. Image control indexing is the most automated of the indexing methods. When the records are microfilmed, an index code number is assigned to each document by a camera attachment; at the same time a high-density light makes a mark (blip) beneath each microrecord. Later the index code number of each document (usually the roll number and the frame number) is registered in an external index for the user to consult. This method of indexing is expensive and requires specialized camera attachments; however, it permits fast access to specific documents, which is very useful in reference work where delays are undesirable.[12]

Aperture cards may have both a printed and a punched-card code index, and microfiche may contain an abbreviated identification name or number at the top of the microform. Retrieval techniques for each of these microforms as well as for automated microfilm retrieval are discussed in the section which follows.

Retrieval Procedures. Finding the stored record is a perennial problem in any filing system. In a microrecord system, however, the number of records may be larger and none of them can be seen without magnification. All retrieval, therefore, requires a reader device.

Retrieval from Roll Film, Cartridges, and Cassettes. A user can scan a film either forward or backward. In a manual system using film that has been flash-target indexed (Figure 10-6), the user can obtain from the index the desired flash area and wind the film until the desired record is located. Time involved may be as low as 60 seconds. Generally, images are stored sequentially along the length of the film, like magnetic tape recordings. Retrieval depends on locating a given serial number position on the film. Additional images are generally placed at the end of the file.

---

[12]Negus and Malkiewick, *op. cit.*, p. 59.

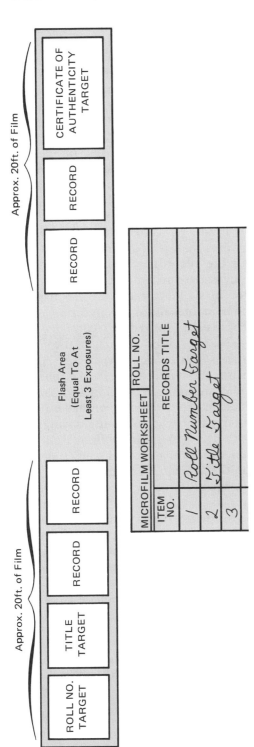

Flash Target Indexing

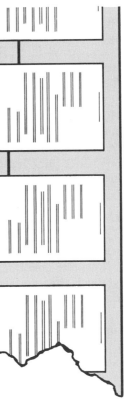

Code Line Indexing

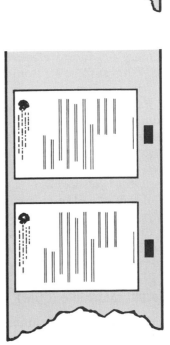

Image Control Indexing

Fig. 10-6
Methods of Indexing Microrecords

Retrieval from Microfiche and Aperture Cards. Because both microfiche and aperture cards are separate units (rather than serial film), both files can be browsed manually like a regular index card file. Both, too, can be automated — microfiche with a separate index of all fiche on file which is scanned by machine; and aperture cards, which are mechanically stored and retrieved like any other punched card (see the section "Retrieval by Punched-Card Machines," page 240, in Chapter 9).

Automated Retrieval Systems. Higher levels of retrieval are available to permit electronic retrieval of data. One such system allows the operator to register in a keyboard the desired frame number obtained from a separate index. The machine advances the film until the frame number matches the preset number and then stops automatically. Another system uses a page search reader-printer to retrieve and view the microrecords. When the records are indexed, they are at the same time catalogued into a small computer-directed magnetic memory for future electronic search. By asking such questions as "How many female employees over 30 years of age have a degree in business administration?" and "How many female employees have indicated an interest in management positions in the firm?," the computer index of microrecords can be searched in seconds and the file numbers of the located microrecords can be displayed on a video screen. Appropriate microforms can then be located and later displayed on the same screen.

Computer Output Microfilm (COM)

Merging the space-saving features of microfilm and the speed of the computer has produced a powerful micrographic service, *computer output microfilm (COM).* The National Micrographics Association defines COM as "microfilm containing data, produced by a recorder from computer-generated electrical signals."[13] Thus, with COM the computer's output is photographed on microfilm for later use in reader equipment. Once the exposed film has been processed, it can be taken to a duplicator which is capable of preparing extra copies of the microrecords.

Finding records in a COM system requires the use of a retrieval code. During the recording process, document numbers are recorded by the COM device in a binary code (the language of the computer discussed in Part 4) adjacent to each filmed document.

Many values accrue to the COM process. For example, when 3,500 documents are reduced in size 48 times by COM and recorded on 16mm microfilm as compared with being printed on computer paper, the following savings are possible: (1) savings in weight — 7 ounces for the microfilm and 40 pounds for the paper printout; (2) savings in postage — 91 cents for mailing the microfilm via first-class postage versus more than $5 for a parcel post mailing of the printout a distance of 1,000 miles; and (3) savings in materials — $4.50 for the microfilm as compared with $35 for one carton of computer paper.[14] Other advantages of COM include bypassing the computer line printer, recording

---

[13]*Fundamentals of Computer Output Microfilm,* (Silver Spring: National Microfilm Association, 1974), p. 3. (The "reverse" of the COM process is CIM, Computer Input from Microfilm, which translates plain language data on microfilm into computer language for storage on magnetic tape as input to a computer.)

[14]*Ibid.*

from 10 to 60 times faster than a line printer, and a low cost of making film copies. In addition, COM serves as an important source of paper savings since, to a great extent, it replaces paper forms and reduces the physical handling of records by as much as 90 percent. COM also provides greater records security and faster access to the records through computer indexing and automated filming operations. Typical business applications include parts catalogs; customer, employee, and vendor lists; and financial records. For managerial control purposes COM is also useful for producing bar charts, scientific plots, and other types of diagrams.

Evaluating Micrographic Services

A person with a knowledge of microfilm applications should be appointed to appraise the efficiency of the microfilm system. Major points in the evaluation should include those listed below:

1. User acceptance and demand for the service.

2. Adequacy of the equipment (sufficient number, properly scheduled and allocated, properly maintained and serviced, and easy to use).

3. Storage (proper environmental controls, effective protective measures, and suitable storage and retrieval devices).

4. Operating conditions (written procedures available for all departments considering microfilm applications; contacts with vendors of equipment and supplies; and effective methods of how to film, store, and retrieve documents).

5. Economies of operation (realistic production standards, and the compilation and use of operating costs of various records storage techniques).

6. Follow-up of the service (periodic evaluation to improve the service to all users.)[15]

Legality of Microfilm. To ascertain the legality of microfilm, administrative office managers should be familiar with both state and federal legislation on the subject. In 1951, Congress passed the Uniform Photographic Copies of Business Records in Evidence Act which established that microfilm copies of business records could be admitted in courts of law if these conditions were met: if the filming occurred in the normal course of business, if the original records were accurately photographed in their entirety, and if they were legible. Since then 48 of the 50 states have enacted their own versions of the act. Most federal and state agencies have their own microfilm regulations concerning the substitution of microfilmed records for hard copies. The Securities and Exchange Commission, for example, allows filming, provided a duplicate of each microfilm is stored separately from the original document. A good guideline to follow is to file a certificate of authenticity (see flash target indexing in Figure 10-6, page 265) as the last document on every microfilm roll. This certificate is an official record of the firm's routine micrographic policy and provides information about the dates and ranges of the records filmed,

---

[15]Persons interested in evaluating present microfilm installations should consult Joseph L. Kish, Jr., "How Efficient is Your Microfilm System," *Business Graphics* (October, 1973), pp. 34, 36.

the date photographed, as well as the signature of the photographer. The firm's legal department should prepare this certificate.

Analyzing Micrographic Costs. The same general cost factors outlined in Figure 9-4, page 227, for administrative paperwork operations also apply to micrographics. The specific factors, however, differ as Figure 10-7 shows.

These major micrographic costs form the basis for evaluating the relative economies of microfilm. With this type of information a break-even point can be determined to justify or to reject microfilming. The break-even point is the point at which the firm "breaks even," that is, the point at which there is no measurable cost advantage in using either type of storage. As shown in Figure 10-8, the cost of microfilming the contents of each four-drawer file cabinet ($178) is compared with the initial cost of the file cabinet ($95) and the cost of space required to store the hard-copy records over the years. "Accumulative

yearly cost" represents the total cost (file cabinet and space occupied by the cabinet) for storing the hard copies. When this yearly cost exceeds $178 (the break-even point), it becomes more economical to convert the hard-copy records to microfilm. A similar type of analysis can be made to determine whether to microfilm internally or use the services of outside agencies.

REPROGRAPHIC SERVICES

In earlier days two processes — spirit and stencil — constituted the bulk of all copymaking in the office and were known largely as *duplicating*. Today, however, the field of duplicating has broadened beyond these two processes, covering offset machines and embodying photographic and telecommunication processes as well. As these processes "serve" to reproduce information for management, they are called *reprographic services* and, for discussion purposes, are classified as duplicating and copying processes in this section.

Equipment Costs
1. Film or file cabinets and shelving
2. Readers or reader-printers
3. Cameras, processors, and duplicators
4. Replacement parts
5. Service charges

Material Costs
1. Paper and carbons
2. Folders and file guides
3. Tabs
4. Microfilm

Personnel Costs
1. Filing time
2. Sorting time
3. Indexing time
4. Searching time
5. Copying time
6. Dissemination costs
7. Microfilming costs

Facilities Costs
1. Overhead
2. Storage area
3. Preparation area
4. Filing area

Source: Alan G. Negus and Edward J. Malkiewich, "The Use of Microfilm as a Creative Systems Tool," *Information and Records Management* (September, 1972), p. 46.

Fig. 10-7
Major Micrographic Costs

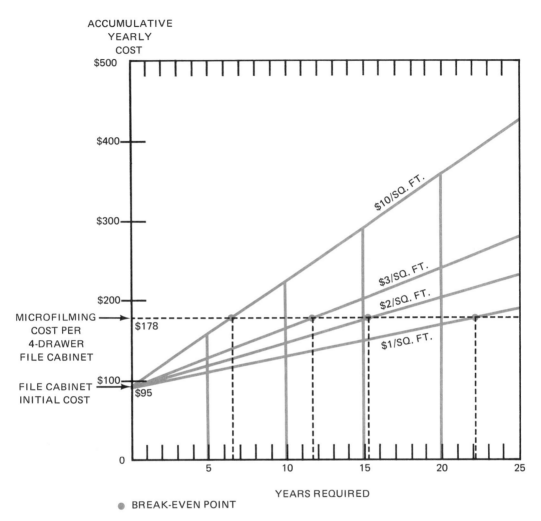

ACCUMULATIVE
YEARLY
COST

$500

$400

$300

$200

$178

$100

$95

MICROFILMING
COST PER
4-DRAWER
FILE CABINET

FILE CABINET
INITIAL COST

$10/SQ. FT.

$3/SQ. FT.

$2/SQ. FT.

$1/SQ. FT.

0

5   10   15   20   25

YEARS REQUIRED

● BREAK-EVEN POINT

Source: Jesse L. Clark and Gloria Wilkes, "Better Record Keeping from Objectives to Working Manual: 2 — The Records Survey: Practical Guidelines for Getting One Going," *Administrative Management* (May, 1973), p. 24.

Fig. 10-8
Break-Even Point Chart Showing
Microfilming v. Utilizing Original Paper Documents

Duplicating Processes

As shown in Figure 10-9 the three types of reprographic machines that make up the duplicating processes are: the spirit duplicator, the stencil duplicator, and the offset duplicator. Often the typewriter and carbon paper are also used to make extra copies of documents as is equipment for duplicating micro-forms.[16] (Automatic typing systems were discussed in Chapter 7 in the section, "Word Processing.")

---

[16]Carbon-copy duplicating is still the most common duplicating method. At the most 10 to 15 readable carbon copies can be made on an electric

Duplicating Process	Copy Range	Machine Speeds (per minute)	Main Advantages*	Main Uses
 Spirit Duplicator	to 400	60-125 cycles	C; COL; EMP; EO; LCC; LMC; S; short runs	"Temporary" runs, forms, general in-house copying
 Stencil Duplicator	60-5,000	60-150 cycles	C; COL; EMP; EO; LCC; LMC; moderate runs	Forms, reports, general copying
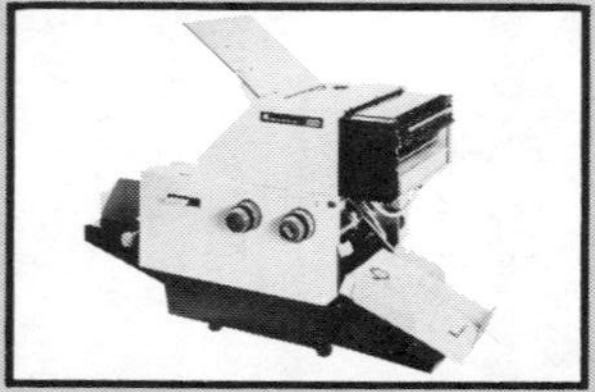 Offset Duplicator	to 20,000 (and to 50,000 with large machines)	60-200 cycles	CQ; EMP; S; long runs	Print-quality work; forms, reports, house organs

*Code: C: Convenience   COL: Color copies   CQ: Copy quality   EMP: Ease of master prepartion   EO: Ease of operation   LCC: Low copy cost   LMC: Low machine cost   S: Speed

Addressograph Multigraph, Multigraphics Division

Heyer, Inc.

Heyer, Inc.

Fig. 10-9
A Comparison of the Duplicating Processes

Spirit Duplicating. For making 400 or fewer copies, *spirit duplicating* (also called *liquid* or *fluid duplicating*, and *ditto*) is the most economical duplication method today. Since alcohol is used as a solvent for the aniline dye used on the special two-part carbon master set, this process is called *spirit* duplicating. To duplicate materials by this process, the two-sheet set (a top or master sheet and a carbon backing sheet) is first prepared by typing, printing, using a thermal copier, or by writing with a stylus, pencil, or ball-point pen. As an impression is made on the face of the master, the back of the top sheet of the set picks up a spirit carbon impression from the carbon backing sheet. The carbon sheet is removed and the master sheet is then clamped on the master cylinder of the machine and the duplicator moistens the master with fluid, which in turn picks up part of the carbon impression of the original master and transfers it onto the copy paper.

Master sets are available in various grades (for long runs up to 400 copies; for medium runs, about 250 copies; and for short runs, about 125 copies) as well as in a variety of colors. Since purple is the most intensive dye, purple carbon gives the greatest number of copies; but red, blue, green, and black are also available. Each color is obtained at the time of preparing the master by changing the color of the carbon sheet. Other features of the spirit duplicating process, such as main advantages and main uses, are outlined in Figure 10-9.

typewriter, fewer on a manual machine. The quality of the carbon paper — some intended for one-time use only — along with the hardness of the typewriter roller and the setting on the electric machine or the touch of the manual machine typist determines how many legible carbon copies can be made.

Stencil Duplicating. In the stencil duplicating process, popularly called *mimeographing*, a stencil is first prepared on the typewriter, with the ribbon in nontype position, or it is written or drawn with a stylus. As the coating on the stencil is penetrated by the typewriter key or stylus point, a porous tissue is exposed which permits ink to pass through. Next the stencil is attached to the duplicating machine; and as the paper is fed through, the ink in the machine cylinder is forced through the openings of the stencil onto the paper. After a "run," the stencil can be stored for reuse at a later time.

Stencils are available in various quality grades and for various purposes. *Photostencils* permit the transfer of photographs, artwork, and drawings; and *electronic stencils*, the automatic copying of straight copy and halftone illustrations by means of an electronic eye that scans the original and cuts the stencil at the same time. Other stencils can be produced by means of the thermal (infrared) process which can accept additional typewritten text. With improvements in preparing stencils as well as in operating the machines (such as automatic inking, paper feeding, and machine stopping), stencil duplicating remains an important duplicating method. This method of duplicating is preferred because of its low cost for moderate-length runs.

Offset Duplicating. This process, sometimes called *multilith*, is the most popular duplicating method for long runs. It offers near-printing copy quality and the capability for quickly producing a large number of copies at a very economical rate. The number of impressions possible can be increased by running two letter-size pages side by side, and one popular model prints both sides of a sheet of paper in a single pass, saving paper and operator time.

The offset principle of duplication is based on the fact that ink and water do not mix. The material to be duplicated is either typewritten, handwritten, or drawn on the offset master or even directly photographed from the original copy. Since water and grease do not mix, the image attracts the ink but the water in the blank spaces repels it, thus making a copy when paper is brought into contact with the image.

Offset machines range from desktop models as shown in Figure 10-9 to large floor presses frequently used in printing plants. Masters are available in a variety of qualities. One large firm gets from 500 to 1,000 copies from each paper master at the rate of .8 cent per copy; for jobs over 2,000 copies, the firm uses aluminum masters capable of making up to 50,000 copies at a cost of .4 cent per copy.

Micrographic Duplicating. One objective of micrographic services, discussed earlier in this chapter, is to duplicate copies of microforms for various users. Duplicate microforms may be produced commercially or internally using one of four special types of duplicators: roll-to-roll, fiche-to-fiche, card-to-roll, and roll-to-card. Fiche-to-fiche duplication is the most commonly used due to the popularity of microfiche.

Copying Processes

Copiers have become indispensable office tools for several reasons. They eliminate as much as 40 percent of a typist's copying work; they are readily available to most office workers; and they are easy to operate. Three basic types of copiers are available: *desk-top*

copiers, for producing a limited number of copies (usually found in smaller firms); *console copiers*, for making copies in large quantities (usually shared by several offices in a firm); and *copier-duplicators*, high-volume units that compete with duplicators. Whether copiers represent the most economical reprographic method depends upon a careful study of the firm's copy needs and a knowledge of the comparative strength of each of the copying processes. The relative advantages and disadvantages of each process are outlined in Figure 10-10.[17]

Diffusion Transfer. This process, also known as *photocopying*, is the basic copying method used in many office copiers. The original document to be copied is placed against a light-sensitive negative sheet and then exposed to light. The original is then removed and the negative sheet placed on a coated light-sensitive positive paper and both are run through a "developer" solution. The two sheets are chemically treated so that the coating on the negative sheet corresponding to the image of the original diffuses into the copy paper (the positive sheet) where it turns black to form a copy.

Gelatin Transfer. In this copying method, also referred to as *dye transfer*, or *verifax*, the original document is placed upon a negative sheet; and as light passes through the negative, it bounces off the unprinted areas of the original and reacts with a chemical coating on the negative. The original is then removed, leaving a negative with a gela-

---

[17]The diazo process is not included in this discussion as it has little general copying application.

tin coating. As the negative comes in contact with the copy paper, the dye from the gelatin is transferred under the pressure of the rollers from the image area of the original to the copy paper.

One negative can be used to make from five to 10 additional copies in rapid succession. However, as the master dries, it becomes more difficult to transfer the chemical; and as more copies are made, the chemical is used up and the copies become fainter. After the first copy is made, each succeeding copy costs considerably less.

Stabilization. This process is similar to both diffusion and gelatin transfer but does not require an intermediate (negative) sheet with a special coating. The original document is exposed to light which is reflected onto a light-sensitive copy paper. The copy paper is

Process	Advantages (A) and Disadvantages (D)
Diffusion Transfer	(A) Produces sharp, high-contrast copies; can copy all colors; machines are compact and relatively inexpensive; equipment requires comparatively little maintenance. (D) Uses wet chemicals; usually involves a relatively large amount of manual operation, although newer models are fairly automatic; copies come out damp and must be dried; usually the cost per copy is relatively high.
Gelatin Transfer	(A) Can make a number of copies (usually up to 10) from a single negative; if several copies are produced from a single negative, the cost per copy is low; can copy all colors. (D) Uses wet chemicals; usually requires a good deal of manual operation, although newer models are more automatic; copies usually come out damp and must be dried; cost of single copy is high.
Stabilization	(A) Requires only one type of coated paper; can copy all colors; reproduces photographs well. (D) Requires wet chemicals; first copy is white on black, unless direct-positive papers are used; copies may gradually deteriorate.
Thermography	(A) No liquid chemicals needed; copies are made easily and rapidly; equipment requires little maintenance. (D) Will only copy inks that absorb infrared radiation — inks containing carbon black or a metallic compound; copies made on treated paper usually darken if exposed to heat; copies are often made on lightweight paper that becomes brittle with age.
Electrostatic	(A) Uses no liquid chemicals; can copy all colors; copies are made on ordinary untreated paper and are permanent; excellent reproduction of printed type. (D) Machine is too expensive for low-volume user; does a fair job of copying photographs and large solid areas; complex machine requires more than usual amount of maintenance; uses a coated drum that must be replaced periodically (usually after about every 40,000 to 50,000 copies).

Source: Reprinted, with permission of the copyright owner, The American Chemical Society, from the July 13, 1964, issue of *Chemical and Engineering News*.

Fig. 10-10

Advantages and Disadvantages of Office Copying Processes

then moved through a developer bath containing a fixing solution, called a stabilizer, which makes the image permanent. The copy is then ready for use after a short drying period. The negative may be stored indefinitely and later used to make as many positives as desired.

Thermography. In this "dry" copying process, also known as *infrared*, *heat transfer* or "Thermo-Fax" (a trade name of the 3M Company), heat is used to form the image. The original document and a heat-sensitive copy sheet are fed into the copying unit which exposes both to infrared rays. The rays pass through the copy sheet and strike the original printed material, which absorbs and holds onto the rays. The heat that is held in the image area causes the corresponding area on the copy sheet to turn dark, thus forming the copy image. A thermographic copier is shown in Figure 10-11.

Only four or five seconds are required for the entire thermographic process. Thermographic copying equipment is relatively insensitive to certain inks and colors. Some copy papers tend to become brittle and to darken when exposed to heat. For speed and ease in making copies, however, the thermographic or "dry" process can be highly satisfactory.

Electrostatic. The electrostatic copying process, for which there are several techniques in use, is based upon the law that opposite charges attract. In one electrostatic copier as the light strikes the original document, the charge remains where the light strikes the printed area. The light that strikes the unprinted areas is dissipated. A black powder, or toner, carrying an opposite electrical charge is then spread over the electrical photograph that covers the plate. The powder adheres to the charged areas and

Fig. 10-11
A Thermographic Copier

produces a visible image, but in reverse. A sheet of paper is next placed above the plate and both pass beneath charging wires. As the paper receives a charge opposite to that of the plate, the powder image leaves the plate and clings to the paper where it is permanently affixed by means of heat.

The initial investment in many electrostatic copiers is high, and for this reason rental arrangements are common.

New Processes. Technical advances in copying processes permit the integration of copying equipment with other types of information-processing hardware. For example, since many kinds of copiers and duplicators can be used to make masters for one or more of the duplicating processes, they are merged together in systems applications. In addition, some copier-duplicator machines combine duplicator speeds with copier quality and operating sim-

plicity. Essentially these machines are copiers that are fast enough to handle work previously undertaken only by duplicators. Required only is the insertion of copy (no special paper is required) and the selection of the number of copies needed, with the machine producing copies at the rate of more than 100 sheets a minute.

Other technological improvements include the capability of producing copies on plain paper, of reducing computer printout to standard letter size, and of reproducing documents on both sides of a sheet of copy paper as well as from bound books and periodicals.

An example of the integration of systems functions is illustrated by the Xerox 400 Telecopier shown in Figure 10-12. By interconnecting the telephone with a facsimile copier, in just four minutes a full page of information with authorizing signatures can be transmitted over regular telephone lines. A related

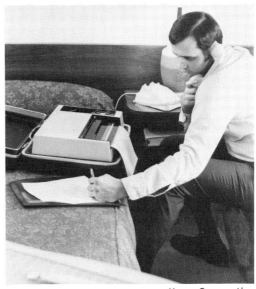

Xerox Corporation

Fig. 10-12
A Telecopier Machine

telecommunication device sends and receives messages without the need of operators, especially after hours, thus reducing communications costs.

Planning and Organizing Reprographic Services

Before installing reprographic services, the administrative office manager should make a careful estimate of the copy needs of the company. This requires that he or she ask each department to furnish data on how many copies of each form, report, and other documents are made; to whom each copy is distributed; how each copy is used and stored; for how long each copy is retained; the condition of each original copy; how frequently copies are reproduced; and what size copy is desired, for reduction and enlargement purposes.

In small firms, one desk-top copier or duplicator may be sufficient to handle the copying volume of the entire firm with no special operator required. Large companies, on the other hand, frequently organize centralized reprographic services departments that utilize many machines and highly trained operators. In some cases copiers and duplicators are placed within individual departments (physical decentralization of machines) even though central control is maintained by reprographic services. Other firms leave both the equipment and its control to the individual departments.

Centralized control of reprographic services is preferred, for it offers several advantages. First, it makes available specialized personnel who can provide high-quality copy work and better care of the equipment. In addition, it permits greater variety of equipment and more flexibility in its use; requires a minimum investment in equipment by reducing the number of duplicate ma-

chines; and provides better scheduling of work, and, ideally, increased productivity. On the other hand, physical decentralization, which is usually self-service, offers each department more flexibility as to what is copied and also reduces travel and turnaround time.

Like other administrative units, a reprographic services department has these managerial responsibilities for organizing the work which it is assigned: procuring efficient personnel and defining their responsibilities, obtaining adequate equipment and space, and developing economical, efficient procedures for providing services to the users. Each of these will be briefly discussed.

Personnel Needs. The responsibilities for operating the reprographic services function normally fall on the administrative office manager or office services supervisor who may supervise the communication services. In a small firm he or she may be assigned many duties and may serve as the supervisor of the duplicating function. In such a setting the day-to-day reprographic work may be handled by secretaries and typists, with commercial printers meeting the larger volume, more complex duplicating needs. In the large firm, on the other hand, a full-time, specialized equipment-oriented supervisor should be appointed. His or her main responsibilities are to select necessary staff, develop production schedules, purchase equipment and supplies, and develop all the necessary operating controls for maintaining a sound reprographic services program.

Selection of Equipment. The selection of equipment involves a great deal more than locating a reliable, low-cost machine. Instead, the initial cost of equipment and its future trade-in value, per-copy cost of equipment operation, as well as maintenance and service contract costs, must be determined. Not only must the factor of low cost be considered but also the equipment selected must be able to produce high-quality copy and maintain required work-load levels for the present as well as the future. Both leasing and purchasing plans should be investigated and the tradeoffs involved in renting or leasing should be compared with equipment purchase.

Worker preferences for machines should also be considered. Such matters as convenience to the worker (fast turn-around time) and reliable maintenance and availability of local service bear close study. Frequently overlooked when equipment is selected are the cost and availability of supplies needed to operate the equipment. Considerable advantage is found in the local purchase of equipment and supplies, especially where service is concerned. Environmental requirements, particularly room temperature and humidity, as discussed in Chapter 6, should also be studied for their effect upon machine operation.

Information on equipment selection is readily available from equipment manufacturers and from professional groups like the Computer and Business Equipment Manufacturers Association and the Administrative Management Society. Managers may also obtain assistance in the careful selection of equipment from such useful publications as *Modern Office Procedures* and *Information and Records Management*, which highlight equipment for information systems.[18]

Planning Adequate Space. Along with maintaining standards of good work layout, as discussed in Chapter 4, the reprographic services center should provide adequate storeroom space for the large quantities of copy paper and supplies required. Other needs include lavatory facilities for cleaning up after operating the machines, darkroom facilities if photographic equipment is used, and acoustical materials to reduce the noise of equipment which can be annoying to office workers in adjacent areas.

Establishing Operating Controls

"Run me off a few extra copies, just in case . . ." expresses a common attitude of office workers toward reprographic services and a lack of understanding of reprographic costs. To overcome these problems, highest priority must be given to setting up effective operating controls that cover personnel and the work procedures. Because of the overall importance of cost control, this topic is treated in a separate section later in this chapter.

Personnel Controls. Only authorized personnel should be permitted to use the reprographic equipment. If not, equipment misuse and downtime can be expected as well as a continuous drain on the budget and the production of unauthorized copies. The most effective use of equipment and supplies can be achieved by training one or more individuals in machine operation and maintenance and in the control of copy quality. The training should emphasize the

---

[18]For a thorough review of the problems involved in selecting copiers, consult Ted Sawyer, "Which Copier Fits the Job?", *Business Graphics* (May, 1974), pp. 34–35. Also valuable is a report on a statewide program on copier management,

Copying — in the State of Washington (Olympia: State of Washington, 1974). Information on this report is available from the Copier Management Center, Department of Printing, P. O. Box 798, Olympia, WA 98504.

costs of reprographic services so that personnel can determine what copies are needed, how well the work is being done, and how much it costs.

Procedure Controls. Personal desires for more copies of documents must be subordinated to organizational needs for information. To do so requires the development of orderly, efficient procedures for performing all phases of the work, for which the following control suggestions should be considered:

1. For authorizing a document to be reproduced use a form like that shown in Figure 10-13, which should be completed by each person requesting copies. This form provides an authorizing signature and other control data regarding volume and cost.

2. For operating the equipment utilize a full-time trained operator if possible; if not, consider a part-time operator for stipulated hours and lock the machine when the operator is not available. Where no operator is assigned, keep the machine under the eye of an office supervisor and post clear instructions on machine use at each work station.

3. For recording usage of equipment keep a log at the machine and require entries for all original or duplicate copies to show who made the copies, for whom, and the quantity. This requirement serves as a control check against the work authorization mentioned above. Periodically examine the logs and furnish summary reports to users and to management for systems and cost purposes.

	REPRODUCTION REQUISITION					
1. Complete form in duplicate. 2. Retain one copy in department.					date	
Copy Number*	Reproduction Method Preferred	No. of Copies	Date Needed	For Rep. Center Use Only		
				Machine Operator	Total Run Time (in hours)	

To be completed by requisitioning department:

Department to be charged: _____   Department code number: _____

For questions, call: _____   Telephone number: _____

Deliver to: _____

Approved by (name, title)

*Number copies if more than one copy is to be reproduced.

(Requisitioning Department)

Fig. 10-13
A Form for Requisitioning Reprographic Services

The use of meter devices for electro-mechanical control over copiers has proved very successful. One such device features a copier attachment for automatic recording of all copies made. This recording is then "fed" into the computer to compile monthly printouts of copies made, lists of users, and total copy costs. Copy costs may also be automatically charged to departments using the machine.

4. Develop standard work methods and copy costs for all reprographic services for the sake of uniformity and efficiency, and allocate charges for all copies made to the requesting department.

5. Group together similar types of copying work to facilitate use of equipment as well as to speed the work. Establish priorities for jobs to be done, and see that delivery dates are met and that the quality of the work is satisfactory.

6. Provide "hands-on" training sessions for all operators (or users, where operators are not available). The experience of operating the copy machine will help employees to estimate a reasonable turnaround time for preparation of copies.

7. Conduct a continuing education program among departments to ensure that only necessary reprographic work is done. These practices in particular should be discouraged: using a copier rather than making two or more carbon copies when an original is typed or using a desk-top copier as a duplicator (or a duplicator as a copier); requesting an unreasonable number of extra ("interest") copies for others instead of circulating one "reading copy" among the staff; reproducing copies of lengthy magazine articles when obtaining additional copies of the magazine would be less expensive; and making copies of materials for personal use.

8. Consider the legality of copied documents, especially copyrighted materials. In 1972 a claims court commissioner ruled that photocopies of copyrighted materials constitute an infringement of the copyright law. These materials may not be copied unless the permission of the publisher or author is obtained. Other materials, such as obligations or securities of the United States government (United States Bonds, certificates of deposit, and paper money are examples), passports, draft registration cards, badges and identification cards of Armed Forces personnel, may not be copied.[19]

Controlling Reprographic Costs

Gone is the day when the costs of extra or unnecessary copies of documents can be ignored. The modern administrative office manager is responsible for a mounting budget for paperwork, which soars in many cases to hundreds of thousands of dollars a year. Good management dictates that a program be set up to control and reduce these costs, starting with a clear understanding of the main reprographic costs and the various methods available for their reduction. Considerable benefit can be derived from studying the reprographic savings programs reported in such periodicals as *Administrative Management* and *Business Graphics* and from reliable sales representatives of equipment manufacturers in the manager's local community.

Reprographic Costs. Two basic categories of reprographic costs are

---

[19]For more information on legal restrictions against reproducing certain materials, the reader should consult General Services Administration, *Copying Equipment FPMR 101-6* (Washington: U.S. Government Printing Office, October, 1966), pp. 6–7.

found: (1) *fixed costs* (that do not fluctuate with changing levels of production) including payroll taxes, heat, light, power, supervision, administrative overhead, insurance, rent or building depreciation, space, and equipment depreciation; and (2) *variable costs* (that tend to change as the level of production changes) involving the costs of power for work produced and the supplies and labor directly related to copymaking. Most of these costs are obvious and should be included in determining per-copy costs.

What is often overlooked, however, are a large number of "hidden" costs that creep into the reprographic operation because they are not directly a part of the copymaking process. These include costs of ordering reprographic supplies and equipment (like getting quotations and dealing with suppliers); storeroom space and shelving costs for storing reprographic supplies; labor involved in stockkeeping and handling invoices and records; mailing costs, since a large portion of the output is mailed; messenger service costs for work that must be delivered; costs of overordering and underordering; costs of the system for charging back all work produced to the requesting department; overtime and borrowed help; and furniture and equipment used by supervisory personnel. In addition, it is wise to add a waste cost caused by overruns, defective work, and excessive paper used in the make-ready operation. When these hidden costs — sometimes adding as much as 100 percent to reprographic costs — are brought to light, a much more complete and successful control of total reprographic costs can be made.

Reducing Reprographic Costs. The following suggestions for reducing reprographic costs should be considered, keeping in mind the types of reprographic processes available within the firm:

1. Select the most suitable equipment for the job to be done. If less than five copies are needed of an original that must be typed, carbon paper is the least expensive production method. If five to 10 copies are needed, in general, a desk-top copier would be more appropriate; and for making more than 10 copies, one of the duplicating processes should be used. The second side of paper should not be ignored.

2. Standardize equipment, methods, and supplies to eliminate an unnecessary variety of machine models from many manufacturers. This permits using uniform supplies bought in large volume from one vendor under quantity purchase discounts. The systems and procedures department, if one exists, should be consulted for advice in increasing the efficiency of reprographic methods, materials, equipment, and personnel. Usually self-service copiers and "captive" departmental duplicating machines should be eliminated and replaced by satellite reprographic centers staffed with full- or part-time operators, messengers, and an office supplies center.

3. From the records of current production of copies compute per-copy costs and make semiannual surveys of anticipated needs of departments. Some firms post usage and cost figures by departments on a monthly cumulative basis compared with the past year's figures. Most workers fail to realize the overall cost of 50,000 copies at 2.5 or 3 cents a copy. This information will help in planning future equipment needs as well as in developing guidelines for copying versus typing carbons versus using each of the duplicating methods.

4. Do not overlook the highly competitive nature of the equipment market and the free services available. Manufacturers' sales representatives can assist office managers in controlling their reprographic costs and can make suggestions for work improvement, as well as provide data on maintenance costs, equipment reliability, and free equipment trial plans. Some vendors offer variable cost plans for leasing metered copying equipment with prices computed in this way: 1–5 copies at 4¼ cents each and 6–19 copies at 1¼ cents each; 20 or more copies — the first copy is metered at 16 cents and the next 100,000 produced monthly at .5 cent each.

5. Make decisions about reprographic services only after first studying all alternatives. The case summarized in Figure 10-14 illustrates this point by comparing Machine A, the firm's present machine, with one recommended for purchase, Machine B. Each year this firm produced an estimated 1,206,400 copies. The anticipated savings of $1,346 would hardly justify the purchase of Machine B as it would take more than five years to cover the investment.

Cost Items	Machine A	Machine B	Difference
Total price................................	$5,000.00	$7,000.00	+$2,000.00
Space requirements.................	200 sq. ft.	250 sq. ft.	+50 sq. ft.
Equipment cost/year.................	$ 440.00	$ 620.00	+$ 180.00
Space cost/year.......................	1,000.00	1,250.00	+ 250.00
Maintenance cost/year..............	1,600.00	1,450.00	− 150.00
Labor cost/year........................	1,869.51	889.80	− 979.71
Supply cost/year......................	2,412.80	1,809.60	− 603.20
Power cost/year.......................	96.51	53.08	− 43.43
Total..................................	$7,418.82	$6,072.48	$1,346.34

Source: Harold W. Nance, "Six Factors to Weigh When Buying Equipment," *Administrative Management* (September, 1971), p. 32.

Fig. 10-14

Comparative Costs of Two Duplicating Machines

1. Differentiate between microfilm and micrographic services. What are the reasons for converting paper records to microform?

2. Identify the various kinds of microforms and compare the relative merits of each.

3. Of all the micrographic equipment, which is the most important from the user's standpoint and why?

4. What types of equipment are typically used for the storage of (a) microfiche, (b) aperture cards, and (c) rolls of microfilm?

5. The term *software* has a special meaning for micrographic services. Define the term and describe its importance to the management of an office.

6. Describe several of the most important managerial problems that stem from a lack of good planning of micrographic services.

7. Outline the main conditions or symptoms in an organization that point to the need for micrographic services.

8. In order to establish efficient operating procedures for micrographic services, what factors must be considered?

9. Three primary indexing methods are used to locate frames on microrecords. Define each method and indicate its purpose and typical use.

10. How does a manual system for retrieving microrecords differ from that of an automated retrieval system?

11. Trace the flow of information in a computer output microfilm (COM) system from the computer to the point of storage.

12. How should an administrative office manager make rational decisions regarding whether to convert to microfilm or retain records in paper form?

13. What basic differences exist in the terms *duplicating* and *reprographic services*?

14. Compare the three duplicating processes (spirit, stencil, and offset) and indicate the relative strengths of each.

15. What factors account for the rapid rise of the office copier during the past decade or two?

16. If you were given the responsibility for selecting copying machines for your firm, what factors would you consider and how would you proceed to acquire the machines?

17. Since per-copy costs of making photocopies seem extremely low to the typical office worker, what measures are available to emphasize the critical importance of reducing copying costs?

18. What advantages accrue to the physical decentralization but organizational centralization of reprographic services?

1. Two business organizations — a bank and a small department store — each maintain an office staff of 10 employees. How and why would the duplicating needs of each firm differ?

2. Anne Estle, administrative services manager for Products Unlimited, asks you to help her organize a study to determine the feasibility of converting paper documents to microrecords. Outline a program for accomplishing this task.

3. The supervisor of the duplicating department of Acker's Mail Order Fashions is often questioned by other departmental managers about the best method of duplicating various communications, some of which are large and some small in volume. Discuss the development of a set of guidelines that describe the relative values and optimum applications for each method.

4. A reprographic services center incurs many operating expenses in the course of its operations. To show management clearly the expenses involved in the work of the center, what type of report would be advisable? What should be its contents?

5. The field of work methods is sometimes called "work simplification" or "efficiency" work. How could such a methods program be applied in the administration of a reprographic services center?

6. Your firm has completed plans for converting to an automated micrographic system in which information retrieval would be achieved by machine with reader-printers available for producing hard copies of records if needed. All departments have given their approval for this conversion except the accounting department head, a key manager, who insists, "My staff cannot function satisfactorily without original records." What arguments should be given to overcome this manager's opposition to the changeover to micrographics?

7. Each of the 10 main departments of the Richmond Electronics Company maintains its own duplicating machine, usually a spirit duplicator, and a copier for convenience. As a result, uncontrolled copymaking occurs in about half of the departments, as indicated by a recent in-house study conducted by a systems analyst. Copying costs have spiraled and complaints are commonly heard in each department. Even though an adequate budget is provided, poor duplicating services are available. The systems analyst has made the following general recommendations to the vice-president of administration:

   a. Initially appoint a full-time supervisor of all reprographic services since the 300 office employees and the large office seem to warrant this move.

   b. Temporarily appoint departmental representatives who will be responsible for controlling each department's copymaking and working with the new supervisor.

   c. Leave the machines in each department, but develop a requisition order form for all copying required.

d. At the end of a six-month period, make a decision as to the organizational restructuring necessary to control reprographic services activities.

Discuss each of the four recommendations as to (1) employee and managerial reactions to anticipate, (2) the wisdom of the organizational changes, and (3) future new personnel to be trained.

8. In the Midway Baking Company some of the office employees use the copying machines to reproduce Christmas letters, wedding announcements, and even recipes clipped from the daily newspapers. As supervisor of reprographic services, what steps do you recommend be taken to stop the unauthorized use of the copying machines?

9. The offices of Cantrell Metals, Inc., require the documents listed below for the month of February. Indicate which of these items might be prepared most economically and efficiently by the office force and which should be provided by agencies outside the office. Also, indicate the type of reprographic service (duplicating or copying) to which each job is best suited.

a. 200 copies of time cards for the office employees. The employee's name, clock number, and date are to be inserted on each card.
b. 20 copies of a two-page bulletin to be sent to each department head.
c. 5 copies of the minutes of the directors' meeting held on February 10, to be sent to board members.
d. 3,000 copies of a two-page form letter to be sent to prospective customers.
e. 500 copies of the eight-page house organ. The company paper, issued monthly, contains snapshots, illustrations, and reading material.
f. 250 copies of notices to stockholders announcing the annual meeting on March 15.
g. 20 copies of a sales analysis report, eight pages in length, for distribution to each of the 20 district sales managers.
h. 20 copies of bulletins to typists suggesting procedures to follow in improving their work. Similar bulletins are issued weekly to the typists who keep them in binders for future reference.

10. Your firm has recently converted to a micrographic system that employs both manual and automated storage and retrieval techniques. While everyone seems to understand how to use the readers for manual retrieval, few understand the more complex automated retrieval. Study the two systems of retrieval and develop a written procedure that management can use to explain microfilm retrieval to users, outlining in simple terms how each system functions.

PRACTICAL OFFICE MANAGEMENT CASES

Case 10-1   Selecting a Duplicating Method

The Crescent National Bank operates from one large, modern urban bank building and 15 suburban branch banks scattered throughout the Greater Boston area. From its beginning Crescent National's management has continued to promote a policy of close personal contact with all its customers, both borrowers and lenders. In fact, one of the standing policies in force through the years, rigidly adhered to by the present chairman of the board, F. Blair Carson, and required of all branch managers, is that top management personally meet and welcome all new customers to the bank. Wherever possible the chairman or his executive vice-president attempts to follow this same practice in the home office. This policy is, of course, admittedly difficult with the great growth in banking services and personnel.

Carson has been in charge of the bank for more than 27 years. During this time he has followed the practice of following up each of the personal welcomes with a short, friendly letter of appreciation to the new customer, normally the next day. The branch managers send out the same letter to each of their new customers from their branches. At the present time the form letter shown in Figure A is being used.

Dear _____:

I was happy to meet you last _____ when you opened a CRESCENT NATIONAL account. I hope that the full facilities of the bank--the savings, lending, and trust facilities and services, especially--have been well explained to you.

The enclosed brochure has been written to give you additional information about our entire organization, including our automatic deposit plan and convenient drive-in facilities. I urge you to study it carefully; and, if you have any questions of any kind, please call me at the telephone number listed on the bank letterhead or call my assistant, _____, at Extension _____.

Sincerely yours,

Enclosure

Fig. A
Sample Form Letter

When the thank-you concept was first initiated, personal handwritten letters were sent. As the banking business expanded, original typewritten letters were sent. Mimeographed letters came into use when the volume increased to its present rate of 185 new customers daily (on the average, about 35 new customers at the main bank and 10 new customers from each of the 15 branch banks).

Carson's administrative assistant, Jan Edmunds, has been asked to look into ways of improving the present stencil-duplicated letter system which requires all branches to maintain stencil duplicators, when in fact this is their main use. Then, too, copy quality varies greatly from branch to branch, partially negating the good image that the letter is intended to create. Her task involves finding answers to these questions:

1. How can an original-looking form letter best be prepared and at what relative cost?
2. What equipment, space, personnel training, and systems changes would such an installation require?
3. How could the insertions of the variable information be made in the form letters?
4. Where can current information on applications of the equipment, initial cost, per-copy cost, maintenance expenses, etc., be obtained?
5. How much time is normally required before such a new system can be installed and functioning satisfactorily?

After carefully examining literature available from manufacturers of office machines and equipment and consulting current office management periodicals and journals, provide answers to the above questions.

Case 10-2   Evaluating Costs of Competitive Reprographic Machines

"Practice what you preach" is an adage that has never been applied in the offices of Management Services Unlimited (MSU), a fast-growing consulting firm located in downtown Chicago. As specialists in manufacturing and information processing systems, the MSU staff has successfully helped their clients to improve production operations, reduce factory and clerical costs, improve customer services, and ultimately improve their overall profit pictures. In fact, MSU's operations have been so successful that the original home office staff of 15 consultants (most of whom had engineering and accounting backgrounds) and 40 clerical workers has expanded into new quarters and now numbers 45 consultants and 150 general office workers. Within the last five years branch offices were set up in six other large midwestern cities.

Ironically, while the firm helped its clients to improve office efficiency, the overall clerical operations at MSU were left to chance. Being a service organization meant that reprographic services were used day and night, and the cost of both equipment and supplies was never questioned. No equipment or supplies standards or cost controls had been developed, nor had any formal operating procedures been put into effect. It was only when the offset duplicator serving the executive offices (including that of the president, Mary Hensley) broke down during the preparation of a report on a multimillion dollar project that the seriousness of the problem surfaced. Hastily, LaVonne Horton, the general office supervisor, called together those of her staff specializing in reprographic work to discuss the problems facing them. The result was a decision to study MSU's total, long-run reprographic needs. Due to the pressing needs of the moment, Horton and her staff were to compare available reproducing machines and procure the best machine possible to replace the scrapped offset duplicator.

The Systems section at MSU's home office verified the need for another offset duplicator; and Horton then called in representatives of four vendors, two of whom were eliminated because their equipment did not qualify for the MSU work. In discussing the copy needs of the firm with the other two representatives, Horton presented this information concerning the average weekly volume of copying:

Documents	No. of Copies Each Week
15 different 2-page bulletins	200 copies each
18 different 1-page forms	500 copies each
10 different 20-page reports	5 copies each

After considering MSU's copying volume, each of the representatives recommended one machine, along with factual information about its purchase price and operating costs. Horton summarized the cost information for the two machines (A and B) as shown in Table A on the next page.

Horton has given this piecemeal information to you to make the necessary computations and compile into a meaningful report so that an objective decision can be made about purchasing the new duplicator. In her discussion with you she requests that the following information be compiled on an annual basis for each machine: (1) net machine cost; (2) cost of space; (3) maintenance cost; (4) cost of supplies; (5) cost of power; and (6) an itemized list of all labor costs involved. Also, the total number of copies made each year should be computed.

COMPARISON OF TWO REPROGRAPHIC MACHINES

Information	Machine A	Machine B
Machine Cost:		
Total Price	$3,600	$4,200
Scrap Value....................................	$500	$700
Depreciation Period.........................	10 yrs.	10 yrs.
Space Required (sq. ft.):		
@ $6 per sq. ft. annually.................	150	175
Maintenance Cost per Year:	$900	$1,000
Labor Cost per Year ($4 per hr.):		
Preparation Time per 100 documents.	2 hrs.	.8 hr.
Load Time per 1,000 copies..............	.04 hr.	.025 hr.
Run Time per 1,000 copies..............	.20 hr.	.15 hr.
Unload Time per 1,000 copies...........	.05 hr.	.025 hr.
Clean-up Time (per week)	1.75 hrs.	.6 hrs.
Supplies Cost per Year:		
Per 1,000 Documents......................	$2.50	$1.75
Power Cost per Year:		
@ $0.03 per Kilowatt Hr...................	20 KW	20 KW

Table A

Compile the report arranged in a format that facilitates cost comparisons between the two machines. Also, recommend to Horton the machine that you believe should be purchased, giving reasons for your suggestions. Subjective features, such as machine design, movability, quietness of operation, and worker preference, should also be discussed in the report.

Part 3

Leadership and Human Relations in Office Administration

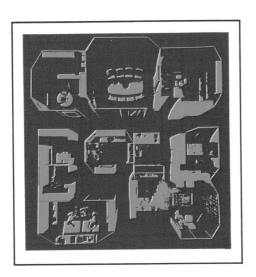

Leading, as a function of management, is concerned with motivating and directing the workers so that the objectives of the organization will be successfully attained. Leadership is present at all levels of the organization — from top-level managers who stimulate, direct, and coordinate the functions of middle managers, to the supervisor of the word processing center who meets his or her daily goals by coordinating and directing the efforts of subordinates.

In exercising the leadership function, administrative office managers place special emphasis upon their human resources, for it is only through people "that things happen." Office managers find that optimum productivity is obtained when they plan and organize their information-management activities around the needs and the talents of their workers and the workers are led, not pushed, into doing their best. To attain the goals that have been jointly established by the office manager and the workers, the office manager must cultivate an environment in which the workers can grow both personally and professionally.

In this third part of the textbook, the function of leading is examined as attention is centered upon these topics: staffing the office, supervising and motivating the office workers; labor-management relations; employee benefits; personnel policies and practices; and training, orienting, and promoting office personnel.

Chapter 11   STAFFING THE OFFICE

Struggling with the problem of how to preserve profits in the face of continually rising personnel costs, administrative office managers find that staffing the office is a vital phase of their daily jobs. Not only must workers be hired but also every effort must be made to keep, to encourage, and to promote these workers. Salary costs, at their highest levels in history and representing an ever-increasing percentage of the cost of products and services, have climbed steadily. The cost of employee benefits (fringe benefits) is about 33 cents of every payroll dollar,[1] which means that, in addition to regular pay, employers spend an average of more than $3,900 annually for benefits for each employee.[2] Another important element that contributes to increased staffing cost is the processing and maintaining of employee records. Marked increases have been noted in the federal, state, and local reporting requirements; equal opportunity compliance records; affirmative action programs; legally required insurance and compensation forms; performance analyses; and job evaluations. All of these record-keeping and forms-completion activities are a substantial charge against a firm's profits.

Recruiting new office personnel has likewise increased in cost. For example,

companies using private employment agencies report that it costs $1,520 to hire a secretary whose annual salary is $7,800; for managers earning $20,000 annually, the cost of hiring is $11,050; for managers earning $30,000 annually, the hiring costs are $18,300.[3] The cost of hiring includes agency fees, interview time, administration (reference checks, medical examination, psychological testing), start-up time (nonproductive time due to unfamiliarity with company methods and products), and, where applicable, relocation expenses. Thus, turnover in an office may represent a loss of at least $1,500 at the secretarial level and between $11,000 and $19,000 for middle- and upper-level managers. To keep turnover at the lowest level is one of the objectives of sound administrative management. Turnover can be kept at a minimum by an efficient selection process, adequate training, and salaries that are in keeping with the skills required and the competitive market conditions.[4]

Obtaining and keeping well-qualified employees for office positions involves a knowledge of the sources of supply, interviewing and testing, maintaining the personnel records required by business and government, and keeping abreast of government regulations

---

[1]"Employee Benefits: Now a Third of Payroll Costs," *Nation's Business* (October, 1976), pp. 36–37.

[2]For the employer's weekly cost of the major employee benefits, see Chapter 14, page 372.

[3]"The High Cost of Hiring," *Nation's Business* (February, 1975), p. 85.

[4]See Chapter 13 for a discussion on how turnover is calculated, reasons for turnover, and how turnover costs may be reduced. The determination of salaries for office personnel is discussed in Chapter 24.

that affect employment processes. In large companies these responsibilities are often assigned to a personnel department, but in small- and medium-size firms the office manager may perform these functions. Therefore, each of these topics is discussed in this chapter. The training, orientation, and promotion of office personnel are discussed in Chapter 16.

SOURCES OF OFFICE WORKERS

The first phase of the selection process is to determine the best sources of employees. Economic conditions, the status of general business activity, and geographic factors affect the relative advantages of the various sources. In the early 1970s unemployed workers seeking employment most frequently applied directly to prospective employers, with the other sources being, in rank order: placing or answering advertisements, using the free services of public employment offices, recommendations of friends or relatives, and placement by private employment agencies.[5] Among the unemployed white-collar workers, however, there was a pronounced use of private employment agencies and newspaper advertisements. This is to be expected since a large percentage of the jobs offered through private employment agencies are of a white-collar nature. Then, too, many employers use private employment agencies to recruit white-collar workers, for the firms find it desirable to have private agencies screen job applicants intensively before referral for the final hiring decision.[6]

The sources used in securing employees vary with different companies, and often, depending upon the type of worker desired, more than one source is used. Administrative managers should be careful in their selection of both sources and employees. Only through a thorough examination of candidates from carefully selected sources can an efficient employment policy be developed that will avoid the mismatching of employees to jobs and the waste of time and money in hiring those employees' replacements.

The selection of the sources of office employees discussed in this section is based on these criteria: economy of time on the part of the employer in interviewing a minimum number of candidates; a prompt and reliable source of qualified workers; reduction of turnover due to careful screening by a reliable source and subsequent elimination by interview; and the creation of a work force that is cooperative, progressive, and happy.

Employment Agencies

In recruiting office personnel, many employers make use of employment agencies, both public and private, for these agencies are in a position to put an employer in contact with a selected number of prospective workers.

Public Employment Agencies. The largest public employment agency is the United States Employment Service (USES), which is supervised by the Department of Labor. Each state has its employment service, sometimes called an employment commission or an employment security agency, which is affiliated with USES. There are USES offices located in every metropolitan area

---

[5]Thomas J. Bradshaw, "Jobseeking Methods Used by Unemployed Workers," *Monthly Labor Review* (February, 1973), p. 35.
[6]*Ibid.*, p. 36.

throughout the country. The full-time state employment offices are generally equipped to offer employers the following services:

1. Recruiting workers in all occupations and meeting employers' personnel needs resulting from attrition, expansion, and staffing of new plants, establishments, and offices.
2. Locating qualified workers — not available locally — through a nationwide interarea recruitment service that includes a professional placement network of selected offices.
3. Selecting the best qualified workers through modern interviewing and testing techniques.
4. Testing and counseling of youths in the fields of work for which their aptitudes and interests best fit them.
5. Giving guidance in resolving employment problems, such as turnover and absenteeism, in maintaining an adequate work force, and assisting in personnel planning by use of job analyses and related techniques.
6. Providing information on labor supply and demand on local, state, and national levels.
7. Initiating training courses to help in alleviating existing shortages of qualified workers and in meeting expected needs for additional trained workers.
8. Relating veterans' service training to civilian occupations.
9. Developing special programs for recruiting older workers, the handicapped, and members of minority groups.

There are no fees for the services provided by USES, and in many localities jobseekers would rather work through USES than pay a private agency fee.

Private Employment Agencies. In competition with public employment agencies are approximately 9,000 privately owned employment agencies. Private agencies charge a fee, depending upon local or state law, which may range from a week's pay to about 10 percent of the employee's annual gross salary. Practices vary according to company policy and geographic location as to whether the fee will be paid by the job applicant or by the employer.

In selecting a private employment agency, the administrative office manager should make sure that the agency is professionally qualified to do its job. Evidence that an agency subscribes to professional and ethical standards may be obtained by checking to see that the agency has membership in its state and national employment agency association. More about the agency's standing and reputation in the community may be obtained from the Better Business Bureau and the chamber of commerce.

Temporary Office Help Services. Temporary office help services "rent out" office workers for varying periods of time such as a day, a week, or two or three months. Use of temporary office personnel has effected significant savings for many firms and enabled them to maintain a lower labor budget without lowering their pay rates.

In utilizing the services of part-time workers, the employer seeking additional help commonly pays a flat fee to the temporary office help service. The temporary employee is interviewed, trained, and paid by the service. The employee's bonding, social security records, tax deductions, accident and sickness insurance, and vacation, if earned, are all obligations of the service. The client-company realizes its savings in the areas of record-keeping costs, payroll taxes, workmen's compensation, vacation and sick time, and use of the employee only when needed. Because of the tremendous increase in the cost of employee benefits, a company is often able to realize considerable savings by relying on temporary help services for its ordinary business situations — not just for emergencies such as peakload periods.

A relatively new development taking place in the use of temporary help services is the Transfer of Personnel plan. Under such a plan the firm recruits its own workers, following its standard personnel practices, and then contracts with the temporary help service to carry the new workers on the temporary service's payroll. Some firms place the new clerical workers they plan to hire on the payroll of the temporary service for a 30- to 60-day probationary period. Thus, a company can retain fully bonded and insured workers during the trial period and the firm's unemployment compensation costs are unaffected if the worker is terminated during the probationary period. One firm that has taken part in the Transfer of Personnel plan cites the following benefits: substantial savings on unemployment insurance costs because of extremely high turnover of trainees; supervisors being able to exercise more discrimination before deciding to make a marginal trainee a member of the permanent staff; supervisors being freer to base their decisions to retain or to terminate more on the actual merit of the trainee than on the potential creation of ill will; reduction of record keeping to a minimum since all payroll accounting is done by the temporary help service; improvement in personnel performance as the trainee becomes motivated to graduate from a probationary status to that of a permanent employee.[7]

In a study of the temporary help industry undertaken by Dr. Paul A. Joray, it was found that an office customer purchases nearly 250 days of temporary office help each year. It was also learned that of the office customers, 70 percent reported that availability of help on short notice was the most important reason for choosing temporary services; 23 percent cited the inconvenience and expenses of hiring and terminating short-term employees as the primary reason for using temporary help.[8] Generally, the survey results indicate that the users feel that temporary help is more feasible than resorting to overtime, spreading the work out among regular workers, or hiring temporary help directly.

The following guidelines are offered to the administrative office manager who is contemplating the use of temporary office help:

1. Determine in advance the hours needed for clerical workload in the department needing help and compare the costs of part-time help on the company's own payroll with that of using temporary help (sometimes these part-time workers are called "temporaries").
2. When ordering help from the service, give a good job description for each position to be filled so that if, for example, a receptionist is needed, a secretary will not be requested.
3. Have the work ready prior to the arrival of the temporary helper by pre-planning complete step-by-step job instructions.
4. Make sure the permanent workers understand in advance that the

[7]For several case histories of firms that have successfully used Transfer of Personnel Plans, see Robert Stover, "Temporary Personnel — More than Just Fill-In," *Management World* (October, 1974), pp. 12–15.

[8]Howard W. Scott, Jr., "The Development of the Temporary Help Industry," *The Office* (December, 1974), p. 20.

temporaries are being brought in for special needs only and not for completing the work of the permanent workers. Ask that the permanent workers be helpful and cooperative in whatever way possible.

5. Make sure that the office equipment is in good working order, supplies are on hand, and space is adequate for the temporaries' needs.

6. Appoint one person to meet the temporary worker, to introduce the worker to others in the department, and to orient the worker briefly to the locations of the lounge, the cafeteria, and the work station.

7. The person in charge of supervising the temporary worker should make sure that the temporary understands the step-by-step instruction sheet by reviewing its contents with the temporary.

8. If possible, employ the temporary helper a day in advance so that he or she can become familiar with the duties of the person being relieved. Company procedures — time for lunch, coffee breaks, handling of personal incoming and outgoing calls, etc. — should be reviewed.

9. If a temporary helper is not producing satisfactorily, contact the service and explain the situation. Usually a temporary can be released after the first four hours and the worker will be replaced by the service.

10. By reviewing the overall performance of each job with the temporaries, ways may be discovered to do the job better and at less cost.

Institutional Agencies. Other sources of office personnel include the nonprofit institutional organizations operated by minority groups, veterans' organizations, churches, charitable organizations, fraternal lodges and clubs, trade associations, and institutions for rehabilitation of physically and mentally handicapped persons, drug addicts, and ex-prisoners. Generally such agencies refer only members of their own groups and charge no fee of the applicant or employer for the services rendered.

Advertising

Before placing advertisements, a careful study should be made of the most profitable form of advertising to use and the most appropriate medium. The type of position to be filled and the local conditions will influence the selection, but a little experimentation will show which is the most satisfactory medium. Care must be exercised in placing advertisements for help wanted to make sure that the wording and the positioning of the advertisements do not conflict with fair employment practices laws, which are discussed later in this chapter. Discrimination statutes prohibit job descriptions in advertisements that show preferences in terms of race, religion, sex, or age. Thus, with respect to age discrimination, expressions such as "young person," "youthful," "teenager," "college student," and "retired person" have been banned.

One disadvantage of placing help-wanted advertisements in newspapers is that a large number of replies may be received, of which it is possible to interview only a few applicants. This method proves very suitable, however, for the firm that has a personnel department adequately staffed to interview, screen, and test applicants.

A source of employees, often aggressive ones, is the "Situations Wanted" columns of local papers. Persons seeking a position often advertise their talents and availability by listing their qualifications in these columns.

In-House Referrals

A firm often obtains satisfactory employees through referral by present employees, company officers, and customers. Great care must be exercised in the use of such in-house referrals, however. If a customer or an officer of the firm recommends a person who is not suitable or qualified for the job, it may cause the firm some embarrassment if the applicant is not hired or is not retained for any length of time. Some firms make a practice of having their employees recommend friends as possible employees because it adds to the prestige of the present employees and creates a good psychological effect. Some firms offer incentives, such as cash payments, United States savings bonds, and company merchandise, for in-house referrals after the newly employed worker has been on the job for a stipulated period of time.

Colleges, Schools, and Their Placement Offices

Many large business firms send representatives to college and school campuses to interview students about possible employment after graduation. In a survey of personnel managers of 100 firms, representing 40 to 74,000 employees, it was found that most personnel managers viewed visitation on college campuses as the best source of young, college-educated talent. These firms also hired more college graduates through college recruitment than all other sources combined. Three sources of college graduates — college recruiting, unsolicited applications, and advertisements — were more important than employment agencies, and about five times as many college graduates were hired through college recruiting as through employment agencies.[9]

If it is not possible to send representatives to college campuses, a firm may write to the placement office of the college, describe the types of job openings available, and ask interested students to submit their personal résumés. Often, however, firms find it difficult to decide from the jobseeker's résumé whether or not to invite the applicant to visit the company. In such cases it may be less expensive to have a company recruiter visit the campus than to have applicants visit the company for interviewing. For those firms that use private employment agencies and pay the agency's fee, campus recruiting may turn out to be less expensive than recruiting through agencies. There are both favorable and unfavorable factors in campus recruitment. One firm, for example, would hire graduates from a certain college only, because the president of the firm was a graduate of that school. Executive prospects coming from one school tend to provide only one viewpoint on managerial problems. While this may supply harmony, it may also lead to stagnation. On the other hand, some firms wish to hire only inexperienced employees so that they may train them in methods peculiar to their work. For these firms, this source may prove helpful, especially if they are hiring inexperienced personnel for long-term employment.

Many private business schools maintain a placement service for their students, some of whom have had office experience. A number of high schools, junior colleges, community colleges,

---

[9]Terry L. Dennis and David P. Gustafson, "College Campuses vs. Employment Agencies As Sources of Manpower," *Personnel Journal* (August, 1973), pp. 721–724.

and universities cooperate with industry by setting up apprenticeship and cooperative work-study programs in which students attend school part-time and work part-time. Some companies sponsor a summer-hire program in which during the junior or senior year the student works for the company during the summer months. If the student's work proves satisfactory, he or she is asked to return the following summer at an appropriate salary increase. Such cooperative training programs develop many good trainees who later become full-time employees of the participating companies.

Other Sources of Office Employees

Additional recruiting sources used by firms include applicants who walk in from the street and apply for a position and applicants who have written unsolicited letters of application. Also, some manufacturers of office equipment have established training schools and placement agencies to supply their customers with well-trained, efficient operators of their equipment.

PROCEDURES FOR EMPLOYING OFFICE WORKERS

The employment procedure in small offices is quite simple compared with that in offices having large staffs of workers. In small offices an interview is usually all that is necessary, followed by a statement that within a few days the applicant will be informed if he or she has been successful. In this way no decision need be reached until a sufficient number of candidates has been interviewed. In larger offices, however, the procedure becomes more formal and perhaps more complicated, since the larger the office staff, the more necessary records become.

Federal, state, and local laws affecting the employment process have stimulated the need for more complete and detailed records of employees. For the medium-size office, the employment records should include, as a minimum, the application blank and the employment record. Where the organization has become so large as to require the special services of a personnel manager, the other forms discussed below will become necessary in order to establish a definite procedure and adequate control over the employment of workers.

The forms used in the offices of most large firms are:

1. Personnel requisition blank.
2. Application blank.
3. Record of interview.
4. Record of employment.

The large amount of clerical work involved in handling all these forms would be justified only in a very large organization. These employment records can be adapted to smaller offices by eliminating all but the basic forms — the application record and the employment record — which, in turn, may be consolidated.

Personnel Requisition Blank

To many people, the application blank is probably the first office employment record of any importance. Its use in large offices, however, is sometimes preceded by the personnel requisition blank prepared by a department head. The latter form specifies the number of persons required and the kind of work to be done. If the office has prepared job specifications, they are studied in order to obtain specific information concerning the job requirements.[10] This is preliminary to any search for a job applicant. If a list of suitable applicants is kept on file, reference is made to this list so that persons may be notified to call for an interview. If no such list is kept, the sources previously mentioned are consulted.

Application Blank

Probably the most frequently used form in the selection process is the application blank. Traditionally, application blanks have served the purposes of aiding in predicting job success and providing information for administrative use. The information called for on an application blank is usually grouped under the headings of personal information, education, business experience, references, and general remarks. In designing their application blanks, employers must be careful to request only data shown to be useful in predicting job-relevant behavior and not to ask questions that may become the basis for charges of discrimination under the fair employment practices regulations. For example, questions that request sex or religion are clearly inappropriate unless it can be shown that they are bona fide occupational qualifications. Questions about race, marital status, and national origin are also unacceptable. Questions on certain touchy areas, such as sexual or religious practices or certain personal characteristics, are doubly dangerous; for not only are they illegal on the basis of their relevance to job requirements,

but they also represent an invasion of privacy.

State departments of labor examine application blanks to make sure they are prepared within the meaning of the law. Whenever there are inconsistencies between federal requirements and state laws, federal requirements may take precedence. For example, in many states the fair employment practices legislation makes it illegal to identify the race of the applicant or employee on individual personnel records. However, federal agencies have found it useful to have this information for studying the possible existence of discrimination in a firm. The federal government may, therefore, request that certain companies maintain such records, with the stipulation that the information will not be used for unfair discrimination.

Careful use of application blanks permits a preliminary screening of applicants for a position, thus saving the time of interviewers. Companies that plan to use the application blank for selection purposes, such as a predictor of job success, should develop a weighted application blank.[11] In developing a weighted application blank, a job analysis study is undertaken to determine the abilities, skills, knowledge, and other characteristics necessary to perform each job. Next, application blank items are selected that do not violate any provisions of the fair employment practices laws. Finally, following the procedures discussed later in this chapter, the validity and reliability of the application blank must be determined, just as with psychological tests.

---

[10]The preparation of job specifications, as part of the total job study program, is discussed in Chapter 22.

[11]Clemm C. Kessler, III and George J. Gibbs, "Getting the Most from Application Blanks and References," *Personnel* (January–February, 1975), pp. 53–62.

The Interview

Social scientists have shown that past behavior and experience predict future behavior and that past learning, acquired habits, and previous accomplishments carry over into the future. Thus, in using the interview and biographical information as aids in selection, interviewers recognize that the typical applicant will continue to behave in familiar ways, ways acquired from previous experience and training.[12] As a result of studying the application blank or the personal data sheet of an applicant, the interviewer can select specific areas to explore more fully or to clarify during the interview. The interviewer should be on guard against arriving at immediate conclusions regarding the personality, intelligence, skills, and abilities of the job applicant. In many instances, especially during the early phases of the interview, job applicants may not show themselves at their best nor show the true kind of face-to-face impact they ordinarily make. Possibly only after an interview has been under way for several minutes and rapport has been built do applicants loosen up and reveal some of their hidden feelings. Thus, the interviewer should try to remain as objective as possible and resist drawing conclusions about the applicant until the interview is well under way and plenty of evidence is available to substantiate the interviewer's feelings.

During the interview the personal appearance of the individual can be evaluated and related to the job opening and to any dress codes that the firm may have established. In many firms dress codes are flexible in relation to the job and the extent to which the job holder meets the public. For example, one insurance company prohibits any of its male employees from wearing beards if they meet and work with the public in the course of their workday. However, in some departments of this firm, such as data processing and accounting, beards are acceptable.

In the process of arriving at an opinion — positive or negative — regarding the suitability of the applicant for the job at hand, the interviewer should strive to preserve the applicant's sense of dignity and self-respect. At the close of the interview, the applicant should be able to leave with a positive feeling toward the company and its position in the community. In some instances, especially where more responsible positions are being filled, it may be advisable to schedule a second interview in order to check on impressions gained during the first meeting and to insure that the applicant still displays interest in the position. During the second interview, senior members of the firm may be called upon to interview the applicant to make sure that the individual is well-qualified for the position.

In eliciting information from the job applicant that relates to education, training, and experience, there are several types of interviews, or approaches, that may be employed. Four of these types are briefly described in the following paragraphs.

The Direct Interview. In this traditional interviewing technique, job applicants are asked direct questions related to their qualifications and ability to fill the job. The direct interview can be completed relatively quickly since a concise answer is required for each specific question. However, use of this

---

[12]For an overview of the approach to developing a validated biographical form, see William D. Buel, "An Alternative to Testing," *Personnel Journal* (May, 1972), pp. 336–341.

method limits the amount of information that can ordinarily be obtained. For this reason, the direct method is most commonly used when screening applicants for jobs of a fairly low level. In using this technique, the interviewer must be careful in wording the direct questions, for oftentimes no more will be learned than a specific answer to the question asked, or in the question, the interviewer will reveal the desired answer. Further, the interviewer must make sure that no questions are asked that pertain directly to race, color, sex, religion, age, or national origin unless the question is directly related to bona fide occupational qualifications.

The Indirect Interview. The indirect, or unstructured, interview rests upon the premise that more can be learned about applicants by stimulating them to talk about themselves than by asking them direct questions. By listening and being patient, the interviewer can learn much as the applicants elaborate on important points, such as why they left their former jobs. During this time the interviewer has an excellent opportunity to determine how well the applicants demonstrate their qualifications and to observe their self-expression, along with other factors such as manners, poise, and dress. The indirect interview is time-consuming and requires an able interviewer who can keep applicants from digressing too far from the subject at hand.

The Patterned Interview. The patterned interview is also known as the guided, standardized, or structured interview. A printed form or questionnaire, containing specific key questions, is used by the interviewer as the questions are asked and the applicant's answers are recorded, either during or immediately after the interview. This technique is especially effective when many people are being screened to fill a number of jobs, usually at a lower level. Time is saved by obtaining the same type of information from all applicants. Also, more than one interviewer may be used at the same time, with the evaluations being compared and reviewed by a senior executive such as the personnel director.

The Stress Interview. The stress, or probing, interview, mainly used by the military and other governmental services, is carried on by one or more persons who fire questions at an applicant, who is kept continuously on the defensive. The objective is to find the applicant's breaking point and to determine how much pressure can be applied. Even in the hands of skilled interviewers, this technique is a highly controversial one, especially when relating its use to business and industry. If not properly handled, the interviewing situation may damage the employer from a public relations point of view, and, of course, ruin the ego of a very sensitive applicant.

Record of Interview. The record of interview contains in an organized form all the information acquired during the interview. The form aids the interviewer in remembering all factors and in making a thorough analysis of the final recommendations regarding an applicant's employment. If the personal nterview has been favorable and there seems to be a possibility of early employment, a subsequent interview may result in further use of the interview record. This brief checkup of the personal characteristics of the applicant is then used in conjunction with the application blank in making a final decision. It should not be assumed, however, that the employment manager, office manager, or interviewer makes the final selection in any but a small number of cases. Usually the interviewer makes a preliminary selection from among all those who apply, but leaves the final selection to the manager in whose department the vacancy exists.

Letters of Reference

Many managers do not place too much confidence in references or letters of recommendation for several reasons. First, if the persons named as references were not likely to give favorable comments, their names would not have been given by the applicant. Second, most people hesitate to write unfavorable letters of recommendation. If information is requested from the references that are listed on the application blank, oftentimes the letters may not be answered. If answered, the letters are often vague, noncommittal, or incredibly glowing.

For those positions in which employees must be bonded, an insurance company will make as thorough an investigation as possible and use formal inquiry blanks for this purpose. Some large public accounting firms use a printed inquiry blank for checking references. Although this is a routine matter, even for some large offices, many firms feel that it should be done, if only for its psychological effect.

When checking references, a telephone call can be effective if the interviewer is careful to establish good rapport with the reference and to ask carefully phrased questions. In the conversation, the interviewer should strive to follow up on every hint or clue, or else there is a risk of accepting biased information. Although long-distance calls may be expensive, they are an excellent means of checking references

when time is of the essence and thorough information is essential.

In many communities there are reporting agencies, generally known as credit associations, that record such information as dates of employment, salaries earned, and civic offices held. Although these agencies are utilized primarily to provide credit ratings to business people, they can be used by the hiring firm to obtain factual, objective information about a prospective employee and to perform special field investigations. Under the Fair Credit Reporting Act of 1971, however, the employer is required to tell an applicant when a retail credit investigation is being made and whether the firm's rejection is the result of the credit check.

Record of Employment

The record of employment consists of a brief personal status and a history of the applicant's employment. In addition to providing personal data and other information usually found on the application blank, this record may provide space for recording such information as the employee's progress, attendance, promotions, and salary increases.

THE USE OF TESTS IN SELECTING OFFICE WORKERS

The use of tests in selecting office workers is not prohibited by government regulations, Supreme Court decisions, or Department of Labor actions. However, those testing practices that have a discriminatory effect upon job applicants are prohibited. Among the charges that have been leveled at testing practices in the past are: (1) many existing tests do not adequately evaluate the capabilities of members of disadvantaged groups, and the disadvantaged may score poorly because of anxiety about the testing situation and because of low motivation; (2) most tests, especially verbal measures, emphasize middle-class concepts and information and are thus unfair to those who have not been exposed to such cultural influences; (3) test scores do not have the same meaning for the disadvantaged as they do for the advantaged; test scores of the disadvantaged, it is held, should be compared only with test scores of others similarly disadvantaged; and (4) test items are often not related to the work required on the job for which the applicant is being considered.[13]

Today, however, as a result of the U.S. Supreme Court ruling in the *Griggs v. Duke Power* case, "Any test must measure the person for the job, and not the person in the abstract."[14] The word "test" is currently interpreted broadly to include any paper and pencil or performance measure used as a basis for any employment decision. Thus, included in today's concept of testing are not only traditional kinds of tests but also the personal history, scored application forms, scored interviews, and interviewers' rating scales. Today *all* aspects of employment procedures are open to scrutiny from the viewpoint of potential discriminatory personnel practices.

---

[13]Jerome E. Doppelt and George K. Bennett, "Testing Job Applicants from Disadvantaged Groups," Test Service Bulletin No. 57 (New York: The Psychological Corporation, May, 1967), p. 2.

[14]On March 8, 1971, the U.S. Supreme Court unanimously declared that practices that act to artificially exclude applicant groups because of race or other factors and that cannot be shown to bear a *predictive* relationship to job performance violate the law. Nothing in the ruling prevents employers from excluding minority members, but if they do, they must be able to demonstrate a substantial relationship between the test scores and critical job performance.

Kinds of Preemployment Tests

The different kinds of preemployment tests may be classified as:

1. *Intelligence tests*, which measure mental and reasoning ability to the extent that the one tested is able and willing to demonstrate it through the medium of a particular test.
2. *Aptitude* and *ability* tests, which attempt to predict the measure of success for applicants with little or no experience for the job and for whom a firm may have to make long and costly investments in training and experience should the applicant be hired.
3. *Achievement* tests, which attempt to measure the degree of proficiency in a given type of work, whether this has been obtained in jobs with other firms or with the present firm, in anticipation of promotion.
4. *Personality*, *interest*, and *attitude* inventories, which measure personality traits.

Test experts are not agreed upon what the tests should indicate. Some professional testers maintain that a battery of tests is necessary in order to test the variety of abilities required for a specific job; others feel that every job can be analyzed into certain basic requisites which can be discovered by a single test. Thus, many offices experiment with a number of the standardized tests on the market and supplement these by tests of their own creation, until experience has shown the testing practices and procedures to be valid and reliable.

Installing a Testing Program

The use of tests in a program of selecting office workers is based upon the two principles listed at the top of the next column.

1. There is need for an unbiased, objective basis for selecting, placing, evaluating, and promoting office employees.
2. Tests are not exclusive devices, but *supplemental* tools in the total assessment of personnel.

Before a testing program can be installed properly, management must be sure that the program can be used successfully. The following conditions seem to indicate when a valid and reliable testing program can be used:

1. A firm either has in its employ or must hire a large number of persons doing similar work for which there are more applicants than positions.
2. An excessive turnover of office workers is traceable to inefficient hiring practices.
3. There is evidence of inefficient work as the result of low aptitude, training, or interest.

Whether the testing program should be part of the personnel manager's activities or should be handled by a professional organization of industrial psychologists depends upon the number of workers that must be hired from time to time. The cost of tests and the trained personnel that must administer and interpret the tests is more than some firms wish to spend. Large companies may develop their own tests or have them designed by a consulting firm of professional testers. The cost for developing a preemployment test, such as intelligence, skills and abilities, aptitude, and personality inventories; standardizing the test; preparing test manuals; and conducting the required validation studies ranges from $25,000 to $250,000.[15] Many companies purchase ready-made tests from one or more of hundreds of test publishers in the United States.[16] In selecting tests from those developed by test publishers, the following factors should be considered: the reliability of the test, its validity, and its validity for different populations (which may or may not be similar to that of the company employee population).

Reliability. A test that is to be used in selecting office workers should have a high degree of reliability. The reliable test should measure consistently whatever it measures in that the same general score can be expected if the test is given to the same person a second time. The information that is published about a test should describe its reliability.

Validity. A test is valid if it can be shown to serve the purpose for which it was intended. For example, the validity of an employment test rests on whether a score on the test predicts a level of performance on the job. If the test predicts performance, the test is valid. If the test does not predict performance, the test is not valid. Through the validation of its tests a firm can determine not only what tests are appropriate to use but also how they should be used. In a survey of the companies represented on the American Society for Personnel Administration-Bureau of National Affairs panel, it was found that more than 40 percent of the small firms and nearly 60 percent of the large companies have validated their personnel tests, and about two thirds of those who have made validation studies

---

[15]Peter Koenig, "Testing: The Industrial Psychologist's Headache," *Management Review* (October, 1974), p. 41.

[16]An invaluable aid in the selection of tests is Buros' *Mental Measurements Yearbook* series, which presents a listing of tests, critical evaluation of the tests, and a directory of test publishers. The *Yearbook* series may be obtained from The Gryphon Press, Highland Park, New Jersey, and from many public libraries.

find that their tests correlate with success on the job.[17]

Tests, such as typewriting and keypunching tests, that have been professionally constructed and can be shown to measure an important aspect of the job are usually acceptable without validation. However, tests not so obviously job-related, such as tests of general mental ability, may be required to undergo validation. To show that its testing practices are job-related, a company may undertake validation studies that are either criterion-related or content-related.[18]

Criterion-Related Validation.

Criterion-related validation is used to determine the validity of those kinds of employment tests that are not samples of the essential job skills. The aim of this kind of validation is to show statistically that a relationship exists between the scores of a group of persons on a test and their subsequent respective performances on the job. The test scores are correlated with important elements of work behavior that are considered to be relevant measures of job performance. Such measures include work proficiency, training time, supervisory ratings, regularity of attendance, and tenure on the job. When a statistically significant showing is made, the test score can be used to predict how that person being tested would perform on

the job for which he or she is being considered.[19]

Content-Related Validation.

Content-related validation is used to evaluate well-developed tests, such as typewriting skills tests, to make sure that the content consists of systematic and logical samples of the knowledge, skills, or behavior essential to the jobs. A content-related validation study requires that each job be analyzed to determine the knowledge, skills, and behavior required for job performance. The test is then examined to show that the factors being tested are realistic, job-related samples.

Differential Validity.

Not only must tests be validated for their job-relatedness, but, wherever technically feasible, they must also be differentially validated by reporting the results separately for minority and nonminority groups. The objective here is to standardize the tests given to whites against normal white scores, tests given to blacks against normal black scores, etc. Thus, employers must validate each test for each minority group to make sure that the test scores fairly predict job success, since it has been established that test validity will ordinarily differ among various ethnic groups.[20]

Tests Based on Expectation of Promotion.

Tests designed to determine an individual's ability to function at a level higher than the entry-level job need not be validated against the entry-level job, provided the new employee will probably within a reasonable period

---

[17]*Personnel Management*, Bureau of National Affairs Policy and Practice Series (Washington: The Bureau of National Affairs, Inc., No. 264, 1975), p. 201:244.

[18]For a very fine presentation of a test validation case study designed to serve as a model for the small company, see Richard J. Walsh and Lee R. Hess, "The Small Company, EEOC, and Test Validation Alternatives: Do You Know Your Options?" *Personnel Journal* (November, 1974), pp. 840–845.

[19]James C. Sharf, "How Validated Testing Eases the Pressure of Minority Recruitment," *Personnel* (May–June, 1975), pp. 56–57.

[20]David E. Robertson, "Employment Testing and Discrimination," *Personnel Journal* (January, 1975), p. 19.

of time and in a majority of cases progress to a higher level. However, an employer may not validate a test against the requirements of a higher level job if the job progression is not so nearly automatic, or if the time span between hiring and promoting is so long that the nature of the higher level job or the employee's potential to fill it may be expected to change significantly in the intervening time.

In summary, even though office managers find that the official guidelines regarding the procedures to be followed in validating tests are not at all clear, it has been clearly established that only properly validated tests can be used and warnings have been given against the exclusive reliance on test results in selection decisions.

Trends in Employment Testing

As a result of the 1971 Supreme Court decision in *Griggs v. Duke Power*, which ruled that employment tests can be used only if they are job-related, there appears to have been a downswing in the number of firms using testing programs of any kind. For example, in one study of companies ranging in size from 780 to over 500,000 employees, it was found that prior to 1971, 53 of the 60 companies were using testing programs at the factory, clerical, or managerial/professional levels. Following the court ruling, however, eight firms (among the smallest of those polled) dropped their testing programs altogether. Evidently these firms felt that validating their testing programs was more trouble than it was worth, and thus they may have decided that it was more feasible to give up testing as part of their selection procedures rather than run the risk of possibly violating the

court ruling. The largest firms surveyed reported that they had administered and properly validated tests in use long before the court ruling. Also noted in the survey was a 25 percent increase in the number of firms validating all of their tests, with a particularly marked increase in the validation of managerial/professional tests. Among the medium-size firms a trend appeared toward an increased use of outside psychologist-consultants as test validators.[21]

The firms sampled predicted that greater reliance will be placed upon good interviewing techniques in the future or, more drastically, the normal selection procedures of the past will be scrapped in favor of a simple probationary period. In his concluding remarks, the author of the study states that it seems likely that tests will continue to play an integral part of the selection process, with much more attention given to validation of the tests, particularly in upper-level occupations.[22]

Another example of the trends in testing is provided by a poll of the testing practices of the firms that make up the American Society for Personnel Administrators-Bureau of National Affairs panel. The following findings came forth: about 45 percent of the companies stated they did not use personnel tests (although in 1963, 90 percent of the firms were using tests); about 50 percent of the small firms and about 60 percent of the large companies were using tests; more than 90 percent of the small and large firms use preemployment tests for office personnel such as typists, clerks, and secretaries; and of those testing, more than 90 percent use standard tests

---

[21]Donald J. Petersen, "The Impact of Duke Power on Testing," *Personnel* (March–April, 1974), pp. 32–36.
[22]*Ibid.*, p. 37.

prepared by companies specializing in publishing tests.[23]

Among the various alternatives to the traditional employee selection practices that have been proposed are: no formal employee selection procedure at all, as in China where no job tests are given but peers are selected for jobs by their peers; testing for competency rather than for intelligence by using tests that measure, for example, one's capacity to learn quickly; developing a hiring system based on an equal exchange between employer and job applicant, with the company stating what needs to be done and the applicant saying what he or she has to offer; and, because people have been deprived of skills to do well on tests, teaching people to do better on tests or encouraging them to take practice tests.[24]

GOVERNMENT REGULATIONS AFFECTING THE EMPLOYMENT PROCESS

With the passage of federal legislation requiring that companies eliminate discrimination from all aspects of employment, a new era in labor relations emerged. To comply with the pertinent laws and the requirements of their companies, today's administrative office managers must be thoroughly conversant with federal, state, and local regulations in order to solve the problems of fair employment and those affecting wages earned, hours worked, and minimum age requirements.

---

[23]*Personnel Management*, Bureau of National Affairs Policy and Practice Series (Washington: The Bureau of National Affairs, Inc., No. 264, 1975), p. 201:244.

[24]Peter Koenig, "Testing: The Industrial Psychologist's Headache," *Management Review* (October, 1974), p. 41.

Civil Rights Act of 1964

For the first time, in 1964, a national policy of fair employment practices was expressed by law. Nearly half of the pages contained in the Civil Rights Act of 1964 affect administrative managers and their responsibility for staffing the office. Although the act contains sections dealing with voting rights; prohibition of discrimination on the basis of race, color, religion, or national origin in hotels, restaurants, and certain other facilities; and the creation of new federal agencies; the present discussion is concerned with Title VII, known as "Equal Employment Opportunity." This section of the act, affecting the hiring practices not only of business firms but also of unions and employment agencies, defines certain actions (or inactions) as unlawful employment practices. For the purposes of the Civil Rights Act, as amended in 1972, an employer is defined as a person engaged in an industry that affects commerce and having 15 or more workers for each working day in each of 20 or more weeks in the current or preceding calendar year. With the passage of the Equal Employment Opportunity Act of 1972, state and local governments became subject to the provisions against employment discrimination contained in the Civil Rights Act. The 1972 act also obligated the federal government to undertake all personnel actions without discrimination. The authority to ensure equal employment opportunity in federal agencies is assigned to the Civil Service Commission.

As a result of the Civil Rights Act and its subsequent amendments and executive orders, if an employer fails or refuses to hire job applicants because of their race, color, religion, national origin, or sex, the action is looked upon as an unlawful employment practice. It is unlawful for an employer to discharge any individual "or otherwise to discriminate against any individual with respect to his compensation, terms, conditions, or privileges of employment" because of that person's race, color, religion, nationality, or sex. Further, an employer is prohibited from limiting, segregating, or classifying employees for the reasons given above if doing so "would deprive or tend to deprive any individual of employment opportunities, or otherwise adversely affect his status as an employee."

Separate provisions bar similar discriminatory practices by employment agencies and labor organizations. Both employers and unions, or joint labor-management committees, are prohibited from discriminating, on the bases mentioned above, against an individual in apprenticeship or training programs, including on-the-job training.

Employers are still permitted to hire and train persons on the basis of either their religion or sex when these are bona fide occupational qualifications (BFOQ) necessary to the normal operations of the business. Thus, if it can be shown that the sex of applicants would prevent them from performing successfully on the job (a BFOQ), then this qualification may be used as a basis for selecting among job applicants. Also, for reasons of national or state security, information about the applicant's national origin and creed may be a BFOQ. However, the task of demonstrating that a discriminatory requirement constitutes a BFOQ rests with the employer.

Employers may not place help-wanted advertisements that specify any preference, limitation, specification, or discrimination based on sex unless sex is a BFOQ. This provision has been inter-

preted to mean not only that the content of classified ads must be free of such preferences but also that the placement of ads in separate male and female columns, when sex is not an occupational qualification for the advertised job, is in violation of Title VII. Employers may legally refuse to employ members of the Communist Party or Communist-front organizations. If the hiring firm is subject to the government security program, it may refuse employment to or may discharge any worker who does not fulfill the security requirements of the governmental position.

Employers may continue to apply different standards of compensation or different terms and conditions of employment, provided such differences are not the result of an intention to discriminate on account of race, color, religion, national origin, or sex. Thus, employers may set their hiring and work standards as high as they please, but they may not enforce them in a discriminatory manner among racial groups. When selecting employees on the basis of tests, employers may administer and act upon the results of any professionally developed ability test, provided the test is not designed or used to discriminate. A "professionally developed ability test" is interpreted to mean a test that fairly measures the knowledge or skills required or which fairly affords the employer a chance to measure the applicant's ability to perform.

Under the Civil Rights Act an Equal Employment Opportunity Commission (EEOC) was created to help enforce the law. The EEOC tries to obtain voluntary compliance with the law before a court action for an injunction is filed. The Commission may seek a temporary restraining order or other preliminary relief where a preliminary investigation determines that prompt action is needed to carry out the purposes of the act. If the Commission cannot reach an acceptable agreement with the party within 30 days, the Commission can file suit in a federal district court. However, where a state or local law forbids discriminatory practices, relief must first be sought under the state or local law before a complaint is filed with the Commission. Beginning in 1974, the EEOC was authorized to institute court proceedings for an injunction if there is reason to believe that any person or group of persons is engaged in a pattern of noncompliance with the law.

If the court finds that employers have *intentionally* engaged in an unlawful employment practice, it can enjoin the employers from engaging further in the practice and order "affirmative action" such as hiring back the aggrieved party with or without back pay. The Supreme Court appears to encourage federal judges to grant back-pay claims where unlawful discrimination has been shown. The Supreme Court has said that Congress intended the equal employment laws to accomplish two major objectives: to eradicate discrimination and to "make persons whole" for injuries caused by past discrimination.[25]

During the 1975 economic recession when the unemployment rate was especially high among women of all races, black men, and black teenagers, minority groups and women saw another discriminatory pattern come about in the discharge practices of firms. As the recession deepened, minorities and women felt discriminated against since they were among the first to be laid off. During the spurt of equal opportunity

employment in the late 1960s and the early 1970s these groups had been the last to be hired. Organized labor has always used the last-hired, first-fired principle as a cardinal rule, for it is the heart of the seniority system. Seniority clauses had been incorporated into labor contracts in the 1930s to protect workers from their bosses and to remove from management the discretion of determining who would be let go in bad times. The Civil Rights Act approves bona fide seniority systems but does not define what is meant by a seniority system and leaves the definition to the courts. In June, 1977, the Supreme Court ruled that unless a seniority system intentionally discriminates in its coverage, it is not illegal. Thus, according to this interpretation, "neutral" seniority systems can legally perpetuate favored employment for white males if the system were operating before the Civil Rights Act took effect.

Executive Orders

Employers not subject to Title VII coverage discussed above may come within the scope of the Civil Rights Act by reason of a contract or subcontract involving federal funds. In a series of executive orders, the federal government has banned, in employment on government contracts, discrimination that is based on race, color, religion, sex, or national origin. More significantly, the orders have been held to require that contractors take affirmative action to ensure equal opportunity.

Executive Order 11246. Executive Order 11246 is the major antidiscrimination regulation for government contractors and subcontractors who perform work under a federal construction contract exceeding $10,000, and for the

[25]"Justices Endorse Back-Pay Grant in Job-Bias Cases," *The Wall Street Journal*, June 26, 1975, p. 4.

United States government itself. The Office of Federal Contract Compliance (OFCC) of the U.S. Department of Labor sets policy and regulations for implementing the Executive Order. OFCC sex discrimination guidelines provide, among other things, that contracts may not advertise for employees under male and female classifications, base seniority lists on sex, deny a person a job because of state "protective" labor laws, or make distinctions between married and unmarried persons of one sex only.

Revised Order No. 4. Revised Order No. 4, issued by the OFCC, requires nonconstruction contractors with 50 or more employees and a contract of $50,000 or more in federal government work to take affirmative action to eliminate the employment barriers to minorities and women. The concept of affirmative action was developed to clarify in a concrete, positive way what firms seeking to do business with the federal government must do to be truly equal opportunity employers. Unless specifically exempted, employers are obligated to specify attainable results-oriented goals and timetables for recruiting, hiring, training, and upgrading minorities and women, where they have tended to cluster in low-paying, dead-end jobs. This order, which has the force of law, has increased opportunities for women to be considered for jobs previously labeled "men only" and to be admitted to training that could accelerate promotion.

State and Local Fair Employment Practices Laws

Most states have adopted fair employment practices laws. Such laws do not supplant Title VII of the Civil Rights Act, since the purpose of the federal law was to encourage more states to adopt such laws and to stimulate increased activity under the laws already in existence. Generally the state fair employment practices laws are aimed at employers, employment agencies, and unions. Employers are forbidden to discriminate in their hiring and firing practices and unions and employment agencies are forbidden to aid or cause such discriminations.

Cities, too, have enacted ordinances that prohibit discriminatory practices in the employment process. One of the most comprehensive and enlightened laws of its kind is the Human Rights Law of the District of Columbia. As shown in Figure 11-1, this law covers discrimination by reason of race, color, religion, national origin, sex, age, marital status, personal appearance, sexual orientation, family responsibilities, physical handicap, matriculation (formal education completed), and political affiliation.

Age Discrimination in Employment Act of 1967

The purpose of the Age Discrimination in Employment Act of 1967, as declared by Congress, is to promote the employment of older persons based on ability rather than age, to prohibit arbitrary age discrimination in employment, and to help employers and workers find ways of meeting problems arising from the impact of age on employment. The law prohibits age discrimination by employers, employment agencies, and labor unions (that are engaged in an industry affecting interstate commerce) against those individuals who are between the ages of 40 and 65 years. No protection is extended directly to individuals outside these age limits.

Equal Employment Opportunity

It is unlawful for any person to practice discrimination in employment in the District of Columbia on the basis of:

Race	**Sex**	**Family Responsibilities**
Color	**Age**	**Physical Handicap**
Religion	**Marital Status**	**Matriculation**
National Origin	**Personal Appearance**	**Political Affiliation**
	Sexual Orientation	

Title 34 of the D.C. Human Rights Law prohibits acts performed wholly or partially for a discriminatory reason:

> "By an employer. To fail or refuse to hire, or to discharge, any individual; or otherwise to discriminate against any individual, with respect to his compensation, terms, conditions, or privileges of employment, including promotion; or to limit, segregate, or classify his employees in any way, which would deprive or tend to deprive any individual of employment opportunities, or otherwise adversely affect his status as an employee; . . ."

Similar prohibitions apply to the services of an employment agency and to membership in a labor organization.

Complaints of possible violations of this Regulation may be filed with:

Government of the District of Columbia ·

Office of Human Rights

District Building, 14th and E Streets, N.W., Room 22, Washington, D.C.
Telephone 629-5331   •   James W. Baldwin, Director

Fig. 11-1
Bases for Unlawful Discrimination in the Human Rights Law of the District of Columbia

Under the law, employers of 20 or more persons are forbidden to fail or refuse to hire, or to discharge, any individual, or to otherwise discriminate against any individual with respect to compensation, terms, conditions, or privileges of employment because the individual's age lies within the specified range of 40 to 65 years. Employers are also barred from using age as a basis for limiting, segregating, or classifying employees in any way that deprives or tends to deprive them of employment opportunities, or otherwise adversely affects their status as employees. The law is enforced in accordance with the powers, remedies, and procedures provided in the Fair Labor Standards Act, which provides for enforcement through suits by individual employees, collective actions by employees, and wage collection suits and injunction suits by the Secretary of Labor. By means of Executive Order 11141, contractors and subcontractors engaged in the performance of federal contracts are prohibited from discriminating against persons because of their age unless age is a BFOQ.

In many cities a concerted drive is being made to find jobs for those over 40 who are unable to obtain work, primarily because of their age. The usual reasons given for not hiring older workers show that they are too slow, too set in their ways, less creative than younger workers, more difficult to train, more prone to absenteeism, and not in as good a physical condition as younger workers. With the exception of the last reason, which is applicable only to heavy physical work, the reasons are mostly myths.

Many businesses fail to make use of the reservoir of talent available through the hiring of older workers. Many older persons find themselves in a position to take seasonal and part-time work, and administrative managers should consider this source of labor when filling those jobs as well as jobs requiring the services of full-time employees.

Vocational Rehabilitation Act of 1973

The Vocational Rehabilitation Act of 1973, covering nearly 12 million individuals of employable age, is designed to provide employment opportunities for qualified physically and mentally handicapped individuals and to eliminate employment discrimination based on a physical or mental handicap.

Federal agency contracts exceeding $2,500 must include an affirmative action clause requiring that the handicapped applicant or employee will be given appropriate consideration and will not be discriminated against because of a handicap. Affirmative action applies both to the initial employment and other considerations such as promotion, training, transfer, termination, accessibility, and working conditions.

Vietnam Era Veterans' Readjustment Assistance Act of 1974

Under the provisions of the Vietnam Era Veterans' Readjustment Assistance Act of 1974, government contractors with federal contracts or subcontracts of $10,000 or more are required to take affirmative action to employ and advance in employment qualified veterans of the Vietnam era and disabled veterans. Employers are also required to list all suitable employment openings with the appropriate local employment service, which will then give referral priority to Vietnam era veterans.

Wages and Hours

The wages to be paid and the hours to be worked by newly employed persons and those presently employed are regulated under federal law by a number of statutes. Those having broadest application to the administrative manager are the Fair Labor Standards Act and the Walsh-Healey Act. The former, commonly known as the Federal Wage-Hour Law, applies to employment in private industry; the latter imposes additional regulations upon employers who are government contractors. Under the Equal Pay Act of 1963, an amendment to the Fair Labor Standards Act, an employer is forbidden to discriminate solely on the basis of sex in the wage rates of men and women doing equal work under similar working conditions. States have clearly defined laws regarding the employment of minors, and the Federal Wage-Hour Law imposes similar restrictions on the employment of minors. These regulations, and others affecting the compensation practices of office managers, are discussed in detail in Chapter 24, in the section "Office Salary Administration."

QUESTIONS FOR REVIEW

1. What services do public employment agencies offer the employer who is recruiting office personnel?

2. What steps should the administrative office manager take to make sure that the private employment agency selected is professionally qualified?

3. In what ways does the use of temporary office help effect significant savings for employers?

4. Briefly describe the main types of employment forms used in the offices of large firms.

5. Why must special care be taken by employers in designing their application blanks?

6. What are the advantages and disadvantages of using the direct interview when compared with the indirect interview?

7. Why do many managers place little confidence in references or in letters of recommendation?

8. Cite several charges that have been leveled against testing practices in the past.

9. How is the word "test" currently interpreted by the courts?

10. What two basic principles should guide the administrative office manager in using tests as an aid in selecting office workers?

11. What conditions are usually present in a firm that indicate the need for a valid and reliable testing program?

12. Distinguish between the testing concepts, reliability and validity.

13. For what reasons should an employment test be differentially validated?

14. What seems to be the trend in the use of employment tests as a result of the *Griggs v. Duke Power* case?

15. What provisions in the Civil Rights Act of 1964 have most relevance for the administrative manager?

16. May an employer hire a person on the basis of sex? Explain.

17. Describe the concept of affirmative action.

18. For what reasons was the Age Discrimination in Employment Act of 1967 enacted?

19. What protection is provided by law to prevent discrimination in the employment of the physically and mentally handicapped? of Vietnam era veterans?

QUESTIONS FOR DISCUSSION

1. On some application blanks there is an essay-type question that often begins, "I would like to work for this company because. . . ." What does the job applicant's answer to this question tell the office administrator in charge of employment?

2. In staffing their offices, some firms encourage in-house referrals. What are some possible objections to this source of job applicants?

3. Some firms have every job applicant fill out an application blank, even though the jobseeker is obviously not fitted for the position. Why is this done?

4. Would it be recommended to ask about a job applicant's arrest record either on the application blank or during the job interview? Why?

5. The proposed 27th Amendment to the U.S. Constitution, the Equal Rights Amendment (ERA), states that: "equality of rights under the law shall not be denied or abridged by the United States or by any State on account of sex." With passage of the proposed amendment, what effects do you foresee on the employment process? on labor legislation?

6. Among the questions appearing on the application for employment form of the van Amstel Company are the following:

   a. Have you ever worked for van Amstel under another name?
   b. Give the name of your church and list the religious holidays you observe.
   c. Indicate the name of your birthplace.
   d. Are you a citizen of the United States?
   e. Indicate the foreign languages you can read, write, or speak fluently.
   f. Are you living with anyone?

In view of federal and state civil rights laws, do you believe that van Amstel is acting legally or illegally in asking each of the questions listed above? Explain.

7. Two years ago you employed Juan Rosario, a 38-year old veteran, as a junior accountant. On his application blank, Rosario indicated that he was a college graduate, with a minor in accounting. Rosario has been an outstanding worker, and you pride yourself on having selected him from among several well-qualified applicants. Two days ago, as part of a security clearance check, you find that Rosario shaved five years off his age when he applied and that he was never graduated from any college. For two days his lying has been gnawing away at you; in spite of his exceptional performance, it is his lying that grates on you and you are seriously considering his dismissal. Explore the pro's and con's of retaining Rosario and anticipate the decision you shall make.

8. Gladys Downs, in applying for a secretarial position with a chemical firm, was instructed on the application form: "Complete this form in your natural handwriting; DO NOT PRINT." In filling out the form, however, she paid no particular attention to these instructions and proceeded to print neatly the answers to all questions. Her application was rejected for "graphological reasons." Downs exploded in front of the personnel manager: "This is not fair at all! I can take shorthand at 100 words a minute and type 90 words a minute. I feel I have a pleasing personality and dress very well. Why should I be turned down because I don't cross my t's to suit you?" As the personnel manager for this firm which relies heavily upon graphology (handwriting analysis) in its personnel selection, how would you explain to Downs the rejection of her application?

9. At the Atlanta field office of the Food and Drug Administration, Gary White felt that everything was proceeding smoothly in the interview process and that the Civil Service job of clerk-typist was his. Toward the end of the interview, White was asked why he had moved from Detroit and was searching for government work in Atlanta. White replied that since he began his undergraduate studies he had been living with his friend, Robert Alms, and when Alms accepted a position in Atlanta, White came along in the search for work. After White told his story about living with Alms and why they had both relocated, he sensed that the interviewer had become aware of White's homosexuality. It seemed as if the interview ended abruptly with the closing words, "We shall notify you after we have talked with several other applicants."

Two days later White learned via the grapevine (from a worker in the field office) that the job had been filled by a person who had scored exactly the same on the Civil Service test as White and who, like White, had no prior experience in office work. White has come to the conclusion that he was barred from employment with the government because of his sexual orientation.

Was the interviewer's line of questioning ethical? Is it legal for the federal government to bar a homosexual from employment?

Assuming that the field office proceeded illegally in its selection process, what steps might White now take?

10. Jean Harper, a black woman, was employed by the High-Line Power Company in 1968, four years after passage of the Civil Rights Act. In 1974, along with several hundred other unionized black men and women, Vietnam veterans, and Spanish-speaking Americans, Harper was let go because of the firm's cutback in production. Along with the others discharged, Harper felt that she had been unduly discriminated against because she was among those most recently hired by the company but among the first to be fired. Representatives of those fired appeared before the state's fair employment practices commission seeking relief.

    Did the company proceed legally in discharging first those who had been most recently employed? Do you believe that the minorities and the women discharged were unduly discriminated against? What alternative solutions do you have to offer to solve the problem of last-hired, first-fired?

11. During her interview for the position of bank teller at the Plymouth Savings and Loan Company, Lenore Zielinski was asked to sign a statement indicating she agreed to undergo a polygraph (lie-detector) test. Zielinski asked the interviewer why the test was required as a condition of employment. The interviewer replied that the objective of having applicants take lie-detector tests is to check their basic honesty and to verify information on the application form such as previous employment, arrest records, and use of alcohol and drugs. The interviewer went on to say that if an unstable person were employed, the company's equipment could be damaged.

    Impatiently Zielinski listened to the interviewer's explanation and then broke in saying, "I refuse to take the test. It's illegal to require me to take such a test in order to get the job. You are invading my personal privacy."

    Is the use of a polygraph illegal as part of the preemployment screening process? Is the company invading the personal privacy of the applicant? Do you believe that the results of polygraph tests are valid predictors of behavioral patterns and personality traits?

12. Friday afternoon Barry Grossbach, office manager of the Cardin Equipment Company, called a local temporary help service and requested a secretary for several days' work during the end-of-the-month rush. Monday morning Eleanor Dickens reported for work. After two days Grossbach found that Dickens was a highly competent worker, got along well with her boss and coworkers, and took on responsibility as if she had been with the firm for years and expected to be there for years to come. Toward the end of the first week of work, a permanent vacancy occurred among the secretarial force and Grossbach approached Dickens with a full-time job offer. He was pleased to find that Dickens liked the company and would like to become a full-time employee.

    Was Grossbach unethical in approaching Dickens with an offer of full-time employment? What steps should Grossbach take now to obtain the services of Dickens on a full-time basis? What are the ethics and business practices involved in hiring a temporary worker on a permanent basis?

PRACTICAL OFFICE MANAGEMENT CASES

Case 11-1   **Discriminating in Departmental Transfers**

Prior to the passage of the Civil Rights Act, it was the policy of the Romo Company to employ minority group workers solely for menial jobs such as sweepers, maintenance personnel, and messengers. Following passage of the act, however, the company abandoned its discriminatory practices and recruited minorities for good jobs with better pay. Such changes in company attitude were readily noted by Bill Horn, a black who had been with the company for over 10 years as a messenger in the mailroom. Via the grapevine Horn learned that a vacancy would soon exist for the job of duplicating machine operator. Immediately Horn contacted the personnel manager, Ed Boyle, and placed his bid for the job opening to guarantee that he would be among the first applicants interviewed.

Boyle was impressed with Horn's qualifications at the time of the interview. It was discovered that Horn had already learned just about all there was to the job of duplicating machine operator, for he often served as "fill-in" when emergencies arose. Horn was hired on the spot at a salary higher than he was receiving in the mailroom and transferred to the new department — the reproduction department. A few weeks later, Horn came into Boyle's office with the following question: "While I was in the mailroom for more than 10 years, I had more seniority than almost anyone else there. Since I am now in a new department, I still have that 10 years' seniority, don't I?"

Boyle replied, "No, Bill, you no longer have your seniority, for it is our policy for each department to have its own seniority roster. Thus, when you transferred out of the mailroom, you lost your seniority. Now you will have to start at the bottom of the ladder in the reproduction department."

Horn, taken aback, retorted: "You know that all those years I was in the mailroom I could have handled the duplicator and have been in the repro department. But because of the color bar, I was stuck on the job as messenger. Now, since I am starting as a newcomer in repro, I may be the first one fired if work slows up. You mean when I accepted this transfer, I lost all my seniority?"

Boyle agreed, "Yes, that's right — company policy, you know. I wish I could help you, Bill, but. . . ."

After telling his story to the civil rights organization to which he belonged, Horn found that the group would hire a lawyer to bring suit against Romo and force the company to restore Horn's seniority. The group's lawyer maintained in court that Horn would have been in the reproduction department for years if it had not been for the company's discriminatory practices. In conclusion, the lawyer stated that the only fair thing for the company to do would be to grant Horn equivalent seniority.

As a representative of the Romo Company, answer the following questions:

1. What arguments can you advance in defense of your firm's practice of not transferring a worker's seniority when that worker is transferred from one department to another?
2. In view of current civil rights legislation, how would you expect the lawsuit to be decided?

Case 11-2 Hiring Part-Time Workers or Using Temporary Help Services

The Bieg Can Company, faced with an upsurge in demand for its glass canning jars and jar lids, has found it necessary in January to increase its full-time production force of 400 by 80 persons. It is anticipated that the increased demand will be firm and the plant workers will become permanent additions to the plant work force. In the office this means that, until several more processing operations are fully automated in the order processing department, six more clerical workers will be needed for three months. With this part-time help, the total number of office workers will be 76. In this department the office employees work a 35-hour workweek and are paid twice a month.

The plant and office are located in a state where the maximum unemployment tax rate is 2.7 percent of the first $6,000 paid each worker. However, because of the firm's excellent past unemployment record and the state's merit rating plan, its state unemployment rate has been reduced to 1.3 percent of the first $6,000 paid each employee. At the present time all workers in the plant and in the office earn more than $6,000 each year. If, however, the firm hires part-time workers and terminates their employment after 10 weeks, it will lose its merit rating and the state tax rate will be increased to 1.5 percent.

Bieg can either hire the six part-time workers and add them to its own payroll or it can obtain the services of six clerical workers from Salomone's Temporary Help Service. Doris Carver, supervisor of the order processing department, has asked you to make a cost analysis of the two approaches available in meeting her department's part-time needs. From the payroll department and conversations with Salomone, you have accumulated the following cost data:

Approach A: Hiring the part-time workers and placing them on Bieg's payroll:

Semimonthly salary of each worker	$365

Payroll Taxes:

Federal Insurance Contributions Act tax (Social Security tax)...	6.05% of gross salary paid, up to $17,700
State unemployment compensation tax............. (The current rate, 1.3%, will increase to 1.5% since it is planned to terminate the services of the part-time workers after three months).	2.7% of first $6,000 paid each worker
Federal unemployment compensation tax..........	0.7% of first $6,000 paid each worker
Workmen's compensation insurance	$0.07 per $100 of gross payroll
Other employee benefits (paid every part-time employee who works more than 20 hours each week):	Estimated at 15% of worker's base salary (covering nonproductive time, holidays, sick leave, etc.)
Hiring costs (advertising and recruiting, testing, screening, interviewing, application forms, reference and credit checks, payroll preparations and processing):	Estimated at $325 per worker.
Separation costs (terminal interview, processing, and termination pay):	Estimated at $300 per worker.

Approach B: Obtaining the six workers from Salomone's Temporary Help Service:

Hourly rate for each worker..................................	$5.20
Other costs (contacts with Salomone, furnishing job descriptions, preparation and processing of monthly checks, etc.):	Estimated at $275 per worker.

Prepare a report for Carver in which you show a detailed analysis of the costs for each of the two approaches and the economic feasibility of the approach you recommend be taken by Bieg Can Company.

Chapter 12

SUPERVISING AND MOTIVATING OFFICE EMPLOYEES

In Chapter 1 it was shown that in the process of managing, the functions of planning, organizing, controlling, and motivating are performed at several levels in the organization, from top management through middle management to supervisory management or operating management.[1] This chapter examines in detail the nature of supervising at the operating management level. At this level the office supervisor plans and organizes work experiences in such a way that both the employees' needs for satisfaction through use of their abilities and the firm's need to be economically effective will be met. The objective of such an integration of needs is to create an organization in which employees, when striving to meet their own needs, are also inevitably making major contributions to the organization's needs.[2] Supervision also involves control — securing actual performance that approximates as closely as possible the desired performance. Finally, supervision is greatly concerned with motivating — moving employees to action to perform the maximum quantity of quality work and to have them happy and satisfied while doing it.

The practical aspects of managing at the supervisory level involve the performance of a certain job by the one *best method* and by the one *best person* in order to obtain the *best results*. A trained supervisor is therefore needed to assure the accomplishment of these three aspects of carrying out a job. The supervisor attempts to achieve these results through careful planning and scheduling, and through effective leadership arising from cooperation; for, wherever more than one person is involved in any job, the best results can be obtained only by the utmost cooperation of all persons concerned.

RESPONSIBILITIES OF THE OFFICE SUPERVISOR

In the small office an office manager directs all the information-processing activities. As the office work expands, a centralized transcription department or a word processing center may be developed under a trained supervisor. Further expansion may necessitate supervisors for centralized departments concerned with records management, computer services, mailing services, and reprographics. Whatever the organization or the number of supervisors, the jobs of office supervision are essentially the same. The jobs require working through and with human beings — superiors, peers, and subordinates — to develop and carry out the plans of office work, to establish systems and procedures that include the measurement of the work,

---

[1]See page 4 and, in particular, Figure 1-1.

[2]David A. Whitsett, "Making Sense of Management Theories," *Personnel* (May–June, 1975), p. 45.

and to improve the work systems wherever possible.

All supervisory positions involve a certain amount of responsibility. This responsibility has direction; that is, there is responsibility *upward* to higher management, *horizontal* to supervisors of equal rank, and *downward* to subordinates. There are also *coordinating* responsibilities for the work to be done, and *self-development* responsibilities as the supervisor prepares for growth and promotion in the business organization. An outline of each of the office supervisor's key responsibilities and its direction is given in Figure 12-1.

MOTIVATION AND HUMAN RELATIONS IN OFFICE SUPERVISION

Men and women do not become supervisors merely because they meet the test of being the best workers and because they know intimately the workings of their departments. In addition to these requisites, supervisors must use the human approach, which means that they must be specialists in dealing with human beings. In their work with human beings, supervisors are continually being appraised as to their genuine value as executives. Determining the work to be done and how to do it is the easiest task of supervision since it deals with the *objective* phase of the position. Most important, however, is the human, or *subjective*, phase of supervision. Herein lies the secret of motivating and leading employees.

Successful office supervisors must possess certain personal qualities if they are to command that respect and loyalty from workers which insure the maximum efficiency in a department. Foremost among these attributes is the ability to treat subordinates as human beings, to be one of the employees without sacrificing any dignity of the executive position. Supervisors cannot be too intimate because with intimacy often comes leniency, and with leniency comes the loss of respect and confidence. Yet, aloofness and a policy of strict discipline are equally poor; the supervisor commands obedience at the cost of cooperation. Between these extremes lies an attitude, a personality, that makes a supervisor a leader rather than a boss; this is the attitude that wins the utmost cooperation.

Impartiality, open-mindedness, and fairness are required of office supervisors in dealing with the everyday problems that at times threaten to disrupt the efficient functioning of their departments. They must be ready and willing to see both sides of problems and to solve them fairly and reasonably so that no bitter resentment remains in those against whom the decision goes. They must be available for advice when approached by subordinates and be patient and understanding in dealing with their individual and personal problems. Finally, good supervisors will keep all promises and "stick up" for cooperative workers when dealing with other departments and with top management.

It is the job of the office supervisor to motivate — to create the enthusiasm and desire to work, and this is best accomplished by treating workers as human beings, not automatons. The following humanizing incentives help to create this enthusiasm and desire: meaningful work experiences; a belief in the importance of the job; good working hours; a comfortable working environment; financial security; congenial working companions; fair treatment from superiors; the opportunity for advancement, to use one's own ideas, and to learn the job; full information via good communication practices; and appraisal of one's performance.

Some office supervisors are able to profit from a self-analysis of their understanding of human relations involved in supervision and of the extent to which they create a "desire to work" on the part of their subordinates. To aid in such a self-analysis, the supervisor may use a checklist and scoring device such as that shown in Figure 12-2, which was published by a firm of personnel development specialists.

In addition to possessing desirable personal qualities, supervisors must see that certain psychological conditions as well as material satisfactions exist in their departments. Several of these conditions and satisfactions are discussed in the following paragraphs; others will be treated throughout the following chapters in this part of the book.

Delegating

Delegation has been defined as:

> . . . the process of establishing and maintaining effective working arrangements between a manager and the people who report to him. Delegation results when the performance of specific work is entrusted to another, and the expected results are mutually understood.[3]

In discussing several leading principles of management in Chapter 3, it was noted that office supervisors have a responsibility to themselves and to their subordinates to delegate effectively the authority and responsibility for the work

to be done. As true leaders, supervisors plan for more efficient operation of their departments by strengthening the confidence of their subordinates and developing their initiative and capability. Supervisors have a moral responsibility to their company to inspire their workers by giving them a chance to assume new responsibilities and to explore new methods on their own. Supervisors must realize that, to a great extent, the future of their company lies in the hands of the men and women who report to them. By effectively delegating the work, supervisors can guide their subordinates to be well prepared to undertake the future responsibilities for the successful operation of the firm.

Unfortunately, however, too many supervisors are unable to delegate, either because they do not fully understand their role and thus do not know how to go about it, or else they are mistrusting of their subordinates' abilities to do the job. Some supervisors simply feel that the work will not be done properly unless they do it themselves. Then, too, some supervisors enjoy doing a task so much that they are reluctant to let someone else handle it. Supervisors also fail to delegate because of several psychological motives — the fear of competition, the fear of losing credit and recognition, and the fear that their own shortcomings and weaknesses will be exposed. Each of these motives is traceable to the basic psychological feelings of fear and insecurity by the supervisor, and many times that fear is the cause of poor-quality work, low-quantity production, and a serious breakdown in morale among the workers in a department.

Similar psychological feelings of insecurity and a lack of motivation may account for a subordinate's resistance to accepting more responsibility. However,

---

[3]Raymond Dreyfack, "How to Delegate — Effectively," from the series *What a Supervisor Should Know About . . ."* (Chicago: Dartnell Corporation, 1964), p. 7.

SUPERVISOR'S RESPONSIBILITIES TO OTHERS
IN THE BUSINESS ORGANIZATION

Upward responsibilities to higher management:

1. Ascertaining and carrying out what management wants done.
2. Keeping superiors informed of what is being done in the department and passing along ideas for improvement.
3. Accepting full responsibility for the work in the department without "passing the buck."
4. Referring matters requiring superior's attention promptly without bothering superiors unnecessarily.
5. Interpreting the employees' needs to management, and vice versa.

Higher Management

Responsibilities

S Supervisor

Horizontal responsibilities to supervisors of equal rank:

1. Cooperating with associates in the same manner that subordinates are expected to cooperate with each other.
2. Helping coordinate the work of the department with that of other supervisors for the good of the firm.
3. Permitting interchange and promotion of goods workers among departments.
4. Accepting full responsibility for work in the department.
5. Trying to understand problems of peers.

Downward responsibilities to subordinates:

1. Aiding in selection of new employees and helping to orient new workers to the job.
2. Training and counseling subordinates to assume greater responsibilities.
3. Assisting each employee to know what to do and how to do it, and checking the results.
4. Evaluating employees periodically and recommending promotions, transfers, dismissals, and salary adjustments.
5. Delegating authority and responsibility in order to develop understudies.
6. Developing harmony, cooperation, and teamwork.
7. Building and maintaining employee morale, handling grievances promptly and fairly.

8. Maintaining discipline and controlling absenteeism and tardiness.
9. Taking a personal interest in employees without showing partiality.
10. Using courtesy, tact, leadership, and consideration in treating employees as human beings.

Supervisor's responsibilities for coordinating office work

1. Planning the systems, procedures, and methods.
2. Distributing the workload fairly.
3. Coordinating the work of different units if this is necessary.
4. Seeing that the work is done correctly and on time.
5. Anticipating difficulties and peak loads in the work.
6. Maintaining the quantity and quality of the work to be done by setting standards.
7. Studying, developing, and using new methods and equipment to reduce and control costs.
8. Training and developing understudies so that absences, overloads, and other interferences with the amount and the flow of work may be handled efficiently.

Supervisor's responsibilities for self-development

1. Constantly analyzing and attempting to improve personality traits such as self-control, analytical ability, personal appearance, confidence of subordinates and others, initiative, punctuality, courtesy, leadership, and fair play.
2. Studying the organization and personnel of the entire firm to develop the maximum of departmental cooperation, train understudies, and study the requirements for the next supervisory job in the line of promotion.
3. Assuming membership and actively participating in professional organizations.
4. Studying up-to-date books, magazines, journals, and other literature that will aid in improving the work in present and future positions.
5. Continuing one's formal education in those areas that will aid in daily work.

Fig. 12-1
The Office Supervisor's Responsibilities

	Yes	No
1. Do you know the first names of your employees?		
2. Do you feel your employees confide in you?		
3. Do you have a below-average absentee rate in your group?		
4. Have you had employees promoted from your group?		
5. Do you try quickly to solve causes of potential grievances?		
6. Do you ever visit a sick employee at his home?		
7. Do you try to handle your employees as individuals?		
8. Do you consider it more important to save an employee than to "scrap" him?		
9. Do you try to sell your people new methods instead of "shoving them down their throats"?		
10. Do you call employees in for face-to-face private discussion when problems arise?		
11. Do you try to understand the employee's point of view when problems arise?		
12. Do you give quick straight answers to employees for their questions?		
13. Do you try to get both sides of an argument before attempting to reach any decision?		
14. Can you discipline an employee and still hold his sincere respect?		
15. Do you treat all your people fairly — without playing favorites?		
16. Are your employees loyal to you — and do they speak well of you?		
17. Do you make yourself clearly understood to your employees at all times?		
18. Do your employees put in a full day's work — no loafing, no too-long coffee breaks, etc.?		
19. Do you have a good safety record in your group?		
20. Do you believe people work for more than money alone?		

HOW TO SCORE

"Yes" to all 20 questions ....Tops
"Yes" to 18 questions ....Excellent
"Yes" to 15 questions ....Good
"Yes" to 13 questions ....Acceptable
"Yes" to 11 questions ....Fair
"Yes" to 9 questions.........................N.G. (not good)

Kelly-Read & Company, Rochester, New York

Fig. 12-2
Human Relations Quotient (HRQ) Checklist for Supervisors

as observed by McGregor in his current view of worker behavior (Theory Y), *depending upon conditions* the average person may find work to be satisfying, will seek responsibility, and will strive to attain the firm's objectives.[4] Thus, it becomes the supervisor's goal to create a work climate wherein subordinates may realize their own goals best and may direct their own efforts toward the aims of the firm.

Supervisors must be willing to share their knowledge and experience with their subordinates. In fact, qualified subordinates should be trained to step into their supervisors' jobs as a result of their supervisors having delegated the work. As supervisors free themselves of work as the result of delegation, they become available for assuming new, higher level responsibilities, all of which may lead to new job opportunities for them. The subordinates who accept responsibilities for the work delegated gain a practical experience in *participative management* — a relatively recent management technique in which the workers are given a voice in determining what they are to do, how they are to do it, and how they are to be appraised. A great motivating force comes into play for the person who is put in charge of a portion of the department's work, given the authority to make decisions that spell success or failure, and then rewarded in terms of what is accomplished. In this way, when subordinates become involved in identifying and solving office problems, more of their personal needs are being met. Thus, participative management brings about increased employee motivation as workers become able to identify more closely with the company, develop

greater team spirit, and, most importantly, work harder to achieve the goals they have helped to establish.

In a study on the use of participative management in supervising office employees, it was found that employee participation was used to the greatest extent in these areas: developing lines of communication within departments, training new subordinates in departments, recruiting candidates for positions in departments, orienting new employees in departments, and establishing procedures for uniformity of work.[5]

When subordinates accomplish tasks and receive credit for doing so, their recognition is also recognition of the supervisors who have enabled them to perform effectively as a result of skillful delegation. If supervisors — often the newly appointed, young executives — refrain from delegating because they fear that to do so would expose their own shortcomings, they must look within themselves and solve the problem by overcoming their own weaknesses. To avoid delegating in order to camouflage their own guilty consciences, supervisors compound the problem — their own problem of weakness and the problem of hindering the progress and cost effectiveness of the company for which they work.

Discipline

The words *discipline* and *disciple* can be traced back to the same root, meaning "to teach so as to mold." Most people, however, think of discipline as reprimanding or punishing, rather than

---

[4]See Chapter 1, page 17.

[5]Zane K. Quible, "Use of Participative Management in Supervising Office Employees," *The Delta Pi Epsilon Journal*, Vol. XVI, No. 4 (August, 1974), p. 15.

teaching or molding. If it is to be effective, however, true discipline should *teach* while at the same time it *corrects*. Discipline should be preventative, not punitive, and should keep employees from making the same mistake twice.

According to one vice-president in charge of personnel, poor supervision accounts for 80 to 90 percent of the disciplinary problems that arise. "Too many supervisors and managers are afraid to discipline, and when they do, they either apologize for it or bellow and rage. A sincere, temperate interview with a supervisor is punishment enough for many employees when they break a rule. Most people want to be good employees and they're more than a little ashamed when they're reminded that they don't always act the way they should."[6]

The need for discipline is often related to factors such as absenteeism, lateness, poor productivity, and quality of output. Behavioral scientists, such as Chris Argyris, believe that such expensive organizational problems as these are associated with employees' boredom and disinterest, which have resulted from underutilization of their abilities.[7] These theorists look upon human talent as a valuable resource and suggest that when human resources, like any other capital resource, are underutilized, the end result is costly and inefficient operation. It is felt by behavioral scientists that employees invest their energies and commitment in their work in about the same proportion as the degree to which they feel that work meets their needs for satisfaction and self-worth. Thus, it is concluded that if the work and the work environment are nonsupportive of employees' needs, the employees withhold their energies and this, in turn, has implications for the organization's cost effectiveness.[8]

Objectivity

The supervisor must be careful not only to avoid playing favorites among employees but also to avoid giving the appearance of doing so. The characteristic of objectivity is one of the most important qualities to be developed by a supervisor for, if once established, it will go far toward overcoming other weaknesses in the supervisor's ability and character.

One of the most effective means of eliminating partiality or favoritism lies in taking from the supervisor the final right of dismissing an employee and in placing this right in a group that is personally disinterested. Such a considerate dismissal policy takes away the chances of arbitrary exercise of power by

---

[6]Warren C. Stevens, "What Do You Do When They're Too Old to Spank?" *Modern Office Procedures* (April, 1964), p. 19.

[7]Argyris, in his theory of maturation, established dimensions of maturity for the human personality. The theory of maturation establishes a basis for certain clashes between business organizations as traditionally structured and the mature human personality as described in the form of a continuum, wherein any individual can be considered in varying stages of maturation on each of the dimension continuums. According to Argyris,

much of the employees' counterproductive behavior (poor productivity and quality, high absence, turnover, and lateness) is a result of the organization's failure to meet individual growth needs rather than an indicator of something wrong with the employees themselves. His thesis is that the root of most difficulties in the business firm is interpersonal rather than technical incompetence. See Chris Argyris, *Personality and Organization* (New York: Harper & Row, Publishers, 1957).

[8]David A. Whitsett, "Making Sense of Management Theories," *Personnel* (May-June, 1975), p. 45.

minor executives. It assures fair consideration to each employee, since the usual procedure is to require the supervisor to submit written charges against the employee whose dismissal is sought. The employee must be given a hearing, and the final decision is left with the committee, not with the supervisor. Ordinarily, such a committee is composed of executives of higher rank than the supervisor. The committee may or may not have employee representation.

Among other means of avoiding favoritism are an equitable distribution of the quantity of work that each employee must complete, efficient records of work performed, and a periodic appraisal of each employee with a subsequent conference and a report to the employee evaluated.

Counseling

Since the personal problems of office workers may affect their efficiency, a supervisor should be available for talking with workers as the need arises or be able to refer a troubled worker to the appropriate person either within or outside the company for help. Some firms that are unable to support a staff counselor or psychologist maintain contact with a specialist in industrial counseling or psychiatry whose services are called upon as needed. Some small firms have set up pools to share the services and the cost of a consultant. Also, industrial psychiatrists may be called upon to conduct group discussions that aid supervisors in anticipating, recognizing, and understanding the needs of their workers.

Office supervisors should be on guard to note any emotional disturbances among workers in their depart-

ments and know how to react to them. The supervisor should watch for symptoms of emotional difficulties such as a marked change in a worker's behavior patterns, as when a punctual worker suddenly develops a high tardiness record. A worker that persistently complains of headaches and nausea may be exhibiting the beginnings of a psychosomatic illness (physical symptoms with an emotional base). A worker who has a series of minor accidents is probably troubled by something; for such accidents may often be the result of inattention, and inattention is a sign of preoccupation. A bigger problem than any of these however, is alcoholism, which may indicate a deeply rooted emotional problem that workers are unable to handle alone. Here, the responsibility of the office supervisor is to help workers recognize their weaknesses and urge them to seek proper professional help before they are dismissed from the company.[9]

How far supervisors should go in talking with employees about their jobs or home difficulties depends upon the perception, sympathy, judgment, training, and counseling experience of the supervisors themselves. In counseling, supervisors should listen sympathetically, for it is only through listening that they can come to understand their workers' problems and learn why these problems are affecting their productivity. There may be occasions when the supervisor can help a disturbed worker by granting a leave of absence or suggesting where assistance may be found. But by all means the supervisor should avoid assuming the role of psychologist or human relations counselor in off-job problems and recommending specific

---

[9]The topic of alcoholism is discussed in further detail in Chapter 15.

courses of action. Most supervisors, even if qualified to do so, do not have the time available to render in-plant counseling services. Also, the emotional problems of subordinates are not the concern of supervisors, except as those problems affect job performance.

When employees seek help on matters relating to their jobs, such as how to improve performance or how to prepare for promotional opportunities, supervisors should feel free to pass along their opinions and recommendations. Supervisors have a responsibility to provide their workers with guidance not only on how they can prepare themselves to meet performance standards but also on how they can acquire the skills and knowledge for advancement.

Performance Appraisal

Much of the office supervisor's counseling is concerned with *performance appraisal*, wherein the employee's work is evaluated and constructively criticized. In appraising the performance of subordinates, supervisors must measure how well the employees have done the work assigned, how well they can do work that may be more demanding, and to what extent they can be depended upon to carry out orders if no one is available to provide close supervision. Such constructive appraisal of employee performance is a valuable tool that can be used by office supervisors to strengthen the superior-subordinate relationship.

The technique of *management by objectives (MBO)* is popularly used in performance appraisal. In management by objectives, a phrase suggested by Peter Drucker, objectives are set forth for every area where performance and results directly and vitally affect the survival and prosperity of the organiza-

tion.[10] These broad objectives are next translated into goals for individual members of the organization. In utilizing MBO in performance appraisal, subordinates and their supervisors mutually agree upon practicable goals to be achieved, which may range from improving one's attendance to redesigning an outmoded data-collection system. The workers set targets for their own objectives and evaluate themselves with respect to their performance in meeting the goals or objectives. Thus, individual workers are encouraged to assume greater responsibility for planning as well as for appraising and measuring their contributions in meeting organizational objectives. This, in turn, aids in meeting the ego and self-development needs of the workers that might otherwise have been ignored. Each goal mutually agreed upon is also evaluated by the supervisor during the periodic performance review, and subordinates are given the opportunity to discuss any problems they might have encountered. At the time of the performance review, new goals are mutually set for the next time period. Thus, the appraisal program emphasizes concrete, measurable goals rather than the traditional, intangible personality traits such as "attitude." Management by objectives, as part of a program of employee evaluation, is discussed in Chapter 24, "Office Salary Administration."

---

[10]For the development and presentation of the concept of management by objectives, see Peter F. Drucker, *The Practice of Management* (New York: Harper and Brothers, 1954). Also see George S. Odiorne, "The Politics of Implementing MBO," *Business Horizons* (June, 1974), pp. 13–21. This article describes the three main approaches used for implementing MBO and illustrates how each approach must be modified by the political constraints that characterize every business organization.

Morale

Morale is the mental state that causes employees to perform their work with a feeling of satisfaction and enjoyment. It is the attitude that creates a feeling of enthusiasm and happiness during and after working hours. The desires, interests, and feelings of most human beings are somewhat alike, and, when supervisors help to satisfy them for employees, the morale of the workers is improved. Improved morale, in turn, results in employees doing more and better work and enjoying life at the same time.

Unless a proper level of morale is built up and maintained, there will be growing distrust and dissatisfaction among employees, who will seek the ways and means, such as calling upon labor unions, to obtain what they need or want. The company and its interest in its workers must be "sold" to the workers by a sincere and continuous effort that takes into consideration the primary and secondary needs of human beings, such as those identified by Abraham Maslow.[11]

Primary Needs. The primary needs consist of basic *physiological needs* (food, water, clothing, shelter, rest, air, etc.) and *safety needs* (security, protection against physical and mental dangers and future deprivation). One thread of continuity cutting across both of these kinds of needs is security, of which job security and personal security are fundamental.

Job Security. Employees should know that their jobs are necessary and

permanent and that they will be provided a basic salary with increments based on performance, promotional opportunities, and seniority. There should be a degree of permanence in the fundamental company plans with which the employees should be familiar. No changes in these plans should be made without giving the employees advance information and an explanation, especially if the plans may affect their jobs.

One of the most effective means of improving morale and meeting the workers' need for job security is to make the company's intentions and motives clear to employees and to keep them informed as to conditions that affect their firm. Bulletin boards, manuals, house organs or newsletters, and other literature descriptive of the company and its processes are effective aids in such a program of communications.

Of prime importance is the necessity of establishing fair and uniform wage and salary rates. Workers are not fundamentally interested so much in their own rates of pay as they are in what wages are being received by workers doing similar work in other offices or by employees doing the same kind of work for about the same length of time in their own departments. As discussed later in Chapters 23 and 24, the pay rates for each job classification should be put into written or printed form so that employees know how far they can rise within any given classification. Workers should be informed as to how standards were developed; nothing is so demoralizing to the morale of a department as a belief that pay rates are determined arbitrarily, that employees doing similar work are being paid widely divergent salaries, and that the pay rates are not commensurate with the earnings of the company.

---

[11]Maslow's hierarchy of needs is discussed in Chapter 1, pages 15–16.

Personal Security. There are certain contingencies in life for which almost everyone tries to prepare. Among these contingencies are the health, employment, retirement, and death of the employee. Business firms, either by choice or through the stimulation of union efforts and contracts, try to recognize these contingencies and do what they can to improve their employees' situations. Many firms attempt to meet the safety needs of their workers by providing employee benefits such as hospitalization insurance for employees and their families, medical service, life and health insurance, pension plans, unemployment compensation, and guidance and counseling. The current status of employee benefits is analyzed in Chapter 14.

As indicated in Chapter 1, once the primary needs have been well satisfied, they no longer motivate. It is then that the higher level needs, the secondary needs, stimulate the worker.

Secondary Needs. These needs consist of *love* (desire for affection, association with others, need for companionship, identification with a group), *esteem* (social approval, self-assertion, self-approval, and sense of integrity), and *self-actualization* (need to achieve one's full potential and need for self-development and self-fulfillment). According to Maslow's theory of motivation, one secondary need does not have to be completely satisfied before the next need emerges. The needs pattern differs from one office worker to the next, and thus supervisors cannot assume that only one approach can be used to motivate all of their subordinates toward attainment of the firm's objectives.

Love. When the worker's need of wanting to feel important and of doing something worthwhile is recognized and fulfilled, a high level of morale is established. Employees should know and feel the importance of their jobs and their work to the firm. Explaining the "why of the job" and showing employees how their efforts contribute to attainment of the company goals are also helpful in creating a feeling of importance. Recognition should be constantly stressed, and, if possible, should be emphasized by developing group or team work.

For example, the Zero Defects plan utilizes what sociologists call *group motivation* to get individuals within a group to assign the same importance to their work activities as they do to their personal affairs. The program is aimed at developing a constant, conscious effort on the part of employees to improve performance continually in accomplishing their jobs so that they will do it correctly the first time. Someone has described the program as the personal search for perfection by everyone. At the Retail Credit Company, Atlanta, where the Zero Defects program is called "Target Zero," the objective is not just to detect errors but to get at their causes and to correct the causes. Error consciousness is encouraged among all employees, and they are encouraged to do their jobs right the first time and every time. As a result of installing the Target Zero program, employees have been able to reduce mismailings by more than 40 percent, thus improving the speed of customer serivce. Also, the handling of the files has attained 98.5 percent accuracy.[12]

Poor supervision causes employees to lose their identity and creates a feeling of lack of importance. Employees

---

[12]"Zero Defects Plan Reduces Mismails by over 40%," *Administrative Management* (July, 1970), p. 52.

feel their lack of importance by their inability to express themselves in connection with their work. Poor supervision becomes evident in public criticism of the employee, playing favorites, lack of friendliness, and lack of understanding the basic human relationships.

Exceptional work and length of service must be recognized by the supervisor if the love and affection need is to be met. So far as exceptional work is concerned, some companies prefer to pay bonuses established on one of many bases, such as units produced or time saved. Other firms use merit rating, whereby outstanding performance is rewarded either by a pay increase within a given job classification or by promotion to a higher classification. Other companies favor incentive wage systems, of which there are scores of basic types and numerous variations, such as piecework payments, differential piece rates, and flat weekly sums plus piece rates. Regardless of the system, the bonus or incentive plan must be fairly established and administered. It should not be changed unless conditions warrant, and then not until the workers have been acquainted with the facts and shown why a change is necessitated.

Length of service is usually recognized by an annual increase in salary or an annual bonus graduated with the length of employment, or by a combination of the two. Some businesses reward long and faithful service by distribution of company stock or by giving employees a share in the profits.

Esteem. This need, which includes both self-esteem and esteem by others, is exhibited by workers in their desire for competence, achievement, and freedom of thought, and in their search for status, prestige, and reputation in the eyes of others. Behavioral scientists feel that management's failure to evolve jobs that utilize fully the talents and skills of workers often makes work a less satisfying experience than it could otherwise be. Thus, for many persons work becomes an unsatisfying, uninteresting experience. "Since these theorists also feel that work constitutes a major potential source of satisfaction and meaning in life for many employees, they conclude that people whose abilities are underutilized suffer a certain amount of psychological damage in the sense that the potential feelings of well-being and self-esteem that can come from doing work that one finds satisfying and meaningful are lost to them."[13]

Self-Actualization. The opportunity for achieving one's full potential is not only part of the element of feeling important in the job and in the firm but also part of the personal self-development of the worker. In the management theories contributed by behavioral scientists, as discussed in Chapter 1, workers are viewed as having great potential and constantly searching for significant ways to develop themselves. It is felt that office workers bring this aspect of themselves to their jobs and that they therefore desire work and work-related experiences that will contribute to meeting this self-actualization need.

A common concept is that employees are motivated only by a concern for what is in the pay envelope. Although money is the oldest motivator and most companies rely heavily on salaries and employee benefits, modern thinkers on the subject of motivation compare the giving of more and more money with

---

[13]David A. Whitsett, "Making Sense of Management Theories," *Personnel* (May–June, 1975), p. 45.

heroin — it takes more and more to produce less and less effect.[14] According to the motivation-maintenance theory offered by Frederick Herzberg, pay is an example of a hygienic (maintenance) factor, one related to productivity but peripheral to the job itself.[15] When a hygienic factor such as pay is felt by workers to be inadequate, the factor functions as a dissatisfier and only has the potential for negatively affecting performance. When the pay factor is present, however, it does not motivate the workers to greater productivity but instead makes it possible for the other set of factors, the motivators, to function. Included in the set of motivators are: an opportunity for workers to say how the job is to be done, recognition of the workers and their accomplishments, a feeling that the workers are using their talents, and a feeling that the workers are developing as individuals. At the core of Herzberg's theory is the concept that the factors which cause employee dissatisfaction are different than the factors which cause employee satisfaction. Thus, supervisors must work on both sets of factors in order not only to avoid discontent but also to provide the best conditions for employee motivation.

Current thinking on motivation includes the assumption that people want to do a good job but that they need to be challenged. Herzberg believes that the only way to motivate employees is to enrich their jobs — to give them challenging and interesting work in which they can assume responsibility. By means of *job enrichment* a job is restructured by building — or vertically loading — higher order responsibilities and

authorities and more challenging content so that an individual has the opportunity for achievement, recognition, and growth that makes a job satisfying and a meaningful experience at which he or she is motivated to perform well. Thus, the individual's accountability for his or her own work is increased as a complete, natural unit of work is assigned to the employee. The worker is then granted additional authority in his or her own activity as new and more difficult tasks not previously handled are introduced to the job.[16]

Interpersonal Communications

Formal written communications and telecommunications, which emphasize the dissemination of information, have been discussed in Chapters 7 and 8 respectively. In this section *interpersonal communications* — between two or more persons — is discussed not only as a medium of transmitting information but also as a means of depicting psychological needs, motives, and feelings, which may often be in conflict with the expressed verbal message.

Interpersonal communications aids in motivating people to perform their jobs in the most efficient manner possible. The establishment of effective

---

[14]Lewis E. Lachter, "Motivation: Old Problem, New Ideas," *Administrative Management* (February, 1969), pp. 22–23.

[15]See Chapter 1, pages 16–18.

[16]For the results of an extensive survey of job enrichment literature in which it is concluded that there are few, if any, genuine cases where job enrichment has been applied successfully to a large, heterogeneous work force, see Mitchell Fein, "Job Enrichment: A Reevaluation," *Sloan Management Review*, (Winter, 1974), pp. 69–88. In his paper Fein shows that most applications of job enrichment either have been common-sense job redesigns or have occurred among such a select group of workers that the success of the program was independent of its content. In order to increase productivity in America, Fein suggests a new approach to job design which balances more thoughtfully both the intrinsic and extrinsic motivational factors.

communications between management and employees is one of the most important and demanding problems of human relations that face business firms today. Communications is not a one-way street from management to the employees or vice versa. To be successful, communications must be two-way — *up* and *down* between managers and employees; and *sideways* among managers, and among employees. Two-way communications is a major factor in the success of many business firms. As the firm, and in this instance the office, becomes larger, the problem of maintaining adequate communications becomes more difficult. In some of the largest firms, the problem of keeping the communication lines open and operating is so important that the employee relations, or labor relations, division conducts periodic employee attitude surveys of what the workers think of their firm, its products, and its management. Playing an instrumental role in effective communications is the supervisor, who serves as a "linking pin," since this person is the main formal channel for both upward and downward communications.[17]

The kinds of information emphasized in effective programs of communications from management to employees are indicated below:

1. Company news and future prospects, such as company goals and achievements, results of sales progress and sales contests, new products, new equipment and methods, organizational changes and reasons for changes, and the financial position of the company.
2. Employee compensation, benefits, and services, such as changes in benefit programs, wage and salary increases, reports of profit-sharing results, and holiday and vacation schedules.
3. Company rules, policies, and programs, such as absenteeism, working conditions and safety, open door policy, EEO programs and achievements, community action programs, and cost and quality control.
4. Promotions and opportunities for training and advancement.
5. Social activities and other items, such as new laws affecting employees, grievances, and job-duty clarification.[18]

In effective communication and employee relations programs, the following kinds of information flow freely from employees to management:

1. The needs and aspirations of the company's employees.
2. The employees' attitudes toward their working conditions, their work, and their work place.
3. The employees' complaints and grievances about work-related subjects.

It should be borne in mind that communication is a highly personal and emotional process. Business offices, like the individuals working therein, have their own individual personalities and what works in one office to improve communications may be only slightly effective or may fail in another office. In many instances it is probable that the lack of good communications lies not in the media or mechanisms of communications but in the communicator. The

---

[17]The linking-pin concept, developed by Dr. Rensis Likert of the University of Michigan, refers to an individual who is a member of two overlapping groups in an organization. The "linking pin" is a superior in one group and a subordinate in the other. See Rensis Likert, *New Patterns of Management* (New York: McGraw-Hill Book Co., 1961), in which a detailed discussion of the linking-pin function of supervision is presented in Chapter 8, pp. 97–118.

[18]"Employee Communications," *Personnel Policies Forum Survey No. 110* (Washington: The Bureau of National Affairs, Inc., July, 1975), pp. 11 and 13.

communicator must be concerned not only with the media of communication but also, and perhaps more importantly, with the emotional reactions, attitudes, and feelings of employees, which play a vital role in any program of communications improvement.

Providing for Two-Way Communications. Several media, each designed for use in keeping the communications lines open between management and employees, are described in the following paragraphs.

Small Group Meetings. Formal meetings with middle managers, supervisors, and workers should be regularly scheduled to convey the importance of keeping open the lines of communication. In small group meetings two-way communications is facilitated, for employees can ask questions and freely discuss. Full explanations, implemented by questions and answers, are an effective means of transmitting messages. Managers and supervisors should also be urged to hold informal discussions with employees, for in a setting of mutual trust and respect, employees are more at ease and seem to relate their feelings more freely. It is surprising how much effect this approach has on the morale of employees, and at the same time managers and supervisors learn what the workers think and how they feel.

Publications. House organs or company publications are used to keep employees informed of the operations, plans, and changes in the firm. The communications should be carefully selected and regularly scheduled. When the publications are sent to the employee's home, the entire family participates in the message, which may be kept for future reference. Pamphlets, booklets, manuals, and posters may be used to in-

form workers of changes in company policies, new methods, products, or future plans. Letters from the president or other officers of the company to the employees' homes are especially effective when a new procedure, product, or equipment is to be used or installed. Employee-association publications may be produced to describe the off-work experiences of workers and to announce company cultural and recreational activities. Motion pictures, radio and television programs, and cassette tapes are useful in explaining company history and the development of new products or services.

Bulletin Boards. Among the various downward communications media, bulletin boards are used by nearly all companies as a means of keeping employees informed. Bulletin boards may be used by firms for posting rules and regulations, recreation activities, safety records, employee illness, job openings, attendance records, new product announcements, vacation schedules, lost and found notices, personal announcements of births and weddings, educational opportunities, and press releases. To be a most effective means of communication, there should be a sufficient number of boards to attract the attention of all employees, the communications posted on the boards should be kept current, and both management and employees should be continuously encouraged to use the boards.

Many companies use information racks with a variety of bulletins to inform employees of the details of company operations and the underlying philosophies and economics of the business. By giving employees the free choice of selecting the information they want from the rack, these firms eliminate the "propaganda" accusation of some employees when the material is given to all workers.

Employee Suggestion Systems.

Employee suggestion systems are used in both business and government offices as a means of building better morale among office workers, getting workers to think more seriously about their jobs, and as a means of upward communications between employees and management. In theory, suggestion systems are excellent. The reasoning that underlies the use of suggestion systems includes: (1) those closest to the work being done are probably best able to understand the inefficiencies and to recommend some changes, and (2) it is wasteful not to use the abilities of all workers to the fullest extent by permitting them to make suggestions and to be paid for these ideas on the basis of their value. In practice, however, the results have not been so successful. Management has not always appreciated the full value of such systems, perhaps as the result of poor planning and organization. This, in turn, often leads to apathy on the part of employees who lose interest in the suggestion system.

Generally all employees are eligible to participate in the suggestion system, with the exception of salaried supervisory employees (excluding officers and heads of departments) who receive awards only for ideas not connected directly with their own departments or fields of activity. It is claimed by some that supervisors submit a better quality of suggestions than their subordinates. This argument seems to have little validity, however. The disadvantage of having both workers and supervisors submit suggestions is that the workers and the supervisors come into competition with one another and as a result, conflicts may arise. The workers may

also think that their ideas are being taken by the supervisors.

The routine for processing and investigating the suggestions submitted varies with companies. Whatever plan is followed, it must be fair and promptly acted upon; otherwise, it will fail because of lack of interest. Many firms have found the unsigned, numbered suggestion blank, with a detachable receipt, most desirable. The suggestion may be placed in a sealed envelope addressed to the suggestion committee and placed in a suggestion box or mailed to the committee. The receipt numbers of the accepted suggestions are posted on the bulletin board, and claims for awards are made on a special award claim form.

The suggestions should be acted upon promptly by the committee so that employees are informed of what happens to their suggestions once they have been submitted. If the suggestions are accepted, the employees making them should be given immediate recognition. If the suggestion is rejected by the committee, a full explanation should be given to the employee.

Some companies, particularly in connection with office work, pay a flat amount such as $5, $10, and up for each suggestion accepted. The awards must be fair. How much satisfaction can an employee get out of a $5 or $10 award if a suggestion saves the company thousands of dollars each year? Other companies — and this plan seems more equitable — pay a percentage of the savings that result from the implementation of the award. When determining the amount of the awards, consideration should be given to whether the idea involves recurring or nonrecurring savings and to the possibility that the idea itself may be superseded later.

The company should show its appreciation of what the suggestions accomplish by giving a certain amount of publicity and recognition for all ideas accepted. Merely sending the employees a check or noting on their personnel records that they have made an acceptable suggestion causes the system to lose much of its morale-building effect. The names of the suggestion award winners, as well as the amount of their awards, can be publicized in company publications and local newspapers. A well-operated suggestion system, although a valuable upward communications tool, is too often neglected or overlooked entirely.

Grievances and Complaints. The handling of grievances and complaints may be considered from two points of view: (1) where the firm has a union contract, and (2) where there is no union of office workers. When the firm has a union contract, specific rules for handling grievances are provided within the contract, as described in the following chapter. For those nonunion offices that do not have a formal arrangement for handling employee grievances, a definite procedure such as the following should be provided for their settlement:

1. Employees should present their grievances to their immediate supervisor.
2. If the grievance is not settled between the employee and the supervisor, it should be presented to an executive or a committee selected to handle employee grievances. The grievance should be taken up by the executive or the committee, meeting with the employee and his or her immediate superior.
3. Provision should be made for a *conciliator*, perhaps a representative of the personnel department or an industrial

relations executive, whose aim is to bring both parties together. The conciliator does not make decisions but works with both parties with the objective of reaching mutual agreement.
4. Final referral is to an *arbitrator* or umpire who must be authorized to make final decisions if the two parties — company and employee — cannot agree. This decision must be binding on all parties.

Terminating the Office Worker's Services

In small- and medium-size companies that have no formal personnel department, office supervisors are occasionally faced with one of their most unpleasant responsibilities — terminating the services of an office worker. In larger firms the responsibility for firing an office worker is usually handled by the personnel department according to a standard procedure. Regardless of the size of the firm, few things in life are as traumatic for the office worker as losing his or her job. Although firing may not be a pleasant task for the office supervisor, if it is done humanely, the supervisor can aid in creating a better organization in the long run.

Basic to the firing of any worker is the existence of a well-planned termination procedure that satisfies the union agreement, if any, and government regulations, such as those described in Chapter 11. Personnel records must be maintained to reflect up-to-date, accurate data so that the cause for termination is well documented. Above all, the termination procedure should be planned to insure a fair hearing for the worker as well as legal protection for the employer.

The firing of an office worker should not come as a surprise to the worker, although there may be an occasion, when for justifiable cause, a worker is fired on the spot. For example, most companies have a policy that if an office employee reports for work intoxicated, the worker is subject to immediate discharge. Prior to most terminations, the worker will have been forewarned by means of periodic performance appraisals and in counseling sessions and meetings with the supervisor. As a result of such prior evaluations and meetings, the worker should know that he or she has not met the company's expectations.

It is important that the termination interview be carefully planned and held in privacy. Some supervisors prefer to schedule the interview near the end of the work day so that the terminated worker does not have to confront his or her peers in the office following the meeting. During the termination interview the worker's nonperformance as compared with expectations should be objectively and honestly reviewed, and the continued failure of the worker to meet goals should be indicated. The worker's strengths and weaknesses can be spelled out by the supervisor and, if possible, the worker may be aided by indicating where his or her strengths may be better utilized elsewhere. The decision to release the worker must be clearly stated, along with the date upon which the worker's duties are to cease. The worker should be informed of the procedure to follow in obtaining his or her last paycheck, and if the company plans to respond to reference checks upon the fired worker, the worker should be so notified. During the termination interview the supervisor must avoid becoming emotionally involved with the worker, personally insulting him or her, or being highly critical of

any personal qualities not within the worker's control. The supervisor should listen carefully for any feedback from the terminated worker that will aid in improving future worker performance in the department.

Ethics and Value Systems

As individuals differ, so do their ethical concepts and value systems. Personal guidelines or policies for everyday ethical conduct, like policies for labor relations, are needed in the office. Like all policies, a code of ethics must be capable of enforcement. Many problems facing today's supervisors — problems that are symptomatic of clashing or poorly understood value systems — come about in an attempt to apply traditional supervisory methods to employees of the new work ethic. To manage effectively, the supervisor must adapt his or her means for achieving organizational goals to the value systems of the people who have the work to do.[19]

Ethics. *Ethics* is the systematic study of that part of science and philosophy which deals with moral conduct, duty, and judgment. A person's concept of what is and is not ethically and morally right stems from deep religious convictions, personal philosophy, and motives.

In a series of interviews, office and business executives were asked to judge the ethics and morality of several questionable office practices, some of which are described below. How does your evaluation compare with that of the executives, which is given in parentheses following each of the practices?

[19]Vincent S. Flowers *et al.*, "Managerial Values for Working," an AMA Survey Report (New York: AMACOM, a division of American Management Associations, 1975), pp. 6–7 and 45.

1. "The employee who punches in another's time card." (Definitely unethical.)
2. "The executive who doesn't want to be bothered and tells his secretary to inform callers that he's not in." (Questionable, but not really immoral. The best solution is to be truthful; have her tell callers that he's too busy to be disturbed.)
3. "Pirating an employee from another company." (It's part of the free enterprise system. If a man wants to work for you, that is his business. However, the company that hires a man away from a competitor solely to hurt the other company is being unethical.)
4. "Taking credit for another employee's idea." (Definitely immoral, unless the idea has been substantially improved upon.)
5. "Padding an expense account." (Very bad. However, some companies with unrealistic rules force their employees into the practice. In that case, it's their own fault.)
6. "Undermining another employee in an effort to get ahead." (When it exceeds the bounds of good clean competition, it's unethical and should be stamped out before it infects the entire organization.)[20]

The inspiration for ethical behavior must originate at the top level of management, filter down through middle management, and permeate the business organization. The best guarantee of high standards of morality in business is that subordinates work under the direction of men and women who themselves have high standards. For at least one third of each working day, supervisors are entering into social relationships with their subordinates. During the remaining two thirds of each day the attitudes, ideals, and beliefs that the employees have formed while at work in the office are being carried back and relayed to society — the families and friends of the employees. Thus, supervisors have a social responsibility to set a good example for their employees. The ethical and moral conduct of supervisors, as leaders, must rise above their own personal and individual motives and needs.

In communicating with their superiors, supervisors should strive to report all the facts honestly, accurately, and objectively. Supervisors must train themselves and their workers to avoid distorting the facts in order to fill a psychological need, for all too often the communications lines become warped by the personality, prejudices, and embellishments of the sender. In reaching decisions, the goal of supervisors should be to discipline their thinking into a logical, orderly, inductive process, rather than impulsively jump to conclusions. In working with subordinates, it becomes easy for supervisors to abuse their authority and prerogative, with the result that employees feel "let down" and unsupported in their actions. To gain employees who will *work with him or her*, a supervisor must *work with them*; be kind, fair, and just; and sincerely praise the satisfactory performance of the workers.

Basic to an ethical and moral conduct is loyalty. Without this fundamental quality, no supervisor, no office, and no business firm can perform at the top peak of potential capability. When office supervisors are unable to bear allegiance to the authority of their firm, they find themselves in a position of conflict and mental torment, which in turn hinders

---

[20]With permission of Warren C. Stevens, Editor, "What's Happened to Morality in the Office?" *Modern Office Procedures* (February, 1964), pp. 19–22. Copyright by the Industrial Publishing Co., Division of Pittsburgh Railways Company.

them from being loyal to either themselves or their company. The only workable solution to the problem of office supervisors who cannot abide by the policies and principles set forth by their firm is to search out another company to which they can give their loyalty.

Value Systems. A *value system* may be considered as the sum of one's moral and social perception of those things that are intrinsically desirable or valuable. As a result of their experiences, education, and the customs and traditions of the culture of which they are members, workers develop and cultivate those values that will satisfy their personal needs. If office workers can look upon their working lives as making a real contribution not only to their coworkers and the firm but also to society, they may find opportunity for satisfying their love, esteem, and self-actualization needs. If, on the other hand, office workers view themselves as being saddled with boring, uninteresting, and unchallenging work, the opportunity for finding satisfaction and happiness and meeting their needs is practically nil.

The Task Force Report, *Work in America*, affirms the findings of other research studies which state that significant numbers of American workers are dissatisfied with the quality of their working lives. Discontent is found at all the occupational levels — blue-collar, white-collar, and middle management — where dull, repetitive, seemingly meaningless tasks offer little challenge or autonomy. This situation has come about not so much because of the great changes in the work itself but because work has not changed fast enough to keep up with the rapid and widescale changes in the value systems, attitudes, and aspirations of workers. Many workers, as a result of their increased

educational and economic status, now find that having an interesting job is as important as the purely economic benefits derived from the job. The Task Force Report confirms that pay is still important, that it must support an adequate standard of living, and that it must be perceived as equitable. However, high pay alone will not lead to job (or life) satisfaction.[21] As Peter F. Drucker so aptly observed, "To make a living is no longer enough. Work also has to make a life.[22]

From its very beginnings the work ethic looked upon all work as a calling forth of people for service and contribution, deserving of respect. With the development of commerce and the revolutionizing of industry, however, value systems began to change and economic rewards became more meaningful. If today there has been a rejection of the work ethic by younger workers, this does not, according to Drucker, represent hedonism (the doctrine of pleasure or happiness being the sole or chief good in life).[23] This thought also appears in a study of the changing success ethic wherein it was noted that the shift in success-related values may be away from the accumulation of material goods that can be readily measured and toward the realization of less tangible objectives upon which no price — in dollars and cents, at any rate — can be representatively placed.[24] Possibly the

---

[21]*Work in America*, A Report of a Special Task Force to the Secretary of Health, Education, and Welfare (Cambridge: MIT Press, 1973), p. xv.

[22]Peter F. Drucker, *Management: Tasks, Responsibilities, Practices* (New York: Harper & Row, Publishers, 1974), p. 179.

[23]*Ibid.*, p. 186.

[24]Dale Tarnowieski, "The Changing Success Ethic," an AMA Survey Report (New York: AMACOM, a division of American Management Associations, 1973), p. 4.

change in values may be explained partly as a reaction against long decades of overworking, and a righting of the balance, and in larger part as a return to earlier elitist work concepts which relate certain kinds of work to nobility or to baseness of the person.[25] It is unlikely that young workers have a lower commitment to work than their elders. Instead, the problem lies in the interaction between work itself and the changing social character of today's generation, and in the failure of decision makers in business, labor, and government to recognize this fact.[26]

In the Task Force Report cited above, among the woes expressed by white-collar workers are the following: (1) offices are often like factories, with work that is segmented and authoritarian; (2) for a growing number of jobs, there is little to distinguish them but the color of the workers' collars; (3) jobs such as computer keypunch operations and typing pools share much in common with the automobile assembly line; (4) the increasing growth in size of organizations that employ the bulk of office workers imparts to the clerical workers the same impersonality that the blue-collar workers experience in the factory; (5) the worker's presence is acknowledged only when mistakes are made or rules are not followed; and (6) lower level white-collar jobs in both government and industry, traditionally held by high school graduates, are now going to those who have college credentials. The

demand for higher academic credentials has not increased the prestige, status, pay, or difficulty of the jobs, however.[27]

Much of the dissatisfaction with job content and supervisory styles expressed among white-collar workers is caused by a mismatching of values. When it is only the value systems of the managers that determine the goals of the firm and the means for achieving those goals, the managers are simply talking to themselves about themselves and designing systems and procedures that appeal only to themselves. Rather, management must attempt to understand other people's value systems and involve them in designing the systems and procedures to be followed.[28] In their study of managerial values, Vincent S. Flowers and his coworkers urge that "the means for achieving organizational goals be adapted to the value systems of the people who have to do the work. Rather than presuming to understand the mix of employee values, management would do better to involve a representative sample of employees in the design of systems, procedures, and jobs. Not only will this make the means of production more efficient, but people at all levels (organizational levels and psychological existence) can benefit from the opportunity to confront, understand, and learn to accept the value systems of others."[29]

---

[25]Drucker, *loc. cit.*
[26]*Work in America, op. cit.*, pp. 49–50.

[27]*Ibid.*, pp. 38–39.
[28]Vincent S. Flowers *et. al.*, "Managerial Values for Working," an AMA Survey Report (New York: AMACOM, a division of American Management Associations, 1975), p. 44.
[29]*Ibid.*, p. 45.

1. Describe the several types of supervisory responsibility. In what directions do these responsibilities flow?

2. "Supervisors must use the human approach." Carefully explain the meaning of this statement and indicate its relevance for the office supervisor.

3. What is delegation? What are the underlying reasons why many supervisors do not delegate?

4. What is participative management? Explain how participative management may serve as a motivating force.

5. Is it possible for supervisors to teach while at the same time disciplining workers?

6. What relationship, if any, exists between the need for discipline and the underutilization of employees' abilities? Explain.

7. How far should a supervisor go in counseling employees about their off-the-job personal problems?

8. Explain how the concept of management by objectives is related to performance appraisal.

9. What is morale? How is morale related to the needs of workers?

10. How may a company provide job security and personal security as it tries to meet the primary needs of workers?

11. In their working lives what do employees search for in an attempt to satisfy their need for recognition?

12. Explain the relevance of Herzberg's motivation-maintenance theory to the concept that the major motivator of workers is the size of their paychecks.

13. How does job enrichment serve as a means of motivation?

14. "Communications is not a one-way street from management to the employees." Explain.

15. Enumerate some of the media available to supervisors who are trying to keep the communications lines open between them and their subordinates.

16. What are the major reasons for installing a suggestion system?

17. Draw a contrast between the role of the conciliator and that of the arbitrator in the handling of grievances and complaints.

18. What points should be kept in mind by the office supervisor who is planning a termination interview?

19. What is the best guarantee of high standards of morality in the business world?

20. What role do value systems play in employees' attitudes toward their working lives?

QUESTIONS
FOR
DISCUSSION

1. Why are studies of employee attitudes toward their work and their supervisor an important phase of office administration?

2. Why is there need for developing a procedure of handling employee grievances and complaints? What is to be gained by having such a procedure when no labor union is involved?

3. Grievances are as much a part of our life as the human race itself and to expect to eliminate them is to wish for a Utopia. Although grievances will never be eliminated, the office manager can take steps, especially in nonunion offices, to reduce and prevent the number of gripes and grievances. Prepare a list of these steps.

4. The supervisor is usually looked upon as "the linking pin." What is the meaning of this statement?

5. Why is conversation not necessarily communication?

6. Why do downward communications frequently create more problems than communications between two persons on the same organizational level?

7. React to the following Principle of Ethics: The ethical standards of any industry are determined by the ethical standards of the individual executives of each member company in that industry.

8. What is an office grapevine? Discuss the pros and cons of trying to eliminate the grapevine.

9. Rodney Pulli, a former high-ranking military officer, was recently employed to head a company in which morale at all levels had slipped considerably in recent months. The board of directors was aware of the morale problem and informed Pulli accordingly. At the first board meeting Pulli indicated that the strength and the success of a business depends 25 percent on the number of employees and 75 percent upon its morale. Furthermore, Pulli stated that the essentials of morale in a business firm are the same as those in the army: (1) respect for the officers or supervisors, (2) discipline, and (3) training.

    Do you agree with the statements made by Pulli? On the basis of these facts, discuss the various methods by which a desirable level of morale may be developed and maintained in a company.

10. Jean Gazzillo, office manager of Baird & Son, is so anxious to do a good job that she always comes to the president before making a decision affecting policy. In the past two months Gazzillo has called upon the president no less than ten times for advice. In nine of these instances, whatever the president recommended seems to have been what she would have done herself. This was found out by a series of questions asked whenever the problem of making a decision arose. What would you do in this instance if you were the president, assuming that Gazzillo is otherwise doing a good job?

11. Pierre Tourneau is manager of administrative services of the Canadian Cutlery Company. He has grown up with the business and has become successful through his own efforts. He has an assistant,

Charles Hachette, who is really the operating manager of administrative services. Hachette has taken several courses in management, has had considerable experience outside the firm, and therefore his ideas seem more progressive than those of Tourneau. In the past, whenever Hachette suggested improvements that could have saved the company money, Tourneau resented the suggestions. He seemed to feel they were a reflection on his lack of training and education. Hachette is anxious to do a good job, does not want to make a change in position, and would like to save the company money if he will not cause himself undue discomfort and embarrassment. Hachette comes to you for advice in handling the situation. Explain what you would do if you were in his position.

12. By means of an employee attitude study, a company surveyed its workers and found that there were two major areas of dissatisfaction — pay and employee benefits. After a study was made of the salaries and benefits in other firms in the community, the company found that its salary ranges were close to the average of the area and that its benefits were better than average in most respects. Management now wants to relay all these facts to its employees. Discuss the various media and techniques that management may use to communicate the results of the community survey and the firm's relative standing.

13. Nancy Wong, recently appointed supervisor of the office services department, has in the past few months found her job very demanding, with the result that she seems to have no time to do anything. It seems to her that she is always attending meetings from which she leaves with more projects to complete. Wong has begun to hand more and more responsibilities to other members of her department, often giving a task to a worker with no more directions than "See so-and-so for more information. She'll give you the details." At times, Wong even delegates the assignment of the projects themselves.

    Wong has given more and more freedom to her assistant, Craig Kennedy, who now issues verbal instructions instead of Wong. Often Kennedy makes decisions on his own when questions arise that Wong is not prepared to answer. Many of the women workers in the department, old enough to be Kennedy's mother, resent taking orders from Kennedy, who is young and has had only a few years of work experience.

    During the past week Wong has found she is so rushed that she must assign various employees to attend project planning meetings in her place. Since these people have no authority, they are at quite a disadvantage and can only listen and make recommendations. The result has been that the meetings are a waste of time and have to be rescheduled when Wong has more time.

    What is the real problem here? As Wong's superior, what steps should you take to remedy the situation?

14. Morris Davidson, a file clerk, has been scanning the list of this month's suggestion awards. He remarks to you, supervisor of the

records management department: "What good is our suggestion plan? None of the awards ever equal the amount of the savings that the company surely realizes. No wonder so few of our workers take part in the plan." Are Davidson's comments legitimate? How would you reply to Davidson?

15. During the past few months Ted Veskosky, office manager of Greenfield Steel, Ltd., has noticed that his boss, Dan Evans, works many more hours than he. On many occasions Evans is at the office an hour or more before the others report in and often he works on Saturdays, in addition to taking work home at night. Veskosky realizes that his boss is a thoroughly devoted, loyal "company man." Veskosky, however, is a thoroughly devoted, loyal "family man."

Evans is well aware of Veskosky's devotion to his family and on several occasions has told him that as long as he is a "family man," he will never get to the top in the company. Although this statement has been made jokingly, Veskosky suspects that his boss is serious. Discuss how Veskosky should go about convincing his boss that he, too, is concerned about the company and that he is loyal, but, on the other hand, that he is married to his family and not to the business as is Evans.

PRACTICAL OFFICE MANAGEMENT CASES

Case 12-1 Analyzing a Supervisory Technique

Peg Zimmerman, formerly an officer in the WAVES, has been employed as supervisor of the word processing center of Yardley Advertising Agency. In this center there are 30 men and women whose work consists of transcribing correspondence and typing various statistical reports. Because of a scarcity of qualified word processors and a lack of adequate supervision in the past, the workers have been coming in at various times in the morning — from 8:35 to 9:15.

Zimmerman decided to "take the bull by the horns" and called the workers together on her first day in the office. Her opening remarks were: "I am Peg Zimmerman, your new supervisor. I have just been released from the WAVES, where I was a lieutenant in charge of 65 women. I hope we get along together; but I expect you to be at your desks each morning at 8:30." The workers smiled. The next day they came in as tardy and as indifferent as before.

1. If you were the supervisor, would you have used the same approach as Zimmerman? If so, what course of action would you take now?
2. If you would not have taken the same approach as Zimmerman, how would you have handled the situation?

Case 12-2   **Overcoming a Communications Breakdown**

Thomas Goldman, supervisor of the information services division of a very large automobile manufacturer, was asked to attend a planning meeting to discuss the development of a new, expanded office services department. Goldman had been aware for the past four months that planning would have to begin shortly on the project, and he had become uneasy because he had heard nothing about it from his boss, Janice Vearling. All the management team who were requested to sit in on the planning session arrived in the board room, and Vearling opened the meeting by announcing the names of the manager and the staff for the new department. Goldman just sat there, utterly amazed, not saying a word. He was taken completely by surprise because he was expecting the discussion to center around who the management team of the new department *should* be, not who it *would* be. Goldman's mind was closed to the remainder of the discussion that took place, for he felt all respect for his judgment was lost and that Vearling had bypassed him prior to making a decision on this important personnel appointment.

When Goldman returned to his division, his assistant, Patrick Skea, knew at a glance that something was bothering Goldman and asked if he could help in some way. Goldman told Skea about the meeting and explained that he just could not understand why he had not been informed prior to the meeting of the selection of the new management team and also why he had not been asked for his recommendations. Skea started to apologize by stating that two weeks earlier while Goldman was out of the city, Vearling had called to ask Goldman for his recommendations on the matter. Skea said that immediately after the call, an emergency had developed in the computer room and he had rushed out, forgetting to make a note of the matter.

Answer the following questions:

1. What mistakes were made in this situation and which individuals were at fault?
2. Explain how each of the mistakes might have been overcome originally by applying workable principles of communications.
3. If you were Goldman, what steps would you now take?

Chapter 13

LABOR-MANAGEMENT RELATIONS IN THE OFFICE

In unionized offices the personnel policies developed by management and the ease with which these policies are administered may hinge upon the degree of acceptance and cooperation forthcoming from the union and its representatives. If the office is not unionized, management must be prepared to deal with any union that may seek to represent the employees in the company. To do so intelligently and to maintain a fair but firm relationship with a union, management must have some knowledge about the objectives and the problems of the unions. Before examining the extent of unionization among office workers, a brief history of the labor movement and a summary of the major pieces of legislation affecting workers are presented. This short excursion into the past will help set the stage for a description of union activities that are taking place in business offices today and of those that may occur tomorrow.

THE LABOR MOVEMENT: AN OVERVIEW

In the late 1700s, long before the mass-producing, assembly-line factories came upon the scene in the United States, workers were grouping themselves together to meet an urgent human need — protection from low wages, long workdays, and intolerable working conditions. The labor philoso-phies of the first organized societies exerted a strong influence on the craft unions and other labor groups that formed later during the early part of the nineteenth century. Following a long period of unemployment and inactivity for labor groups, as a result of the financial panic of 1837, trade unionism (unions of local trade groups or societies) revived with the discovery of gold in California in the 1850s. Workers' demands still lay in the areas of increased wages and shorter workdays. With the Civil War came the need to increase the output of plants, for the period was marked by the building of railroads and the establishment of modern factories in the Midwest. In 1869 the Noble Order of the Knights of Labor was formed, uniting mining and railroad workers with all the craft and kindred workers to combat the employers' opposition to unionization by means of lockouts and blacklists. However, in spite of the craft and railroad strikes, the unified opposition of employers led to the defeat and dissolution of most unions.

In 1886 the American Federation of Labor (AFL) was formed under the dynamic leadership of Samuel Gompers. Gompers' goals, applicable to all workers in their particular crafts, included bringing about economic changes by: abolishing child labor, shortening the workdays, improving working conditions, and providing collective bargaining for workers. The decade 1890 to 1900, with its severe depression and general unemployment, was not favorable to the growth of unions. Following 1900, the membership of unions increased as unionism penetrated many unorganized industries, making notable advances in the coal industry. With the outbreak of World War I in 1914 and the resulting rise in productive capacity, the number of organized laborers grew rapidly, reaching 5 million in 1920. After the war, with the liquidation of war industries, the depression of 1921, and employer opposition to organized labor, the unions began to lose members. The labor movement was further weakened as a result of the Great Depression following the stock market crash in 1929.

With the New Deal legislation of the 1930s union membership rose rapidly, numbering 9 million by 1940. World War II further stimulated the growth of unions, and by 1945 the total membership numbered 15 million. Since 1945 union membership (including public and professional employee associations) has grown to about 24.2 million in 1974, which represented about one fourth of the nation's total labor force. In 1974 unionized white-collar workers (clerical workers, professional and technical workers, managers and administrators, and sales workers) numbered nearly 6 million, or about one fourth of all union members.

In 1938 led by John L. Lewis, the Congress of Industrial Organizations (CIO) was founded, with the aim of unionizing all workers in mass-production industries, with no restriction as to trade or craft. The growth of the CIO membership and the development of new local unions came into direct competition with the AFL unions; as a result, jurisdictional strikes broke out in which each union sought control over certain work operations and jobs. Violence erupted between both unions, and costly, prolonged strikes were forced upon employers. The early disputes between the AFL and the CIO unions were characterized by the presence of radical elements that began to bore from within the labor movement. Along with other disruptive conditions, the desire to purge their ranks of these extremist elements led to the merging of the two unions in 1955 under the name of AFL-CIO.

Early Labor Legislation

By 1920 most states had adopted workmen's compensation laws that provided for the payment of benefits to employees injured while on the job or to the dependents of those workers who are killed on the job. The Railway Labor Act of 1926, amended several times since, provides for mediation, voluntary arbitration of wage disputes, and compulsory investigation by the National Railroad Adjustment Board before a strike can be called. If the Mediation Board cannot settle a dispute, the matter is referred to the President of the United States, who appoints a fact-finding committee. The Davis-Bacon Act of 1931 specifies the payment of certain prevailing wages, as determined by the Secretary of Labor, on federal construction projects. The Norris-LaGuardia Anti-Injunction Act of 1932 defines and limits the powers of federal courts that issue injunctions in labor disputes by explaining when and under what circumstances injunctions may be issued. This act made unenforceable in federal courts the "yellow-dog contracts" in which a worker agrees not to join a union as a condition of employment.

To put people back to work at a decent living wage following the depression years, the National Industrial Recovery Act (NIRA) was passed in 1933. The NIRA attempted to equalize wage differentials geographically and to prescribe equal wages and salaries for the same work in all areas. All attempts failed, however, and in 1935 the United States Supreme Court ruled that the NIRA was unconstitutional since it was based upon an unconstitutional delegation of legislative power.

Until the passage of the National Labor Relations Act (Wagner Act) in 1935, union organization was at a standstill. This act prohibited employers from interfering with the formation or administration of any labor organization. The act gave to employees "the right to self-organization, to form, join, or assist labor organizations to bargain collectively through representatives of their own choosing." *Collective bargaining* is defined by the act to include three duties: (1) the duty of both the employer and the representative of the employees to sit down at the same table and work to achieve a mutually acceptable labor contract, (2) the duty of both sides to work sincerely and honestly toward a labor agreement — to bargain in good faith, and (3) the duty to limit the bargaining to wages, hours, and other terms and conditions of employment. Over the years, however, this subject matter has been dramatically expanded to include wages and employee benefits, grievance procedures, arbitration, no-strike clauses, length of contract, management rights, discipline, seniority, and union security. Thus, as a result of the Wagner Act, collective bargaining was made an instrument of national policy, and the way was paved for labor to organize and to bargain collectively.

The Social Security Act of 1935, amended many times since its passage, is one of the most important laws that protects workers who are out of work through no fault of their own. In addition to providing assistance to unemployed workers qualifying under the act, insurance is provided for retirement, survivors, and disability benefits, and health insurance for the aged (popularly known as Medicare). The Walsh-Healey Public Contract Act of 1936 establishes minimum wages and maximum hours for work done on government contracts amounting to $10,000 or more, with the Secretary of Labor deciding the minimum wages that contractors are to pay. The Fair Labor Standards Act of 1938, commonly called the Wage and Hour Law, provides a 40-hour workweek for employees in firms engaged in interstate commerce. Covered employees receive a minimum wage and payment of time and one half for all hours worked over 40 in one week. The act also prohibits, with certain exceptions, the employment of minors in order to protect their health and safety.

The most far-reaching piece of labor law in the United States was the Labor-Management Relations Act (Taft-Hartley Law) of 1947. During World War II, employers and unions cooperated with governmental agencies in carrying out the war in accordance with the National Labor Relations Act. After the war, however, there was strong public agitation to amend or change the act because it prohibited employers from performing certain labor practices and did not provide for unfair union practices. As a result, the National Labor Relations Act was amended by the Taft-Hartley Law. Some of the more important provisions of the Taft-Hartley Law with which the office manager should become familiar are given as follows:

1. The National Labor Relations Board is the quasi-judicial agency that hears testimony, renders decisions, determines the collective bargaining unit or agency, and prosecutes unfair labor practices.
2. Unfair labor practices on the part of the employer and the union are enumerated, some of which are listed in Figure 13-1.
3. Both unions and employers can be sued for violation of the labor contract. The *labor contract* is a private agreement entered into by the employer and the employees for the purpose of regulating certain work-related conditions. The provisions of the contract are binding on both sides for a mutually acceptable period of time and are enforceable through procedures such as mediation and arbitration, or finally through state and federal courts. In *mediation*, an impartial third party tries to bring both sides to a point of common agreement. In *arbitration*, labor and management agree to submit the issue in dispute to an individual arbitrator or a board of arbitration that renders a decision binding upon labor and management.
4. A 60-day notice must be given to either party before the normal termination of a labor contract, and the Federal Mediation and Conciliation Service must be notified within 30 days after the 60-day notice if no agreement is reached.
5. Union shop agreements must be in accordance with prevailing state laws and are void where prohibited by state laws. A *union shop agreement* requires that after a worker has been hired, he or she must join the union within a specified period of time or be fired. (Twenty states have right-to-work laws that ban contracts which make union membership or the payment of fees a condition of employment).
6. Nonpayment of dues under an authorized union-shop contract is the only cause for loss of good standing with the union for which the employer can be compelled to discharge or fire an employee.
7. Union dues check-off (deducting of union dues from paychecks by the employer and remitting of collections to the union) requires the written consent of the employee.
8. An individual employee can present grievances directly to his or her supervisor, but the union representative must be informed and be given an opportunity to be present.
9. Supervisors may be unionized, but the employer does not have to recognize or bargain with them since they represent management.
10. Employees may decertify (eliminate) the union selected to represent them, but only during the 60- to 90-day period at the end of the contract.

After the Taft-Hartley Law had been in operation, the need for certain changes in its provisions became apparent. As the result of the investigations into corrupt practices occurring within the field of union-management relations, the Labor-Management Reporting and Disclosure Act was passed in 1959 to: protect the rights of individual union members, protect the equities of members in union welfare funds, and prevent racketeering or unscrupulous practices from being committed by certain employers and union officers. One of the most important provisions of this act, also known as the Landrum-Griffin Act, is the Bill of Rights of Union Members, which requires that every union member be given the right to: (1) nominate candidates for union office, (2) vote in union elections or referendums, (3) attend union meetings, and (4) participate in union meetings and vote on union business. Under the act unions

By the Employer	By the Union
(a) Cannot interfere with or restrain employees from joining a union.	(a) Cannot coerce or restrain an employee who does not want to join a union.
(b) Cannot dominate or influence a labor organization.	(b) Cannot coerce or restrain an employer in the selection of the parties to bargain in the employer's behalf.
(c) Cannot discriminate against employees because of union membership.	(c) Cannot charge excessive or discriminatory union initiation fees.
(d) Cannot terminate employment or discriminate against employees for testifying before the National Labor Relations Board or any other agency in connection with the Taft-Hartley Law.	(d) Cannot refuse to bargain collectively with an employer.
(e) Cannot refuse to bargain collectively with the duly chosen representatives of the employees.	(e) Cannot practice "featherbedding" — making employer pay for services not rendered.
	(f) Cannot persuade an employer to discriminate against any employee.
	(g) Cannot attempt to force recognition from an employer when another union is already the certified representative.

Fig. 13-1
Unfair Labor Practices

are required to file a financial report with the Secretary of Labor each year and employers must report any expenditures that are made in attempting to persuade employees to exercise their bargaining rights.

The Wagner Act of 1935 applied only to workers in private enterprises. Under a presidential executive order in 1962, which was followed by similar legislation in the states during the 1960s, collective bargaining rights were granted to government employees.

Recent Labor Legislation

In Chapter 11 several federal and state laws were described as marking the beginning of a new era in labor relations. A summary of the major federal laws follows:

1. *Equal Pay Act of 1963*, an amendment to the Fair Labor Standards Act, providing that no employer may discriminate solely on the basis of sex in determining the wage rates of men and mining the wage rates of men and women who are doing equal work under similar working conditions.

2. *Civil Rights Act of 1964*, in which one section — Title VII, Equal Employment Opportunity — provides that employers, unions, and employment agencies may not discriminate in their hiring and training practices on the bases of race, color, religion, national origin, or sex.

3. *Age Discrimination in Employment Act of 1967*, which prohibits age discrimination by employers, unions, and employment agencies against those individuals who are between the ages of 40 and 65 years.

4. *Vocational Rehabilitation Act of 1973*, designed to provide employment opportunities for qualified physically and mentally handicapped persons and to eliminate employment discrimination based on physical or mental handicaps.

5. *Vietnam Era Veterans' Readjustment Assistance Act of 1974*, requiring government contractors to take affirmative action to employ qualified veterans of the Vietnam era and disabled veterans.

In addition to these labor laws, another piece of legislation that has far-reaching effects upon labor-management relations is the Occupational Safety and Health Act of 1970 (OSHA). This law was passed by Congress to insure American workers a safe and healthy work place. For many years there has been much public concern for wildlife and environmental pollution, but the far greater health and safety hazards to human beings in the work place have been greatly ignored. By 1970, the yearly job-related accident toll was estimated at 2.2 million injuries, 400,000 illnesses, and 14,500 deaths.[1] The Occupational Safety and Health Administration, established by the act, was directed to encourage states to develop and operate their own job safety and health programs, which must be at least as effective as the federal program. Funds were also provided by Congress for financing, planning, and operating the state programs.

OSHA requires that an employer furnish a place of employment free from recognized hazards that are likely to cause death or serious physical harm. Under the act employers are required to keep records of work-related deaths, illnesses, and injuries; maintain records of employee exposure to materials that are potentially toxic; and notify employees of their exposure to such materials when the toxic effects exceed the set standards. Trained safety inspectors, employed by the government, have the responsibility for enforcing the extensive standards, which cover most aspects of the job environment. For example, each of the following kinds of office environments described in Chapter 6 is covered by these standards:

1. *Surface environment* — exact specifications for aisle widths, stairs and ladders, entries and exits, rest rooms and lunch rooms, and other walking and working surfaces.
2. *Seeing environment* — specifications for lighting levels and regulations that apply to electrical groundings and hook-ups.
3. *Hearing environment* — restrictions upon permissible noise levels (decibels) at place of work in relation to duration of the exposure. As indicated in Chapter 6, the level of 90 db. is acceptable for an exposure period of eight hours.
4. *Atmospheric environment* — specifications for vents and ventilation and limits for air contaminants, fumes, and, as mentioned above, exposure to toxic chemicals.

In addition to routine, unannounced visits by OSHA inspectors, inspections may be requested by workers who spot on-the-job safety and health hazards. Although an employee who has filed a complaint may keep his or her name confidential, the employee is given protection by the act, which states that no employee shall be discharged or in any manner discriminated against by the employer because a complaint has been filed.

TRENDS IN LABOR-MANAGEMENT RELATIONS

Increasingly, labor and management are entering into agreements that include broadened provisions aimed at meeting the workers' needs for job and personal security by protecting the workers against unemployment of all kinds, shrinkage of the purchasing power of the dollars earned, and the

---

[1]John H. Stender, "OSHA and Management: Alliance for Safety," *Managers' Forum* (June, 1975), p. 1.

uncertainties of old age. Some of the efforts that have been made to insure jobs and income and to maintain employee benefits include: guarantee against job or income loss; cost-of-living escalator clauses that protect the workers' purchasing power by tying increases in wages and salaries to an index that measures increases in the cost of living; protection of pensions against inflation; supplementary unemployment compensation for employees who lose their jobs; guarantee of income for workers required to take lower paying jobs; provision for retraining; provision for transfer to other plants and payment of relocation expenses; agreements that provide workers with notice of plant closing or other major changes that affect the workers' earning capacity; and expanded benefits packages to include employer-paid dental-care programs, extended medical coverage, improved sickness and accident benefits, and additional vacation and holiday time. There appears to be growing acceptance of the philosophy that layoffs resulting from technological innovation should be handled exclusively through attrition.

Joint Labor-Management Committees

Use has been made of labor-management committees in a wide variety of industries in an attempt to ease collective bargaining and to find solutions to many labor problems ranging from minor grievances to the installation of automated systems and procedures. For example, a cooperative undertaking has occurred between one company and the union as a result of the firm's concern with productivity and the union's concern with combatting worker boredom. The company and the union have joint-

ly announced their commitment to elevate the status of the individual worker and enrich jobs while working to maintain productivity.[2] By means of exploring mutually the changing trends in manufacturing processes, working conditions, and employee benefits, such committees are able to lay the groundwork for early settlement of labor-management difficulties rather than waiting until the contract expires.

The Shortened Workweek

A labor-management bargaining issue that has received much attention in the past few years is the length of the workweek. In 1969 the president of the United Steelworkers reported to the convention of the AFL-CIO Industrial Union Department that 1974 was the target for getting the whole union onto the four-day week.[3] Four years earlier at the meeting of the Office & Professional Employees International Union in San Francisco, the union had urged that locals press for a 32-hour, four-day week under a three-shift arrangement that would keep office operations staffed Monday through a full day on Saturday. Howard Coughlin, president of the Office & Professional Employees International Union, anticipated a four-day week in the 1970s, as the result of social forces that had been in motion for many years. Coughlin noted that the workweek for white-collar workers has continued to change, having declined three hours each decade since 1900 until it reached 37½ hours in the eastern United States. The three-shift workweek

---

[2]*Management in Practice* (October, 1974), p. 1.

[3]Kenneth E. Wheeler, "Small Business Eyes the Four-Day Workweek," *Harvard Business Review* (May–June, 1970), p. 143.

plan of Coughlin would embrace one shift of persons working Monday through Thursday, another from Tuesday through Friday, and a third group from Wednesday through Saturday. In this manner, a business firm would have the advantage of six days' work at straight-time rates.[4]

Taking an opposite stand, the editors of *Administrative Management* magazine cited the foreseeable shortage of competent workers and the added element of cost and disagreed that the anticipated four-day workweek would be widely observed within this decade.[5] Other authorities, such as Riva Poor, in her book *4 Days, 40 Hours*, stated that the four-day week would become widespread before too long.[6] As a result of her extensive study of firms in the United States, Poor predicted that the four-day week would sweep the country — and much faster than the five-day week had replaced the six-day week, a move that spanned some four decades between 1908 and the end of World War II.[7]

The 4/40 Workweek. The *4/40 workweek* is a fixed work schedule that consists of four work days during the week, each of which is 10 hours in duration. The 4/40 workweek represented a radical departure from previous trends, since historically labor unions and other groups have tried to reduce *both* the number of days worked each week and the numbers of hours worked each day. This form of shortened workweek was originally introduced by management, primarily in small and medium-size nonunion firms, as a means of providing their workers with a benefit not found in larger companies. The objectives of introducing the 4/40 workweek were to increase production and profits, to improve morale, to decrease costs and overtime requirements, to reduce absenteeism and turnover, to improve employee recruitment, and to obtain better utilization of equipment by reducing the number of start-ups and shut-downs.

In its 1971 study of the four-day week, which included several combinations such as 4/35, 4/37, and 4/40, the American Management Association found from the presidents and other executives of the 811 firms answering the survey that 5 percent were on a rearranged workweek and that 18 percent were planning or evaluating a four-day week. In those companies that were on a four-day week, 38 percent reported an overall decrease in operating expenses, while 11 percent of the firms experienced higher costs; production was increased in 62 percent of the firms; efficiency increased in 66 percent of the companies; profits increased in 51 percent of the firms. Although many observers estimate the failure rate for the four-day week at 10 to 15 percent, the AMA survey detected a failure rate of only 8 percent. In those firms with rearranged workweeks, the major problem area appeared to be the increased difficulty in scheduling the work. Increased fatigue in relationship to overall productivity, one of the prime concerns of many critics of the four-day week, was mentioned in the AMA survey by only eight respondents as being the principal disadvantage.[8]

---

[4]"A 4-Day Work Week Is Inevitable," *Administrative Management* (May, 1970), pp. 22–23.

[5]"4-Day Week Soon? We Doubt It," *Administrative Management* (May, 1970), p. 17.

[6]Riva Poor (ed.), *4 Days, 40 Hours* (Cambridge: Bursk and Poor Publishing, 1970), p. 37.

[7]"The Leisure Class — Firms, Workers Cheer as the Four-Day Week Makes Some Inroads," *The Wall Street Journal*, October 15, 1970, p. 1.

[8]Kenneth E. Wheeler, Richard Gurman, and Dale Tarnowieski, *The Four-Day Week* (New

A few years later in another study of the four-day workweek, the Bureau of the Census studied a sample survey of 47,000 households as part of its 1973 and 1974 Current Population Survey. This study found that the five-day workweek still dominated the work schedules of wage and salary workers and that workweeks longer than five days are still much more prevalent than workweeks shorter than five days. In May, 1974, 1.1 million workers, or 2 percent of all full-time wage and salary workers, were regularly working less than five full days a week. Wage and salary workers who regularly put in 5½, 6, or even 7 days a week were far more numerous. Totaling over 9 million employees, they accounted for 16 percent of all full-time workers. Almost 49 million full-time wage and salary workers, or four fifths of the total, usually worked five days each week in 1974.[9] Similar findings were revealed two years later in May, 1976, when the Bureau of Labor Statistics reported that about 1.3 million workers were putting in 35 or more hours weekly in less than five days. This study confirmed that although the four-day workweek has been discussed as an energy-saving device and as a booster of employee morale, there has been little growth in the number of employees on shorter weeks.[10]

The Census study found that the five-day workweek is encouraged as a result of collective bargaining premium-pay (overtime) provisions which combine with legal restrictions. Among those laws that encourage a limit on the daily hours by requiring premium pay after eight hours a day are the Contract Work Hours and Safety Standards Act and the Walsh-Healey Public Contract Act, which apply to most workers in firms holding government contracts. However, some companies that are required to pay overtime rates for any hours worked over eight each day reduce the base pay so that the weekly pay plus overtime remains the same as before. Although most labor officials oppose four-day workweeks that increase the daily work time beyond eight hours, the Census study showed that union members were as likely as nonunion members to be working under such schedules.

Outlook for the 4/40 Workweek. When the 4/40 workweek came upon the scene, many employees were dissatisfied with their working lives and were eager for a change — any change — to relieve their status quo. Thus, the new revolutionary concept was greeted with great enthusiasm as an antidote to worker boredom and alienation. Although there are a considerable number of successful applications, the initial impetus to convert to the 4/40 workweek seems to have faded and much of the enthusiasm has waned. The 4/40 will not disappear from the horizon, but, instead, will become one of the several approaches for workers and management to consider as they strive to meet their own needs and those of the firm.[11]

York: American Management Association, 1972), pp. 2–14.

[9]Janice N. Hedges, "How Many Days Make a Workweek?" *Monthly Labor Review* (April, 1975), p. 30.

[10]"The Four-Day Workweek," *Bulletin to Management*, The Bureau of National Affairs (Washington: U.S. Government Printing Office, March 31, 1977), pp. 4–5.

[11]See B. J. Hodge and Richard D. Tellier, "Employee Reactions to the Four-Day Week," *California Management Review* (Fall, 1975), pp. 25–30, for a study of how 223 employees in 12 companies throughout the United States perceive the four-day week. This study concluded that: no matter how employees were classified (sex, age,

As an early supporter of the 4/40 workweek, management consultant Kenneth E. Wheeler prescribed the compressed workweek for certain firms, mainly smaller companies that could more easily adjust their production schedules. Today, however, Wheeler's philosophy is that most firms ought to retain the five-day week or adopt a flexible system where workers select their own schedules.[12] Although the 4/40 may be the answer for some small- and medium-size firms working on two shifts, it is doubtful over a long period of time that either morale or productivity is increased as a result of converting to the 4/40. Over a short period of time, because it meets some workers' needs by allowing them more time for family and leisure, the 4/40 does tend to raise the morale level. As the novelty begins to wear off, however, it is doubtful that morale will remain at a high level. As one critic has stated, "Purely from a behavioral scientific and theoretical perspective, the major reason for instituting the 4/40 workweek, to improve morale,

is of dubious validity."[13] Not every firm that converts to a rearranged schedule has found it a blessing, for at least 10 percent of those that convert go off the schedule, sometimes because management decides the change is not paying off in greater efficiency per payroll dollar and sometimes because workers, especially those with families, have difficulty in adjusting either at home or at the work place.[14]

It is generally believed that, with a compressed workweek, productivity will increase. However, in a pilot study of 16 firms on either a four- or a three-day workweek, it was found that while productivity did increase in some firms, there was no change in others, and a decrease in the remainder.[15] Similar effects upon productivity were reported in the AMA survey which found that in two thirds of the firms, productivity increased; in almost one third of the companies productivity remained about the same; and in three percent of the companies productivity decreased.[16] As the hours worked each day increase on routine jobs, the level of enthusiasm and the efficiency of many workers begin to decline, and productivity decreases.

Companies considering a conversion to the 4/40 express concern about whether a schedule that provides three days off a week will lead the workers to moonlight — to take a second job —

etc.) they are substantially more satisfied with their jobs as a result of the conversion to the four-day week; the most common positive effect of the four-day week was the more (and better arranged) leisure time afforded by the longer weekend; and the most common negative effect was the general dislike of the longer workday.

The results of another survey of 98 persons' reactions toward the four-day week are reported by Thomas A. Mahoney, Jerry M. Newman, and Peter J. Frost, "Workers' Perceptions of the Four-Day Week," *California Management Review* (Fall, 1975), pp. 31–35. The results of this study of employees working both four- and five-day schedules and of employees contemplating the four-day week do not provide support for arguments in favor of the four-day week that are based upon alleged job dissatisfactions. It did not appear that employee reactions to the four-day week are related to their jobs or satisfaction with their jobs, but, rather, the reactions are more a function of perceptions of and demands for leisure.

[12]J. Carrol Swart, "What Time Shall I Go to Work Today?" *Business Horizons* (October, 1974), p. 23.

[13]Martin J. Gannon, "Four Days, Forty Hours: A Case Study," *California Management Review* (Winter, 1974), p. 76.

[14]A. H. Raskin, "Whatever Happened to the 4-Day Week?" *The New York Times*, January 19, 1975, p. 20.

[15]John J. Macut, "Measuring Productivity under a 4-Day Week," *Monthly Labor Review* (April, 1974), p. 56.

[16]Kenneth E. Wheeler, Richard Gurman, and Dale Tarnowieski, *The Four-Day Week* (New York: American Management Association, 1972), p. 19.

thus becoming more fatigued, with their health and productivity affected. When employee attitudes toward the 4/40 workweek were studied, Poor found that of the major disadvantages cited by workers in 13 firms, nearly one half cited fatigue.[17] The Census survey indicated that workers on four-day weeks were roughly twice as likely as all full-time workers to hold a second job.[18] Since moonlighting does seem to increase among workers on four-day workweeks, under such conditions fatigue can certainly be a major problem.

Employers may expect a decline in absenteeism as the 4/40 workweek is adopted, since workers have three days to take care of all personal obligations and thus will be more reluctant to take off a 10-hour day than an 8-hour day. While some managers have reported a decline in absenteeism, others observe that absences returned to their normal levels after the novelty of the 4/40 schedule wore off. The Census survey showed that four-day workers were about as likely as five-day workers to be absent and the data did not indicate that four-day weeks are effective in reducing absenteeism.[19] Turnover, too, is generally thought to improve as a result of the conversion to four-day workweeks, but the pilot study, referred to earlier, found little confirmation of this fact among the firms studied.[20] The office manager who is faced with a conversion to the 4/40 workweek may experience other potentially negative aspects. One such aspect is the difficulty in scheduling the work,

especially if the office workers spend much of their time dealing with outsiders such as sales representatives and shipping and receiving personnel who work a five-day week. Also, the office supervisors may find themselves working extra long hours.

The Census survey concluded by noting that there had been a slower growth in the number of firms with four-day workweeks from 1973 to 1974 than from 1970 to 1973.[21] One of the major causes of the decreased rate of growth has been the introduction from Europe of a different type of workweek — the flexible hour system — which is discussed next.

Emerging Patterns of Work Schedules

Office managers, workers, and unions are actively engaged in discussing and experimenting with new organizations of working schedules that represent permanent shifts away from the traditional five-day, 9 to 5, 40-hour week. In addition to the fixed work schedule, such as the 4/40 workweek, the other kinds of work schedules being used in the United States and abroad include: (1) staggered, (2) flexible, and (3) variable, each of which is described in the following paragraphs.

Staggered Work Schedule. Under the staggered work schedule system, groups of workers arrive at their work places at different times, according to a master plan. Once the hours have been set, they do not change and all employees work a predetermined number of hours during the workday. Individual workers have no more control over the starting and quitting time of their work than with the fixed work schedule.

---

[17]Riva Poor (ed.), *4 Days, 40 hours* (Cambridge: Bursk and Poor Publishing, 1970), p. 111.
[18]Janice N. Hedges, "How Many Days Make a Workweek?" *Monthly Labor Review* (April, 1975), p. 32.
[19]*Ibid.*, pp. 33–34.
[20]Macut, *op. cit.*, p. 55.

[21]Hedges, *op. cit.*, p. 33.

The Staggered Work Hours Program, designed to encourage the voluntary staggering of workers among Manhattan firms, has been adopted by more than 400 lower Manhattan firms, representing more than 220,000 employees. The objective of the program is to persuade business and government offices to switch from the customary 9 to 5 schedule so that a more even distribution of commuting times may be obtained. The program was an immediate success in alleviating commuter tie-ups, reducing waiting times for elevators, and lessening lobby congestion in large office buildings, with the result that the program has been expanded to include the midtown Manhattan work district.[22]

Flexible Work Schedule. Flexible work scheduling had its birth in West Germany in 1967. Its introduction in Europe has been spearheaded by Switzerland, where an estimated 15 to 20 percent of all industrial firms utilize a flexible schedule.[23] In West Germany more than 3,000 companies, involving over one million employees, use some form of flexible hours.[24]

The *flexible work schedule*, also known as *flextime* and *gliding time*, re-

places the fixed times of worker arrival and departure and divides the working day into two different types of time: core time and flexible time. During *core time*, a number of hours is designated during which all employees must be present for work. *Flexible time* is the time employees may choose for their arrival and departure times from the office. Under a typical plan each worker elects to come in at any time from 6 to 9 a.m. and leave at any time from 3 to 6 p.m. The only fixed hours (the core time) when all workers must be on the job are the peak workload hours 9 a.m. to 3 p.m. The two requirements of the plan are that all employees be present during core time and that required hours be accounted for on a daily basis. Beyond this, working hours can be selected to meet the individual needs and requirements of each firm. Lunch periods may vary both in duration and the time at which taken. If employees work for a company where overtime pay requirements pose no problems, they may carry over hours from one day to the next or even between pay periods.

Since flexible work scheduling, in contrast to the fixed 4/40 workweek, permits employees to have some say about the conditions and processes affecting their work, the workers are actively engaged in participative management, as discussed in Chapter 12. When employees make the decision to work longer hours when there is more to do and then take time off when things are slow, they have the opportunity to either contribute to or withhold their contributions from meeting the organization's goals, for the availability of this "free"

---

[22]Cynthia J. Fields, "Staggered Work Hours — A Roundtable Discussion," *Personnel Journal* (February, 1975), pp. 80–82.

[23]Martin J. Gannon, "Four Days, Forty Hours: A Case Study," *California Management Review* (Winter, 1974), p. 78. An especially comprehensive study of flexible work scheduling in Swiss firms is detailed in Heinz Allenspach, *Flexible Working Hours* (Geneva: International Labour Office, 1975).

[24]Alvar O. Elbing, Herman Gadon, and John R. M. Gordon, "Flexible Working Hours: It's about Time," *Harvard Business Review* (January–February, 1974), p. 18. In this article the authors maintain that some form of the flexible working hours system so popular in Europe may well become standard for United States companies. They describe the benefits of adopting the system and

some of the problems involved in implementation and suggest that the issue of trust is at the bottom of both.

labor force, when needed during peak hours, is under the workers' control.[25] Flexible working hours also appeal to the workers' needs for more responsibility, allowing them more autonomy on the job.

Illustrative Flexible Work Schedules.

To show the variations that may exist in flexible work scheduling, three systems are briefly described.

In a study of flextime scheduling conducted by the Social Security Administration's Bureau of Data Processing, an experimental group of clerical workers were allowed to establish their own work hours, after consulting with their supervisors, so that they worked an eight-hour day between 6:30 a.m. and 6 p.m. Workers were permitted to vary their shifts, day by day, so long as they put in eight hours and their schedules conformed with the workloads of the Bureau. Although no advance notification to the supervisors regarding starting times was required, at least one supervisor was on duty for the entire workday.[26] The Bureau's test study brought forth the following results: generally increased productivity and improved workflow with a drastic decline in overtime, more job satisfaction, caring for children made easier, accuracy of work improved, getting to work made easier, and more time was available to spend with families.[27] The only problem encountered was in scheduling the shifts of supervisory personnel to pro-

vide supervision for the entire period between 6:30 a.m. and 6 p.m. As a result of this study, the government plans to extend the flextime system to other Social Security Administration units.

One of the most liberal flexible hours plans is found in the East Hanover, New Jersey, offices of Sandoz-Wander, a subsidiary of a Swiss drug firm. Here the office employees can carry over or owe hours from week to week. With a regular workweek of 37½ hours, an employee can work 40 hours a week and accumulate 2½ hours of carryover time each week (at regular pay), with a maximum total of 10 hours carryover time. Thus, subsequent workweeks can be shortened by the amount of time the worker has "banked." In reverse, a worker can work less than the 37½ hours and thus owe the company time which can be made up in subsequent weeks.[28]

In the offices of Pitney Bowes, a manufacturer of business equipment, employees start to work any time after 7 a.m. and may work up to 6 p.m. The only time they must be on the job is during the core period of each day, that busy time when each department needs its full staff. Employees may put in more than the regular 7½ hours one day and have corresponding time off another day for their personal needs. Each worker records his or her arrival time by inserting a plastic "key" in a timing device that records the amount of time the employee works during the week, not the daily hours worked.[29] Flextime was found unsuitable for those employees

---

[25]Alvar O. Elbing, Herman Gadon, John R. M. Gordon, "Flexible Working Hours: The Missing Link," *California Management Review* (Spring, 1975), p. 51.

[26]*Bulletin to Management*, The Bureau of National Affairs (Washington: U.S. Government Printing Office, January 2, 1975), pp. 4–5.

[27]"Federal Offices Try Flexible Hours," *The Office* (December, 1974), p. 70.

[28]"New Points in Time, Rather Come in Later, or Go Home Earlier? More Bosses Say OK," *The Wall Street Journal*, July 13, 1973, p. 25.

[29]"Workers Set Own Hours, 'Work Harder,'" *The Cincinnati Enquirer*, January 26, 1975, p. 8-E.

who spend much time outside the office and, because of federal regulations pertaining to daily overtime pay, the scheduling cannot be extended to manufacturing employees involved in government contracts.

Benefits and Weaknesses of Flexible Work Schedules. Feedback from the flextime systems found in the United States and in other countries forecasts a wide use of flexible work scheduling. Because of the newness of the approach in the United States and the lack of research, a firm contemplating conversion to flextime should proceed cautiously by analyzing its own work requirements and its employees' needs within the climate of the organization. When the German approach to flextime is instituted in English-speaking countries, it must be done in a democratic way, according to the manager of a Chemistry Department in England, who went on to say, "Only when you get the employees to realize it's their system and they're running it for their own benefit, will it work.[30]

Some of the primary benefits and potential disadvantages of flexible work scheduling for the company, the workers, and for society are discussed in the following paragraphs.

For the Company. Companies that have converted to flextime note significant gains in productive hours, for regardless of the starting time, employees still put in a full day or a full week of work. Absences of less than half a day as well as full-day absences are reduced, for flextime overcomes the necessity of taking sick leave to care for personal business affairs. The output per hours

worked increases because employees gain more satisfaction, which typically means better production. Employees who perform better early in the day (or later in the day) are enabled to come in early (or late) and be at work during their most productive hours. Workers become more inclined to stop work only after they have completed a task, thus reducing the start-up time on the following day and avoiding downtime at the end of the workday.

In working with flextime scheduling, supervisors more actively delegate responsibilities and provide understudy training in order to provide coverage during the lengthened workday. Companies find that they can attract more and better job applicants, for the choice of work schedules appeals to jobseekers who want to select the most advantageous means of transportation and starting times to suit their own life styles. The successful operation of flextime confirms that workers do respond in a positive and responsible manner when they are treated as mature adults with individual differences. Thus, in working with flextime, supervisors learn that motivational tools such as job enrichment must be realistically applied.

Among the possible disadvantages of converting to flextime is the added cost of providing more extensive external and internal communications. For example, can telephone coverage be adequately planned over the longer workday? Meetings outside the core-time periods tend to be called less spontaneously (a possible blessing in disguise) and thus require more advance planning. Some companies experience difficulty in maintaining adequate supervision to make sure that all functions are covered during the workday when other people in the company are depending on

---

[30] J. Robert Moskin, "Flextime," *Réalités* (November, 1972), p. 29.

them. Because of the longer hours of operation, there is an increase in energy costs. Additional costs may be incurred, too, in the purchase of special time-recording equipment. Finally, some supervisors feel that they are not doing their jobs well if they lose control over subordinates who arrive earlier or stay later than they.

For the Workers. When working under flextime employees are able to participate more in the decision-making process and thus become positively motivated as a result of exercising more responsibility in the performance of their work, in selecting alternative courses of action, and in exerting more control over their work situations. Thus, a higher level of morale and increased job satisfaction should follow, giving evidence of the real value of job enrichment. The success of flextime, as a motivator, is due to the employee, not the employer, in making the decision whether or not to change the hours of the workday and by how much.

Employees report a reduction in early morning stress and tensions. Not having to report in at a fixed time, they do not fret when caught in the morning traffic jams. Their commuting time is reduced by selecting hours that avoid peak traffic periods. Workers are able to plan their day to obtain a better mesh of work and home life and leisure-time activities. Not fearing reprimand or the loss of pay, workers can handle their emergencies and personal problems and plan for after-work activities with less effect on the work situation.

On the other hand, workers may be pressured to work longer days when the workload is heavy, without getting overtime pay. Regarding the use of special time-recording equipment, some workers feel that time mechanisms to measure accumulated hours are a step backward toward time clocks. Many workers, however, find that the timing devices are an easy way to keep track of the hours that have accumulated. At the White Plains, New York, office of the Nestlé Company, employees do not punch time clocks. Management works on the premise that the honor system for employees is the best approach since flexible hours are to the employees' advantage and they will work to make the system work.[31]

For Society. As more and more firms convert to flextime, the miles of jammed highways and the number of frustrated motorists should be reduced since the commuting load is distributed over a longer period of time each day. Existing transportation facilities should be better utilized, since the same, or a less amount of, public transportation would be sufficient to meet demand by making more trips with the same vehicles. A more uniform use could be made of business and recreational facilities, which should experience less severe peak periods since workers have more time to shop, to visit the doctor, to play golf, etc.

Where employees are represented by a union, the union contract will have to be taken into consideration because unions are concerned that flexible scheduling will not mean the loss of overtime pay. If productivity is increased, the unions may press for the workers to share in this increased productivity. In Europe, most unions have supported the flexible working hours. In some cases, however, union officials opposed the introduction of the flexible

---

[31]*Management in Practice* (August, 1972), p. 37.

working hours only to be pressured into active support of the schedules by the members themselves.[32]

Variable Work Schedule. The most flexible of all working arrangements, the *variable working hours plan* does not specify a core time. Under this plan employees work whenever they wish and may take time off without specific permission so long as their functions are covered in their absence. One of the most advanced examples of variable work scheduling is found in the German time-recording meter assembly plant of the Hengstler Gleitzeit (gliding time) Company, where 100 employees schedule their own workdays. They all have keys to the plant and can let themselves in at any hour and turn on the assembly line.[33]

Each of the developments in the labor movement and the trends in labor-management relations are of prime concern to the administrative office manager. Of increasing importance, however, is the challenge of the onward drive by unions to organize the white-collar workers in government, trade, transportation, public utilities, finance, insurance, real estate, and other services.

UNIONIZATION OF WHITE-COLLAR WORKERS

The increased activity of unions during the period of labor legislation, as described earlier, has helped to swell union membership to more than 24 million workers. Although the number of organized workers has risen, union membership has declined as a percent of the nonagricultural work force, from 29.8 percent in 1962 to 24.5 percent in 1974. The unionization of workers could not help but affect office employees. More than one third of the gain in membership has been among government employees and white-collar workers. The increased participation of women in the labor force, together with the overall gains in organizing white-collar workers, has resulted in a larger proportion of women in organized labor. In 1974 women accounted for 25 percent of national union and employee association membership.[34]

The more than 42 million white-collar workers (15.1 million clerical workers, 12.7 million professional and technical workers, 8.9 million managers and administrators, and 5.5 million sales workers) in the United States offer a fertile field for unionization, especially since only about 6 million of them were white-collar union members in 1974.[35] In the 1977–78 Salary Survey conducted by the Administrative Management Society among 6,778 companies in the United States and Canada, representing more than 506,000 clerical and data processing employees, 90.7 percent of the firms in the United States did not have an office union; 5.4 percent reported that part of their office employees were unionized; and 2.1 percent reported an office union.[36] Little appreciable change has been noted in the extent of office unionization among the companies surveyed during the past several years.

[32]Alvar O. Elbing, Herman Gadon, John R. M. Gordon, "Flexible Working Hours: The Missing Link," *California Management Review* (Spring, 1975), pp. 28 and 33.

[33]*Ibid.*, p. 19.

[34]"Union, Employe-Group Rolls Rose 4.8% to 24.2 Million Between 1972 and 1974," *The Wall Street Journal*, August 13, 1975, p. 4.

[35]*Ibid.* Also see "Current Labor Statistics," *Monthly Labor Review* (June, 1976), p. 77.

[36]*Office Salaries Directory for United States and Canada, 1977–78* (Willow Grove: Administrative Management Society), p. 38.

In Chapter 2 it was pointed out that 53 percent of the projected labor force of 108 million in 1985 will be represented by white-collar workers. If this projection comes true, unions will be experiencing a decided decline in the number of blue-collar, unskilled, and production employees from whom they have traditionally drawn their strength and support. If the unions are to remain economically viable and retain their influential force on the political scene, they must continue to actively recruit white-collar workers. In 1976 the unions set a record in organizing white-collar workers by winning bargaining rights for about 24,500 employees, with almost 10,000 of the newly organized workers engaged in health care.[37]

Some 40 unions, such as the Office & Professional Employees International Union; the United Office and Professional Workers of America; the Retail Clerks International Association; the American Federation of State, County, and Municipal Employees; and the American Federation of Government Employees, are predominantly or wholly white-collar unions. Several blue-collar unions, such as the United Steelworkers of America, the Teamsters union, and the International Union of Electrical Workers, are trying to increase white-collar membership. In 1976 the most active organizers of white-collar workers were the Teamsters, Service Employees, and the Retail, Wholesale, and Department Store Unions.[38] It is felt by some that the smaller independent unions offer the best chances for long-range growth among office workers, for these unions are generally more informal and office oriented than those of the larger organizations.

Why White-Collar Workers Join Unions

With so many office jobs having become more routine, production-oriented, and depersonalized as a result of today's computerized information systems and company growth, many jobs have become akin to factory production work. There have been changing patterns of values, attitudes, and expectations among office workers, as indicated in Chapter 12, and as a result the unionizing of office workers is stimulated. Also the shortsightedness of management at times in its failure to provide satisfactory working conditions, adequate compensation, and employee benefits has added impetus to the formation of white-collar unions.

The main reasons offered by white-collar workers for joining unions are:

1. Discontentment over earnings and the relatively weak economic position of workers. For example, in a Princeton University study prepared for the Council on Wage and Price Stability, it was found that union members averaged 16 percent more in pay than comparable nonunion workers in 1975.[39]
2. Worker insecurity in that office workers feel there is no guarantee they will not be laid off arbitrarily, especially in periods of recession.
3. Poor handling of grievances by management, which all too often takes a "don't care" attitude.
4. Importance of employees' work not recognized by the company, which,

---

[37]"Labor Letter," *The Wall Street Journal*, May 31, 1977, p. 1.
[38]*Ibid.*

[39]"Union Wages Up, But Not Inflationary," *Bulletin to Management*, The Bureau of National Affairs (Washington: U.S. Government Printing Office, July 15, 1976), p. 2.

instead, looks upon workers as commodities to be bought and sold in the market place.

5. Inadequate channels of communications between both the employees and management.

The Opinion Research Corporation, in its study of the attitudes of clerical employees toward management, has found evidence that the traditional clerical loyalty to management is breaking down. Results of the study show that there has been a marked and growing dissatisfaction among clerical workers in the following three areas: (1) basic employment conditions (pay, benefits, job security, and working conditions); (2) personnel practices; and (3) communications.[40] Unless office managers commence to act now, clerical discontent will continue to increase and possibly history will repeat itself, with management losing out to the unions, a situation that occurred when the discontent of factory workers emerged in the 1930s.

At the low and middle levels of management, changes in life styles, value systems, attitudes, and expectations have produced pro-union sentiment. For many of the same reasons offered by clerical workers, some middle managers, frustrated and discontented with corporate life, have expressed their willingness to join a managers' union. Middle managers, too, look for more job security (especially in periods of prolonged recession), higher salaries, and better employee benefits. In its survey of more than 500 business firms, the American Management Association found that nearly one half of the middle managers favor a change in current

labor laws that would compel employers to recognize and bargain with manager unions in business organizations where managers elected to organize. Although union membership might not satisfy the deeper longings and needs of middle managers, 75 percent of the managers surveyed endorsed the idea of informal associations for supervisors and middle managers. These associations would be on an individual company basis and would meet periodically with corporate top management to discuss conditions of employment affecting supervisory and managerial personnel.[41]

James L. Hayes, president of the American Management Associations, has stated that if management development on the middle-management level is not taken more seriously than it is at present, he would not be surprised by the coming of management unionization. Hayes feels that employees would seldom need to express their grievances through collective means if organizations were effectively managed, if managers understood people and their needs — individually and collectively. Noting that in most organizations the needs for individual achievement and corporate objectives run on different "tracks," Hayes commented: "We must make the two more compatible. The two must share a common objective, a common mission."[42]

The Role of the Office Manager in Office Unionism

There are many arguments both for and against unionism, none of which seems absolutely unbiased. However, it

[40]Alfred Vogel, "Your Clerical Workers Are Ripe for Unionism," *Harvard Business Review* (March–April, 1971), p. 50.

[41]Alfred T. DeMaria, Dale Tarnowieski, and Richard Gurman, "Manager Unions?" an AMA Research Report (New York: American Management Association, 1972), p. 1.
[42]*Ibid.*, p. 17.

is no longer a question of being for or against a union for office workers. Rather, it is a question of what the office manager will do about the formation of office workers' unions or attempts to unionize office workers. What the office manager does about office unions involves these time-related factors: (1) before union activity starts, (2) while attempts are being made to organize the workers, and (3) after the workers become organized.

Before Union Activity. Long before any union activity might have started among a group of office workers, the office manager should have been studying working conditions in the office and comparing them with those conditions found in unionized offices. Wherever possible, conditions should be improved to equal or surpass those that prevail in unionized offices. But these conditions and the attempts of management must be properly presented to the workers, using the various communication media described in Chapter 12, pages 334–336. In one instance a firm was paying higher salaries than those offered by unionized companies in the area, but still dissatisfaction with salaries existed among the employees. This dissatisfaction was not due so much to the company's salary structure as to the employees' lack of reliable information from management about its wage and salary program.

Among the questions to which the administrative office manager must have answers are the following:

1. Do the working conditions in the office create a desirable level of morale? If not, how can they be improved?
2. How can the work be made more challenging and rewarding by enriching and redesigning the jobs?

3. How can the company become more responsive to employee needs for job security in the areas of salaries, promotional opportunities, vacations, suggestion plans, recreational programs, and other employee benefits? Virtually all surveys have concluded beyond any question that the prime reason white-collar employees vote for union representation is the desire to gain higher pay as a direct response to an unsatisfactory existing salary schedule.[43]
4. How can the personnel administration program and its policies be improved to provide fair, perceptive, and impartial supervision? Research has shown that a formal grievance procedure, whereby employees can air their complaints to higher management (see Chapter 12, page 336), has been a key factor in preventing white-collar unionization.[44]

While Attempts Are Being Made to Organize. If a firm is not able to provide its office workers with salaries and benefits equal or superior to those offered by unionized offices, then it must expect that in many cases the workers will seek unionization. Thus, the office manager becomes faced with the problem of how to deal with a union. If the company does not have its own legal staff, the firm should obtain competent legal counsel from the outside so that the firm will be advised regarding its statutory rights and obligations and thus avoid possible charges of unfair labor practices. Supplementing such legal help, the office manager should be familiar with labor legislation and current labor relations practices.

In many instances when attempts are being made to organize, one or more

---

[43]Erwin S. Stanton, "White-Collar Unionization: New Challenge to Management," *Personnel Journal* (February, 1972), p. 122.
[44]*Ibid.*

disgruntled workers contact a union organizer, who is invited to come in to evaluate the situation. Where the opportunity presents itself, the organizer seeks to acquire signed authorization cards from 30 percent of the employees so that the union can petition the National Labor Relations Board for an election. The *authorization card* states that the employee who has signed it authorizes the named union to represent him or her in collective bargaining. If the union organizer acquires cards from 50 percent plus one of the employees, the union can demand that the employer recognize the union as the bargaining agent and bargain with it. In this case the National Labor Relations Board certifies the labor organization and the process is complete. Many employers do not voluntarily accept the signed cards as proof of union interest, however, for they feel they should have an opportunity to tell their side of the story to the employees. In this case the regional office of the National Labor Relations Board sends an investigator to the scene to determine if sufficient interest exists among the workers to form a union. If so, the potential bargaining unit is determined and an election is called so that the employees may vote for or against the union.

Prior to the election free discussion is encouraged, but there are many rules surrounding an election and any violations constitute unfair labor practices. If over 50 percent of the employees voting choose to join a particular union, the labor organization is certified, and the employer must bargain with the organization in good faith. The employees are next classified by salary and job and a list of specific proposals covering work-related items such as wages, hours, and benefits is prepared. After the proposals have been approved by the workers, management is presented with the suggested changes. At this stage of the unionization process, a bargaining committee made up of the employee representatives and a business agent from the union meet with management to draw up the contract. After the contract has been approved, shop stewards are appointed for the various office departments and a grievance procedure is established.[45]

Any worker or group can request that another election be held at any time 12 months after the first election. If the employees vote against the labor organization, it is decertified, or eliminated. The employer, however, cannot make such a request or even encourage it.

After the Workers Become Organized. Once the union has been established, management and the employees should work toward realizing the objectives of the firm and those of the union, which will be attained only through harmonious labor relations. New relationship patterns come to be developed between the company and the new union, with a more formal, rigid, and legalistic system of relationships emerging. As a result, management will find itself much more restricted in future actions and in its decision-making processes. To create positive union-management relations, management must maintain open lines of communications between all parties involved in the collective bargaining relationship and make sure that the contract is

---

[45]For exceptionally fine descriptions of a typical union campaign, see James O. Dunn, "Union Campaign — Organizer vs. Supervisor," *Personnel* (August, 1970), pp. 15–24, and (January, 1972), pp. 8–15; and Rose Clavering, "The Unionizing Drive: What's Fair, What's Legal?" *Supervisory Management* (September, 1975), pp. 25–34.

uniformly interpreted and applied by all supervisors and middle managers. Finally, companies can establish rapport and create the best morale-building relationships by working with the union and not against it. At the same time, however, both management and employees must remember that the employees are still employed by the company, and that it is the company that hired them, pays them, and expects their support.[46]

----

[46]Michael J. Shershin and W. Randy Boxx, "Building Positive Union-Management Relations," *Personnel Journal* (June, 1975), pp. 326–331. In this article the authors present their recommendations for improving union-management relations and establishing stable industrial relations policies.

QUESTIONS FOR REVIEW

1. What are the major provisions of the National Labor Relations Act of 1935?

2. What are the three duties prescribed by collective bargaining for employers and representatives of their employees?

3. The Labor-Management Relations Act of 1947 enumerates certain unfair labor practices. What are the unfair labor practices (a) on the part of the employer and (b) on the part of the union?

4. What requirements are imposed upon employers by the Occupational Safety and Health Act to ensure that workers have a safe and healthy work place?

5. For what purposes are joint labor-management committees formed?

6. In relation to length of workweek, what were the findings of the Bureau of the Census study conducted in 1973 and 1974? What appears to be the future of the 4/40 workweek?

7. Describe how a staggered work schedule operates.

8. Compare and contrast the flexible work schedule and the variable-work schedule.

9. When employees work under flextime, how are they taking part in participative management?

10. What are the benefits and weaknesses of flexible work schedules from the viewpoint of (a) the company and (b) the employees?

11. What are the main reasons advanced by white-collar workers for joining unions?

12. Compare the role of the office manager in office unionism under each of the following situations: (a) before union activity, (b) while attempts are being made to organize, and (c) after the workers become organized.

QUESTIONS FOR DISCUSSION

1. A nonunion company is planning to install a formal grievance procedure as a means of curing employee dissatisfaction while at the same time keeping the union out. What problems may face the nonunion firm under such conditions?

2. A labor lawyer has stated that the supervisor is the most essential person in management when it comes to deciding whether a company is going to be organized by a union. What arguments can you advance to support this statement?

3. Alice Canter, an office employee, was injured on the job when she slipped and fell on the highly waxed tile floor. She is now threatening to sue the company, claiming that she was hurt because the firm failed to comply with OSHA safety standards. Can Canter bring suit against her employer? If so, how should she proceed? If not, is Canter entitled to any aid in the form of money?

4. Flextime is still in its infancy as a work concept in the United States and its future is unknown. Both management and organized labor view flextime as part of a broad picture of changing work conditions. Assuming for a moment that flextime were to become the standard form of workweek in the United States by 1986, what changes would you expect to see in work conditions?

5. Schweizer & Sons has just won a union representation election by a very small margin. Management now intends to increase wages and salaries, to improve certain employee benefits, and to accomplish other aims listed by the union in its leaflets distributed prior to the election. Evaluate the wisdom of such a move by management at this time.

6. The Kekaha Supply Company has had a coffee break in its offices both in the morning and in the afternoon for the past 12 years. Recently there seems to be evidence of some unionizing interest in the office that has worried the office manager, Lani Honomu. In an effort to discourage the unionizing activities, she has told the employees that if they join a union, the coffee breaks will be discontinued. This did not deter their efforts, nor the formation of their union. Discuss the actions of Honomu in light of modern labor-management relations.

7. The office force of the Sauer Company consists of 49 women, who are supervised by John Proudfoot. Early one Monday morning Proudfoot's secretary rushes into his office and breathlessly reports: "I've just heard from Lois Smith that we are going to have a union in here." Proudfoot coolly replies, "Forget it. These women don't want a union. They're only working for pin money to help out at home. Besides, the bulk of them will only be with us until they marry or start raising a family." As Proudfoot's secretary, how do you perceive your boss and his statements?

8. An election date for union representation has just been set for the offices of the Davis Tire Company. The company has decided that

merely because it lost the first round, it need not lose the next — the election. Feeling that working time is for work, the company has decided to institute a "no solicitation, no distribution" rule governing all union activity. The company has notified its employees that there are to be no oral communications or distribution of union literature during lunch breaks or rest periods. Is the company proceeding legally or has it engaged in an unfair labor practice?

9. How do you react to each of the following comments about the subject unionism:

   (a) Unions are "for the birds" — for people without much education who can't stand on their own two feet.
   (b) Unions may be a necessary evil, despite the strikes and all. If the company recognized individual worth, the union would not be needed.

PRACTICAL OFFICE MANAGEMENT CASES

Case 13-1   Wearing Blue Jeans on the Job[47]

The supervisor could not restrain an involuntary gasp when she walked into the switchboard room. There was operator Flora DeWitt attired in a tattered, faded, soiled pair of blue jeans. "Really now, Flora!" she exclaimed. "You ought to know better than to dress like that. We won't have it here."

"I don't see anything wrong with it," Flora pouted. "Hardly anybody sees us switchboard girls at work. Jeans make me comfortable."

"It's a dreadful way to dress for work," the supervisor rejoined. "Don't let it happen again."

Flora resumed wearing conventional dress the following day. Her conversion lasted two weeks. Then she came to work again in blue jeans — even dirtier and more torn than her previous pair.

When the supervisor spotted Flora this time, she made short shrift of her. "I have only one thing to say to you," she snapped. "You've forfeited your job. Go home!"

The blue jeans enthusiast did not go home; she went straight to her union. "Get that job back for me," Flora demanded. "That old battleax of a supervisor is still living in the 1890's."

A grievance proceeding was promptly started. Before an arbitrator, Flora explained:

1. Modern young people dress very casually. Wearing jeans that are somewhat faded is a mark of my generation.

---

[47]*White-Collar Management* (New York: Man & Manager, Inc., April 15, 1975), Issue 1222.

2. What conceivable difference can it make to my employer if I wear them? I'm invisible to people whose calls I take on the switchboard. Visitors to the telephone room are few and far between.
3. It's unreasonable for the company to interfere with my desire to be comfortable.

Management rejoined:

1. Wearing jeans is a violation of a long-standing company rule. Flora was told about it when she came to work for us.
2. The switchboard area is not isolated from the public. Customers, salesmen, and delivery personnel often pass through it. We want them to get an impression of employee neatness — not the slovenliness that Flora indulged in.
3. Nor can she claim that we acted precipitantly. She was warned that there would be trouble after she committed her first offense.

Prepare a report in which you discuss the following questions:

1. What is your reaction to the manner in which the supervisor first disciplined DeWitt? Would you have proceeded differently in criticizing her? If so, how?
2. Was DeWitt right or wrong — do employees have the right to wear blue jeans on the job?
3. What do you see as the most pressing problem of labor-management relations in this case? What approach would you take in solving this problem?

Case 13-2   Cussing Like a Man[48]

Fem liberation advocates have been grabbing plenty of headlines — and getting results. State laws designed to protect the "weaker" sex have fallen by the wayside as more women take their places on an equal foot with men in industry.

"Shop talk" wasn't encouraged at Formsby Electronics, but neither was it discouraged. The rough banter between workers was an accepted fact of plant life — with one exception, the assembly room where the women worked. Any man entering that sanctum was careful to curb his tongue. After all, there were ladies present!

Then the job barriers fell, and the female workers branched out from the assembly room to all parts of the plant. At first the men felt uncomfortable working next to women. It's tough not to rip off an oath when your finger gets nicked or a tool drops on your toe.

But the women soon put the men at their ease. The men were shocked — but secretly pleased — to discover that an occasional

---

[48]*Employee Relations in Action* (New York: Man & Manager, Inc., September, 1973), Issue 453.

profanity didn't bother the women. The ladies were quite capable of responding in kind and even, on occasion, doing the men one better.

Before long profanities were flying as thick as ever — the women happily contributing their share. How did management feel about this? It didn't say — until there was a showdown with Martha Tipton, when she took an active part in organizing the workforce to join a union.

Martha spent every free moment buttonholing workers and urging them to sign authorization cards. Some of the employees were anti-union — and Martha suspected that one of them, Tim Henshaw, was spying on her for the front office.

One day she loudly and profanely berated Henshaw in front of everyone. This purple-prosed tirade was overhead by the foreman, who bustled over to see what the commotion was about.

"I'm sick and tired of this *blankety-blank* brown-noser!" Martha was screaming, her finger pointed at Henshaw. "That SOB is always sneaking over to the Plant Manager to report on me!"

"And I'm sick and tired of your dirty mouth!" the foreman interrupted. "Martha, you're fired!"

Martha made a beeline to the union to complain: "They say they fired me for swearing! That's a lot of crap. Those so-and-so's canned me because I'm pushing for the union."

The union filed an unfair labor practice charge against the company, and the case came up for a hearing before the National Labor Relations Board. A witness who testified to Martha's propensity for profanity was asked on cross-examination:

"Does any other employee — male or female — use as much obscene language as Martha Tipton?" — to which he replied: "Mostly all of them."

Discuss each of the following questions:

1. Do you expect that the company won or lost the case? On what grounds?
2. Does a female employee have the right to use excessive profanity the same as a male worker?
3. Would your answers to Questions 1 and 2 be the same if Tipton had been employed in the office rather than in the plant? Explain.

Case 13-3 Installing a Ladies' Room for an All-Male Staff[49]

The last lap of the tour of inspection by the representative of the Occupational Safety & Health Administration (OSHA) took him to a small, outlying building on the grounds of the Flonnet Company.

---

[49]*White-Collar Management* (New York: Man & Manager, Inc., January 1, 1975), Issue 1215.

"Who uses this building?" the OSHA man inquired as he came near.

"A small group of engineers and draftsmen," the Flonnet official replied.

A dozen men looked up as the pair entered the building. After checking safety and health facilities, the OSHA man asked a question which astonished the Flonnet official.

"I see you have a washroom for the men but where's the ladies' room?" he queried.

"We don't have any here because there's an all-male staff in this division," was the answer.

The OSHA representative consulted his rule book. "The rules require equal lavatory facilities for men and women," he commented.

"Even if no women work here? That's ridiculous!"

"I'm a stickler for the rules," the inspector said. He hit the Flonnet Company with a violation. The company appealed the violation to OSHA's Review Commission which referred the matter to an Administrative Judge.

At the hearing, the OSHA inspector cited a regulation which "requires separate toilet facilities for men and women." He opined, "that regulation states my case for me. Flonnet's one-toilet building violates the law."

In reply the Flonnet official exclaimed:

1. Of what possible use would a ladies' room be in an all-male department?
2. At most it would be a curiosity — a subject of sick jokes.
3. I can't imagine that the regulation the inspector cites applies to a situation which prevails in our little building.

Discuss each of the following questions:

1. Would you expect the Review Commission to dismiss the charges against the Flonnet Company? Explain.
2. Can the Flonnet Company use the absence of a ladies' room as an excuse for not hiring a female in the all-male department?

Chapter 14   **EMPLOYEE BENEFITS FOR OFFICE WORKERS**

The term *employee benefits*, also known as *fringe benefits* describes any benefits, services, or compensation that employees receive over and above their regular wages or salaries. The term fringe benefits is really a misnomer, for supplementary or indirect compensation to workers that amounts to about 33 percent of every payroll dollar can scarcely be called a "fringe" or a peripheral item. (The determination of direct compensation — the regular wages and salaries paid office workers — is discussed in Chapter 24.)

In 1975 business firms spent an average of $76.62 a week for each employee for extra benefits, reflecting a 165 percent increase in the costs of the benefits since 1965. Of all employee benefits, the social security taxes paid by the employer are the most expensive item. In its 1975 study of employee benefits, the Chamber of Commerce of the United States found that the weekly cost of social security taxes for each employee amounted to $12.23; followed by private pensions costing $11.92 per week; insurance (life, accident, hospitalization, etc.), $11.19; and paid vacations, $11.15. This same study showed that the non-manufacturing firms that were the most liberal in providing benefits were, first, the public utilities; followed by miscellaneous industries such as mining, transportation, research, and hotels; then, banks, finance, and trust companies; then, insurance companies; then,

wholesale and retail trade, excluding department stores; next, hospitals; and, finally, department stores.[1]

Why do companies provide such extensive and costly benefits for their office workers? In this chapter the reasons for providing employee benefits will be briefly explored, and then the nature and extent of employee benefits will be discussed by examining (1) those benefits that affect the health and welfare of office workers, (2) those benefits representing wages paid for time not worked, and (3) a variety of benefits called employee services, which are generally made available voluntarily by the employer at little or no cost to the employee. The concluding section of the chapter deals with recent developments in providing relatively new kinds of benefits for the office worker.

WHY COMPANIES PROVIDE EMPLOYEE BENEFITS

Employee benefits are extended to office employees for a number of reasons besides the legal requirements to do so. The cost of employee benefits, which today form an integral and indispensable part of the total compensation package, continues to mushroom. A company generally looks upon the cost of employee benefits as an investment in

---

[1] "Employee Benefits: Now a Third of Payroll Costs," *Nation's Business* (October, 1976), pp. 36–37.

attracting and retaining desirable workers. The success of this investment depends to a great extent on whether there is a need and desire for the benefits and whether the employees understand and appreciate the value of the benefits provided. As pointed out later in this chapter, employees must be given the facts about the benefits that are available in order to evaluate what the benefits mean to them as individuals and to understand fully the efforts made by the company on their behalf.

Labor costs may be reduced by the company as a result of its payments for employee benefits. The indirect compensation to employees coming from benefits may help promote the idea of the company family and thus increase productivity through greater employee loyalty and dedication, with less absenteeism and employee turnover.[2] The productive time of workers may be controlled better by providing company-subsidized parking and eating facilities than if the employees are forced to satisfy such needs on their own. Benefits such as vacation time and annual credits toward retirement act to reduce turnover because of their tie-in with length of company service.

Employers are not faced with payroll taxes on compensation that is paid in the form of benefits, which is undoubtedly a primary reason for the growth of employee benefits as a form of compensation. Employee benefits can be the least costly method which companies use to reward their workers by rank or experience or to hide the true compensation levels of certain employees from other employees, or from stockholders, regulatory bodies, or taxpayers.[3]

The availability of employee benefits aids a company in partially meeting its workers' needs of job security and job satisfaction. However, not all employee benefits are positive motivators, as viewed by Frederick Herzberg and discussed in Chapter 12. The addition of a new benefit to the company's benefit program does not necessarily bring forth a corresponding increase in productivity; or if any increase can be detected as the result of the newly added benefit, it is doubtful that the increase will be apparent for any prolonged period of time. Benefits, as a hygienic factor, may function as dissatisfiers and negatively affect performance. If the workers believe that their benefits are inferior to those enjoyed by workers in other firms, productivity may be affected adversely.

Benefits are also extended to office employees in an attempt to prevent unionization, as the result of labor-management bargaining sessions, or because the pressures of other firms in the community may have forced the granting of the supplementary payments.

BENEFITS AFFECTING THE HEALTH AND WELFARE OF OFFICE WORKERS

Among those benefits provided by the employer that affect the office worker's health and welfare are: social insurance, group life insurance, hospital and surgical insurance, major medical insurance, sick leave, maternity leave, disability income, pension plans,

---

[2]Dan M. Bechter, "The Elementary Microeconomics of Private Employee Benefits," *Monthly Review*, Federal Reserve Bank of Kansas City, (May, 1975), p. 7.

[3]*Ibid.*

profit-sharing plans, employee stock purchase plans, and several miscellaneous employee insurance programs. Each of these benefits is discussed in the following paragraphs.

Social Insurance

Employer contributions for social insurance have been increasing tremendously over the past decade, with the largest and most rapidly growing component being old-age, survivors, disability, and health insurance (OASDHI). Social insurance includes employer contributions for not only OASDHI benefits but also unemployment compensation, workmen's compensation, state and local employee retirement, federal civilian employee retirement, railroad retirement, cash sickness compensation, and veterans life insurance. Because of the limitations of space, only the first three of these benefits are discussed here.

OASDHI Benefits. As briefly mentioned in Chapter 13, the social security program was planned by the federal government to provide economic security for workers and their families. Under the Federal Insurance Contributions Act (FICA), a tax is levied on employers and employees in most industries to be paid to the federal government. Amendments to FICA provide for a two-part health insurance program, commonly known as Medicare, for the aged and the disabled. The Hospital Insurance plan is financed by a separate tax on both employers and employees. The Supplementary Medical Insurance plan is voluntary and is financed by those who desire coverage, with a matching payment by the federal government. Benefits from the OASDHI program are payable monthly to workers who qualify under the provisions of the law.

While near-universal retirement coverage has been attained under the social security system, the benefits are much less than satisfactory. Benefits have been increasing partly because of the steady upward drift of wages and prices; but they have not grown as rapidly as prices and thus have declined in real terms during some periods of inflation, thereby threatening the living standards of the retired. Social security benefits are tied into an automatic escalator which is geared to the cost of living. As that cost goes up, so do the benefits — and so do the taxes of middle- and high-income workers and their employers.

In 1967 the employer's contribution for OASDHI benefits was 4.4 percent of the first $6,600 earned by each worker, or $290.40. Of course, each worker paid a matching amount. Ten years later in 1977 the employer's contribution was 5.85 percent of the first $16,500 earned by each worker, or $965.25. In 1979 it is estimated that the taxable wage base will be $19,200 and the maximum tax paid by both employees and employers will be $1,161.60.

Unemployment Compensation Benefits. The purpose of unemployment compensation insurance is to provide funds at the state level for compensating unemployed workers in that state. Employers are faced with two unemployment compensation insurance taxes — federal and state. The state unemployment taxes are used exclusively for the payment of unemployment compensation benefits. The tax paid to the federal government is used for paying state and federal administrative expenses. In 1977 many employers subject to the Federal Unemployment Tax Act

(FUTA) paid a state unemployment compensation tax of 2.7 percent on the first $4,200 of wages paid each employee during the year, or $113.40. The unemployment compensation tax paid to the federal government amounted to .7 percent of the first $4,200 of wages paid each employee during the year, or $29.40.

Workmen's Compensation Benefits. By means of workmen's compensation insurance, employees and their dependents are protected against losses due to injury or death incurred during employment. The cost of the workmen's compensation insurance premiums is borne by the employer. Benefits are paid to the injured workers, or to their survivors in the event of death, by the state, by the insurance company, or by the risk-assuming employer according to the kind of insurance plan adopted.

The insurance rates are based upon the total gross payroll of the business and are usually stated in terms of an amount for each $100 of weekly wages paid to employees. The premium rates vary among types of jobs and vary in amount with the pay rate involved. For example, the rate for office workers may be $0.06 per $100 of payroll, while the rate for machine-shop workers may be $1 per $100 of payroll. If the employer's accident experience is low, the rates may be reduced to a certain minimum. In 1975 the weekly cost of workmen's compensation for each employee, on the average, was $2.71.[4]

Group Life Insurance

Group life insurance, protection that covers all employees of a single firm, is designed to provide benefits should the

worker die or become totally disabled. The amount of coverage may be equal to the office employee's salary or some fraction or multiple of it. Group life insurance is term insurance that expires when the worker leaves the company unless steps are taken to convert it into a private policy. The tendency today is for the employer to pay the entire premium for the office worker's life insurance coverage.

The morale-building effect of a group life insurance plan cannot be overestimated, for this benefit relieves the employee of a certain amount of worry and insecurity. In many cases the group life insurance plan provides for total and permanent disability benefits, accidental death and dismemberment coverage, as well as modest amounts of life insurance for the employee's survivors. Companies usually provide reduced amounts of life insurance for retired employees, especially after they reach age 65 or 70.

Hospital and Surgical Insurance

Hospital and surgical insurance affords office employees protection by covering all or the major part of the hospital, surgical, and medical expenses for employees and their dependents. This type of benefit is so common that almost all firms have established group medical insurance plans for their workers, either paying the costs entirely or having the employee contribute part or all of the costs at reduced rates. Retired workers and their dependents are usually covered under such plans, at least until they reach age 65 when they are eligible for Medicare.

Proposed Health Insurance Protection. When most workers are faced with a layoff, they lose health insurance

---

[4]"Employee Benefits: Now a Third of Payroll Costs," *Nation's Business* (October, 1976), p. 37.

protection for themselves and their families, either immediately or within a month of the layoff. For those whose coverage extends into the layoff, the health insurance benefits usually cease within three months of layoff.

Various plans for national health insurance have been proposed. Under one proposal, every resident of the United States would be covered for all hospital and physicians' services, as well as for eyeglasses, hearing aids, dental services up to age 15, mental health care, preventive care, and rehabilitation care. The program would be federally administered, providing what is commonly referred to as "cradle to grave" insurance. Under this plan health care would become a matter of right, and the present government health care programs, such as Medicare and Medicaid, would be totally or substantially replaced by the new coverage. Financing for this program calls for a tax on employee wages and unearned income, a tax on employers' payrolls, and a levy on the earnings of the self-employed, with these payments to be matched by federal general revenues. Another similar plan would set up a privately administered insurance program that would require employers to provide health insurance for their employees. The federal government would provide coverage for the aged, low income, unemployed, and medically indigent persons. Employers would pay at least 75 percent of the premium costs, while employees, who would have the option of whether or not to participate in the plan, would pay the balance, treating the payment as a tax deduction.

Health Maintenance Organizations (HMO). Under the Health Maintenance Act of 1973 employers of 25 or more employees who are subject to the Fair Labor Standards Act and who now provide payments for health insurance to their employees are required to offer them the option of membership in a qualified Health Maintenance Organization. A *Health Maintenance Organization*, also known as a group practice prepayment plan, not only finances health care but also guarantees to deliver health care through services which it organizes and for which it accepts a predetermined payment.

The purpose of HMOs is to provide prepaid health maintenance by offering preventive health care to members. Thus, the present health insurance trend, which, because of limited coverage, encourages workers to postpone or avoid regular checkups, would be reversed. As a result, an employer participating in an HMO program may have a healthier workforce.

Major Medical Insurance

Many companies have expanded their group hospital and surgical insurance coverage by providing *major medical insurance*, which protects employees against catastrophic medical bills resulting from serious accidents or prolonged illness. According to a survey conducted by The Conference Board among 1,800 firms, about 95 percent of the companies have major medical insurance programs for office employees.[5] In most of these plans the company pays the full cost of the employee's own health insurance while the costs for coverage of dependents are generally shared by the company and the employee.

---

[5]"Employee Benefits Rose 28% in Past Decade, Conference Board Says," *The Wall Street Journal*, February 18, 1975, p. 19.

Under most major medical insurance policies, coverage ceases after a lifetime maximum, often $10,000 to $25,000, has been reached. Other policies set a maximum payment for each disability period. Most plans require the workers to absorb a certain dollar amount before they are paid anything, with deductibles of $50 to $300 each year being the most common. Most often major medical plans pay 80 percent of the charges above the deductible amount, up to the maximum amount provided.

Sick Leave

Most firms have a company-paid *sick leave plan* that provides office workers with continuing income during short periods of illness. To become eligible for sick leave coverage, a minimum service requirement is usually specified, with the most common service requirement being two or three months. Often the service requirement is tied in with the end of a probationary period for new employees. The amount of paid sick leave provided office workers ranges from 5 to 15 days each year, with the number of days often varying with the employee's length of service.[6] Many firms provide for the accumulation of sick leave days from year to year and often permit the sick leave to be used for maternity reasons.

Maternity Leave

Formal policies covering maternity leave apply to office employees in 91 percent of the firms surveyed by the

Bureau of National Affairs. Where no maternity leave policy exists, the maternity benefits are provided under a sick leave policy, as described above. The survey noted that the majority of firms with maternity leave policies have no specific service requirement for eligibility, that about one third of the companies have a limit on how long a pregnant employee can continue working, and that in about 30 percent of the firms there is no specific maximum length of leave for office workers. Often the decision on length of leave is handled on an individual basis, with a doctor's statement that the employee is medically able to return to work being required.[7]

Disability Income

Many office workers are covered by short-term sickness and accident disability insurance plans. Such plans provide continuing income for the workers who are unable to return to their jobs after they have exhausted their sickness and accident benefits. Five states (California, Hawaii, New Jersey, New York, and Rhode Island) and Puerto Rico along with the railroad industry have laws requiring employers to protect their workers against short-term nonoccupational disability.

There is a growing trend to recognize the coverage of more and more physical and mental ailments under disability insurance plans. For example, in some states it has been ruled that pregnant workers are entitled to disability pay under company insurance programs. The courts of appeal have decided that a company's policy of denying insurance benefits to employees disabled by pregnancy and requiring them to return to

[6]*Paid Leave & Leave of Absence Policies*, Personnel Policies Forum Survey No. 111 (Washington: The Bureau of National Affairs, November, 1975), p. 4.

[7]*Ibid.*, pp. 13–14.

work within a specified period of time following childbirth discriminate against women in violation of Title VII of the Civil Rights Act.[8] These decisions mean that pregnant workers must be granted leaves of absence and they are entitled to reinstatement without loss of seniority and other benefits when they return to work. However, at the federal level the Supreme Court ruled in 1976 that private employers may exclude pregnancy in their sickness and accident plans without violating the Civil Rights Act.

Long-term disability income insurance, often an extension of the short-term program, has increased dramatically. In The Conference Board survey cited earlier, it was found that 72 percent of the firms have long-term disability income insurance plans for managers and 62 percent have plans covering office employees.[9] Long-term disability income insurance usually provides a benefit equal to 50 or 60 percent of the pay for the worker who is medically determined to be totally disabled. The period of payment may range from a few years to age 65, or for life, depending upon the design of the plan. The benefits paid under the plan are usually reduced by any social security benefits or other statutory disability benefits received by the worker.

Pension Plans

Since in many instances social security benefits are inadequate for retired employees and their dependents, many firms modify their pension plans to supplement the government benefits, thus maintaining the interest of their employees in long-term employment with the firm. A survey conducted by the Bureau of National Affairs shows that nine out of ten of the firms questioned provide retirement benefits under a pension plan. Although benefit formulas and eligibility rules vary, the coverage is about the same for production workers, office employees, and managers. Most of the plans in the firms surveyed are single employer and are financed by employer contributions; only one fourth of the plans involve employee contributions.[10] When employees contribute toward the cost of their retirement benefits, the contributions are usually expressed as a percentage of earnings, such as three to seven percent.

Over the years pension plans have been substantially liberalized, and in the better plans pensions are based on the worker's highest earnings and not on the average salary paid. Modern pension plans also provide for earlier vesting. *Vesting*, which refers to how many years are needed for a worker to earn equity in the pension plan, entitles workers to full or partial benefits at some future date if they leave the company before retirement. Once vested, a worker has a right to receive a pension at retirement age, based on years of covered service, even though the worker may not be working for the firm at that time. Most pension plans provide for vesting after the worker has been covered under the plan for a specified number of years, although some plans also have a minimum age requirement. Today many

---

[8]The Civil Rights Act of 1964 and other government regulations affecting the employment process are discussed in Chapter 11.

[9]"Employee Benefits Rose 28% in Past Decade, Conference Board Says," *loc. cit.*

---

[10]*Pensions & Other Retirement Benefits*, Personnel Policies Forum Survey No. 103 (Washington: The Bureau of National Affairs, October, 1973), p. 1.

plans provide 100 percent vesting after 10 years' service, regardless of age.

Most plans provide for retirement before the normal age, which is typically 65, if the worker meets certain age and service requirements. Often in these cases the pension benefits are reduced. However, in its 1974 study of 149 major pension plans, the Bureau of Labor Statistics found that one half of the plans provided unreduced benefits before the common retirement age of 65.[11]

If the office worker is forced to retire early because of a disability, a pension benefit is still provided. If an eligible employee dies before retirement, the spouse receives a payment based on the worker's length of service with the company and the extent of vesting.

As a result of the Employee Retirement Income Security Act of 1974 (ERISA), workers covered under its regulation receive greater protection, a vested right toward their pensions, and assurance of better management of pension funds. Employees are encouraged to participate earlier in private retirement plans since generally all employees are eligible to participate in a plan after they are 25 years old and have worked for an employer for one year. Seasonal and part-time employees, defined by ERISA as those who work 1,000 hours or more during the year, must be covered by a plan after a year of service. However, if the plan gives full vesting as soon as the employees join it, the workers need not be covered by the plan until they have completed three years of service.

Vesting standards have been established under ERISA whereby workers who participate in a plan do not lose all of their benefits because of punishing forfeiture standards or inadequate fund resources. To protect against potential benefit losses because of a plan's termination, ERISA set up a government insurance program, the Pension Benefit Guaranty Corporation, to pay any benefits that could not be met with funds from the plan.

A high standard has been imposed upon the operation of pension plans, for it is mandatory that all information concerning the operation of the employer's pension plan, other benefit plans, and the amount of the worker's accrued benefits be fully disclosed and communicated to the workers. Also, the act established a limited form of portability whereby workers are allowed to transfer, tax free, some of their pension benefits to other plans, if all parties are agreeable. Or, workers may transfer their vested benefits into individual retirement accounts on a tax-free basis to be held for their retirement or until they join a new company plan that is willing to accept the transfer.

Profit-Sharing Plans

Under *profit-sharing plans* the benefits received by eligible workers are based on a percentage of the company's profits for the year. (As noted later in Chapter 24, profit sharing may be tied in with a company's group financial incentive plan). Employees can receive cash shares of the profits at regular intervals, or they can defer or postpone their shares, which will be invested by the company and paid to them upon their retirement, termination of employment, or death (in which case the value of the employees' shares are paid to their beneficiaries). The cash shares received by workers represent immediate spendable

---

[11]Evan L. Hodgens, "Key Changes in Pension Plans," *Monthly Labor Review* (July, 1975), p. 22.

assets and are taxed as regular income. The deferred shares are invested by the company and the workers do not have to pay any taxes until they actually receive the money. Thus, workers are enabled to defer their income from years of high earnings to years of lower earnings such as at time of retirement. Some plans provide that part of the profits may be paid directly to the workers in the form of cash, with the rest placed in a trust fund under a deferred-payment plan.

Profit-sharing plans are more frequently found in small companies; in larger firms the plans are more likely to be in addition to, rather than instead of, pension plans. In the Bureau of National Affairs survey, it was found that about one fifth of the firms have deferred profit-sharing plans.[12]

In the profit-sharing plans of some companies, a predetermined percentage of profits is set aside each year, while other firms use a sliding scale for determining the amount of profit to be shared. To guarantee the stockholders a return on their investment or to retain funds for company growth, some firms may first deduct from their annual profits a basic minimum return on the invested capital before calculating the share to be distributed among the employees. To provide a real incentive for employees, the profit-sharing plan must provide a sufficiently large payment to the workers but still permit the company to retain earnings for future growth. The most successful deferred profit-sharing plans produce, on the average, 8 to 15 percent or more of the employee's annual pay.[13]

[12]*Pensions & Other Retirement Benefits, loc. cit.*

[13]"How Much Do 'Fringes' Boost Your Pay?" *Supervisory Management* (April, 1973), p. 41.

In one firm that has been paying a profit-sharing bonus to its employees for a number of years, the amount of the annual bonus varies each year according to the profits earned. The amount of bonus is calculated as a percentage of each eligible employee's straight-time salary at the rate in effect on the last pay period in June of the year in which the bonus is paid. In computing the amount on which the bonus is paid to an employee, deductions are made for nonpaid absences, regardless of their nature, during the year. Employees must work three years on a permanent basis before they can participate in the bonus.

Employee Stock Ownership Plans

Stock ownership plans are intended to interest the employee in the success of the company. Most companies have two different types of stock ownership plans for their employees: the stock option which is usually offered only to top management and key personnel, and the stock purchase plan which is available to all employees.

Stock Option Plan. The stock option plan may be offered in lieu of additional remuneration and gives the executive an opportunity to purchase a specific number of shares of stock in the firm by a specific date at a given price which is normally lower than the market price. In some stock option plans participation is based on job function, job performance, and length of service.

Stock Purchase Plan. In an employee stock purchase plan an employee who meets certain service requirements is given the opportunity to purchase shares of the company's stock. To pay for the shares, the employee usually authorizes payroll deductions in advance.

The price of the shares may be set on the date the employee signs up for the plan or on the date the stock is actually purchased. In either case, the price is usually lower than the current market price. Most firms limit stock purchases to a stipulated percentage, such as 10 percent, of the employee's annual salary.

Miscellaneous Insurance Programs

Recent studies indicate the emergence of several new types of benefits, each designed to provide additional health and welfare security for office employees. For example, dental insurance plans, the fastest growing employee benefit according to the Conference Board, were found in 19 percent of the 1,600 firms surveyed in 1975; in most plans the premiums were entirely company-paid.[14] Group automobile insurance plans, most of which are employee-paid, were found in 12 percent of the companies responding to the 1975 Noncash Compensation Survey conducted by Hays Associates.[15] Among other relatively new benefits are insurance covering the purchase of drugs and medicines, which is found in about 12 to 16 of the firms; and eye-care insurance in about three percent of the companies.[16]

WAGES PAID FOR TIME NOT WORKED

Some benefits received by office workers represent wages earned for time not worked. Among the major benefits of this nature are: vacations, coffee breaks and rest periods, holidays, and Christmas bonuses. In addition, there are several other minor benefits such as jury duty pay, time off for voting, and military training leave that are granted some office workers.

Vacations

Virtually all white-collar workers receive a one-week paid vacation after six months of service and two weeks' vacation with pay after one year of employment. Most office employees receive three weeks' vacation after 10 years and four weeks' paid leave after 15 years of service. However, in its annual salary survey the Administrative Management Society noted a definite trend in office workers receiving three weeks' paid vacation after five years of service.[17] Office workers in some Western European countries fare somewhat better than workers in this country, however. For example, in France everyone receives four weeks' vacation; office workers in Western Germany usually get a month off; and in Britain, nonmanual workers usually receive more than three weeks' vacation.

The company-wide vacation shutdown, once very common in so many firms, is seen less frequently. Few employers allow their workers to carry over vacation time from one year to the next. Also, most employers stipulate that the vacation time actually be taken away from work rather than the employee requesting extra pay in lieu of the time off. In 1975 the average weekly cost to

---

[14] "Open Wide," *The Wall Street Journal*, March 2, 1976, p. 1.

[15] "Editor to Reader," *Personnel Journal* (May, 1976), p. 208.

[16] See *Pensions & Other Retirement Benefits*, op. cit., and *Bulletin to Management* (Washington: The Bureau of National Affairs, May 1, 1975), p. 8.

[17] *Office Salaries Directory of United States and Canada, 1977–78* (Willow Grove: Administrative Management Society), p. 38.

employers of paid vacations for each employee amounted to nearly $11.15.[18]

Rest Periods

Coffee breaks, rest periods, wash-up time, and other on-the-job time paid for — but not worked — averaged 17 minutes a day in 1975 and cost the employer an average of $7.85 a week for each worker employed.[19] The purpose of providing coffee breaks and rest periods is to increase the productivity and efficiency of workers, which should be so communicated to the workers and so understood by management. Such paid rest periods are not a charitable contribution to paternalism. The rest periods should be scheduled at such intervals and for such length of time as seem most successful. They should be administered with the same regularity and control as arrival in the morning and departure at night. Otherwise, their purpose is defeated by creating more wasted time and decreased production in the office than if they were never provided.

Underlying the provision for rest periods is the principle that certain types of work, being repetitive, soon become monotonous. This monotony increases fatigue, which in turn slows down production. The work output of employees performing motor-skill tasks such as typewriting and keypunching varies at different times throughout the day. After workers start in the morning, they tend to increase their productivity. Physiologically the ability of the worker's muscles to function increases as the body adjusts to the activity. Psychologically warming up involves a

change in attitude and attention. As workers become more absorbed in their work, an increase in productivity results. There is a similar warm-up period following the lunch break. The initial warm-up period is followed by a period of high productivity; but as work continues, the performance begins to fall off and continues to decrease to the end of the work period. In the first graph of Figure 14-1, the morning's maximum productivity is usually higher than that reached in the afternoon; and the afternoon warm-up period starts at a higher performance level than the worker's initial efforts in the morning. Also, in the afternoon the downward trend often begins earlier and the productivity usually falls to a much lower level by the end of the afternoon.

To be most effective, rest periods should be introduced just before performance begins to drop from its maximum. The typical work curve shown in the second graph of Figure 14-1 indicates that most motor-skill tasks require only two official work breaks each day to maintain high-level performance. Most office activities have natural breaks, and many tasks require only intermittent attention of the worker. It is recommended for an eight-hour day that the breaks be placed between the second and third hours in the morning and between the sixth and seventh hours in the afternoon. For a limited number of activities such as visual inspection of punched cards, that require a high degree of concentration, two work breaks each day may not be sufficient to maintain an acceptable level of performance. Whether or not rest periods are the answer to the problems of fatigue and slowdown of production is not conclusive. The fact that in this way management shows concern for the well-being of its employ-

---

[18]"Employee Benefits: Now a Third of Payroll Costs," *Nation's Business* (October, 1976), p. 37.

[19]*Ibid.*

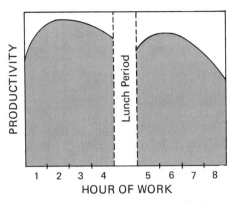 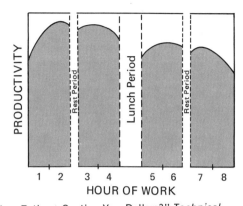

Source: I.L. Bosticco and Robert B. Andrews, "Is Worker Fatigue Costing You Dollars?" *Technical Aids for Small Manufacturers* (Washington: Small Business Administration, January–February, 1960).

Fig. 14-1
Typical Work Curves for a Motor-Skill Task Without and With Rest Periods

ees may be the most important aspect of the rest period.

If an office employee earns, on the average, $140 during a 40-hour week and spends 20 minutes a day on work breaks, about 83 hours — more than two workweeks — during the year are spent away from the work place. The cost of this lost time is about $290! When employee's long lunches, leaving work early, tardiness, sick days for nonsickness, extensive socializing with coworkers, and inattention to the job at hand are added to rest periods, the costs to business are a staggering sum!

Most companies provide work breaks and many firms pay at least part of the cost of snacks. In many small offices, workers are permitted to take their breaks whenever they have a chance. In larger firms, the workers may alternate the times of their breaks so they are not all absent from the office at the same time.

The negative attitudes of some office managers toward rest periods may be caused by their inability to control the breaks or because they do not know

how to control them. The amount of control that the office manager can exercise over the breaks is related to where the employees get their refreshments. In the small office, it is much more difficult to control the length of the break if employees must leave the premises at break time. In large offices, the employees may have access to vending machines and cafeteria services. Some firms are able to control the work break problem by permitting their employees to eat and drink at their desks because it is felt that if the coffee is drunk while the employees are at their desks, the workers will lose less time.

Although most office managers feel that rest periods are desirable, they object to the abuse of the privilege. Some office managers excuse the lack of rest periods by stating that the freedom enjoyed by most office workers makes such breaks unnecessary.

The following guidelines should govern the granting of rest periods:

1. For some types of office work, rest periods are absolutely necessary.

2. Rest periods should be scheduled when they will be most helpful — not too early in the morning and not too late in the afternoon. The work breaks should be scheduled so that not all employees are absent from their desks at the same time. Such an approach tends to discourage the overly long "talk" sessions that commonly characterize many breaks.

3. Definite time limits should be set for the length of the breaks and these limits should be observed. Habitual offenders should be reprimanded and, if necessary, discharged. The inability of a few to abide by the rules only sets a poor example for the others.

4. Supervisors should be held responsible for the abuse of rest period privileges.

5. If possible, facilities should be provided for getting coffee and snacks in the office so the employees do not have to leave the premises.

Holidays

In its annual salary survey the Administrative Management Society found that more than one half of the firms grant nine paid holidays.[20] Along with the traditional six holidays (New Year's Day, Independence Day, Labor Day, Thanksgiving, Memorial Day, and Christmas), other days such as Good Friday, Christmas Eve, the day after Thanksgiving, Washington's Birthday, New Year's Eve, Veteran's Day, and the employee's birthday are becoming recognized more frequently as paid holidays. In its 1975 Noncash Compensation Survey, Hay Associates found that the number of paid holidays cluster in the nine to eleven-day range and that more than one half of the responding firms gave from two to four "floating holidays" that can be taken at different times each year or at the employee's convenience.[21]

Christmas Bonuses

Many companies give Christmas bonuses to their office employees as a gesture of goodwill; other firms base their bonuses on merit, granting them only to workers who have made an extra effort or exceeded predetermined quotas during the year. A popular bonus in smaller firms is a percentage of the worker's annual earnings, such as two percent, or one week's pay, while sometimes more is given by larger companies. Although a bonus is a gift, employees quickly begin to expect it. When business is bad, however, bonuses have a way of shrinking or disappearing altogether. Giving a worker a cash bonus that is less than the amount received last year tends to cause ill will and misunderstanding and can seriously endanger morale.

In a union office the employer may be committing an unfair labor practice if a bonus is unilaterally withdrawn. If the Christmas bonus is a gratuity representing a goodwill gesture and has no relationship to the employee's job performance, hours worked, seniority, or position, then the bonus is not a bargainable item. In such cases the employer can withdraw the bonus for economic reasons without prior notification or bargaining. If, on the other hand, the bonus is part of wages or a condition of employment, good faith bargaining is required preceding the withdrawal of such a benefit.

---

[20]*Office Salaries Directory of United States and Canada, 1977–78* (Willow Grove: Administrative Management Society), p. 38.

[21]"Editor to Reader," *Personnel Journal* (May, 1976), p. 207.

Other Benefits

When office employees are called to *jury duty*, some may receive full pay from their employers in addition to their jury fees. Usually, however, if employees are paid jury fees, this amount is deducted from the pay they receive from the company.

Over half of the states have laws allowing employees to take *time off from work to vote*. Most state laws provide that employees who are entitled to vote in an election may, upon application to their employers, absent themselves from work for a specified period, without penalty or loss of pay. The state laws that cover time allowed for voting provide for time off ranging from one to four hours, and in a growing number of states time off to vote is granted only if there is insufficient time outside working hours.

Employers cannot refuse to grant office employees time off to meet their *military training obligations*. The majority of the firms surveyed by the Bureau of National Affairs treat the required summer training programs as paid leave. In these companies the employees usually are paid the difference between their regular pay and what they receive as base pay from the military. In other companies not having a policy regarding military training leave, employees may use their vacation period for military training and receive accrued vacation pay in addition to their military pay.[22]

Most companies also provide office workers paid *funeral leaves*, usually of three days' duration, for family members; many firms also grant paid *leaves for family illness* and paid *leaves for "personal" reasons* other than personal illness or illness in the family.[23]

SERVICES FOR EMPLOYEES

A variety of services for office employees relating to their health, education, work-day meals, transportation, and financial problems are found in today's business firms. The employee services discussed in this section generally are made available voluntarily by the employer, with some or no cost to the employee.

Food Services

Providing food services is becoming an important part of office administration. In the larger firms, company-operated cafeterias supply either free or low-cost meals to their employees. In many lunchrooms catering companies have installed vending machines, with employees securing their meals at a lower cost and the company paying the difference. Such a service is a supplemental and indirect wage benefit. Company-provided food services are particularly applicable in large cities, where a deluge of several thousand employees from one building seeking meals in a variety of restaurants is not conducive to the best physical and mental well-being of the employees. Also, in the suburbs where the office building may be located far away from restaurants, lunchroom facilities have become a necessity.

Social and Recreational Programs

The social and recreational programs in many large companies consist mostly of picnics, employee parties,

---

[22]*Paid Leave & Leave of Absence Policies*, Personnel Policies Forum Survey No. 111 (Washington: The Bureau of National Affairs, November, 1975), p. 11.

[23]*Ibid.*, pp. 8–10.

group tours or trips, and bowling and softball teams. With the additional leisure time resulting from a shorter workweek and flexible work schedules, there is a trend toward providing more interest programs, sports, and hobbies for the entire family. Some of the types of activities that have become a part of company social and recreational programs are: chess or checkers, bridge, concerts, golf, basketball, baseball, fashion shows, dancing, crafts, glee clubs, fishing, theater parties, and sports car racing clubs. The scope is almost limitless. Good recreation planning should provide organized activities for those employees who prefer to spend their leisure time in individual or small-group pursuits.

Most firms feel that the improvement in employee morale is worth whatever it costs to achieve. In its survey the Bureau of National Affairs found of the companies studied that the median cost of the social and recreational program per employee is $6 a year.[24] In some companies employee associations bear some or all of the expenses of the recreational program, while in other firms the costs of recreation may be partially defrayed by other sources of revenue such as income from vending machines located throughout the offices and plant.

Educational Assistance

Many firms provide some type of educational assistance to their employees, with the result that office workers can continue to grow professionally and to prepare themselves for maximum flexibility of career pursuit and for future promotion to supervisory and middle management positions. In its study of 620 firms in the United States and Canada, the Administrative Management Society found that over 90 percent of the companies provide educational assistance and about three fourths support studies that are job related, either directly or indirectly. Less than 10 percent of the firms permitted employees to enroll in courses nonrelated to their present jobs.[25]

For courses that qualify for assistance, over 50 percent of the firms reimburse the employee 100 percent for tuition costs; nearly 15 percent of the companies pay 75 percent or 50 percent of the tuition costs; a little more than one percent of the companies pay less than 50 percent of the tuition. When assistance is related to the grade obtained in the courses, much variation in reimbursement practice is noted. For example, 12 firms indicated 100 percent tuition reimbursement for an A grade; 75 percent reimbursement for a B; and 50 percent reimbursement for a C. Slightly less than 50 percent of the respondents did not pay for books, but here again considerable variation in practice exists. One firm paid a maximum of $10 toward books, while another paid up to $20 for the textbooks for each course.[26]

Some companies provide for furthering the education of their employees within the firm's own classrooms. For example, one utility company in Florida

[24]*Social, Recreational & Holiday Programs*, Personnel Policies Forum Survey No. 109 (Washington: The Bureau of National Affairs, March, 1975), p. 1.

[25]"Going Back Means Moving Up," *Administrative Management* (May, 1971), pp. 61–63. In addition to giving results of the survey, this article describes the tuition policies of three firms wherein (a) an "A" merits a refund of 90 percent, (b) full tuition is paid for a degree, and (c) the educational program pursued must be related.

[26]*Ibid.*, p. 62.

has established its own "college" which is taught by employees for employees. The "college" grants credits and "degrees" in much the same fashion as a university. The company offers 40 courses on all educational levels, ranging from advanced physics to speed reading. Further discussion of company schools as a means of training and upgrading skills is presented in Chapter 16.

Office managers should be concerned about the quality of the return being realized from their company's investment in programs of educational assistance. Among the measures that are available to evaluate the values received by the company are: employee performance appraisals, studies of promotion patterns, surveys of the employees' superiors, and interviews with and written reports from employees who have taken courses. In a survey of the tuition aid plans of 283 large corporations, it was found that 92 percent of the firms contacted were benefiting from their tuition aid plans; according to their records and experiences, employees who took advantage of the tuition aid plans usually advanced in their organizations more rapidly than those who did not. Other evidence offered by the firms to substantiate the value of their tuition aid plans included: increased employee concern and involvement in their own self-development because of the firm's concern and support; improved organizational climates favorable to improvement and innovation; and improved quality of work performance because of better employee knowledge and skills gained through off-the-job courses.[27]

Miscellaneous Services for Employees

A wide variety of other services is offered office employees in today's business firms. In its 1974 survey of more than 200 companies (of which nearly one half were large organizations with 1,000 employees or more, and slightly more than one half were small firms with less than 1,000 employees) the Bureau of National Affairs reported the extent of several employee services as summarized below.[28]

Parking Space. When parking space is provided by the company, employees are saved the cost of renting their own space, a saving which is probably between $20 and $50 a month. Parking lots or garages are provided in more than 80 percent of the companies and in nearly all of these firms there is no charge to the employees.

Company Medical Facilities. First-aid stations are provided in three fourths of the companies, while sick rooms are found in more than half of the firms. Also, in more than half of the firms the medical staff consists of full- or part-time doctors and full- or part-time nurses.

Preemployment Physical Exams. Eighty percent of the firms provide preemployment physical exams and 20 percent of the companies give periodic exams to all employees.

Counseling or Referral Programs. About one fourth of the firms provide counseling or referral programs for alcoholism, emotional illness, and

[27]Charles E. Watson and Alexis L. Grzybowski, "What Your Company Should Know about Tuition Aid Plans," *Business Horizons* (October, 1975), p. 80.

[28]*Services for Employees*, Personnel Policies Forum Survey No. 105 (Washington: The Bureau of National Affairs, March, 1974), p. 1.

personal problems. Counseling or referral programs for drug-abuse problems are found in one fifth of the companies.

Financial Services. The most frequently available financial services to employees are those provided by credit unions, which are found in more than 60 percent of the companies. A *credit union* is a financial institution, chartered by the state or federal government, that is organized to assist a homogeneous group, such as the employees of a firm, in saving money and lending it to one another.

Discounts on Products or Services. About one half of the firms give employees a discount on company products or services, with discounts ranging from 10 to 100 percent.

Child-Care Services. Child care, a relatively new employee service, is found in only six percent of the companies which participated in the study.

RECENT DEVELOPMENTS IN PROVIDING EMPLOYEE BENEFITS

Employee benefits, as a percentage of total compensation, have been increasing faster than wages and salaries, although these benefits are not always motivators for all office workers. Even though studies show that employee benefits are important, there is considerable question about the degree of motivation; the amount of increased satisfaction, longevity, and production; and the decrease in turnover that accrues from benefits. Today employee benefits appear to be neither inducements nor rewards but a condition of employment and an integral part of the total compensation package. Paying wages and salaries in kind, rather than in money, is a trend that appears to have no apparent end. Recent developments that broaden further the base of employee benefits are discussed in the following paragraphs, along with a few new benefits that are appearing upon the office scene.

Flexible Benefits Program

Under a *flexible benefits program*, also called the "cafeteria" or "market basket" approach, employees choose which benefits they wish by determining how many dollars will be allocated each type of benefit from the total amount of compensation due from their employers. In some instances employees have the option of giving up certain benefits and being reimbursed for them in the dollar amount instead.

Based on the findings of behavioral scientists, a flexible benefits program assumes that employees are better motivated and more satisfied if they take an active role in developing their own benefit arrangements. Thus, employees may construct a package of salary and benefits that most precisely meets their preferences as dictated by age, family situation, tax bracket, health condition, and spending needs. One of the few companies that have installed flexible benefits programs is the TRW Systems Group, which reports that more than 80 percent of its 11,000 workers have joined the program since it began in late 1974. Each year in this company the workers can select from four levels of company-paid, hospital-medical coverage, eight life insurance plans, and 18 supplemental accident policies, as well as buy other coverage separately.[29]

---

[29] Reported in *The Wall Street Journal*, June 17, 1975, p. 1.

No conclusive results are available from the very few companies that are experimenting with flexible benefits programs and it will probably be several years before the value of such programs as a motivator can be measured and assessed.[30]

Time Off for Social Work

Several companies have established programs whereby employees are granted extended leaves of absence in order to make personal contributions to society. Often, such leaves of absence are without pay, but in some cases a full year's leave with pay is granted. The main purpose of the programs appears to be one of enabling the firm itself to respond to social needs.[31]

One of the first companies to grant workers time off for social work was Xerox Corporation. Under this company's plan any employee with three years' service, regardless of job status, is eligible to spend up to a year working on self-selected social welfare projects outside the firm. Applicants may propose almost any kind of social service in almost any location, sponsored by a public or a private nonprofit organization. Some of the projects selected in the past include youth counseling, training minority workers, and assisting in the rehabilitation of drug addicts, alcoholics, and convicts. The volunteers are guaranteed their salaries while away and a return to a job of at least equal status when their assignments are finished.

Prepaid Legal Service Plans

Prepaid legal service plans, similar to those in the health-care industry, are still a benefit of the distant future, although it is expected that more unions will be pushing for the establishment of such plans. Under such a plan prepaid legal advice would be provided union members by lawyers who would be paid through employer contributions to a special fund.

Under the open-panel plan, the insured employees seek their own lawyers as the need arises and are reimbursed in whole or in part by the plan. The closed-panel plan involves a contract between the plan members and preselected lawyers who agree to provide legal services for members in exchange for a specified fee.

Paternity Leave

Paternity leave for new fathers is commencing to appear in some labor agreements. Such leave, paid or unpaid, gives more fathers time to be with their new children. The United States Department of Labor, in its contract with union employees, grants paternity leaves

---

[30]Thomas E. Wahlrobe, "The Cafeteria Approach to Employee Benefits," *Administrative Management* (December, 1974), p. 48. See also Robert V. Goode, "Complications at the Cafeteria Checkout Line," *Personnel* (November–December, 1974), pp. 45–49. In these articles the authors raise serious questions as to whether flexible benefit plans will ever work, at least for most employers. In "Editor to Reader, *Personnel Journal* (January, 1977), pp. 6–7, TRW reports that the problems related to cafeteria-style compensation are not insurmountable and that employees can learn to make complex decisions and learn what their benefits are all about as a result of having to decide something about those benefits. In the article, "Introducing Cafeteria Compensation in Your Company," *Personnel Journal* (March, 1977), pp. 124–131, the author points out that only two companies — TWR and Educational Testing Service — have implemented true cafeteria programs; others have merely adopted a cafeteria approach.

[31]David Clutterbuck, "Whatever Happened to 'Time Off for Social Responsibility?' " *Management Review* (April, 1974), p. 47.

up to 30 days' duration to males when their children are born. The leave may be either charged against annual leave or taken without pay.

Career Apparel

Providing wearing apparel for workers is becoming an important employee benefit in many companies. It is estimated that one million workers are wearing career apparel, and that by 1980 over two million people will be using coordinated clothing.[32] Over a two- or three-year period the apparel costs a company between $150 and $200 for each worker. In some programs, employees pay for the cost of all their wearing apparel, while in other plans the firm may provide the initial wardrobe, with additional or optional items being paid for by employees. In other instances the cost of apparel is evenly divided between employee and employer.

Companies that provide career apparel as an employee benefit cite the fol-

---

[32]Howard A. Wolfe, "Career Apparel Is an Important Benefit Today," *The Office* (August, 1975), p. 66. See also "An Office Career Apparel Program," *The Office* (August, 1975), pp. 32 and 35.

lowing benefits: decreased absenteeism and turnover, greater job efficiency and esprit de corps, and a reduction in recruiting efforts as a result of more walk-in applicants.

Communication of Employee Benefits

Employee benefits, those newly emerging as well as those that have been granted for decades, must be communicated to and understood by the workers. Not only must companies bring their employee handbooks up to date to comply with the Employee Retirement Income Security Act of 1974 but also they must make sure that employees are aware of the cost of the benefit programs and appreciate the firm's willingness to incur these costs in order to provide wide-range protection for their workers. The most frequently used procedures for communicating newly added benefits and changes in benefits are the written media discussed in Chapter 12 — pay inserts, letters to employees' homes, articles in employee publications, and meetings, especially small group information sessions.

QUESTIONS FOR REVIEW

1. What reasons are cited by management for extending employee benefits to office workers?

2. How may employee benefits function as dissatisfiers?

3. How is the cost of OASDHI benefits financed?

4. What kind of protection do employees gain from workmen's compensation insurance?

5. Briefly describe the most common practices for providing insurance benefits to office employees.

6. How does the Employee Retirement Income Security Act of 1974 contribute to the employee's well-being insofar as pension plans are concerned?

7. Distinguish between profit-sharing plans that provide cash shares and those that provide deferred shares. What is the major advantage of each type of plan?

8. Explain how a stock option plan operates.

9. What is the most common practice regarding paid vacations for office workers?

10. If providing coffee breaks and rest periods is not a charitable contribution to paternalism, what are the reasons for providing them?

11. How common is the practice of providing rest periods for employees? What principles should be followed in scheduling rest periods?

12. An employer may be committing an unfair labor practice if a Christmas bonus is unilaterally withdrawn. Explain.

13. What is the nature of the educational assistance provided office workers in many firms?

14. How does the operation of a flexible benefits program provide increased employee motivation?

QUESTIONS FOR DISCUSSION

1. Do you believe that employee benefits motivate office employees to higher productivity? Explain.

2. As a company continues to prosper, is it better to (a) expand the amount of benefits that employees are presently receiving, (b) offer additional benefits, or (c) plow the money back into the company on the grounds that the firm is already providing reasonable benefits?

3. In order for a firm to get a fair return on the dollars expended in its benefits program, the administrative office manager, along with other managers, must be sure that workers understand the benefit program and are often reminded of the value they are receiving in addition to their direct compensation. Develop a program of informing employees about the benefits received, indicating the various communications media that you might use.

4. The Stelzer Brothers Electronics Company has grown during the past several years from its two-man beginning to a firm now employing 150 people. The company is not security-minded, and in the early years offered only those employee benefits required by law. Today many outsiders are amazed that the firm has been able to hold its employees and to avoid unionization, since no benefits other than the usual paid vacations, holidays, and group life insurance have been provided. The company now wants to provide some additional benefits, but it does not wish to appear too paternalistic. What are the most meaningful benefits you believe that the company should now offer?

5. At the Brinkerhoff Research Center food services are provided under a contractual arrangement with a catering firm. During the past six months the cost of coffee and doughnuts has increased to such an extent that the workers have begun to complain. The company does not want to give up its practice of granting coffee breaks to its workers, but at the same time the firm is financially unable to subsidize the food service. What suggestions do you have for the company whereby the employees can retain their coffee breaks without the firm becoming financially involved?

6. During his two weeks' vacation Paul Lightcap was forced to leave the motel at the seashore and undergo an appendectomy at a nearby hospital. Upon returning to work, Lightcap indicated to the office manager that, in view of his hospitalization, the company should reschedule his vacation date and treat his former two weeks' vacation as sick leave. As office manager, how would you answer Lightcap?

PRACTICAL OFFICE MANAGEMENT CASES

Case 14-1   Granting Time Off with Pay "When and If Possible"[33]

In common with virtually every other collective bargaining agreement in the area, the contract covering office workers in the headquarters of a trade association gave employees up to three days off with pay to attend funerals of parents, children, in-laws, husbands or wives. If the death involved a person not that closely related, management did not pay for time lost and usually frowned upon the employee taking time off, even at his or her own expense.

The union wanted to broaden the list of relatives in the family death clause, but management refused. Finally a compromise was reached: the clause remained the same, but the new contract contained some additional language to the effect that, "when and if possible," time off with pay would be given for attending the funerals of persons who were not close blood relations.

When a clerk in the accounting department learned that an uncle had died, she asked for a half-day off and was refused. "We're awfully busy right now with year-end payroll and accounting work," the department head said. "If we let you go, we'd have to get help from a temporary agency or put employees on overtime. It just isn't possible."

"I don't care what it costs," the girl replied. "He was my favorite uncle. I couldn't look my relatives in the face if I didn't show up at the funeral. They would never understand me." So, without permission, she stayed away from work. She was not only docked for the lost hours, but suspended for three days as a disciplinary penalty.

When the matter eventually came to arbitration, management argued:

1. We agreed to give time off with pay when an uncle dies "when and if possible." That means when and if we can do it without adding to costs. Her absence added to costs.
2. An employee who thinks she has been wronged is supposed to obey orders and file a grievance later. Taking time off when she was told not to justified discipline even if she were correct in her view of what the contract requires.

The union's arguments also numbered two:

1. The "when and if possible" language has nothing to do with costs. The grievant should have been given the time off no matter what it cost the company, as long as it wasn't absolutely impossible to do so.
2. If the grievant had followed the usual procedure of obeying first and grieving later, there would have been no way for an arbitrator to correct the wrong done her in her family relationships. She took the only course she could.

Discuss each of the following questions:

1. In refusing the accounting clerk time off with pay, did the department head violate the intent and purpose of the new contract language?
2. Do you accept the statement in the grievance procedure that a worker should obey first and grieve later?
3. Assuming you were the department head, how would you have proceeded in handling the request of the accounting clerk?
4. Assuming you were the arbitrator, would you vote for or against the employee? Why?

Case 14-2   Unilaterally Withdrawing a Benefit[34]

For a number of years, the company had permitted employees to leave company premises during their 15-minute morning and afternoon coffee breaks. But after some difficulty with workers who overstayed their breaks, management upgraded the company lunchroom to keep employees in the building during breaks.

Most workers stuck to their old routine, however; the lunchroom was hardly used at all. A few weeks later, the personnel director called a meeting. "As you know," he said, "we've made a lot of

---

[34]Morris Stone, "If You Were the Arbitrator," *Supervisory Management* (March, 1974), p. 21.

improvements in our lunchroom. Because it's now a pleasant, convenient place in which to take coffee breaks, we've decided to discontinue our old policy of letting you leave the building." Many employees were clearly disgruntled, and several of them voiced their disapproval. But the personnel director was adamant.

The workers decided to consult their union representative. "Nothing in the contract says that a coffee break has to be taken on the premises," he said. "They can't punish everybody for the mistakes of a few people who stretch their breaks. We'll file a grievance."

The case eventually went to arbitration. At the hearing, the union argued that management had no right to discontinue a practice of long standing without discussing it with their workers. The company maintained that it had the right to make reasonable regulations governing the conduct of workers during breaks.

Prepare a report in which you:

1. Evaluate the approach used by the personnel director in discontinuing the old practice of permitting employees to leave the building for coffee breaks. If you disagree with how the personnel director proceeded, indicate how you would have solved the problem of dealing with the workers who overstayed their breaks.
2. Present your arguments for either the union or the company and decide which is the "winner."

Chapter 15

PERSONNEL PRACTICES AFFECTING OFFICE EMPLOYEES

Along with the basic principles of effectively supervising and motivating an efficient work force discussed in Chapter 12, administrative office managers should be familiar with the current practices regarding personnel problems that occur in the office. A knowledge of how other managers solve their problems aids office managers in improving the quality and quantity of their work and in motivating their subordinates to create a better work environment. The office personnel practices discussed in this chapter are grouped under the following headings: practices affecting the physical and mental well-being of employees, and practices relating to special personnel problems.

PRACTICES AFFECTING THE PHYSICAL AND MENTAL WELL-BEING OF EMPLOYEES

Each day office managers, supervisors, and department heads are faced with a multitude of problems that affect their employees' physical and mental well-being. Each problem requires a fair and equitable hearing and a decision that will be satisfactory to both the manager and the worker. Some of these problems are quickly disposed of by reference to the employee handbook or the company's policy manual. Other problems may require further study and consultation with the employee before a decision can be made.

Alcoholism

Alcoholism is a progressive disease characterized by the excessive, repetitive, and uncontrolled consumption of alcohol. The disease cannot be cured, only arrested. Alcoholism is not only a social and physical problem, but also it is generally considered to be a psychiatric one. It ranks behind heart disease and cancer as America's third greatest killer disease. An *alcoholic* is a person who is powerless to stop drinking and whose normal living pattern is seriously altered by drinking. Alcoholics cost employers about $13 billion dollars each year in lost work time, health and welfare services, property damage, medical expenses, workmen's compensation claims, and insurance.[1] Of the more than 78 million workers in this country, the National Council on Alcoholism estimates that six percent are alcoholics in varying degrees and, on the average, an alcoholic costs the employer an extra sum equivalent to 25 percent of the worker's salary. Surveys at a number of companies show that alcoholic employees are typically aged 35 to 50; about

---

[1]John Cunniff, "Firms Take a New Look at Cost of Alcoholism," *Bucks County Courier Times*, August 14, 1975, p. C38.

half are women; 25 percent are white-collar workers, 50 percent graduated from, or at least attended, college; and 45 percent are professional or managerial personnel.[2] The National Council on Alcoholism estimates that one out of 12 managers is an alcoholic.[3]

Alcoholism has become a serious concern in collective bargaining, and it is expected that more union-management committees will be working together to develop rehabilitation programs for alcoholic workers. Such programs are designed to recognize alcoholism as a compensable illness, like any other sickness, under the company health insurance plans, which includes payments of bills for hospitals, detoxification centers, rehabilitation centers, and counseling programs. In its company-wide recovery program, General Motors reports that it has helped more than 7,000 employees through its more than 100 union-management alcoholism committees operating in plants around the country and in Canada.[4]

Companies should develop a straightforward policy regarding alcoholism with the aim of correcting behavior problems in their employees before they become unemployable. The company should look upon alcoholism as it would any other disease that affects an employee's output or behavior while at work. In those firms that have instituted some kind of rehabilitation program, the plans usually operate along the lines of the three-step program advocated by the National Council on Alco-

holism: (1) education, (2) early detection of the alcoholic by the supervisor, and (3) referral to a treatment center.

Education. The firm must get across to its workers the fact that alcoholism is a disease and will be treated as such. As the past president of the National Council on Alcoholism, Merle Gulick, emphatically stated: "The biggest thing about alcoholism is to get it out in the open. Everyone in the company must be convinced it is a disease."[5]

At Union Carbide, which follows the Council's recommended rehabilitation program, all supervisors are given a statement that reads in part:

> Alcoholism is a disease in which alcoholic consumption is interfering with an individual's normal process of behavior and living. The supervisor must be alert to the earliest signs that alcoholism is interfering with work performance and insist that immediate corrective action should be taken.[6]

Many myths and misunderstandings surround the subject of alcoholism and obstruct the development and operation of treatment programs. The facts on the subject must be given to employees through such media as visual aids, group meetings, and articles in company news organs and other publications. Further, there is need for a continuing flow of reliable information, which may be obtained from the sources given later in this section.

Early Detection. The responsibility for detecting an alcoholic problem lies with the immediate superior, usually the supervisor. Supervisors should be

---

[2]"Business' Multibillion-Dollar Hangover," *Nation's Business* (May, 1974), p. 66.

[3]Thomas J. Murray, "The Fight to Save Alcoholic Executives," *Management Review* (September, 1973), p. 42.

[4]"Alcoholism Getting Spot in Bargaining," *The Pittsburgh Press*, June 15, 1975, p. A-25.

[5]Susan Margetts, "The Staggering Cost of the Alcoholic Executive," *Management Review* (July, 1968), p. 33.

[6]*Ibid.*, p. 34.

aware of what signs may denote a case of alcoholism and be alert as to how the effects of alcohol cause an employee to behave. A close study and understanding of the employee's behavioral patterns and visible signs of alcoholism during its several phases, as shown in Figure 15-1, must be undertaken by the supervisor. The supervisor must remember, however, that alcoholics strive to hide their problem from others and even deny it to themselves. Thus, the early detection of alcoholics is often the most difficult phase of the rehabilitation program.

Supervisors should not try to make a medical diagnosis of their employees' alcoholic problems nor delve into the employees' private lives unless invited to do so. Supervisors should, however, discuss with the employees their poor performance on the job and make it clear that unless their performance improves, or unless the employees try to solve their problems by treatment, their jobs are in jeopardy.

Referral. If the company retains a counselor or a physician either on a full-time or a part-time basis, the alcoholic worker can be referred to the counselor by the supervisor. Often the company counselor is a recovered alcoholic whose function is to persuade the employee to accept suitable treatment, which may be through a lay group such as Alcoholics Anonymous, a professional agency, or a hospital detoxification center. The task of the counselor is to impress upon workers that their undergoing and responding to treatment is the only way to avoid endangering their jobs — a most effective tool in motivating the alcoholic worker to accept treatment. In companies where there is a treatment policy in force, the National Council on Alcoholism reports a recovery rate ranging between 60 and 80 percent.[7] A study by the National Industrial Conference Board, in which authorities emphasized that alcoholism is never cured but only arrested, showed that some 60 percent of those who accepted treatment were helped and were able to hold their jobs.[8]

If the firm does not retain a company doctor or counselor, the supervisor can obtain help and information from the following sources:

The local Alcoholism Information Center or local Council on Alcoholism; or the National Council on Alcoholism, Two Park Avenue, New York, NY 10016

The local Central Office of Alcoholics Anonymous; or General Service Board of Alcoholics Anonymous, P.O. Box 459, Grand Central Station, New York, NY 10017

The Al-Anon Family Groups Headquarters, 115 East 23d St., New York, NY 10010

The Family Service Agency in the community

The state agency concerned with alcoholism, which may be an independent commission, or a division within the State Department of Public Health, or Department of Mental Health

Local AFL-CIO Community Services Committee; or AFL-CIO Department of Community Services, 815 16th St., N.W., Washington, DC 20006

Drug Abuse

Another problem that may face the office manager is drug abuse, which for many of today's work force threatens their work performance and continued employment. A *drug abuser* is one who

---

[7]Murray, *op. cit.*, p. 41.
[8]AMemo, *Administrative Management* (April, 1970), p. 96.

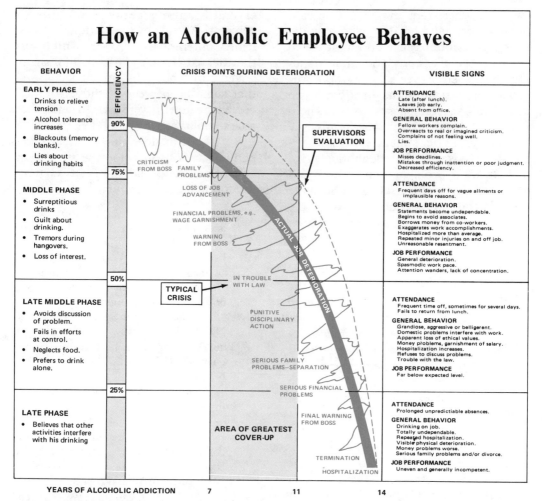

How an Alcoholic Employee Behaves

BEHAVIOR	EFFICIENCY	CRISIS POINTS DURING DETERIORATION	VISIBLE SIGNS
EARLY PHASE • Drinks to relieve tension • Alcohol tolerance increases • Blackouts (memory blanks). • Lies about drinking habits	90% 75%	CRITICISM FROM BOSS FAMILY PROBLEMS	**ATTENDANCE** Late (after lunch). Leaves job early. Absent from office. **GENERAL BEHAVIOR** Fellow workers complain. Overreacts to real or imagined criticism. Complains of not feeling well. Lies. **JOB PERFORMANCE** Misses deadlines. Mistakes through inattention or poor judgment. Decreased efficiency.
MIDDLE PHASE • Surreptitious drinks • Guilt about drinking. • Tremors during hangovers. • Loss of interest.	50%	LOSS OF JOB ADVANCEMENT FINANCIAL PROBLEMS, e.g., WAGE GARNISHMENT WARNING FROM BOSS	SUPERVISORS EVALUATION **ATTENDANCE** Frequent days off for vague ailments or implausible reasons. **GENERAL BEHAVIOR** Statements become undependable. Begins to avoid associates. Borrows money from co-workers. Exaggerates work accomplishments. Hospitalized more than average. Repeated minor injuries on and off job. Unreasonable resentment. **JOB PERFORMANCE** General deterioration. Spasmodic work pace. Attention wanders, lack of concentration.
LATE MIDDLE PHASE • Avoids discussion of problem. • Fails in efforts at control. • Neglects food. • Prefers to drink alone.	25%	TYPICAL CRISIS IN TROUBLE WITH LAW PUNITIVE DISCIPLINARY ACTION SERIOUS FAMILY PROBLEMS—SEPARATION SERIOUS FINANCIAL PROBLEMS	**ATTENDANCE** Frequent time off, sometimes for several days. Fails to return from lunch. **GENERAL BEHAVIOR** Grandiose, aggressive or belligerent. Domestic problems interfere with work. Apparent loss of ethical values. Money problems, garnishment of salary. Hospitalization increases. Refuses to discuss problems. Trouble with the law. **JOB PERFORMANCE** Far below expected level.
LATE PHASE • Believes that other activities interfere with his drinking		AREA OF GREATEST COVER-UP FINAL WARNING FROM BOSS TERMINATION HOSPITALIZATION	**ATTENDANCE** Prolonged unpredictable absences. **GENERAL BEHAVIOR** Drinking on job. Totally undependable. Repeated hospitalization. Visible physical deterioration. Money problems worse. Serious family problems and/or divorce. **JOB PERFORMANCE** Uneven and generally incompetent.

ACTUAL JOB DETERIORATION

YEARS OF ALCOHOLIC ADDICTION   7   11   14

Source: "Booze and Business: Can Your Employees Mix Them?," *Administrative Management* (December, 1969), p. 21. Reprinted from *Administrative Management*, Geyer-McAllister Publications, Inc.

Fig. 15-1

How an Alcoholic Employee Behaves

exhibits strong psychological dependence on drugs, often reinforced by physical dependence when certain drugs are being used. This person has been on drugs for some time and presently feels that he or she cannot function without them. The annual economic cost of drug abuse has been estimated at $10 billion, but no one has adequate information to determine just how much a

problem drug abuse presents in the business office.[9] Dr. David H. Goldstein, professor of environmental medicine at New York University Medical Center, in an interview reported by *The New York Times*, stated that: ". . . drug

---

[9]"Mental Illness Is Reported Main U.S. Health Problem," *The New York Times*, August 3, 1975, p. C49.

addiction is a problem of great gravity to industry. It robs an employee of the motivation to do his job, makes a thief of him because his salary is too small to pay for increasing drug needs, and turns him into a security risk."[10]

Some findings support the relatively widespread illegal use of drugs and narcotics in business and industry. In a survey by Chicago's Industrial Relations Newsletter, the conclusion was reached that three out of every four plants with 50 or more workers have a serious drug problem.[11] Newspaper columnist Sylvia Porter has written that "one out of eight employees has had a drug experience and one out of four job applicants has experimented with drugs."[12] In a 1971 study conducted by the Research Institute of America and published by the New York Chamber of Commerce, it was found that of the 80 corporations studied, 90 percent reported some incidence of drug abuse on their premises; those that reported no incidence were for the most part small firms, with very low turnover. The firms that did note drug abuse also reported sharp increases in absenteeism, turnover, and theft.[13] In a nationwide study of 222 firms, published by *The Conference Board Record*, more than one half of the companies indicated that they were aware of a drug problem in their organizations. Most of the firms noted that the instances of drug abuse had been minor.[14] For sever-

al years the American Management Association has been surveying a large number of firms and asking if there is a drug problem in each firm. In 1967, seven percent of the firms indicated they had a drug problem; by 1970, the number of firms replying affirmatively had skyrocketed to 41 percent.[15] Most studies reveal that the hardened drug users in business are usually in their early 20s and have low-echelon jobs. Most activity seems to be centered on campuses, the major employment market for business offices, and in commune-oriented neighborhoods of the nation's largest cities.

A knowledge of the above facts alone should motivate the administrative office manager to realize and to understand the potential threat of the use of drugs to employees and to their continuing employability. In dealing with drugs in the office the office manager should follow a three-step program similar to that described in the preceding section dealing with alcoholism.

Education. Cooperative education efforts with the community and its social agencies possibly represent to business the one major means of halting the spread of drug usage. Some firms have undertaken broad educational programs aimed at initially preventing the use of drugs or narcotics, supporting the principle that the only real cure for an addict — one who is physically dependent on drugs — is never to start using drugs. Other companies conduct special drug seminars for their supervisors and set up programs for spotting drug-using personnel. Information that can be distributed in the office about drugs and

[10]David Sohn, M.D., "Screening for Drug Addiction," *Personnel* (July–August, 1970), p. 22.

[11]"The Rising Problem of Drugs on the Job," *Time* (June 29, 1970), p. 70.

[12]Joseph G. Zalkind, "Is Your Office Part of the Drug Scene?" *Administrative Management* (October, 1970), p. 41.

[13]Jerome Siegel and Eric H. Schaaf, "Corporate Responsiveness to the Drug Abuse Problem," *Personnel* (November–December, 1973), p. 8.

[14]*Ibid.*

[15]"The Drug Sickness: No Company Immune," *Nation's Business* (November, 1972), p. 20.

narcotics may be obtained from the following sources:

Local or state narcotic education centers, or the Drug Enforcement Administration, U.S. Department of Justice, 1405 I Street, N.W., Washington, DC 20537

American Pharmaceutical Association, 2215 Constitution Avenue, N.W., Washington, DC 20037

National Clearinghouse for Drug Abuse Information, 5454 Wisconsin Avenue, Chevy Chase, MD 20015

Clinical Research, National Institute of Mental Health, Department of HEW, Lexington, KY 40501

United States Public Health Service, Office of the Assistant Secretary, 5600 Fishers Lane, Rockville, MD 20852

Detection. Detecting the on-the-job user and addict, again the major responsibility of the supervisor who is closest to the worker, is a much more difficult task than spotting the alcoholic. The addict's symptoms are not always apparent, even to the trained observer. The chart in Figure 15-2 shows the most common symptoms of drug abuse. However, these are not the only signs that may occur. The reaction to a drug usually depends on the person, his or her mood and environment, and the dosage taken.

Company officials should be very cautious about accusing employees of drug usage or addiction or even searching their lockers and personal belongings, for an error in judgment can lead to a costly lawsuit including both the supervisor and the employer. Those in charge of interviewing should be alerted to the telltale signs that may indicate a drug problem. In the case of a suspicious situation, the application form should be carefully scrutinized and searching questions asked about gaps in employment history, frequent job changes, and reasons for leaving former jobs. Previous employers and references also should be contacted directly.

Referral. A modern, enlightened approach in the referral of drug users and addicts appears in the Statement on Company Position on Narcotics and Dangerous Drugs of one of the country's major mutual life insurance companies.[16] A portion of this statement appears below:

Persons in management and supervisory positions are expected to, and all other employees are urged to, bring immediately to the attention of the Personnel Department the names of employees known to be or believed to be actively and illegally using, transporting, selling, or promoting the use of narcotics or dangerous drugs on company premises; or where apparent use of narcotics or dangerous drugs outside of working hours have a direct effect on the employee's performance on the job.

Such referrals will be discussed and handled on a confidential individual basis. Our primary objective is to help the employee. However, we must recognize the serious nature of the problem, and at times it may be necessary to provide corrective measures, discipline or termination of the employee(s) involved as the facts may warrant.

In its "Guidelines for Supervisors" this insurance company advises its supervisors not to become involved in a counseling relationship with any suspect employees. As the law stands, accusing an individual of illegal use of drugs is a cause for libel, and both the supervisor and the employer may be sued. Trying to counsel a drug abuser may cause a supervisor to become involved in the abuser's personal problems

---

[16]Company name withheld by request.

Fig. 15-2
Common Symptoms of Drug Abuse

Drug Enforcement Administration

Symptom columns (read diagonally, left to right):

SMOKED · SNIFFED · INJECTION · ORALLY · ABDOMINAL CRAMPS · NAUSEA AND VOMITING · DISTORTION OF SPACE OR TIME · INSOMNIA · INCREASED APPETITE · LOSS OF APPETITE · RUNNY EYES AND NOSE · INFLAMED EYES · UNUSUALLY BRIGHT SHINY EYES · DILATED PUPILS · CONSTRICTED PUPILS · INCREASED SWEATING · DEPRESSED REFLEXES · HYPERACTIVE REFLEXES · DIZZINESS · IMPAIRMENT OF COORDINATION · STAGGERING · TREMOR · LAUGHTER · SLURRED SPEECH · RAMBLING SPEECH · TALKATIVENESS · CONFUSION · IRRATIONAL BEHAVIOR · PANIC · HALLUCINATIONS · DEPRESSION · EUPHORIA · ANXIETY · BELLIGERENCE · IRRITABILITY & RESTLESSNESS · EXCITATION & HYPERACTIVITY · DROWSINESS

Legend: ● HOW TAKEN ◉ SYMPTOMS OF WITHDRAWAL ◉ SYMPTOMS OF ABUSE

DRUG	SLANG TERMS
MORPHINE	M, dreamer, white stuff, hard stuff, morpho, unkie, Miss Emma, monkey, cube, morf, tab, emsel, hocus, morphie, melter
HEROIN	Snow, stuff, H, junk, big Harry, caballo, DooJee, boy, horse, white stuff, Harry, hairy, joy powder, salt, dope, Duigi, hard stuff, schmeek, shit, skag, thing
CODEINE	Schoolboy
METHADONE	Dolophine, Dollies, dolls, amidone
COCAINE	The leaf, snow, C, cecil, coke, dynamite, flake, speedball (when mixed with Heroin), girl, happy dust, joy powder, white girl, gold dust, Corine, Bernies, Burese, gin, Bernice, Star dust, Carrie, Cholly, heaven dust, paradise
MARIHUANA	Smoke, straw, Texas tea, jive, pod, mutah, splim, Acapulco Gold, Bhang, boo, bush, butter flower, Ganja, weed, grass, pot, muggles, tea, hash, hemp, grifo, Indian hay, loco weed, hay, herb, J, mu, giggles-smoke, love weed, Mary Warner, Mohasky, Mary Jane, joint sticks, reefers, sativa, roach,
AMPHETAMINES	Pep pills, bennies, wake-ups, eyeopeners, lid poppers, co-pilots, truck drivers, peaches, roses, hearts, cartwheels, whites, coast to coast, LA turnabouts, browns, footballs, greenies, bombido, oranges, sweets, beans, uppers
METHAMPHETAMINE	Speed, meth, splash, crystal, bombita, Methedrine, Doe
BARBITURATES	Yellows, yellow jackets, nimby, nimbles, reds, pinks, red birds, red devils, seggy, seccy, pink ladies, blues, blue birds, blue devils, blue heavens, red & blues, double trouble, tooies, Christmas trees, phennies, barbs
OTHER DEPRESSANTS	Candy, goofballs, sleeping pills, peanuts
LYSERGIC ACID DIETHLAMIDE (LSD)	Acid, cubes, pearly gates, heavenly blue, royal blue, wedding bells, sugar, Big D, Blue Acid, the Chief, the Hawk, instant Zen, 25, Zen, sugar lump
PEYOTE	Mescal button, mescal beans, hikori, hikuli, huatari, seni, wokowi, cactus, the button, tops, a moon, half moon, P, the bad seed, Big Chief, Mesc.
PSILOCYBIN	Sacred mushrooms, mushrooms
DIMETHLTRYPTAMINE (DMT)	DMT, 45-minute psychosis, businessman's special

and certainly will make it more difficult for the supervisor to reflect accurately the facts in succeeding discussions with the Personnel Department.

In a survey conducted by *Industrial Relations News* among 108 firms employing from 275 to over 80,000 workers it was found that only 34 percent of the companies have a formal policy on the use of drugs.[17] In slightly more than half of the companies having such a policy, the penalty for those violating the organization code on drugs is immediate dismissal. In a few other companies the firm takes an additional step of referring the employee to a rehabilitation agency. These firms do not dismiss the worker unless rehabilitation efforts fail.

Some of the treatment techniques available to the drug abuser include: the Methadone maintenance program under which controlled doses of Methadone are given to the addict under a doctor's care (Methadone is a synthetic drug that helps to end an addict's craving for heroin); the therapeutic center concept, whereby addicts help each other overcome the habit by living together and undergoing a series of reinforced job stages that prepare them to return to normal living; and suicide prevention programs where addicts can call and receive a sympathetic hearing from trained personnel.

Mental Illness

According to the National Institute of Mental Health, mental illness is America's primary health problem, afflicting at least 10 percent of the population and accounting for an economic cost of $21 billion each year. Of the 20 million persons who suffer from some

form of mental illness, only one seventh receive psychiatric care.[18]

Generally most companies have well-established and fairly liberal policies for dealing with mental illness among their office workers. Firms rely primarily upon employee magazines, reading rack material, special literature, and films which describe the various kinds of mental illnesses and identify the sources of help available to troubled workers. In detecting employees with mental problems most firms place great emphasis upon observations made by the supervisors, who focus their attention on the workers' job performance and changes in behavioral patterns, such as increased absenteeism. Because of their pivotal role in identifying workers who may have mental problems, supervisors should be provided with information that will help them recognize mental illness and be able to refer the worker to a qualified person or agency, such as a nurse-counselor, psychiatrist, psychologist, family doctor, hospital, or clinic.

The absence of job satisfaction has been found to be related to a variety of mental health problems such as psychosomatic illnesses, low self-esteem, anxiety, worry, tension, and impaired interpersonal relations. The work environment factors that correlate with these mental health problems are low status, little autonomy, rapid technological change, isolation on the job, responsibility for managing people, shift work, and threats to self-esteem inherent in the appraisal system. It has also been noted that workers with personality disorders (including alcoholism and drug

---

[17]Sohn, *op. cit.*, p. 26.

[18]"Mental Illness Is Reported Main U.S. Health Problem," *The New York Times*, August 3, 1975, p. C49.

abuse) may find that their psychiatric disorders stem partially from job insecurity, unpleasant working conditions, or hazardous work.[19]

Work, looked upon for centuries as a form of rehabilitation, may be the best therapy for mentally ill persons; but unless job satisfaction is made possible as part of such therapy, work will only compound the workers' difficulties. Here, as pointed out in Chapter 12, it is the responsibility of the office supervisor to plan and organize work experiences so that both the employees' needs for satisfaction through use of their abilities and the firm's needs to be economically effective will be met.

Safety in the Office

Office hazards cause accidents which are costly both to management and to employees due to loss of time, loss of production, and loss of income. To reduce the number of deaths and disabling injuries that occur on the job each year, the Occupational Safety and Health Act of 1970 was enacted. This act, which was discussed in Chapter 13, imposes safety and health standards upon businesses involved in interstate commerce.

Every accident has a cause, and since it is the problem of management (long recognized by state workmen's compensation laws) to furnish a safe place in which to work, managers should attempt to reduce hazards. To provide a scientific plan of safety administration in the company requires a recognition on the part of management that potential hazards may lurk at each em-

ployee's work place. Someone should be assigned the responsibility for establishing a company-wide safety plan and conducting a safety campaign. There should be a coordinated system of establishing and enforcing safety rules, of recording and analyzing accident data, and of using the results to track down unsafe employee practices as well as potential hazards.

Office employees should be informed of the types of accidents that may occur. For example, very often an employee may open two or more drawers of a file cabinet at the same time, forgetting that such an action may cause the file to topple over. As the result of investigating such an accident and determining its causes, the office manager may decide to tape a warning sign on the top of each file cabinet or line the cabinets back to back and bolt them together, thus preventing their toppling over.

Each department supervisor should be required to complete a written report at the time of each accident so that the person in charge of safety administration will be able to analyze the causes and to improve the safety conditions. By means of a standard reporting system, the safety administrator can compare the effectiveness of the firm's safety program with that of other companies in the same industry.

All the hazards that cause office accidents are too numerous to list. There are, however, some simple basic precautions that every office manager should insist upon in order to reduce the number of accidents:

1. Treat floor surfaces with a nonslip finish.
2. Adjust springs on doors to prevent them from banging into persons, and

---

[19]*Work in America*, Report of a Special Task Force to the Secretary of Health, Education, and Welfare (Cambridge: The MIT Press, 1973), pp. 82–85.

avoid having employees go through swinging or revolving doors too quickly.

3. Instruct workers in the proper use of desk drawers to avoid banging into open drawers.

4. Instruct workers in the proper use of filing cabinets to prevent a cabinet from tipping or falling on a person who may open more than one drawer at a time.

5. Place pencil sharpeners so that they do not injure persons passing by.

6. Check the surfaces of all desks, tables, and chairs to prevent injuries from splinters or rough edges.

7. Check electrical cords and connections for machines and equipment to eliminate fire and shock hazards.

8. Check the spring adjustments of swivel chairs to avoid accidents of upsetting and injuring employees.

9. Avoid placing loose or movable materials on top of filing cabinets or lockers so the objects cannot fall on employees.

10. Check the level of illumination along stairways and consider the painting of walls in a bright color to make the stairways more visible.

11. Provide handrails on either side of stairways and a handrail approximately in the center of very wide stairways.

12. Prohibit smoking in those areas where flammable fluids, such as solvents, are being used.

13. Make sure that exit doors are properly marked and left unlocked.

14. Provide one fire extinguisher for every 3,000 square feet of floor space. Extinguishers should be a foam, loaded stream, or multipurpose chemical type located no more than 75 feet from the farthest point of the area covered.

15. Provide a first-aid kit in a central location.

16. Where smoking at the desk is permitted, be aware of the possibility of fire resulting from hot ashes being dumped into a wastebasket. Should a fire start in a wastebasket, an effective method of containing the fire is to place another wastebasket over the top of the first.

Smoking in the Office

The problem of employees smoking in the office and its effect upon their productivity must receive the attention of the office manager because smoking affects the health, morale, and efficiency of those being supervised.

Office workers and supervisors who argue against smoking in the office say that smoking is unhealthy, it pollutes the air, and it is unfair to the nonsmoking coworkers whose eyes and throats become irritated. Others look upon smoking in the office as an unbusinesslike practice that makes a poor impression on the public. Also, some believe that the worker who smokes is impairing his or her efficiency. Finally, there are those who point out that the nonsmokers' rights to breathe clean air, free from harmful and irritating tobacco smoke, have become recognized by a number of actions. For example, federal regulatory agencies require no-smoking sections on interstate planes, trains, and buses; and some states and municipalities have banned smoking in public buildings.

On the other hand, there are those who would permit smoking in the office. These workers and their supervisors state that nonsmokers are exposed to smoke in many other places besides the office. The argument is advanced that few office workers come directly in contact with the public, and, furthermore, visitors may smoke when they come into the office. Many office workers object to the fact that executives in their private offices can smoke but the office workers cannot. If smoking makes an unfavorable impression on the public in the general offices, why not in the private offices? Also, it is felt that there is a very small fire hazard in most offices, and smoking can be prohibited in hazardous areas. Finally, many office workers find that their efficiency improves, rather than decreases, with smoking. If smoking is permitted only in the lounges and the lunchrooms, the workers become nervous at their stations and their efficiency decreases.

In view of the reports of the relationship of smoking to health hazards, companies have tried by means of films, posters, literature, and financial incentives to encourage employees to stop or reduce their smoking. Other attempts to solve the issue of smoking in the office include: restricting employee smoking to nonwork areas such as the lunchrooms and the employees' lounges; permitting a moderate amount of smoking by present employees who feel they cannot quit, but imposing a no-smoking rule for all new employees; establishing no-smoking sections in company cafeterias and employee lounges and posting "No Smoking" signs at the office workers' desks; and transferring a nonsmoker from an area where smoking is permitted to a smoke-free environment. Other firms have altered their smoking privileges in order to improve production by permitting employees to smoke while working, to reduce the time wasted for smoking breaks, and to abolish smoking rules that formerly discriminated against women.

PRACTICES RELATING TO SPECIAL PERSONNEL PROBLEMS

In this section several practices pertaining to special personnel problems arising in the office are investigated. Most of these problems are directly related to the element of cost and their effective solution requires expert leadership by office managers and their first-line supervisors.

Tardiness and Absenteeism

Tardiness and absenteeism are serious problems for the office manager, particularly in times when there are many jobs available. In some firms the workers do not even bother to notify the company when they are to be absent. Such conditions seriously impair the efficiency and morale of the office.

Tardiness. Tardiness, which is really a form of absenteeism, is usually handled by a written or an oral reprimand, pay deductions, temporary layoff, or discharge, if habitual; postponement of scheduled salary increases until improvement is shown; loss of work-break privileges; and a deduction of points in the merit rating of the employee. One of the simplest methods of controlling tardiness is not to tolerate it. In many instances this will work, but there may be extenuating circumstances, such as transportation delays, automobile breakdowns, and strikes, that mean breaking the rule. A better approach is to place tardiness on a cooperative basis so that all departments work together and perhaps compete for the best record of punctuality. Usually there are a few chronic offenders, and these can be dealt with accordingly. Most workers try to be punctual, but their efforts are nullified by the few who arrive late because of indifference or lack of effort.

Tardiness in the office is traceable more often to laxness in discipline than to any other cause. Of course, supervisors themselves must set the proper tone by arriving promptly for work. The practice of many companies in not tolerating tardiness except under emergency conditions proves that it can be controlled. Further, the use of flexible work schedules, as discussed in Chapter 13, minimizes, if not eliminates, the problem of tardiness.

Absenteeism. The absence of certain key workers may interfere seriously with the work of others in the office unless there are "floating" replacements. Some offices have all their employees indexed so that their capabilities for performing other jobs are known; thus, employees can readily be transferred to take over the jobs of the absentees. But the problem is one of management and must be studied more carefully. The office manager should analyze the problem of absenteeism by finding out:

1. The extent of absenteeism.
2. The causes of absenteeism.
3. The cost of absenteeism.
4. The action to be taken to reduce and to control absenteeism.

Extent of Absenteeism. In 1973 the median monthly absenteeism rate of 136 small and large corporations was 4 percent, according to a survey by the Bureau of National Affairs.[20] This absenteeism rate means that for every 25 workers in a firm, the company is carrying one extra employee to take care of the average absence. Assuming an hourly salary of $4 and taking employee benefits into consideration, the one extra worker may be costing the firm at least $11,000 each year.

To obtain the facts on absenteeism may be very simple. When workers have been absent from their jobs for one full day or longer, they should be required to report to the office manager or the personnel office before returning to work. Thus, a record may be kept of the absentee time and the reasons for it. Such a record should be placed in the personnel files of the employees affected so that it may be considered when opportunities for promotion and salary increases arise. The individual absentee records can be combined to give an absentee record for the entire company, or for each department, that will show the total days of absence during the year, a classification of the reasons for absences, and the frequency of times absent by each employee. Determining the frequency of times absent for each employee aids in locating and controlling chronic absentees who exhibit a pattern of being ill or having a headache on Friday afternoons or Monday mornings.

Causes of Absenteeism. Sickness and on-the-job accidents are the most common causes for absenteeism, and the theory has been advanced that perhaps 80 to 90 percent of all accidents are psychological in origin. Some employees seem to avoid working on the slightest pretext of illness; others work when they are so ill that they should stay at home. It is estimated that alcoholics are absent from their jobs 16 times as often as nonalcoholics.[21] Sometimes economic conditions, age, sex, and marital status are factors in absenteeism. Studies indicate that those who save more,

---

[20]*Employee Absenteeism and Turnover*, Personnel Policies Forum Survey No. 106 (Washington: The Bureau of National Affairs, May, 1974), p. 1.

[21]"Business' Multibillion-Dollar Hangover," *Nation's Business* (May, 1974), p. 66.

own their own homes, and live in better locations have fewer absences than those who do not. Similarly, the chronic absentees tend to be younger than those workers who have regular attendance. A Labor Department study showed that women generally had a higher absenteeism rate than men; married women have a worse record than single women; divorced men had a lower rate than the supposedly more stable married men.[22] Industrial physicians and psychologists report that there is much feigned illness, and some blame that on the liberal sick-leave policies of companies.[23]

New employees are often found among the most chronic absentees, perhaps because of dissatisfaction with their jobs. This points to the need for careful selection of employees, proper assignment to jobs, the enrichment of jobs, and effective supervision and motivation that pays more attention to the psychic satisfactions of work. If management were to realize how much it costs to hire and train each office worker and how much the company loses if a worker leaves and must be replaced, perhaps a more careful matching of workers with job openings, together with appropriate supervision, might result.

Cost of Absenteeism. The cost of absenteeism for the individual firm can be computed as shown below. In this example for an assumed 400-employee firm, the annual cost of absenteeism is $102,400.[24] This amount does not include lost production, overtime costs, employee benefits, etc., which could easily double the final expense.

Total sick days paid previous 12 months .	3,200	Based on 400-employee firm with average of 8 days' absence per employee
Average daily pay multiplied by total sick days..	× $32	Based on average daily pay of $32
Annual cost of absenteeism to firm......	$102,400	
Total accrued 5-year expense	$512,000	

Action to Be Taken. What can be done about the absenteeism problem? Penalties, fines, and incentive bonuses have not produced the desired effects. Penalties and fines with their demoralizing effects create hard feelings and dissatisfaction; incentive bonuses are usually only temporary in effect. But most of all, it should be remembered that only a small number of workers are chronic offenders, and each of these individual cases should be studied in solving the problem. In the case of chronic absenteeism, surveys by the Bureau of National Affairs indicate that the traditional three-step disciplinary technique — warning, layoff without pay, and finally discharge — is enforced by many companies.[25]

Prior to taking disciplinary action when workers are excessively absent, supervisors should freely talk over job

---

[22]Leroy Pope, "Managers Join Day Off Binge," *Bucks County Courier Times*, January 28, 1974, p. 4, and *The Wall Street Journal*, October 16, 1973, p. 1.

[23]Pope, *loc. cit.*

---

[24]"How to Cut Absenteeism and Turnover," *Administrative Management* (March, 1971), p. 65.

[25]Robert L. Caleo, "Absenteeism," *Administrative Management* (June, 1963), p. 23.

problems with their workers to discover why the workers are remaining away from their jobs. Reference to the causes of absenteeism may indicate the cure. Every effort should be made to reduce the absences caused by illness and on-the-job accidents. A good medical department available to the office may help. An educational campaign to maintain the health and safety of employees may be undertaken. For example, providing vitamins and free flu shots have been successful in some offices in reducing substantially the absences caused by illness during winter and spring months. Rest periods, good lighting, air conditioning, music, and noise control may also be effective in reducing absenteeism. Further reduction in and control over absenteeism may be obtained by converting to a flexible work schedule, as evidenced by the experience of those firms mentioned in Chapter 13.

Standards can be established for the amount of absenteeism that will be tolerated, under normal circumstances, as the result of various kinds of illnesses. In establishing its standards, one company looks upon eight or more *absence periods a year* for an employee as excessive and classifies any such worker as a chronic absentee. Some firms define a chronic absentee as one who is away from the job four days or more each month, without excuse, for two successive months.

Departmental supervisors should be held accountable for the attendance record in their departments. To do so, supervisors must be provided with guidelines for discplinary action to impress upon employees the need for good attendance. When it comes to taking disciplinary action, decisions are often made on the merits of each case — the employee's seniority, work record, and su-

pervisor's recommendations. Many firms penalize employees for excessive absenteeism by deducting pay for excessive days absent. In the investigation of absences, some firms conduct their investigations in subtle ways, while others ask the office workers to bring in proof of legitimate absence, such as a physician's statement. Others telephone employees who are absent and inquire as to their state of health.

Turnover

Unless there is some strong reason to the contrary, *turnover* — the amount of movement of employees in and out of the organization — is a measure of the efficiency with which personnel policies and practices are being carried out. As indicated in Chapter 11, recruiting, interviewing, testing, placing, orienting, training, and supervising a newly hired secretary may cost more than $1,500. When a company loses a supervisor, the cost of replacement may be as great as $11,000; and for a middle manager, the cost may be almost $20,000. Since some firms experience turnover rates as high as 20 percent or more among office workers, excessive turnover exerts a strong influence upon the profit picture of the firm.

Turnover Rate. Most turnover falls in the "controllable" category, with the remainder being caused by death, accident, retirement, sickness, military service, or pregnancy. The *turnover rate*, expressed most often in terms of the number of separations from the payroll, is computed as follows:

$$\frac{\text{Total Number of Separations for the Time Period}}{\text{Average Employment for the Time Period}} \times 100 = \% \text{ of Turnover}$$

In 1975 the Administrative Management Society conducted a turnover study among business firms, educational and service organizations, and government offices in the United States and Canada. The findings of this survey that have significant implications for the administrative office manager are listed below:

1. The annual turnover rate for 1975 was 14 percent, which means that for every 100 office workers in the firms surveyed, 14 left their employment during the year.

2. The highest rate of turnover (19 percent) was in the classifications of advertising, printing, and publishing; construction, pulp and paper; and service businesses. The lowest rate (7 percent) was in the public utility grouping.

3. The turnover rate was little affected by the size of office and geographical location. The highest turnover rate, 19 percent, occurred in offices with 26 to 100 and 101 to 250 employees. The lowest turnover rate, 7 percent, occurred in offices with over 5,000 employees. The highest rate was found in the West Central United States, while the lowest rate was in the Western United States.

4. For nonexempt workers (those receiving overtime pay for hours worked over 40 each workweek) the turnover rate of 18 percent was twice that of exempt workers, 9 percent.

5. Terminations decrease dramatically after five years of service. Of those who terminated their jobs, 80 percent had served less than five years with the firm; those who had served five years and over accounted for only 20 percent of the turnovers.[26]

Reasons for Turnover. Among the total number of exempt and nonexempt workers surveyed by the Administrative Management Society, the strongest reason for terminating their jobs was to find another job (30 percent); the second major reason for separation was dismissal from the job (15 percent).[27]

Analysis of the major reason for separation — to find another job — shows that the two main causes are the desire for better salaries and for better jobs. This would seem to indicate that if higher salaries were paid, more promotional opportunities were made available, and if the level of job satisfaction could be improved, there would be about 45 percent less turnover. Thus, there is need to evaluate the present salary structure, employee benefits program, promotional opportunities in the firm, and job content. Opposing this reason for separation is the large number of employees who are discharged for incompetency during the early years of their employment, which may be due to faulty selection, improper job training, and unsatisfactory working conditions. If job dissatisfaction and personality conflict account for a large number of separations, attention should be paid to job content and counseling, and consideration should be given to the possibility of transferring desirable employees to other departments.

Exit Interviews. At the time of terminating an employee's services, an *exit interview* may be conducted to make sure that the real reasons for termination are known. During such interviews, there should be a warm, supportive atmosphere in which the interviewer refrains from criticizing or arguing as the

---

[26]"1975 AMS Office Turnover Survey," *Management World* (September, 1976), pp. 3–5.

[27]*Ibid.*

employees give their reasons for leaving. Copies of the exit interview should be made available to interested executives so they may be kept informed of the reasons for separation.

Post-Exit Interviews. Some companies make use of a *post-exit interview* in which a written questionnaire and a letter are sent to former employees asking their opinions of the company and their reasons for selecting work else-

where. The former employees are asked to be frank in their replies, and if they wish they may omit their signatures on the questionnaire forms.

Reducing Turnover Expense. The turnover expense may be calculated for an individual company as shown in the example below, which assumes a 400-employee firm and an average cost of employee separation amounting to $850.

Total number of employees separated in past 12 months.............................	56	based on 400-employee firm with 14 percent turnover (1973 rate)
Average cost of employee separation ..	× $850	
Annual cost of turnover.......................	$47,600	
Total accrued 5-year turnover expense..	$238,000	

To reduce excessive turnover expense or to control a presently satisfactory turnover rate, the office manager should make sure that in the selection process, the nature and the responsibilities of the job are carefully explained to each job applicant. The job should not be "oversold," nor should it be "undersold." Job applicants should be presented a realistic picture of the job at the time of the interview, and if they have any reservations about the work to be done, they can be investigated prior to employment. Employees must be carefully matched to the jobs by following the workable employment procedures outlined in Chapter 11, and opportunities must be provided the workers to achieve what they expected when they were hired. After the employees have been carefully evaluated and selected, provisions must be made for their orientation and training, as described in the following chapter.

Employee Theft

Employee theft has reached an all-time high and is growing at the rate of 15 percent a year; the thieves are not typical crooks but, by and large, are trusted employees whose opportunities for theft are great, whose methods are less subject to scrutiny, and who are often the last to be suspected.[28] Clerical employees steal millions of dollars each year by taking advantage of their companies' indifference to the pens, pencils, stationery, staplers, and typewriter ribbons that find their way into the employees' homes and into the classrooms of the employees' children. Control over theft and fraud is a problem in human relations, ethics, and value systems, as discussed in Chapter 12; and the attitude and policies of management con-

---

[28]Donald F. Morgenson, "White Collar Crime and the Violation of Trust," *Personnel Journal* (March, 1975), p. 154.

tribute to the problem. If managers and supervisors are indifferent toward the rules that have been established and if the atmosphere is one of "Who cares?," the office can become a school for dishonesty.

Studies on work motivation show that how workers perceive their company is related to whether or not they will steal.[29] Thus, if employees believe that their company is exploiting them in their daily relationships, the employees will tend to steal more. Such workers are searching for an equitable return for the contributions they feel they are making. Sometimes employees who are overlooked or slighted may become frustrated and try to work out a balance between how they behave on the job and what benefits they receive. Often the workers will attempt to remedy the supposed inequity by slowing down their rate of output by not working up to their capacity, wasting time in idle gossip, and taking prolonged work breaks — all of which are forms of "stealing."

Some guidelines that the administrative office manager should follow in developing an effective control system to insure employee honesty are listed below :

1. Department heads should be assigned the responsibility for developing and enforcing a program of control over the purchase and issuance of supplies. The supplies needed by each department should be estimated and planned for in preparing the annual budget for each department, as discussed in Chapter 25. Budgeting a dollar estimate will impress upon workers the cost of the supplies and create greater respect for usage. Supplies should be ordered in bulk only a few times during the year in order to reduce the number of orders and the opportunites for employees to "pad" the orders. Requisitions for supplies should be signed by a department head or someone so authorized. When delivered, the supplies should be turned over to the department head so that he or she may acknowledge their receipt and safeguard them by placing the items in a department storage cabinet.

2. All job applicants should be screened by investigating their references and any gaps in their employment history. If applicants for positions of trust and those who are promoted to such positions are required to fill out bonding questionnaires, the bonding company will investigate the person's character references. Psychological as well as financial benefits will be realized from bonding employees, for experience shows that employees who know they are bonded are far less likely to steal than those who are not bonded or do not know they are covered by a fidelity bond. For the relatively inexpensive premiums, the psychological benefits are enormous.

3. Any employee leaving the firm should be required to report to an executive outside the former employee's department to make sure that the employee's name is removed from the payroll. Otherwise, an unscrupulous person might continue to issue checks in the name of the former employee and cash them with a forged signature.

4. Realistic performance standards should be set. If the standards are not realistic, and employees cannot achieve the goals, quotas, or benefits,

---

[29]Salvatore Didato, "Giving Employees a License to Steal," *The New York Times*, November 9, 1975, pp. 3–16. This article describes industrial psychologist Laurence Zeitlin's concept of "controlled theft," which requires that a company determine how much it can tolerate in losses and then allow a controlled amount of theft, all in an attempt to increase employee motivation and to keep labor turnover costs down.

they are faced with two alternatives —
to fail or to be dishonest. Periodic unannounced spot checks should be
taken upon employee performance at
all levels in the office. Employees
should be informed that such checks
are a normal part of internal control.
Spot checks may be made more effective by introducing deliberate errors as
a means of detecting indifference and
inefficient performance. All critical
areas of office operations — cash handling, disbursements, and safeguarding
of important records — should be inspected and reviewed periodically.

5. The enforcement of policies should be
   uniformly fair and firm at all levels.
   Double standards of enforcement and a
   vacillating approach on the part of the
   office manager will break down the
   discipline and morale quickly and less-
   en the employees' respect for management and company procedures.

Nepotism

Nepotism is the showing of favoritism in the employment of relatives.
Many critics of management look upon
nepotism as unprofessional, but their
beliefs appear to be contradicted by the
actual practices of companies. Businesses may look upon nepotism as undesirable, but this attitude changes when the
business executive is confronted by a
specific case and makes a decision.

Firms that practice nepotism believe
that the employment of a relative, compared with a nonrelative, gives them an
employee who is more loyal and dependable. At the top managerial level, especially in close corporations, the employment of a relative may assure continuity
of the business and an effective perpetu-
ation of the corporate policies. The rela-

tive placed in a junior executive position need not be concerned with
"making points with the boss" and can
thus concentrate on developing his or
her potentialities to the utmost. Some
employers feel that relatives working in
the same office share a strong sense of
responsibility in their work, take more
interest in the company operations, and
are likely to "fit in" better — all contributing to an improved level of morale.

In other companies the practice of
nepotism brings about problems. Often,
the hiring of relatives creates jealousy
and resentment among the employees.
Employees ask themselves, "What's the
use of trying?" and as a result the level
of morale sinks. The hiring of relatives
may also tend to discourage outsiders
from seeking employment in a "family-
togetherness" company. Then, too,
some firms have found that if relatives
are employed and later prove to be unqualified for the job, they cannot be discharged or demoted as readily as non-
relatives.

In some offices the employment of
husband and wife makes for a close-
knit, harmonious working group, while
in other offices the employment of a
married couple may bring about marked
personality conflicts, especially when
both the husband and wife work in the
same department or are in direct supervisory relationships. Some companies
do not permit husbands and wives to
work in the same office, while other
companies take no action to discourage
office romances and if marriage results,
permit both parties to continue working.

In connection with the employment
of relatives and married women, the provisions of the Civil Rights Act of 1964,
discussed in Chapter 11, must be kept in
mind. It has been ruled by the Equal
Employment Opportunity Commission

that it is legal for a company to have a policy against hiring a person whose husband or wife already is on the company's payroll. However, this rule must apply to male and female workers alike. It is illegal for a company to have a policy against hiring married women unless the same rule is applied to the employment of married men. Also, to discharge women when they get married is illegal unless there is a similar rule for male workers.

Receiving Personal Mail at the Office

The problem of employees receiving personal mail at the office, like most of those mentioned in this chapter, is influenced by the size and the location of the office, and sometimes by general working conditions. In the small office, greater freedom is allowed in receiving personal mail at the office. In larger offices, however, it is necessary to impose rules because the volume of personal mail may interfere seriously with the efficiency of work in the mailing department.

Some firms state as a policy that personal mail should not be sent to the office. Some firms reserve the right to open all mail sent to the firm, even though addressed to a particular individual, unless marked "Personal." This is done on the assumption that any mail sent to the office is business mail. Although the propriety of this action may be questioned, it can readily be appreciated that where there is a large number of office employees, the receipt of a large volume of personal mail seriously interferes with and delays the work of the mailing department. Some office managers claim that employees waste too much time in the office or in the lounges in reading personal mail that is received at the office.

Many office managers prefer to ignore the problem of employees receiving personal mail at the office until such a time as it seems to become annoying or interferes with the work. The problem may then be handled in one of several ways:

1. If the firm has an employee handbook, a paragraph may be inserted to the effect that the firm does not approve of having personal mail sent to the office.
2. All personally addressed mail may be opened but not read.
3. On all incoming personal mail, small stickers stating "Personal mail should not be sent to the office" may be attached.
4. A notice may be posted on the bulletin boards to the effect that personal mail should not be sent to the office.

Personal Use of the Telephone

Personal telephone calls prevent the firm from receiving its business calls and actually obstruct the business of the firm. At the outset it should be stated that no firm would object to receiving urgent or emergency telephone calls for an employee, but it is the other personal calls that pose the problem.

One way in which the problem of personal telephone calls may be handled is to have the number or the nature of the incoming call noted by the switchboard operator on a specially printed form. When the employee goes to lunch or takes a work break, the notation is given to him or her so that the call can be returned. In this way the office work is not interrupted.

The office manager or the department supervisor should talk with those who persistently abuse the privilege to the extent that the work flow is interrupted. The offenders should be told that all personal calls should be made before or after office hours or during the breaks. If these efforts do not succeed in solving the problem, the switchboard operator may be asked to supply a list of those employees who make personal calls on company time. Such a list can be used by the office manager or the supervisor to justify a probation period or a termination, depending upon the circumstances.

The mildest way of handling the personal telephone problem is, as in the case of personal mail, to have it noted in the employee handbook or posted on the bulletin boards, thus attempting to discourage the use of the telephone for personal matters. If the office staff is large enough, public telephones may be installed in several locations for employee use.

Collections in the Office

A practice found in many offices is the collection of money to provide gifts for office employees or members of their families. Many firms feel that this is not a problem of management. Others feel that such collections interfere with the morale and efficiency of office work because collections are made too often and disrupt the work flow, the amounts collected are too large, and the funds collected are used for purposes that show partiality. The purposes for which collections are made include: marriage of an employee, departure of an employee, death of an employee, death in the family, illness of an employee, birth in the family, illness in the family, employee

birthday, service anniversary, and military service.

In the offices of a printing company in the Midwest, an envelope is routed to all office workers, supervisors, and executives at the time of an employee's illness or death. Workers voluntarily contribute whatever amount they wish. If the amount collected should be insufficient to purchase the desired gift or floral arrangement, the deficit is made up by the company. Any amounts collected in excess of that required to purchase a gift are retained in the collection fund and are used at the time of the next collection.

Another type of office collection is that which is taken for donations to charitable organizations. Rather than permit numerous charity drives to be undertaken throughout the year, many firms limit their office collections to one or two voluntary drives each year and select as the recipient of the funds a combined-type charity such as the community chest or the United Fund, each of which helps as many worthwhile causes as possible.

Many charitable organizations provide individual collection envelopes. Some organizations provide punched-card forms upon which employees record their pledges and indicate whether they wish to pay the donation in full at the present time, whether they prefer to be billed at home in installments, or whether they prefer to have their contributions deducted periodically from their payroll checks.

Giving and Receiving Gifts

On many occasions, especially at Christmas time, companies are faced with the problem of giving and receiving gifts. Some firms establish a policy of accepting no gifts that are likely to obligate the employee or the company, and to give only nominal or token presents that are not likely to embarrass the recipient. Other firms donate to charities the money that would have been spent on Christmas gifts for their customers and clients. The charitable organizations then send notices to the donor firm's clients, advising them that gifts have been made in their name and by whom. Rather than exchange Christmas cards among the workers, supervisors, and officers, some offices ask the employees to contribute to a charitable organization the amount that they ordinarily spend on Christmas cards and postage.

In its survey of standards and practices regarding business gifts, *Administrative Management* found that about two thirds of the responding companies have no formal rules for employees about the acceptance of gifts. Of the one third that do have either a written or a semiformal policy, about one half state that absolutely no gifts at all are to be accepted from outside companies. A number of these firms also state that any employee found accepting a gift of any kind is subject to immediate dismissal. The survey revealed a definite trend away from giving gifts at all, for a large majority of the respondents reported that they do not give gifts to customers or business associates. About one third of those surveyed reported that they give

away promotional items of nominal value (anything under $10).[30]

Office Parties and Picnics

Closely related to the practice of giving and receiving gifts at Christmas is the policy to be established with regard to Christmas parties in the office. According to a Bureau of National Affairs survey, company-sponsored Christmas parties are held in 46 percent of the responding companies, and holiday celebrations on the job, such as informal employee parties preceding Christmas or New Year's Day are permitted in 48 percent of the firms. Alcoholic beverages are permitted at these informal parties more often in small firms and in nonbusiness organizations than in large or business firms.[31]

The annual company picnic, or outing, is still fairly popular. In the Bureau of National Affairs survey referred to above, more than one half of the companies participating in the survey regularly organize such an outing.[32] The strongest element that supports continuance of annual outings is tradition.

---

[30]Dwayne Meisner, "'Tis the Season for Yuletide Graft — uh, Pardon — Gifts," *Administrative Management* (December, 1973), pp. 22–23.

[31]*Social, Recreational, & Holiday Programs*, Personnel Policies Forum Survey No. 109 (Washington: The Bureau of National Affairs, March, 1975), p. 12.

[32]*Ibid.*, p. 6.

QUESTIONS FOR REVIEW

1. Describe the three-step program recommended by the National Council on Alcoholism in working with the alcoholic in the office.

2. What role does the office supervisor play in working with alcoholic employees?

3. What steps should an office supervisor take in dealing with a worker who is suspected of being a drug abuser?

4. How is job satisfaction related to problems of mental health?

5. What steps should be taken in developing a scientific plan of safety administration? What role should the office manager play in such a program?

6. In view of the government reports that link smoking with unhealthful effects upon the body, how can the office manager defend smoking in the office?

7. Explain why tardiness in the office is traceable more often to laxness in discipline than to any other cause. How can the administrative office manager reduce or, better yet, eliminate tardiness?

8. What should be the role of department supervisors in controlling absenteeism in their departments?

9. Explain how personnel turnover is calculated.

10. How should the office manager proceed to reduce excessive turnover expense?

11. Describe an effective control system aimed at insuring honesty among office employees.

12. What is nepotism? How is nepotism affected by the provisions of the Civil Rights Act of 1964?

13. What approaches may be followed in controlling excessive personal use of the telephone in the office?

14. Should management be concerned with the practice of collecting money to provide gifts for employees? Why?

15. What is the prevailing practice regarding the accepting and giving of gifts?

QUESTIONS FOR DISCUSSION

1. Since the average annual turnover rate for female office workers is twice that of male office workers in the Troust Company, the office manager has concluded that male personnel are more stable employees. What is your reaction to this statement? What, if any, are the fallacies in the office manager's reasoning?

2. The management of D'Ambrosio Soup Company has decided to authorize a charity contribution and is considering the use of a "Buck of the Month Club" to obtain the funds voluntarily through payroll deductions. Employees who care to contribute will grant management the right to deduct $1 from their paychecks each month. What is your reaction to the use of the "Buck of the Month Club" plan? If you react negatively to this proposal, what other approach would you recommend management take to obtain the funds?

3. One writer states that American management generally clings to the pessimistic view that people will take days off no matter what management does. Management cannot stop them, short of firing, and this would mean increased turnover. Management just pays them for so many sick days a year and hopes for the best.

   In your opinion, do these statements accurately portray American management? What evidence can you cite to the contrary?

4. Personality disturbances, ranging from anxiety and psychosomatic illnesses to severe mental disorders such as schizophrenia are common causes of absenteeism. Emotional sickness is believed to provoke more absences than any other illness except the common cold. One large insurance company reports that out of the 120,000 employee visits made to its medical department each year, 200 or 300 result in recommended psychiatric treatment.

   What steps should the office manager take in dealing with the psychoneurotic or maladjusted employee, who as a result of his or her absenteeism, is really costly to the organization?

5. A midwestern newspaper reported that a 22-year-old secretary in charge of a $300 petty cash box secretly withdraws $100 every Friday to bet on horses, ball games, and fights. No guilt for wrongdoing is felt by the secretary who reasons that all money borrowed from the petty cash fund is eventually returned and no harm is done to the newspaper. Do you agree that the secretary is doing nothing wrong? How can management anticipate and prevent such a practice as this secretary's?

6. Joe Tipp has been employed as an accountant in the North American Company for more than 20 years. Over the past few years Tipp has developed a drinking problem to the extent that after his "liquid" lunches, he is often unable to do his job well. When the situation gets out of control, Tipp's supervisor, Helen Charles, talks frankly with Tipp about his drinking; and after each meeting, Tipp seems to work well for about three or four days — but then back to the bottle! Tipp refuses to join Alcoholics Anonymous and Charles is reluctant to recommend discharge in view of Tipp's long record of service. What approach do you recommend that Charles use?

7. In the offices of Bledsoe Sports, Inc., there had been an increasing amount of smoking on the part of secretaries and accountants during working hours. Dawn Gruley, the office manager, felt this was unbusinesslike and was causing excessive pollution of the air. Therefore, she decided to curtail all smoking in the offices and to set aside a special area in which all smokers would take their breaks. Following Gruley's announcement regarding nonsmoking, production among the secretaries and accountants fell about 30 percent. Discuss Gruley's method of handling the smoking problem and indicate how you would recommend the problem be handled.

8. In the Dedulin Medical Center there are several employees who frequently make local outgoing personal calls on office time. Since they can dial outgoing numbers directly from their desks, the situation is

rather difficult to control, especially since personal calls cannot be distinguished from business calls without listening in. As office manager, discuss how you would solve this problem.

9. The Ermentrout Realty Company has recently tried to better its office environment. First, it improved the appearance and comfort of the employees' lounges by installing new furniture; one of the office employees was delegated to make the purchases. Then it was decided to provide 15-minute rest periods twice a day. Soon the employees had burned cigarette holes in the cushions of the new furniture and otherwise damaged it. Furthermore, shortly after the rest periods were started, many employees persisted in returning to their desks 20 minutes after they had left, instead of at the end of 15 minutes.

   Discuss the weaknesses of management in planning and implementing its personnel procedures to improve the office environment.

10. George Laffeter, executive vice-president of the Shelby Company of New York City, is becoming concerned about the increasing number of his middle managers who are having a cocktail or two during their lunch. He is also aware that a couple of his managers must have a "fortifier" before coming to work in the morning. Although Laffeter has never seen any of his subordinates "tipsy," he firmly believes that drinking during lunch (or the first thing in the morning) causes a person to slow down mentally. Laffeter feels that drinking during the workday is totally undesirable and he wants his managers to discontinue the practice.

    Is Laffeter justified in telling his managers not to drink during the day? If so, how do you recommend that he proceed in telling them? Do you believe that Laffeter will be able to abolish his managers' custom of having a cocktail or two at lunch?

11. Anna Ling, office manager of Fen-Tung Industries, Inc., is aware of the company policy that forbids any form of gambling on the company premises. However, each year Ling sees (and occasionally participates in) World Series and football pools being organized by the office workers. As Ling, how would you defend such pools in view of the company's policy against gambling? Is it dishonest or unethical for Ling, as a manager, to participate in any of the pools?

12. Ramona Moreno, manager of employee services, is concerned about the latest group insurance claim submitted by Joss van Riel, one of the firm's junior accountants. The company has a policy of discharging any employee who is dishonest and Moreno believes that van Riel has been less than honest when he submitted the claim for his wife's illness. Van Riel stated on the claim form that his wife was not covered under any other plan, although Moreno and several other workers feel certain that van Riel's wife is covered under the insurance plan provided by her employer. Since the company has a nonduplication of benefits clause in its contract, it appears as if van Riel is attempting to collect twice because his wife is covered under her employer's plan. If you were Moreno, how would you proceed in talking with van Riel about his dishonest actions?

PRACTICAL OFFICE MANAGEMENT CASES

Case 15-1   **Employing a Vice-President's Son-in-Law**

The Whitehorse-Hamilton Corporation is considering hiring the son-in-law of one of the vice-presidents for the position of administrative office manager. The son-in-law, Brendon Mulvey, is as well qualified for the position as any other person who has been interviewed. The position involves planning and control responsibilities in areas where services and technology are undergoing great change.

Management wants an executive who can "grow with the job," for the position is expected to increase rapidly in scope and status. There is a chance, however, that any person employed will not be the right one for the job tomorrow because of changing trends and problems. Although the company has employed relatives of executives for other managerial posts in the company, there is no consensus that employing a relative for the administrative management job will work equally well.

The four executives who have the responsibility for making the final decision have evaluated the situation as follows:

1. Marilyn Averre, the mother-in law of Mulvey, feels that since her son-in-law is well qualified for the position, he should be hired.
2. R. D. Bullock, the vice-president in charge of personnel, also feels that Mulvey should be hired. But Bullock is aware that the position is subject to much stress and change. Therefore, he feels that special measures must be taken to see that Mulvey's performance is evaluated objectively and impartially. Bullock firmly believes that if and when Mulvey should fail to measure up to the job, he should be replaced immediately.
3. Marlene Miller, the vice-president in charge of finance, feels that nepotism in a situation such as this is too much of a gamble. She sees that the son-in-law may not measure up and, as a result, the company will be faced with a messy and extremely unpleasant decision.
4. You, as the president of the company, are trying to reconcile the different points of view and reach a decision.

      You hold a great deal of admiration and respect for the ability of Averre, but you know that this is no guarantee that her son-in-law will perform equally well. Still, as you realize, there is a family tie here. And if you vote against Mulvey, what will be the effect upon Averre?

      You appreciate Bullock's point of view and agree wholeheartedly that if Mulvey is employed, his performance must be evaluated objectively and his rating must not be influenced by the position of his mother-in-law. But, you ask yourself, how can a *relative's* performance be evaluated *objectively*?

      Miller has made a good point, too, for you recall that 10 years ago the former president's son-in-law was hired and turned out to be a misfit. It was a sticky situation and the company had no alternative but to let the son-in-law "gracefully resign." After that, things were never the same with the former president, up until the day he retired.

After listening to Averre, Bullock, and Miller evaluate the capabilities of Mulvey and express their viewpoints on nepotism, you realize that the next step is up to you — to cast your vote. What will your vote be? How would you justify your position to each of the three vice-presidents if you were asked to do so? How would you proceed to evaluate objectively the performance of an executive's relative?

Case 15-2 Solving the Sweet Smell Problem[33]

Harold London found a note on his desk Monday morning that had curtly ominous overtones: "See me in my office as soon as possible. T.C." It was from Ted Curry, the executive vice-president, a man with whom Harold had a stable, amicable relationship. But he was not used to getting abrupt notes from Ted, so he went to see him immediately.

"What's up?" asked Harold, trying to keep from sounding apprehensive.

"Something important, Hal. Sit down." Ted was troubled. "You've been in charge of the mailroom operations for five years now, and I've never had any reason to fault your decisions seriously. But this new development troubles me."

"I don't understand," said Hal, though he was beginning to suspect the problem.

"I've heard, and occasionally seen, that a group of your boys, a clique, seems to take their breaks surreptitiously, and in out-of-the-way places, like distant closets. I've also heard that the reason is because they're smoking marijuana. How about it, Hal?"

"You may be right, Ted. I can't honestly say I'm their confidante."

"But have you confronted them with the idea? Have you asked them outright?"

"No," Hal answered directly, "and I'm not sure it's a good tactic."

"Why not? And what would you suggest in lieu of it?"

"To answer the first question, there are several reasons we can't ask them outright if they're smoking grass. One is that they probably would lie, for fear of being fired. Another is that I'm not eager to be guardian of their morals, especially since break time is strictly their own. Oh, I know that it's illegal, and the company could get into trouble even though we don't control their breaks, but still, we

---

[33]AMS News (Willow Grove: Administrative Management Society, April, 1971), p. 6.

would be discriminating against them because of their more vulnerable positions."

"What does that mean?" Ted wanted to know.

"You know as well as I do," said Hal, "that there are a couple of younger men under you who have spoken openly about the effects of pot, and who may have tried it themselves. Do I have to name names?"

Ted looked thoughtful. "I know," he said finally, "but if they've stepped out of line, they haven't done it in here. And I wouldn't say that they condoned its use, just discussed it. You're right that we can't be everyone's guardian, but you're also right that the weed is illegal. We just can't take the risk that it is being used on company property, even if not on company time."

Discuss your approach to solving this problem, including the role that values and company policies play in the situation presented.

Chapter 16

TRAINING, ORIENTING, AND PROMOTING OFFICE PERSONNEL

So that office workers can function effectively in an environment with ever-changing technology and changing employee needs, companies spend a great deal of time, energy, and money annually for training and development programs. Well-defined recruiting, hiring, and orienting procedures may be established, but the process cannot end there; for even the best office workers can grow stale, especially today when employees' knowledges and skills are outdated quickly. Thus, each worker must be provided with opportunities for continuing growth and development. To accomplish this goal of learning and improved performance, companies, looking upon themselves as educational institutions as well as producers of goods and services, maintain formal training and development programs to equip their personnel with the knowledge and skills needed for growth. As indicated in Chapter 14, more and more companies, by means of company-financed tuition plans, acknowledge the importance of continuing education as a lifelong process by encouraging and guiding their workers in furthering their education.

TRAINING

Training is the process of exposing trainees in a systematic way to a series of events, experiences, and materials that, in themselves, comprise opportuni-

ties to learn.[1] What takes place within the trainees, that is, what changes occur in their behavioral patterns and attitudes, is known as *learning*. The money that a company spends for training pays dividends as a result of fewer errors, greater production, and less turnover. Eastman Kodak Company estimates that perhaps 10 percent of a person's time over the years is spent learning about the job and keeping abreast of new developments. This firm believes that it should earn as good a return on its training investment as it does on any other investment it makes.[2] Like any business activity, training has no value unless it aids in achieving the goals of the organization by contributing to better performance. Training helps attain a firm's goals directly by increasing production, improving the quality of work, and reducing costs; and indirectly by improving the skills and attitudes of workers and by increasing their knowledge and experiences.

Before any training program can be undertaken, the question to be answered is: "What are the goals of the training to be offered?" The objectives of the entire training program, its courses, and its instructional content must be clearly and

---

[1] "Examine Both Hardware and Software You Need," *Administrative Management* (March, 1970), p. 86.

[2] From information supplied by Robert M. Jacobs, Company Training Development, Eastman Kodak Company, March, 1970.

carefully identified in order to show their relation to the objectives of the firm. Included among the goals of office training programs are: to provide *initial* or *entry* training by means of which employees qualify for entry-job assignments, to provide *upgrading* training for employees already in an occupation to improve their knowledge and skills in that occupation, to provide *promotional* and *developmental* training to qualify workers for the added responsibilities and challenges of higher positions, and to provide *retraining* of those workers whose job assignments change.

The objectives of training are derived from what is actually required for performance of the jobs to be filled. The objectives must be communicated to the trainees, and each unit of instruction must be based on the knowledge and skills already possessed by the trainees before the training commences. Therefore, the new materials must be within the reasonable achievement level of the trainees.[3]

Principles of Office Training

The office training program may be looked upon as a subsystem of the major business system, personnel, as discussed in Chapter 17. Along with the other subsystems of personnel — hiring, orientation, evaluation, and operating a suggestion system — the effectiveness of the office training subsystem depends upon the extent to which management is committed to support the program, the proper assignment of responsibility to line managers, and the care and skill with which the training program is planned, implemented, and evaluated.

Principle of Commitment. *Management must be committed to providing an organizational climate that is conducive to continued learning and growth.*

Without the support of top management, office training efforts are likely to have little lasting impact. The quality of the training program is greatly influenced by top management, which sets the policies designed to support the training effort. The goal of such policies is to create a climate that will lead to the healthy personal and professional development of all office workers who participate in the training program.

Principle of Responsibility. *Line managers must be assigned responsibility for organizing and administering the office training program in their own departments.*

Office managers must accept as one of their prime responsibilities the training and development of their subordinates, and must be willing to be appraised as to how well they carry out this responsibility. Although office managers may aid in planning, conducting, and evaluating the training activity, their greatest contribution lies in helping their subordinates apply to their jobs what they have learned from training. To do so, office managers should work with their subordinates to set specific performance goals, measure and discuss the results obtained, and provide opportunities and guidance for overcoming the workers' shortcomings and for building on their strengths.

The responsibility for an effective training program rests with the line managers who may assign individuals to

[3]Blair J. Kolasa, *Introduction to Behavioral Science for Business* (New York: John Wiley & Sons, 1969), pp. 192–198.

certain training duties, employ professional training specialists, or use training consultants. In large firms the office manager is usually provided staff assistance to facilitate the administration of the office training program. Staff training personnel may aid in planning and coordinating the various aspects of the training program and in training the instructors and the trainees. In smaller firms an office supervisor is usually personally responsible for training subordinates in acquiring the skills and knowledge needed to perform their jobs. Usually the supervisor does not have the assistance of a training specialist. If help is needed, the supervisor will have to call upon another supervisor or personnel representative or will have to seek help from outside the company.

Principle of Planning. *The successful planning of an office training program depends upon how accurately the needs of the organization are identified and how the objectives of training are specified.*

With its investment in an office training program, a company expects that the funds will be spent on the right people in the right positions and functions and that the resources will be used to achieve the goals of the firm. Thus, effective planning requires that adequate emphasis upon training be properly placed within the organization. The specific experiences, abilities, and knowledge needed for the successful performance of each job should be determined and clearly stated by undertaking a program of job analysis, as explained in Chapter 22. Next, an inventory of the abilities, experiences, and knowledge presently possessed by workers may be determined through observations, interviews, tests, and written reports prepared by the workers. After

the needs of the jobs have been determined and compared with the present inventory of worker abilities, experiences, and knowledge, the differences can be identified and specific training objectives, oriented toward meeting the needs of the trainees, can be stated. Thus, the training objectives express the gap that needs to be bridged between both present performance and expected performance.

Principle of Implementation. *The office training program should be implemented to meet the needs that have been identified and the training objectives that have been established.*

The person charged with responsibility for implementing the office training program should prepare a plan that:

1. Specifies the training objectives.
2. Outlines the scope and subject matter of the program.
3. Identifies the training methods and techniques that may be employed.
4. Describes the types of trainees and instructors who will be involved.
5. Assigns responsibility for developing training materials and course outlines.
6. Provides for top management's review and approval of the training program.
7. Provides for periodic follow-up to evaluate the effectiveness of the program.

Principle of Evaluation. A *sound office training program provides for periodic evaluation and measurement of its effectiveness.*

The results of any office training program — initial training or promotional training — must be evaluated in order to determine the extent to which the objectives of the training function were achieved. The company should be able to determine whether the time and money spent on training, like any other investment, are yielding profitable results; whether better results could be obtained from the same dollars spent for training; or whether the goals of the company could be better attained by some means other than training.

For certain clerical tasks such as keypunching, billing, and filing, direct measures of output can serve as a measure of the skill level attained. Or production figures based on the percentage of workers that meet standards or accomplish the task within the time required to do the job may be used. In Chapter 23 it is pointed out that performance standards, created through a work measurement program, are one means by which the effectiveness of new office employees and their rates of learning may be measured. By means of standards it is possible to determine at what point in the training process trainees should be able to handle a normal workload on a full-time basis. Indirect measures of the effectiveness of training include the savings realized as a result of error reduction, lower absenteeism, and decreased turnover. More difficulty in evaluating the effectiveness of training occurs in the human relations or social skills training, for the outcomes of desirable attitude development and modification of behavioral patterns are less easily identified, let alone reviewed and measured.

To evaluate and measure the effectiveness of an office training program, the person in charge of the training program should take each of the following steps:

1. Check the results of the training against the objectives of the program.
2. Establish standards of learning time against which the progress of trainees may be checked.
3. Develop data on trainee performance before, during, and after training.

4. Obtain reactions from the trainees, preferably in writing, about what they liked in the training program, what they disliked, and suggestions for improvement.
5. Keep records on the progress of each trainee.
6. Test trainees on the abilities, skills, and knowledge acquired.
7. Provide for the instructor to rate each trainee during and at the end of the training program.
8. Follow up on the trainees by periodically observing the long-range effects of their training.

Psychological Factors in the Learning Situation

To develop an effective office training program — one in which the trainees will learn to the fullest extent — attention must be given to several essential psychological factors in the learning situation. Often a well-planned training program suffers simply because one or more of these factors has been overlooked or was not adequately provided.

As indicated earlier in this chapter, learning is any change that occurs in the previous behavioral patterns and attitudes of the trainees. The product of such learning is called a *habit*. The psychological factors that surround the learning situation, which leads to the development of desirable work habits, should be reviewed by office managers and supervisors not only to refresh their own knowledge, but also to help others in their group who may be providing training.

Motivation. The basic factor upon which all learning is built is motivation, for without it, little, if any, learning occurs. Thus, office trainees must be properly motivated so that they recognize a need for acquiring new information, developing new skills, or improving skills. Further, this desire to learn — to satisfy a felt need — must be maintained throughout the training sessions. In earlier chapters it has been stressed that office workers are motivated by certain needs, but workers differ from one another in the relative importance of these needs at any given time. Among those needs that can be satisfied through training activities are the needs for safety, recognition, esteem, and self-actualization. Thus, those responsible for training must recognize the workers' needs and use them as a basis for motivating the employees.

In motivating office workers the trainer must set performance standards that are realistic and attainable during the training sessions. For example, in the mailing department of a company an average, fully qualified clerk can manually fold letters and circulars at the rate of 1,000 an hour. However, during the program of training new mail clerks, the trainer erroneously adopted a standard of 1,500 folds an hour. Trying to meet such an unrealistic performance standard, the trainees became frustrated, anxious, and confused, all of which caused stress and hindered learning.

Knowledge of Results. The motivation of the trainees should be maintained by advising them of their progress throughout the training period so that they are able to appreciate their accomplishments. Thus, feedback should be structured into the training program. A knowledge of results is a strong incentive at all stages of the learning process, but such feedback is especially needed after the initial enthusiasm of the learning situation has diminished.

The person in charge of training should inform the new learners that their rate of improvement during the practice sessions on a complex task is not expected to be steady. At first, improvement is rapid, with a considerable portion of the total task being mastered in the few first trial sessions. However, each of the following trial sessions contributes decreasingly to the learning process.

The trainees should also anticipate those occasions in many learning situations when progress does not occur. On these occasions the trainees are said to have reached a *plateau* — a period of time or a level of learning where there is no observable improvement or where the rate of increase in learning levels off. Although reaching a plateau seems unavoidable, the trainees should understand its nature and function so that while the plateau lasts, their discouragement and anxiety will be reduced. Reaching a plateau may result from ineffective work methods, or it may come about because of reduced motivation. With proper guidance by the trainer, the real cause of the plateau may be found, and the trainees can be aided by suggestions for incorporating new work procedures or by the establishment of new incentives.

In a training course involving printed materials, such as a seminar on how to improve one's skill in preparing written communications, frequent tests are generally better and will produce more effective learning than merely one end-of-course test. In demonstrating a task, such as how to calculate the extensions on a shipping order and prepare the sales invoice, the trainer can reinforce learning by checking the amount the trainee understands at regular, short intervals rather than checking the entire task at the end of a long time period.

Reinforcement. A *reinforcer* is a condition following a response that results in an increase in the strength of that response. Once the desired behavior occurs, it should be reinforced so that the probability of its recurrence is increased. Reinforcement of learning is generally most effective if it occurs immediately after a correct response has been made, such as the proper performance of a task. Examples of possible reinforcers are: approval and recognition from the trainer, the trainee's personal feeling of accomplishment that follows good performance, self-satisfaction in arriving at a correct answer, information about one's progress and achievement, additional assistance or support provided by the trainer, and monetary rewards. As pointed out on several occasions in this textbook, especially in Chapter 12, managers and supervisors too often rely upon money as a reinforcer when other less tangible factors prove more important in meeting employees' needs.

The person charged with the responsibility for office training must recognize which reinforcers are operative and most effective in a particular situation. An example of the effective use of reinforcement by a trainer in a large insurance company is illustrated by the trainer's practice of evaluating the written tests taken by correspondence secretaries who were undergoing remedial training in medical terminology. The trainer was aware that the numeric grade recorded on the test papers served satisfactorily as a reinforcer for most of the trainees. In other instances, however, the trainer realized that reinforcement came about as a result of writing a few words such as "Well done" or "Fine improvement" on the test papers. The trainer also knew that for a few excep-

tional workers, a verbal "pat on the back" was all the reinforcement needed.

Practice. Few, if any, office trainees would hope to learn how to type by merely reading a book on the subject; most know that the development of typing skill depends upon active participation — practice. In acquiring information from a textbook, a similar requirement for practice is needed, although it is less likely to be applied by the learner. Reading through this textbook will result in some recall as evidenced by tests later on, but the same amount of time divided between reading and self-recitation (practice) with the book closed should significantly increase the amount of recall. Self-recitation should improve motivation since the learner will be able to observe progress, have an opportunity to correct any misunderstandings on the spot, and devote extra time to the more difficult sections of the book. Above all, the learner is practicing recall, which is the desired response.

Office trainees should be given frequent opportunity to practice their job tasks with relevant learning materials, and in the same manner that they will ultimately be expected to perform their work. For example, the payroll clerk who is being taught to operate an electronic calculator should have ample opportunity to practice on the machine using payroll problem exercises. The practice exercises should be instructor-directed experiences, and the trainer should point out any possible pitfalls that the trainee should guard against. It is important that the trainee perform correctly and develop good work habits.

Massed vs. Distributed Practice. In planning the courses of instruction for an office training program, it must be decided whether the practice sessions will be massed, such as two highly concentrated three-hour periods, or distributed, such as six one-hour periods. Usually practice that is spaced out over several periods, with rest or other activities intervening, will result in more rapid learning and more permanent retention than if the same amount of practice is concentrated in a single period. The amount of time devoted to practice in each session determines the effectiveness of training. Each practice session should be sufficiently long so that warm-up may be provided to overcome any initial period of inefficiency. Massed practice tends to favor a repetition of errors, while distributed practice favors the disappearance of errors and the likelihood of developing correct responses. Rest periods enable the trainees to recover from fatigue and to maintain a higher level of interest.

A student's cramming for examinations is an example of intensive massing of practice. Although it cannot be stated that forgetting is unusually rapid after cramming, generally more learning is accomplished if the same amount of study is spaced out over a longer interval.

Whole vs. Part Learning. To determine whether learning by parts or learning by the whole is the most efficient approach to learning a task, the nature of the task must be studied. If the task can be broken down successfully into component parts, it probably should be broken down to facilitate learning; otherwise, it probably should be taught as a unit.

Often a trainer is an experienced worker who may think of the task in larger units than the trainee can readily grasp. A good trainer knows how to break down the instructional units of information into the appropriate size for the learner. The trainer must then arrange the units of information into their proper, logical sequence. In a small office the supervisor-trainer may present some phase of his or her job in the order in which the supervisor performs that job. However, a new worker does not learn in that same order and thus may become frustrated and confused. A good supervisor-trainer knows how to organize the information into a logical learning sequence by proceeding from the known to the unknown and from the simple to the complex. This means that the training should begin where the trainee is at present and not where the trainer has determined the trainee should be.

Most office tasks can be broken down into parts that lend themselves to further analysis. By analyzing the most effective manner for completing each part of the task, the trainer provides a basis for giving specific instruction. For example, keypunching consists of several skills, each of which is part of the total process. The trainee commences by learning the proper use and reach of each finger; then, with practice, the individual finger movements become integrated into a total pattern. This practice of moving the individual fingers is an example of learning by parts.

Individual Differences. In planning the office training program, the supervisor should give special consideration to the capacity of the trainees — their intelligence, aptitudes, and interests. Variations in individual ability must be recognized in order to structure a learning situation that will allow each individual to proceed at his or her own rate. The extent of individual differences among the trainees affects the type and amount of instruction required to attain the learning goals as well as the training methods and techniques by which the materials to be learned are presented.

To provide for individual differences in the training program, sometimes the trainees are grouped according to their capacity to learn as determined by test scores. The test scores provide a basis for offering a different or an extended type of instruction to meet the varying needs of the groups. Further, the trainer may find that in teaching one group of workers how to learn a complicated procedure or how to master a complex skill, the language level must be kept relatively simple, the learning materials or skill broken down into easy learning segments, or the training spread out over a relatively long period of time.

Outcomes of Effective Office Training

The principles of office training and the factors at work in the learning situation are directly related to the major objective of the office training program — to develop office personnel who have learned to work differently through improved performance and who are actually using the new learning on the job. With the attainment of this goal, the following outcomes will become evident.

An Improved Competitive Position for the Firm. Office workers who have participated in training and development programs aid in maximizing the profits of and thus improve the competitive position of their firm. The training experience helps the workers satisfy their own needs to do a good job and reach a high level of productivity, thereby increasing production and reducing

costly errors. As a result of the improved performance of its employees, a firm is able to realize additional economies in the production of its goods or services. Closely allied to this outcome are the cost-reducing factors of standardization and uniformity of output, both of which characterize the end results of effective training.

Office Employees Prepared for Promotion. Having undergone promotional training that utilizes the best available methods and techniques, office personnel are prepared to take advantage of promotional opportunities in their firm. Thus, when there is a change in business conditions, such as expansion, qualified workers are available to fill the newly created positions. Also, if employees are trained for promotion, the illness, death, reassignment, or resignation of other workers will have little effect upon the smooth operations of the business.

More Self-Confident Office Employees. Well-trained, confident office workers lessen the need for close supervision. Training increases the self-confidence of workers, which means that well-trained employees will ask fewer questions and will cooperate more readily with their coworkers. As a result, the burden of the supervisor is reduced and the morale of all workers should be improved.

More Effective Employee Appraisal. Training that is relevant to the real world and geared to the individual needs of office workers enables superiors to more effectively appraise employees' capabilities. This, in turn, helps to insure the proper placement of employees in the organization. Thus, turnover caused by unsatisfactory adjustment to the job should be reduced. Also, employee interest in the job should be increased because of a more thorough understanding of the work and its relation to that of other employees.

Types of Training

Training, as a form of practical education, is essentially of two types: (1) initial or entry training for new employees and (2) promotional training.[4] In both types of training, most of what an employee learns in the work situation is learned in a job environment of superior-subordinate relationships.

Initial or Entry Training. Initial training for new office employees is often given on the job by coworkers, department heads, or first-line supervisors. *On-the-job training* enables the office trainee to acquire the knowledge and skills needed to perform a job while using the actual equipment and materials required by the job. On-the-job training is especially well suited for teaching relatively simple clerical operations such as the opening and sorting of incoming mail. Initial training may also be given in the facilities of the training department of the firm; in a company school operated by the firm's training department that cooperates closely with the firm's offices; in conjunction with public institutions such as high schools, trade and vocational schools, junior and community colleges, and four-year colleges and universities; and in cooperation with private institutions such as business colleges.

In an Administrative Management Society survey of administrative managers, it was found that most managers feel that the following knowledge and skills are best learned in a formal company training program or through on-the-job training: human relations, oral communications, supervision, and office organization and planning. Skills such as accounting and business mathematics are best taught in the university. Generally the survey noted that the skills and knowledge which were thought of as being best presented in formal college programs were least likely to be selected as being best taught in an on-the-job training program, and vice versa. Subject matter such as economics was generally considered to be in the college domain, while skills such as the operation of duplicating equipment and office machines were overwhelmingly favored for on-the-job training.[5]

Instructional Staff. Those who are assigned responsibility for the training program of a firm should possess human relations ability, leadership ability, and technical ability. Those in charge of training, whether a first-line supervisor or a training director, must know enough about human nature, behavioral patterns, and attitudes to realize that the trainees should be accepted as they are. In trying to adapt new employees to work situations, even the most skilled trainer cannot completely remold personalities or alter significantly the behavioral patterns of the employees. The trainer can, however, create an environment in which an employee accepts the need for an attitude change in himself

---

[4]The following discussion pertaining to the instructional staff and the methods and techniques of initial training applies equally to upgrading training and retraining.

[5]Harold T. Smith, "Favor On-Job Supervisory Training," *Administrative Management* (August, 1970), p. 53.

or herself. The teacher should have had experience in exercising the managerial functions of planning, organizing, leading and controlling in order to develop the skills, attitudes, and work habits of the trainees. The instructor in a training program must be technically competent, through appropriate education and experience, in order to command the respect of the trainees and to impart to them the knowledge and skills required to qualify them to produce a quality product or service.

Possibly the most important part of the overall training picture is the supervisor and the manner in which this person handles responsibility. The supervisor's subordinates must be permitted to apply their knowledge and skills and to be independent and professional; otherwise, the supervisor will become an obstacle to their effectiveness as well as to his or her own. At the Eastman Kodak Company where many training specialists are employed at various points in the organization, the company is adamant on the principle that the responsibility for training rests with the line superior.[6] This responsibility cannot be delegated to any other person, regardless of the specialized skills that person may have. The training department has the task of providing staff assistance to the supervisor, who conducts the training rather than personnel in the training department. The responsibility of the supervisor goes beyond conducting courses, however. It is the supervisor's job to be alert to the training needs of the workers and to the opportunities for meeting these needs. The supervisor's job is to see that the training which can-

not be provided personally is provided from some other source and to follow up on the training when it has been completed.

Training Methods and Techniques. The following factors should be taken into consideration when selecting a particular method or technique of training office workers: the number of trainees and their location; their similarities and differences in education, experience, abilities, functions, and occupational levels; the abilities of the trainers; and the cost of the method selected in relation to the results expected. Of major concern in the selection of any training method or technique is the kind of change that the training is intended to bring about. The objective is not necessarily to select the "best" method but to identify, adapt, or invent a method that best fits the situation.[7] The purpose of the training, whether to increase knowledge, to improve skills, or to influence attitudes and change behavior, strongly influences the method or technique to be selected.

As indicated earlier, a primary means of training new office employees is on-the-job training, by means of which a new office worker learns about his or her job by working at the job on a one-to-one basis under the direction of a coworker, a first-line supervisor, or a department head. On-the-job training is commonly used in teaching the skills needed to perform operative and clerical tasks. Other methods of one-to-one training include job rotation and understudy. In conjunction with these training methods, initial training, upgrading,

[6]From information supplied by Robert M. Jacobs, Company Training Development, Eastman Kodak Company, March, 1970.

[7]Frank E. Fischer, "Training," *Handbook of Business Administration* (New York: McGraw-Hill Book Co., 1970), pp. 11-86–11-87.

and retraining programs make use of programmed instructional materials, television, and computer-assisted instruction. Each of these methods and techniques is briefly described below.

Job Rotation. The *job rotation* method exposes trainees to a number of functions in a relatively short period of time by rotating them through the various departments of the company or sections of a department. Trainees may be assigned to each job solely as observers or they may be assigned a specific responsibility at each job so that they become personally involved in the operations and learn a set of skills as they move from one job to the next. For example, one company in recruiting general clerical, stenographic, and secretarial workers does not hire the employees for any specific jobs but instead assigns them to a training center. The new employees are "fed out" on various temporary jobs from one department to another, always returning to the center for further training until a position opens up for which the worker is qualified.

Understudy. In the *understudy* method a new employee is assigned as the assistant to a coworker or a department head who discusses the problems of the department and from time to time delegates certain responsibilities to the trainee. The understudy-superior relationship provides an opportunity for close and continuous shaping of behavior within the work environment, but the value to be gained from this training method depends upon the teaching or coaching ability of the person to whom the understudy is assigned.

Programmed Instruction (PI). *Programmed instruction* is a method of self-instruction in which the training material is presented in small bits of in-

formation that are logically structured so that the learner proceeds in a step-by-step sequence from the basic elements of a skill or concept to the more progressively difficult material. Programmed instruction materials are effectively used where specific skills and knowledge, such as how to fill in sales report forms properly and uniformly or how to understand the technical processes of photocopying equipment, are to be taught.

Programmed instruction *textbooks and workbooks* may have several advantages over conventional textbooks. It is often contended that PI textbooks give the trainees more motivation to learn and enable them to learn faster and retain more of what they learn.[8] Such learning materials appear to be popularly used in large organizations that have many employees to be trained or with employees who must learn a great amount of technical information at frequent intervals. However, before PI textbooks and workbooks are adopted, their cost of preparation (which may be relatively great) and their effectiveness should be evaluated in relation to other training methods.

Although many PI materials are presented in textbook or workbook form, they can be prepared in other forms. For example, by means of a *teaching machine*, the learner progresses step by step through carefully programmed material, immediately reinforcing his or her learning before proceeding to an advanced concept or aspect of a skill. The teaching machine, an electromechanical tabletop device, allows the trainees to read the programmed material, requires them to answer questions at various intervals, scores their responses to questions, and instructs them in further

---

[8]*Ibid.*, p. 11-88.

completion of the program. The main disadvantage of this teaching method is that there is no instructor to clarify concepts that are not clearly understood.

Television. Television, which was discussed earlier in Chapter 8, offers many potential advantages in the development of initial training and retraining programs. Videocassette films can be easily used, and training sessions can be repeated at various times during the day or evening. Several companies may share the cost of producing a training program that meets their common needs and thus be able to obtain outstanding instructors, who otherwise would be unable to come into the firms one at a time to participate in a training session.

Before deciding to use television as a supplemental training medium, all cost factors — equipment, trained personnel, and installation — should be carefully evaluated and compared with the benefits expected since a sophisticated television installation can become quite expensive.

Although television may be a valuable supplemental training technique, it cannot replace the personal aspect of training. The greatest limitation of television as a training medium is its inability to interact with the people being trained.[9]

Computer-assisted Instruction (CAI). By means of *computer-assisted instruction* several trainees may have simultaneous access to a computer, usually through a terminal input-output unit such as a typewriter console or a display panel. Lessons consist of explanations or lectures with questions and quizzes programmed on the computer so that an immediate response or reinforcement is available by communicating with the computer. The trainees are informed by the computer of the accuracy of their answers, told where and how to proceed next, and informed of how well they are doing. CAI, which is based on programmed instruction concepts, enables the instructor to retrieve information rapidly about a trainee's performance and to revise the lesson materials easily when required.

Promotional Training

Having a definite plan for promoting and transferring qualified office workers to supervisory positions improves the morale in all departments. Nothing is more discouraging to conscientious employees, who have worked many years for a company, than to learn that persons outside the organization are given preferential consideration when promotions are to be made or higher positions filled.

Office workers who aspire to attain supervisory and middle-management positions include many different types, and there is ample room for individual style. In evaluating office workers as potential supervisors, the possession of the traditional characteristics and abilities is less important than evidence of what they have been able to do with them to date.[10] The outstanding candidate for promotion in general can demonstrate

---

[9]Anthony Tiano, "TV for Training Need Not Be a Big Production," *Administrative Management* (November, 1975), p. 50.

[10]Reprinted by permission of the publisher from *Developing Tomorrow's Managers Today* by Francis W. Dinsmore, p. 112, © 1975 by AMACOM, a division of American Management Associations. The traditional characteristics and abilities sought in a candidate have been defined as analytical ability, communication skills, ability to work with others, leadership, resourcefulness and ingenuity, decision making, and drive and determination in following through.

that he or she is rapidly developing the following characteristics and abilities in his or her areas of primary interest. He or she:

1. Is strongly motivated to achieve excellence and has demonstrated a consistent ability to do so.
2. Has a curious, probing mind and can use it to generate original ideas and to reach well-reasoned conclusions.
3. Is a resourceful self-teacher who has learned from experience to make himself or herself as effective as possible.
4. Has tended to seek a role as a leader, effectively setting goals and motivating others, and maintaining a strong sense of responsibility for results.
5. Thinks a problem through, decides, takes action, and stays involved.
6. In conversation, is responsive and demonstrates clarity of thinking and persuasiveness.
7. Has demonstrated a scope of interests and abilities which provide an adequate basis for a genuine and lasting interest in the type of work applied for.

Promotional training may be provided by many forms of formal education. For example, promotional training may be carried out entirely by the company, or the company may cooperate with nearby educational institutions in providing evening classes in areas such as credit management, business communications, and data processing applications. Supervisors may take advantage of home-study courses and executive development programs offered by the American Management Associations, which sponsor courses for managers of small businesses, and the Administrative Management Society, which offers a series of advanced management training courses. The training may be given for a short, intensive period during each year, such as an annual two-week seminar. Some firms engage management

consultants to conduct such intensive courses. Others conduct courses in supervision in company-supervised schools and in group conferences. In developing the skills needed by middle managers and top-level managers, it is questionable to what extent these skills are provided through formal education. Most of the top and middle managerial skills are acquired through on-the-job training, by understudying superiors, or through self-study and self-development.[11]

Instructional Staff. Line management, assisted where necessary by staff personnel, should be in charge of the promotional training program. The training program should be carefully organized and planned so that potential supervisors and middle managers obtain full knowledge of the work to be done and its place in the total organization. A knowledge of what work is to be done and how it is to be done can be obtained by experience in the departments, by a study of the operations manuals that many firms have developed, or by working on studies with a system and procedures department, if the firm has one. Information relating to company policies, rules, regulations, authority, and responsibility may be obtained from company manuals, organization charts, and personal consultations with senior executives.

Training Methods and Techniques. In addition to the one-to-one training methods and techniques used in initial training programs, many methods and techniques of group instruction

[11]Robert F. Pearse, *Manager to Manager: What Managers Think of Management Development* (New York: AMACOM, a Division of American Management Associations, 1974), p. 24.

are used in promotional training of prospective office supervisors. Most of these methods have been used for many years in universities, in management education centers, and by professional organizations. The methods and techniques of group instruction used most frequently are described below:

1. *Conference method* or *discussion group*. The head of the group leads the discussion by trainees. The discussion leader may instruct the trainees who are present to learn, or the leader may guide the trainees to reach a decision partially or entirely by themselves. The conference method is effectively employed in training prospective supervisors in human relations and in changing group attitudes and behavior by making use of case histories, followed by on-the-job coaching by and understudying of a leader skilled in human relations. The conference method is generally more costly than the lecture method and requires greater sensitivity and skill on the part of the discussion leader.[12]

2. *Lecture method*. In this nonparticipative, one-way communication technique, the head of the group, instructor, or training specialist is able to impart much factual information to large groups in a relatively short period of time. Of all the various training methods, the lecture method is probably the least expensive, easiest to use, and most universally used and understood. The lecture, whether it is presented in person, on film, or by television, is limited in its ability to influence attitudes and shape behavior since the method cannot discriminate among the needs of the trainees. Further, the trainees receive

little motivation, for they are unable to participate actively in practicing what they are taught.

3. *Role playing*. This training technique, also known as "play acting," "reality practice," and "psychodrama," calls upon potential supervisors and the other trainees to act out their own roles or those of others under simulated conditions. The supervisor may assume the role of a higher level executive and then "act out" a solution to problems that would face the executive on that level. Other trainees act as observers, and afterward their immediate superior or training specialist evaluates the performance.

4. *Decision simulation*. Originally designed for use by top and middle managers, this method, commonly known as "business games," is based on a model of the actual business or one of its functions. Competing groups of supervisors, who assume certain roles in the management of the company, are given a description of a mythical business firm and then asked to perform tasks and make decisions, often with the aid of a computer. The decisions to be made may be related to improving the company's position by taking such actions as cutting costs, improving production, and increasing sales.

   Although the business game furnishes insights into organizational behavior, promotes teamwork among participants, and teaches at the behavioral rather than the verbal level, the method is characterized by several disadvantages. For example, the trainees may concentrate more on "winning" instead of learning and thus become preoccupied with beating the computer or their competitors rather than taking the time to analyze the results they obtained; further, the business game distorts reality by grossly oversimplifying it, with the result that the participants find it difficult to apply to their own work the

---

[12]Frank E. Fischer, "Training," *Handbook of Business Administration* (New York: McGraw-Hill Book Co., 1970), p. 11-90.

lessons they have learned in the game.[13]

5. *In-basket training.* In this simulation technique the prospective office supervisor is given a brief description of a higher ranking position, after which the trainee is "promoted" to that job and given a representative sample of the problems — usually memos and correspondence — as they might arrive in the mail. Within a specified period of time, the trainee must make all decisions and solve all problems, ranging from taking action on reports and letters to settling conflicts among coworkers.

6. *Case studies.* Prior to the meeting of the training class, the supervisor-trainee is given a written case history of a problem or situation that exists or has existed in the business firm. After the background information available for decision making has been studied, the trainee presents a solution to the problem in class. The trainees then evaluate the decisions reached by each other and learn to relate the solutions to the enterprise as a whole and to perceive the interrelationships of people and events. After having evaluated their own decisions, the trainees may be told what actually took place in the business firm. Although there is rarely a single solution to a case problem, trainees can gradually develop insights into management behavior as a result of having analyzed and discussed several possible solutions.

   The case method of instruction has been criticized primarily because it demands too little of the learner and because it tends to equate the ability to verbalize about a problem with the ability to solve that problem. The use of case studies is also criticized because of the frequent use of cases that seem irrelevant, incompletely presented, and removed from the real, immediate situation.[14]

7. *Incident process.* The group of potential supervisors is given a series of incidents that occur in a mythical company, but only a minimum of related information is supplied. The supervisors themselves must obtain all additional data needed and then make the decisions. The objective of this training technique is to teach the supervisor-trainees how to examine all facets of the incident and to engage in research by gathering data from many sources.

8. *T-groups or sensitivity training.* This method, also known as *laboratory training*, places the supervisor in a controlled environment with a small group of people who are strangers to each other. A consultant, with particular sensitivity and a high degree of skill in using this training technique, sets the stage for the unstructured group discussion and interaction during which the people talk about the behavior of the group as a group and the behavior of individuals as they relate to the group. Each individual is judged by the group for his or her strengths and weaknesses, as a personality, as a manager, as a leader, as a speaker, and as someone who is attempting to get a job.[15] An atmosphere of mutual confidence and respect must be established at the beginning, for the criticism may often be bitter when prejudices and shortcomings are laid bare.

9. *Grid® team training.* This training approach is associated with the

---

[13]*Ibid.*, pp. 11-92–11-93.

[14]*Ibid.*, p. 11-91.

[15]"How AMA Trains Managers," *The Office* (March, 1970), p. 62. See also Edgar H. Schein and Warren G. Bennis, *Personal and Organizational Change Through Group Methods: The Laboratory Approach* (New York: John Wiley & Sons, 1965).

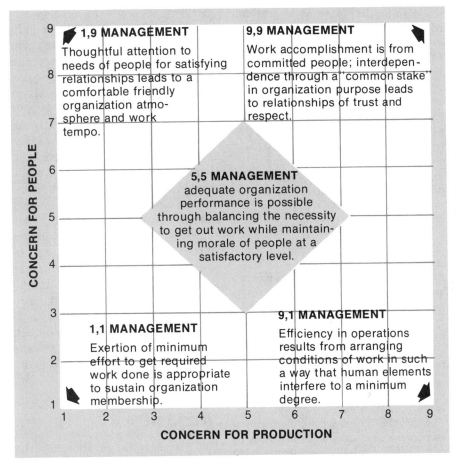

Source: From *The Managerial Grid*, by Robert R. Blake and Jane Srygley Mouton. Houston: Gulf Publishing Company, Copyright © 1964, page 10. Reproduced with permission.

Fig. 16-1
Managerial Styles of the Managerial Grid Program

Managerial Grid concept, wherein managers identify their own managerial styles by plotting behavioral patterns on a set of coordinate axes.[16] As shown in

Figure 16-1, five principal managerial styles are shown on the two axes, one of which represents "concern for production," and the other, "concern for people." The two numbers identifying each approach indicate the extent of the manager's concern for production and people, respectively. Thus, a "2,8 managerial style" represents a relatively low concern for production and a high concern for people. The objective of

[16]Robert R. Blake and Jane S. Mouton, *The Managerial Grid: Key Orientations for Achieving Production Through People* (Houston: Gulf Publishing Company, 1964). See also Robert R. Blake, Jane S. Mouton, Louis B. Barnes, and Larry E. Greiner, "Breakthrough in Organization Development," *Harvard Business Review* (November–December, 1964), p. 133.

this training technique is to provide managers with a conceptual tool by means of which they can learn to integrate and balance their concern for production and their concern for people.

10. *Transactional Analysis (TA)*. This communication improvement technique is used as an analytical tool to train customer-contact type employees and more recently to help the manager understand the more complex phenomena in management — the behavioral interactions between manager and employee.

TA is described by Dr. Thomas A. Harris, who has explored the subject of TA in great depth, as a method for examining a transaction between two people "wherein I do something to you and you do something back" and determining which part of the multinatured individual is "coming on."[17] In practical application of TA, managers analyze their daily transactions with employees and identify the ego states from which both parties are interacting. Managers are made more comfortable, confident, and effective as they better understand themselves, employees, and interactions with others. They become aware of ego states and seek the proper ego state when interacting with employees, all with the goal of better understanding and motivating their employees.

To keep their trainees motivated and to minimize boredom, companies provide diversity in their training programs by using one or more of the ten training methods and techniques de-

scribed above. Varying degrees of success are experienced by companies, and some tend to report biased interpretations of the results received from their promotional training programs. For these reasons the individuals responsible for implementing a firm's promotional training program must make sure that the methods and techniques selected are in accord with the content of *their* company's training program and the needs of *their* trainees. A trainer must guard against adopting in its entirety another company's approach to training merely because a particular method brought forth excellent results in the other firm. This trainer must remember that the success of any training method selected is measured by the results obtained in *his or her own company* — a desired change in the behavioral patterns and attitudes of the firm's trainees and improvement in their performance.

ORIENTING

In the field of administrative office management, *orientation* refers to a carefully planned, systematic, and effective introduction of new workers to their jobs so that they may start working with a minimum of delay, misunderstanding, and error. Orientation covers many topics, such as: company history and organization, including that of the department in which the new employee is working; products manufactured or services rendered; kinds of customers and services rendered them; compensation plans and pay periods, including overtime arrangements; payroll deductions; employee benefits such as group life insurance, hospitalization, cafeteria services, and recreational programs; vacation schedules, holidays, and rules of

---

[17]Thomas A. Harris, M.D., *I'm OK — You're OK, A Practical Guide to Transactional Analysis* (New York: Harper & Row, Publishers, 1969), pp. 12–13. TA was first introduced by Eric Berne, M.D. See Eric Berne, *Transactional Analysis in Psychotherapy* (New York: Grove Press, 1961) and *Games People Play* (New York: Grove Press, 1964).

conduct; suggestion plans; and promotion plans.

Orientation As Part of Vestibule Training

Sometimes orientation is provided as part of the new worker's *vestibule training*, which takes place in an area away from the site where the job is normally performed. In this area, the trainee's future work station, including a duplicate of any equipment to be used, is simulated. Vestibule training is often used in those situations where the trainees have no knowledge of the jobs to be performed, where there are stringent demands on either quantity or quality of work to be produced, or where the initial slowness of the trainees would seriously interfere with the orderly flow of work in the department. By means of vestibule training the trainee is provided with the basic information necessary for a complete knowledge of the job and understanding of the practices and procedures of the firm before the worker begins the job. Companies that provide vestibule training are required to invest a considerable sum of money in equipment and a staff of trainers, with the expectations that these costs will be offset by improved performance on the job.

The Induction Checklist

In their vestibule training, many firms use an employee handbook that contains general company policies and information. Supplementing the employee handbook is the *induction checklist*, which contains items that the supervisor should cover when introducing a new employee to his or her job. The induction checklist is one of the most effective means of making sure that new employees are properly introduced to the firm and to their jobs.

The two-page induction checklist shown in Figure 16-2 provides for an orientation program extending over a period of about two weeks. This carefully planned program leaves a more lasting impression than merely reading a handbook and thus is more effective in "breaking in" new employees. Furthermore, using this checklist insures a complete orientation in all the details of the firm's policies and procedures. Sometimes the checklist is followed up by a formal induction class in which is discussed company-wide information such as company history, products and services, systems of evaluating employees, salary increases, promotion plans, and social activities.

The Sponsor System

Many companies find the sponsor system to be an effective technique for orienting new employees. Under the *sponsor system*, each new employee is assigned to a present worker who takes care of the new employee, acquaints him or her with the duties of the job, and answers questions. Not only does the sponsor system relieve a supervisor or department head of part of the orientation procedure, but it also gives the sponsors an added sense of responsibility and aids in their self-improvement. The sponsor selected to orient a new employee should have a job similar to that which will be assumed by the new worker, a complete knowledge of company policies and department operations, a pleasant outgoing personality, and an interest in people and their problems.

Sample Induction Checklist

FOR USE BY SUPERVISORS AS A GUIDE IN INDUCTING NEW EMPLOYEES

One of the most effective tools which can be used in inducting new workers is the induction checklist. Its primary value lies in the fact that it spreads induction over a number of days, giving the new employees a chance to absorb and digest the various facts and figures, rules and policies they should know. With the use of a checklist like this one, the employer can be certain that the new workers are getting all the information about the company they need in order to do a good job. And it helps the supervisor present the information in a logical, orderly manner.

Supervisor_____   Date_____

For Employee_____   Dept._____

BEFORE WORKER ARRIVES

Check when completed

_____ 1. **Prepare Future Associates** (by individual or group conference) If
     a. The job is different
     b. The person is different
     c. If someone could have been promoted from within

_____ 2. **Have Desk and Supplies Ready**
     a. Have workplace arranged as you want it kept (inspect personally)

_____ 3. **Alert Job Instructor**

_____ 4. **Arrange for Luncheon Escort**
     a. Escort will explain location of rest room and other facilities (show employee)

FIRST DAY

_____ 1. **Review the Job**
     a. Confidential aspects
     b. Stimulate job enthusiasm and satisfaction in a job well done
     c. Explain work to other sections (give copy of job description and organization manual)
       1. The way work originates
       2. Where it goes
       3. Relation of the job to other jobs in section
       4. Relation of the section to division
       5. Relation of the division to company
       6. Let employee know you are depending on him or her
       7. Give assurance employee will learn quickly

_____ 2. **Explain Hours of Work** (give copy of company manual of personnel policies)
     a. Starting and quitting time
     b. Hours per week
     c. Rest periods
     d. Lunch period
     e. Not to leave desk or put away work until bell rings

_____ 3. **Review Compensation**
     a. Amount
     b. When paid
     c. Cost of living allowance
     d. Mention deductions
       1. Income tax
       2. Social Security
       3. Retirement (if applicable)
     e. If applicable, review company's retirement plan (give copy of retirement plan)
     f. Emphasize value of fringe benefits paid by company (give copy of Group and U.C.D. cost to company)
     g. Salaries must be kept confidential
     h. Cashier not permitted to cash checks
     i. Right reserved to deduct for absence

Check when completed

_____ 4. **Discuss Attendance Requirements and Records**
     a. Filling out time card (show card and demonstrate)
     b. Method of reporting tardiness (stress honor system)
     c. How and to whom absence is reported
     d. Stress punctuality
     e. Explain effect of good attendance and punctuality on employee's record

_____ 5. **Has the Employee Any Questions?** (ask)

_____ 6. **Explain Induction Quiz**
     a. Voluntary; will be given if employee chooses at end of first 10 days

_____ 7. **Introduce to Immediate Associates**
     a. In department and supervisors and others in related departments

_____ 8. **Introduce to Workplace**
     a. Workplace to be in order as employee expects to keep it
     b. Stress good housekeeping

_____ 9. **Have Chair Adjusted**

_____ 10. **Give Job Instruction** (use job breakdowns or manuals if available)
     a. Prepare
     b. Tell
     c. Show
     d. Practice
     e. Check
     f. Explain what to do about any idle time
       1. Report to supervisor for more work
       2. Emphasize this is not a reflection on employee, but responsibility of management
     (Have a trainer well prepared and temperamentally suited to teach)

_____ 11. **Discuss Work Instructions**
     a. Majority will come from supervisor
     b. Occasionally from department head
     c. Question any orders received from fellow-workers — check with supervisor
     d. Stress that all instructions should be clearly understood

_____ 12. **Explain Learning Aids**
     a. Examples of work (show employee)
     b. Job instruction breakdown, if available
     c. Special terms used, including abbreviations

_____ 13. **Encourage Employee to Ask Questions**
     a. They aid in learning
     b. They help develop judgment

_____ 14. **Explain Where to Store Work Overnight** (show)

SECOND DAY

Check when
completed

_____ 1. **Explain Performance Review** (show the form and illustrate with examples)
 a. Important to employee
 b. Raises depend upon work, attitude, length of service

_____ 2. **Explain Quality and Quantity of Work**
 a. Production standards, if any
 b. Importance of accuracy
 c. Quality before quantity
 d. Speed will come with experience

THIRD DAY

_____ 1. **Explain Telephone Technique, if Employee Conducts Company Business on Telephone** (give copy of telephone company booklet)
 a. Speak clearly
 b. Give your name when answering
 c. Take messages in writing for those not present
 d. Deliver messages before you forget
 e. Find numbers in company directory

_____ 2. **Give Reasons for Rules, Policies and Plans**
 a. To make cooperation easier
 b. To result in greater efficiency
 c. To avoid duplication of effort

_____ 3. **Explain Voluntary Disability Plan and Company's Group Insurance Plan** (give copy, if not already included in company manual)
 a. Sign up employee for group insurance

_____ 4. **Has Employee Any Questions?** (ask)

FOURTH DAY

_____ 1. **Give Employee Opportunity to Say How He or She Is Getting Along**

_____ 2. **Explain Use of Medical Facilities**
 a. Reason for compulsory physical examination
 b. Report to company doctor at any time ill — with knowledge of supervisor

_____ 3. **Discuss Suggestion System** (show current scoreboard on bulletin board)
 a. How it encourages initiative and ideas
 b. How awards are made
 c. How to submit
 d. Should be well thought out ideas
 e. Must sign suggestion form
 f. All suggestions are thoroughly considered

_____ 4. **Explain Messenger Service**
 a. Messengers work on regular schedule (show message carrier envelope and illustrate how to fill out)
 b. Don't expect special service
 c. Don't make a messenger of yourself

FIFTH DAY

_____ 1. **Discuss Personal Telephone Calls**
 a. Can be made during working hours if urgent
 b. Incoming calls only when urgent

_____ 2. **Explain Policy on Donations**
 a. No solicitors allowed in building
 b. Start no subscriptions without approval

_____ 3. **Discuss Departmental Policies Which Are in Addition To (But Not in Conflict with) Overall Company Policy**

_____ 4. **Has the Employee Any Questions** (ask)

SIXTH DAY

Check when
completed

_____ 1. **Explain How to Get Additional Supplies**
 a. On requisition, on approval of department head
 b. Don't visit supply department
 c. Explain conservation of supplies

_____ 2. **Discuss Personal Mail**
 a. Best to have sent to home
 b. Deposit outgoing letter in box outside of building (or in lobby)
 c. Company does not pay postage
 d. Can get stamps from cashier
 e. Do not write personal letters on company time

SEVENTH DAY

_____ 1. **Explain Change of Address**
 a. Company must have complete record
 b. Notify personnel department of changes
 c. Same for telephone number

_____ 2. **Explain Company Educational Program** (give copy of plan)
 a. Tuition, if any

EIGHTH DAY

_____ 1. **Explain the Employee's Association**
 a. Membership advantages
 b. Dues
 c. How collected

_____ 2. **Explain Company Library**
 a. Free to use it
 b. Where located

_____ 3. **Describe Company Magazine** (give copy of latest issue)

NINTH DAY

_____ 1. **Describe Vacation Plan** (show copy of schedules)
 a. Explain vacation system
 b. How length of vacation is determined
 c. The part seniority plays
 d. The part convenience to section plays
 e. Time selected must be approved by department head
 f. Subject to change for good of company

_____ 2. **Explain Company's Bulletin Boards**
 a. Do not post anything on it without approval
 b. Watch it for current announcements

TENTH DAY

_____ 1. **Explain that Patience and Understanding are Important Qualities to Develop** (give examples)
 a. Employee will work with all types of persons as to age training, education, experience, background

_____ 2. **Encourage Employee to Talk Things Over with Immediate Supervisor**

_____ 3. **Department Manager is Glad to Talk Things Over When Necessary and with Knowledge of Immediate Supervisor**

_____ 4. **Administer Quiz** (get written answers)

_____ 5. **Review Employee's Public Relations Influence**

ELEVENTH DAY

_____ 1. **Review Quiz Results**

Employee's Induction Completed: ....
                                         Department Manager Signature

Instructions: Upon completion of this checklist, return it to Personnel Department for inclusion in employee's personnel file.

Fig. 16-2
Induction Checklist

PROMOTING

To be successful, a promotion plan must be definite, systematic, fair, and adhered to uniformly. The basis of promotion is the functional organization chart, developed after a systematic job analysis, as described in Chapter 22. Each employee should understand his or her position, the line of promotion, the requirements for the next job, and the salary. A promotion plan must have the confidence of the employees. To provide for promotions that are based upon objective data and not solely upon personal opinion and assessment, the personnel department should keep complete files of personal data on all employees — their age, marital status, education, experience, special abilities, and physical condition. The personal data sheet should be supplemented by the history of employment record. Regular entries should be made on the personal data sheets — not too much to make the work cumbersome but sufficient to present an unbiased, factual basis for promotion. Such personal data should cover absences from work, tardiness, suggestions offered by the employee to the firm, disciplinary action taken, and most important, periodic evaluations of the worker.

Promotion Trials

Some firms have adopted the civil service concept of *promotion trials* for positions that are frequently vacated. Any promotions in position or changes in responsibility are made with the consent of the person being transferred who has the privilege of returning to the former job and salary if desired, after a probationary period. A promotion should always carry with it an adjustment of compensation, which should

never be less than the minimum salary for the position in the new classification or rank.

Evaluating Employees' Promotion Potential

Some firms look to the outside for professional help in obtaining an objective evaluation of their employees' potential for promotion. Management consulting firms may be called upon to test employees and to conduct interviews in an attempt to determine which employees possess the abilities and characteristics for promotion. In addition to the use of tests and interviews, one management consulting firm gives a personality index test that enables the consultant who is evaluating the test results to obtain a better understanding of the employee's attitudes and opinions and whether or not they will be of benefit to the company. The consulting firm looks upon the personality index as a means of validating the findings it has obtained by use of other appraisal techniques.

In large companies, psychological tests are sometimes used to observe and to evaluate rank-and-file workers in order to locate future managerial ability. Other criteria, such as recommendations of supervisors, seniority, and excellence of technical skills are also given appropriate weight in locating supervisory and managerial ability among nonsupervisory workers.

Seniority As a Basis of Promotion

Seniority is frequently a basis of promotion and probably should be since it is based upon the principle that those who have served loyally for a long period merit recognition. The philosophy of basing promotions upon seniority tends to stabilize employment and to reduce turnover. Seniority must not, however, be adhered to rigidly because it is an arbitrary check on the younger worker and, if continued, may result in a somewhat stagnant staff. New ideas and ability must be given recognition, even at the expense of seniority. Otherwise, the younger and perhaps more creative and aggressive employees will seek work with a competitor or perhaps start in business for themselves, with either action possibly being detrimental to the firm.

Horizontal Promotion

An employee may have reached a certain level in his or her department at which the future is not too promising because there is little turnover and the department is not expanding. It would therefore be wise to transfer such a capable worker to another department where promotional opportunities are greater. This type of transfer is really a form of promotion — a *horizontal* promotion — though there may not be any increase in salary or rank. It is a promotion because in the new position there will be an earlier chance for advancement. Horizontal promotion should be recognized and given emphasis among employees so that it is fully appreciated.

Transfers

Transfers and promotions are closely related, although not all transfers are promotions. For instance, transfers may be necessary because an employee has been improperly matched to the job. In some firms a misfit employee would be discharged. The more intelligent way of handling such a situation, however, is to transfer the employee to a position for which he or she is better suited and where the worker's capabilities may be challenged. This can be done only where the firm has a staff sufficiently large to absorb the transferee.

There are a number of sound reasons for transfers. The one indicated above stresses the policy of the firm by which the constant fear of being discharged is removed from the minds of the new employees. Such a policy creates in the workers a more wholesome attitude toward the firm and toward their work. Moreover, the company does not incur the expense of hiring workers who later turn out to be unsatisfactory.

The fundamental purpose of transferring employees is to stimulate them out of the monotony, and perhaps inefficiency, in which their long service may have placed them. Some firms believe in the practice of developing understudies and therefore have a regular schedule of transfers so that resignations, promotions, reassignments, deaths, and illnesses of employees do not seriously affect the office work. There is always someone who can step in and do the work. This policy also stimulates the worker. Few workers will feel that their services are indispensable or that "the firm cannot get along without them."

Other firms have rush and slack periods either during the month or during certain periods of the year. By having a series of employee transfers, workers obtain experience in a variety of positions, thus enabling the office manager to shift workers during the busy seasons.

QUESTIONS
FOR
REVIEW

1. Distinguish between the concepts of *training* and *learning*. What is the relevance of this distinction for the office manager who is in charge of training new office workers?

2. As the result of effective training and development of its office workers, what benefits may a company receive?

3. Contrast the role of the office manager in a large firm to that of the office supervisor in a small company in organizing and administering the office training program.

4. How should the administrative office manager proceed in evaluating the effectiveness of the firm's office training program?

5. How important is knowledge of results in an office training program?

6. Which kind of practice — massed or distributed — usually results in more rapid learning and more permanent retention of the learning materials? Explain.

7. What are the outcomes of effective office training? Which of these outcomes do you rank as the most important? Why?

8. Of the three abilities that should be possessed by the person in charge of training, which do you look upon as being most vital? Why have you assigned this ability number one ranking?

9. Define the role of the supervisor in an effective office training and development program.

10. Contrast the job rotation and the understudy methods of training.

11. Which of the methods and techniques of promotional training are participative? Which of the methods is the least expensive and easiest to use?

12. What is orientation?

13. What advantages can be cited for on-the-job training as contrasted to vestibule training?

14. How is the use of an induction checklist related to the orientation process?

15. Explain how a sponsor system operates.

16. What are the characteristics of a successful promotion plan?

17. To what extent should seniority be considered in the promotion of office personnel?

18. A horizontal transfer may, in effect, be a promotion. Explain.

QUESTIONS
FOR
DISCUSSION

1. In the employee handbook prepared by the Malek Book Company, the following statement is made: "All new employees are placed on an official three-month trial basis." Is the company able to discharge a worker after one month if that person proves to be unsatisfactory by the end of that time? Discuss.

2. Should office training and development programs be discontinued during a recession when few or no employees are being added to the work force and when few promotional opportunities are available? Explain.

3. A weakness of many promotional training programs is that employees are often trained for advanced positions which are not available when the training courses are completed. Do you agree with this statement? Explain.

4. In many offices the responsibility for initial orientation and training is assigned to the "older" office workers. Unless considerable care is exercised in using this approach, what kinds of problems often emerge?

5. Evaluate the following statement: "You could dispose of almost all of the leadership training courses for supervision in American industry today without anyone knowing the difference."

6. If a company is interested in furthering the education of its employees and is willing to pay part of the costs, the firm must supervise its employees' study. How can such supervision be undertaken?

7. What disadvantages may a company experience by having its initial training program for typists and stenographers conducted at a nearby community college? Under what conditions do you think a cooperative program of training between a business firm and a community college is desirable?

8. Philip Stoddard, head sales correspondent in the Order Processing Department of the Havas Ball Bearing Company, has been qualified for the past six months for promotion to a supervisory position in the Sales Department. However, Stoddard's boss, Luisa Oliver, refuses to let him be promoted out of her department, claiming that the Order Processing Department's operations would be hurt by his loss. How would you solve this problem?

9. As part of its employment procedure, the McGinnis Copper Company includes a testing program to determine whether or not applicants will be hired and also to determine their potential for promotion. Employees are not considered for promotion unless they attain a stipulated score on the tests. What is your reaction to using test scores as the major determinant of an employee's promotion potential?

10. Some firms encourage their supervisors and executives to teach courses in nearby colleges and universities, especially in the evening. Do you consider this a desirable practice? Explain. Other companies prohibit their employees from engaging in any kind of "moonlighting," including teaching. Do you consider such a restriction to be in the best interests of the firm? Explain.

11. Joyce Melendez has just been graduated from high school and has accepted the job of correspondence secretary in the home office of the Walsh Tire Company. This is her first job and she has had no

business experience other than one semester's cooperative work experience as part of her course requirements. It is your plan, as manager of office services, to have each new worker such as Melendez properly oriented and trained before actual employment begins. Your budget allows you to pay all new workers the minimum hourly wage during the initial training period. The home office, with its 400 office workers, has an annual turnover of 20 percent. Outline a complete plan for orienting and training all new office workers.

12. In the Fritz Piano Company, the administrative office manager is also the assistant to the president. The firm gives an orientation handbook to all new employees in the office as well as in the plant. The handbook covers all the points the firm wishes to communicate to new employees, but the workers tend to forget or to ignore some of the items that management considers very important. Discuss the procedures that you as the administrative office manager might follow to impress upon all employees the importance of remembering the contents of the orientation handbook.

PRACTICAL OFFICE MANAGEMENT CASES

Case 16-1   Deciding Whom to Promote[18]

Upon the resignation of George Lovett, unit supervisor in the clearing area of a large brokerage firm, Section Head Bill Dunham was faced with a dilemma.

In line for the promotion were two senior clearing clerks — Dan Wilbur and Mary Longgood — who had joined the firm at the same time and were equally skilled in performing their jobs.

Naturally, however, the position of unit supervisor required supervisory skill, and Bill felt that Mary outshone Dan in this area.

Mary got along extremely well with her coworkers and seemed quite capable of assuming a leadership role. Dan, on the other hand, was introverted and shy. He came to the office each day, did his job, and went home — usually without saying three words to his colleagues. But he was competent and he did know the clearing operation backwards and forwards.

Despite such diligence on Dan's part, it seemed clear to Bill that he should give the promotion to Mary. The only thing that was stopping him was Mary's home situation. She was married to a salesman in the computer business, and her husband had already been transferred to four different cities in the 12 years they had been married. Bill couldn't help wondering if another relocation would soon take place.

---

[18]Reprinted by permission of the publisher from *Supervisory Management* (February, 1972), pp. 43–44, © 1972 by American Management Association, Inc.

The employee promoted to unit supervisor would have to undergo an extensive training program, and Bill didn't want to give the job to Mary if there were any chance that she would be leaving the firm in the near future.

Bill decided to bring his doubts into the open and explain the situation to Mary. He called her into his office, told her that she was the number one candidate for the job, and asked if she felt that her husband would be transferred in the next year.

"I will level with you, Mr. Dunham," she replied. "My husband and I really don't know if or when we'll be asked to move. We could be in this city another five years or we could be relocated tomorrow. I would like to have the job more than anything, and I certainly feel that I could handle it. But in all fairness, I must tell you that I will always have to put my husband's career ahead of mine."

Mary had just gotten the words out of her mouth when Bill's telephone rang. It was Clearing Department Manager Peter Morris, asking if Bill had made a decision on the promotion. When Peter heard that a decision had not been reached, he replied: "I hate to put pressure on you, Bill, but I have to have the name of the new unit supervisor by nine o'clock tomorrow morning."

Consider these questions — and ask your own:

1. Should Bill give the job to Mary?
2. If so, or if not, is there anything he should say to her?
3. What, if anything, should he say to Dan?

Case 16-2   Developing a Remedial Training Program

Joseph Fioravanti has been employed for two months in the accounts payable department of an office machines manufacturing firm. During the past three weeks you, as supervisor, have been conducting a random sampling check of the quantity and quality of output in the accounts payable department. With the exception of Fioravanti, all workers are producing at or close to the standards set earlier in the year by the firm. Along with numerous errors, Fioravanti's work is characterized by low output, often 25 percent less than that of other accounts payable clerks in the department.

Today, as you examine a sampling of Fioravanti's work for the past week, you begin to think about the need for installing some sort of remedial training for persons such as Fioravanti, whom you wish to retain in your employ.

Determine the need for a remedial training program by answering the following questions:

1. How can I as Fioravanti's supervisor check his work to determine if the poor performance is due to inadequate training or to some other cause?
2. If my checking should indicate that Fioravanti has been inadequately trained, how do I go about introducing a remedial training program?
3. If my investigation indicates that Fioravanti has been adequately trained, what do I do next?

Case 16-3   Improving the Orientation Procedure

The headquarters office of the Witzky Insurance Company, located in a suburb of Seattle, employs 800 office workers. Although the company pays above-average salaries, the turnover of office workers has been very high, often reaching 24 percent among the newly employed. In four of the departments, the turnover has been greater than in others. Management has assumed that the high turnover rates have been due to faulty supervision and improper selection procedures.

Recently an investigation has indicated, however, that those hired were properly qualified for the work for which they were selected. Exit interviews with a number of those who had left resulted in the discovery that they felt lost in the company and did not know too much about what they were to do nor whether their work was satisfactory.

A management consulting firm which was called in suggested that perhaps the orientation procedures were faulty and that the supervision of the new employees was inadequate, especially in the four departments mentioned. It was recommended that an orientation checklist be used. When this recommendation was passed along to the supervisors, they objected vigorously. They said that the checklist would not help and, besides, they did not have time to do the additional clerical work.

Prepare a report to the president of the company in which you, as office manager, answer the following questions:

1. How would you handle this situation from the viewpoint of top management?
2. What would you do about implementing the consulting firm's recommendation that an orientation checklist be used?
3. Assuming that the checklist is an effective tool, how will you go about "selling" its use to the supervisors?

Part 4

Controlling Administrative Office Operations

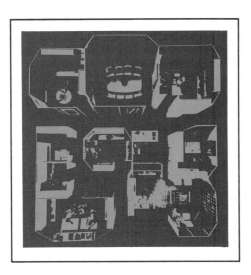

Controlling, the underlying theme of this last part of the textbook, is the managerial function concerned with ensuring that operating results conform as closely as possible to the plans made for the organization. The functions of planning and controlling are closely related in that both functions directly influence the attainment of an organization's goals. Thus, the office operations of a firm are set into motion as a result of managerial planning; the operations are kept "on the right track" by means of the control process.

In the process of controlling, the principal steps are to establish standards, to measure performance, to evaluate performance, and to render long-term appraisals. Throughout this part these steps are examined in relation to the role they play in controlling office costs. First to be explored is the topic of office systems, the analysis of which is designed to reduce the cost of the information-management function without impairing its effectiveness in helping the organization achieve its goals. Next, the opportunities for cost reduction and control of information processing are examined as they relate to three levels of office systems — manual, mechanical, and electronic. Attention is next focused upon studying and evaluating office jobs, measuring the work, setting standards of performance, and determining an equitable salary compensation plan. Finally, the last chapter of this textbook describes how, through a program of budgetary control, the company maximizes its competitive position by intelligently planning and controlling the acquisition and use of its resources.

Chapter 17

OFFICE SYSTEMS

Within recent years the term "system" has become universally recognized in business, industry, government, and education, as witnessed by frequent references made to such terms as accounting systems, production systems, political systems, and instructional systems. Much of the impetus for this rapid growth in systems springs from the computer and its related components. In Chapter 2, for example, automation was discussed in terms of a management information system (MIS) where the responsibility for the processing and control of data in large firms is vested. The small firm, too, even though usually without automated equipment, is as dependent upon systems as the large firm; and for this reason efficient managers and their employees in all types and sizes of firms must understand and apply systems concepts in their respective jobs.

What are systems and their related procedures and methods? What purpose do systems serve, and how do they operate in a firm? In what ways does a company organize its systems function? How are existing systems studied and new systems designed and installed so that the work of the office is performed more efficiently? How important are people in the age of systems? All of these questions and other related ones are discussed in this chapter as they relate to the management of an office. Primary attention will be centered on the manual systems of processing information in the office, leaving the discussion of the mechanical and electronic systems for Chapters 19, 20, and 21.

THE SYSTEMS FUNCTION

The effective administrative office manager, along with other members of the management team, realizes that a firm's success depends on its operating efficiency — that the work to be accomplished must be carefully planned, organized, and controlled. In keeping with Leffingwell's principles of effective work cited in Chapter 1, the administrator must decide what work is to be done, how it is to be done, who will do the work and at what time, and also how to provide the resources necessary to get the work done. Finally, the manager must evaluate the completed work.

To assist all departmental managers to provide improved methods of operation, a systems function has emerged in the organization. In the office, for example, most work is composed of a pattern of office systems, procedures, and methods. The term *system* refers to a set of related elements that interact to achieve some planned objective. For the office manager, these elements are the personnel, data, forms and related records, and the machines and equipment involved in completing a major phase of office work. For example, there is the sales system that involves the forms, personnel, equipment, and records necessary to complete a sale from the time an order is received until the goods are shipped and payment is received. A similar system is developed for handling purchases. Sometimes the system, such as the cost accounting system, may be an auxiliary control function of the business.

Each system is composed of a number of procedures. A *procedure* is a planned sequence of operations for handling recurring business transactions uniformly and consistently. For example, in the sales system there are procedures for processing an order, shipping the goods, accounting for the shipment, receiving payment for the sale, handling claims and adjustments, and analyzing the sales.

For each operation or step within a procedure, there is a method for accomplishing that phase of the work. A *method* is the manual, mechanical, or electronic means by which each operation is performed. Thus, in a sales order-processing procedure there are various methods for acknowledging the incoming order, checking the credit status of the customer, preparing the sales invoice, and distributing the copies of the invoice. The skills and preferences of the workers as well as the cost and availability of equipment account for the various methods employed in each system.

Major Systems and Procedures of Business

The routine operations of most firms are organized around the basic functions that are required to achieve the objectives of the firm. The major functions of business organizations involve purchasing, sales, production, finance, cost accounting, and personnel.

Each of these basic functions is frequently considered as a system, as illustrated in Figure 17-1, to accomplish certain planned objectives. In turn, when each of these major systems is analyzed, it is found to comprise a series of detailed procedures or steps for achieving the desired purpose in the most efficient way. Throughout all these systems there are a large number of clerical or office services upon which the various departmental managers must depend. Office services, such as word processing, reprographic and micrographic services, and records management are examples of systems for which the typical office manager has company-wide responsibility.

Objectives of Office Systems

The systems function has developed from the scientific management contributions of Frederick Taylor and the application of these contributions to factory work, as discussed in Chapter 1. In fact, many of the first improvements in office operations were achieved by applying Taylor's principles of industrial engineering to office systems work.

Presently, however, the scope of systems work extends into many new areas involving the complex interrelationships of an entire organization and the whole administrative process in such firms. In the office, for example, systems studies include such topics as layout and the flow of work, forms design and control, records management, reports management, procedures development, work measurement and standards development, equipment utilization, methods analysis, and personnel utilization. To undertake studies of this magnitude, which go beyond the simple paperwork surveys, analysts must understand the

Major Systems of Business	Procedures
Purchasing	Requisitioning the purchase Requesting quotations from suppliers Placing the order Receiving the goods Accounting for purchase and payment of goods Returning unsatisfactory goods
Sales	Receiving the order Processing the order Shipping goods Accounting for sales Accounting for receipt of payment Processing sales returns and allowances
Production	Designing the product or service Scheduling production Specifying the required components Developing the production system Evaluating the product quality
Finance	Preparing payrolls Preparing financial reports Borrowing money from banks Paying dividends and debts incurred Preparing tax reports Receiving cash
Cost accounting	Computing material costs Computing labor costs Computing manufacturing overhead costs Inventory procedures
Personnel	Hiring procedure Orientation procedure Training procedure Evaluation procedure Discharging procedure Operating a suggestion system

Fig. 17-1
The Major Systems and Procedures of Business

philosophy, objectives, and thinking of management.

A well-designed office system has the objective of coordinating the interactions of people, equipment, time, and money in order to increase productivity and at the same time reduce costs. For the office manager this means eliminating as much unnecessary information and as many unessential business forms and records as possible. More specifically, the system should achieve the following objectives:

1. Furnishing the best information to the right people at an appropriate time, at the least cost, and in the right amount so that an improvement in decision making will result.
2. Eliminating the duplication of work.
3. Ensuring safer, less fatiguing work.
4. Eliminating the waste of time, energy, and materials, and thereby increasing the productivity of workers and capital.
5. Improving customer service.
6. Mechanizing the repetitive, routine tasks where possible when automatic equipment will do the work more quickly, more accurately, and at a reduction in cost that will pay for the equipment in a year or two. (This objective is analyzed in Chapter 19 through the illustration of several basic accounting systems.)
7. Establishing a uniform procedure to follow for each similar transaction. When such procedures are based upon a standard time allowance for identical manual and machine operations, wasted motion, delays, and errors in the smooth flow of work are reduced or eliminated.
8. Fixing responsibility for satisfactory work performance.
9. Training that is simplified and more effective because the workers are trained in "the one best way" to perform each office job.

10. Developing a climate that is receptive to change — a change for the better through a more analytical approach to problem solving. Thus, improvements are constantly made, which eliminate the weakness found in so many offices — i.e., that because a job was always done a certain way, this is still a satisfactory way. Systems and procedures analysis stresses the philosophy that, when something has been done in a particular way for five or more years without change, it is likely that a better way can be found.

The area of systems work is known by many names. Most frequently it is called *systems analysis*; other names used are *systems and procedures analysis, procedures analysis, methods analysis, systems engineering*, and less frequently by an outmoded term, *work simplification*.[1] The systems objectives outlined in this section serve as the foundation for the discussion of systems analysis in the remainder of this chapter as well as in the following chapters on forms management, mechanization of accounting systems, and data processing systems.

SYSTEMS CONCEPTS

The systems that are common to most offices may appear on the surface to be extremely simple; but this is a deception, for behind the scenes is a complicated network of procedures, methods, and data-handling operations. The

---

[1] For office managers and other personnel interested in the field of general systems including manual systems, the Association for Systems Management (ASM), 24587 Bagley Rd., Cleveland, OH 44138, offers considerable assistance. The ASM provides regular seminars on systems analysis through its chapters, which are located throughout the country; special monographs on systems efficiency; and a monthly publication, the *Journal of Systems Management*.

payroll system is a good example of this complexity, for it involves dozens of possible withholding items, a confusing array of tax regulations, and a variety of continually changing reporting procedures that complicate the preparation of payroll records.

To understand the systems at work in efficient offices, the following systems concepts will be discussed: (1) a basic systems model that explains the overall operation of any system; (2) systems relationships ranging from total systems to their subsystems; (3) the idea of a data base; and (4) the various systems levels found in the office. Emphasis will be placed on the manual system and the needs of the small office for effecting systems improvements.

The Basic Systems Model

The term "model" as used by management planners has several meanings.

In one sense a model explains a process or an operation in its most general form, free of the many details that prevent an easy understanding of the complex functioning of an entire system. In another sense, the word represents an ideal form of that operation, such as a model office or a model worker.

One of the best ways of understanding complex systems is through the use of a basic systems model. A *basic systems model* represents a general explanation of an operating system to which more concrete details can be added when a specific system is studied. Figure 17-2 describes the following general elements or parts of any system, regardless of the system's size or complexity: input, process, output, and feedback or control. *Input*, the first phase of any system, puts the system into operation and is illustrated by the introduction of raw materials into a manufacturing process or by the arrival of the morning mail in

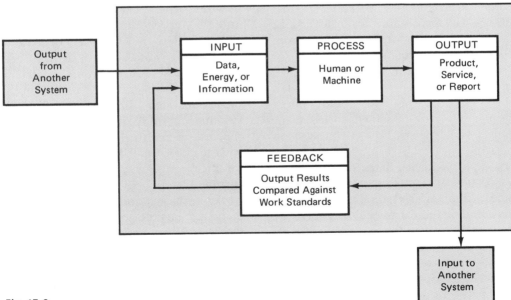

Fig. 17-2
The Basic Systems Model

an office. *Output*, on the other hand, represents the ultimate objective or goal of a system — that which results after the input element has been "put into motion." Unprocessed sales data are converted into a finished report (the output) by that phase of the system called *process*. Thus, processing, which occurs between the input and output stages, changes the form or makeup of the input elements into output elements, and in so doing adds value to the input and makes it more useful to the firm. Classifying, sorting, filing, and calculating are all common processing activities.

At this point, however, the systems model is not complete, for it lacks a regulating force — *feedback* or control. The purpose of feedback is to determine if the output of the system has been produced within established or tolerable limits. Feedback seeks to compare "what is" (the systems output) with "what should be" (the standards of performance set for the system). Later, some "activator" — a person or a machine — is responsible for adjusting or correcting the amount of deviation from the standard expected.

A sales system illustrates each of the elements found in the systems model. The sales orders regularly coming into a firm as input are classified, sorted, computed, and typewritten — all processing activities — which result in two forms of output: a formal sales report as well as invoices for customer payment notices. Thereafter the sales quota (the standard of performance) expected of each sales worker can be compared with the actual sales. If the sales quota is not met, corrective action in the form of a more intensive sales training effort is "fed back" into the system as new input for the next sales period; if the quota

has been met, no corrective action is necessary. In the same way the invoice file copies feed back information for use in the preparation of customer bills and for documentation purposes in the accounts receivable department. Examples of several common systems are shown in Figure 17-3.

The Total Systems-Subsystems Relationship

Effective management requires office executives to understand that their work is made up of various systems, all of which integrate into a *total system* — the company-wide information network. Office managers must know which systems are the framework of their office organizations, and what procedures make up each of these systems. The office managers are in much the same position as a physician who must know that the human body (the total system) is made up of a larger number of systems such as the circulatory system, the nervous system, the respiratory system, and the reproductive system, and that each of these is composed of a large number of *subsystems*. Furthermore, each of these subsystems is related to the other subsystems and "leans" on the other subsystems in order that the total system can fulfill its mission. Such is the case in the total system of the firm, with the personnel function responsible for hiring workers, the production department responsible for assigning the workers' duties, and the payroll department responsible for compensating the workers. These various subsystems support the main objective of the firm — to manufacture the products sold by the firm for a profit.

With the advent of electronic data processing and its application to the

Systems Examples	Systems Elements			
	Input	Process	Output	Feedback (Control)
1. Sales	Sales data	Classifying, sorting, filing orders, billing	Invoice, sales report	Comparing sales with sales quotas, setting new quotas, invoice file copies
2. Production	Raw materials, labor, energy, blueprints	Production operations	Automobile	Quality control, work standards, worker morale
3. Word processing	Dictation, instructions	Typing	Letter, memo report	Proofreading, line counts of work
4. College student*	Food, rest, books, motivation	Studying, learning, testing, grading, counseling	Diploma, degree	Employer and alumni reaction to education

*The fourth example deals with the human factor and qualifies as a system because it includes all the elements found in the basic systems model.

Fig. 17-3
Systems Elements with Common Examples

functional aspects of business operations, the total systems concept has taken on increasing importance. Under this concept the necessary operating documents, records, and reports are linked together and presented simultaneously as part of the company-wide information network, as discussed in Chapter 2. At the same time management is provided with control information that permits the making of timely decisions. The total systems concept results in more effective management since it not only takes into consideration the present operating procedures and methods but also projects the probable effect of expanded or reduced operations. Furthermore, in place of a number of independent operating systems, the total systems concept stresses the interrelationships of all business operations, all of which are made possible by the use of electronic data processing.

If developed and used properly, the total systems approach to managerial planning, organizing, controlling, and leading should result in great economies.

Data Base

One of the major responsibilities of any system is to provide immediate access to the information in the files. This requires that the files be carefully designed and the locations of stored records be known at all times. The data base concept is one answer to a more efficient use of the files.

A *data base*, sometimes called a data bank, is a central master file containing information about a firm in a readily accessible form. Normally it represents a total package of information from such areas of the firm as accounting, marketing, engineering, production, personnel, and research and development in one large library of files arranged so that duplication of such files throughout the firm is avoided. Such information is "captured" only once, giving organization-wide access to the files. With a data base in operation much manual effort is eliminated, and the total file space is reduced as duplicate files, previously maintained by the individual departments, can be eliminated. Updating the files when new transactions occur as well as extracting information from such files is made easier because transactions come into the system at one point only.

The data base concept is largely an ideal, which for most firms is still far from reality. It requires extensive automated equipment to handle the information within a firm, and the concept demands a very rigid discipline of the workers who store the information, as there is a natural tendency to create departmental files for the sake of worker convenience. Also, a data base is impractical for old, established organizations where work patterns are firmly entrenched and in which departments will not release their records for a central file. The fundamentals of a computer data base are treated in Chapter 21.

Systems Levels

Information-processing systems may be classified in terms of complexity or processing power and, thus, in terms of the degree of automation involved. In this section, three levels of systems are discussed: (1) manual systems, (2) mechanical (sometimes called electromechanical) systems, and (3) electronic or automated systems.

Manual Systems. In an age when the computer continues to make greater inroads into the production of goods and

services including information, it is understandable that the electronic system represents to many people the most common and the most efficient method of processing data. However, such is not the case, for there are many systems in which manual or hand processing is clearly preferable.

In a *manual system*, the earliest and still most prevalent type of system, the human being is the data processor. Such a system is illustrated by the preparation of paychecks in a small firm. In the manual system people in the payroll unit receive input data through their senses, usually the eyes, from the information appearing on time cards. The data are then sent to the brain for storage via the nervous system, with the brain acting as the control unit. The brain also acts as a processing unit by performing such data processing operations as arithmetic calculations (adding, subtracting, multiplying, and dividing); storing these results; comparing one number or word with others (as in the case of proofreading); and finally producing output such as paychecks, payroll registers, and tax reports. Output in the manual system is provided on the basis of the set of instructions or "program" that is stored in the payroll clerk's brain or perhaps contained in a procedures manual.

In the earliest manual systems all tools for processing data (pencils, pens, and rulers) and the journals and ledgers for storing information were actually operated by hand. Under such a system information appears in a human-readable form and changes or corrections are easily made. Such manual methods may be quickly adapted to various working conditions and to the exercise of judgment in making decisions from the data. However, there are certain weaknesses in the manual system. The human mind is subject to fatigue and boredom, which frequently cause from 5 to 10 percent error in computations and related clerical tasks. Too, the mind is slow in performing arithmetic calculations and, because of the impact of the emotions, may find it difficult to apply the rules of logic.

For most of the past 100 years machines have assisted in the operation of the manual processing system. Such machines as typewriters, adding and calculating machines, dictation and transcribing machines, and the telephone have become handy office tools, each performing a single processing function. Later came more specialized multifunction machines, such as the accounting machine, that can perform calculations, print out the results on forms, and retain data in one or more storage registers for future use. Such machines offer greater speed and accuracy; but at the same time their use is limited to the imagination, experience, and control of human beings. The final output in a manual system can be no better than the human condition — both psychological and physical — will permit.

Mechanical Systems. *Mechanical systems*, sometimes called electromechanical systems, are most frequently illustrated by the machines that make up the punched-card data processing system. These systems have been widely used for the past 40 to 50 years and represent a more powerful and more automatic means of processing information than the manual system. Chapter 20 discusses this level of system in detail.

Electronic Systems. The *electronic system*, as illustrated by the computer, operates at the speed of light and therefore has great processing speed as well as many other information-handling ca-

pabilities. In this system as well as in the mechanical system, however, many activities are not convertible to machine processing and hence require the presence of manual systems. Examples are the human functions, such as customer relations, keypunching, completing source documents, solving human relations problems, and making decisions from data based on intuition and common sense. In Chapter 21 the limitations and strengths of electronic systems are explored more fully.

ORGANIZING THE SYSTEMS FUNCTION

The most common approaches for organizing the systems function are:

1. Employing a firm of management consultants or systems analysts to make special studies of office systems, procedures, and methods.
2. Developing an internal staff of systems analysts whose services are available to the entire organization.
3. Assigning responsibility for systems improvement to the office manager.

The organizational approach used for studying and improving systems will be determined by the size of the office and the attitude of management toward this phase of work. Whatever the subdivision of office work may be, the office manager must realize that the analysis of office systems and procedures requires the support and approval of top management if new or improved systems are to be successfully installed and operated. Thus, before a program of systems analysis can be undertaken, top management must be sold on the merits of such a program.

Not only must the program of systems analysis be recognized by top management, it must also be recognized by the company as a whole. The entire company must participate in recognizing, defining, analyzing, and solving problems, and in implementing the recommended changes that are aimed at increasing company profits. Through the issuance of company regulations or instructions, proposals for systems improvement must be "sold" to the employees so that they will understand that in most instances they will not lose their jobs, their skills and abilities will be used more effectively, and they will not receive less pay.

Use of Consultants

There is an ever-increasing number of consulting firms engaged in systems analysis. Many of them are industrial engineering firms that specialize in factory layout, machines, and methods, but with separate departments for office systems. Others specialize solely in the study of office functions, such as office personnel and telecommunications. The management consulting firm is hired by a company in much the same way the company would hire auditors or lawyers to render special services and to give expert advice.[2]

The advantage of employing an outside consulting firm is that the recommendations are made by a group of experts who, because of their experience with other firms, can bring in many new

---

[2]For an interesting discussion of how to select the best consultant for the firm's needs and the kinds of help that can be expected from the consultant, see Robert I. Weil, "How To Select a Management Consultant," *Administrative Management* (November, 1966), pp. 59–60. Additional ideas on the best use of outside consultants in the small firm are discussed at length in Gary A. Studer, "Systems Analysis for the Small Company," *Management World* (February, 1976), pp. 9–10.

ideas. Because the consulting firm is an outsider, it is able to study the systems with an objectivity that management does not possess. However, management, as the client, does not give up its responsibility for final acceptance, modification, or rejection of the recommendations made by the consulting firm. Management must, on the other hand, be prepared to cooperate to the fullest extent with the consulting firm by giving it total access to company data, policies, and employees.

Use of Internal Systems Staff

Large firms with the capability of staff specialization find the creation and constant use of an internal systems staff an absolute necessity as the work systems become more complex. If the firm is especially large with many branches, such as General Electric and the Ford Motor Company, a centralized systems staff may be set up to coordinate the work of the decentralized staffs that can deal more effectively with the systems found in each division. On the other hand, firms that are served by the corporate staff in one central location (and this would include those smaller firms capable of maintaining a small central systems staff) can view the organization as an entity and maintain adequate systems service for each of the individual departments.

There is no set rule that dictates the size of an internal systems staff. Some corporate managers estimate that an adequate systems staff is one percent of the clerical personnel employed by the firm. Others feel that there should be one analyst for approximately every 200 office workers. The size of the systems staff should be determined by the results that are expected of the systems unit — supplying management with better information and at the same time producing sufficient savings in order to justify its own existence.

For an effective systems program in the firm a definite organizational responsibility must be established for the systems staff. If the staff is to represent the corporate viewpoint and interpret top-level directives and, at the same time, receive proper recognition for the importance of systems work, it should report to a person at the upper management levels. Studies of firms — such as insurance, banking, and public utilities — that employ a large number of office workers indicate that the head of the systems department reports to the executive officer as follows:

Executive Officer	Approximate Percentage
President or vice-president	35% of the firms
Controller (chief accounting officer)	30% of the firms
Treasurer	20% of the firms
Department heads	15% of the firms

The systems staff should be available to all departments of the firm. This method permits the development of experts for various types of work and provides an excellent training ground for future executives. Because of the specialized nature of its work, such a staff unit will strive constantly to seek out and recommend areas where systems improvements can be made. The disadvantages are that there may not be enough work to keep the staff busy and that some executives may look upon staff analysis as a reflection on the work of the executive whose department is being studied. Then, too, top management sometimes feels that the intermediate or

supervisory managers are being paid to do the work that such a staff organization would be called upon to do.

The Office Manager's Role in Systems Work

In a small company there may be no one available for full-time systems work; yet the systems function must be carried on. Since the main aim of systems is to improve the flow of information — and the office manager is a specialist in information management — it is logical that systems work in the small firm be assigned to, or assumed by, the person holding the office manager's position. To fulfill this responsibility the office manager must, of course, possess the attributes that characterize an effective systems analyst: a logical, analytical, perceptive mind; an inventive, imaginative nature; sound judgment; and a thorough understanding of the total firm and its information needs.

The advantages of selecting the office manager to assume the part-time job of analyst are: it is a less expensive method, it can be used by small as well as by large offices, and the office manager is closer to the work than anyone else. The main disadvantage is that the office manager may be so busy with other work that the systems work may be neglected. Another disadvantage is that the employees working under the direction of the office manager may resent his or her efforts more than those of a staff group or an independent management firm. Then, too, the office manager may not be aware of modern systems methods and, therefore, may follow an established routine rather than inaugurate changes.

The office manager who is responsible for the systems function may obtain much help from active membership in the Association for Systems Management and the Administrative Management Society. (These associations sponsor meetings and conventions and publish several monthly and annual publications.) There are many firms, such as Moore Business Forms, Inc., Uarco Incorporated, Standard Register Company, and Shaw-Walker Co., which specialize in the design and preparation of forms to be used in certain systems. Other companies manufacturing office machines and equipment will aid in the design or adaptation of a standard system to their equipment. Among these are IBM, Burroughs Corporation, NCR Corporation, Sperry Remington, and the A. B. Dick Co. Through contact with such firms, many office managers are able to study and improve their present systems and to adapt a system used by some other firm.

CONDUCTING SYSTEMS STUDIES

Some of the world's great philosophers have described successful people as those who can solve problems to their own satisfaction and to the satisfaction of others. In the same way, senior management members, looking back on long, successful business careers, describe success in management in terms of satisfactory problem solving. Thus, it would seem that effective office management is really solving problems that occur in office systems and procedures.

Too often, however, an office manager discovers a problem only when something goes wrong. It seems that no one realizes that a problem exists until something fails to perform properly; and even in such a case, what may appear to be the problem (such as not enough space for office employees) may be only

a symptom. The real problem may be the absence of a records retention system that results in the use of excessive amounts of space for the files, thereby crowding the workers.

The staff in charge of office systems must be alert to internal problems throughout the office systems as well as those problems which involve the external environment (the business community and the customers or clients). A well-planned program of systems studies should be developed by the staff unit. Of special importance in such a program is the mental attitude of the analyst. Systems studies require of the analyst a keen analytical skill and an objective viewpoint that sets aside preconceived ideas about the area of study and which relegates personal considerations to the background. For these reasons it is important that a problem be carefully defined, that clear-cut objectives be formulated, and that the systems approach to problem solving be carefully followed. In this section each of the required steps in the systems study cycle will be discussed briefly. Areas of application in office systems will then be treated in the following section of this chapter.

The Systems Approach

In the age of systems, the scientific method for solving office problems discussed in Chapter 1 is still in widespread use. This problem-solving technique centers on the careful definition of a problem and the development of reasonable solutions to the problem. Since the primary objective of systems analysis is problem solving, analysts have taken the scientific method, adapted it to their needs, and called it the *systems approach* to problem solving. Utilizing the systems approach, the analyst employs the scientific method in addition to these unique systems steps:

1. Identifying the work problem and all its components, noting the interrelationships of all parts and how each contributes to the total work system. Systems studies are far more concerned with interrelationships in the work system than was true of the early scientific management studies.
2. Clarifying the objectives for which the system is designed. Systems analysts emphasize the great need for developing and writing objectives or unit goals so that all workers involved understand what is expected of them. The management-by-objectives (MBO) technique is useful in this respect.
3. Noting the effect of *synergism* in the system. (This term describes the fact that interrelated parts produce a total effect greater than the sum of each of the parts when working independently. An example would be a symphony orchestra operating in concert.) What this really means in the office is that more can be accomplished through harmonious group-work relationships than through working as individuals.
4. Considering all problems from a systems point of view, that is, considering the input, processing, output, and feedback or control factors involved in any problem.

The impact of any proposed changes in an office system must be weighed carefully because of the large or long-term investment involved. An office manager may purchase an expensive machine only to realize later that it cannot handle the load for which it was designed and requires considerably more worker retraining, maintenance costs, and space than were initially considered. Such a disaster might have been foreseen if a feasibility study had been made prior to the purchase.

Thus, before contemplating a full-fledged systems study, a feasibility study should be undertaken. This planning method may be described as a "look before you leap" approach to systems work in order to determine the possibility of improving an existing system at a reasonable cost.[3] In general, two types of feasibility studies are made, each of which is a slight variation of the other: (1) a general feasibility study that recommends for or against a full systems study; and (2) a specialized study such as determining whether a computer system is feasible for the firm, looking at the use to which a computer will be put, and identifying the best computer for the job. This latter type of study along with guidelines for making such a study was discussed in Chapter 2. These same guidelines can be modified for use in the general systems studies described in the following sections of this chapter. Both studies employ the same set of steps of the systems study cycle.

The Systems Study Cycle

Ideally, each systems study should be a part of a carefully planned program covering a long-term period of company operation. Such a plan should have the approval of top management and each of the managers of the departments under study. With such a plan each unit can budget time and money and prepare the personnel to assist the systems staff.

---

[3]For a comprehensive discussion of feasibility studies, see John M. FitzGerald and Ardra F. FitzGerald, *Fundamentals of Systems Analysis* (New York: John M. Wiley & Sons, 1973), Chapter 2; *Business Systems* (Cleveland: Association for Systems Management, 1970), Chapter 13; and Victor Lazzaro (ed.), *Systems and Procedures: A Handbook for Business and Industry* (2d ed., Englewood Cliffs: Prentice-Hall, 1968), Chapter 13.

Realistically, such a plan is too often pushed aside by the pressing problems of everyday work operation. Requests for studies originate from managers who have problems in need of solution and which they cannot solve in their own units with their own staffs.

Whether the study is a part of a long-term plan or the result of a pressing and unexpected problem, a cycle or pattern of systems steps to follow is described below:

1. *The request for conducting the systems study is made by a department to the systems staff.* The systems staff may then conduct a feasibility study to determine the probable value of the study. During this time the problem is redefined: objectives established (such as lowering costs, improving the data flow, strengthening operating controls, better meeting customers' requirements, or automating a phase of a system). The study is broken down into major phases (personnel, equipment, layout, and procedures), and a schedule or timetable developed for each phase of the study.

2. *Data are collected in order to solve the systems problem.* During this phase of a study it is important to explain to the employees involved why the study is being done and what data are needed from them. The facts are recorded on questionnaires, preferably during personal interviews. Frequently charts, such as the organization chart discussed in Chapter 3, are used to pinpoint the organizational role and interrelationships of all workers involved, as well as charts for showing work flow, space utilization, worker motions, and work sequence and travel time involved. (Charting is discussed in more detail in a later section of this chapter.) Experienced analysts may visit other companies having similar information needs and solicit advice from systems specialists and machine

equipment vendors having expertise with the type of problem under study.

3. *Systems analysis, the most important phase in the complete systems study, is then carried out.* Analysis of the data that have been organized according to the objectives of the study must relate all the facts — their causes, effects, and interrelationships. This means that the analyst must pose and answer all questions that relate to the problem. One effective questioning framework uses these questions: *What* work is being done? *Where* is it being done? *Who* does the work? *When* is it being done? *How* is the work being done? The analyst then determines *why* each phase of the existing system operates as it does. Often it is necessary to discuss the facts collected with line people to determine the accuracy of the data and to agree on possible solutions.

4. *A new systems design is formulated and a proposal for a revised or a new system is developed.* Such a proposal is usually a joint effort stemming from suggestions of the departmental personnel involved and management that understands the nature of the problem. The proposal must consider possible effects on employees (whether anyone will be laid off, how much retraining will be required, or what interdepartmental transfers or upheavals may be generated by the study); on profits (how the proposed system may affect salaries, space, material and supplies, overhead costs, cost of capital, and profits earned on capital invested as well as on equipment required); on work schedules; and on customer service. While there is no set rule for answering these kinds of questions, experienced analysts find the use of a checklist covering each of the many elements of systems studies a very useful technique.[4]

---

[4]For a very useful systems analysis checklist, see *Business Systems, op. cit.*, pp. 72–83. This checklist covers environmental considerations; organizations, policies, and directives; work flow

5. *The systems proposal, when approved by management and the department concerned, is implemented.* Good planning and persuasion are required to sell a departmental staff on making a change in their systems operation, for the jobs and personal security of the workers are at stake. An effective approach for selling the new system is for the analyst to work with departmental personnel during the entire study period, thereby gaining their confidence. The report presenting the proposal should be carefully prepared in clear-cut form, with emphasis on the anticipated savings and advantages and relating expected results to profits and income to be realized for the company. If a large-scale study is involved, sometimes dual (or parallel) operations are conducted, which allows the old scaled-down system to operate alongside the new system until all of the problems or "bugs" have been removed at which time the old system is completely phased out. Periodically the new system should be evaluated for its benefits and costs, and modifications in the systems operation made where necessary.

This orderly cycle of steps is commonly followed in studying each of the office systems discussed in the following section.

MAJOR AREAS FOR OFFICE SYSTEMS STUDIES

The main purpose of studying office systems is to improve the level of *productivity* in the office. By studying the

and systems interrelationships; staffing and workload; standards and specifications; methods; facilities and equipment; timing and scheduling; transport, posting, and retention; forms, reports, and documents; general systems and analysis; the universal "why"; and appraising changes. The checklist can be easily modified to meet the needs of the individual office.

various aspects of work flow in the office it is possible to reduce the time required to complete the work; therefore, a greater volume of work can be done by the same personnel without increasing costs. Thus, higher productivity should result in *cost reduction.*

Analyzing and improving office systems may involve one or more elements of the various managerial and clerical systems in the office, with the actual number of elements depending on the availability of the staff and the time and money available for the study. The study may involve the forms, records, and other documents used; the space requirements of the system; the equipment used; the personnel required; worker methods involving motion and time studies of the repetitive aspects of the clerical work surveyed; and finally, the overall costs incurred in operating the system.

Studying the Forms Used

The paperwork involved in office systems occupies the center of the stage in a systems study, because all key transactions involve information that is recorded on business forms. The business form may seem like an inexpensive piece of paper, yet it accounts for a tremendous amount of office costs and affects the efficiency of a great number of office workers. Repeated studies show that it is not the cost of printing the form that is so expensive but rather the cost of handling, transporting, and filing the copies of the form. It has been estimated that it costs from $25 to $30 to use a form that costs $1 to print. The number of forms and the number of copies of each form as well as the design and control of forms used require constant study. The management of forms design and the control of their cost are discussed in detail in Chapter 18.

Analyzing office systems through the study of forms involves eliminating those forms and the numbers of copies not required, combining as many forms as possible, simplifying the forms both in content and in method of preparation, and studying the route taken by the forms as well as the final disposition of each copy. This analysis may be accomplished by one or more of the following tools:

1. A *written procedure* in outline form with information compiled from the systems survey.
2. *Flowcharts* that provide a medium of effective communication between management and the operating personnel with reference to forms, procedures, and personnel methods.
   (a) A *block diagram* showing the number of copies of a form and their disposition.
   (b) *Procedure flowcharts* of the sequence of office operations. These may be constructed either horizontally or vertically and do not require specialized symbols for understanding or interpretation.
   (c) *Flow process charts*, sometimes called process flowcharts, showing either the present or suggested flow of work; or both the present and the improved suggested flow of work.
   (d) *Information-processing flowcharts* used to record the flow of work and the various steps involved in either manual or machine systems for processing data.

Each of these tools used to study the forms and information flow is discussed in the following paragraphs.

Analysis by Written Procedure. The written procedure is a simple outline of the steps involved in the flow of work; it describes verbally the number of copies of the forms used and their disposition. Figure 17-4 outlines the processing of a sales order by a wholesaler's office staff and includes references to communications (business letter, credit rating manual, and financial statements) from other systems that are required to handle the detailed operations of this procedure.

Analysis by Flowcharts. Many varieties of charts have been developed to present the flow of office work. Some of the charts consist of simple blocks or rectangles and do not require special training of the user; others use special symbols that must be studied at length in order to be understood by the reader. Some use descriptive titles and illustrations combining the geometric symbols with words.

Block Diagram. To illustrate the block diagram for studying forms and their flow through a firm, the purchasing system of a business firm is shown in Figure 17-5. The block diagram shows the number of copies prepared of a purchasing requisition, a purchase order, and a receiving report; their movement throughout the firm; and the final disposition of each copy. The block diagram, which uses no special symbols, represents a simple version of the data processing flowchart illustrated in Chapter 21.

Procedure Flowchart. The procedure flowchart, or management-type flowchart, is also easily understood since it does not use any special symbols. The chart may be read from left to right or from top to bottom. This chart has been widely used in systems studies by such well-known firms as Moore Business Forms Inc. and Standard

Processing a Sales Order

I. The order clerk receives the order by mail, telephone, telegraph, or in person.
   A. Two copies of the order are prepared on the company's preprinted order forms.
   B. The original copy goes to the credit manager.
   C. The duplicate copy is filed.

II. The credit manager checks the credit rating of the customer.
   A. In the case of an active account the credit manager:
      1. Notes on the back of the sales order the information needed to show the condition of the account.
      2. Inquires of the accounts receivable clerk the current status of the customer's account (account balance).
   B. If the account is in satisfactory condition, the credit manager approves the sales order by:
      1. Affixing a signature on the sales order.
      2. Sending the approved sales order to the billers.
   C. If the account is past due, the credit manager:
      1. Writes a letter to the customer, carefully stating the condition of the account and asking the customer if orders may be sent COD until the account balance is brought to a satisfactory credit standing.
      2. Files the sales order for which payment has not been received in the unfilled sales order folder. The original letter is mailed while the duplicate letter is filed.
   D. In the case of a new account, the credit manager:
      1. Refers to the credit rating manual of Dun & Bradstreet or some other agency.
      2. Refers to companies giving credit information service.
      3. Sends the customer a letter stating that the order is receiving prompt attention but that further information is being requested as part of the customary routine of opening an account.
      4. May analyze the financial statements of the new customer and may establish a credit limit.
      5. May refuse to extend credit based on the findings from various sources.
      6. If the credit rating is OK, the order is approved and sent to the biller.
      7. If the credit rating is not acceptable, a letter is sent asking the customer whether a COD shipment is acceptable.

Fig. 17-4
A Sales Order Procedure for Analyzing the Flow of Work

Register Company, because of its simplicity in presenting and promoting office systems. Simple line drawings or photographs of the equipment used in the procedure studies may be used to complete the picture of the flow of work. The procedure flowchart follows the trail of the data used in the procedure whether the data are on printed forms, punched cards, punched paper tapes, or magnetic tapes. The procedure flowchart in Figure 17-6, which illustrates the steps involved in a purchasing system, provides an alternate method of charting the system that was block diagrammed in Figure 17-5.

Flow Process Chart. The flow process chart is one of the most widely used tools for studying office work. Through its use, it is possible to record office systems and procedures in easily understood "picture" form, for the chart uses certain standardized symbols that make the presentation and reading of charts — and hence the analysis of procedures — easier and more effective. Since the flow process chart aims at simplifying office work, it is often spoken of as a *work simplification chart*.

The symbols and definitions used in flow process charting and illustrated in

Figure 17-7 were developed by the American Society of Mechanical Engineers for engineering use and later adopted by the Administrative Management Society for use in office systems and procedures analysis. These symbols

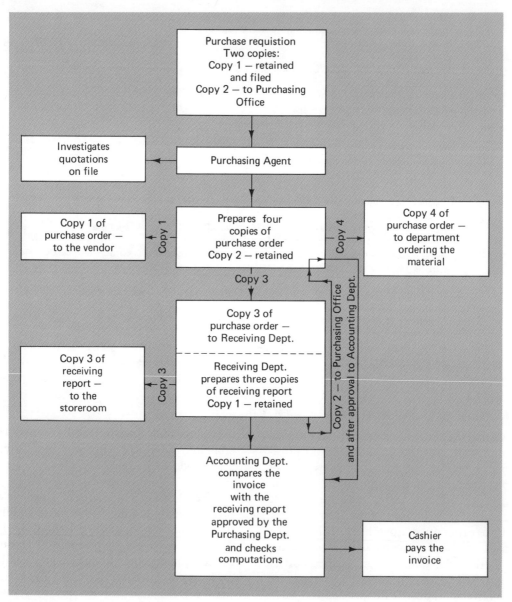

Fig. 17-5
A Block Diagram of a Purchasing System

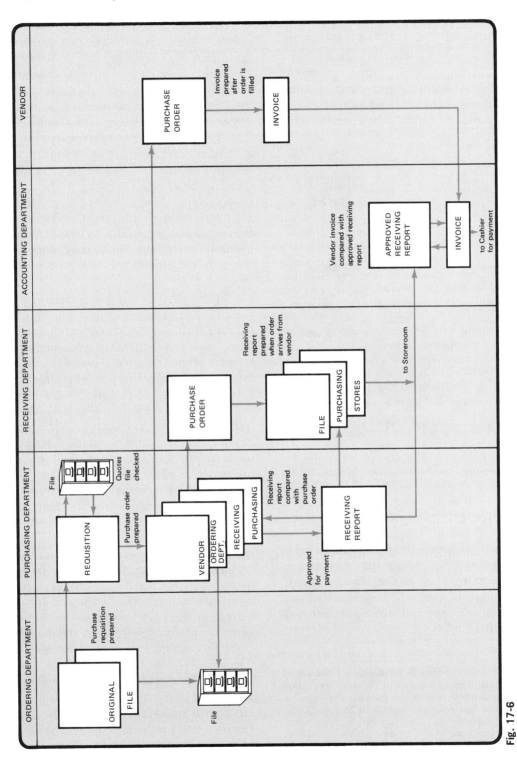

Fig. 17-6
A Procedure Flowchart of a Purchasing System

are now part of the "Method of Charting Paperwork Procedures" developed by the American National Standards Institute, although various office equipment and forms manufacturers and systems consulting firms vary the format of the charts and the symbols they use.[5]

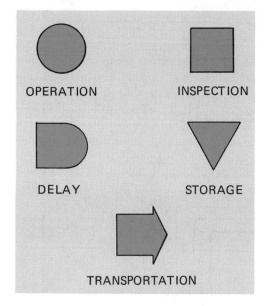

Fig. 17-7
Standardized Flow Process Chart Symbols Developed by the American National Standards Institute

Figure 17-8 shows a flow process chart of the present and the proposed methods of handling an incoming check in a branch bank. Note that with an investment of $100 in the installation of the proposed method, the estimated net saving for the first year amounts to $9,900.

---

[5]The Administrative Management Society is no longer actively engaged in the development of standards. Standards developed in the past by AMS are now referred to as ANSI Standards and are available through the American National Standards Institute, 1430 Broadway, New York, NY 10018.

Information-Processing Flowchart. Many systems analysts prepare flowcharts with special symbols to indicate the origin of a clerical operation, the different copies of each form used, the flow of the form or the work, and the disposition of each copy of the form. The use of the various symbols provides a standardized method of communication but requires the reader to be familiar with the symbols. Similar to the flow process charts are information-processing charts used by office machine manufacturers, and especially by systems analysts in recording the flow of work in manual and automated data processing systems.

In the past the manufacturers of office machines and forms and other firms involved in systems and procedures work have used different types of symbols for preparing their flowcharts. This lack of uniformity often resulted in confusion and misinterpretation when persons attempted to read the charts. Also, with the advent of automated data processing, many of the symbols formerly used in manual systems proved inadequate for a clear understanding. To overcome this condition, a committee composed of representatives from commercial and industrial firms, as well as the government, developed a uniform set of symbols known as the American Standard Flowchart Symbols for Information Processing. By means of these standardized symbols, all types of information-processing systems — from the simplest manual system to the highly complex computer systems discussed in Chapter 21 — can be charted.

The American National Standards Institute's symbols and their definitions are shown in Figure 17-9. The first six symbols are commonly used in preparing concept charts that present the

FLOW PROCESS CHART

IDENTIFICATION

SUBJECT CHARTED: Check in branch bank	CHART NO. 0000
DRAWING NO. / PART NO.	TYPE OF CHART: Material
POINT AT WHICH CHART BEGINS: Receipt of batch from main office	SHEET NO. 1 OF 1 SHEETS
LOCATION: Rack Dept.	CHARTED BY: John Spear DATE 8-18-
POINT AT WHICH CHART ENDS: Filing of checks	APPROVED BY: S. Brown DATE 8-19-
LOCATION: Accounting Dept.	

QUANTITY INFORMATION
- 100 checks make one block
- YEARLY PRODUCTION: 3,600,000 checks
- COST UNIT: 1 check

SUMMARY

TOTAL YEARLY SAVING—DIRECT LABOR
UNIT COST DIRECT LABOR & INSP. $10,000.00
DISTANCE TRAVELED IN FEET
INSTALLATION COST OF PROPOSED METHOD $ 100.00
ESTIMATED NET SAVING—FIRST YEAR $ 9,900.00

	PRESENT METHOD NO.	TIME IN hrs.	PROPOSED METHOD NO.	TIME IN hrs.	DIFFERENCE NO.	TIME IN hrs.
	.545		.425		.120	
	321		156		165	
OPERATIONS	10	.4355	7	.3220	3	.1135
TRANSPORTATIONS	8	.0120	4	.0055	4	.0065
INSPECTIONS	4	.0975	4	.0975	0	.0000
DELAYS	5	.2850	4	.1750	1	.0500
STORAGES	1	.0000	1	.0000	0	.0000

PRESENT METHOD

QUANTITY UNIT CHARTED: 1 block

DESCRIPTION OF EVENT	DIST. MOVED IN FEET	UNIT OPER. TIME IN hrs.	UNIT TRANSP. TIME IN hrs.	UNIT INSPECT. TIME IN hrs.	DELAY TIME IN hrs.	STORAGE TIME IN hrs.
to Rack Dept. by messenger.	36		.0004			
Blocks proved on hand adding machine. Corrections made on form.		.0850				
to "coop" sorting rack by "proofing check"	33		.0012			
await sorting					.0050	
sorted by ledger		.0206				
await proofing					.0850	
to proofing desks	33		.0012			
ledger totals run on hand adding machine and compared with block total		.0600				
to storage table by "proofing clerk"	18		.0007			
placed on storage table by ledger breakdown		.0050				
await pickup by bookkeepers					.0500	
to bookkeeper's work station	75		.0028			
sorted by account name		.0360				
sight pays ledger file				.0075		
balances prelisted on extended sheets		.0400				
machine post amounts and prove total		.0750				
await microfilming					.0600	
to microfilm machine by operator	63		.0034			
microfilm		.0300				
to cancelling machine by micro. op.	6		.0002			
perforate to cancel		.0080				
to bookkeeper by micro. op.	57		.0021			
await filing					.0500	
filed by account name by bookkeeper		.0570				
in file.						

PROPOSED METHOD

QUANTITY UNIT CHARTED: 1 block

DESCRIPTION OF EVENT	DIST. MOVED IN FEET	UNIT OPER. TIME IN hrs.	UNIT TRANSP. TIME IN hrs.	UNIT INSPECT. TIME IN hrs.	DELAY TIME IN hrs.	STORAGE TIME IN hrs.
to Rack Dept. by messenger.	20		.0007			
blocks proved on automatic adding machine. Corrections made on form. Sorted by ledger		.0425				
await proof					.0850	
ledger totals run on automatic adding machine and compared with block total		.0345				
await pickup by messenger					.0500	
to bookkeeper	75		.0028			
sort by account name		.0150				
sight pays ledger file				.0975		
balances prelisted on extended sheets		.0400				
machine post amounts and prove total		.0750				
await pickup by messenger					.0600	
to microfilm operator	30		.0010			
microfilm and perforate to cancel		.0380				
to bookkeeper by messenger	30		.0010			
await filing					.0500	
filed by account name by bookkeeper		.0570				
in file						

Fig. 17-8
Flow Process Chart of Present and Proposed Methods for Handling an Incoming Check in a Branch Bank

overall picture of an operation. Along with these symbols the remaining 13 are used to prepare detail charts showing the broad concepts of what is done and how it is done.

To overcome the necessity of the reader having to understand each of the engineering symbols used in the symbol-type flowcharts, some firms have developed a modified hybrid chart that

1. Input–Output Symbol – This symbol represents the input-output function (I–O), i.e., the making available of information for processing (input), or the recording of processed information (output).

2. Processing Symbol – This symbol represents the processing function, i.e., the process of executing a defined operation or group of operations resulting in a change in value, form, or location of information, or in the determination of which of several flow directions are to be followed.

3. Annotation Symbol – This symbol represents the annotation function, i.e., the addition of descriptive comments or explanatory notes as clarification.

4. Flow Direction Symbol – This symbol represents the flow direction function, i.e., the indication of the sequence of available information and executable operations. Flow direction is represented by lines drawn between symbols. Normal direction flow is from left to right or top to bottom.

5. Connector Symbol – This symbol represents a junction in a line of flow. A set of two connectors is used to represent a continued flow direction when the flow is broken by the physical limitations of the flowchart.

6. Terminal Symbol – This symbol represents a terminal point in a system or communication network at which information can enter or leave; e.g., start, stop, halt, delay, or interrupt.

7. Punched Card Symbol – This symbol represents an I–O function in which the medium is punched cards, including mark sense cards, partial cards, stub cards, etc.

8. Magnetic Tape Symbol – This symbol represents an I–O function in which the medium is magnetic tape.

9. Punched Tape Symbol – This symbol represents an I–O function in which the medium is punched tape.

10. Document Symbol – This symbol represents an I–O function in which the medium is a document.

11. Manual Input Symbol – This symbol represents an I–O function in which the information is entered manually at the time of processing, by means of on-line keyboards, switch settings, push buttons, card readers, etc.

12. Display Symbol – This symbol represents an I–O function in which the information is displayed for human use at the time of processing, by means of on-line indicators, video devices, console printers, plotters, etc.

13. Communication Link Symbol – This symbol represents an I–O function in which information is transmitted automatically from one location to another. The symbol is always drawn with superimposed arrowheads to denote the direction of data flow.

14. On-line Storage Symbol – This symbol represents an I–O function utilizing auxiliary mass storage of information that can be accessed on-line; e.g., magnetic drums, magnetic disks, magnetic tape strips, automatic magnetic card systems, or automatic microfilm chip or strip systems.

15. Off-line Storage Symbol – This symbol represents any off-line storage of information, regardless of the medium on which the information is recorded.

16. Decision Symbol – This symbol represents a decision type operation that determines which of a number of alternate paths is to be followed.

17. Predefined Process Symbol – This symbol represents a named process consisting of one or more operations or program steps that are specified elsewhere, e.g., subroutine or logical unit.

18. Manual Operation Symbol – This symbol represents any off-line process geared to the speed of a human being.

19. Auxiliary Operation Symbol – This symbol represents an off-line operation performed on equipment not under direct control of the central processing unit.

Fig. 17-9

American National Standards Institute's Flowchart Symbols for Information Processing

uses both symbols and descriptive words. Such a chart is shown in Figure 17-10.

Studying the Space Used

In earlier chapters the effective use of the space environment was discussed in detail. Chapter 4, for example, treated the ways in which office layout can contribute to a more productive office operation. Chapter 5 explored another side of the physical environment — the office furniture and equipment that are used in the work systems; and Chapter 6 analyzed the combined psychological and physiological aspects of the office environment.

In addition to the environmental studies of office space, it is necessary to give attention to the flow and frequency of movement of each of the forms and of the workers who transport the paper throughout the office. This may be accomplished by studying the office layout, preparing a separate before-and-after layout chart for each important office system or procedure, and drawing lines to indicate the movement of the various business papers throughout the organization. Office layout charts should be prepared for those transactions that occur most frequently. The direction and distance of the movement in the office will point out waste motion and needless backtracking. Measuring the distance traveled before and after the changes in office procedures are made will indicate the distance and time saved in performing certain office activities.

An effective example of how to rearrange an office so that there is a minimum of movement of forms and personnel is shown in the before-and-after illustrations in Figure 17-11. A study of the two illustrations shows the waste that had formerly taken place in steps, time, energy, and money. Each order, which previously traveled 162 feet, now travels only 35 feet. Auxiliary forms, once traveling 80 feet, now travel only 35 feet. A significant reduction in costs including worker travel time was achieved in the new layout as a result of reducing by more than 50 percent the total floor space required for the processing of orders.

Studying the Equipment Used

Equipment analysis closely parallels the feasibility study treated in Chapter 2. In automated systems as well as in manual systems, many basic operations are performed on data for which machines and related equipment are available. Throughout the data processing cycle — starting with the creation of a document — there are many activities, such as recording, transcribing, listing, posting, reproducing, storing, and calculating data, which utilize mechanical equipment in the typical office. Some activities — such as classifying, indexing, and summarizing — are largely mental in nature and thus are not machinable. Others, such as sorting and communicating, may, on occasion, use machines to ensure an efficient office operation.

A large selection of equipment is available for use in the various office operations. An analysis of the systems equipment needs and the comparative costs and advantages of the various methods of performing work — manual or machine — should be undertaken in conjunction with the suggestions made in Chapter 5.

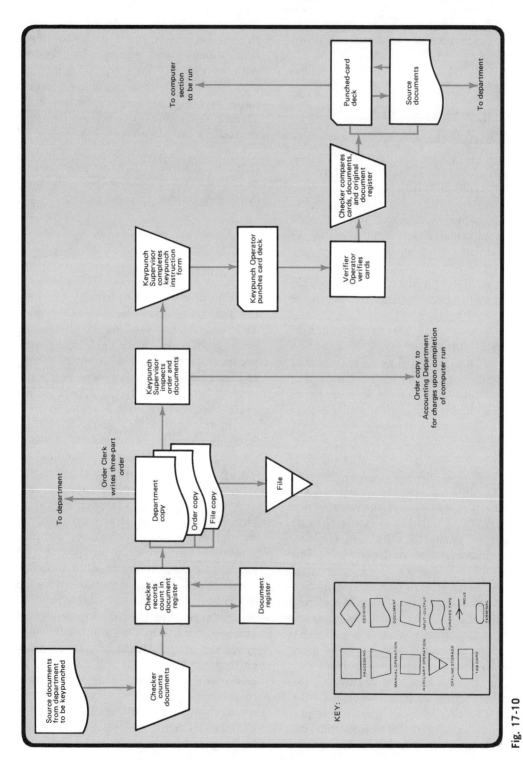

Fig. 17-10

A Special-Symbol Flowchart of a Procedure for Processing Departmental Orders for Keypunching in a Firm's Data Processing Department

Office Layout Chart *before* Study

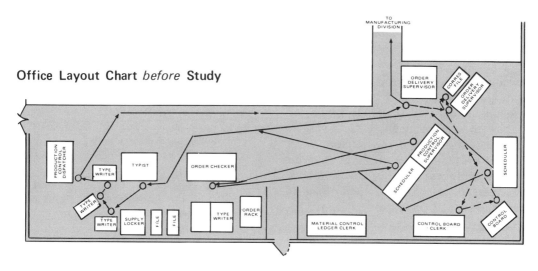

The proper arrangement of desks in sequence, consistent with the flow of personnel and paperwork, corrected the "before" situation. Total floor space was reduced from 960 to 460 square feet.

Office Layout Chart *after* Study and Changes

Fig. 17-11
Before-and-After Office Layout Charts

Standard Register Company

Studying the Personnel Performance

"The worker can *make* or *break* the system" is a frequent remark of experienced managers, for they know the importance of people in the successful operation of any system. Thus, before any systems change can be considered — or for that matter before any system can be studied — the role of the personnel in the department under study should be given the highest priority. Involved in a total personnel study are such areas as job analysis and evaluation, work incentive plans, work methods and motion economies, overstaffing, morale problems, evaluation of personnel policies, working conditions, training programs, and employee development. The analyst should investigate causes of job dissatisfaction, poor work coordination, and irregularities in working conditions so that the human link that controls the system is as effective as possible. The important role of people in the system is discussed further in the last section of this chapter, "The Human Factor in Systems."

Studying the Systems Costs

Systems analysts must be highly cost conscious. In their work they must learn to estimate the many costs of a complex system as well as the probable benefits that such a system provides. With such information, management is in a position to evaluate these cost benefits in terms of their overall effect on the total organization.

A cost analysis of office systems may be accomplished in several ways:

1. All systems costs must be identified before a systems study can be made. For both the current system and any new system proposed, the following costs should be determined: (a) salaries; (b) space costs; (c) costs of supplies and inventories, including the cost of business forms; (d) overhead or indirect costs such as office maintenance services, insurance, property taxes, heat, light, and power; and (e) costs of implementing the system. This final category includes costs of moving equipment and people, renovating costs (repainting, relocating telephones and electrical outlets), furniture costs, and costs of converting the files to a new system and of removing the current system.[6]

2. After the systems costs have been pinpointed, the benefits anticipated from the improved system should be determined. While the key benefits expected from an improved system are usually measured in dollars, there are many noneconomic benefits that should also be considered. Such a list includes better public relations stemming from faster response time to inquiries from customers; more prompt deliveries to customers; higher employee morale and a more stable office force; a better controlled inventory of forms and supplies; fewer rejects in the work produced due to quality control of the office product; and better managerial control over the total office operation.

3. A general survey of the office information system should be undertaken

---

[6]Most of the important costs involved in a systems study are outlined in the discussion of feasibility studies in Chapter 2. There are, however, other facets of systems costs that should be studied, including the *payback period* (the number of years required to accumulate earnings sufficient to cover the systems costs); *the marginal efficiency of investment* (the rate of return that a potential new system is expected to earn after all of its costs other than interest expense are covered); and *opportunity costs* (the costs of using a resource for one purpose rather than for another). For a comprehensive analysis of the implementation, investment, and operating costs involved in a system, see John M. FitzGerald and Ardra F. FitzGerald, *Fundamentals of System Analysis* (New York: John Wiley & Sons, 1973), Chapter 10.

using a questionnaire such as the one shown in Figure 17-12. In one such survey, data were collected from three sources — from the worker, from the supervisor, and from an unbiased person's observation of the physical aspects of the department. Personal interviews were used to supplement the questionnaires. Five office employees with previous experience in analysis collected information from personal interviews supplemented by the completed questionnaires. From such a survey, analysis is made of such factors as (a) the data generated by the office force, its usability and cost of collecting, producing, storing and moving; (b) the clerical force — its increase over the past few years; the distribution of work and related job analyses; overstaffing; (c) character of the work performed by the office force — assignments made; efficiency of procedures and methods; interruptions in flow of work; number and frequency of reports prepared and their purposes.

4. By studying the flow of work through the office, shorter routes can be established so that less time will be required for completing the work, thus saving many dollars in office costs.

5. By using a suggestion system, many workers may recommend changes that will simplify office systems and procedures. When the ideas for improvement are considered and accepted, the morale of workers improves and a greater spirit of cooperation develops between the department heads and the workers.

One large organization employed a systems analyst to study the actual distance traveled by each letter entering the office. It was found that at the time this study of "letter-traveling" was made, the total distance traveled was about three miles — from the time the letter entered the office to the time that action on the letter was completed and it was placed in the file. It was also found that the number of clerks who processed the incoming letters could not be reduced, but the location of their desks in relation to one another could be vastly improved. Upon completion of the study, changes were made in the various steps involved and then the distance traveled was charted again, from the standpoint of continuity in moving forward and in actual distance both between desks and in total distance. It was discovered that the traveling distance of each letter could be reduced from three miles to approximately one fifth of a mile. When this reduction is multiplied thousands of times each month, the ultimate results in increased production, efficiency, and reduced costs are tremendous.

THE HUMAN FACTOR IN SYSTEMS

In addition to studying the specific tasks that workers perform in office systems, there is a broader, more basic need for teamwork and close cooperation between systems people and managers. Operating managers, as users of the services of a systems staff, have the knowledge of the departmental systems to help the systems staff establish effective policies, procedures, and methods in the operating departments. Systems personnel are the specialists in systems improvement from whom the new systems designs will come. The success of a systems program is closely tied to the close participation between the two groups in the design, implementation, and operation of all systems.

The most important activity taking place in the office system is the behavior of the people working together. The

Job Survey

Department _____ Your Name_____

Division or Group _____ Date_____

Name of Desk or Job _____

Purpose

    The purpose of this set of questions is to aid you in writing a description of what you do. The collection of this information into a permanent form will not only be helpful to you but will aid your department head and the personnel department. Your department head will be able to plan better the future work of the department, while the personnel department will obtain information of value to it in future selection as well as in training and promotion throughout the company.

General Directions

    Answer all questions in detail. When you 'ave finished the description, ask yourself this additional question, "If I knew nothing about this particular job, but were given this survey to read, would I get an accurate picture of the work?" If there is any additional information, it should be given in answer to Question 13. In case sufficient space has not been allowed, please use a regular 8½ × 11 inch sheet, marking it so that the information can be readily identified, and attach the sheet to the survey forms.

1. Who is your immediate supervisor? _____

2. List your regular duties in the order of their importance and show approximately how much time is spent on each one. An easy way would be to make a brief statement starting with a verb in the present tense, such as "Type daily sales reports," "Clear orders," etc. The time element is an important one and should be based upon what you consider as an average. The time unit for daily duties can probably be best expressed in "minutes a day," while the less frequent work might be expressed in "hours each month." List the various parts of your job under the following headings and show the time required for each item at the right-hand side of the sheet.

    a. *Daily*. Those which occur regularly every day.

                                                              Minutes
                                                              a Day

    b. *Periodic*. Those which occur regularly at longer intervals, say weekly, monthly, etc. State the number of times the work is done during an average month.

                                        Total Hours   Approx. Times
                                          a Month   a Month

    c. *Special*. Work done in spare time, of an unusual nature, or not provided for in advance.

                                          Total Hours   Approx. Times
                                          a Month   a Month

    d. *Recurrent*. Those which are not regular and which occur less frequently than daily but cannot be listed under the other headings.

                                          Total Hours   Approx. Times
                                          a Month   a Month

3. What duties shown under the last question come directly to your desk, are handled on your own initiative, and leave your desk without being checked by some other member of your department, thus making you responsible for the entire job while it is in your department? ___
_____

4. Are you held responsible for supervising the work of others? _____
   a. If so, of how many? _____
   b. List the names of their jobs. _____

5. List all machines you are required to operate, such as a typewriter, a calculator, etc., and estimate the amount of training or speed required to do your work. _____

6. Where does your work come from? _____

7. Where does it go after it has been handled? _____

8. Is there anything about your job which requires special physical qualifications? For example, are you required to stand, walk, or operate some machine all day? _____

9. Do you have business contact (daily, weekly, etc.) with
   Employees _____   By phone _____
   Customers _____   Correspondence _____
   Executives _____   Personal _____
   General Public _____   Telegraph _____
                                     Other _____

10. What is the minimum amount of education (in years, months, etc.) and kind of experience, whether obtained here or elsewhere, necessary to start on your job?
    Education _____
    Experience _____

11. With the proper qualifications, what is the minimum time (in days, weeks, etc.) it would take for a new worker to become sufficiently acquainted with the duties of your present job to handle the work alone?
    _____

12. Peculiarities of the job.
    a. Is accuracy or speed the more important? _____
    b. Are there periods when your work is increased beyond the usual amount? _____
    c. Is your work checked before leaving the department?
    _____
    d. Are there written instructions for this job? _____
    e. Would it be helpful to have written instructions?
    _____
    f. What would be the result of errors in your work?
    _____
    g. What specialized abilities or knowledge are required?
    _____

13. Additional information: _____
    _____
    _____

Fig. 17-12
Questionnaire Used to Collect Systems Study Data

office manager and the office staff represent the key input to any office job; and, accordingly this group has a great impact on the output produced by the office. Managers and their workers bring *individual inputs*, such as the skills, knowledge, status, motives, needs, attitudes, and values to any task. Groups of individuals bring *social inputs*, such as group cohesion, group norms and ideas, and group conduct regarding what is acceptable behavior, to their work. For example, an administrative office manager has a very positive effect on his or her staff by the manner in which the staff is directed. Similarly, a group of typists in a word processing center, if unhappy with the type of supervision provided, may reduce their daily output of correspondence to show their dissatisfaction.

Human needs must receive first consideration in any systems study. By understanding and applying the philosophies of the behavioral school of management discussed in Chapter 1, effective managers consider *employee goals* and *company goals* in systems planning. Thus, job satisfaction for the worker and profit making for the firm become the basic objectives of any system.

QUESTIONS FOR REVIEW

1. Explain the relationship that exists among a system, a procedure, and a method.
2. Why is it necessary for administrative office managers to understand fully the systems function in their organizations?
3. What are the objectives of office systems?
4. Define the term *model*. Why are models used in the study of office systems?
5. What is the connection between the various subsystems in an organization? How do these subsystems affect the output of the total system?
6. Describe the purpose of a data base. How practical is such a concept in the present organization of a firm?
7. Trace the flow of information from input through feedback in a manual system. What advantages and disadvantages does such a system have?
8. What advantages accrue to management as the result of constantly studying office work?
9. Compare the use of a management consulting firm with the development of an internal staff of systems analysts as a means of studying the office systems of a firm.
10. What are the advantages and disadvantages in assigning the major responsibility for office systems analysis to the office manager?
11. What is the systems approach? How does it differ from the concepts developed by the scientific management school of thought?

12. What is the basic systems study cycle with which the office manager must be familiar to perform the analyst duties efficiently?

13. Describe briefly the tools employed in studying office systems.

14. Identify the principal costs incurred in designing and operating an office system. What benefits to the organization can be cited to compensate for these costs?

15. Why is the human factor considered the key to the effective operation of any system?

QUESTIONS FOR DISCUSSION

1. An office manager believes that worthwhile systems improvements can be made by the office staff through the brainstorming technique, without the need for expensive outside consulting help. Investigate the nature and purpose of brainstorming and suggest how such a technique might be used in conjunction with the improvement of office systems.

2. One of the means of studying office systems is by analyzing the procedures involved in the system. Discuss some of the problems of gathering data on existing procedures and of converting these data into written form for purposes of systems analysis.

3. Many office administrators report serious bottlenecks in their systems as a result of having all employees start working at the same hour in the morning and stop at the same hours for lunch and for closing. Discuss some of the major inefficiencies that may occur under such conditions and recommend steps to alleviate these common problems.

4. In the Rayder Tool Company no micrographic equipment is available and no program for converting paper records to microform is planned for the immediate future. The records manager, Beryl Manson, has to contend with more and more crowded conditions in her records department, even though there is considerable unused space available in the accounts payable department located next door. Unknown to the accounts payable supervisor, Manson has measured the unused space in the accounts payable office, has obtained estimates of the cost of filing cabinets for the space, and has drafted a report to her superior recommending that the records department be assigned the extra space presently unused by accounts payable. She reasons that the accounts payable department has a stable size staff, is presently forwarding its inactive records to the records management department for retention purposes, and that the extra space will not be used by accounts payable anyway. What potential problems might occur in connection with this proposed reallocation of space? How should Manson proceed in order to apply the systems approach to problem solving?

5. The president of the Wilson Trucking Company agreed to hire a systems analyst on a full-time basis as long as twice the analyst's salary of $20,000 could be saved for the firm each year as a result of systems analysis. During the first three years the systems savings amounted to $40,000, $45,000, and $47,000, respectively. During the fourth year the savings fell to $17,500. The analyst was aware of the conditions under which the hiring took place; and since the annual savings did not exceed the salary provided, the analyst was dropped from the staff.

   Discuss this policy of employing an analyst and the procedure for discontinuing these systems services from a managerial point of view.

6. The Darcy Manufacturing Company has on its systems staff a work methods specialist who has already saved the firm $20,000 through sound systems redesign and who is confident that the program can be expanded to save the company even more. Before agreeing to an expanded program, the firm is interested in the answers to two questions:

   a. How many people can be placed on the systems staff before the point of diminishing returns is reached?

   b. If the systems department is enlarged as proposed, should an expert from the outside be employed, or can the same results be obtained by training or teaching the line people in the organization?

   Discuss the answers to these questions.

PRACTICAL OFFICE MANAGEMENT CASES

Case 17-1 Organizing the Systems Department in a Small Firm

During the past 10 years the office staff of the Partridge Company, a small service business with one central office location, has increased from 45 to 150. With this rapid growth in the office staff, however, there has been no corresponding increase in office supervision, and the office systems have become unworkable. The president has announced plans to decentralize the company operations by opening three branches in nearby suburbs and transferring some of the home-office staff to these new offices.

As office manager in charge of all 150 office workers, you have repeatedly complained to the president about the need for a small internal systems unit to study the overall efficiency of the firm's office systems on a continuing basis. The president has tentatively agreed to set up a systems department to coordinate the work of the home-office and branch-office operations under the new decentralized plan, pending a report from you on how to handle the organization of the systems unit.

On the basis of this information, prepare a report to the president in which you suggest how you would determine answers to these "organizing" questions:

a. Who should be in charge of the systems department?
b. Who and how many should staff the department?
c. How would the costs of operating the systems be justified?
d. How would the functions of the home-office and the branch-office systems be coordinated?
e. What priority list of systems studies should be developed?
f. What steps should be taken in order to obtain acceptance of the new systems program?

Case 17-2 Analyzing an Incoming Order Procedure

Stilwell's is a music store with a small retail outlet and a growing mail-order business for musical instruments and related supplies. The office manager, who has a clerical staff of three to handle the routine office duties, is constantly studying the systems, procedures, and methods in order to seek improvement. Recently the office manager became concerned with some serious bottlenecks found in the procedure for processing incoming sales orders and made repeated observations of the system in action. As a result of this study, the following data were collected.

Orders are received by the receptionist-clerk either by telephone or by mail on a formal sales order form. Several sections of this form are apparently never used. The bookkeeper — and sometimes the receptionist-clerk — checks the credit standing of the customer. If the credit is satisfactory, the order is priced by the receptionist-clerk and sent to the Shipping Department. Next, notification of shipment is sent from the shipping clerk to the general clerk, who computes and checks the invoice totals. The general clerk also is responsible for preparing the invoice. The completed invoice is sent to the receptionist-clerk for comparison with the original copy of the incoming sales order. Three copies of the invoice are distributed as follows: (1) the original copy is mailed to the customer by the general clerk; (2) the second copy is sent to the bookkeeper for posting to the Accounts Receivable records; and (3) the third copy is sent to the receptionist-clerk, who is responsible for the files.

As office manager of Stilwell's, prepare an appropriate chart from among those discussed in this chapter to show the present flow of work in the order processing procedure. Through the use of the charted data, analyze the present procedure, and point out "gaps" in the information collected as well as opportunities for improving the paperwork, the flow of work, and the utilization of machines and personnel. Also, indicate what additional systems information would be required before any full-scale systems revision can be considered.

Chapter 18   **FORMS MANAGEMENT**

At the heart of office systems is a vast network of forms, records, and reports that holds people, machines, and entire divisions together and enables them to function as coordinated units. Statistics show that business forms alone constitute between 75 and 80 percent of a manufacturing company's paperwork load and as much as 90 percent for banks and insurance companies.

Because office forms are necessary to gather the data that are later incorporated into business reports, forms are usually considered the most basic systems tool in the office. Also, because of the staggering volume used and because their effectiveness in the system is too often assumed, forms constitute the principal source of paperwork problems and the greatest potential for cost reduction.

Everyone in the company — from the office messenger to the corporate president — uses forms daily. Because of this universal use and because the efficiency of all personnel is directly affected by the quantity and quality of forms, management has a twofold responsibility toward forms: to understand the purpose and function of forms and to ensure that these paper tools contribute to the achievement of the systems objectives discussed in Chapter 17. To this end *forms management*, a company-wide program for planning, organizing, operating, and controlling the total forms system, has been developed. The basic principles of forms management

along with effective forms design and control practices are discussed in this chapter.

THE NATURE OF OFFICE FORMS

A *form* — sometimes called a "printed form," a "business form," or an "office form" — is a specially designed paper having *constant* information printed on it with space provided for the entry of *variable* information. For example, on a bank check form, the word "dollars" is preprinted on the form as constant information, while the handwritten entry of the amount represents the variable information. Forms are used in business systems to simplify and standardize office work and to accumulate and transmit information for historical or reference purposes.

Forms may be classified according to the business functions for which they are used, such as purchasing forms, sales forms, personnel forms, and accounting forms. A second classification of forms is that of external forms and internal forms. *External forms* are those sent to customers, creditors, and others outside the organization with whom a firm does business. Such forms include sales invoices, statements, checks, and purchase orders. *Internal forms* — those created by employees and used solely within the business — may be subdivided into memorandum forms, such as requisitions, and time tickets used for conveying information to other employees; accounting records, such as journals and registers; and report forms used for presenting data gathered from other records.

A simpler and perhaps more useful classification of forms is single copy or multiple copy. *Single-copy* forms are commonly used within one department for intradepartmental needs. *Multiple-copy* forms, on the other hand, are made up of an original and one or more duplicate copies. Multiple-copy forms are used to transmit information outside the "creating" department, or to provide additional records.

PRINCIPLES OF FORMS MANAGEMENT

So that forms may serve as fully productive parts of an office system, a full-fledged program of forms management is commonly instituted. Forms management considers the basic functions of the business and the role that forms play in these functions. In a typical business that lacks a sound program for managing forms there are many duplicate and overlapping forms; unnecessary forms which create much needless clerical work and many files of unused papers; poorly designed and inadequately stored forms; no formalized reproduction methods or procedures; and minimal control over the inventory of forms. With the absence of controls over their use, forms reduce the efficiency of the workers and increase the clerical expense considerably.

A sound forms management program is built upon four basic principles: the principle of use; the principle of standardization, which pertains to the physical characteristics of the form; the

principle of effective design; and the principle of centralized control.[1]

Principle of Use

Forms follow functions; that is, forms should come into existence only when there is a justified need for their use.

This principle is basic. The job to be accomplished must first be planned and approved and then the form can be developed. A form should be used:

1. Whenever certain information must be recorded for use in the business system, such as orders, requests, and instructions.
2. When the same type of information must be recorded repeatedly. With the constant information preprinted on each copy of the form, time is saved in information processing.
3. When it is necessary to have all information recorded in the same place on

---

[1]The management of business forms is a high-priority item in all administrative systems programs. Associations, such as the Administrative Management Society and the Association for Systems Management, periodically offer publications and seminars on improving the performance of forms, along with other systems-improvement topics. Other groups, such as the Business Forms Institute and the Business Forms Management Association, specialize in forms management work. For more information on the development and operation of a total forms management program, see Roy F. Pemberton, "Organizing the Forms Management Program," *Information and Records Management*, (August, 1975), pp. 8, 44, 46; Jesse L. Clark, "The Forms Management Program — An Overview," *Information and Records Management*, (September, 1975), pp. 8, 55, 56; J. W. Morris, "The Systems Approach to Forms Management," *Information and Records Management*, (November, 1975), pp. 32, 34; Frank M. Knox, *The Knox Standard Guide to Design and Control of Business Forms*, (New York: McGraw-Hill Book Co., 1965); and *Forms Management*, published in 1969 by the General Services Administration of the U.S. Government and available from the Superintendent of Documents, Washington, DC 20402.

each copy of the form, as in the case of duplicate copies. This arrangement serves as a check on the completeness of the record and ensures identical information on all copies.

4. When it is desirable to fix responsibility for work done by providing spaces for signatures of those responsible for the work.

Principle of Standardization

The physical characteristics of the paper used in all forms should be standardized to improve operating efficiency and reduce costs.

Standardization of forms affects primarily their physical characteristics — size, quality of paper stock, color, and printing styles.

Size of Forms. Standards should first be set for the size of office forms, and the number of approved sizes used by a business firm should be kept to a minimum. Since forms are printed on standard-size sheets of paper stock, odd-size forms increase printing costs because of the waste incurred in the surplus paper trimmed off the standard-size printing sheet. Odd-size forms also contribute to increased office costs in that such forms make the filing and handling tasks more difficult, often requiring the purchase of odd-size envelopes or containers for transmittal through the mail. Before the size of any form is selected, a study should be made of the envelopes, file cabinets, and the mechanical equipment to be used with each form.

The individual or committee in charge of forms management should be familiar with the data in Table 18-1, which shows the size of forms in inches and millimeters that can be cut without waste from standard-size sheets of paper stock. This table also shows 25 different

sizes of forms, some of which are not practical for office use. For example, the smallest sizes are odd sizes that cannot be used in the common index card files. In determining the size of a form, analysts adopt form sizes that can be cut without waste from the standard-size printing sheet — 17" × 22" or 17" × 28".

Quality of Paper Stock. A second factor affecting the standardization of office forms is the quality of paper stock. The durability and ease of handling the forms, as well as the length of time that the forms may be kept, are determined by the quality of stock. Paper stock is sold by the ream and in multiple packages of reams by the carton. The weight is figured by the ream in 17" × 22" size. For example, a ream (usually 500 sheets) of 17" × 22" paper which weighs approximately 20 pounds is called substance 20, or 20 lb. stock. When using the metric system, the basic weight of paper is expressed in grams per square meter (g/m^2). Thus, the metric equivalent of 20 lb. bond (17" × 22" basic size) is computed by multiplying 20 (the number of pounds per ream) by 3.76 (the number of grams per square meter), resulting in 75.2 or 75 g/m^2 when rounded. Commonly used weights for three kinds of office paper stock are shown in Table 18-2.

For multiple-copy forms, weight is particularly important because it determines the number of copies that can be made in one writing. The weight of the stock used also affects mailing costs.

The physical handling that a form will receive must also be considered in deciding upon the quality of stock to be used. Normal treatment, such as that given an invoice form, can be provided for by using a relatively inexpensive, all-sulphite (nonbond) paper. On the other hand, company stationery, such as letterhead sheets and matching envelopes, are usually printed on more expensive cotton-content bond paper which is a hallmark of quality and prestige for the firm. Extremely hard treatment received by some factory orders requires a tough sheet with great tensile strength so that the paper will not crack after many foldings. Some forms, such as shipping tags, are printed on cloth. Sometimes it is advisable to provide a strong, compact case with a celluloid facing to protect such forms.

STANDARD FORMS SIZES

Size of Form*		**Cuts Without Waste from Standard Sheet Measuring:		Number Obtained from Single Standard-Size Sheet	Number of Single Forms Obtained from One Ream of Paper
inches	millimeters	inches	millimeters		
2¾ × 4¼	70 × 108	8½ × 11	216 × 279	8	4M
2¾ × 4¼	70 × 108	17 × 22	432 × 558	32	16M
2¾ × 8½	70 × 216	8½ × 11	216 × 279	4	2M
2¾ × 8½	70 × 216	17 × 22	432 × 558	16	8M
3½ × 4¼	89 × 108	17 × 28	432 × 711	32	16M
3½ × 8½	89 × 216	17 × 28	432 × 711	16	8M
4¼ × 5½	108 × 140	8½ × 11	216 × 279	4	2M
4¼ × 5½	108 × 140	17 × 22	432 × 558	16	8M
4¼ × 7	108 × 178	17 × 28	432 × 711	16	8M
4¼ × 11	108 × 279	8½ × 11	216 × 279	2	1M
4¼ × 11	108 × 279	17 × 22	432 × 558	8	4M
4¼ × 14	108 × 356	17 × 28	432 × 711	8	4M
5½ × 8½	140 × 216	8½ × 11	216 × 279	2	1M
5½ × 8½	140 × 216	17 × 22	432 × 558	8	4M
5½ × 17	140 × 432	17 × 22	432 × 558	4	2M
6 × 9	152 × 229	19 × 24	483 × 610	8	4M
7 × 17	178 × 432	17 × 28	432 × 711	4	2M
7¼ × 10½	184 × 267	22 × 34	558 × 864	9	4½M
8½ × 11	216 × 279	17 × 22	432 × 558	4	2M
8½ × 11	216 × 279	22 × 25½	558 × 648	6	3M
8½ × 14	216 × 356	17 × 28	432 × 711	4	2M
8½ × 22	216 × 558	17 × 22	432 × 558	2	1M
8½ × 28	216 × 711	17 × 28	432 × 711	2	1M
11 × 17	279 × 432	17 × 22	432 × 558	2	1M
14 × 17	356 × 432	17 × 28	432 × 711	2	1M

Table 18-1

Adapted from Hammermill Paper Company

*Metric sizes are stated in millimeters as recommended by the American Paper Institute.
**In some sizes a small "trim" may be allowed, and a form may be permitted to be a small fraction of an inch under the stated dimensions.

The manner in which the form is filled in determines the finish of the paper to be used. Forms completed in ink must be of nonabsorbent paper that will withstand erasures and will prevent the ink from "bleeding." Forms filled in by means of spirit duplicators and other reprographic equipment must be sufficiently absorbent so that the inks will dry quickly and not offset on each succeeding sheet being duplicated. Continuous multiple-copy forms are usually printed on a lighter weight of paper with a medium finish to secure copying legibility. If the finish is too hard, however, the fibers will be so flattened that they will not readily receive the carbon image. If the finish is too soft, the surface of the paper will be rough, which results in poor copying qualities with part of the copy being clear and other parts indistinct.

Most business forms are printed on the *commercial writing class* of papers, a group of writing papers commonly used in ordinary business transactions and

GUIDE TO OFFICE PAPER WEIGHT

Type	Bond				Ledger				Copy		
Weight*	24 (90)	20 (75)	16 (60)	13 (49)	9 (34)	32 (120)	28 (105)	24 (90)	11 (41)	9 (34)	7 (26)
Letterhead	x	x							x	x	x**
General Typing		x	x							x	x
Interoffice		x	x	x	x					x	x
Legal Documents	x										x
General Ledgers						x	x				
Bookkeeping Machines						x	x	x			
Data Processing Continuous Forms											
1st sheet			x	x							
2d–4th copies										x	x
5th–7th copies											x
Form Sets											
3-part form 1st sheet		x				x					
2d and 3d sheets			x					x			
5-part form 1st sheet			x				x				
2d–5th sheets				x	x					x	x

Table 18-2

Adapted from Modern Office Procedures

*The first weight shown indicates pounds per ream; the second weight, shown in parentheses, indicates grams per square meter.
**Depending on number of carbon copies made.

for advertising purposes. The types of paper falling under this heading are bond, copy or onionskin, ledger, index, and more recently a new category, recycled paper, each of which is described in the following paragraphs.

Bond. Bond paper is traditionally used for letterheads, office forms, and certificates where fine appearance and durability are essential. Bond paper is more durable than other commercial writing papers because its fibers are stronger. Bond paper usually has definite writing and erasing qualities, cleanliness, uniformity of finish and color, and freedom from fuzz. Thus, bond papers are more expensive than other commonly used papers.

For many years it was felt that some rag content was required for high-grade business papers. Today, however, many papers made without a rag construction possess all the necessary qualities for normal office use, including letterhead stationery. Sulphite and sulphate papers, for example, are made entirely of wood dissolved into pulp by chemical processes. Sulphite bonds are available in a variety of colors and finishes, and today these bonds represent the standard office papers for typewriting and handwriting. Where durability and permanence are important factors, cotton fiber bonds should be used. For example, in the manufacture of insurance policies, legal forms, and other permanent records, a 100 percent cotton fiber bond is commonly specified. Since the life of paper is dependent upon its use, it is difficult to estimate how long paper will last. However, papermaking authorities state that 50 percent cotton fiber paper should have a 35- to 50-year life.

Erasable bond is a special type of paper that permits errors in freshly typed material to be corrected quickly and cleanly with an ordinary pencil eraser. Once the typing has "set," however, it stays on the paper permanently.

Copy. Copy paper is a general term that describes a group of lightweight writing papers such as onionskin and manifold papers that are used for making carbon copies. Onionskin paper is a lightweight writing paper that is thin, partly transparent, and often highly glazed. It is very durable and may be used for permanent records where a minimum of bulk is desirable. Generally either a 9 lb. or an 11 lb. onionskin, or tissue, is used for carbon copies. If the number of carbon copies required is greater than 5, the tissue weight may be reduced to 7 lb. stock in order to permit good reproduction on all copies. Manifold paper is a lightweight writing paper which, when used alternately with carbon papers, produces multiple copies of handwritten or typewritten work with either an unglazed or glazed finish.

Ledger. Ledger paper is commonly used for systems work since it has a good writing surface for any type of ink or pencil and a card-like finish that stands a lot of abuse. Ledger paper withstands erasing and creasing, and both sides may be ruled clearly and distinctly. Loose-leaf records should be printed on heavier ledger paper than the bound-book type. Generally the most used type of ledger paper is a hard-surface stock in weights from 24 to 40 lbs.

Index. Index papers, the "heavyweights" of office papers, are used for machine-posting records, punched-card systems, index files, and library files. Index papers have the same smooth finish as ledger stock, but are tougher and more rigid. Common weights of index papers are 43, 53, 67, and 82 lbs.

Recycled. Although paper manufacturers have been recycling papers for more than 100 years, recently there has been an increase in the use of recycled paper in all phases of office work. Many firms sell their waste paper to paper manufacturers where it is reduced to a pulp state. New fiber is then added to produce recycled paper at a cost lower than paper manufactured entirely from original wood pulp. Buying such paper not only helps to reduce paper costs but also aids in environmental control.

Color. Colors used on office forms should be standardized. The use of carefully selected colors expedites the routing, sorting, and filing of forms. Forms may be color coded to indicate departments, branches, or other divisions to which copies are to be sent or in which they are to be used or stored.

Printing Styles. Printing styles should be standardized since a uniform typography improves the appearance and readability of forms, thus reducing the possibility of error.

Principle of Effective Design

Sound forms design, based upon the use of the form in the system, ensures the effective flow of information in the firm.

The designers of forms must know how the form functions in a system (that is, what information is needed, by whom, and in what order) as well as the physical requirements of the form. Such physical factors as the size of the form, its quality, and color must be combined with the functional needs of the form when the design process is considered.

In large firms, the responsibility for forms design may be assigned to forms analysis and design specialists who work with the central systems staff. In smaller firms that do not have a full-time systems staff, the responsibility for designing forms rests with the office manager, who may call on forms manufacturers, such as Standard Register Company and Moore Business Forms, Inc., for assistance. A comprehensive discussion of forms design and its impact on the office system appears on pages 465–473.

Principle of Centralized Control

The entire life cycle of the form, including its approval, design, use, and replacement, should be centrally controlled.

Too many offices create new forms and perpetuate all the old forms without seriously questioning their need. This problem can be avoided by providing a system of forms management under the direction of a central office administrator, such as the records manager in large firms or a files supervisor in the small firm. Various aspects of a centralized forms management program are discussed later in this chapter.

GUIDELINES FOR DESIGNING OFFICE FORMS

In planning office forms the forms designer has the same type of responsibility as the architect of a building. Both individuals are primarily concerned with *function*, that is, how the form or building will be used and what is required to make it work or function effectively. Thus, the forms designer must have access to the data compiled in systems studies, as discussed on page 465, in order to find answers to the who, what, when, how, where, and why questions concerning the form's use.[2] Forms design, as an outgrowth of systems analysis, evolves as the analyst considers the needs of the person preparing the form, the ultimate users of the filled-in form, the printer or reprographics department manufacturing the form, and the personnel and equipment involved in mailing and filing the form.

A well-designed form is easy to fill in and easy to read and use. Moreover, it clearly defines what information is needed in its preparation and simplifies the task of data handling. Thus, the well-designed form creates a better attitude on the part of the users, and, as a result, their efficiency increases and costs decrease.[3] To ensure that these general design requirements are met, there are a number of specific guidelines that must be considered. The designer must provide a logical arrangement for entering data on the forms, determine the capabilities of the procedures and equipment that will be used with the forms, include adequate forms identification, and specify clear instructions for printing and using the forms.

The metric system of measurement, discussed in Chapter 4, has many implications for effective forms design. Designers of forms should have a working knowledge of this sytem of measurement and should maintain adequate records on form sizes and weights for both the metric and English measurement systems — sizes in inches and millimeters, and weights in pounds and grams as shown in Tables 18-1 and 18-2. The Metric Information Office of the National Bureau of Standards is the primary source of metrication information in the United States. Additional information on the metric system as it affects paperwork is available from stationery stores and from representatives of forms manufacturers.

Sequence of Data Entered

As forms are designed, the designer should give attention to the logical sequence and arrangement of the items to be entered on the form. Not only must there be a minimum of fill-in, but also a minimum of delay when entering each item of data; constant zigzagging up and down or back and forth on the form must be avoided. If several departments use similar information on the forms, the sequence of the data should be identical so that only one form is required and so that comparisons and use will be facilitated. In an automated office, making the sequence of data on the forms to be keypunched the same as the sequence on the punched cards speeds up the keypunching process. Wherever possible, information should be grouped by the use of ruled lines and white space between the groups. An example of such

---

[2]For information about general forms design, especially for forms used in manual systems, see *Forms Design*, September, 1960, one of a series of Records Management Handbooks developed by the National Archives and Records Service, Office of Records Management, General Services Administration, Eighth Street and Pennsylvania Avenue NW, Washington, DC 20408. An excellent discussion of the more specialized principles for designing forms used in automated systems can be found in Alan Daniels and Donald Yeates (eds.), *Systems Analysis* (Palo Alto: Science Research Associates, Inc., 1971), Chapters 3–7; and in H. N. Laden and T. R. Gildersleeve, *Systems Analysis for Computer Applications* (New York: John Wiley and Sons, 1967), Chapters 9–10.

[3]William V. Nygren, "Forms Design: It's More Than Appearance," *Information and Records Management* (August, 1975), pp. 10, 25–26.

grouping appears in the "Ship Via" and the "Terms" sections of the form shown in Figure 18-1.

Use in Procedures and Equipment

Most of the office forms in use are integrated with people, record-keeping procedures, and various types of processing and filing equipment. For this reason the capabilities and limitations of existing and planned procedures, machines, and equipment should be studied by taking inventory to determine how each will be used with the forms. All equipment that performs a function in the system or procedure — such as typewriters, accounting machines, file cabinets, and collators — must be included in the inventory. An overlooked item may create a bottleneck that will slow down the operation of a fast-moving, efficient system. For each procedure and item of equipment, the following information should be listed in the inventory:

1. The maximum and minimum dimensions of paper stock that the equipment will handle.
2. The maximum and minimum weight of paper stock that the equipment will handle.
3. The direction of feed of paper into the equipment. In the manufacture of paper, the fibers line up with the direction in which the paper machine moves. Thus, the paper is said to have a *grain direction*. Grain direction is highly important where automatic office equipment is concerned. In specifying the paper stock to be used for forms, a grain direction should be selected to parallel the direction of feed into the equipment. If the grain direction runs at a right angle to the feed, the paper will curl and snag, thus slowing down or stopping operations.

In some cases very sensitive equipment may be damaged. If a form is to be stored in a stand-up file, the grain direction should be "on the vertical" in order to give support. If, however, such a form is to be used with automatic equipment, the feed direction should take priority. When a binder is used in manual posting, the grain direction should parallel the binding edge. Papermakers usually indicate the grain direction by underscoring the dimension that runs the same way as the grain. For example, 25 × 38 means that the grain runs parallel to the longer edge. For technical specifications concerning the paper stock, the forms design staff should consult the representatives of the forms manufacturers. Usually their advice is provided without cost to the customer.

4. The method of feed of paper into the equipment. Office or accounting equipment that prints on a cylindrical surface, such as a typewriter roller, will usually handle up to 36 lb. ledger paper. Sample stock should be checked to make sure that the printing is legible and that the machine does not jam. Equipment that prints on a flat surface will print on most all weights of ledger paper stock.
5. The amount of margin to be provided at the top, bottom, and sides of the form. Margins are affected by the type of filing equipment used, such as a vertical file, where the main data unit in the form name or number filed is typically located in the upper right-hand corner of the filed record; or in a visible (cardex) file, where the name or number by which the record is filed may appear at the bottom of the card form.
6. The space required for entering each digit or letter, either by handwritten or machine-printed methods. A simple, yet effective technique for providing an adequate amount of space is the 3 × 5 spacing method. The *3 × 5 spacing*

method (with *three* vertical writing lines per inch and *five* characters per horizontal inch such as measured on a standard typewriter) provides good all-purpose spacing for most forms that are handwritten, typewritten, or both.[4] It will also work well with many automated systems forms where the number of characters printed per inch must be measured in relation to each piece of printing equipment. For the recording of numbers, vertical columns should be provided for easy tabulation on the machine used. On some of the more complex printing equipment, the vertical and horizontal spaces can be easily adjusted by the manufacturer's representative to increase or decrease the number of lines or spaces per inch in order to permit more working space on each form. However, the well-designed form should not be based on getting the most copy on the sheet, but rather on making the form benefit the user as much as possible.

Identifying the Form

Every form should be assigned a name and a number by the forms designer. This type of identification assists the workers in referring to forms in everyday departmental use; facilitates the sorting, storing, and reordering of forms; and helps in preparing written procedures in which the forms play a part. By using both a name and a number, a cross check is maintained over the common errors made in the transposition or omission of numbers in clerical procedures. Also, each copy of a multiple-copy form should have a name designating the main user of each copy, as shown in Figure 18-1. In this illustration of a combined purchase order

and vendor's check, the form has a name that depicts its function (single shipment purchase order) and above it a number (4715) that was assigned by the forms designer for company-wide control. In addition, there is a sequential number (10347) preprinted on the form for each consecutive purchase order written, and this number serves as a further control for later reference in the purchasing and accounting systems. The distribution of each copy is indicated at the bottom of the form as follows:

Original purchase order and check. Note that the purchase order and check bear the same preprinted control number, 10347.

Receiving Copy, sent with original purchase order and check to vendor, who returns Receiving Copy with shipment. Receiving Copy is then referred to accounting department to match and file with Accounts Payable Copy.

Accounts Payable Copy, referred to accounting department for accounts payable record keeping and control.

Purchasing Department Copy, retained as a follow-up and file copy.

Requestor's Copy, returned to department that initiated request for goods.

Some firms use a letter to identify each department and a number for each form originating within that department. For example, *A* may be used for the Accounting Department, *P* for Production, *S* for Sales, and *O* for Order. As a further aid in identifying and distributing copies of forms, manufacturers of forms make available a wide variety of colors of paper stock.

Using the Form

In order that the form may be properly filled in and forwarded to the point

---

[4]Nygren, *op. cit.*, p. 10.

of destination, the designer must provide instructions for entering the data as well as for distributing each copy. Short "fill-in" instructions, such as "prepare in duplicate," are normally located at the top of the form, while brief instructions for distributing the form may be inferred from the departmental copy designations shown in Figure 18-1. When instructions are lengthy, the reverse side of the form may be used, as is the case with complex legal requirements accompanying many purchase orders. The instructions should be clearly worded so

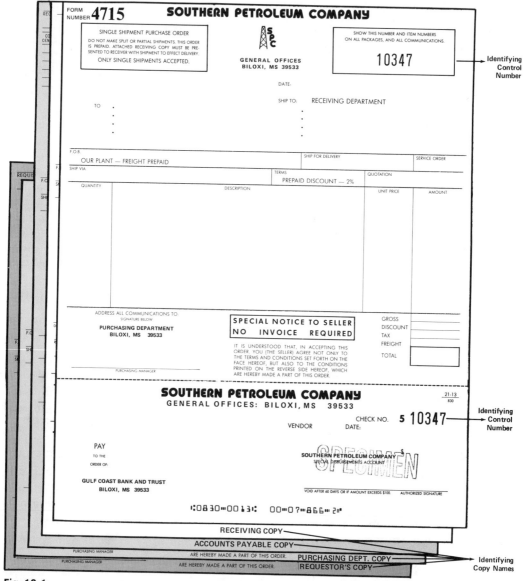

Fig. 18-1

Identifying Names and Number of Copies to Facilitate Sorting and Control

the people who will have to use the forms can understand them.

Printing the Form

To avoid needless expense and delay in forms printing, the forms supervisor must be certain that the design of the form is correctly composed and laid out and that the printer (for external printing) or the reprographics department (for internal printing) has clear and complete instructions of what is to be done. It should be noted that the pricing structure in the paper industry is based on standard units such as reams, cartons, cases, 5,000 and 10,000 lb. lots, and carloads. Fractional quantities will cost extra as will several small orders rather than one large order.

The use of a checklist simplifies and standardizes the ordering of forms from outside printers or internal printing departments. Such a checklist, as shown in Figure 18-2, can be used before placing a printing order for a new form or for an old form to be reprinted. Often additional information is added to the checklist, especially data on the quantity of the form used each month, where the form is stored, what quantity should be maintained in inventory, and who should be contacted for reordering, revising, or eliminating the form.

Analysis of Good Forms Design

The report of cash form shown in Figure 18-3 was designed for use in a banking organization. The forms manager studied the form's use and revised its design; in final form it illustrates the essentials of good forms design. Because of this fact, the form promotes economy, efficiency, and convenience, as can be noted by analyzing the following applications of good forms design:

1. The size $5\frac{1}{2}'' \times 8\frac{1}{2}''$ cuts without waste from standard-size printing sheets. (The illustration in Figure 18-3 has been reduced to fit the textbook page; thus, this point cannot be observed on the reproduced form.)

2. An original and four copies of this form are prepared. Therefore, substance 16 bond is used to permit legibly typed carbon copies. (This point cannot be observed in Figure 18-3.)

3. The firm name and address do not appear on the form. For internal forms such as this, such company information is unnecessary and space consuming.

4. The titles of all persons who may receive a copy of the form are printed in the upper left corner. The distribution of each copy is indicated by placing a check mark in the appropriate box alongside the person's title. An alternate plan would be to print on each copy the title of the person receiving a copy. Also, by using a different color paper for each copy, the forms can be identified and distributed promptly.

5. Double horizontal rules are used at the top and bottom of each box section. The vertical rules are of a different weight so that the form is divided into logical sections. This makes for easier reading and rapid comprehension of the facts presented.

6. The type selected is easy to read but is not so large as to draw attention from the more important typewritten or handwritten information.

7. All rules are unbroken and clean. Careful craftsmanship makes the form neat and easy to read. Neat forms design encourages neatness by the users.

8. The horizontal lines are spaced six to the vertical inch, the same as the vertical spacing on a typewriter, thus

HAMMERMILL FORM ORDER SHEET • PART 1

FORM PLANNING CHECK LIST

A quick and easy method of checking the efficiency and economy of any form — new or old — before placing your printing order. Read the text at the bottom of this sheet.

NECESSITY | OK | ?

1 Has the entire system been checked and would a written procedure for the use of this form help put it into more efficient operation?

2 Are all copies of the form or report necessary?

3 Have the actual users of this form been consulted for suggested improvements, additional requirements and possible eliminations?

4 Can the data furnished by this form be combined with some other form or can some other form be eliminated or consolidated with it?

5 Has everyone responsible for the form or the form system approved it?

PURPOSE | OK | ?

6 If form is to be sent from one person to another, are proper spaces for "to" and "from" provided?

7 Will routing or handling instructions printed on each copy be helpful?

8 Should this form be consecutively numbered, or have a place for inserting a number?

9 If this is an Outside Contact Form, should it be designed to mail in a window envelope?

10 If this form is to take information from, or pass information to, another form, do both have the same sequence of items?

11 Have we taken into consideration the number of forms which will be used in a given time (4 to 12 months) — the possibility of changes, and how long the form will remain in use?

SIZE AND ARRANGEMENT | OK | ?

12 Is the size right for filing, attention value, ample room for information and to cut without waste?

13 Is all recurring information being printed so that only variable items need be filled in?

14 Has space been provided for a signature?

15 Is spacing correct for handwriting or typewriting? (The Hammermill Form Layout Sheet will help check this.)

16 Are the most important items, which should be seen first, prominently placed? (Near the top, if practicable.)

WORDING | OK | ?

17 Does the form, by title and arrangement, clearly indicate its purpose?

18 Is there a proper space for the date?

19 Is the form identified by company name and firm name or code number to aid reordering?

20 If this is a revised form, can it be distinguished from the previous form?

PAPER AND PRINTING | OK | ?
(Specifications)

21 Should the form be on colored paper to speed up writing, distribution, sorting and filing; to designate departments or branch offices; to indicate days, months or years; to distinguish manifold copies; to identify rush orders?

22 Have we specified paper which will be thoroughly satisfactory, economical enough for form use, consistent in performance and surely available for later reorders?

23 Is proper weight of paper used for original and each carbon copy? (Bond Substances 13, 16 and 20. Ledger Substances 24, 28 and 32. Mimeo-Bond Substances 16 and 20. Spirit and Gelatin Duplicator Substances 16 and 20.)

24 Are detailed specifications complete? (Paper, type, ink, rules, punch, perforate, score, fold, gather, pad, carbon sheet, stitch, etc.)

25 Can other forms, printed on the same paper as this one, be ordered now to reduce production costs?

26 Have requirements been estimated correctly and is the quantity to be ordered most economical? (Consider probability of revision and rate of use.)

Pt. #   **REMARKS** ON POINTS QUESTIONED (?)

Date_____19_____   Signed_____

HOW TO USE THIS FORM

Run through this list and appraise a new or revamped form point by point with an initial (rather than a check mark) either in the column headed "OK" or "?." This will help in working out the most efficient form size and specifications and the best working arrangement of items and copy.

Points marked (?) for further study can then be appraised systematically and discussed with those who will regularly use the form. Findings and further details can be elaborated upon in the column for "Remarks" at bottom of the second column.

To pin down responsibility, the person or persons giving the final OK should place their initials opposite the remarks. The whole Check List should be filed with a copy of the form for future reference.

Hammermill Paper Company

Fig. 18-2
Hammermill Form Planning Guide

saving typing time. Otherwise, the typewriter would have to be adjusted for each line. Usually three vertical spaces are used for a box which may contain either typed or handwritten data.

9. No horizontal rules are used for recording amounts, since such lines are confusing and unnecessary on most typewritten forms. In order to make reading easier on very wide forms, faint horizontal rules may be used as a guide for the eye.

10. The banks are grouped by cities and the cities are listed alphabetically. This permits a quick analysis of the

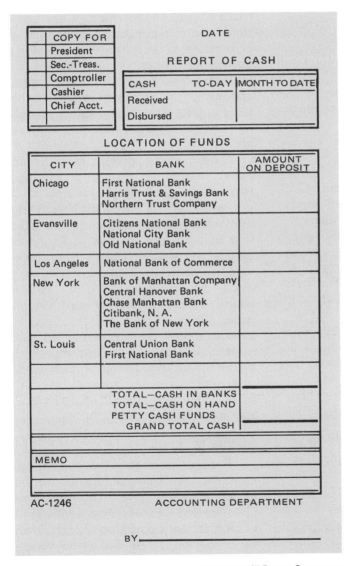

Hammermill Paper Company

Fig. 18-3
An Example of Good Forms Design

funds in each location.

11. The side margins have been kept narrow to provide all available space for actual use.
12. Additional spaces are provided for extra bank names, when needed.
13. Space for writing memos is provided for the bank officers who frequently make such notes. If a place is provided for this writing, illegible scribbling is reduced.
14. The form bears a proper name and number to facilitate reordering, handling, and storage.
15. Ample space has been provided for the signature of the person issuing the form.[5]

KINDS OF OFFICE FORMS

The standardization of forms size mentioned earlier in this chapter carries over into other aspects of forms management. A forms analyst and designer should understand the standard printing processes, including the reprographic services discussed in Chapter 10, as well as the kinds of office forms available for use in various office systems.

Forms manufacturers classify office forms by physical construction, such as flat forms, specialty forms, and forms for automated systems. In the design of each kind of form, a major aim is to plan for one initial recording of all data that will be used throughout the remaining data processing operations. This write-it-once principle of effective office systems is explored in Chapter 19.

Flat Forms

The most commonly used type of office form is the *flat form*, a single sheet of paper. This form is the simplest and

———————————
[5]With permission of the Hammermill Paper Company.

easiest of all forms to design and reproduce, and may be printed by the company's printing or reprographics department. The most standardized kinds of flat forms, such as sales tickets, may be purchased from a stationery dealer or a forms manufacturer.

Single-sheet flat forms can be prepared by hand or machine. When additional copies are required, carbon paper is inserted between the copies. Many businesses continue to use carbons for preparing five or six duplicate copies and rely on an office copier for making more copies. Thus, the data are recorded only once, saving time and copying errors.

The use of a plastic film carbon paper results in a tougher quality, longer-lasting, more smudge-free product, although its cost may be slightly higher than regular carbon paper. This type of hard-finish carbon paper works particularly well under the heavy-pressure use in electric typewriters. To produce the blackest "writes" when handwritten forms are prepared, carbon paper that has a high degree of carbon deposit should be selected so that the same carbon may be used several times before discarding. The carbonless form, discussed in the next section, may also be considered by office managers where its special features are useful.

Specialty Forms

Forms that require special equipment for their manufacture or use are called *specialty forms*. In this forms classification are carbonless forms, spot-carbon forms, continuous forms, unit set or snap-out forms, and a wide variety of miscellaneous forms requiring special printing processes. Figure 18-4 shows those specialty forms that are in common use.

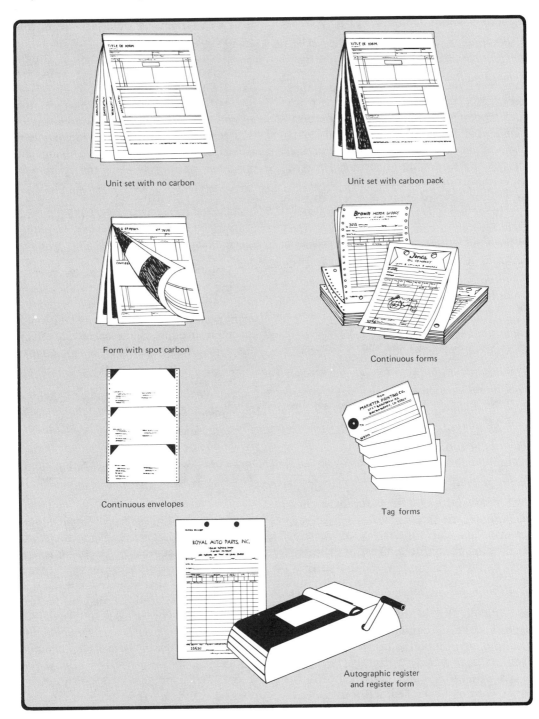

Unit set with no carbon

Unit set with carbon pack

Form with spot carbon

Continuous forms

Continuous envelopes

Tag forms

Autographic register
and register form

Fig. 18-4
Varieties of Specialty Forms and Specialized Forms Equipment

Carbonless Forms. The type of form used and the equipment with which it is used determine the method of obtaining copies. Modern technology has developed many and varied paper treatments that permit impressions from copy to copy without the use of carbon. The image is made when special coatings on the back of one sheet and the face of the following sheet are brought together under pressure. Carbonless paper can be used in typewriters to obtain up to eight legible copies; by hand, up to four copies may be prepared with a ball-point pen; and with an impact printer in the computer system, the maximum is five copies.

Carbonless business forms offer the following advantages to the user:

1. No smearing or smudging of copies.
2. No soiling of hands or clothing.
3. No time wasted with insertion or removal of carbons.
4. No need to dispose of used carbon sheets.
5. Erasures are easily detected.

Each of these advantages is of major importance to the business forms user. Smearing and smudging, for example, become a serious problem when forms are handled many times, as in certain accounting procedures. Shuffling flimsy carbon paper is not only hand-soiling but time-consuming as well. In many government offices, security requires the burning or shredding of used carbon paper. Since carbonless forms use no carbon of any kind, this time-consuming problem is eliminated. Finally, because of its chemical coatings, carbonless paper cannot be erased without detection. Improper or excessive erasures tend to remove the chemical coatings and prevent retyping of information in this area. In many business firms this may be an important safety feature.

Because of their special chemical composition, carbonless forms are usually more expensive than comparable carbon forms — sometimes costing an additional 20 to 30 percent. However, this cost may be offset by two costs that are often overlooked in planning the purchase of forms — the transportation cost from the forms manufacturer's plant and the cost of storing the forms. Since carbonless papers weigh less and are less bulky, some economy is to be realized from their use.

Spot-Carbon Forms. By carbon coating only certain areas on each copy of a form, confidential or unneeded information will not be readable on each subsequent copy of the form. In effect, this type of form withholds or conveys information to individuals or departments as the needs of the information system dictate. In purchasing spot-carbon forms from forms manufacturers, the forms designer must make sure that the location of the carbon spots has been carefully specified. (See Figure 18-4 for an illustration of a spot-carbon form.)

Continuous Forms. Forms constructed in a prearranged manner with perforations separating each form are known as *continuous forms*. Printed forms, such as invoices and special accounting forms, are designed in continuous, single- or multiple-copy sets arranged in proper numeric order. Letterheads and envelopes are also used in continuous strips, varying as to paper weight, size, and fastening techniques, to speed up the correspondence process. The principle underlying the use of continuous forms is based upon the automatic feeding of prearranged sheets.

Often such forms are perforated with holes or slots on each side, which permits fastening the forms to an aligning device on the writing machine. The result is an accurate registration across and down each form set and the elimination of the need for aligning each form in the machine.

Two kinds of continuous forms are in use — the fanfold and the separate strip form. The *fanfold form* has alternate edges that are held together, without pasting or stapling, for subsequent handling. The *separate strip form* is composed of sheets that are printed and arranged separately in long strips, but the multiple copies are not attached to each other.

The use of continuous forms saves the time of employees concerned with their completion. The greater the number of copies to be made at any one given time, the greater the savings in the worker's time. Any comparison must therefore consider the usual manual operations of collecting, inserting, removing, and separating the sheets when noncontinuous forms are used as compared with the use of automatic bursting machines for the separation of sheets of continuous forms. This savings in oper-

ations is then multiplied by the number of copies to be made.

The manufacturers of continuous forms have had time-study engineers make stopwatch studies comparing the time used for completing loose, unassembled forms with the time required for using continuous forms with preassembled carbons. As shown in Table 18-3, their results point up the wasted time each week caused by inserting carbons between sheets, jogging into alignment, inserting in the typewriters or billing machines, straightening in the machines, removing from the machines, and taking out the carbons.

The wasted time can be translated into the dollar cost of unproductive labor as shown in Table 18-3. Based upon a 40-hour week, with allowance for small waste from the use of fanfold forms, the cost of wasted time is given at three salary levels for every 1,000 forms — under the assumption that 1,000 sets of forms are prepared during the week.

Against the savings to be realized from the use of continuous forms must be charged the cost of a continuous forms machine, such as an autographic register, and the higher cost of forms

WASTED SECONDS AND UNPRODUCTIVE WEEKLY SALARY COSTS FOR EACH SET OF FORMS

Number of Parts Per Set	Seconds Wasted Per Form	Hours Wasted Per Week*	Weekly Salary (40-Hour Week)		
			$140	$150	$160
2	14	3.89	$13.62	$14.59	$15.56
4	32	8.89	31.12	33.34	35.56
6	50	13.89	48.62	52.09	55.56
10	85	23.61	82.64	88.54	94.44
12	102.5	28.47	99.65	106.76	113.88

Table 18-3

*Based on 1,000 forms in use per week.

printed in continuous sets. For some types of continuous forms work, a simple attachment to the typewriter costing less than $50 can be used. In automated systems using continuous forms, a more expensive device must be purchased to hold the fanfold arrangement of continuous forms; and a burster may also be required for the separation of multiple-copy forms and the carbon sheets. If the cost of this equipment is prorated over its life, however, the equipment cost is negligible. Therefore, the savings effected through decreasing the time spent by employees in preparing the forms must be compared with the higher cost of the continuous forms used and the equipment required to use such forms, before the office manager makes a decision as to which kind of forms should be used.

Comparatively speaking, for forms having the same printed matter, the continuous forms are slightly more costly than those that come unassembled. However, use of continuous multiple-copy forms frequently brings about an improved system. More copies of a form may be prepared and used, and the necessity of having several persons prepare closely allied forms is avoided. For example, before one firm installed its automated accounting system, an order clerk prepared an acknowledgement of each order. Subsequently, the shipping department prepared the original bills of lading, the memorandum copy of the bill of lading, and the shipping order. Finally, the invoicing department prepared a series of four invoices. After a study of the system and slight modification of the forms, it was possible to prepare in one writing all nine copies, thus saving the time of the order clerk and the shipping department clerk.

Unit-Set Forms. Instead of using continuous forms, many firms choose unit-set forms because more copies can be made simultaneously and some of the copies may be longer than others. *Unit-set forms* (sometimes called snap-out forms), such as those shown in Figure 18-4, are preassembled with one-time carbon paper interleaved between the perforated sheets which permits easy removal of the nonperforated carbons. Unit sets are also constructed using carbonless or carbon-coated papers. Such forms are specialized and expensive to print, but they are justified by the great savings realized in the typist's time, as illustrated in Table 18-4.

Other Specialty Forms. While the specialty forms previously cited do not cover completely the many forms available to business, those shown in Figure 18-4 are commonly used. Spirit-process masters, offset masters, and

TIME SAVED USING UNIT-SET FORMS

Number of Parts in the Form	For Average of Five Lines of Typing	For Average of Ten Lines of Typing	For Average of Fifteen Lines of Typing
2	38%	23%	17%
4	55%	38%	30%
6	64%	47%	37%
8	70%	54%	45%
10	74%	59%	50%

Table 18-4

Uarco, Incorporated

stencils, which were discussed in Chapter 10, may also be used as forms. This is accomplished when lines and alphanumeric information are preprinted on these duplicating-machine masters for the later entry of variable information. The master can then be "run" on the appropriate duplicating machine for producing a much larger quantity of forms than would be possible if carbon sheets were used for preparing multiple copies of forms on a typewriter or billing machine. Other specialty forms used in automated data processing systems are discussed in the next section.

Forms for Automated Systems

With the emergence of the punched-card and electronic data processing systems, additional demands were made upon the design and control of forms. In both systems, input machines such as the optical character reader or card reader may read data from paper forms or tab cards and ultimately print out information on another set of output forms. In some cases, the systems demand human processing, which in turn requires the handwritten entry of data. The forms most often used in automated systems are: continuous forms, discussed in the previous section; tab cards; two-wide forms; and MICR and OCR forms.

Tab Card Forms. Tab card forms are used as input and output documents in punched-card and electronic data processing systems. The tab card forms must conform to the machine requirements of the system in which they operate, but they can be designed for a wide variety of functions. As shown in Figure 18-5, tab card forms are produced (a) in continuous form (one- or two-wide) for high-speed continuous writing in single- or multiple-copy, (b) in tab card sets with a side stub, (c) in single tab card form, and (d) in "piggyback" form which provides a means for automating those applications requiring added form space for recording supporting data.

Two-Wide Forms. As shown in Figure 18-5, two-wide invoice forms can be printed for each customer. A copy sent to the customer and a copy retained by the office are printed at the same time by utilizing the continuous-form, fanfold design technique. The simultaneous printing of two-wide forms, such as a payroll check and the employee's earnings statement, has greatly increased the capability of the computer-controlled output printer for printing of data at great speeds. In addition to printing economy, the forms-handling costs after machine processing are significantly reduced.

MICR and OCR Forms. In manual systems as well as in most automated systems, the forms designer is responsible for providing printing that is human-readable. With the steady progress made by computer technology, most automated systems utilize hardware with *machine-readable* capabilities, as found in the MICR and OCR processes illustrated in Figure 18-5.

MICR (Magnetic Ink Character Recognition) is a system developed by the American Bankers Association. MICR is used by banks to interpret and process numeric data that have been recorded in special magnetic ink characters on checks and other business papers. Automatic equipment is used to read, sort, and transmit to a computer the data printed on the business forms for further processing, such as the

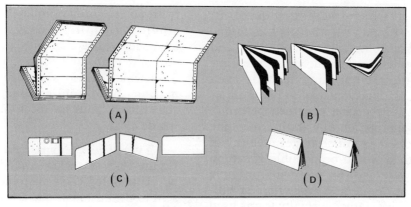

Tab Card Forms

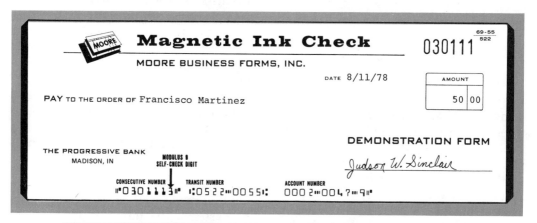

MICR and OCR Forms

Fig. 18-5 (page 1)
Forms for Automated Systems

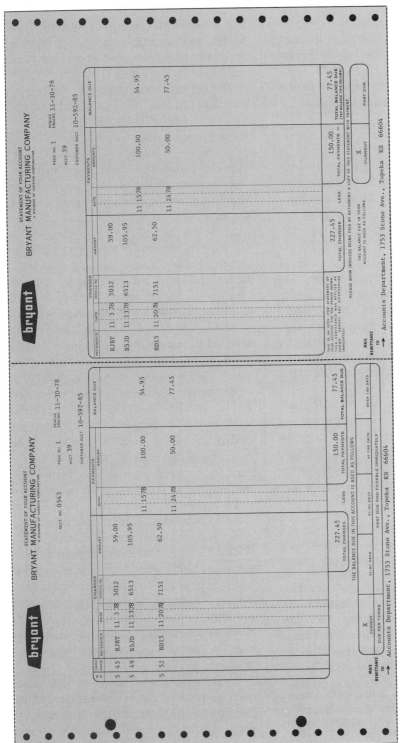

Fig. 18-5 (page 2)
Forms for Automated Systems

preparation of customer bank statements. Examples of such MICR characters in Figure 18-5 are the bank's Federal Reserve number, the customer's account number, and the amount of the check, recorded in machine-readable form.

OCR (Optical Character Recognition) is a related scanning system of reading numeric and alphabetic data that have been printed in a distinctive type style on business forms and records. As each character is read from the business document, it is translated into electrical impulses that are transmitted to the computer for processing. Optical readers have been developed that can also scan and read handwritten data to a limited degree. One type of optical scanner can read handwritten numbers and pencil-written marks in predefined areas on business forms for direct feeding into and subsequent processing of the data by a computer.

The development of MICR and OCR equipment was dependent upon the ability of the forms industry to provide printed forms that the machines could read. The printing of such forms requires precision manufacturing equipment and quality papers and inks.[6]

THE FORMS MANAGEMENT PROGRAM

In Chapter 17 it was pointed out that all aspects of the office system must be managed in order that the system attain its objective of providing information to management. Since business forms are an important phase of the of-

fice system and since the proliferation of forms has increased the problems of maintaining office efficiency and holding costs in line, it is the responsibility of the office administrator to establish a practical system for managing the creation and use of forms. A *forms management program* has as its objective the elimination of unneeded forms, the design of forms for their most efficient use, the most economical distribution of the forms to avoid needless waste and expense, and an organized and continuous review of all company forms. For such a program to be effective, top management must know the importance of forms and their use, the costs involved, and the inefficiencies of overlapping and duplication that normally arise without control, and must give its continuing support to the control program.

Well-qualified personnel must be available for the forms management program. Such a program cannot be carried out as a "side job" or on a part-time basis in the large firm. The job requires dedicated people who understand the company's information flows and its information needs. In addition, forms personnel must possess a knowledge of paper, graphics, printing, postal and legal regulations, forms inventory control, and records management. With such an array of qualifications required, there is little probability of one individual being proficient in all areas. Thus, large-scale forms management programs are organized into groups of functions, such as design and printing, with individuals specializing in each functional group.

The nature and scope of the forms management program are influenced by the unique qualities of the business organization — especially its size — and the willingness of its management to

---

[6]The American National Standards Institute has developed a standard type font (X3.17-1966) for designing OCR forms. For more information on this standard and other OCR forms requirements, write to the American National Standards Institute, 1430 Broadway, New York, NY 10018.

support an ongoing forms management effort. The number of forms used daily and the cost of their use determine the feasibility of establishing a centralized forms management (sometimes called a forms control or forms administration) department. Such a unit usually reports to the systems and procedures department. In the small office the office manager is the logical person to assume the management and control of office forms. Frequently such managers will delegate the design of forms to a supervisor who has an understanding of the information needs of the entire firm as well as the necessary authority to enforce the regulations pertaining to the creation and control of all forms.

Each of the steps to be taken in managing the entire life cycle of office forms is described in the following paragraphs. An abbreviated version of a written procedure relating to this same cycle is shown in Figure 18-6.

Collecting Forms and Usage Data

In starting a forms management program, first it is necessary to collect a copy of every form presently used by the firm. Along with a copy of the form, information should be obtained regarding the form's use by each department. Flowcharts, similar to those shown in Chapter 17, may be used to record the flow of information and the distribution of the form throughout its cycle. This initial collection will provide information about the units or departments using the form and the relative frequency with which each form is used — daily, weekly, or monthly. Information should also be gathered on the method of preparation (machine or handwritten), the number of copies made, and the destination of each copy. A personal visit to each department provides an opportunity for the analyst to explain the

FORMS MANAGEMENT PROCEDURE

1. The requesting department contacts forms management for assistance in the analysis, development, design, approval, and acquisition of all printed forms.
2. On being advised of a need for a form, forms management determines if an existing form will satisfy the requirement.
3. If no suitable form exists, the requestor is asked to "rough out" the form needed and to explain the function it will fulfill. Two samples of each design are prepared, one blank and one filled in, and then routed through a forms coordinator to forms management.
4. Forms management reviews the request, analyzes the need, coordinates the final

design, the printing specifications, and usage with the user and/or the forms coordinator.
5. Forms management works with the purchasing department to procure the forms, either internally through in-house printing or externally from a vendor.
6. The requestor is advised through the forms coordinator when the new form is ready.
7. Thereafter, inventory control notifies forms management when reorder points are reached and, based on whatever schedule has been set up, reviews the form at specified intervals.

Fig. 18-6
A Procedure for Managing the Life Cycle of the Form

overall purpose of the forms management program, shows how the program will ultimately benefit each departmental employee, and permits the employees to offer suggestions for improving the forms system. Copies of standardized questionnaires to assist in the collection of forms and usage data are available in systems and data processing textbooks as well as from representatives of the forms manufacturers.

Analyzing the Use and Distribution of Forms

The forms collected in the initial survey can be arranged in various ways. The most basic organizational plan is to list all forms by name and then cross reference them to their appropriate form number. In order to eliminate all nonessential forms or nonessential parts of forms, a functional file is often set up in which all forms having identical or similar functions (such as recording, listing, ordering, requesting, and registering) are grouped together. With such forms groupings it becomes easier to spot duplicate forms and opportunities to consolidate and standardize forms.[7]

The elimination of forms requires tact by the individual responsible for forms management. By questioning individuals using the forms and following the distribution of each form copy to its final user, it will be found that some forms should be discarded, some redesigned, and others retained.

By the use or lack of use of forms and their cost of printing and preparation, a department head will readily understand why a form should or should not be eliminated. Sometimes by slightly changing an existing form it is possible to use one form to replace several others. Such consolidation decreases the number of forms and reduces the printing costs.

The adoption of standards will systematize the work and simplify the supervision and control of the use of forms. Among the recognized standards are: (a) use of identifying numbers where sequential control is necessary as in the case of vouchers, invoices, and checks; (b) use of appropriate descriptive titles, such as acknowledgment of order, invoice, and routing slip, to avoid misuse and to facilitate operating use; (c) uniform placement of items that occur consistently on a large number of forms; (d) arrangement of items in order of preparation and observation or reading; and (e) footnote dates and quantities of original printing or revisions.

Approving Requests for Forms

A sound forms management program requires a definite procedure for initiating all new forms and for revising of existing forms that may require reprinting. As indicated previously, such a procedure must take into consideration the systems department, the department requesting the form, and the forms manager. A typical procedure followed by large firms with central control of forms includes (1) a formal written request for a new form or a revised form, (2) a central control log showing the date and nature of the request and its ultimate disposition, and (3) the preparation and issuance of the accepted form.

---

[7]Frank M. Knox has, for several decades, represented the foremost authority in cost reduction through forms control. The functional-index concept which he developed is described in detail in his comprehensive forms management text, *The Knox Standard Guide to Design and Control of Business Forms* (New York: McGraw-Hill Book Co., 1965), Chapter 2.

Printing the Forms

The final step in the forms management cycle is procuring the form that has been approved. This phase of the program requires of the manager a thorough knowledge of printing and reprographic processes and a constant study of the most economic quantity of the form to be printed and stocked at any time. The decision on the quantity to be ordered is influenced by the rate of use and the possibility of future forms revisions, as offset by the fact that the larger the quantity printed, the lower the cost.

Reducing the Cost of Forms

The modern organization has developed an insatiable appetite for information carried on paper. Typical of the paper flood that gluts business offices are some statistics compiled by the Commission on Federal Paperwork whose mission is to trim the federal paperwork load.

A Commission staff report points out that a typical small business with 50 workers or less must complete at least 75 government forms a year; that major pharmaceutical firms report that 50 cents of every prescription cost is due to federal regulatory compliance requirements; and that the government estimates that federal paperwork adds $4 a day to each patient's costs in a hospital. The present 8,000 varieties of federal forms evolve into 10 billion copies of forms each year which cost the taxpayers 40 billion dollars annually to mail, process, file, fill out, and store.[8] Further,

with a higher degree of accountability expected in business and government, records are kept longer, which adds to the costs of the paperwork system.

The State of California, through its General Services Department, has recognized the dire need for controlling the relentless growth in forms. In a study of paperwork proliferation in that state, it was found that there are 75,000 forms being used by the state government with as many as 21 different forms used to provide the same kind of legal notice. From such a study a Forms Management Center for the state was set up to oversee the forms used by state agencies. Other states have followed the same pattern as private business in order to control the number of forms in use and, along with them, their staggering costs.

Suggestions for reducing the cost of forms overlap to some extent the suggestions for improvement of office systems discussed in Chapter 17. Nevertheless, the following factors may be considered as important methods for reducing the cost of forms and related paper supplies:

1. Centralize the responsibility for approving new forms as well as for improving old forms and for eliminating unnecessary forms. Forms managers should be alert to unnumbered and temporary forms that are "bootlegged" within departments, never reaching a forms manager's desk. By supervision of departmental copies and duplicating machines, these unauthorized forms will diminish in number.

2. Establish standard procedures for all phases of the forms management program including clear-cut guidelines about the physical (paper and ink) costs of printing the form and the

[8]For a more comprehensive treatment of the mounting paper costs in offices of all sizes, see "The Commission on Federal Paperwork," *The Office* (February, 1975), pp. 39–40, 42; and "New Hope for a Real Federal Paperwork Cutback," *Nation's Business* (April, 1976), pp. 24, 27.

more important functional (labor) cost involved with the form's use.

3. Group forms by category — tags, snapouts, and continuous forms — to take advantage of opportunities for cost reduction through large-quantity buying. Similarly, design continuous tabulating forms to be printed *two up*, or two to a sheet as shown in Figure 18-5, on the computer-printer.

4. Print low-usage flat forms with a firm's own duplicating equipment. For runs in quantities of less than 10,000, internal printing is more economical than using the services of an outside small-lot printer.

5. Use white paper wherever possible rather than colored paper. The routing or distribution of each form can be printed on all-white paper.

6. Standardize on forms, letterheads, and envelope sizes, which reduces the number of different items in use, allows sizable purchase discounts through quantity buying, and simplifies warehousing problems. Some firms reduce forms warehousing, inventory control, and forms printing costs by establishing a vendor warehousing and printing program in which a qualified forms vendor stores company forms and distributes them to locations at a minimum percentage of the printing cost.

7. Considerable savings can be made in careful forms design. Money can be saved by furnishing a master or negative of the form to the printer; by considering the need for printing forms on two sides, and by avoiding the use of a department name, employee name, or similar information that may cause a form to become obsolete or restrict its use to a specific department or office. Also, it is important to be sure that all copies of a form are necessary, as extra copies add to the cost of printing, stocking, filing, and distribution.

8. Consider postage costs when specifying the weight of forms and stationery. Through the course of a year the use of a 20 lb. rather than a 36 lb. weight stock will result in considerably lower postage costs. Also, select paper stock carefully, using recycled paper for internal forms.

9. Insist on good housekeeping practice, such as maintaining supplies stockrooms or storage cabinets in an orderly and efficient fashion. Check all drawers often to avoid accumulation of unused forms and supplies.

10. Reuse as many of the stationery and forms supplies as possible. Use the reverse side of an incoming letter for the carbon copy of the reply, which saves the cost of the second sheets and reduces the number of items to be filed. Also, use the carbon paper as long as it produces legible copy. Envelopes left unsealed may be used repeatedly for interoffice mail.

11. Prepare departmental supplies budgets and compare with actual costs of supplies used. Where a centralized forms management program is in effect, the costs of all forms and supplies should be charged to the using department where such costs should be justified.

Because the individual office form and supply items cost so little, many office employees and office managers are prone to overlook the total amount involved over the period of a month or a year. This means that much waste occurs because of lack of supervision or control. Unless the supervisor is interested in economy and cost control, the employees in his or her department will not pay much attention to better ways of doing the work.

FORMS MANAGEMENT IN ACTION

Forms management functions as a phase of systems and procedures analysis, as explained in the preceding chapter. Thus, a change in forms may involve a change in systems and procedures, such as the case when two forms have been combined into one and the new forms processing and storage are centered in one location rather than two. When a form is redesigned for more efficiency in use, the effect is more clerical efficiency in terms of entering and reading the data on the form, and the overall information system is not affected. The following illustrations are but a few examples of the great savings achieved by firms having effective forms management programs.

In a study of its purchasing procedures, a major university found that more than 75,000 purchase orders were issued each year and that approximately 80 percent of these involved amounts of $100 or less. It became apparent that the clerical effort expended was definitely out of proportion to the amount of money being controlled. After a careful study it was decided to combine a check and a purchase order into one form so that the supplier could be paid at the same time the order was placed. The new purchase order form which is used for all purchases of $100 or less enables the university to reduce its keypunching time and the use of punched cards by 75 percent, to eliminate checkwriting through the combined writing of the check and the purchase order, to reduce the overall accounting time, and to receive additional discounts given by suppliers who are, in effect, receiving cash often before the merchandise is shipped.

One large airline, by studying the forms and the procedure followed in issuing passenger tickets, was able to save $60,000. This saving was brought about by abolishing 78 ticket forms and reducing the range of time for issuing tickets from five to 15 minutes to one minute or less.

One corporation redesigned four sets of forms, each previously written separately, into a single form which in one writing produced a label, an invoice, an acknowledgment, and production records. The savings in dollars was tremendous, even though the newly designed forms cost more for each set. This change also involved a slight modification in office procedures and the elimination of three workers.

Another service-oriented firm having computer capabilities maintains for each form an index record that is stored on magnetic tape and used in a word processing typewriter. The system stores 9,000 records and permits immediate access and reporting on all phases of the form cycle including the latest inventory figures and an overall picture of all forms activities. Group purchasing of commercially printed forms results in large savings and more productivity in scheduling forms printing in the in-plant print shop. The only out-of-pocket cost is the information-retrieval cartridge required for using the magnetic tape equipment.

By having a specialist in charge of all forms design and analysis, one firm was able to reduce by 35 percent the cost of the printing and the use of 750,000 tags. Similarly, the incorrect specification of 20 lb. paper for a form that was to be prepared in seven copies almost caused an expensive mistake in this firm.

A new forms design alone can also effect astounding savings. One government installation filling in 400,000 copies of one form each year observed that eight minutes were required to fill in the form. By redesigning the form, only four minutes were required, thus saving 20,500 hours of worker time during the year. A specialized type of motion analysis, as applied to the typewriter, was used in this case.

One of the most futuristic — and potentially important — applications of forms management employs the computer in the layout and printing of forms. In this application the layout of the form is programmed and stored in the computer. Whenever information that is being processed by the computer is to be printed out on a form, the program for the layout is called forth to print out the form at the same time that the information on the form is being printed. In essence, this operation results in instantaneous forms printing and forms fill-in. Also, it eliminates most of the forms production cycle as well as the costs of purchasing and storing forms.

The tangible cost of forms used in administrative systems amounts to thousands of dollars annually in even the smallest firms. When the intangible costs of using or processing forms are considered, additional costs amounting to many times the initial cost of the forms are involved. In each of the examples of forms management in action reported in this section, the individual forms costs were low, but the volume of forms used was so great that dramatic overall savings resulted when better forms supervision was introduced. The largest portion of such savings is the time required of the office worker, the most expensive resource in any office.

QUESTIONS FOR REVIEW

1. What are the four principles of forms management with which the administrative manager should be familiar?

2. Explain what is meant by standardization of business forms.

3. What factors should be studied and analyzed before the size of a form is determined?

4. Describe briefly the main types of paper that make up the commercial writing class.

5. In order to label a form "well-designed," what characteristics should such a form possess?

6. Why is grain direction important in the design of office forms to be used on automatic machines?

7. Explain how a form name and number can serve dual purposes — identification and control — at the same time.

8. What are the principal kinds of forms? For what kinds of work can the use of each kind of form be justified?

9. What steps should be taken in order to implement a forms management program?

10. Cite at least five suggestions for reducing the cost of forms and related paper supplies.

1. If you were appointed supervisor of a forms management program, what preliminary steps would you take to plan the overall operations? What basic questions would you ask in making a functional analysis of the business forms in your firm?

2. It has been stated that the chief savings in the cost of multiple-copy forms is not in the cost of the paper and ink on the forms but in other kinds of savings. Explain.

3. Several days a week you have lunch at a nearby restaurant that is noted for its excellent food but "lousy" service. Because the location is so convenient and the quality and quantity of food is so good, you continue patronizing the restaurant. One day during lunch the restaurant owner, Tony Pirelli, who knows of your expertise in forms management and office systems, chats with you about the customer-service problems in his business and asks you to "take a close look at how we're doing things — and let me know how much I owe you." You agree to undertake such a project and report to Pirelli, suggesting how he can improve his operating efficiency, especially the flow of information within the restaurant. How would you proceed with such a study? What techniques for information gathering and analysis would you employ? What role would office forms play in such a nonoffice situation? How would you determine a fair charge for your services? Utilizing the systems study techniques discussed in Chapter 17, discuss each of the preceding questions.

4. The invoice form shown in Figure A has been handed to you for criticism and suggestions for improvement. The actual size of the form is 7 × 9 inches. Using the principles of forms design that are presented in this chapter, indicate the good and poor features of this form.

5. A forms manufacturer has given you the completed design for the invoice form illustrated in Figure B. Prior to releasing the form for printing, you want to give the layout a final critical inspection. The actual size of the invoice is 7¼ × 10½ inches. Five copies of the form are to be completed in one writing for each shipment. The copies are to be identified by means of red type at the bottom of the form as follows: (1) Original Invoice, (2) Duplicate Invoice, (3) Remittance Copy, (4) Numerical File Copy, and (5) Alphabetical File Copy. Each copy is to be printed on a different color of paper stock. Consecutive invoice numbers beginning with 0001 will be preprinted in red at the time of printing.

    Examine the form carefully and indicate whether or not there are any last-minute changes that should be made before the final design is released for printing.

6. Luisa Perez is the newly employed office manager for the Sanchez Company. When she discovered that the company prepares a spirit master for duplicating 15 copies of its receiving reports, she asked for an explanation as this seemed an unusually large number of copies. The reply from the receiving department was, "We always

did it this way, even though there are extra copies. We don't want to change for fear that the extra copies will be needed. After all, it's just as easy to run off 15 copies as it is 10."

A subsequent study made by the office manager indicated that only six copies of the receiving report were needed, but that seven copies could be prepared in one typing.

(a) What are the probable reasons for the initial adoption of the inefficient procedure?
(b) What plan should have been followed when first installing the receiving report procedure?
(c) Give your recommendations for correcting this inefficient procedure.

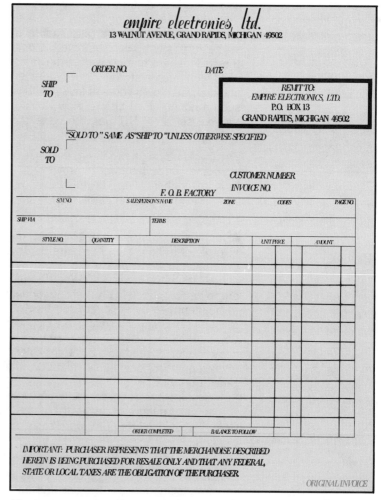

Fig. A
Example of Invoice Form

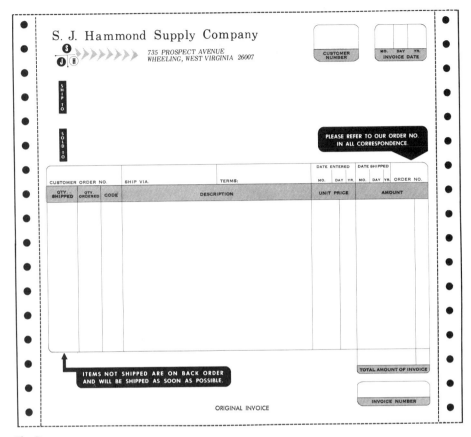

Fig. B
Completed Design for Invoice Form

PRACTICAL OFFICE MANAGEMENT CASES

Case 18-1 Converting to a Dual-Measurement System of Forms Management

As assistant office manager for the Buena Vista Food Wholesalers, you are responsible for all company forms. Your company has recently announced plans to develop branches throughout Central America with operations, including forms management, to be coordinated from the El Paso, Texas, headquarters office. This means that all forms data must be maintained in both metric and English measurements, as the entire Central American area utilizes the metric system while the United States offices retain the English measurement system. In order to meet the needs of a dual-measurement system, some immediate steps must be taken to develop the present forms systems to include metric data as such data affect all forms and the machines and equipment in which the forms are used.

Compile a short report in which you show both metric and English measurement data as they relate to the following needs of forms systems: (a) forms sizes for the five most frequently used forms; (b) space guidelines for designing forms with both vertical and horizontal spacing for handwritten and typewritten entries; (c) forms filing data for standard- and legal-size file cabinets and an estimate of the quantity of papers to be stored per inch or centimeter of space; and (d) measurement suggestions for setting up the most common types of paper documents such as instructions for business letter placement, manuscripts, tabulations, envelope address locations, and post card sizes.

Case 18-2 Consolidating Shipping and Billing Forms

As a manufacturer of custom-built home and office clocks, the Imperial Clock Company of Shelby, Ohio, presently uses three separately prepared forms to complete and ship an order. These forms are:

1. Shipping Label — one copy prepared by the shipping department from information provided by the stock control department. The copy is attached to each express package or parcel post package.
2. Invoice — prepared in quadruplicate in the billing department from information received from the shipping department.
3. Packing Slip and Shipping Memo — numbered consecutively and prepared in triplicate by the shipping department from information received from the stock control department. The Shipping Memo is sent by first-class mail to notify the customer of the shipment of the order; the Packing Slip accompanies the order.

Recently a small forms management program was installed in the company with a forms supervisor in charge of all company forms. Immediately the supervisor conducted a survey of all company forms; and upon analyzing their use, discovered a proliferation of forms and duplicate effort involved in processing the orders for clocks and supplies. Giving the order processing and billing procedures first priority, the supervisor found that, on the average, about 200 orders are shipped each day; and each of the three forms used for shipping, billing, and customer notification of shipment is typed in a separate department. After examining completed copies of the three forms, the supervisor noticed considerable duplicate information on the forms, with much of the following data commonly required by each of the three departments (the figure in parentheses indicates the number of digits or letters required for recording a typical "size" data item):

> order number (6); date (14); customer order number (5); sales representative name (14); customer name and address (50); how shipped (10); terms (16); quantity ordered (3); quantity shipped (3); back ordered (3); description (30); unit price (6); total amount (8); sales tax (5); invoice total (9).

After considerable discussion with manufacturers of business forms and with the departments involved, the forms supervisor feels that all three forms can be consolidated into one multiple-copy form and prepared in one location — the order processing section — in one single writing on typewriters equipped to handle continuous forms. From that location copies of the form could be distributed to the shipping department for labeling purposes and for inserting packing slips with the shipment. Also, the invoicing department would receive appropriate copies for completion of the billing procedure. Thus, no major overall systems changes would be required, for the consolidation of forms would affect only the forms and files involved.

As a junior forms analyst, you are asked to determine the main needs of each internal department of the company, as well as the information needs of the customer in order to recommend an improved forms procedure centered around a consolidated form.

After studying the information needs of the order-processing procedure, prepare a report that includes:

1. A sketch of a suitable multiple-copy form for use in the order-processing procedure of the company with suggestions for efficient preparation of the form.
2. An analysis of possible effects of the forms consolidation upon other elements of the office system. For example, there may be systems costs involved in making this forms change.

The discussion of systems studies in Chapter 17 as well as the material on effective forms design in this chapter should be considered carefully in developing a solution to this case.

Chapter 19

MECHANIZATION OF BASIC ACCOUNTING SYSTEMS

The application of laborsaving machinery and equipment to industrial processes doubtlessly accounts for the great growth in industrial societies throughout the world. Machines offered certain advantages over the employment of additional workers; and when combined with human labor, machines were able to raise productivity levels and effect great economies in the production of goods and services.

The earliest large-scale applications of machines to work processes occurred in factory operations, such as the steel mills in Pennsylvania and later the automobile plants near Detroit. Many office operations were also mechanized very early as the amount of information processing increased and as technology provided the machines to handle the repetitive office tasks. Such common machines as typewriters, dictating and transcribing machines, reproducing machines, and the various telecommunication devices have been cited previously for their important role in general office operations, largely in handling written and oral communications.

In addition to the widespread mechanization of communication operations, there is another major phase of office work involving the basic accounting systems of the firm in which machines have been successfully employed. To understand the nature of accounting systems one must remember that, in theory, the entire firm may be considered as a total system, as discussed in Chapter 17. In reality, however, the principal functional areas (such as marketing, finance, and accounting) are usually treated as the main operating systems of the firm. In turn, each system is divided into smaller units, or subsystems, that have all the basic characteristics of the "parent" system and hence are also called systems.

Four common accounting systems for which the administrative office manager has a major responsibility are: (1) order processing and billing, (2) payroll accounting, (3) purchasing and receiving, and (4) processing invoice payments to vendors. To a large extent each of these systems deals with numeric input data that must be processed in line with the output requirements of the system. In this chapter these four basic accounting systems are discussed in order to acquaint the students of administrative office management with the variety of basic accounting operations that fall under the jurisdiction of an office executive. Furthermore, many of the common computing and accounting machines and equipment are described in relation to their application in the basic accounting systems where the volume of data to be processed does not justify a computer. Through the use of mechanization in these systems, a major portion of the office work can be performed more rapidly, more accurately, and more economically.

GUIDELINES FOR MECHANIZING ACCOUNTING SYSTEMS

The effective office administrator is a successful allocator of resources, or in other words, one who has mastered the art of getting more productivity from the resources assigned to the office. This requires that the office administrator keep informed about the people, machines, and information needs as well as the continually rising costs of performing the work. In turn, such a manager must constantly search for better methods and equipment available for performing office work.

The successful use of machines in the communication and information storage and retrieval functions has been discussed in Part 2. However, mechanization has achieved its most rapid success in the data processing function, which for the business community has largely come to mean the efficient processing of numeric accounting data. The effective processing of accounting information is of special concern to top management, for such information involves the financial resources flowing into and out of the firm and upon which the firm depends for its survival. This places a strong responsibility upon the office manager to develop and maintain effective accounting systems and to consider mechanization of the accounting systems wherever feasible.

A bewildering array of machines supplied by dozens of companies make up the office machines industry. In fact, the number of new machines and machine improvements is overwhelming, even for the most specialized persons in the office. Moreover, there must be considered a host of machine services, supplies, and systems, which serves to compound the problems of arriving at "quick-and-easy" machines applications in the office. Thus, machines cannot be looked upon in isolation but must be viewed in a systems context as one key factor in a complex multifactor information system. Beyond the punched-card and electronic data processing systems there is a huge market for unsophisticated, easy-to-use devices for the many accounting operations in small companies and in decentralized locations — such as branch offices and warehouses — of large organizations.[1]

Why Mechanize?

This basic question has faced office managers since the earliest mechanical device was designed for processing data. Present-day managers of all types and sizes of offices assume that mechanization is necessary, but frequently they must deal with the puzzling questions of when to mechanize and to what extent. Answers to such questions become increasingly difficult as the line of demarcation between the noncomputer systems and computer systems becomes less distinct. Thus, overlaps in areas of application exist, and these are confusing to the manager who is considering the use of machines.

In general, machines are preferred for processing accounting data when

---

[1]Because of the great number of office machines on the market, the high degree of competition among machines manufacturers, and the difficulty of developing a clear perspective on machines use, office managers must compare competitive machines and study their applications before making decisions about acquiring new machines. To develop such perspective, see Carl Heyel, *Computers, Office Machines, and the New Information Technology* (Toronto: The Macmillan Company, 1969), as well as the "Tools of Administration" series of articles which appear regularly in *Administrative Management*.

they can perform the work more quickly and accurately, in better form for human use, and at a lower cost than by manual methods. While a few would argue with the general advantages of employing machines under certain conditions, such benefits are difficult to measure. Thus, the following specific reasons for mechanizing accounting systems, which point out more tangible benefits of mechanization, are especially valuable to the office manager:

1. Clerical labor costs may be reduced. For example, an electronic calculator costing less than $300 may save an hour of computing time each day for a $20,000-a-year office executive. Thus, the calculator will pay for itself in a few months.

2. The output produced by the machine is usually more legible, neater, and more accurate than if processed by human means. This machine advantage springs from the fact that machines are wholly physical devices while people as data processors are combinations of physical and psychological forces. Machines are not hindered by all the attitudes, stresses, fatigue, motivations, and skill levels inherent in people.

3. For many applications, such as performing arithmetic calculations, machines are much faster than workers. Solving square-root and multiple-digit multiplication problems dealing with decimals is extremely simple when electronic computing devices are used, but they are time-consuming and often difficult for the office worker to solve. Thus, large volumes of information can be handled in a shorter period of time and, at the same time, improve the operating efficiency of the accounting systems.

4. Since much of the work in accounting systems is routine and repetitive, methods and procedures can be standardized, thus permitting the office to handle large volumes of data by the use of machines. With standardization machines can be transferred from one department to another without the need for retraining personnel for the work which was mechanized and other work which was not.

5. Machines are effective space savers. They have become increasingly compact, with more processing power being built into smaller units, as is the case with the small electronic calculators. Compactness also permits building a lighter weight machine which promotes portability and more widespread use throughout the office. Thus, lower idle time for the machine results.

6. With the advent of electronics, noisy machines with typebars and mechanical computing and printing features have been replaced by quiet and easy-to-operate "touch-key" machines. These reduce both office noise and operator fatigue.

7. The operating limitations of machines, such as lines of output per minute, length of printing line, and the number of computations per second, can usually be determined, which simplifies the task of machine application. This machine advantage is especially helpful to the office manager who must evaluate today's information-processing needs in terms of the volume of work expected several years ahead.

While the advantages cited above should be verified by the office manager before machines are chosen, occasionally the mechanization of accounting systems saves nothing for the company. This happens when mechanization merely substitutes machine costs for the costs of clerks doing manual work. Such was the case in a payroll department where 25 clerks were busy twice a month around payday, but in the intervening period they had little to do. The payroll calculations previously accomplished by the payroll clerks were then mechanized and handled by the data processing department, but all of the clerical workers were retained in the payroll unit. Thus, the cost of mechanization added to the total cost of payroll preparation. Part of the reason for this ineffective overall system, although the machines were effectively used, was a human problem — the supervisors' perceptions of their status, which to them was reflected in the size of their office staffs.

Before mechanizing accounting systems, the reluctance of supervisors and their workers to mechanize should be explored and their job security assured. The accounting systems should also be studied to make sure that there is a clear-cut gain to be achieved by mechanization. The basic philosophy that must prevail is that it is not too difficult to change a mechanical process, but it is difficult to change people. Since it is people who direct the work performed in an office, their feelings, work habits, and work preferences should be carefully considered.

Office Manager's Role in Mechanization

A recurring theme throughout this book is the need for holding all office costs in line. When machines are considered for the various accounting systems within the organization, office managers must be both cost-conscious and machines-conscious and must understand the accounting systems sufficiently well to know when machines, rather than human labor, can be used most effectively and economically. As a

rule, to obtain the type of information required to make wise machine-selection decisions, the office manager must study the accounting systems following the guidelines for conducting systems studies that are outlined in Chapter 17. Such studies will normally involve the office manager in three decisions: (a) a determination of the need for certain types of mechanical equipment; (b) a comparison of the merits and costs of the various makes of similar equipment; and (c) a determination of the advisability of purchasing or leasing the equipment, as discussed in Chapter 5. This last decision is one of growing importance that has developed only in recent years when almost any type of equipment may be leased.

In the area of supervision, the personnel problems facing the office manager have become more challenging and varied. The characteristics and attributes of machine operators are not the same as those of other office personnel. The training and background of data-processing personnel present problems unlike those encountered elsewhere. One life insurance company spent a long time learning that the most efficient keypunch operators were those workers whose education did not take them beyond the lower high school grades. In some firms having centralized office management and control in the home office, with merely remote transmission and machine operations in the branch offices, the branch office supervisors have been placed on a higher managerial level and have entirely new responsibilities.

The rapid changes being brought about in the field of administrative office management by the newer methods, equipment, and materials involving automation necessitate that the office manager of the future be a more responsible executive — one whose duties will require a great amount of study, experimentation, and understanding of the total information system of the firm. Frequently in making decisions regarding the mechanization of accounting systems, many departments as well as the needs of customers and vendors are involved, which enlarges the scope of the manager's responsibilities. When the firm's machine capabilities are not adequate to handle all of the accounting work to be done, the office manager must be alert to the opportunities available for external processing of data discussed in the following section.

Using a Data Service Center

A *data service center* is an independent profit-making organization specializing in the processing of data for customer firms. The center is used by a firm with large-scale data processing equipment during peak-load periods when the firm's equipment is not adequate to handle all its needs. Other firms turn to the data service center to obtain the advantages of low unit-cost computing without getting involved in a major capital investment and the personnel problems entailed.

Data service centers may be independent service bureaus or, as is frequently the case, large commercial banks that rent out their excess computer capacity to others and perform data processing services. The services provided by these centers range from specialized systems that concentrate on payroll and related accounting systems work to elaborate personnel recordkeeping and information retrieval. For example, a leading New England real estate firm with branches throughout a six-

state area uses a service center for "instant" retrieval of available property listings throughout the region. For accounting systems, service centers specialize in such work as payroll, accounts receivable, order processing, sales analysis, and inventory control.

For the small business, data service centers fill a very crucial processing need. The advantages of using the services of such a center are:

1. No large investment in computers, auxiliary hardware, or other expensive equipment is required by the firm.
2. The work is done accurately and according to a prearranged turnaround time by the center.
3. Frequently there is a savings in the unit cost of processing data because of the skilled technical personnel and the efficiently programmed procedures and appropriate equipment. Accurate records on processing times and cost are provided, thereby furnishing better information for controlling costs to the customer.
4. There is a savings in payroll taxes and costs of employee benefits because the office staff is reduced.
5. A maximum of convenience is provided the customer. In some cases the data to be processed are picked up at the customer's office and the processed output is delivered back to the office at a specified time. In other cases the data may be deposited in a drive-in type of facility where the finished processed reports may be picked up later. The input of data to the center is usually simple and relatively inexpensive.

The costs of using data service centers will vary, depending on the nature and extent of the work performed. Information on such centers may be obtained from the representatives of machines manufacturers as well as from the "yellow pages" of the telephone directory in the larger cities. With the great expansion in data service centers throughout the country — numbering almost 2,000 — a national association was organized to establish ethical and professional practices in data service work, and to ensure that member companies maintain high standards of service and a uniform degree of operations. This association is called The Association of Data Processing Service Organizations (ADAPSO).

The variety and number of mechanized accounting systems applications found in offices seem almost infinite, and each has its own unique features. However, the basic accounting systems discussed in the following sections of this chapter are common to most organizations and have many common systems characteristics. An understanding of each system is facilitated by utilizing the input-process-output analysis provided by the systems approach. Important points to study, in this order of importance, are the objectives or the desired output of each system, the required input records and input data, and the most effective processing means for meeting the system's objectives.

ORDER PROCESSING AND BILLING SYSTEMS

The major source of income and working capital in business organizations is the revenue received from the sale of goods and services to their customers. The growth in sales volume coupled with a corresponding number of information-handling problems in order processing and billing point to the need for an effective system of accounting for all orders received and all customers billed.

The order processing and billing system is dependent upon accurate, timely data as input to the system from the various departments of the firm or from the customers directly. The departments involved and the forms used in order processing and billing systems are determined by the nature of the business, whether it be retailing, wholesaling, or manufacturing either for direct-to-consumer sales or for sales to wholesalers. The departments usually involved are: (1) the sales order department, existing either as two separate divisions (order processing and billing) or as a combined unit; (2) the warehouse and shipping department; and (3) the accounting and control departments. Commonly used forms are: (1) the sales order, (2) the shipping form, (3) the sales invoice, and (4) accounting records. In the mechanized systems in small firms, the forms may be prepared separately in the various departments, or they may be prepared as a part of *prebilling*, whereby the customer's invoice and its copies, together with the shipping order forms, are prepared simultaneously; or there may be a combination of these two methods. The forms may be handwritten or prepared on mechanical devices, but in all cases the objective of the overall system must not be overlooked. This objective is to utilize the most efficient order processing system to account for all sales beginning with the receipt of the order and ending with the production of management control information, including the invoice and accompanying accounting records.

In small companies simple manually operated computing and accounting machines are the only equipment needed in order to perform the billing function internally. When an outside data service center is hired to perform this work, this same equipment is usually sufficient to prepare the data as input to the center's computer. The data service center provides weekly or monthly reports to the small business firm and individual statements to be mailed to the company's customers. On these statements the unpaid items are listed by date and invoice number, regardless of how old the unpaid items happen to be. The company is also given printouts that show all unpaid items by date and invoice number, and the total sales for each of the last 12 months. A weekly or monthly summary report provided by the data service center shows the schedule of accounts receivable by age with supplementary information, such as credit limits, and how much of the outstanding account balance is current. Special reports are also prepared that list all customers' names by volume of business with the company, sales and returns for the month and the year, and salespersons' commissions.

Separate Order Processing and Billing Systems

A customer's order for goods or services usually follows one of the following patterns. A customer may send his or her order to the firm by letter or on a preprinted form, or the order form may be prepared by a salesperson who sends the form to the office, or the order may be given by telephone to a clerk in the order department. In most firms the customer's order must be approved by the credit department, after which the order department reviews the order for completeness and verifies the shipping instructions.

When separate order processing and billing systems are followed, separate forms are commonly prepared for the shipping order, the shipping report, and the sales invoice, as follows:

1. Shipping orders are prepared in the office and sent to the warehouse or shipping department. The number of copies prepared varies with the type of business organization and its products. As a minimum, three copies are usually prepared: the original copy and the packing slip, which are sent to the shipping department; and a file copy, which is retained in the office.

2. In the shipping department the packer prepares a separate shipping report. Three copies are ordinarily prepared: the original, which is sent to the office for pricing the shipment; the packing slip, which is included with the shipment; and a copy that is filed in the shipping department for any future reference.

Meanwhile the shipping department selects the goods ordered and prepares them for shipment. Where necessary, bills of lading may be prepared in quadruplicate. Two copies, an original and a duplicate, go to the transportation company; one copy is sent to the customer along with the invoice; and one copy is retained in the office.

3. The office (or billing department) receives a copy of the shipping report, together with a copy of the bill of lading.

If a complete order has been shipped, the shipping order is priced and sent to a billing clerk for calculating totals and the addition of freight and other charges where necessary. If the order was only partially filled, a back order or follow-up must be prepared to be used with the subsequent shipment, which will follow the same routine outlined above.

Billing clerks then prepare copies of the invoices. The number of copies again is affected by the type of business and its products. Four copies are usually the minimum number — one sent to the customer, one filed for future reference, one sent to the accounting department, and one retained in the billing department.

In the accounting department the invoice copies become the source or input documents for recording the sales and updating the accounts receivable ledger. If necessary, sales analyses by product, by department, by salesperson, or by geographical area may be developed from the invoice copies and incorporated into the records.

Figure 19-1 illustrates this separate order processing and billing system.

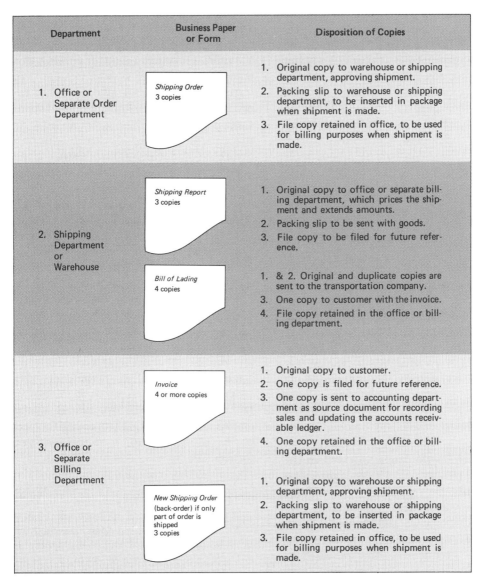

Department	Business Paper or Form	Disposition of Copies
1. Office or Separate Order Department	*Shipping Order* 3 copies	1. Original copy to warehouse or shipping department, approving shipment. 2. Packing slip to warehouse or shipping department, to be inserted in package when shipment is made. 3. File copy retained in office, to be used for billing purposes when shipment is made.
2. Shipping Department or Warehouse	*Shipping Report* 3 copies	1. Original copy to office or separate billing department, which prices the shipment and extends amounts. 2. Packing slip to be sent with goods. 3. File copy to be filed for future reference.
	Bill of Lading 4 copies	1. & 2. Original and duplicate copies are sent to the transportation company. 3. One copy to customer with the invoice. 4. File copy retained in the office or billing department.
3. Office or Separate Billing Department	*Invoice* 4 or more copies	1. Original copy to customer. 2. One copy is filed for future reference. 3. One copy is sent to accounting department as source document for recording sales and updating the accounts receivable ledger. 4. One copy retained in the office or billing department.
	New Shipping Order (back-order) if only part of order is shipped 3 copies	1. Original copy to warehouse or shipping department, approving shipment. 2. Packing slip to warehouse or shipping department, to be inserted in package when shipment is made. 3. File copy retained in office, to be used for billing purposes when shipment is made.

Fig. 19-1

Separate Order Processing and Billing System

Separate order processing and billing systems involve a large amount of duplication of effort, writing, and forms. There may be reasons for requiring such a system, however. The customer's product specifications may be complex and yet not have to be shown on the sales invoice. Many orders may not be shipped complete at one time and therefore require rather involved back-order or follow-up procedures. Sometimes the seller is permitted to substitute other merchandise for that ordered; thus, the customer's order and the sales invoice will not be identical. But a separate order processing and billing system must be considered inefficient, except where its installation is absolutely necessary.

Unified Prebilling Systems

In contrast to the separate order and billing systems discussed previously, *unified prebilling systems* are designed so that in *one* writing the shipping order, the shipping report, the customer's invoice, and in some cases, the sales journal entry are prepared. This system presupposes that the firm has on hand the required merchandise to fill the orders so that there will be few, if any, back orders. Also, the forms must have been carefully designed so that the information can be recorded on all forms in one writing.

Sometimes the steps followed in the unified prebilling system are modified so that only the shipping order and the shipping record are prepared in one writing; the invoice and the sales journal entry are completed in a second writing. To reduce the time required in completing the various forms, most firms use forms that are preassembled with one-time carbon paper. Increased

use is also being made of carbonless and carbon-coated paper in the construction of preassembled forms, in the form of packs, or in continuous feed forms.

The Write-It-Once Order Processing and Billing System

The *write-it-once* order processing and billing system makes use of duplicating or reproducing equipment and specified procedural steps for using this equipment. In this system a stencil or translucent paper for photographic reproduction contains the basic or constant data that will appear repeatedly on the customer's order, the production order (if the firm manufactures the goods before shipment), the invoice, and the sales journal. The variable data are inserted later by hand or by typewriter. The various forms used must be carefully designed so that all the same information will appear in the same location on each form; so that information which must not appear or some forms will be blocked out; and where an order is only partially filled, so that the master stencil can be reused for future completion of the transaction.

Figure 19-2 illustrates the write-it-once principle applied in the order processing and billing system for a manufacturing concern. In this system which employs duplicating equipment for preparing multiple copies of the required forms:

1. A master stencil is prepared from the customer's order.
2. Using the stencil and the appropriate forms with areas properly blocked out so that unwanted data do not appear on certain copies, the following forms are prepared: a production order to manufacturing departments; order acknowledgment; labels for shipment; packing

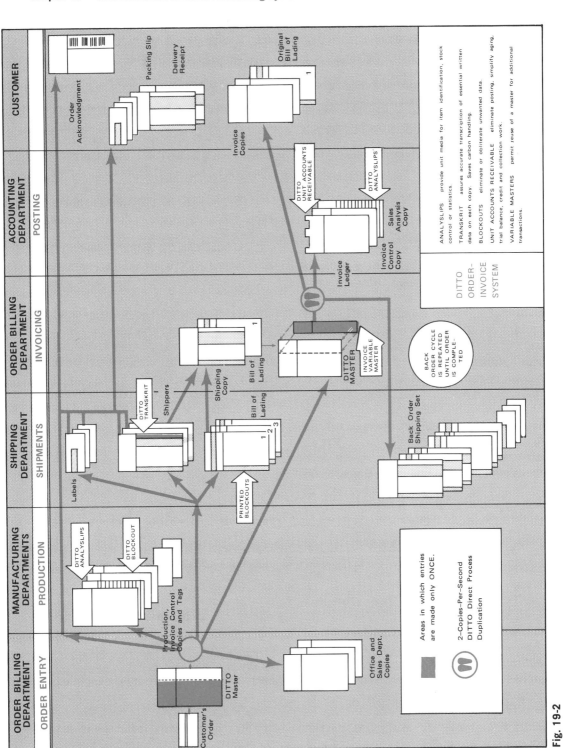

Fig. 19-2
Write-It-Once Order Processing and Billing System Using Ditto Direct Process Method of Duplication

slip; bill of lading; invoice copy for Accounts Receivable Ledger; a similar invoice copy for Sales Analysis; and the invoice for the customer.

3. In the event of partial shipment, a new master stencil is prepared to cover the back order, and the steps in the system are repeated until the order is shipped in full.

Cycle Billing

For many years the public utility companies and large retail stores with many customers buying on credit were faced with a tremendous volume of work in sending out statements at the end of each month. Such a regular billing operation resulted in an overload of work during the latter part of each month, while during earlier parts of the months the staff experienced a slack in their work. To overcome this regular peak-and-valley workload, an ingenious office employee developed an improved billing system known as *cycle billing*, which distributes evenly throughout the month the work connected with the preparation and mailing of monthly statements of account. Cycle billing has proved to be an effective accounting technique and is used today by many public utilities, retail stores, banks, telephone companies, and stock brokerage and industrial firms.

To overcome the difficulty of peak loads at the end of the month and to obtain a more uniform distribution of work throughout the month, firms using cycle billing divide their customers' accounts alphabetically into groups. There may be as many as 16 or 20 groups, each of which should be about equal in size in order to balance the work among the billing department personnel. Each

group represents a cycle and covers certain letters of the alphabet and certain days of the month. For example, statements to customers in the alphabetic group A–B may be sent out on the first mailing day of each month; and on the next mailing day, statements are mailed for the C–D group, with the system continued during the entire month until the last cycle — the W–Z group — is completed.

Following the closing day for each cycle group, a single billing operation is performed. Statements for all active accounts may be thus produced in one high-speed run. With the division of the accounts receivable ledger into several independent, alphabetic groups and the closing of each of these groups at a different time during the month, the daily work load is spread more evenly throughout the month, which reduces the need for overtime and extra part-time workers. Collection schedules, cash intake, and all supporting operations flow more evenly.

PAYROLL ACCOUNTING SYSTEMS

Payroll accounting is a highly specialized part of the overall accounting function for which efficient systems must be developed for every organization. It is important that all workers be paid on time, and that their paychecks and the corresponding payroll records for the company be prepared as accurately and as inexpensively as possible. With governmental agencies making increasing and more frequent demands on business firms for payroll and tax records, the time and money expended for payroll work is of vital significance to the office manager.

There are many variables in payroll accounting systems. Some of these arise as a result of the type of business activity, and others as a result of the type of wage-payment plans, incentives, and bonuses. The payroll system for a life insurance company or a bank that has mostly clerical workers paid on a weekly or semimonthly basis is much simpler than that of a manufacturing concern paying some of its workers on a piecerate basis, others on an hourly basis, and office employees on a weekly basis. Furthermore, there are certain legal requirements as to minimum wages and hours, income tax and social security deductions, and unemployment compensation and disability insurance taxes that must be taken into consideration in the preparation of payrolls. It becomes apparent that computing all the deductions and taxes, with different limitations on the amount taxable in any one year, makes the payroll system complicated and expensive. It also indicates that in most cases mechanical equipment must be used, for such equipment will permit simultaneous preparation of the forms and will accumulate the various totals from one pay period to the next, all automatically. Systems such as these are particularly suited to electronic computer operations, as described in Chapter 21.

Because of the mounting costs and requirements of payroll accounting work, it has become increasingly important for the office manager to inaugurate systems and procedures that will do the work more quickly, more accurately, and at less cost. To be able to do this, the office manager should become familiar with various methods and procedures that can be used in payroll accounting systems. As in the case of order processing and billing systems, payroll systems may also be automated when the volume of work involved in payroll preparation and reporting consistently overloads the internal system. Data service centers are well equipped to handle payroll accounting and can provide about 95 percent of the data processing work required by law for reporting purposes. Typical services provided by such centers include the writing and signing of payroll checks; preparing the payroll register; reconciling the payroll account with the bank statement; preparing and filing the various payroll tax reports; and preparing, as needed, job or departmental cost reports.

A Basic Payroll Accounting Systems Model

The payroll operation in an organization may be viewed as a special application of the basic systems model discussed in Chapter 17. To better understand the essential role of mechanization in a payroll system, a similar systems model — in this case designed specifically to explain the payroll function as an operating system — is illustrated in Figure 19-3.

In this illustration two common bases for paying employees are noted: *hourly pay*, with combined time and payroll deductions data accumulated on a time card, such as that shown in Figure 19-4, to be verified by the timekeeping department and forwarded to the payroll department for processing. (Similar processing steps are followed for employees on the piece-rate method of payment.) *Salary pay* is a second method of payment in which employees — frequently managers, supervisors, and most office workers — are paid a set weekly or monthly rate. To improve the efficiency of the overall payroll operation, mechanization has been applied to the input of data (the recording of time on the employee time card) as well as to verifying and computing processes outlined in the process block of the systems model and discussed in the following section.

Types of Payroll Accounting Systems

In this section several typical payroll accounting systems are described and illustrated. Each of the systems makes use of one or more of the following accounting records and simple mechanical devices and equipment:

1. Combination time record and payroll journal.
2. Accounting board.
3. Unit control.
4. Addressing system.

Additional equipment, such as the computing and accounting machines required to process the payroll data, are treated in a later section of this chapter.

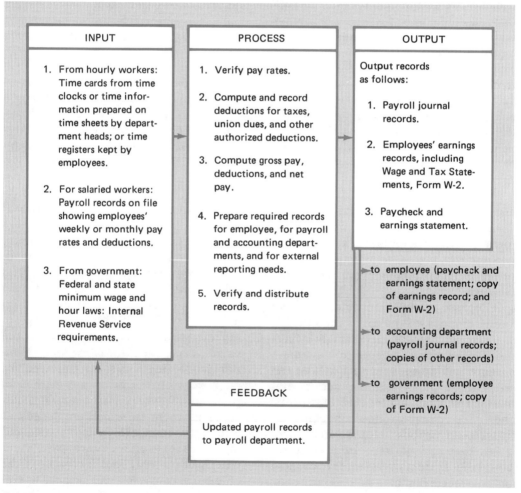

Fig. 19-3
A Basic Payroll Accounting Systems Model

NO. **12**

NAME Perry R. Archer PAY END JUL 1 19--

REG. TIME HRS. _40_ RATE _3.90_ AMT. _156.00_
OVERTIME HRS. _2_ RATE _5.85_ _11.70_

TOTAL EARNINGS _167.70_

FED. W. TAX _10.40_
STATE W. TAX _1.68_
F. I. C. A. _9.81_
INS. _.90_
OTHER _____ TOTAL DEDUCTIONS _22.79_

AMOUNT DUE _144.91_

Days	MORNING		AFTERNOON		OVERTIME		Daily Totals
	IN	OUT	IN	OUT	IN	OUT	
1	MO 7 59	12 03	1 00	5 05			8
2	TU 7 50	12 04	12 59	5 07			8
3	WE 7 51	12 01	12 50	5 04	5 29	7 35	10
4	TH 8 00	12 02	12 58	5 03			8
5	FR 8 00	12 05	1 01	5 06			8
6	SA						
7							

Fig. 19-4
Employee Time Card

Combination Time Record and Payroll Journal. One of the simplest types of payroll accounting systems utilizes a combination time record and payroll journal similar to the one illustrated in Figure 19-5. In small firms this payroll record is commonly prepared by hand. The record may be used with or without time cards. Although this system is simple, it is laborious; and its use is recommended only where the clerk responsible for preparing the payroll records has sufficient time left over to do other work.

Accounting Board. The *accounting board*, often called the *pegboard*, utilizes carefully designed handwritten forms prearranged in shingle-like fashion for the simultaneous preparation of the payroll journal, the individual employee's earnings record, and the pay envelope or the payroll check. This simplified manual system requires that the forms necessary for preparing the payroll records mentioned previously be designed so that, in one writing, identical information appears in the same location on each form. Thus, by use of

PAYROLL REGISTER

FOR WEEK ENDING _January 17_ 19_ _

No.	NAME	Marital Status	No. Exemp.	M	T	W	T	F	S	RATE PER HOUR	AMOUNT	Hours	RATE	AMOUNT
				TIME RECORD						**REGULAR EARNINGS**		**OVERTIME EARNINGS**		
1	10 Adams, Ralph C.	M	3	8	8	8	8	8	4	3 10	1 24 00	4	4 65	1 8 60
2	12 Archer, Perry R.	M	4	8	8	8	8	10		3 90	1 56 00	2	5 85	1 1 70
3	13 Atwater, Betty C.	S	1	8	8	8	8	8		4 75	1 90 00			
4	23 Baker, Lloyd J.	M	2	8	8	8	8	8	8	3 60	1 44 00	8	5 40	4 3 20
5	24 Barrett, Ann P.	S	1	8	8	8	0	8		4 70	1 50 40			
36	Totals										24 9 7 20			26 5 50

Fig. 19-5 (left page)

Handwritten Time Record and Payroll Journal

carbon paper, spot-carbonized forms, or carbonless paper, only one writing is necessary to prepare all records simultaneously through the use of the equipment shown in Figure 19-6. The accounting board system is simple in concept and easy to use. Also, it is inexpensive to purchase and maintain and yet has the advantages that more expensive machine methods provide in simultaneously preparing several records. The accounting board can also be effectively used in other accounting systems applications, such as accounts receivable and accounts payable, where several records using identical data may be prepared at one writing. By using this system, small and medium-size businesses can benefit from the economies and accuracies of mechanized accounting equipment without having to buy expensive machines or employ specially trained operators.

Unit Control. Under the *unit control* or *ledgerless accounting* system, these procedural steps are followed. Multiple copies of the paycheck or pay envelope are prepared by hand or on the typewriter. One of the multiple copies is then filed by employee name and serves as a record for the later preparation of the employee's annual withholding tax statement. A second copy may be summarized weekly and used as the payroll journal, while a third copy may be filed by check number (if the employees are paid by check.) Because of the number of separate forms that must be used, this manual system is usually restricted to firms having few employees.

Addressing System. Addressing equipment is most commonly associated with the preparation of permanent mailing lists for the repetitive addressing of large numbers of envelopes and cards. However, the equipment used for such large-volume addressing operations may be combined with other recording functions to print identifying information on time cards, paychecks, and other payroll records and reports. Through the use of the Addresserprinter, one form of addressing system illustrated in Figure 19-7, basic employee information and

DEPT. ACCOUNTING – 10

TOTAL EARNINGS	DEDUCTIONS					Check No.	NET PAID	TAXABLE EARNINGS		
	FICA TAX	GROUP INS.	FED. INCOME TAX	STATE INCOME TAX	OTHER		AMOUNT	FICA	FUTA	
142 60	8 34	90	8 80	1 43		898	123 13	142 60	142 60	1
167 70	9 91	90	10 40	1 68		899	144 91	167 70	167 70	2
190 00	11 12	1 10	31 40	1 90		900	144 48	190 00	190 00	3
187 20	10 95	1 10	20 20	1 87		901	153 08	187 20	187 20	4
150 40	8 80	90	22 20	1 50		902	117 00	150 40	150 40	5
2762 70	161 62	14 70	279 60	27 63			2279 15	2762 70	2762 70	36

(right page)

Fig. 19-5
Handwritten Time Record and Payroll Journal

payroll data are integrated into an effective mechanized payroll system.

At the heart of the Addresserprinter system is the master record of information contained on the one-piece metal plate, which is prepared on a machine called the Embosser. The metal plate contains constant information such as the name, address, date, employee and social security numbers, and other required payroll data. Once embossed on the metal plate and verified, this payroll information becomes an original source record from which data may be repetitively transferred to any payroll record, such as the time card, wage and tax

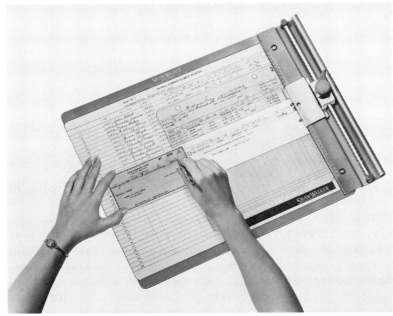

The Shaw-Walker Co.

Fig. 19-6
Accounting Board

Pitney-Bowes

Fig. 19-7
The Addresserprinter

statement, and the Form 941A shown in Figure 19-8 or imprinted on any other record with complete accuracy. Increased flexibility in the use of the metal plates is obtained by extracting and imprinting only certain desired information from the plates.

Because of its relatively high operating speed, the Addresserprinter is adaptable to small as well as large payrolls. Furthermore, the equipment may be used for many applications other than payroll accounting — compiling membership lists, cutting stencils to be used in imprinting addresses on outgoing packages, imprinting customers' names and addresses on ledger cards that are later reproduced to serve as monthly statements, writing insurance annuity and installment checks, and preparing statistical reports.

PURCHASING-RECEIVING SYSTEMS

The *purchasing system* is responsible for selecting the best sources of goods and services for a firm and for the placement of orders for goods and services when needed. As a companion function, the *receiving system* is responsible for the physical verification of the quantities of goods and services actually received as orders are filled and for the recording of quantities and costs of the goods and services. Together the purchasing-receiving system constitutes an important specialized branch of the basic accounting systems found in organizations and one in which the mechanization of the repetitive, routine paperwork operations can save time and reduce administrative costs.

One of the critical subsystems in the purchasing area involves the collection of data to be processed, duplicated, and distributed to all departments concerned. With the use of the *diazo copying process*, similar to those copying processes discussed in Chapter 10, many copies of anything written, typed, printed, or drawn on *translucent* paper can be reproduced in seconds from the same original source documents. Since most repetitive writing appears on forms created for internal use, the company forms should be initially printed on translucent paper or card stock in order to utilize this particular copying process. The procedural steps followed in implementing a typical purchasing-receiving system that employs the diazo copying process are listed below and illustrated in Figure 19-9.

1. The purchase order is typed on a multiple-copy form, signed, and distributed to the vendor; the purchasing, receiving, and accounts payable departments; the requestor; and the numeric file.
2. The Receiving Copy of the purchase order, containing columns for recording multiple receipts, is filed. Each receipt against the original purchase order is recorded successively on this translucent form, thus eliminating a separate receiving report form for each receipt of goods.
3. When the first shipment arrives, the receiving clerk pulls the translucent form out of the file, verifies the contents of each package received, and fills in only the receiving information at the bottom of the form. There is no need to transcribe the vendor's name, descriptions, codes, and other information since it has previously been

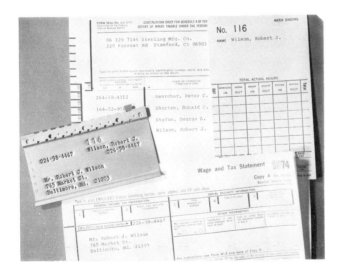

Pitney-Bowes

Fig. 19-8
Payroll Records Imprinted from the Addresserprinter Plate

1. Typing Purchase Order

Purchase order is typed on a multiple-part form, then signed and distributed to vendor, purchasing, receiving, accounts payable, requisitioner, expediter, and numerical file.

4. Producing Receiving Reports

After receiving data are entered, the form is inserted into a Bruning machine together with a sheet of Bruning paper. Copies are made on white and color-tinted paper for material identification, accounts payable, purchasing, and for any other departments or individuals concerned. The flexible Bruning process permits making additional copies when needed, such as for special purchases involving research personnel.

2. Filing Receiving Copy

This copy of the purchase order contains columns for recording multiple receipts, thus eliminating a separate receiving report form for each receipt of goods. Each receipt against the original purchase order is recorded successively on this translucent form.

5. Matching, Auditing and Preparing for Payment

In the accounts payable department, the Bruning receiving copy is matched with a copy of the purchase order and the vendor's invoice. If all items are in agreement, the invoice is OK'd for payment. The job of sorting and matching can be eased by using color-tinted paper (such as green for the original purchase order and pink for the Bruning receiving copy).

3. Recording First Receipt

Receiving clerk pulls translucent form out of the file. After verifying contents of each package, clerks fills in only receiving information at the bottom of the form. There is no need to transcribe vendor name, descriptions, codes, and other order information, because it is already in the purchase order section of the form.

6. Recording Successive Receipts Against Same Purchase Order

For each successive receipt of goods against the same purchase order, the same translucent receiving form is again pulled out of the file and receiving data is added to the previous record. Bruning copies are made and distributed as before. Latest receiving reports is a complete file in itself, showing all receipts to date.

Source: Taken from "Bruning for Business, A Guide to Paperwork Simplification," with permission of the Bruning Division of Addressograph-Multigraph Corporation, Schaumburg, IL 60196.

Fig. 19-9

Procedural Steps Followed in Using the Diazo Copying Process in a Purchasing-Receiving System

recorded in the purchase order section of the form.

4. After the receiving data are entered, the form is inserted into the copying machine, and copies are made for distribution to the proper departments and individuals.

5. In the accounts payable department, the reproduced Receiving Copy is matched with a copy of the purchase order and the vendor's invoice. If all items are in agreement, the invoice is approved for payment.

6. For each successive receipt of goods against the same purchase order, the same translucent receiving form is again pulled out of the file and receiving data are added to the previous record. Copies are made and distributed as before, with the latest receiving report representing a complete file in itself, showing all receipts to date.

As a result of employing the diazo copying process as part of the purchasing-receiving system, the following advantages are realized:

1. The transcribing of purchase order details by the receiving clerk to a separate receiving report form is eliminated. Handwriting is reduced to recording the receiving information only.

2. A translucent receiving report form (prepared as part of the purchase order) that can accommodate multiple receipts against a single purchase order is provided. The translucent form can be used for reproducing any number of receiving report copies.

3. Incoming materials are quickly moved to their point of use, and at the same time prompt notification of receipt of goods and services is given to the purchasing department.

4. Maximum control over all operations — from purchase to payment — is ensured.

INVOICE-PROCESSING SYSTEMS

In an accounts payable operation, the processing of vendors' invoices for payment requires frequent references to related filed documents, such as invoices, purchase orders, and receiving orders. Direct examination of one or more of these source documents is needed to reconcile any discrepancies between what was ordered from the supplier and what was received; to account for differences between prices quoted and prices billed; and to answer questions about important purchase information, such as the status of open orders, delivery dates, and shipping information.

Frequently these references to filed documents are time-consuming, even resulting in delay in making payments when the records are not immediately accessible. Further, such file references require the use of expensive clerical help. To reduce the cost of retrieving accounts payable documents and to expedite the rapid processing of invoices for payment, many firms have turned to mechanization of their invoice-processing systems through the installation of micrographic machines. Such a machine system for photographing, storing, and retrieving information in microrecord form, a topic which was discussed in Chapter 10, may be readily adaptable either to computerized operations or to less sophisticated nonautomated accounts payable operations.

One type of simple mechanized microfilm system is designed for storing and retrieving vendors' invoices and does not require the use of a computer in its operations. Such a system operates as follows:

1. After the incoming invoices have been approved for payment and the pay date added, they are microfilmed in random

sequence. As the invoice is automatically fed into the microfilmer, an identifying code number is first imprinted on each invoice, and then the invoice passes into the microfilmer for photographing. As the document is photographed, a code is simultaneously recorded on the film alongside each document. As many as 3,000 invoices, each sequentially numbered, can be recorded in this manner on a 100-foot role of 16mm microfilm. Each invoice is tied into a code that becomes the key to retrieving a specific image after the film has been processed and loaded into film magazines.

2. After each batch of invoices has been microfilmed, the invoices are put through the normal accounting procedures to create payment checks for the vendors. The imprinted numbers on the invoices are entered into the paying process and thus appear on any listings or registers such as the voucher register or the check register. The sequential imprinted numbers provide the control index by means of which any particular invoice can be located on its roll of microfilm which is housed in the information retrieval center.

3. After the invoice has been paid, it may be destroyed or sent to the vendor with the check in payment of the amount due. The microfilm record provides the complete information required at any time.

4. When a microrecord is requested, the appropriate film cartridge is selected from the film file in the information retrieval center and placed in a retrieval terminal, as shown in Figure 19-10. The proper sequential index number is keyed into the retrieval unit, the start button is depressed, and the film advances automatically. By means of the previously recorded codes, the number of images is counted until the desired

Eastman Kodak Co.

Fig. 19-10

A Stand-Alone Terminal Used to Retrieve Information on Vendors' Invoices in an Invoice-Processing System

invoice number is reached. At this point the film stops and the image of the requested invoice appears on the visual display screen of the reader. The entire retrieval operation takes about five seconds. If needed, a readable-size facsimile print can be made which is delivered in seconds by the retrieval unit.[2]

MACHINES USED IN ACCOUNTING SYSTEMS

Throughout the history of the office, machines and other devices have been applied to the solution of mathematical problems. The spectrum of machines ranges from the hand-operated abacus, still used frequently in the Orient, to the wide variety of electronic computers that have revolutionized the data-processing world. In between these widely varying machines systems are two general-office machine groups — basic computing machines and basic accounting machines. Each of these machine families and their applications to basic accounting systems are discussed in this section.

Basic Computing Machines

In each of the accounting systems discussed in this chapter, the various kinds of basic computing machines shown in Figure 19-11 are ordinarily used. At one time, however, the most common type of computing machine found in the office was the *adding machine*. This machine was available in a number of different makes and models and was used primarily for addition and

subtraction. A second type of computing machine is the *calculator*, which performs each of the four basic arithmetic operations, but is designed especially for high-speed multiplication and division.[3] Prior to the development of electronic circuitry, such as that found in electronic computers, most of the basic computing machines were constructed with mechanical rotating "counting" wheels for performing the arithmetic operations. Many were hand-operated, although electrical models have been most popular because of their greater speed of operation.

With the application of electronics to the counting process in computers, the technology of high-speed, compact circuits was adapted to the basic computing machines. The result has been a series of drastic changes in the nature and availability of those machines, and the gradual obsolescence of some of the time-honored computing machines, especially the adding machines and the mechanical calculators. However, no matter how sophisticated the data processing system, there is a need for some basic computing machines in every office. Many of these machines are used to provide the input for computer systems as well as to perform some of the tasks that do not lend themselves to computer applications.

The basic computing machines may be classified as follows: listing and non-listing, full-keyboard, and ten-key.

---

[2]The operation of the microfilm system is adapted from Kodak's Recordak Microfilm System, "Accounts Payable," with permission of Eastman Kodak Company, Business Systems Markets Division.

[3]The American National Standards Institute defines calculating machines as devices having manual means for entering numerical data and intended primarily for multiplying or dividing; however, they may be used for adding or subtracting. There are two major classifications of these machines: printing calculating machines and nonprinting calculating machines. Business organizations typically shorten these terms to printing calculators and calculators.

Courtesy of
Sharp Electronics Corporation

Electronic Printing Calculator

Victor Comptometer Corporation

Electronic Display Calculator

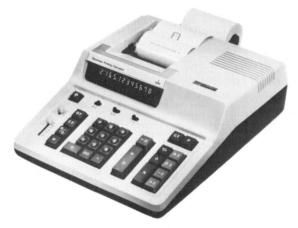

Courtesy of
Sharp Electronics Corporation

Combination Electronic Display and Printing Calculator

Fig. 19-11
Basic Computing Machines

Hewlett-Packard

Programmable Calculator

Listing and Nonlisting Machines. A *listing* machine not only records the individual numbers of a problem in the internal register of the machine but also prints these numbers on a paper tape. Verifying the accuracy of the answer is thus simplified since the individual numbers and the totals appear on the tape along with identification information, such as a date or account number, if desired. Some listing machines, such as the full-keyboard listing machine and the ten-key listing machine, are used most frequently for addition purposes; others, particularly the mechanical and electronic printing calculators, perform all arithmetic operations and are used for a wide range of office problems involving credit balance, negative multiplication, automatic squaring, and carrying constants in their internal registers.

A *nonlisting* machine, such as the electronic calculator, is not equipped with the paper tape but records the numbers only in the register of the machine with answers appearing in the dials or visual display screen. Nonlisting machines are claimed to be much faster than listing machines, thus making it feasible to do the problem a second time for the purpose of verifying. The most common nonlisting machines have been the *rotary* calculator (with answer dials on the machine's movable carriage) which is now largely outdated by the electronic calculator; and the key-driven calculator (on which calculations are performed by depressing the keys), which is especially well adapted to problems requiring fast addition and multiplication. While both of these machines are no longer manufactured, many are still in use, with the rotary calculator primarily used for complex multiplication and division problems.

Full-Keyboard and Ten-Key Machines. A *full-keyboard* machine may have from five to 20 columns of numbers, with each column containing keys from 1 to 9. A zero is automatically registered in any column in which no number key is depressed. Such a machine provides full visibility of the numbers entered on the keyboard. Common examples of full-keyboard machines are the full-keyboard adding machines, rotary calculators, keydriven calculators, and the accounting machines described later in this chapter.

The *ten-key* machine has a keyboard that consists of one set of keys numbered 0 through 9. The digits of a number must be entered in the order of their occurrence. Zeros must be entered whenever they occur, but some ten-key machines have double and triple zero keys that speed the entry of large numbers. The ten-key model is especially adaptable to "touch" operation and has wide application in solving mathematical problems containing many digits. Typical of the ten-key machine are the ten-key adding machine, the mechanical printing calculator, and the full range of electronic calculators. Because of their overwhelming dominance in the computing machine field, electronic calculators are treated individually in the next section.

Electronic Calculators. Electronic calculators have revolutionized the field of basic computing machines in the same way that computers have monopolized the field of large-scale data processing. The electronic calculator is a miniature desktop computer that performs operations electronically rather than mechanically. The machine operates at the speed of light and is completely silent. One of the major advantages of this machine is its excellent performance as the result of no moving parts that wear out and cause inaccuracies.

The three types of electronic calculators that are discussed in this section include the two electronic desktop calculators and the programmed calculator. A miniature version of the desktop machine, the small pocket-size "hand-held" electronic calculator, is not included in this discussion.

Electronic Desktop Calculators. In a few short years electronic desktop calculators, examples of which are shown in Figure 19-11, have become the most common and highly regarded computing machines for general-office use. In addition to the general advantages cited previously for using electronic calculators, the desktop units possess other desirable features. Electronic calculators have storage memories or registers that enable the machines to hold and store many different totals for continuous use in operations, thus eliminating the possibility of error in manually reentering or transferring amounts. Also, they are equipped to perform many special functions, such as square root, automatic rounding of numbers, credit balance, storage and recall of constants, and automatic decimal placement that are valuable for general-office and accounting systems use. Because of their increasingly low purchase cost, their ease of operation, and low maintenance costs, electronic calculators have become an essential computing tool.

Electronic desktop calculators are usually classified by their mode of output. One type, known simply as the *electronic calculator*, has a display screen much like the cathode-ray tube display described in Chapter 8. Another type,

called an *electronic printing calculator*, performs its computing operations at noiseless electronic speeds and prints out on a paper tape which is actuated mechanically with relatively noisefree performance. Another machine combines the display screen with the tape and thus offers the operator a choice as to which mode of output to use. Electronic printing calculators cost more than those with display units with comparable features but have the added advantage of providing a record of the calculations made.[4]

Programmed Calculators. In terms of processing power, complexity, and cost, programmed calculators represent a more advanced step in the development of desktop calculators, combining the keyboard of a calculator with the power of a small computer. Programmed calculators are available in *preprogrammed* models in which the operator has only to push a key, such as for extracting a square root, to execute the internally stored program. More common are the *programmable* calculators with input devices for entering an operator-written program into the storage register of the machine to be executed as the problem data are entered for later output on a display screen or on a paper tape. For business problem-solving, the simplest level of programming has the operator depress a number of preprogrammed keys which access a prestored program in memory to solve a problem. With some experience the operator can

---

[4]An excellent digest of information on the many calculators available is the "Tools of Administration" series appearing regularly in *Administrative Management*. For an overview of this rapidly expanding machines area, see Rick Minicucci, "The New Calculators — They Print, They're Programmable," *Administrative Management* (July, 1976), pp. 28–30, 32, 34, 36.

prepare his or her own programs or rely on the manufacturer's program library, often stored on punched cards or magnetic cards, for entry into the machine. Programs that are stored on cards are available for such business processing tasks as loan amortization, interest calculations, invoicing, discounting, standard deviation, and metric conversion, and are stored externally to be reused whenever the repetitive processing operation is required.

Basic Accounting Machines

Accounting machines, also known as *bookkeeping machines*, not only record entries in ledger accounts and journals but also perform many of the simpler arithmetic operations of the basic computing machines discussed earlier. Furthermore, accounting machines extend balances and provide direct and indirect methods of verifying the accuracy of the amounts recorded. For such jobs as billing, payroll, and general ledger record keeping, managers with a medium-to-high volume of accounting work require one of several types of basic accounting machines. They can choose electromechanical accounting equipment, or equivalent electronic machines below the small business computer level, such as those machines described in this section.

Although the trend is toward the replacement of electromechanical accounting machines by electronic units, there is a large market remaining for the electromechanical units that are particularly well-suited for those small business operations considered uneconomical for a computer. Two types of units are found: the numeric accounting machines, sometimes called posting machines, and the alphanumeric accounting machines.

Numeric accounting machines are full-keyboard adding machines with date keys and are capable of horizontal addition and subtraction operations. Numeric accounting machines are used wherever the accounting operation does not require a completely itemized alphabetic description, such as the posting of ledger cards involved in updating a customer's account and preparing the statement of account. In a payroll operation they are used to prepare the payroll journal, the paycheck or envelope, and the employee's earnings record.

More frequently, alphanumeric accounting machines are used to improve the efficiency of the accounting system. An *alphanumeric accounting machine* is a typewriter-calculating machine with a dual alphabetic and numeric keyboard. This type of machine is widely used in accounting work requiring the typing of names, descriptions of transactions, and the computation of numeric data common to billing and payroll systems.

Electronic Billing Machines. Although widespread use of electromechanical alphanumeric accounting machines continues, all of the major manufacturers of these machines have converted entirely to electronic models for reasons cited earlier. An example of such an electronic system that is specially designed for customer billing is shown in Figure 19-12. This simple system combines an input-output typewriter with alphanumeric capability and an electronic processing unit to type and compute the numeric data. The billing program is stored in the processing unit along with the individual customer data that have been stored externally on magnetic cards and inserted into the typewriter for use in the program. Once the program has been activated, the constant items are printed out automatically

Monroe, The Calculator Company

Fig. 19-12
An Electronic Billing System with Input-Output Typewriter and Production Unit

along with all calculations, automatic spacing, and preparation of totals. As shown in Figure 19-13, only the individual items to be billed need be entered by the typist. Such a system offers great speed and accuracy; and because of its simplicity, no knowledge of programming is required. The equipment is relatively inexpensive compared with machines in the minicomputer class and is capable of reducing labor costs and collection delays to a significant degree.

Electronic Accounting Computers. A more automated application of accounting systems is the *dual-pass* payroll and departmental labor cost analysis system which uses the electronic accounting computer shown in Figure 19-14.[5] In the first pass of this operation the basic payroll and time data are taken from employee time cards. For each cost center or department in which the employee has worked during the pay period, the computer operator simply enters into the keyboard the rate of pay, the distribution code for the department to be charged, and the hours worked by type of work. The computer automatically calculates regular and overtime earnings using the

---

[5]This special-purpose electronic accounting computer illustrates the type of accounting machines that have replaced the electromechanical machines discussed earlier. A detailed explanation of general-purpose computers, which are used not only for accounting applications but for many other applications as well, appears in Chapter 21.

internally stored processing instructions and stores in the computer memory the regular and overtime hours and the totals accumulated for each cost center. The output of the operation is a labor distribution report by employee, including a one-line summary of total earnings for each employee. Upon completion of the processing of all employee data, the operator depresses a key and the computer automatically prints the departmental labor cost analysis that has been stored within the computer. This analysis contains total hours as well as regular and overtime charges by each department.

To prepare the payroll for the second pass of the operation, the operator enters into the keyboard the employee number and the "to-date" information from the employee ledger and lists the total regular and overtime hours and earnings from the employee's summarized payline on the labor summary. As a double check for accuracy, the employee's pay can be recomputed using the time card as a basic source document. With this payroll data, the computer calculates gross pay, federal withholding tax, the amount withheld for social security, and city or state withholding taxes, after which deductions

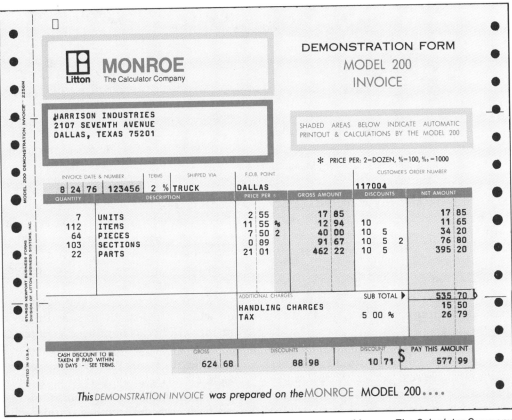

Monroe, The Calculator Company

Fig. 19-13
A Customer Invoice Prepared on an Electronic Billing Machine

Fig. 19-14   *Burroughs Corporation*
An Electronic Alphanumeric Accounting Computer

are listed and net pay computed. Once the payroll is completed, the computer automatically prints payroll totals for posting to the general ledger. Examples of the labor summary, departmental distribution of costs, and the various payroll records produced by this dual pass operation are shown in Figures 19-15 and 19-16.

This automated application simplifies payroll preparation if the employees work in many cost centers during a pay period, or if the pay computation involves different or complex rates. It also provides a high degree of accuracy in both payroll writing and labor analysis as well as automatic forms spacing and placement of forms under the control of the computer's program. Program-select keys allow the operator the option of choosing alternate programs or subroutines for processing various other types of accounting work.

Such electronic accounting systems are widely used in all sizes and types of business. The accounting computer described in this section is designed with great flexibility in that it can serve in a stand-alone capacity (that is, without the need for other supporting machines) or can be connected to other equipment in a large computer system, as discussed in Chapter 21.

LABOR SUMMARY

NAME	RATE	DEPT	OT HRS	CO	REG HRS	REG ERN	OT ERN	OTHER	CO
	2.8600	2			12.50	35.75			
	2.9600	3			7.25	21.46			
	2.6800	5	1.25	3	6.25	16.75	5.03		
	2.6800	8			14.00	37.52			
1045 S F HELTON			1.25		40.00	111.48	5.03		
	2.4600	7	2.50	3	28.00	68.88	9.23		
	2.5600	9			12.00	30.72			
1076 D JENSON			2.50		40.00	99.60	9.23		
	3.0600	12			6.50	19.89			
	3.0600	15	1.00	3	8.00	24.48	4.59		
	3.1600	19			5.50	17.38			
	3.1000	14			12.00	37.20			
	3.1600	16			8.00	25.28		2.50	6
1537 F DREWS			1.00		40.00	124.23	4.59	2.50	
	3.8800	5			5.00	19.40			
	3.8800	12	1.50	3	7.00	27.16	8.73		
	3.6300	1			3.50	12.71		7.25	9
	3.5600	18	.50	3	3.75	13.35	2.67		
	3.7525	11			20.75	77.86			
1234 J BLEEG			2.00		40.00	150.48	11.40	7.25	

DEPARTMENTAL DISTRIBUTION

TOTALS	DEPT NO.	OT HRS.	REG. HRS.	REG. ERN.	OT ERN.	OTHER	TOTAL
	1	2.50	93.00	359.52	14.53	7.25	381.30
	2	3.50	118.10	444.83	20.34		465.17
	3		62.25	238.78		12.50	251.28
	4	2.00	65.25	257.90	11.84		269.74
	5	1.25	83.25	286.60	5.00		291.60
	6		15.00	57.82			57.83
	7	3.00	53.00	165.12	12.09		177.21
	8		29.00	95.21			95.21
	9		57.50	206.24			206.24
	10		85.00	327.68			327.68
	11		66.25	253.26			253.26
	12	1.50	28.50	104.75	8.70		113.45
	13		17.50	67.46			67.46
	14		14.00	44.12			44.12
	15	1.00	8.00	24.40	4.57		28.97
	16		23.00	77.26		2.50	79.76
	17	1.25			6.49		6.49
	18	.50	6.75	24.09	2.67		26.76
	19	1.25	11.50	40.01	7.09		47.10
	20		12.25	46.31		8.50	54.81
		17.75	849.10	3121.37	93.32	30.75	3245.44

Source: Adapted from "Payroll Accounting with Burroughs L-4000 Accounting Computer," Burroughs Corporation.

Fig. 19-15
Labor Summary and Departmental Distribution Costs
Prepared on an Electronic Accounting Computer

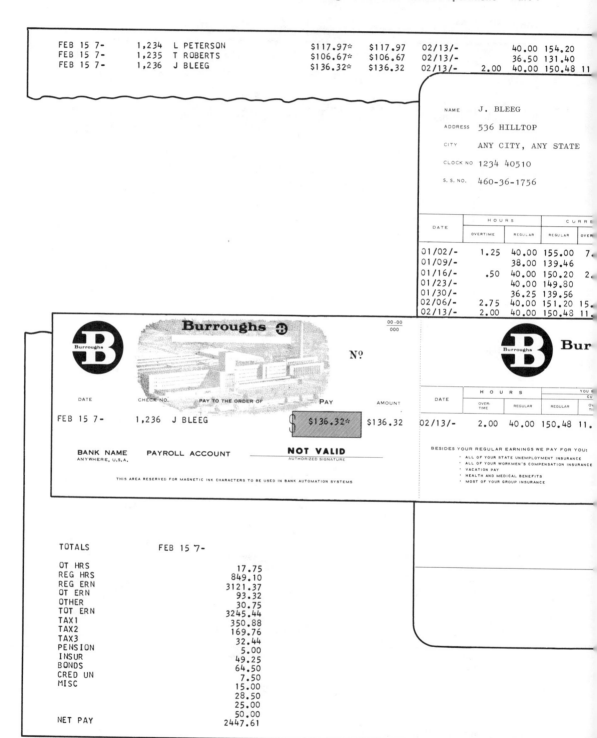

FEB 15 7-	1,234	L PETERSON	$117.97☆	$117.97	02/13/-		40.00	154.20	
FEB 15 7-	1,235	T ROBERTS	$106.67☆	$106.67	02/13/-		36.50	131.40	
FEB 15 7-	1,236	J BLEEG	$136.32☆	$136.32	02/13/-	2.00	40.00	150.48	11

NAME   J. BLEEG

ADDRESS   536 HILLTOP

CITY   ANY CITY, ANY STATE

CLOCK NO   1234 40510

S. S. NO.   460-36-1756

DATE	HOURS		CURRE	
	OVERTIME	REGULAR	REGULAR	OVER
01/02/-	1.25	40.00	155.00	7.
01/09/-		38.00	139.46	
01/16/-	.50	40.00	150.20	2.
01/23/-		40.00	149.80	
01/30/-		36.25	139.56	
02/06/-	2.75	40.00	151.20	15.
02/13/-	2.00	40.00	150.48	11.

Burroughs

00-00 / 000

N°

PAY TO THE ORDER OF   PAY   AMOUNT

| DATE | | | |
| FEB 15 7- | 1,236 | J BLEEG | $ $136.32☆ | $136.32 |

BANK NAME   PAYROLL ACCOUNT
ANYWHERE, U.S.A.

NOT VALID
AUTHORIZED SIGNATURE

THIS AREA RESERVED FOR MAGNETIC INK CHARACTERS TO BE USED IN BANK AUTOMATION SYSTEMS

Bur

DATE	HOURS		YOU	
	OVER-TIME	REGULAR	REGULAR	OV
02/13/-	2.00	40.00	150.48	11.

BESIDES YOUR REGULAR EARNINGS WE PAY FOR YOU!
* ALL OF YOUR STATE UNEMPLOYMENT INSURANCE
* ALL OF YOUR WORKMEN'S COMPENSATION INSURANCE
* VACATION PAY
* HEALTH AND MEDICAL BENEFITS
* MOST OF YOUR GROUP INSURANCE

TOTALS   FEB 15 7-

OT HRS	17.75
REG HRS	849.10
REG ERN	3121.37
OT ERN	93.32
OTHER	30.75
TOT ERN	3245.44
TAX1	350.88
TAX2	169.76
TAX3	32.44
PENSION	5.00
INSUR	49.25
BONDS	64.50
CRED UN	7.50
MISC	15.00
	28.50
	25.00
	50.00
NET PAY	2447.61

4.20	19.79	7.40	1.54			7.50				117.97	920.08	123.14	44.16	9.20	127963
1.40	13.61	6.31	1.31		2.50		1.00	10		106.67	955.96	118.53	45.89	9.56	134671
9.13	16.25	8.12	1.69	1.75	5.00					136.32	1089.52	97.01	52.30	10.90	145135

EMPLOYEES EARNINGS RECORD

1

FIXED DEDUCTIONS

___TAX	___TAX	OTHER	PENSION	INSURANCE	BONDS	CREDIT UNION	MISC. CODE	PERIODS
							9	1ST PERIOD
							10	2ND PERIOD
							11	3RD PERIOD
							12	4TH PERIOD

EXEMPTIONS   5

DEPARTMENT

RATE

DATE

CODE:
UNION DUES - 9
UNITED FUND - 10
ACCTS. REC. - 11
ADVANCES - 12

S ROSS PAY	DEDUCTIONS									NET PAY	TOTALS TO DATE				
	___TAX	___TAX	OTHER	PENSION	INSURANCE	BONDS	CREDIT UNION	MISC.	CODE		EARNINGS	___TAX	___TAX	OTHER	PROOF FORMULA
62.26	15.01	7.79	1.62		1.75	5.00				131.09	162.26	15.01	7.79	1.62	57086
39.46	11.04	6.69	1.39		1.75	5.00				113.59	301.72	26.05	14.48	3.01	70458
62.52	15.06	7.80	1.63		1.75	5.00		5.00	9	126.28	464.24	41.11	22.28	4.64	85821
49.80	12.77	7.19	1.50		1.75	5.00				121.59	614.04	53.88	29.47	6.14	100093
39.56	11.06	6.70	1.40		1.75	5.00				113.65	753.60	64.94	36.17	7.54	113473
66.79	15.82	8.01	1.67		1.75	5.00				134.54	920.39	80.76	44.18	9.21	129204
69.13	16.25	8.12	1.69		1.75	5.00				136.32	1089.52	97.01	52.30	10.90	145135

Ⓑ

N⁰

	TO YOUR GOVERNMENT ACCOUNTS			YOU HAVE REQUESTED THESE DEDUCTIONS						NET PAY
	DEDUCTIONS									
TOTAL	___TAX	___TAX	OTHER	PENSION	INSURANCE	BONDS	CREDIT UNION	MISC.	CODE	
169.13	16.25	8.12	1.69		1.75	5.00				136.32

CODE
UNION DUES - 9
UNITED FUND - 10
ACCTS. REC. - 11
ADVANCES - 12

DETACH AND RETAIN FOR YOUR RECORDS

THE FOLLOWING RECORDS ARE COMPLETED
DURING THE PAYROLL WRITING:
1. CHECK
2. EMPLOYEES STATEMENT OF EARNINGS
3. EMPLOYEES LEDGER
4. PAYROLL JOURNAL
5. CHECK REGISTER

Burroughs Ⓑ

Source: Adapted from "Payroll Accounting with Burroughs L-4000 Accounting Computer," Burroughs Corporation.

Fig. 19-16
Payroll Records Prepared on an Electronic Accounting Computer

1. How can an administrative office manager be considered a "resource allocator?"

2. What factors must be considered by an office administrator in deciding whether to mechanize an accounting systems function?

3. What psychological roles do office supervisors play in the mechanization of office procedures?

4. Cite some of the principal advantages of a data service center for a small business.

5. Under what circumstances should a data service center be used for accounts receivable work?

6. In recent years the write-it-once principle has been developed by firms manufacturing basic accounting machines. Explain how this principle has been applied effectively to payroll accounting operations.

7. What basic principle of work accounts for the effective application of cycle billing?

8. Identify the main elements in a basic payroll accounting systems model.

9. Under what conditions can the accounting board be effectively used in payroll and other similar accounting functions?

10. In addition to their work in handling large-volume mailings, addressing machines are used in basic accounting systems. Indicate how such machines can be assigned to multiple tasks in the organization.

11. Describe how the diazo copying process can be used to eliminate repetitive paperwork operations in a typical purchasing-receiving system.

12. What major advantages characterize a stand-alone microfilm system for handling accounts payable records?

13. Within the past few years revolutionary developments have occurred in the basic computing machine field. Cite several of these developments and their effects on computing work in the office.

14. What are the main classifications and advantages of each of the basic computing machines?

15. Under what conditions should you choose an alphanumeric accounting machine rather than a numeric machine?

1. Arthur Wilcox, an administrative office manager, is frequently faced with the problem of mechanizing certain phases of his office work. On what considerations should he base his decision to mechanize or not to mechanize?

2. Using one of the flowcharting techniques discussed in Chapter 17, chart the procedural steps involved in the order processing and billing system outlined on pages 524–525. With the completed chart as a source of information, analyze the routing of information through the various departments, and point out potential opportunities for mechanizing the system charted.

3. The Superior Petroleum Company is considering a plan to simplify its purchasing system for those orders whose total does not exceed $250 on any given invoice. Under such a plan the company would send the vendor a check in full payment, less the discount if applicable, whenever the company places an order that does not exceed $250. Thus, certain accounting entries would be eliminated. Discuss the advantages and disadvantages of such a plan.

4. The accounting staff of the Tan-Tara Country Club is limited to one person, Beverly Naber. Each month Naber has the job of preparing and mailing the monthly statements to the 2,000 members. During a typical month the club members sign approximately 15,000 credit receipts which must be tabulated and then posted to their accounts. Ordinarily this job requires two weeks' time, along with 60 hours of overtime work each month.

   Discuss how cycle billing might be used by the club to reduce its work load at the end of each month. What kind of computing machine might best be used in the processing of members' accounts? Is there an application for an electronic accounting machine in this billing system? Explain.

5. A steady stream of requests for additional computing machines has been coming to the desk of Julie DeRosa, the supervisor of the Administrative Services Department of Handcraft Toys, Inc., and the person responsible for the selection and purchase of all office machines. Not only does DeRosa face the eventual problem of an unending number of machine makes and models from which to choose and salespersons to interview but also she has received a confusing variety of machine requests, some clearly without foundation, from the various department heads. For example, the payroll department wants their obsolete rotary calculator overhauled and a new ten-key adding machine purchased. Those in the billing department want printing calculators, and the accounting department has requested the purchase of a reliable, used, full-keyboard adding-listing machine inasmuch as these machines are no longer being manufactured. One of the assistant managers in the sales department recently saw an electronic desktop calculator and a programmable calculator being demonstrated at a business equipment show and has recommended one of each type of machines be purchased for the sales department. The chief cost accountant has even suggested that the company adopt a policy for providing "hand-held" electronic calculators as standard equipment for each work station.

   Because of the varying requests from each department, DeRosa is a bit confused. She does not want to antagonize any of the departments by purchasing machines that they may not consider suitable for their work, yet the budget is limited to the purchase of about five machines.

Discuss how you would handle this situation if you were DeRosa and indicate the type of computing machines you would recommend be purchased for each department. Show reasons for your decision.

PRACTICAL OFFICE MANAGEMENT CASES

Case 19-1   **Improving the Payroll Accounting System**

The Lee Canning Company has a processing plant in which there are 450 employees, most of whom are paid at the rate of $3.50 an hour for a 37½-hour week, with time and one half for all over-time work. At present a staff of five clerks is required to calculate earnings on the time cards, prepare the payroll sheets, post employee's earnings records, prepare the periodic statements of earnings for the governmental agencies and the statements of earnings given to employees at the end of the year. The average weekly salary of each clerk is $175.

The office manager is eager to improve the payroll accounting work in the firm. Presently the clerks use payroll tax tables and obsolete rotary calculators in their work. It is felt that further mechanization of their payroll work will reduce costs. After giving the matter attention and talking with several systems analysts, the office manager has concluded that the two best ways in which to improve the present payroll accounting system are:

1. Install one electronic accounting machine that will prepare the payroll, the earnings record, and the paycheck in one writing. The machine will cost approximately $20,000. One clerk, instead of the present five, would be required to handle all payroll work.
2. Install an accounting board system that will not require any investment in machines. Three clerks would be required to prepare all payroll records. The investment in forms and three accounting boards would be approximately $700.

Discuss the system you recommend the office manager install and indicate the approximate savings to be realized in each case.

Case 19-2   **Using a Data Processing Billing Service**

Nuts and Bolts, a hardware wholesaler, averages $10 million in sales annually, with 4,000 customers and 7,200 sales transactions per month. The company classifies its sales under six major headings, two of which have their greatest volume in September and

October. Presently two clerks calculate all invoices from the shipping or delivery slips, and three clerks prepare the invoices and the monthly statements as a combined operation. They average 15 invoices an hour in an eight-hour day. The salaries of the clerks are $165 each week, or a total weekly payroll of $825.

You have been considering having the billing and the sales analysis work performed by a data service center. Your studies indicate that you would still need the two clerks to do the computing that precedes the billing, as under the present order processing system. However, only one clerk would be required to prepare a specially coded printing calculator tape that would be sent to the data service center for their work. A printing calculator tape would also be prepared for the daily cash receipts from customers. The initial investment in the calculator with a special tape attachment would be approximately $1,000.

The center will supply your firm with monthly detailed statements that would be mailed to your customers. The center will also supply a monthly ledger card for each customer to show the status of the account (including the previous balance), render monthly sales analysis reports by product line, and prepare customer delinquency reports. For this service the bureau charges $750 a month.

On the basis of this limited information, you are asked to report on the probable savings that may be realized from using the data service center. Your report should also indicate any possible disadvantages in the use of the service.

Case 19-3   Analyzing a Small-Scale Order Processing-Billing System

The Novy Calendar Company is a small-scale printer of custom-designed calendars for a highly specialized, exclusive market. Its sales transactions average 35 orders each day and have stabilized at that figure for the past two or three years, in keeping with the desires of its owner-founders to "stay small and give personal, customized service." Thus, the order-billing system in operation is largely manual in nature with the usual communication and computing tools required to do the routine jobs.

The company uses a combined order processing-billing system whereby an order is filled directly from a copy of the invoice. When an order is received in the sales department, the order clerk prepares a prenumbered invoice unit-set of five copies arranged with preassembled one-time carbon paper. The five copies are distributed as follows:

1. Original invoice — held for mailing to customer after goods have been shipped.
2. Acknowledgment of order — sent to customer when invoice is prepared.
3. Duplicate of invoice — held in follow-up file.
4. Inventory copy — routed to storekeeper for entry on inventory records.
5. Shipping room copy — sent to shipping clerk.

Unit prices and extensions are not shown on any copies at the time the invoices are prepared but are inserted on all necessary copies after the order has been shipped. Other information, such as the quantity ordered, the description of the order, and the shipping terms, is entered on the invoice set when the sales order invoice is initiated by the sales order clerk.

During the past year and a half, several critical invoicing problems have been brought to the attention of the sales manager, Barb Wyant. However, Wyant is a sales promotion specialist, not a paperwork expert, and mentions that she has no "real feel" for the manner in which the present system is operating, let alone make changes in it. Besides, the present system has been in operation for 10 years without change. For these reasons, Wyant wants a thorough study made of the entire order processing-billing system.

With the information provided, you are asked to prepare a report documenting the present system and making recommendations for improvements in the system. In your report include:

1. A flow process chart of the present system.
2. An analysis of the weaknesses of the present system.
3. A flow process chart of a proposed system that would correct the shortcomings of the present system.

The suggestions for conducting systems studies and for charting the flow of information, as discussed in Chapter 17, will be useful in developing a solution to this case.

Chapter 20

PUNCHED-CARD DATA PROCESSING SYSTEMS

Much of the progress that has been made in the automation of office work is linked directly to the successful application of data processing machines. As noted in Chapter 2, business firms have come to realize that the quantity of information needed to conduct normal operations requires more energy and control and lower unit costs of production than can be provided by human efforts alone. Thus, office managers have adopted efficient machine power on a wide scale in the same way that industrial managers mechanized their work on a widespread basis during the nineteenth century in order to increase the productivity of goods and services.

In the systems discussed up to this point, an office system was described as a combination of personnel, forms, records, and equipment organized to meet a common objective. In the early office the systems work was largely accomplished through manual means supplemented by the use of mechanical equipment, such as the various communication, computing, and accounting machines. In general, however, these machines were used separately to perform individual functions and were not tied together in any meaningful framework.

During the past several decades a more complex, *unified* set of machines has been developed for the office. These machines represent the core of data processing systems, which are used to maintain control over the various re-

sources of the firm such as capital, labor, time, space, and operating costs, that are considered crucial to the firm's survival. Because of the dominance of machines in these work areas, the systems are often referred to as automated systems; that is, data are processed with a minimum of human effort and intervention because the systems are largely self-regulating. There are two types of automated systems for processing data. One is the punched-card system, which is discussed in this chapter, and the other is the electronic data processing system, which is discussed in the next chapter.

HISTORY OF PUNCHED-CARD DATA PROCESSING

In their search for better methods of processing data, managers have continued to look for a system that would eliminate many of the weaknesses of the older manual systems and the partially mechanized systems. In such nonautomated systems there was much repetitive work performed by many clerks who were solely responsible for copying and recopying the same items of information. In many cases the full-time sorting, filing, and copying tasks were hardly appropriate for office workers with considerable creative talent. Moreover, because of the increased volume of such processing, the repetitive, standardized nature of these relatively simple office tasks, the serious rise in the costs of processing data, and the time required for completing the processing steps, the development of a more highly automated system for processing data became essential. Such a revolutionary development came near the end of the nineteenth century with the invention of punched cards.

In preparation for processing the data compiled from the census of 1890, Herman Hollerith, a statistician, developed a series of devices that have become known as *punched-card* or *unit-record* machines. These machines utilize machine-readable cards which are compatible with, and used in, the other machines making up the punched-card machine group. Information is coded and recorded as holes in punched cards, and once stored in this manner, can be processed repeatedly without further recording. This development, which was simple in concept but at that point difficult to implement in operating systems, permitted the census of 1890 to be processed in two and one-half years. This was less than one third the time required to complete the 1880 census, despite the fact that the population of the United States had increased from 50 to 63 million from 1880–1890. By recording much of the business data just once; by providing a means of reading the coded data by each of the punched-card machines; by carefully planning a system in which the machines could properly function; and by assigning the routine large-volume processing tasks to machines rather than to people, great improvements were made in the processing of data for use in managing organizations.

Other benefits stemmed from the punched-card system. The size and makeup of the paper records flowing through the system were standardized, making automatic data handling possible since information appears in uniform locations on all punched-card forms. Too, data can be selected out and printed in human-readable form by the machines, which promotes legibility and flexibility in the reporting process.[1]

For several decades punched-card systems functioned very satisfactorily as the most sophisticated means of processing data. In the mid-twentieth century, however, the electronic computer was developed, which has had a very profound impact on punched-card systems. To understand the many relationships between the two levels of systems, it is important to get a firm grasp on the basic nature of the unit-record concept, to see how punched-card machines gradually evolved into stand-alone systems, and to appreciate the present role of punched cards in the world of business data processing. Each of these matters is discussed in the following paragraphs.

The Unit Record Concept

A *unit record*, as noted in Chapter 2, is a punched-card form in which all data concerning each item in a transaction are punched into one card. Thus, when a customer orders three different types of merchandise, such as two 4-drawer

---

[1]Punched paper tape employs many of the concepts and techniques found in punched-card data processing systems. It is frequently produced as a byproduct of some other machine operation, such as the teletypewriter discussed in Chapter 8. For more information on the role of punched paper tape in data processing systems, see Elias M. Awad, *Business Data Processing* (4th ed.; Englewood Cliffs: Prentice-Hall, 1974), pp. 241–243; and S. J. Wanous, E. E. Wanous, and Gerald E. Wagner, *Fundamentals of Data Processing* (Cincinnati: South-Western Publishing Co., 1971), pp. 98–100.

file cabinets, five executive desks, and one conference table, each of the types of merchandise ordered is defined as a *unit*; and a separate card or unit record is punched for each type of merchandise listed on the invoice. Data processing personnel call this type of unit record a *detail card*, for it contains all the detailed data about each type of merchandise ordered such as the customer's number, date, invoice number, salesperson's number, quantity ordered, stock number of the item, price, and total amount. Also, a separate type of unit record, called a *master card*, is punched which contains information about the customer which does not change frequently, such as the name of the customer, the customer's account number, and the mailing address. Thus, the master card may be used over and over again without repunching this constant information. For the total sales transaction mentioned here, three detail cards are punched — one for each type of item — and are used with the master card to prepare the invoice. Later, the same three detail cards can be used again to update the inventory records without additional punching.

The unit record system of utilizing one card for each item of the transaction quickly became an accepted way of recording data for business processing. Prior to the development of punched-card data processing, source documents, such as purchase orders or sales orders, typically showed several transactions on the same form. Under such conditions it was impossible to group the forms by type of transaction. Considering the order for office equipment discussed earlier, before the advent of the unit record principle, it would have been impossible to compile a machine-run report on the sales of office desks while at the same

time compiling a separate report on the sales of four-drawer file cabinets since both items would have been recorded on the same order form. With the unit record system of punching a separate card for each item of record, new flexibility was provided the manager. Cards could be grouped and regrouped into a wide variety of reports to provide managers with more information than ever before, and the information could be processed entirely by machine without the need for additional manual recording.

Punched-Card Data Processing Stand-Alone Systems

An effective means of understanding the basic operation of punched-card data processing is to consider it as a complete, stand-alone, or independent data processing system consisting of four basic parts as shown in Figure 20-1. Normally the system is put into motion by the arrival from various departments of batches of source documents, such as time cards and sales orders, in handwritten or typewritten form. The data on these documents constitute the input to be converted into machine-language code by the keypunch. After the punching is completed, the data are checked for accuracy either visually or by a machine called a verifier, after which the card is certified to be accurate and ready for further processing.

Once the data have been converted into machine language, the cards can be "read" by each of the other machines in the punched-card system in the following manner: As a card is fed through one of the processing machines, each card column passes under a separate sensing device, usually a wire brush. If there is a punched hole in any card column, the brush makes contact with a roller known as the contact roller, which emits an electrical impulse that the machine is able to read or sense and then process. If no hole appears in a column, no contact is made between the brush and the roller and no electrical impulse is created; thus, no processing can take place. This basic principle of "hole or no hole" in a card column suggests a simple two-state condition in information processing, which will be developed more fully in Chapter 21 in discussing the role of the binary system in electronic data processing systems.

Figure 20-1 identifies an array of machines and processing operations available for handling punched cards. Usually processing consists of recording, sorting, classifying, summarizing, calculating, reporting, and storing operations. Regardless of which processing machine is being used, each machine must first read the card and then perform the specialized function required

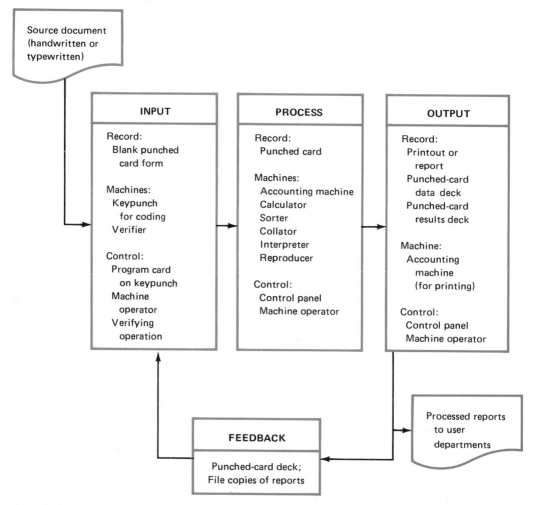

Fig. 20-1
A Punched-Card Data Processing Stand-Alone System

in line with the desired output of the system. Also, the provision for control should be noted in this system as a means of regulating the results of each phase of the system. Typical control elements include the program card for performing automatic punching and skipping tasks on the keypunch; the verifying operation to ensure accuracy of all the encoded data; the external, changeable control panels similar to a telephone switchboard that are wired to instruct the machines on what functions to perform; and in all cases, the machine operator attending each machine. In most routine operations, the deck of coded punched cards is retained in the data processing department for later use while the decoded, plain-language reports are forwarded to the individual departments.

The basic system discussed in this chapter operates in a stand-alone manner and utilizes electromechanical machines to perform very simple operations. The most frequent pattern is to keypunch random, unordered data into cards; sort the cards; and then print out a listing of the newly arranged cards to meet some management information need. Another common processing requirement makes use of the accounting machine to perform simple arithmetic functions, such as addition and subtraction in an inventory control system, and addition, subtraction, and multiplication operations in a simple payroll system. Because the machines are electromechanical, they are relatively slow processors, usually operating at a rate of several hundred cards per minute. In turn, each processing requirement, such as sorting, duplicating, and calculating, requires a separate machine which further slows the processing operations, delays the use of the information, and in-

creases the unit costs of producing the information. Because many of these functions can be performed with much more effectiveness by the electronic computer, the stand-alone, punched-card data processing system has decreased in importance and number, although many of its individual punched-card machine units still furnish valuable service to the computer system.

Punched-Card Oriented Computer Systems

Analysts specializing in data processing systems contend that the traditional stand-alone, punched-card installation is being squeezed from both sides — from the top by computers and from the bottom by the new forms of electronic accounting machines discussed in Chapter 19. However, the use of punched cards in computer systems is still widespread, as Chapter 21 indicates. In such systems, the punched card serves as a familiar, useful input record to the computer where all processing takes place at electronic speeds. Upon completion of the processing operations, the punched card may be used again, this time as an output record for storing the results of the computer-processed operations and for later reentry into the computer system.

BASIC PUNCHED-CARD DATA PROCESSING SYSTEMS CONCEPTS

Most of the mystery surrounding the punched card vanished long ago. In every household and office there is evidence of this data medium serving an important function. Examples are almost infinite and include payroll checks and earnings statements, utility bills, insurance payment notices, record club invoices, and course registrations in many universities and colleges. Part of the reason for this acceptance and understanding of the punched card is the fact that, in addition to the punched holes appearing in the tangible card record, the machine system provides a sufficient amount of decoded, plain-language information on the card itself to make any individual understand its basic function. However, students of admistrative office management need to know more about the system than the general public. Administrative office managers frequently serve as architects of information systems and thus must understand the capabilities of the entire data processing system, including the hardware. This requires a study of the card itself as well as the equipment within which it is used, both of which are discussed in this section.

Punched Cards

As the first step in the punched-card system, the data on a source document are transcribed in punched cards. In both punched-card and computer systems, punched cards are recognized as a desirable medium for the input of information, with the nature of the card varying according to the equipment used. Three kinds of punched cards are discussed in this section — the traditional 80-column card, the newer 96-column card, and mark-sensed cards — as well as related paper records employing some type of perforations or punches for the recording of data.

The 80-Column Card. At one time both 80- and 90-column cards were used in punched-card systems — the 80-

column card with IBM systems and the 90-column card with Univac systems. With the discontinuance of the 90-column card and equipment designed for its use, the 80-column card has become the most common type of punched card in data processing systems and the one that is designed for use with the standard IBM punched-card equipment discussed in this chapter. Figure 20-2 shows the code for recording digits, letters, and special characters on an 80-column punched card. Each of the digits 0 through 9 is represented by one punch in the appropriate column. Thus, a two-digit number requires a punch in each of two adjacent columns, and a three-digit number requires a punch in each of three adjacent columns. When recording alphabetic data in punched cards, two punches are made automatically in each column — with one of the punches from the zone area (a 12, 11, or 0 punch as required) and the other punch from the digit area. The 0 may be used either as a digit or as a zone punch in the same column with a digit to code certain letters of the alphabet or special characters. Thus, as shown in Figure 20-2, the letter A is recorded by a punch in the 12 position and a punch in the 1 row. The letter J is recorded by a punch in the 11 position and a punch in the 1 row, and the letter S is recorded by a punch in the 0 position and a punch in the 2 row. Special characters are recorded by one punch or a combination of two or three punches in each column.

To conserve space on the punched card, alphabetic data are often abbreviated or represented by a numeric code, and marks of punctuation may be omitted. For example, the name Williams Company, Incorporated, may be abbreviated and punched as Williams Co Inc, or assigned a customer number such as

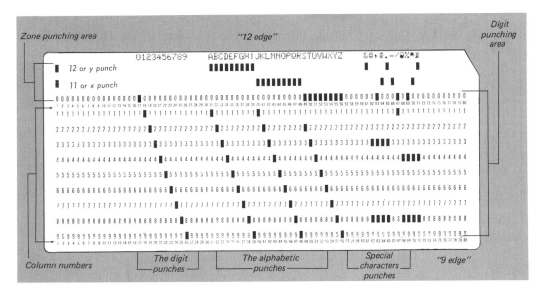

Fig. 20-2
Digits, Letters, and Special Characters Recorded on an 80-Column Punched Card

79180. The names of the months are coded from 01 through 12; thus, a date such as December 15, 1978, is punched as 121578.

The nature of the final reports to be completed or the forms to be filled in determines the amounts and kinds of data to be punched into cards. The cards must be properly planned to accommodate all the data to be recorded and to make sure that on all cards the data will be recorded in the same location. The punched card is actually a business form, and thus the 80 available columns on a card are laid out in sections, called *fields*, according to the principles of forms design discussed in Chapter 18. Accordingly, each field is assigned a sufficient number of columns for recording the greatest number of digits or letters to be accommodated in that field. In the punched card shown in Figure 20-3, columns 18 through 23 are set aside as the Date field. The recording of a date, after it has been coded, will not require

more than six columns. The invoice number 9893 is recorded as 09893 in columns 24 through 28, the Invoice No. field. Since successive invoice numbers will shortly require five columns for their recording, the need for an extra column has been anticipated in laying out the field. In a similar fashion, a business must anticipate the greatest number of digits or letters to be accommodated in each of the various fields such as Stock Number, Unit Price, and Amount.

In addition to serving as a principal input medium for data to be processed, punched cards cause other data processing functions to be performed in the punched-card system. The following list summarizes the main processing operations that may be expected from the total punched-card data processing system:

1. Data punched into cards can be added to, subtracted from, multiplied by, or divided into another amount.

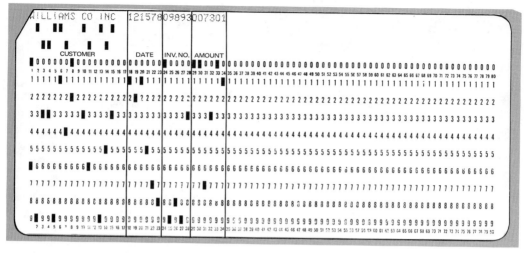

Fig. 20-3
Sales Data Recorded on an 80-Column Punched Card

2. Punched data can be listed, reproduced, or selected out of a group of cards.

3. The contents of an entire card or of one or more card fields may be printed on another punched card.

4. The card can be filed or posted automatically.

5. An automatic balance forward can be computed and punched or printed on another card.

6. One card can reproduce itself and print selected information on the edge of the reproduced card.

7. A coded punch can be produced from a pencil mark on a card.

8. A total can be printed.

9. One card or a portion of a card can be compared with a like area in another related card record, and on the basis of such comparison make a machine "decision," such as including or excluding a card from a group of cards in a deck.

The 96-Column Card. In 1969 IBM introduced a small business computer called the System/3 which utilizes a 96-column punched card. Figure 20-4 shows the card with data punched as round holes in three sections, called *tiers*, with each section containing a maximum of 32 characters. The 96-column punched card provides space for recording 20 percent more information on a card that is about one third the size of the 80-column card. On the 96-column card, data can be punched in the lower part of the card and printed on the upper part.

The 96-column card uses the Extended Binary Coded Decimal Interchange Code (EBCDIC), which is a computer data code. To understand this code it must be noted that each card column is composed of six punching positions labeled B, A, 8, 4, 2, and 1. The B and A punching positions are the zone portion of a character, not unlike the zone punch for coding alphabetic characters on the 80-column card. The 8, 4, 2, and 1 positions are the digital portions of the code, and together with the punching code positions provide a maximum of 64 different punching combinations for representing data on the card. Data are punched into the 96-column card by means of a data recorder,

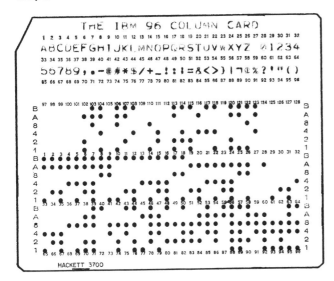

Fig. 20-4
Alphanumeric Codes on the 96-Column Punched Card

rather than the customary keypunch, and the cards are forwarded to a card reader for entry of the punched data into the computer.

Mark-Sensed Cards. Mark-sensed cards are specially designed cards used for recording information with an "electrographic" (graphite) pencil. The cards, although containing less than 80 vertical marking columns, are very similar to the 80-column punched cards since the digit positions are the same on both types of cards. Mark-sensed cards are processed on equipment that senses and converts the graphite marks into punches. Mark sensing is a variation of the optical character recognition concept (discussed in Chapter 18) in which OCR equipment reads pencil marks made in specific positions on a form.

Meter readers commonly use mark-sensed cards to record readings as they go from meter to meter. When the cards are returned to the offices of the utility, the same cards, or new ones, are punched automatically. The mark sens-

ing of data is usually limited to the recording of numeric data containing few digits, as shown in Figure 20-5. Although alphabetic information can be recorded on the cards, a user such as a meter reader would have to carry the alphabetic code for reference in order to mark such information on the cards. Therefore, alphabetic information recorded on mark-sensed cards is usually confined to items containing but a few letters of the alphabet. Many companies adapt mark-sensed cards for their special needs.

Other Punched Records. In addition to the punched cards used in large-scale data processing systems, other records are processed using similar punched-card principles. Examples are perforated cards, which are manually punched for conversion to regular punches for a punched-card data processing system; the punched tags that are attached to merchandise in retail stores and which are used for inventory

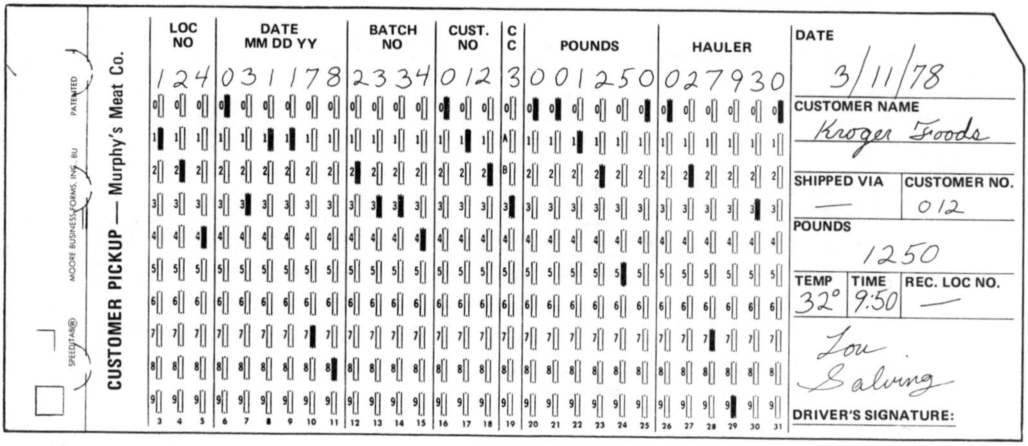

Fig. 20-5
Mark-Sensed Card

Moore Business Forms, Inc.

control purposes; and the marginal punched cards frequently used in manually operated systems.

One of the most commonly used marginal punched card systems utilizes the Keysort card. The Keysort system is a mechanical and manually operated system for sorting data recorded on specially designed and coded cards. After the data are recorded on a Keysort card, the card is punched, or notched, along the four edges so that it may be accurately sorted into any required order. It is ideal for analytical work applied to sales, orders, payrolls, costs, inventories, vouchers, and checks.

In punching the card to designate a number, a group of four holes is required for each digit in the numeric code. If the numeric code uses a units digit only, a group of four holes is required. The holes have the numeric values of 7, 4, 2, and 1. By using the holes in each group of four singly or in combination, it is possible to designate all numbers from 0 to 9. Note in Figure 20-6 how the code for Instructor No. 14 has been punched along the top edge of a college grade report card. On the right

edge of the card is the coded three-digit course number, 742.

Sorting of cards is accomplished by manually using a long, specially designed "needle." This needle is passed through the holes in the stack of cards designated by the code of the classifications or sorts desired. When the needle is raised, the cards in the classification sought fall from the stack of cards being sorted since the edges of the holes representing the classification sought have been notched out. An instant check of accuracy of the cards sorted is always available, since a missorted card shows up as a break in the line of notches.

Basic Punched-Card Equipment

The makeup of a punched-card machines installation will vary to a considerable degree. If the system is a stand-alone type as outlined in Figure 20-1 and not integrated with a computer system, a basic configuration, or "mix," of machines must be provided. If, however, the main processing power is provided by a computer, a considerably different mix of machines is required. Because

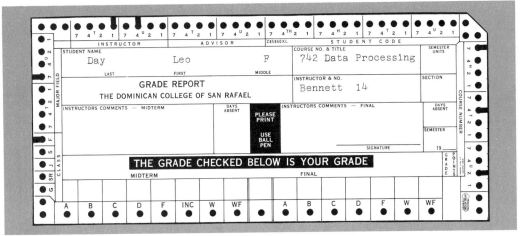

Kimball Systems Division, Litton Industries

Fig. 20-6
A Marginal Punched-Card Record

punched-card-oriented computer systems are discussed in Chapter 21, at a point where the essential computer concepts required to understand the operation of such a system are explained, discussion in this chapter is restricted to stand-alone punched-card systems.

While there are many machine functions possible in a punched-card system, certain functions may be considered basic to most applications. As explained earlier, typical functions are the recording of unordered data by the keypunch; the sorting of the random data into an orderly sequence (such as alphabetic or numeric order) on the sorter; and performing simple calculations, such as addition and subtraction, as well as printing out the results on the accounting machine. To ensure the accuracy of the data before sorting, a verifier may be used, although this operation is not vital to the operation of the system. These essential machines in a stand-alone punched-card system are shown in Figure 20-7 and are discussed in the following paragraphs. The main

functions of the peripheral punched-card machines are explained in a later section.

The Keypunch. Data are first encoded on punched cards by means of a *card-punch machine*, commonly called a *keypunch*. The keypunch operator reads the data from a handwritten or machine-written form, the *source document*, and registers the data into the keyboard for automatic punching of the cards. While this operation is essentially manual in nature, similar to typewriting, as mentioned earlier it has been automated to the extent that a program card may be used to machine-punch master information or to perform automatic skipping or duplication of information from the master program card to the card being prepared. Small manually operated keypunches are available to record data at the point of origin as in a warehouse, in a manufacturing plant, or in a house-to-house milk-delivery truck. Most portable keypunches record numeric data only and do not print as they punch.

Photo Courtesy of IBM

Keypunch

Photo Courtesy of IBM

Verifier

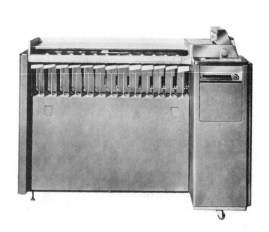

Photo Courtesy of IBM

Sorter

Photo Courtesy of IBM

Accounting Machine

Fig. 20-7
Essential Machines in a Stand-Alone Punched-Card Data Processing System

The Verifier. Since the use of punched cards usually involves a large volume of data to be processed and since most of the cards will be used over and over again, it is essential that the data be punched accurately. Therefore, a *verifier* is used by a second operator to check the work of the keypunch operator. The verifier, shown in Figure 20-7, is similar in appearance to the keypunch; but instead of punching holes, it electrically senses whether a discrepancy exists between the keys being depressed and the holes punched in the card during the keypunching operation. If such a discrepancy exists, the machine locks and a hole is punched in the top of the card above the incorrectly punched column. If the card is correctly punched, a hole is punched in the right edge of the card. On some models of the keypunch, the verifying and punching operations can be combined in one unit.

Punched cards may also be verified by reading the data printed at the top of the card during the punching operations and comparing the printed data with that appearing on the source document. An informal "sight verification" is sometimes used by holding up to the light several cards requiring identical information. If the light shows through, it is assumed that the information on the cards is identical and thus accurate. More convenient types of punched-card verification, as found in computer systems, are explained in Chapter 21.

The Sorter. After the punching operation has been completed, the cards are usually in miscellaneous, random order. The next step in the punched-card system — and usually considered the most frequent of all punched-card tasks — is the rearrangement or sorting of the cards in sequence by some desired classification. To arrange the cards in the desired order, whether it be numeric or alphabetic, requires the use of the *sorter*. (See Figure 20-7). This machine sorts cards by sensing the position of the holes in appropriate columns, one column at a time, and depositing the cards in the appropriate sorter pockets. For example, if the data in a two-digit field — columns 20 and 21 — are to be sorted in numeric order, first the punches in column 21 of the cards — the units column — would be passed through the sorter during which time a "9 punch" in that column would be directed to the 9 pocket, an "8 punch" to the 8 pocket, and so on. Next the newly rearranged deck would be sorted on column 20 of the card — the tens column — during which time the same deposition of cards would occur. The result would be a deck of cards arranged in ascending numeric order, a common sorting operation.

The Accounting Machine. The major processing unit in the punched-card machine system is the *accounting machine* (Figure 20-7), also known as the *tabulator* or *tab machine*. The accounting machine accepts input data from punched cards, and through the use of an external removable control panel wired for each job, processes the data. The output of such processing is the printout or printed report in various formats.

To perform these various functions, an accounting machine is made up of three units: a reading unit which senses the holes in the cards and passes this information to the calculating and printing units in the form of electrical impulses; a calculating unit, for performing the various addition and subtraction operations and the related accumulating and totaling of numeric data read from the punched holes; and a printing unit. This last unit prints the summarized data resulting from the calculations on forms, such as a wage and tax statement (Form W-2), employee's earnings paycheck, sales invoice, expense distribution sheet, or almost any other report or record requiring printed and numeric data. The accounting machine positions continuous paper forms automatically to the line where the data are to be printed. It can also punch summarized data into cards when it is connected with another machine capable of *summary punching*.

Peripheral Punched-Card Equipment

To provide more flexibility in processing data by the punched-card system, peripheral equipment is available to perform the following operations: (1) print information on a punched card; (2) duplicate or reproduce the data in punched cards, (3) collate the cards when more than one type of card is used for a data processing operation, and (4) perform calculating operations.

The Interpreter. Whenever a visual check must be made of the data punched into a card or if the card is to be used as a business form, an *interpreter* is used to print the information that is punched on the card. The machine translates or interprets the punched holes and then prints this information on the card, usually at the top edge.

The Reproducing Punch. A *reproducing punch*, or *reproducer*, is used to punch automatically the data from one deck of cards into another deck of cards. For example, the reproducing

punch is used in extracting constant data from a deck of prepunched master cards for use in a subsequent accounting period; as in the preparation of weekly earnings or detail cards from a deck of employee master cards; or subscription renewal cards for magazine publishers; or billing cards for public utility companies. Firms using the reproducing punch for billing operations often send out a punched-card bill with a 22-column stub. When customers remit their payments they also return the stub, which is used to reproduce automatically an 80-column card for mechanized cash accounting.

In other forms of duplication mark-sensed cards may be reproduced into punched cards, several detail cards may be punched from one master card (*gang punching*), or prepunched sales tickets may be fed through a specially designed machine and converted to standard punched cards for processing.

The Collator. Sometimes the data required for a printing operation must be obtained from two or more punched cards. For example, in preparing a Form W-2, the name and address may appear on one card, followed by other cards showing the social security number, the gross earnings, and the taxes withheld. To use the punched-card machines most effectively, each series of cards must be arranged in the same sequential order. This arrangement can be accomplished by feeding the cards through a *collator*, which is similar to a four-pocket sorter. The collator performs four functions — merges the cards, matches the series of cards, checks the sequence, and makes special selections where desired.

The Calculator. Mathematical calculations in a punched-card data processing system are performed by means of a *calculator*, or *calculating punch*. The difference between a calculator and an accounting machine is that the calculator can perform all mathematical operations whereas the accounting machine can perform addition and subtraction only. The calculator makes computations from two or more punched cards and punches the results in one of the cards or on a following summary card. Because this machine as well as the other punched-card machines are operated electromechanically, its speed of operation is slow. Except for its use in stand-alone systems, the calculator has been replaced by the electronic computer, which is clearly superior in speed, accuracy, and lower unit costs of processing data.

Summary of the Punched-Card Systems Cycle

Because of the need to understand the total environment in which their departments operate, modern managers find it useful to view the punched-card method of processing data in a systems context, such as that shown in Figure 20-1, noting the required inputs and processing operations essential to provide the output desired by their departments. In a related way Figure 20-8 shows in diagrammatic form the various phases and equipment in a stand-alone, computer-independent system discussed in this chapter. The steps commonly involved in each of the phases of such a system are summarized as follows:

Input:

1. Source data are brought to the punched-card installation and converted into punched-card form. Keypunches range from simple portable units to the printing keypunch, which

may print information on the cards as it punches.
2. The verifier is used to ensure the accuracy of the data input. In this machine, data from the source document are registered and compared against the keypunched data on the appropriate card.

Processing:

3. A sorter is used to group cards in sequence within desired classifications prior to use on other data processing machines.
4. A collator is used to merge or combine newly punched cards with an existing file of cards into one file of a given sequence.
5. A reproducing punch, like an automatic copier, automatically transfers data from a set or deck of source cards into another set.
6. Arithmetic operations (addition, subtraction, multiplication, and division) are performed on the calculator. Cards punched by the calculator can be fed into the accounting machine to obtain final printed reports.

Output:

7. The accounting machine, or tabulator, sums up automatically the data recorded on cards and prints various reports. It is also used in the processing phase for performing addition and subtraction operations.

Control:

Although the system's control phase is not pictured in Figure 20-8, it is certainly implied. The outcomes of the system are regulated through the wired control panels on the reproducing punch, the collator, and the calculator, as well as through the program card on the keypunch. In addition, there are control keys and selector switches on each machine that are monitored by the careful machine operator.

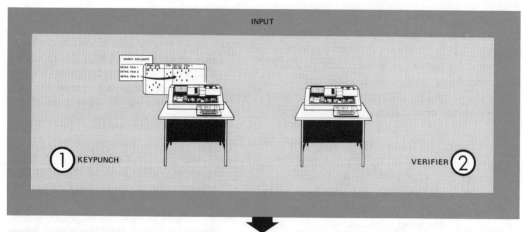

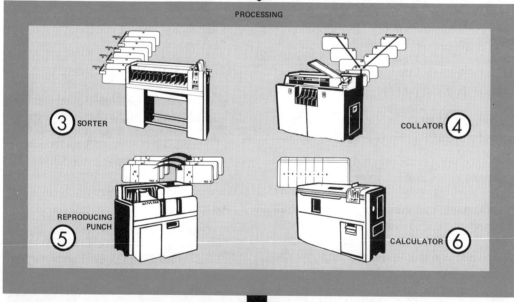

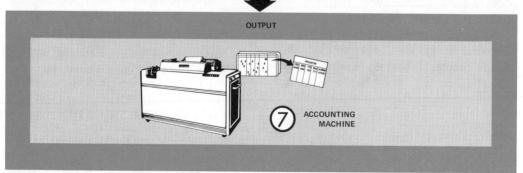

Fig. 20-8
Basic Steps and Equipment in the Punched-Card System

AN ILLUSTRATIVE PUNCHED-CARD SYSTEM — PAYROLL ACCOUNTING

In companies where the volume of payroll accounting operations is too great to consider the mechanized systems discussed in Chapter 19 but too limited in size for a full-fledged computer system, punched-card systems have traditionally been used. Such a payroll system serves as a good illustration of the true advantages of a relatively automated system for processing information over the manual systems. The payroll system is typically one of the first systems automated in a firm and also the most universal and most essential system found. At the same time, the limitations in processing and reporting power become readily apparent, pointing to the need for more powerful equipment to handle the increasingly greater information needs of the competitive business firm.

This section presents a systems flowchart that illustrates a broad overview of the application of punched-card equipment to a payroll system in a hypothetical firm, the Gerber Company. Subsequently, the basic input documents are analyzed in terms of the machine processing required to provide the payroll accounting reports needed by the firm.

A Systems Cycle of Payroll Accounting

The basic steps of a punched-card system, as outlined in Figure 20-8, become more understandable when they are converted to an actual systems application — payroll accounting. The procedural steps involved in a payroll accounting system for the Gerber Company follow the regular payroll cycle which is illustrated in Figure 20-9. In this system most of the processing work, including the printing of records and reports with any desired combination of totals and balances for the system, is performed automatically on punched-card equipment.[2]

It should be noted that the desired output of the payroll system consists of three reports: the paycheck; the statement of gross earnings, deductions, and net earnings; and the payroll register. To provide this basic payroll information, it is necessary to introduce new gross earnings data for each employee and "pull" from the files the previously updated payroll master cards and payroll deduction cards, already in punched-card form, for all employees. Once these decks of cards have been merged in the collator, a new master deck is available for performing the necessary addition and subtraction operations on the accounting machine and for printing out the reports previously identified. If the need had arisen for multiplication and division operations in this system, the use of the punched-card calculator would have been required.

Each of the general steps charted in Figure 20-9 is explained in detail in the following paragraphs which describe the various records processed in this system.

Payroll Master Card

In converting information to punched-card form, the first step is to prepare for each employee a *payroll*

---

[2]The symbols used to construct the chart in Figure 20-9 have traditionally been limited to punched-card systems charting. However, other standardized symbols, such as those designed for use in information processing systems, as shown in Figure 17-9, page 472, would also be useful for charting this payroll accounting system.

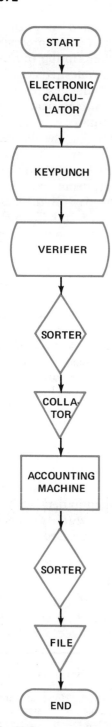

Payroll accounting systems cycle begins with the completion of each pay period.

Time figured from weekly attendance time cards and gross earnings determined.

Gross earnings payroll cards punched.

Cards verified against source documents.

Gross earnings cards sorted in ascending sequence by employee number.

Payroll master cards and payroll deduction cards merged with gross earnings cards.

Net earnings computed and following reports printed out: payroll check; statement of gross earnings, deductions, and net earnings; and the payroll register.

Punched-card decks (gross earnings cards, payroll master cards, and deduction cards) sorted by groups.

Reports distributed as required and punched-cards decks returned to file.

Payroll accounting systems cycle completed.

Fig. 20-9
A Punched-Card Payroll Accounting System Cycle

master card that contains all constant payroll information — name, social security number, clock or badge number, marital status, and hourly rate or salary. Data for preparing the master card may be obtained from personnel records, such as a notification of employment form and from the employee's earnings record. Additional information, such as date of birth and date employed, which may be needed by the personnel department, may be included.

Ordinarily, to speed up the payroll accounting operation, a numeric code is assigned to all information punched into the master card that is not originally recorded in numeric form, except the employee's name, which is retained in its alphabetic form. For example, rather than punching Tool Designer as the job occupation for which the employee was hired, this occupation may be assigned a code number such as 25, and that number would be punched into the card. However, the date of employment, such as November 16, 1963, would be retained in its original numeric form and punched as 111663. In the payroll master card shown in Figure 20-10, the employee's name has been punched in columns 1 through 12. However, since some employee's names will require more columns than these, in the initial planning stages it was decided to set aside columns 1 through 24 for recording employee names. At the time of punching this name into the card, the keypunch also printed or "interpreted" the name in the columnar heading at the top of the card. Other information recorded in the card and the fields occupied by these data are as follows:

Columns	Description of Data	Data Recorded
25–33	Social security number	077 05 2831

Columns	Description of Data	Data Recorded
34 and 35	Occupation code number	25
36–41	Hourly rates	
	Regular	400
	Overtime	600
42 and 43	Tax code (the first number indicates marital status; the second, the number of exemptions)	24
44–46	Employee department number	133
47–49	Employee clock number	258
50–55	Date hired	11 16 63

Deduction Card

After the master card has been prepared, the next step is to create a *deduction card* for each employee to cover those payroll deductions requested by the employee. The employee usually signs an authorization form covering deductions to be made from earnings for such items as savings bonds, hospitalization insurance, charitable donations, lunch tickets, and union dues. In the payroll deduction card shown in Figure 20-11, the employee has authorized the monthly deduction of $5 from his paycheck to cover the purchase of U.S. savings bonds. Such deduction cards, based upon authorization forms completed by the employee, can be predetermined by the payroll department and kept in the master file for reuse at each pay period.

Time Card

Under any payroll system, the basis for all payroll computations is the time and attendance record. In some systems, time and attendance records may be kept manually. In many payroll systems, however, mechanical equipment is used to record time on the job. Figure 20-12 shows one type of weekly attendance card commonly used with a punched-card payroll accounting system. A sec- ond type of time card is illustrated in Figure 19-4, page 531.) Attendance time is the basis upon which the employee's pay is figured, except when piecework or incentive plans are used. When an incentive or piecework plan is used, the employee's pay is calculated on the basis of units produced.

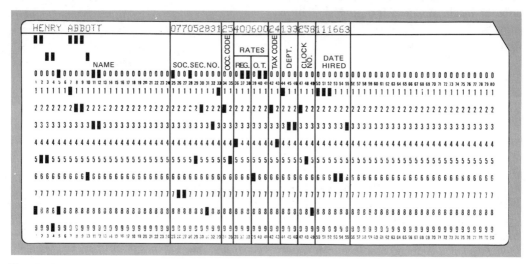

Fig. 20-10
Payroll Master Card

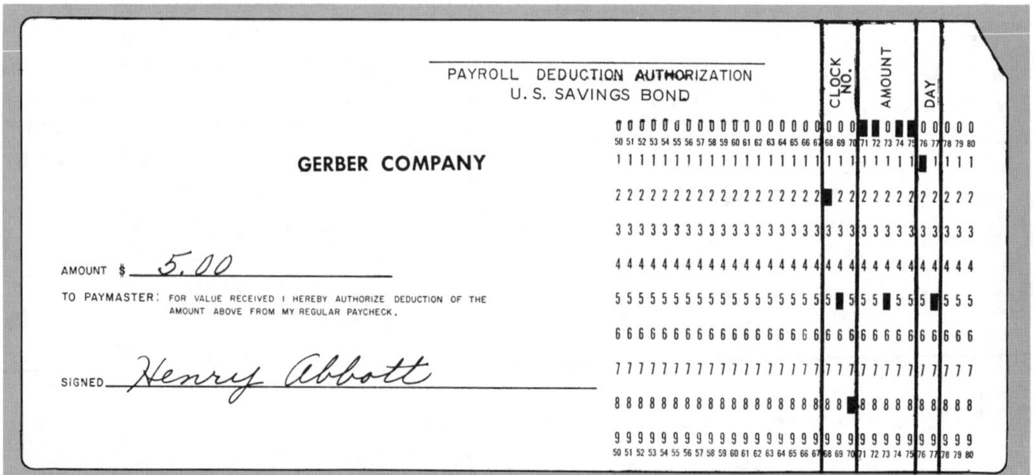

Fig. 20-11
Payroll Deduction Card

The time card may be either a "daily" time card or a "pay period" card, such as that shown in Figure 20-12. At the end of the pay period, the attendance time is figured and multiplied by the hourly rate to determine gross earnings. The extension of hours times rate may be accomplished on desk calculators or on other automatic equipment that is a part of the punched-card system. These data are then punched into a *gross earnings* card, similar to that shown in Figure 20-13.

Output Records

The master card, the deduction cards, and the gross earnings card are then merged to prepare automatically the payroll register. As shown in Figure 20-14, the payroll register lists each employee's department number, clock number, hours worked, earnings, deductions, and net pay.

The file of punched cards may then be used to prepare automatically the payroll checks. If payments are made in cash, the data recorded on the payroll envelopes may be obtained from the payroll register. Statements of gross earnings, deductions, and net earnings may also be printed at this time. For example, usually a separate register is compiled for each type of deduction. Thus, the preparation of a register showing total withholding taxes becomes invaluable for reference purposes and for a basis of remitting to the appropriate government agency money deducted from employees' wages.

In addition to the output records described for this payroll accounting system, it is possible to prepare automatically the following records and reports, which play an essential role in the control of payroll accounting operations:

1. Employees' pay statements.
2. Social security statement.
3. Federal, state, and local income tax reports.
4. State unemployment compensation wage reports.
5. Deduction registers.
6. State workmen's compensation reports.

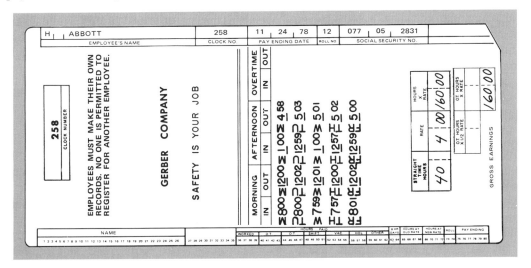

Fig. 20-12
Weekly Attendance Time Card

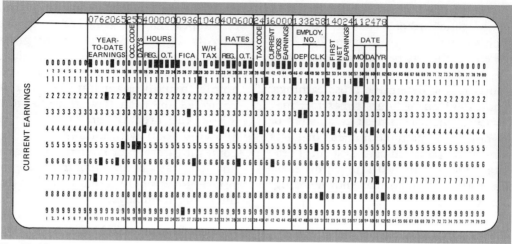

Fig. 20-13
Gross Earnings Card

Additional reports more related to managerial control than to the accumulation of accounting data may be obtained. For example, from the information punched into the payroll master card, deductions cards, and gross earnings cards, management is able to obtain such data as the average hourly earnings per employee, average number of hours worked, labor turnover, departments in which turnover is excessive, number of employees contributing to charitable organizations, and amount of absenteeism.

AN ASSESSMENT OF PUNCHED-CARD SYSTEMS

When a data processing system is evaluated for its effectiveness as a service function in an organization, it is important to consider objectively the benefits and limitations of such a system. In such an assessment, the past records of the system are examined — what work was accomplished, how well it was done, and how much it cost.

Based upon present needs and long-term expectations of the firm, attempts are made to project, as accurately as predictions will permit, future processing needs for the system.

Based upon the analysis of data processing by punched-card methods discussed in this chapter, the benefits and limitations of the punched-card system will be summarized briefly in this part. Also, the emerging role of the punched card in the applications of future systems will be explored.

Benefits and Limitations

At the time of its development, punched-card equipment became highly popular for data processing applications having a large volume of simple, repetitive transactions. The system provided considerably more speed, accuracy, and ability to handle large volumes of data compared to manual and simpler mechanical methods. All of these benefits resulted from the versatility of the punched card as a common-language,

SHEET 1 OF 6														

GERBER COMPANY

PAYROLL REGISTER

DATE Nov. 24, 1978

NAME DESCRIPTION	EMPL. NO. DEPT.	CLOCK	TAX CODE	DAYS	BASE RATE	HOURS REGULAR	OVERTIME	CURRENT GROSS EARNINGS	DEDUCTIONS F.I.C.A.	WITH. TAX	OTHER	CURRENT NET PAY	YEAR TO DATE EARNINGS	F.I.C.A.	WITH. TAX
HENRY ABBOTT	133	258	24		4 00						5 00				
SAVINGS BOND				5		40 0		160 00	9 36	10 40	5 00	135 24	7 620 65	445 81	498 80
MARTHA ADMAN	131	100	23		3 80						7 50				
SAVINGS				5		40 0	2 0	163 40	9 56	13 30	7 50	133 04	7 979 80	466 82	614 10
GERALD ALTON	131	145	24		4 15						5 50				
SAVINGS											5 00				
SAVINGS BOND				5		40 0	2 0	178 46	10 44	12 40	10 50	145 12	8 302 16	485 68	589 40

Fig. 20-14
Payroll Register Automatically Prepared from Punched Cards

machine-readable record and as an effective input-output and storage medium.

Once the data have been accurately punched into a card, they can be processed repeatedly in a great variety of applications. Unlike the data processed by manual and mechanical methods, punched-card data do not need to be "recaptured" or rewritten for each new cycle of the system, as the discussion of the payroll master card confirms. The card's use as a unit record increases the flexibility of processing a greater number of reports, since single or unit transactions can be easily grouped or isolated automatically.

The system, however, is not without its limitations. In the stand-alone systems discussed in this chapter, punched-card systems employing electromechanical machines operate at processing speeds of several hundred cards a minute, which is a snail's pace compared with the billions or more of operations per second of which the computer processor is capable. In a punched-card system, several machines must be used because each machine performs its own special function. The system operates in a *batch mode*; that is, cards are processed in groups or decks or batches, which results in peak-and-valley workloads during which time the cards are physically carried by the operator from one machine to another before processing can take place. Also, no internal storage of operating instructions is possible.

Emerging Applications

In the past, business data processing by punched-card methods has been applied successfully to many well-recognized systems. Some of the applications include payroll accounting highlighted in this chapter, personnel records, material accounting and control, accounts payable, billing, sales accounting, inventory control, and many other specialized areas of accounting. Where the volume of work to be processed was not large enough for a computer system, punched-card systems have been widely used. Recently, however, the electronics technology has provided new processing systems in which the speed and accuracy of the computers are combined effectively with punched-card input and output media to bring about a "marriage" of the most beneficial aspects of the punched-card system and the overwhelming advantages of the computer. These punched-card oriented computer systems are explored in detail in the next chapter.

Predictions are that the punched card as now employed in computer systems will continue to be widely used.

The punched-card system started the automated data processing movement and still retains many advantages with its tangible, understandable unit record. Then, too, there are hundreds of thousands of punched-card machines performing satisfactory services in data processing installations in business, making it highly unlikely that the demise of the punched card is at hand.

QUESTIONS FOR REVIEW

1. What data processing problems were solved by the invention of the punched-card system?

2. Why is a punched card called a unit record? How does this "unit" concept influence the effectiveness of the card in an information system?

3. Briefly describe each of the four basic parts in a punched-card data processing system.

4. What is meant by the term "stand-alone" as it is applied to punched-card data processing systems?

5. In what respects does a punched-card-oriented computer system differ from a punched-card stand-alone system?

6. Explain the use of mark-sensed cards in punched-card accounting.

7. Identify the basic punched-card machines and describe the main function(s) of each.

8. How does a collator differ from a sorter?

9. In what ways does the concept of control enter into the design and operation of a punched-card data processing system?

10. What three types of punched cards are commonly used in a typical punched-card payroll accounting system? For what reason is each type of card prepared?

11. What are the main benefits and limitations of punched-card systems? In what respects can these limitations be corrected by computer-based systems?

1. Some writers state that keypunching is out of date and that the efficient organization today demands more sophisticated, automated approaches to data preparation, such as optical scanning. Others argue that for the small firms with standardized data processing routines, keypunching remains a very efficient procedure. What evidence can you cite to justify these two points of view? How can the keypunch machines effectively compete with more automated data-entry devices?

2. "Frequently installations of punched-card equipment have been made that have proven impractical." What are some of the systems limitations of punched-card machines with which the administrative office manager should be familiar?

3. Keysorting is a manual process used in some accounting work. It is also considered an adjunct to the records management function in the office. Indicate how both accounting and records management may be expedited by means of keysorting.

4. Why have punched-card systems been retained in modern offices now that computer systems are available for all types of information processing and all sizes of offices?

5. The punched-card system for processing data has been termed a batch-processing system in which the machines are subject to peak-and-valley scheduling of work. To reduce the "valley" period, that is, the time when these machines are idle, what measures would you recommend?

6. Because of your experience as an office manager in the successful selection and maintenance of basic computing and accounting machines, Julia Barta, the vice-president of administration of your firm, has asked your advice on the selection of punched-card equipment for a new branch plant being planned. Barta is aware of the machine manufacturer's policy of either selling or leasing the equipment, but she has neither the time nor the information-processing experience to make such a procurement decision on punched-card equipment. Which approach would you recommend to Barta — purchasing or leasing — assuming that the equipment will be used as a stand-alone system to record and report on sales and inventories for the products manufactured and sold by that branch? Defend your answer.

7. Your company is firmly committed to the continued use of keypunch machines as data-preparation devices for its computer system. Accordingly, it has established a policy of placing such machines in the various decentralized offices where large volumes of data are generated so that the punched-card data can be transmitted over telecommunication lines to the home office in Indianapolis. As the administrative office manager for the Topeka branch office, you must begin preparations for the arrival of several keypunch machines in

your office and for a data set (discussed in Chapter 8) to be used in conjunction with these machines to transmit data to the home office. To incorporate these machines into your office operations, what overall questions of a systems nature must be answered? What problems do you foresee in terms of basic logistics (space, personnel, and the like)? What training needs do you perceive and what training assistance should you be prepared to request from the central-office systems staff to minimize the problems of converting to the new system? Discuss answers to these and other related questions that could be expected to develop in this situation.

PRACTICAL OFFICE MANAGEMENT CASES

Case 20-1   Mechanizing the Processing of Customers' Orders

In the order-processing system of T. Wong Imports, Inc., the following clerical procedures have been in operation:

1. As customers' orders are received, they are edited, specifications are approved, and shipping dates are assigned by the sales coordinator. Orders are then forwarded to the Order Department and each customer's master card is pulled. A separate master card is on file for each customer for each product purchased.
2. From the customer's order and the master cards, a 9-part order form is prepared on electric typewriters. After being carefully checked, the copies are distributed to the various destinations. Two copies are retained in the Order Department, one filed by scheduled shipping date and the other by customer name.
3. After the material has been shipped, the Traffic Department returns one copy of the order form to the Order Department as notification of shipment. The copy filed by scheduled shipping date is pulled from the file and destroyed. The copy filed by customer name is pulled and sent to the Accounting Department along with the Traffic Department copy.
4. The Accounting Department prices and extends the order, computes the sales representative's commission and calculates the freight allowances. After checking these computations, a 5-part invoice is prepared on electric typewriters. One copy of the invoice is sent to a code clerk who codes the entire invoice for keypunching. The punched cards are used later in preparing various statistical reports.

After much study, the company realizes that there is too much wasted effort involved in manual work, especially repetitive writing. As office manager, you are responsible for exploring the possibility of applying a greater amount of mechanization, such as the mechanized accounting systems or the punched-card systems discussed in Chapters 19 and 20, respectively, to as many of the order-processing procedures as possible. Prepare a report in which you provide the information listed at the top of the next page.

1. A chart of the present system along with an analysis of the problem areas that might be corrected by a higher degree of mechanization in the order-processing system.
2. A realistic proposal for integrating the processing of customers' orders into a more effective system. Provide cost estimates for any major changes recommended in the system.

Case 20-2 Applying Punched-Card Data Processing to a Branch Payroll

The main plant and the home office of Perfecto Prefab Homes, Inc., with a staff of 2,500 employees, are located in Madison, Wisconsin, less than 200 miles from both of the firm's branch plants. A plant employing 450 workers is located in LaCrosse, Wisconsin, and another plant employing 390 workers is located in Waterloo, Iowa. Presently the processing operations of the two branch payrolls are completely independent of each other and of the main office.

In the home office the punched-card processing department in which the Madison payroll is prepared has been replaced by a small-scale computer system. Since there was little trade-in value to be realized from the punched-card machines, management retained these machines and has suggested that perhaps either or both of the branch offices might utilize the equipment to improve the efficiency of their payroll operations. Only a keypunch, a verifier, a sorter, a reproducing punch, and an accounting machine would be transferred to a branch office.

The long-established custom of this firm requires that employees be paid each Wednesday for the preceding week's work. The company is seeking to reduce payroll costs and at the same time maintain accuracy and promptness in payment. Presently both payrolls are prepared manually using the accounting board system, which is slow and requires considerable overtime work each week. Under such a system the cost of payroll processing has been getting out of line.

As the newly employed office manager in the home office, you have been asked to study the feasibility of converting the manual system of preparing branch-office payrolls to a branch-office punched-card accounting system. Another possibility would be a centralization of the payroll accounting operations in Madison through the use of punched-card data preparation in the branch offices. In your report, present a reasonable description of the most feasible plan to follow along with the equipment, forms, procedures, and personnel required to implement your recommended plan.

Case 20-3   Designing Forms for a Punched-Card System

As assistant to the office manager of Empire Electronics, Ltd., you have specialized in the design of handwritten and typewritten business forms used by the company. Up to the present time, all of the major processing systems, such as purchasing and billing, have utilized efficient clerical personnel and manually operated machines to handle the routine processing tasks. Now, however, with the growth in sales and the expectations of even greater expansion in the future, it has become apparent that the office work, like the various manufacturing processes, must become more highly automated.

A decision has been made to purchase a small-scale computer system that accepts punched-card input records, with the first application to be made in the order-processing system. Thus, the basic invoice form (See Chapter 18, Figure A, page 514) must be converted to a machine-prepared invoice form and the necessary card input forms must be designed to provide the information for the invoice. This will require a review of typical order-processing procedures and the types of data that are processed in order to determine the following: (1) the essential *master* information (customer name, customer code number, customer address, and the like); (2) the typical *detail* information involved in each transaction (invoice data, style or stock number, quantity purchased, and the like); (3) a reasonable size of punched-card field for each item of information; and (4) a logical sequencing of fields so that the sequence of data on the original source document and the sequence on the card form are the same.

Prior to developing the new machine-system records, you have studied the order-processing files and have found the following information:

The firm's biggest customer is the Barlow Manufacturing Company, located at 3728 South Michigan Road, Kalamazoo, Michigan, 49056, Customer No. 08367 (although the firm's customers can soon be expected to number in the hundreds of thousands); invoice numbers require larger fields than customer numbers as many orders come from "repeat" customers; unit prices of products are exclusively below $1,000; records show that no orders have been received for quantities of more than 100 of each item; and the maximum number of items listed on one invoice is 10.

Using the systems information cited above and blank punched cards or card layout forms if available, you are to design the following records for use in the new machine system planned for order processing:

1. A machine-prepared invoice form that will be created for the new system to replace the old handwritten form mentioned previously.

(See Figure 20-14 for an example of a report form that has been prepared by a machine printer.) On your report or output form for the invoice include sample information recording the sale of three items of merchandise sold to the Barlow firm identified above.

2. An 80-column master card for customers such as the Barlow Manufacturing Company.

3. An 80-column detail card illustrating the recording of one of the items sold to the customer. On the card layouts show the interpreted (printed) data and the related punches for encoding those data in each column used on both the master and the detail cards.

The careful application of the principles of forms design presented in Chapter 18 as well as a consideration of the size and sequencing of punched-card fields will be required in order to complete this case satisfactorily.

Chapter 21   ELECTRONIC DATA PROCESSING SYSTEMS

Part 4 has described a succession of developments in the field of information processing, starting with the manual machines discussed in Chapter 19, progressing to the punched-card systems explained in Chapter 20, and finally reaching the most sophisticated electronic levels treated in this chapter. With this array of information-processing power, management has been offered increasingly better means of meeting its insatiable demand for more accurate, up-to-date information.

Electronic data processing (EDP) refers to the use of a computer in the processing of data that have been converted into a machine code consisting of electrical impulses. In addition to the computer, other equipment and procedures are required to convert human-readable data into a form that the machine can use for processing and for later conversion of the coded data into a language useful to management. The combination of equipment (*hardware*), the procedures and instructions (*software*) required to make the machines work, and the personnel needed to operate the system is called the *electronic data processing system*. Because of the dominance of the computer in this system, the term is usually shortened to *computer system*.

The development of computers and electronic data processing systems has been acclaimed as the most important technological development of the 20th century. This sweeping claim is sup-

ported by ample evidence that the computer has greatly extended the human ability to analyze, compute, and communicate, and as a result greatly accelerated the progress of business and of society. Several years ago, a group of sociologists studied the effects of computers and telecommunications on the quality of life, the allocation of national resources, and the adequacy of our present institutions to accommodate them. According to this study, from 1950 to 1975 the industrialized world was the center of a major social transition from an industrial society to an "informational" society in which information processing, rather than industrial production, became the dominant labor activity. The cause of this shift to a new type of production is the computer, whose basic industry is now the world's fastest-growing business.[1]

All types and sizes of business either employ computers directly or utilize computer services in some capacity. Every person as a private citizen is touched by the computer's product. In the office, especially, where the principal product is information, a quiet revolution has been created by this information-processing marvel. Work processes

---

[1]This information is abstracted from the findings of a study entitled "The Information Sector of the Economy," conducted by Edwin Parker, Center for Interdisciplinary Research, Stanford University, Palo Alto, CA 92605 and presented at the 1975 Paris Conference on Computer/Telecommunication Policies.

and methods of organization have changed; new work skills have appeared; a host of new items of equipment and auxiliary services and new professions have been created. Each of these developments has affected directly the responsibilities of administrative office managers and their staffs. Too, each of these developments has alerted the managers of offices to the need for understanding more fully what a computer is, how it functions in an information system, and most important of all to the office manager, how it can process information more effectively. It is the purpose of this chapter to provide this basic background about the computer and to explain in a nontechnical language how it functions as a systems tool.

THE EVOLUTION OF COMPUTERS IN BUSINESS

According to a study made by the Research Group of Predicasts, Inc., Cleveland, Ohio, the computer industry has grown so remarkably fast that by the end of its third decade in 1980, there will be 800,000 computers operating in over 60 countries, compared with fewer than 10,000 in 1960 and about 100,000 in 1970. The value of this hardware (including all items of equipment in the computer system) is expected to rise from just under $35 billion in 1970 to $160 billion by 1980, which represents an annual growth rate of nearly 17 percent. The industry is dominated by United States firms, such as International Business Machines Corp. (IBM), Burroughs Corporation, Control Data Corp., NCR Corp., and the Sperry Univac Division of Sperry Rand Corporation; but this dominance is being eroded by increased competition from combinations of American, European,

and Japanese firms.[2] IBM alone accounts for about three fifths of the installed equipment in the United States and abroad.

The evolution of the computer has been marked by extremely rapid changes in the hardware and software and the successful application of these developments to information systems, as the following discussion of early and modern computers shows.

Early Computers in Business

The early computers in business span two generations of machines. The first generation of business computers began with the development of UNIVAC I in 1955 to process business information at the General Electric plant in Louisville, Kentucky. First-generation machines were quite large, produced enormous amounts of heat because of their use of vacuum tubes, and thus required a great deal of air-conditioning. Primarily these machines used punched cards as their input-output records, and the programs and data to be processed were stored on magnetic drums and cores. The development of temporary storage devices, known as *buffers*, facilitated the rapid sequencing of the input, the output, and the movement of data and instructions within the computer so that the computer could engage in processing operations at the same time it was receiving new data and transmitting processed data to an output

---

[2]Reprinted with permission from *Data Management*, official publication of Data Processing Management Association (October, 1974), p. 38. This periodical is a monthly publication of the Data Processing Management Association, 505 Busse Highway, Park Ridge, IL 60068, an organization dedicated to the improvement of data processing systems in organizations.

medium. Later in this period magnetic tape was developed as an effective input-output medium. Most firms utilized the early computers to convert from their existing manual and mechanical accounting and punched-card systems in order to obtain savings in the number of personnel required to do the work, to secure increased accuracy, and to provide for greater processing capacity that would handle anticipated increases in their workloads.

With the replacement of vacuum tubes by transistors and other solid-state devices in 1959, a second generation of computers was born. Transistorized circuits were much smaller, generated little heat, were less expensive, and required much less power than the vacuum-tube circuits. In addition, transistors offered the advantages of reliability and speed, since transistors last indefinitely and are characterized by fast switching ability.

During the second computer generation there were considerable improvements made in the storage of data. For example, high-speed magnetic tape units with massive amounts of data stored on reels of magnetic tape for later processing became the primary input and secondary storage media for major computer systems; removable disk packs were developed to permit nearby storage of data; and magnetic cores were used as the primary internal storage medium. From a systems standpoint, the concept of modularity (the building-block principle) was developed, whereby small- and medium-size computer systems could be expanded with compatible equipment into large systems. During this time most of the large-scale, stand-alone punched-card systems were replaced by electronic computers in business data processing operations.

Coming upon the scene was the first application of on-line, real-time data processing to new management information systems and computer applications in the area of operations research. As a result of such real-time systems, data could be fed into the computer for processing and returned in time for the user to have immediate access to the processed information, thus facilitating timely decision making.

Modern Computers in Business

Two computer generations also characterize the modern computer period. The third generation was introduced in 1964 with the marketing of the IBM System/360 computer, which featured the replacement of transistors by miniature integrated circuits in which all the circuit elements were contained on a tiny silicon wafer or chip. These circuits were smaller, more reliable, and significantly faster than those used in second-generation computers. Other developments in this computer generation were major improvements in all the components of the system, which resulted in increased speed, more storage, greater reliability of the input-output devices, and more frequent use of magnetic disk units. Also emerging were the concepts of time-sharing and multiprogramming, which are explained in a later section of this chapter.

IBM, always a leader in data processing, continued to operate as a trendsetter with its 1970 announcement of the System/370, which marked the beginning of the fourth generation of computers. Changes in this period were more evolutionary than revolutionary in nature and largely involved improvements in hardware and software. Hardware developments included microscopic integrated circuits, so small that in the System/370 the tiny silicon chips containing the circuits included 8 to 16 times the number of circuits used in the System/360 series. Again, the trend toward increased miniaturization continued, thus reducing the size and power requirements of the new computers and at the same time greatly increasing their processing speed. Other impressive fourth generation developments are *microprogramming* — in which the programmer uses the basic, built-in instructions of a computer to construct other instructions — and *virtual memory*, which allows secondary storage devices apart from the computer to be treated as an extension of the primary storage.

During this latter period, most of the remaining full-scale, punched-card installations were eliminated. Many small computer systems were produced at extremely low prices, considering their processing power, so that electro-mechanical punched-card machines were relegated to the role of supporting the input-output functions of card-oriented computer systems.

A new type of memory, called *bubble memory*, promises to compete successfully with magnetic disks as an effective form of storage in a computer system. The bubble device, a one-inch square package that stores 92,000 bits of data in the form of magnetic bubbles which move in thin films of magnetic material, uses far less power and five percent of the space of a disk and operates at speeds up to 75 times as fast as disk storage. Bubble memory can be used to turn handheld, programmable calculators into minicomputers and may also be used with portable computer terminals, word processing systems, and minicomputers to provide reliable, low-cost, mass computer storage.

COMPUTER FUNDAMENTALS

The staff of systems personnel and programmers in a firm are responsible for designing and operating the computer system, and therefore must understand the technicalities of the machine and its systems components. On the other hand, the users of computer services — the departments of a firm — require a relatively nontechnical type of computer knowledge. Departmental personnel must understand how the computer system functions; what the computer can do for their units; and then be able to evaluate its benefits and costs to their departments. As a specialist in information management, the office administrator must be especially sensitive to this powerful data-processing machine and clearly understand its basic characteristics in order that the office system may function as efficiently and economically as possible.

Basic Characteristics of Computers

While the computer systems found in today's business organizations vary considerably from firm to firm and from manufacturer to manufacturer, all computers have many common characteristics, such as the following:

1. The *electronic circuitry* which provides the modern computer with fantastic processing speeds and great computational capabilities. Earlier computing machines were electromechanical and dependent in large part upon the physical rotation of counting wheels.

2. An *internal memory* which can store both data and instructions (the stored program). This enables the computer to "remember" the details of instructions and proceed automatically from one instruction to another.

The computer's internal storage is subdivided into many small sections called *storage locations*, each of which has a special numeric address much like the address given to a residence in a city. When this address is known, the alphanumeric data "residing" in each storage location can be located easily by the computer. The illustration of computer storage shown in Figure 21-1 helps one visualize how either the data or the instructions may be stored in any storage location within the computer. Note that "I" represents a stored program instruction; "D," a stored data item, such as $5, the pay rate; and the one- or two-digit number, the hypothetical address of the storage location. The internal memory of a computer is measured by the number of storage locations available, that is, by the size of internal storage. A computer described as having 16 K memory refers to approximately 16,000 storage locations. (The letter *K* is an abbreviation of the word *kilo*, or 1,000).

3. The *great internal operating speed*. While a punched-card sorter can process cards at the rate of 800 cards per minute, some computers are capable of recalling information from internal storage at a rate that is measured in microseconds (millionths of a second), others in nanoseconds (billionths of a second), and more recently, in picoseconds (trillionths of a second). For example, within the half second it takes to spill a cup of coffee on the floor, a large computer can debit 2,000 checks

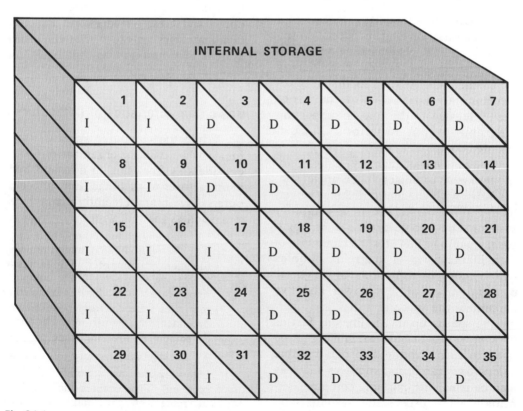

Fig. 21-1
A Conceptual View of Primary Storage Locations for Data and Instructions in the Computer

to 300 different bank accounts; examine the electrocardiograms of 100 patients and alert a physician to possible trouble; score 150,000 answers on 3,000 examinations; figure the payroll for a company with 1,000 employees; and have spare time remaining.

4. The *ability to perform mathematical operations and to exercise machine logic.* Stated simply, the computer can perform the arithmetic operations of addition, subtraction, multiplication, and division. Also, it can identify whether a number is positive, negative, or equal to zero, and can determine whether two numbers, when compared, are equal to, higher than, or lower than the other. Thus, the computer is said to have a logical ability when it makes comparisons of numbers and on the basis of such comparisons can change from one set of operations to another.

5. The *automated control of input and output.* The computer has the capability of automatically controlling the flow of data and instructions from various input devices. Thus, the computer can perform many steps without the need for human operators, thereby decreasing labor costs and increasing the production of work in the office.

Classifications of Computers

Computers may be classified by type, by purpose, and by size. Each classification is discussed briefly as it relates to the computers used in business information systems.

Type. Electronic computers are grouped into analog and digital categories, that is, by the type of data processed. *Analog computers* are used primarily in scientific research to perform arithmetic operations by *measuring* changes in a continuous physical phenomenon, such as electronic voltage, speed of sound, and air resistance. A slide rule is an example of an analog device. *Digital computers*, on the other hand, *count* numbers or digits. Thus, a digital computer performs arithmetic operations and comparisons of numbers and other characters that have been numerically coded. Digital computers can process both numeric and alphabetic data. Because of the fact that the majority of the data processed in business is alphanumeric, the digital computer is the most common type of computer used in business information systems.

Purpose. A second computer classification relates to the purpose for which the computer is intended. A *special-purpose* computer is designed to process one or more specific applications, and in some cases all or part of the operating instructions are built into the electronic circuitry. Examples of such devices are airline reservation computers, industrial process control computers, and special accounting computers. *General-purpose* computers, on the other hand, are designed to process a wide variety of applications. Usually these applications can be processed merely by changing the program of instructions stored in the machine.

All of the computers described in this chapter fall into the general-purpose, digital computer classification and are referred to as *business computers*. These computers are designed to process the large volumes of alphanumeric data required by payroll, billing, inventory, and other typical business systems applications. Contrasted with business computers are the *scientific computers*, which are designed for high-speed processing of numeric data involving complex mathematical calculations but smaller volumes of input and output data than are required for business processing.

Size. Computers may also be classified by *size*, which refers to their ability to process differing volumes of data or handle special types of computational problems. The various sizes are minicomputers, small-size, medium-size, and large-size computers. In the following paragraphs each of these class sizes is described, with major emphasis given to the minicomputers for the reasons cited.

Minicomputers. *Minicomputers* are very small computers that can perform all of the functions of a general-purpose computer; however, they are limited by their small internal storage and restricted capabilities for the input of data and the output of records. As the newest general type of computer on the market, the minicomputer is suitable for most business tasks (accounts payable, sales systems reporting, interest computations, and the like) that are too complex for the desk calculator but too simple for the large-scale computer. To an increasing degree minicomputers are being used for common business applications as well as input-output terminals for large computer systems or for handling communications between terminals and large central computers. In other cases — and this is the most common type of application — minicomputers work independently of the central computer as stand-alone systems within departments.

The cost of minicomputers ranges from under $5,000 to over $100,000; but due to improvements in hardware technology, minicomputers come surprisingly close to the capability of the larger computers. Because of advances made in microtechnology, a machine with a 4 K internal storage that cost $25,000 in

1965 could be purchased for only $1,900 in 1974.[3]

Beside their undisputed cost advantage, minicomputers can relieve the operational load on the main computer and provide convenience and economy to a department that previously had to wait for heavy-priority loads to be run on a central computer or in a service center. The result is more operating independence since the machine is under the user's control. Since many minicomputers are stand-alone machines in organizations not having large programming staffs, the software may be obtained from firms that specialize in writing minicomputer programs for business applications, or from the machine manufacturer. The latter arrangement is called a *turnkey service*, in which the manufacturer is fully responsible for installing a complete, ready-to-work system.

Figure 21-2 shows the tiny Hewlett-Packard 21MX minicomputer, selling for $5,500 and offering 4 K memory, and the IBM System/32, with 16 K memory and a potential of 5 million units of external disk storage. The IBM System/32 is compact (the "works" are in a desk), the rental price is low (usually about $1,000 a month), and the programming support is usually supplied in advance since the System/32 is sold for specified applications.[4]

----

[3]For a comprehensive analysis of the emerging role of minicomputers in business, see Gerald J. Burnett and Richard L. Nolan, "At Last, Major Roles for Minicomputers," *Harvard Business Review* (May–June, 1975), pp. 148–156. The authors present important management considerations regarding the minicomputer and excellent comparisons of the capabilities of minicomputers, medium, and large computers.

[4]With the increasing success in reducing electronic circuitry to smaller and smaller sizes, processors for computers have been produced successfully on small boards or chips. Smaller than

Hewlett-Packard, Inc.

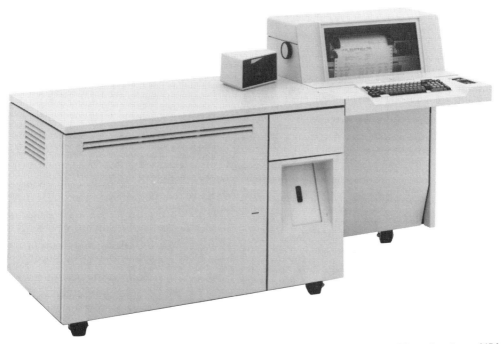

Photo Courtesy of IBM

Fig. 21-2
Two Sizes of Minicomputers Used in Business Data Processing

Small Computers. The line of demarcation between computer sizes becomes more blurred as the capabilities of minicomputers are expanded. However, *small computers* are usually considered as larger and more versatile than minicomputers, and have greater storage and input-output capabilities. Included in this category are the computer systems that utilize punched-card input and the 96-column card discussed in Chapter 20. Such a computer is the IBM System/3 that rents for less than $1,000 a month and which is discussed later in this chapter.

Medium-Size and Large-Size Computers. Since medium- and large-size computers are larger and faster than the smaller computers, they can handle more input and storage devices and produce more output. Large-size computers have even faster processing speeds, greater storage capacities, and a wider selection of input and output devices than medium-size computers. The large-scale system is utilized to handle complex data processing assignments requiring hundreds of remote terminals and the simultaneous processing of many programs under the direction of a highly specialized systems and programming staff.

THE COMPUTER SYSTEM

A computer system is a complex mixture of equipment, instructions, and

---

the minicomputers is a new group called *micro-computers*, made possible by the development of *microprocessors* as the data-handling unit in the smallest size of computers. For a discussion of microprocessors, see Dan M. Bowers, "Systems-on-a-Chip: Part 2 — Microprocessor Scorecard," *Mini-Micro Systems* (July, 1976), pp. 42–47. This monthly periodical was formerly named *Modern Data*, which indicates the significant trend in the computer industry toward increasingly smaller, less expensive hardware.

effective ideas for integrating these systems elements to maximize the processing of data in an organization. While there are secondary systems elements, the primary elements to consider in the computer system are the systems components, principally the equipment or hardware; certain concepts upon which modern computer systems are based; and the programming function that is required for people to communicate with the computer.

Components of the Computer System

Although a computer system performs the same basic operations as the punched-card system discussed in Chapter 20, the manner by which these operations are performed in the two systems differs markedly. Figure 21-3 illustrates the various components of a computer system, the processing functions to be performed, and the equipment required to perform the functions. Each of the systems components will be examined in detail in the following section.

Input. Input to the computer system may by divided into two forms: the *program* or sequence of instructions telling the computer what operations to perform and in what sequence; and the *data* to be processed. Specially trained technicians, known as *programmers*, plan the conversion of unprocessed data onto a medium such as punched cards, punched paper tape, or magnetic tape, that is acceptable to the computer.

For example, in an analysis of sales, the data may be partially stored on a tape prepared from the invoices and partially stored on a tape prepared from the shipping records. The data on the two tapes must be correlated and arranged in their proper sequence. Similarly, in the processing of payroll data, one tape may show the hours worked and the hourly rates; another, the social security status and related data; and another, the withholding tax deductions. Reading the information in proper sequence into the computer is part of the input operation and also part of the second phase, processing.

The following forms of input or *data entry* may be used in a modern computer system:

1. *Punched cards*, with the data being prepared on a keypunch machine and later transferred to the computer by means of a card reader. Although the keypunch is antiquated, noisy, and inconvenient, it still accounts for two thirds of the data-entry equipment. However, it is gradually being replaced by the more sophisticated devices described below.

2. *Punched paper tape*, using a code with five to eight channels. Paper tape is typically encoded as a byproduct of

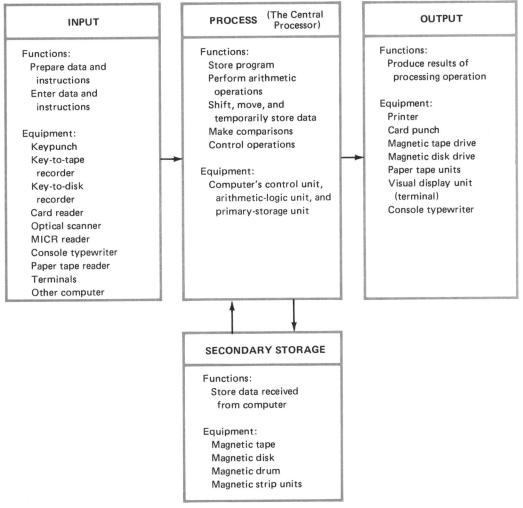

Fig. 21-3
Data Processing Functions and Equipment in a Computer System

some typewriting operation, such as the teletypewriter discussed in Chapter 8. Data on punched paper tape are translated into computer language by means of a paper tape reader.

3. *Magnetic tape*, upon which data are recorded as magnetized spots to create the electrical impulses. A tape unit may be used to translate the data from magnetic tape into the computer language. Or by means of a key-to-tape input device, as shown in Figure 21-4, the data are entered directly onto the magnetic tape for immediate processing by the computer. In key-to-cassette input, the data are recorded on a small magnetic tape cassette and later converted to full-size magnetic tape for ac-

ceptance by the computer. Strips of magnetic tape may be attached to the back of business records. These input records are called *magnetic stripe cards*, and are used in computer terminals to authorize credit and transfer funds. The magnetic stripe is also used on the back of ledger account cards to facilitate posting to accounts payable and accounts receivable records. Magnetic tape possesses most of the advantages of punched cards and punched paper tapes; but, in addition, magnetic tape may be erased and reused.

4. *Magnetic disks*, thin metal disks coated on both sides with a recording material. Data are recorded on a disk in the form of magnetized spots located in

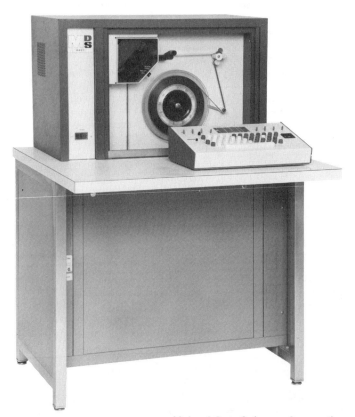

Mohawk Data Sciences Corporation

Fig. 21-4
A Key-to-Tape Input Device

concentric tracks on each recording surface. To enter data as input to magnetic disks, the key-to-disk device has been developed and is designed especially for input-preparation systems utilizing many keyboard stations either on-line, that is, connected to a computer, or off-line. One of the most recent versions of key-to-disk input is the *diskette*, or *floppy disk*, which is a small, plastic, magnetic disk that resembles a phonograph record. The floppy disk can hold as much data as are stored on three thousand 80-column punched cards and is easily filed or mailed. To use the diskette an operator inserts the diskette into a slot on the keyboard and terminal station, such as shown in Figure 21-5, after which the data are registered in the keyboard. The data are then verified through display on the visual display screen, and recorded on the diskette for later transfer to magnetic tape by a data converter or read directly into the computer.

Use of magnetic disks as input media permits *random access* — the retrieval of data from any portion of the record. When other input media such as punched cards, punched paper tape, or magnetic tape are used, it may be necessary to sort through a deck of cards or unwanted portions of tape in order to locate the desired data.

5. *Optical scanners* that read printed or handwritten documents, such as credit cards, and that transmit the data directly to a computer, bypassing data entry by human operators.

6. *Magnetic ink character readers* that read symbols specially printed in magnetic ink on "turnaround" documents, such as bank checks, that are designed to be returned to the sender.

7. *Console typewriters and data terminals*, which are used for manual, direct keyboard input of data, for updating data already stored in the computer, and for querying the computer. The console typewriter is located in the midst of the computer hardware while the data

Photo Courtesy of IBM

Fig. 21-5
A Key-to-Disk Input Device

terminals may be located nearby or frequently in more remote locations. Terminals, which were illustrated in Figure 8-7, page 206, are commonly used as interactive devices on both small and large computer systems. A more recent development is the *intelligent terminal*, which has the added features of a processing unit and memory and is capable of editing, recalling constant information, and error detection, independent of the computer.

8. *Point-of-sale (POS) equipment*, such as the cash register, that utilizes optical character recognition (OCR) fonts for imprinting and machine reading of journal tapes or low-cost cassette magnetic tape records to speed the collection of retail sales data and the automation of subsequent processing operations. POS systems are discussed later in this chapter.

Processing. The main work area in the computer is called the *central processing unit* (CPU), and within this area are the three operating units outlined in Figure 21-6. Both data and instructions enter the *primary storage* unit (also called the *main memory* or *main storage*) before the processing begins; or they may be stored in *secondary storage*, such as magnetic tape and magnetic disk units that enlarge the storage capacity of the computer system. However, the contents of secondary storage cannot be processed without first being brought back to the primary storage unit.

Flow of Data. To be processed, the data held in primary storage must be transferred to the arithmetic-logic unit where processing takes place. A common example of business data processing is an hourly payroll run in which the four arithmetic processes are employed as well as the logical processes of comparing numbers, such as comparing

year-to-date earnings of an employee with the maximum earnings permitted for social security computations to determine whether a deduction for social security is required. Thus, the processor, by making comparisons, can test for various conditions during processing and follow certain alternate routes in the computer program. The function of the control unit is explained in a later section.

The sequence of processing steps within the CPU is indicated by the numbers appearing in Figure 21-6. No such sequence has been indicated for the control unit as it regulates the computer during all phases of the processing operation.

Representation of Data. Within a machine system, the data to be processed must be represented in some form in order that the machine can manipulate the characters in line with the output desired. Prior to the advent of electronic circuitry, computing machines, such as adding machines and rotary calculators, were electromechanical and processed numeric data in the same way that the office worker does — using the ten-position (0–9) decimal system to solve computational problems. Such a system was slow and when possible was replaced by a much more simplified numeric system utilizing two states. This concept was introduced in Chapter 20 in the discussion on the "hole-no hole" coding system used in recording data on punched cards.

In the computer, data are represented in a similar two-state form: either the presence (one state) or the absence (a second state) of electronic signals in certain sections of the circuitry. This is the so-called *binary code* in which all letters and numbers to be encoded are represented by two symbols, "0" and "1," in various combinations. Thus, a computer's electrical pulses may be either in a conducting or nonconducting state, while internal storage devices, such as magnetic cores, may be magnetized in either a clockwise or counterclockwise direction. More simply, the two symbols may be considered as indicating a "pulse," and "no pulse," or an "on" and "off" state. The "on" state indicates the presence of a number (1)

while the absence of a pulse (the "off" state) indicates the absence of a value, or 0.

Since the binary system has but two symbols, 0 and 1, as opposed to the decimal or ten-position system, the binary system is inherently simpler. When the binary code is used, all numbers, letters of the alphabet, and special characters are expressed as a combination of either zeros or ones, and each character is called a binary digit, or more commonly

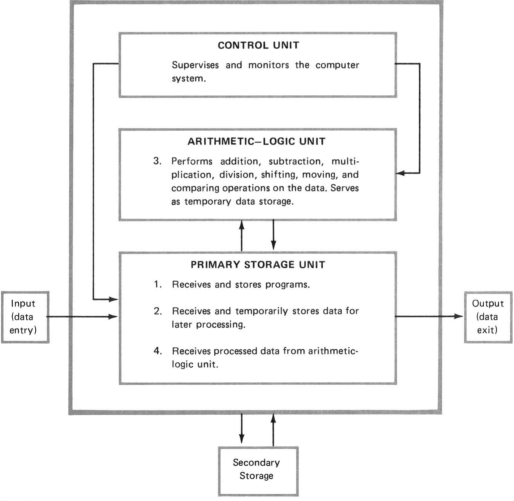

Fig. 21-6
The Central Processing Unit of the Computer

by the contraction "bit." In pure binary notation the value of a digit is doubled each time it is moved one place to the left, as shown below. Higher numbers are expressed by adding additional digits to the left.

Decimal Digit	Four-Digit Binary Notation	Digit, Letter, or Symbol	Six-Digit Binary Notation
	8421	1	00 0001
0	0000	2	00 0010
1	0001	3	00 0011
2	0010	A	11 0001
3 (1+2)	0011	B	11 0010
4	0100	C	11 0011
5 (1+4)	0101	%	01 1100
8	1000	$	10 1011

Combinations of decimal digits, letters of the alphabet, and special symbols such as "%" and "$" are expressed in an alphanumeric code by providing additional binary digits. For example, using six binary digits, the code for "4%" is "00 0100 01 1100" and the code for the letter "A" is "11 0001." Note that each digit, letter, or symbol in this code requires six binary digits. The first two digits are comparable to the zone punches on the 80-column card; the last four digits have the same binary values as found in the four-digit binary example.

For arithmetic computations, most computers use a version of the *binary-coded decimal* (BCD) system in which only the first four binary positions are used. Therefore, any decimal number can be expressed by stringing together groups of four binary digits. To illustrate, the decimal number "4609" is expressed in BCD form in this way:

Decimal Number	4	6	0	9
BCD Number	0100	0110	0000	1001

In pure binary this number would be expressed as 1001000000001; thus, the BCD system is easier for humans to read. The most current computers use a version of the BCD code called the Extended Binary Coded Decimal Interchange Code (EBCDIC), explained on page 562, Chapter 20. More detailed information on the various codes used in computer systems may be found in data processing textbooks and the technical manuals of computer manufacturers.

Storage. As pointed out in Figure 21-6, primary storage and secondary storage are the types of storage found in the computer system. *Primary storage* is located within the central processing unit and is used to store all data and instructions prior to their use in processing or until the program calls for the processed data to be "read out." The data, as instructed by the program, move back and forth between the primary storage unit and the arithmetic-logic unit. The primary storage of many modern computers consists of tiny doughnut-shaped rings called *cores*, as shown in Figure 21-7, each of which is capable of storing either a binary one or a binary zero value. A specified number of adjacent bits, when considered as a unit, is known as a *byte* and makes up each position of storage. Cores are arranged on a screen of wires, and each core has an X and Y wire running through it at right angles. To record a "1" value, one half of the total required current is sent through the X wire from left to right and the other half of the required current through the Y wire from top to bottom. To record a "0" value in a core, an opposite current flow is sent through the X and Y wires.

In any computer system, one of the major considerations is the *access*

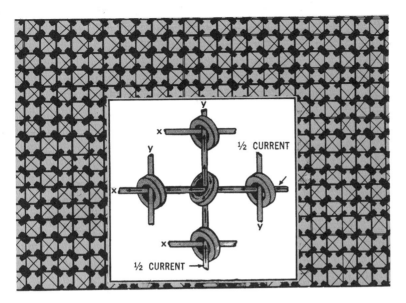

Fig. 21-7
Internal Storage by Means of Magnetic Cores

time — the speed with which the data and the instructions can be retrieved from their location in the memory unit and transported to the desired location. The data stored in the computer are not erased when they are transported to another location nor when they are "read out"; the data are erased only when the computer is given instructions to store new information in the same location as the old data. Because of the speed of access to data in magnetic core storage and its storage capacity, core storage is often the most economical means of storage in terms of cost per machine calculation.

When data are stored in *secondary storage*, that is, external to the computer, they are retained in the form of punched cards; punched paper tape; or on magnetic media such as disks, tape, or magnetic cards, ready for re-entry into the computer as desired. The storage of data in magnetic tape files is shown in Figure 9-6, page 231.

Control. The *control unit* interprets the instructions recorded on the input media, directs the various processing operations, and checks to see that the instructions are properly carried out. The control unit directs the receipt of information in the storage unit, stores the intermediate results of the operations, and releases the information as needed in the arithmetic operations.

Output. After a program has been run, the results of the computer operations, the *output*, are communicated to its user. The instructions fed into the computer indicate the location in the storage unit of the output that is to be printed out, where it is to be printed, and the manner in which it will be printed. If the end use of the processing is a formal report or a business document, the results will be printed in planned report form or on a business form such as a statement or a check. If the output is to be used in subsequent processing, it may be recorded as secondary storage on punched cards, magnetic tapes, or magnetic disks to be used later in the input unit for further calculations.

The major kinds of output devices are:

1. *Printers* that produce single or multiple copies of the information generated by the computer and at printing speeds ranging from 10 to 2,000 characters per second or up to 2,500 lines per minute. Some electronic printers may operate at faster speeds for use with business forms and gummed labels, and eliminate the noise associated with the mechanical output equipment in which hammers strike the paper. The console typewriter can be used either as a printer or as a remote terminal when it is linked on-line to a computer console.

2. *Visual display terminals* or cathode ray tube devices that provide information on television-like screens. The terminal serves as a device for communicating data to and from the computer, as discussed in Chapter 8.

3. *Voice response units* that generate the human voice from a prerecorded set of words stored in memory. These units represent the most convenient means of accessing data for certain kinds of businesses such as airlines, transportation companies, and financial institutions, as discussed later in this chapter.

4. *Special-purpose output devices*, such as computer output microfilm (COM) discussed in Chapter 10. Another specialized output device is the *graph plotter*, which produces graphic drawings under the direct control of a computer. In essence, the plotter is simply a paper-holding drawing board with a mechanical pen suspended over it for making various lines in different locations as directed by the computer. Plotters are used increasingly in civil engineering, drafting, and in medical research.

Computer Systems Concepts

The components of the computer discussed in the preceding paragraphs are, in essence, hardware items — machines and devices that have been programmed to initiate, operate, and complete the processing of data by the computer. Before such equipment can be put to work, an understanding of some of the most basic systems concepts surrounding the computer system should be developed so that the administrative office manager and managers in other areas of the firm may be able to make wise decisions regarding the most efficient, economical means of processing data.

File Maintenance. *File maintenance* is the process of keeping current the files of recorded data. In a computer system, the magnetic tape and magnetic disk files are routinely updated to reflect the most current condition possible. A department store, in handling its accounts receivable, updates the accounts of all customers to allow for payments against their outstanding balances as well as increases in the amounts owed because of additional purchases on credit. File maintenance is one of the most common applications of the computer in business data processing.

Data Base. With the tremendous processing power of computers and their merger with telecommunication devices that transmit information over great distances at the speed of light, it is possible to centralize in one physical location a collection of files. As discussed in Chapter 17, a data base is a library of interrelated data files that is concentrated in one area, which is accessible via telecommunication devices to employees throughout the firm. The advantages of a data base include the elimination of duplicate files and the related manual storage and retrieval tasks; the provision for a single information source that furnishes complete, accurate data storage and retrieval; and a great reduction in the computer processing time. The disadvantages that may be found in a data base operation include problems of security (protecting the confidentiality of the stored data); the question of economics (the technology and file maintenance procedures required are very expensive); the difficulty of sharing departmental information for integration into a centralized data file; and finally, the company-wide problems that are generated when unreliable equipment causes work stoppages and a drop in office productivity.

Source Data Automation. To get the information into digital form, the computer system requires, on the average, six to eight persons — someone to write the original information and someone else to copy it. Later, various persons review the data for keypunching, after which an operator punches the data into cards. Still later, the data are verified and eventually fed into the computer. Obviously, this is a time-consuming, costly process. To overcome the weaknesses of such a "batch" system, the concept of source data automation is employed.

Source data automation (SDA) is simply the conversion of data to a machine-readable form at the point where the data originate, rather than later at some centralized location. This concept covers a wide range of devices — optical character readers, magnetic stripe encoders and readers, point-of-sale systems, tag readers, and the whole family of machines that involve keying in data on tape, disk, diskette, and cassette. It should be noted that source data automation is usually concerned with replacing the keypunch function in a data processing system and thereby speeding up the "capture" of data, improving the accuracy of the data base, and saving money for the user.[5]

An increasing number of SDA applications are found. Examples are an optically readable sales invoice to be returned by the customer with a check, the mark-sensed form to be filled in by a student taking an examination, the Universal Product Code (UPC) marking on a can of mushroom soup to be machine read at a supermarket checkout counter, or the tag attached to a pair of socks that will be removed by the retail clerk when the item is sold. In each case a sensor (detecting) device is matched to the input documents and the coded information is read and processed according to the instructions contained in the computer system.

Programming the Computer

The "director" of a computer system is its internally stored program. To program the computer, the first step is to define and analyze the particular problem that the program is to solve. Next, the programmer systematically charts

[5]The problems of developing an effective source data automation program in business are analyzed in the following two articles: Malcolm L. Stiefel, "Source Data Automation: Part 1," *Mini-Micro Systems* (May, 1976), pp. 58–62, 64–69; and Malcolm L. Stiefel, "Source Data Automation: Part 2," *Mini-Micro Systems* (June, 1976), pp. 38–43. In the first article, the author develops an interesting conceptual view of both closed-loop and open-loop systems.

the problem solution and translates the solution into a suitable programming language. Each of these steps will be described briefly in this section.

Analyzing the Problem. The first step of programming involves the activities of analysis and synthesis, which precede the writing of the actual program. It involves studying the problem and developing a general scheme for solving the problem. Both systems analysts and programmers may work on this phase of the study. Once the overall strategy is developed for solving the problem, the programmer determines the specific steps required to program the computer.

Developing the Problem Solution. Programming involves the preparation of instructions broken down into sequential steps so that every eventuality can and will be considered. Otherwise, the final output will be incorrect, thus involving much expense and delay. From the analysis performed during the systems analysis phase, the programmer prepares a *block diagram*, or computer system flowchart, as discussed in Chapter 17, showing the sequence of steps and the machine decisions required to complete the program. Figure 21-8 illustrates a block diagram for solving a simple inventory problem that involves computing and printing a report of inventory valuation for a manufacturing organization. It should be noted that the input in this case is derived from a punched-card reader. The simple arithmetic operations are performed within the CPU's arithmetic-logic unit, as are the test or logical functions (appearing in the diamond-shaped symbols) in which the computer makes internally programmed decisions independent of the operator.

Writing and Testing the Program. After the charted solution has been tested for validity, each of the steps in the chart is converted into computer language statements using one of the languages discussed in a later section of this chapter. The program is tested by running it on a computer with actual data to make sure that the program works and to provide for all predictable contingencies. At this stage, *debugging* — the process of making corrections in the program — starts. Debugging is a critically important step in the programming process, sometimes consuming as much as 25 percent of the time the programmer spends working on the program. As soon as the program is debugged, it is recorded on the available input media discussed earlier for transmission of the program to the computer.

An Illustrative Program. As a relatively simple example of the kind of work involved in programming, the problem of taking a physical inventory of stock on hand will be analyzed, presented in a step-by-step form, and illustrated by means of a block diagram. In this example, it will be assumed that after the inventory has been taken, the following data are to be recorded in punched cards: (1) part number, (2) inventory count in units, and (3) unit price. This group of cards becomes the *data deck*. The program that is developed from the block diagram is also recorded in punched cards and becomes the *program deck*. In order to use these two card decks, the following steps are involved in completing the problem:

1. The program deck is fed into a card reader from which the data on the cards are transmitted to the computer for storage in the internal memory unit.

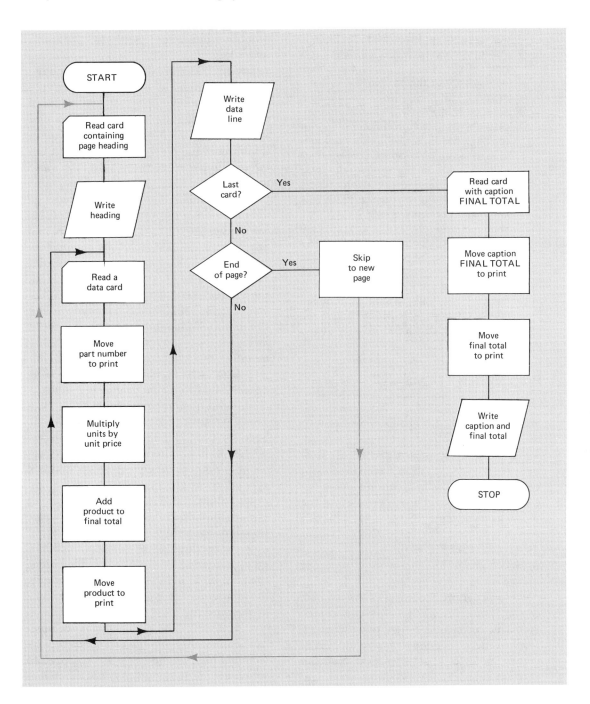

Fig. 21-8
Block Diagram for Solving an Inventory Problem

2. The data deck is sorted into part number order, after which the deck is fed into the card reader one card at a time, as the program states, for temporary storage of the data in the internal memory unit.

3. As shown in Figure 21-8, the program calls for the computer system to print the page heading, read a data card into internal storage, perform the necessary calculations in the arithmetic-logic unit, print these calculations along with other data, test to see if the last card has been processed, and if so, print the final total and stop. If it is not the last card, the computer must test for the end of the page; and if it is not the end of the page, the computer reads another card into storage and repeats the process. The routine is changed when a new page is needed and when all the cards have finally been processed.

Programming Languages

A computer system may be considered analogous to a group of workers in an office. For all of them to work together effectively as a unit, there must be present a common language that each understands and can interpret accurately in the course of completing the work assignments. Similarly, when a computer system performs its data-handling activities, it requires a programming language for communicating with all the units in the system.

To program a computer in its own binary-code or *machine-oriented language* using symbols that represent different orders or commands to the computer is a tedious process. Such a process requires the programmer to remember the codes for all the steps in an operation as well as the storage locations of all the data and program instructions. To overcome the difficulties

involved in writing a program in actual machine language, synthetic programming languages, which represent a cross between the normal human language and the numerical language of the machines, were developed. At first, some of these languages were restricted to one application and to one brand of system, which prevented an easy interaction between different brands of computers and thus caused major rewriting of programs when changes in hardware occurred.

The development of higher level languages, which are independent of any computer on which they run and require of the programmer no particular understanding of the machine code or the characteristics of the computer used, was a giant step forward in simplifying the programming function. A *higher level language*, as contrasted with the machine-oriented language, utilizes instructions that combine several machine operations in one programming instruction, which simplifies the task of program writing. Once the program has been written, it is fed into the computer where it is finally translated into machine language by a *compiler*, which is a special program provided by the computer manufacturer. Note that under all circumstances the computer can operate only in machine language; and that even with the use of higher level languages discussed in the next section, the computer converts the higher level language to its own language before processing the data.

Because of the great number of business applications that are shared by firms as well as the expertise required to write efficient programs, an extensive number of ready-made programs have been developed by computer manufacturers and by firms specializing in software applications. These well-planned software packages enable the user to obtain full computer capability.

Several of the most common compiler languages are described very briefly below. They include the principal languages used in commercial applications: COBOL and RPG; FORTRAN, a universally used language with some business applications; and BASIC, a widely used, time-sharing language for interaction with the computer system. Figure 21-9 illustrates several commands written in three different languages to show the relative readability of the various languages.

COBOL. *COBOL,* an acronym for *Common Business-Oriented Language,* is the most widely used language for business data processing. It is an English-like language which offers to the user readable and understandable program details. It is designed specifically to handle the input, processing, and output of the large volume of alphanumeric data files that are characteristic of business data processing applications. COBOL is usable on any manufacturer's equipment and has been adapted to minicomputers. The programmer prepares the instructions in COBOL, which are then converted into the computer's numeric-code language by the COBOL compiler provided by the manufacturer.

RPG (Report Program Generator). This popular business programming language was originally designed to generate programs that produced printed reports. A later version, RPG II, has been developed for use in report preparation, file maintenance, and other business applications on small computers. RPG is easy to learn and simple to use. Using abbreviated English terms

and special source statements called *specifications,* the programmer sets up a program that describes the form of the input data, the input and output devices that are to be used, the calculations that are required, and the format of the output reports. For example, the computation C + A times B might take the following form on an RPG calculations sheet:

Factor 1	Operation	Factor 2	Result Field
A	MULT	B	C

With the total program specifications punched into cards and transmitted to the computer, the RPG compiler generates a machine-language program that compiles the data processing operations and produces the required reports.

FORTRAN. *FORTRAN,* whose name was created from the two words FORmula TRANslation, was developed to aid in the programming of scientific, mathematical, and engineering problems. FORTRAN relies largely upon mathematical notation, such as $=$ for EQUALS and $+$ for PLUS and $\star$ for MULTIPLY as shown in Figure 21-9. Although it has some application in business data processing since many business problems can be expressed in mathematical equations, FORTRAN is not suitable for the extensive processing of alphanumeric data files stored in secondary storage devices. For this reason, *PL/1 (Programming Language-1)* was developed as a general-purpose language that could be used for both business and scientific applications. Due to its more limited use, however, PL/1 is not covered in this book.

BASIC. The term BASIC is derived from the words *Beginner's All-Purpose Symbolic Instruction Code* and is a widely used language in time-sharing. Resembling ordinary mathematical notation, such as the FORTRAN statements, BASIC has a simple English vocabulary and few grammatical rules. The language is versatile, for it can be quickly used for business and scientific problems. With BASIC a person can "converse" with the computer system that includes a time-sharing terminal by executing the following steps:

1. The user dials the number of the computer facility and types in basic

Operation to be Performed	Programming Language	Programming Language Statements*
Addition	COBOL FORTRAN BASIC	ADD HOURS TO TOTAL-HOURS. C = A + B LET C = A + B
Multiplication	COBOL FORTRAN BASIC	MULTIPLY HOURS BY RATE GIVING GROSS- PAY. [OR, COMPUTE GROSS-PAY = HOURS * RATE.] C = A * B LET C = A * B
Input	COBOL FORTRAN BASIC	OPEN INPUT HOURS-FILE, RATE-FILE, OUTPUT GROSS-PAY-FILE. READ CARD. READ HOURS-FILE RATE-FILE AT END. GO TO FINISH. 01 READ (1, 02, END = 06) A, B 10 INPUT A, B
Output	COBOL FORTRAN BASIC	FINISH. MOVE GROSS-PAY TO OUTPUT-LINE. WRITE OUTPUT-LINE AFTER ADVANCING 2 LINES. CLOSE HOURS-FILE, RATE- FILE, GROSS-PAY-FILE. STOP RUN. 06 STOP 07 END 60 END

*The two-digit numbers preceding FORTRAN and BASIC statements represent arbitrary statement numbers assigned by the programmer for reference use within the program.

Fig. 21-9
Business Data Processing Statements Written in Three Programming Languages

identification data, such as a user number and a required password.

2. The computer system verifies the identification information, after which the user types in the BASIC program with the final command "RUN."
3. Assuming an error-free program, the program is executed and the answer is printed out on the terminal for action by the waiting user.

EVALUATING COMPUTER SERVICES

The administrative office manager, like other departmental managers, is a user of computer services. In order to make the most effective use of the various computer services offered, the office manager must understand what types of applications are most feasible for converting to the computer system, when to use a data service center to handle the firm's computing needs, and how to appraise the computer services of the manager's firm. Each of these aspects of computer service appraisal is discussed briefly in the following section.

When to Use a Computer

Office managers have historically been considered as experts in the selection and use of basic computing machines. With the minicomputers that are dedicated to one type of operation, such as accounts receivable, this same condition may still be true. For the larger, general-purpose computers, however, office managers must have available sufficient systems information to make intelligent decisions on which general office operations to computerize and which operations to perform using manual or mechanical methods. By and large, systems specialists agree that a computer is used most efficiently in processing oper-

ations that have one or more of the following characteristics:

1. Large volumes of data input, many reusable data files, and frequent references to the files.
2. Speedy processing and accurate reporting requirements.
3. Repetition of the processing runs. Thus, a standardized operation is required that calls for frequent reruns of the computerized system (such as the weekly payroll system or a daily inventory update).
4. A high probability of reducing the unit cost of processing the data.
5. Continuous need for current management information. For example, time-sharing systems permit managers to retrieve real-time data from the system at lightning speed in order to appraise the firm's situation and make immediate decisions. Inventory control and financial reporting systems frequently require such information.
6. Where future expansion in information processing seems likely. In such a case, a computer system can be modified by the addition of new processing and storage equipment.

Frequently a computer system can offer unexpected advantages to a department. By reducing the amount of dull, repetitive manual work, extra time is provided for more creative efforts, such as designing new programs or improving the basic methods of workers. In addition, the use of a computer outside the department relieves the office manager from the recurring problems involved in selecting, maintaining, and updating office equipment. Space in the office may be reclaimed for more productive work; and because of the lower unit costs of processing data by computer, departmental budgets may be lowered. With the accurate accounting for time and run costs made possible with each computer operation, the office manager can maintain more precise cost records of processing data than was true in pre-computer days.

When to Use a Computer Data Service Center

With the advent of the minicomputer that can be located in a department, the need for an outside service center to handle the department's data processing may be reduced. However, such a facility offers benefits worth considering, sometimes at costs lower than are possible within the small firm. One advantage of a service center is the strength of its staff, including the widespread work experience and technical expertise available for developing various programs. Another is the immediate availability of efficient programming packages and the existence of back-up equipment if needed. Provisions for the cost of data center services, the turnaround times, the methods and frequency of delivery, and performance guarantees should be spelled out in the agreement with the data center. In Chapter 19 additional values of a data processing service center were discussed at length, all of which apply to data processing by computer.

What to Expect of a Firm's Computer Services

When a manager assigns the main data processing operations of a department to the firm's computer center, a high degree of confidence is placed in the computer center. In order to be sure that such confidence is justified, the computer center must maintain a high level of work performance for its customers, the user departments. This requires setting up standards that meet these typical expectations of the computer user within the firm:

1. The firm's computer services should include reasonable assistance with the problems of the user department. Basic documents, such as bank checks, payroll checks, purchase orders, and invoices should carry preprinted numbers to facilitate accounting for all such records.
2. Effective data preparation should be provided. Controls should be designed which allow input checking at each step of preparing the data (recording, punching, and verifying), which in turn eliminate the chance of transcription errors and ensure accurate output.
3. All source documents brought by the user department to the computer installation should be identified and counted. Frequently a receipt is issued indicating the date and some type of identification for all such documents (such as document count, first and last document number, if consecutive, and the total number of the documents in the batch.)
4. Standard procedures should be available for returning the documents to the originators for correction before processing.
5. Controls within the computer program should provide further assurance of accurate processing. For example, a computer can determine that a customer number is incorrect — that it has no corresponding customer name; or the computer can calculate the sum of a group of debit items and the sum of a group of credit items and compare these sums for equality.
6. Users require reasonable turnaround times with little variation from one processing period to another. When such variation occurs, major adjustments in the systems of user departments are required, which in turn cause problems of employee morale and delay the completion of work.

7. Department managers look for ways of reducing processing costs as well as efficient processing procedures. In 1952 the cost of performing 100,000 multiplications on a computer was $1.26; and six years later it was 26 cents. In 1975, this figure had dropped to one cent.[6] This same reduction in the cost of processing data is expected to be demonstrated in departmental processing jobs, which should be charged to the departments involved.

With the passage of time office managers make additional applications of the computer to their department's data processing operations. Although the majority of such operations are still directly related to the routine processing of business data, new inroads are being made by more sophisticated analytical techniques that assist the decision maker. In a study completed at The University of Iowa, a random sample of 150 office managers from the 1,500 leading firms in the United States expressed a strong interest in the use of management science techniques, such as queuing theory, linear programming, and related topics. Such areas were unknown or of little interest to many a decade ago. As a result of changing developments in information processing and in their positions, the participating managers recommended for study the areas of computer-related training outlined in Table 21-1 on the following page.[7] Note the low rank order given to punched-card

equipment, formerly rated near the top in terms of office managers' interests.

ILLUSTRATIVE COMPUTER SYSTEMS

The following descriptions of computer systems tie together the principles and concepts of punched-card data processing presented in Chapter 20 and the preceding discussion of computer concepts in this chapter. While there are many medium- and large-size computer systems in operation, there is a marked trend in the computer industry toward the expansion of the smaller systems. Further, with the simplicity and power of the minicomputers and microcomputers, such machines have brought about a new concept called *distributed processing*, in which the computing equipment is decentralized within the firm. In essence, the computer's capability is being distributed to those departments or branches in which it is most critically needed. Under such circumstances, it is likely that the office manager will deal directly with small-size computers, the type of computers emphasized in this chapter.

Burroughs Corporation's L-9900 Magnetic Record Computer

The Burroughs L-9900 Magnetic Record Computer, a minicomputer, enables the user to read, store, and retrieve data on magnetic memory records and to produce a variety of accounting records and comprehensive management reports. Data on the magnetic memory records are provided in both printed and electronic forms. The memory records may be randomly accessed from an unlimited file for automatic updating or for immediate visual reference. Thus, users

---

[6]Excerpted from *Administrative Management*, copyright © 1975 by Geyer-McAllister Publications, Inc., New York.

[7]Alden P. Talbot, "A Comparison of the Computer Needs of Office Managers in Computer-Using Companies with the Computer Course Requirements in Office Management Curriculums in NABTE Schools" (Doctoral Dissertation, The University of Iowa, 1976), p. 87.

AREAS OF COMPUTER-RELATED TRAINING RECOMMENDED BY A NATIONAL SAMPLE OF 150 OFFICE MANAGERS

Recommended Areas of Study	Percent of Office Managers
Computer Capabilities	85.33
Interpretation of Computer Output	72.67
Computer Operations	55.33
Preparation of Computer Input	48.00
Flowcharting	44.67
Operations Research	40.00
Decision Tables	35.33
PERT	33.33
Punched-Card Equipment	27.33
Programming the Computer	26.67
Linear Programming	22.00
Keypunching	20.67
Queuing Theory	15.33

Table 21-1

can refer to the magnetic memory records visually, use them as input to the computer for updating accounting records, and process them for many types of reports useful for effective management control. Data stored electronically in the memory contribute directly to speed, accuracy, and processing productivity. For example, when preparing sales invoices and updating the accounts receivable file and inventory records, the customer's name and address are read from the customer's memory record and automatically printed in the "Sold To" portion of the invoice. The inventory memory record provides product description, pricing, discount, and other data for automatically completing the invoice. At the same time, the customer's and the inventory memory records are updated automatically.

Functional Units. The magnetic record computer, shown in Figure 21-10, operates with a variety of input and output peripheral devices that increase the flexibility of accounting and man-

agement reporting. The automatic magnetic record feeder-stacker as shown in the figure provides for the automatic feeding and alignment of magnetic records during the processing of accounting jobs, such as payroll. This device also allows for the automatic processing of magnetic memory records for management reports.

For the input of information, readers include magnetic tape cassettes (located in the "window boxes" at the left of the machine), punched paper tape, and punched cards. A terminal display device may also be used to input data. Devices for output include magnetic tape cassettes, punched paper tape, punched cards, and line printers.

The computer is programmed internally and has large-scale integrated circuitry, a type of "chip" memory as discussed earlier in the chapter, advanced logic for decision-making ability, and fourth-generation techniques called micrologic interpreters. These interpreters consist of strings of microinstructions stored in the computer's memory and provide complete internal control of computation, print formatting, printer positioning, forms movement, and the input and output of data by means of a console.

Software. A wide variety of standard application programs, written in COBOL, are available for such businesses as manufacturing, contracting, credit unions, hospitals, and banks, as well as for use in government.

IBM System/3

Small computers are usually general-purpose digital computers with a memory of up to 65,000 characters, and some even offer remote communication capabilities. For the small business this type of computer is justified on the basis of its ability to provide better control over a firm's data processing operations. Larger businesses install small computers as terminals to larger systems, especially in situations requiring some type of decentralized processing capability. Among the various small computers is the IBM System/3, which is discussed in the following paragraphs.

Functional Units. The IBM System/3, shown in Figure 21-11, is designed to handle business applications, such as accounts receivable, inventory control, sales analysis, and general ledger. The central processing unit

Burroughs Corporation

Fig. 21-10
Burroughs Corporation's L-9900 Magnetic Record Computer

Fig. 21-11
IBM System/3, a Small Computer System

consists of primary core storage with 8,192- to 32,768-byte capacity, an arithmetic-logic unit, a control system (for sequencing instructions and initiating communication between the primary storage and the input-output devices), an inquiry-control console, and an optional dual-program feature. This dual-program feature allows the concurrent loading and running of two independent programs. For example, when one program is undergoing an input or output function, the CPU is processing details for the other program, thus putting the CPU to more efficient use. Input-output equipment includes card units, printers, and disk-storage units. The card unit is capable of multiple functions; it can read, punch, collate, sort, and print cards without operator handling. The line printer, which operates at rates of 100 to 200 lines per minute depending on the unit, is similar to a ball-element typewriter and is capable of both input and output functions — for data entry, for inquiry, for operator commands, and for use as a second printer.

On-line storage in the System/3 consists of a disk unit having 2.45 million characters of storage and an average

access time of 153 milliseconds. Additional disk storage can be added to the system to increase the amount of storage and the access time. Off-line devices available to the system include sorters using photoelectric sensing elements and a magnetic character reader designed to process up to 500 checks and other related bank documents per minute.

Software. The programming language for System/3 is RPG II, a modification of the basic RPG language discussed earlier in this chapter. Preprogrammed packages are also available for use in this system.

A System/3 Application.[8] In the design and implementation of any business data processing system, information from one subsystem may often be used in another subsystem. While applications like billing and accounts receivable can stand alone, it is more efficient

---

[8]Adapted from *Guide to Order Writing, Billing, Inventory, Accounts Receivable, and Sales Analysis* (International Business Machines Corp.: June, 1970), pp. 1–13.

and profitable to combine them wherever possible. For example, in sales and distribution accounting, the four interrelated applications are: order writing and billing, inventory accounting, accounts receivable, and sales analysis. Figure 21-12 shows these basic applications and their interrelationship. Information on stock shipments can be used to maintain records in inventory accounting; charges billed to customers can be posted directly to accounts receivable; and detailed records of all sales made are essential to sales analysis. The use of a computer in the order writing and billing application sharply reduces the clerical functions otherwise required for processing in each of the other three areas.

As a batch of customer orders enters the system, a 96-column card is prepared for each item on a customer's order. In this way a card deck is punched and fed into the System/3 computer for the preparation of the customer's invoice and subsidiary documents, such as the invoice register, which is a summary listing of all invoices that have been printed, and the invoice summary card, which shows only the total amount billed to a customer rather than a listing of all items sold. Subsequently, the invoice summary cards are used as input in the preparation of the accounts receivable transaction register and the customer statements. In the meantime, the item transaction record cards are "rerun" — in the one case to process stock status reports for inventory accounting; and in the other, for analysis of sales by salesperson, by type of product sold, and by customer.

When a firm outgrows the capabilities of its punched-card system, the System/3 with its card input-output capabilities serves as a natural follow-up

because of its greater computing power and flexibility. Also, more powerful models of this system with data communication devices are available, which provide even more processing capability to the firm.

EMERGING COMPUTER APPLICATIONS

Beyond the widespread use of the computer in the so-called bread-and-butter applications in business, such as payroll accounting and inventory accounting, a host of new and exciting computer applications is announced from time to time. Such applications extend into the repetitive-work areas formerly dominated by workers, and thus remove from them much of the boredom which routine, repetitive work creates. Too, such applications integrate more and more departments within a firm, firms within an industry, and industries within an economic system, which facilitates the making of decisions in all areas.

Since the computer not only performs calculations on numeric data but also performs other important operations such as storing and moving alphabetic data, it has the potential for broader applications in information systems. Several of the most promising applications are discussed in this section. Each is largely limited to the imagination of the systems staff and to the firm's ability to afford the systems hardware and software required.

Data Communications

As described in Chapter 8, data communication services are used in a wide range of computer systems, such as

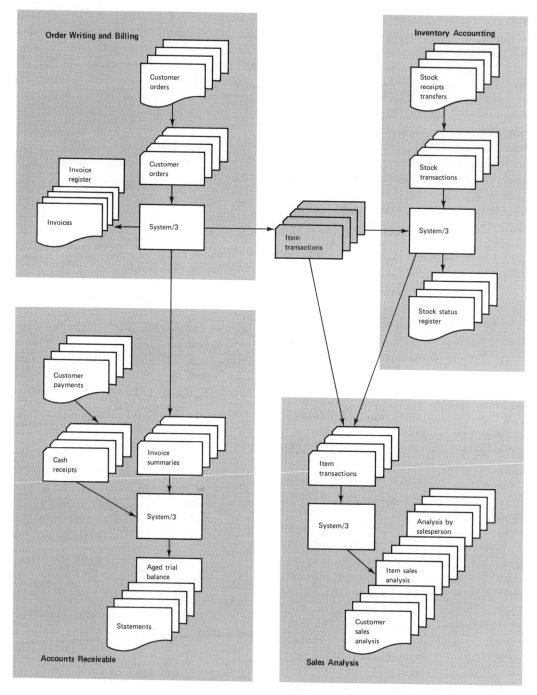

International Business Machines Corp.

Fig. 21-12

Sales and Distribution Accounting Applications Using the IBM System/3 Computer

computer time-sharing, inquiry processing, and data collection. An example of each of these applications is illustrated in the data communications network of Ramada Inns, Inc., a motel chain controlling almost 700 motels with more than 100,000 rooms. Through the use of terminals located throughout the country, incoming reservations are received from customers who use the toll-free telephone number. A reservationist clerk receives the calls and uses a terminal to communicate directly with the firm's central computer in Omaha. There the computer searches a disk file on the availability of rooms, and displays on the terminal screen the room availability in the requested hotel by room type and price. The clerk then confirms the reservation with the customer. If a reservation is made, the room is taken off the availability list, and the computer transmits the confirmed reservation to the proper terminal at the hotel. A related procedure involves terminal-to-terminal transactions where a guest at one hotel may request a reservation at any other hotel in the chain. Within a minute or two the request is transmitted to the computer, the disk file is scanned, and the computer transmits the confirmation back to the originating hotel where it is printed on-line and handed to the customer. Within business firms, similar integration of departmental functions is maintained through terminal-to-computer communication with a central data base.

Special Computer Applications

Within the space limitations of this text it is impossible to describe fully the growing list of special computer applications. However, the following very brief remarks show not only the variety

but also the broad, sweeping areas that have been adapted to computer processing.

Computer Output Microfilm. In the area of micrographics, the computer is combined with a recording device to photograph on microfilm the computer's output for later use in microform readers. As discussed in Chapter 10, page 266, this process, called COM, offers rapid storage of the photographed records, automatic coding and counting of microrecords, and fast access to the microfile.

Electronic Funds Transfer. Within the banking industry, *electronic funds transfer (EFT)* is a reality. EFT is a kind of electronic money transfer system; it permits consumers to transact nearly all their banking business with electronically coded plastic cards which are inserted in computer terminals located in very convenient places, such as supermarkets and post office branches. These terminals take the place of branch bank offices and are an added convenience to the depositor. EFT systems spring from earlier versions of cashless transactions, such as the pay-by-phone system, which uses a computer to electronically pay monthly bills received from the telephone company, department store, or gas station. Each payment is entered through a push-button telephone that is used to call a computer in a central location. The simplicity and the ease of using the system permit retailers to arrange credit transactions from their stores and customers can do the same from their homes. Such systems can reduce the edge of rising costs, growing personnel demands, and increased inefficiencies in managing administrative operations. Further, they eliminate mailing costs and the most expensive element — paper — and thus place the cost burden upon the least expensive element, the hardware.

Point-of-Sale Systems. In each of the examples cited in this section, information was received, stored, and processed for typical office operations. Although these applications are becoming very common, the computer may be used wherever information must be processed. In the supermarket, for example, the introduction of the *Universal Product Code (UPC)*, identified by thick and thin vertical lines, appears on about 75 percent of all supermarket items. At the checker's station such items are passed over a computer scanner which reads the UPC markings, registers the prices, and issues a printed tape at the end of the transaction. Also in growing use are point-of-sale (POS), or electronic cash register, systems. In these systems the POS stand-alone terminal or cash register may be able to process a variety of management reports, check credit status, or handle billing and merchandise-ordering functions.

Computerized Word Processing. Most of the computer applications in this section deal largely with numeric

data. However, the processing of words, as outlined in Chapter 7, page 175, may also be facilitated by the use of a computer. Computerized word processing combines a compact central processor with a number of interactive terminals for achieving the input and output of data, and for data storage on disk, tape, or magnetic card records. For communication systems requiring "canned" paragraphs, form letters, legal documents with variable fill-in information, or long reports requiring editing followed by a complete printout, the minicomputer is a highly effective word processor.

Another kind of word processor, the "talking" computer, has been developed. In such an audio-response system the procedure is simple: Users dial the computer on their telephones, and the computer answers. Mail-order firms use audio responses stored in computer memory to allow customers to enter orders over the telephone while an artificial computer voice verifies the order. An air-freight firm makes similar use of an audio-response system to let customers check the status of shipments. In this system a computerized voice response might be: "Shipment number 1245 was delivered on March 20."

QUESTIONS FOR REVIEW

1. What effects has the computer had on the makeup of present-day society?
2. What are the major characteristics of early and modern computers in business?
3. List the main characteristics that digital computers have in common.
4. How does a digital computer differ from an analog computer? Why are digital computers more commonly used in business?

5. Cite several reasons for the fast growth of minicomputers in business data processing.

6. (a) Describe the five components of a computer system.
   (b) With which of these components is the programmer's work most closely related?
   (c) With which is the administrative office manager most concerned?

7. Compare the advantages and disadvantages of punched card and magnetic tape when used as input media.

8. Explain the major differences between the primary storage and the secondary storage of data in a computer system.

9. What is the purpose of the logic unit in the computer's central processor?

10. Briefly describe each of the major kinds of output devices and the output media produced.

11. Define source data automation and indicate how it offers systems advantages to the office manager.

12. Trace the path of data and instructions from the input to the output phases of the computer system. In so doing, indicate the various forms of storage employed for the data and the instructions.

13. Compare machine-oriented programming languages with the so-called higher level languages in terms of ease of use in programming a computer.

14. What characteristics should a system possess in order to make computerization feasible?

15. What services should a department manager expect from a firm's computer center?

16. What are some of the uses of the magnetic memory records produced by the Burroughs Corporation's L-9900 Magnetic Record Computer?

17. What role does the punched card play in the IBM System/3?

18. Cite three recent applications of the computer to business systems in which the computing and the communication functions are merged.

QUESTIONS FOR DISCUSSION

1. An EDP system is highly technical in nature and requires the services of a specialized staff to make it operate effectively. At the same time the computer users represent a group of specialists in their own functional areas. What types of human relations problems can be anticipated in such a situation, and how can these problems be averted?

2. What is the relationship of the programmer to the systems analyst in an electronic data processing system?

3. To replace the use of a central computer to handle its large billing operation, the Apex Company has obtained a minicomputer to be located in the billing department and dedicated solely to the billing operation. What changes in the operating procedures of the billing department would be necessitated by the acquisition of this new machine?

4. How does a computer system handle exception routines — that is, deviations from the standard operating procedures in a system?

5. The purchase of a computer system requires the investment of large sums of money. What type of financial return should management expect on such an investment?

6. The Kenzi Construction Company of Seattle has commercial building projects going on all across the country. For example, on the Denver job alone there are 200 workers on the payroll. To save time and cost, the company is considering the use of a teletypewriter hook-up for the preparation of daily payroll records in the main office where there is punched-card equipment capable of card-to-tape and tape-to-card preparation of data for the computer. In the meantime the telephone company has recommended converting to a telecommunication system, using portable terminals at the construction sites to transmit payroll data to the main office. However, this approach would require a change in computers, as the present computer does not have communication capabilities. Indicate the course of action that you would recommend.

7. The Namura Elevator Company has installed a computer system at a cost of $250,000 to assist in the maintenance of company records. One of the system's major uses is to "watch over" the 35,000 inventory items, which requires about 2,000 inventory entries into the computer daily. This massive inventory, which is valued at more than $5 million, is necessary because no two elevators are exactly alike, and the firm must be prepared to service any elevator that it has installed. Discuss the reasons for justifying this general-purpose type of computer installation as well as other alternatives for controlling the inventory system by computer.

PRACTICAL OFFICE MANAGEMENT CASES

Case 21-1   **Developing a Systems Model for Internal Telecommunications**

Baumgartner Engines, Ltd., has achieved a tremendous engineering breakthrough in the development of a reliable, low-cost engine with a very low fuel consumption. Because of the widespread uses and worldwide acceptance of this engine in business, industry, and in the armed services, the firm has expanded from the main plant in Richmond, Indiana, to five branches in other sections of the United States as well as to foreign sales offices and assembly centers in Belgium, Iran, Japan, and Brazil. A global network has been set up which provides all branch plants with on-line communications to the corporate management staff and to the main-office data base.

While the information processing system between the main office and the branch plants makes extensive use of computer terminals, no such integrated system is found within the main office and plant. Rather, departments such as accounts payable, accounts receivable, inventory control, payroll, and personnel utilize the services of the central computer installation on a batch-processing basis. Thus, batches of records (source documents) are sent to the computer center for processing on a daily, weekly, or monthly basis with the output later "hand-carried" to the respective user departments. The result is slow turnaround time, inefficient use of staff due to the peak-and-valley workloads, excessive production of paper records, and less-than-desirable service to customers.

The Vice-President of Administrative Services, Dave McDaniel, was responsible for setting up the efficient corporate network of telecommunications. McDaniel has discussed with you, his assistant, the need for achieving the same type of processing efficiency within the main office and plant, as the computer system can accommodate additional terminals and thus could overcome many of the problems of batch processing. As a first step, McDaniel has obtained the approval of top management to set up a model telecommunication system using terminals on an experimental basis in one department; and if after a trial period of operation, the test system is considered satisfactory, most of the other 12 departments in the main office would be connected on-line to the computer center.

In his conversations with you, McDaniel has mentioned the following information about the status of the company's plans for the model telecommunication system:

1. The first application on the departmental terminals is to be the storage and retrieval of large-volume, active files, using magnetic disk storage devices. The tasks of adding, updating, and deleting records from such files are to be processed on the terminals provided within the department, thereby eliminating much of the batch processing work.

2. In the test department, a ratio of one terminal for every 10 workers is planned. Such a device would give the workers access to the calculating power of the computer as well as to the stored records controlled by the computer. Hard-copy output would be available upon demand through the computer's printing devices.

3. Physical and psychological factors as they relate to the work and to the workers must be given prior attention. In addition, work flow

within the department as well as into and out of the department must be studied. This type of information would be available from the test department.

4. Orientation and training needs of the workers can be handled by the staff in the computer center. However, the present procedures for batch processing the department's work must be converted to a new on-line system yet to be devised. Thus, a realistic time schedule must be set up before the new system can be installed.

5. No departments have been contacted about serving as the test department.

McDaniel places in your hands the entire responsibility for planning, designing, and implementing the model system and for gaining the support of the test department. He and Leslie Parker, the manager of the computer center, feel that the inventory-control department is the most feasible application for such an on-line system because of the great number of inventory files maintained and the frequency of change in the files. They stress to you that other departments in the firm have similar processing needs, and that only the data among the departments differ to any degree. Thus, a prototype or model system should be designed, tested, and installed in the inventory-control department for later use by the other departments as the processing needs require and as the available funds permit.

Using the systems approach to problem solving discussed in Chapter 17, construct a model (an overall blueprint) of a data processing system in which terminals connected on-line to the computer replace the batch method of processing data. In the model identify all of the important factors such as the hardware, software, space, and human needs, the information needs of management, interdepartmental problems involved in a systems change, and the time and training resources required to put the new system into operation. While the first specific application of this model concerns inventory control, keep in mind that your final objective is a written report to McDaniel in which you show clearly a general plan for converting batch processing to an on-line system in all departments, including inventory control. A judicious use of flowcharts as shown in Part 4 of this textbook will facilitate the presentation of your solution to this case.

Case 21-2   Solving the Human Problems of Changing to a Minicomputer System

You have recently been employed as the assistant manager of the purchasing department of your firm after completing three years' work as a systems analyst in another firm. In your previous position you had an opportunity to work with the data processing staff, especially the programmers; and primarily for this reason you were hired, since a new minicomputer is being acquired in your department. The new machine system is to be used solely for the processing of data related to the purchasing function, which was formerly handled by the firm's central computer.

It has been assumed that you can handle all the details of operating the new minicomputer system, which involves a turnkey machine. However, in case assistance is needed, Terri Clemens, the operations manager of the central computer center, is available to help you. Also, Clemens has offered to provide an orientation session to your staff to simplify their transition to the new system.

The staff of ten in the purchasing department consists of the manager who is away on sick leave for four months, you, four women whose average age is 51, three men in their mid-40s, and one young woman, a general clerk, just out of high school. None of the group has had any direct experience with a computer, for under the old system the approved typewritten purchase requisitions were forwarded in batches to the computer center for order writing and later return of several copies of the purchase order printout to the department. All the staff secretly have feared the new machine, although they have not openly conveyed their feelings to you.

As soon as the minicomputer arrived, Clemens came to the purchasing department and demonstrated the computer's operation. A few minutes later she gathered the staff around her and explained the machine's functions in technical computer language. As soon as she finished, this dialogue between Clemens and Marti Wolfson, a spokesperson for the group, followed:

Clemens: You won't have any trouble adjusting to this machine. It's preprogrammed and will run by itself. All you have to be able to do is read. After watching the demo I just gave, any second grader could operate it within 10 minutes.

Wolfson: But this is all new to us. What should we do to understand the machine?

Clemens: Just study the manual. When you interface with a computer, no one knows all the answers right away. Relax; it's not going to get your jobs. It'll just make them easier.

Wolfson: All of us tried to read the manual, but it was so technical that we couldn't even understand the new vocabulary. All of us in the department are interested in making the new system work. Can't you give us any specific suggestions for learning the new machine system?

Clemens: I don't think the manual is difficult to read. It isn't for me. Probably you haven't given yourselves enough time. I'd recommend getting in there and "playing around" with the machine. That's what I did and it worked for me, didn't it?

After Clemens returned to her office, you face a staff that is dejected and angry, and one that expects reasonable answers to their questions.

In a brief report outline an appropriate course of action for resolving the new human relations problems present in your office. Indicate to what extent you would draw on the technical competence of Clemens in the future as well as on the human skills and experience of your departmental staff.

Chapter 22

ANALYZING OFFICE JOBS

To control effectively the information-management activities of his or her firm, the administrative office manager must know what systems and procedures are carried out, what jobs and personnel are required, what qualifications are necessary to hold the jobs, the relative value of each job to the firm, and how much should be paid the holders of the various jobs. As a program of administrative office operations, the study of office jobs has as its aim the accomplishment of work in the one best way by the best qualified persons, and at the fairest wage or salary that will produce the largest volume of satisfactory work. The various components of a job study program may be outlined as follows:

1. *Job analysis:* The process of gathering information and determining the principal elements involved in performing a specific job.
2. *Job description:* An outline of the information compiled from the job analysis, presented in an organized form that identifies and describes the contents and essential requirements of a specific job or position.
3. *Job specification:* A detailed record of the minimum job requirements explained in relation to the job factors (skill, effort, responsibility, and working conditions) so that the job can be easily rated during the job evaluation process.
4. *Job evaluation:* The process of appraising the value of each job in relation to other jobs in order to set a monetary value for each specific job.
5. *Work measurement and setting work standards:* The procedure of determining the time required to accomplish each job or task and of determining criteria by which the degree of performance may be measured.

The first four phases of a job study program are explained in this chapter. The measurement of office work and the setting of work standards are described in Chapter 23.

JOB ANALYSIS

A program of office job analysis may be used for several purposes. In the area of job evaluation, the analysis of office jobs is a prerequisite to ascertaining job requirements, working conditions, health and safety requirements, and standardization of job terminology. In the appraisal of employees, job analysis is used to determine the qualifications of employees and to facilitate their promotion, counseling, and transferring from one job to another. Job analysis is also fundamental to the preparation of specifications for the recruitment, selection, placement, training, and guidance of employees. When properly undertaken, job analysis places a firm's office personnel practices on a positive antidiscrimination basis and aids in meeting the demands and requirements of federal legislation such as the Equal Pay Act of 1963, the Civil Rights Act of 1964, and the Age Discrimination in Employment Act of 1967. These acts, as explained in Chapter 11, make it mandatory that all job applicants be accorded equal treatment, regardless of race, color, religion, sex, national origin, and age. The acts place particular emphasis upon an evaluation of the skills required by the job and an upgrading of those persons who merit promotion, free of discrimination.

It is necessary not only to know what type of person should be employed in each job, but also to select a worker in terms of the education, experience, age, and other qualifications necessary to perform that job. In job analysis all the elements involved in performing a specific piece of work are determined. The difficulty in analyzing jobs accurately is the problem of defining a "piece of work." Building a 20-story building is a piece of work as is the sharpening of a pencil. The term *job*, as used in this book, means the work performed by an individual and the relationship of that work to the work produced by all other workers in the company.

Job analysis leads to standardization and simplification of jobs and stabilization of office work. As a result, office work is performed according to the instructions of the office manager, who has the facts of job analyses to back up his or her decisions. Job analysis improves the office manager's ability to control operations, for once a job has been standardized, it is easier to measure the output of employees in similar positions. Thus, as a result of job analysis, wasted motion, such as that found in operating calculating machines and in filing correspondence, may be eliminated. The office manager can follow up the job analysis by testing the basic production for certain kinds of jobs and setting up bonuses or other incentives for increased output.

Job analysis supplies information that improves the work of the personnel department. Employers seek the best qualified individuals and consider their

offices as the training ground for future executives. Should the work of any department lag, it may be because the best qualified employees are not in that department. This, in turn, may be the result of faulty selection of workers. It may be that the department head and, therefore, the personnel department did not have complete, detailed information on the requirements of the position, thus causing a poor selection of workers. To gather information about a job, a job analysis must be made.

METHODS OF GATHERING JOB INFORMATION

The study of office jobs rests firmly upon obtaining reliable information. The office manager, or the individual charged with analyzing jobs, must decide which method of gathering job information will be most effective at a minimum cost. The principal methods of obtaining job information are described on the following pages.

Questionnaire Method

Office managers, personnel managers, and management consultants have developed and used a variety of questionnaires whereby the employee who is most familiar with the job does most of the clerical work involved in this method of job analysis. Some of the questionnaires consist of only a series of four or five questions; others may use three or four pages of questions. Whatever the form of questionnaire, its results must be edited, organized, and interpreted in the form of job descriptions or specifications that provide management with a knowledge of what the job requires of the jobholder.

For the simpler form of questionnaire, which may be used in small firms, two groups of questions may be given. In the first group of questions, the employee is required to give information such as the following:

Description of duties.
Special knowledge required for job.
Experience required to qualify for job.
How long a period of time must be spent on the job before the employee considers himself or herself capable of working without supervision.

In the second group of questions the employee is asked to indicate:

Daily routine tasks performed.
Work performed weekly.
Work performed monthly.
Special work performed.
Other job-related information.

If the office force is made up of a large number of employees, a much more detailed questionnaire may be prepared, such as the prose form of questionnaire illustrated in Figure 22-1. At PPG Industries Inc., the job description forms are given to employees and they are asked to write up their jobs in accordance with the instructions on the form. Each employee's write-up is revised and edited by the employee's immediate superior and submitted to a trained job analyst. The analyst obtains any additional information necessary to prepare the job analysis and indicates the presence or absence of, degree of, and frequency of characteristics required by the job if such is not indicated in the job description.

The possible disadvantages that characterize the questionnaire method of gathering job information include the difficulty in designing a questionnaire that is sufficiently thorough to obtain all the data required by the job analyst. There is the temptation to ask for so much information that the question-

naire becomes top-heavy, complex, and often confusing. The data provided may be misleading or incomplete because employees do not take time to complete the form correctly. Some employees are not necessarily skilled in properly analyzing their jobs and thus may exaggerate the importance of their jobs. On the other hand, employees may underemphasize those phases of their jobs that occupy a fairly large percentage of their total work time. The personal touch, which characterizes the interview method, is entirely lacking since the employee is called upon merely to fill out a questionnaire. Unless the questions are precisely and clearly worded, it may be difficult for the worker to communicate and for the analyst to interpret the information supplied. Finally, in order to obtain reliable and valid results, the completed questionnaire requires careful analysis and editing, all of which represent a costly means of obtaining job information.

Against all these possible disadvantages must be weighed the major advantage of being able to obtain information rapidly by means of questionnaire, at least when compared with the time-consuming chore of personally interviewing each worker. The questionnaire method does serve as a starting point in job analysis, however, and is often supplemented by means of the interview, the observation method, or a combination of methods.

Interview Method

The interview, which requires the job analyst to spend time in talking personally with the employee and the employee's supervisor in order to gather information about the job, is often costlier than the questionnaire method. However, for some types of job analyses, the

PPG INDUSTRIES

JOB DESCRIPTION (PLEASE TYPE)

JOB TITLE

DEPARTMENT

NAME OF EMPLOYEE

DATE

INSTRUCTIONS: *JOB TITLE - Enter here the name by which the job is called.*
                    DEPARTMENT - Enter here the General Office Department in which the job is located.
                    DATE - Enter here the date on which the Job Description was approved.

PART I - DESCRIPTION OF DUTIES - This portion of the job description is to be a series of numbered statements, each of which describes a task or major step of the job.

    1. Introduce each task or major step with an action verb and follow it by a concise statement that tells what you are doing and, where appropriate, include an account of how the task or major step is done.

       There is additional space on the backside for the completion of the Description of Duties if needed.

    2. Tasks or major steps are to be written in descending order of frequency of performance, i.e., the task on which the most time is spent is to be listed first and the task on which the least time is spent is last.

    3. Minor steps or tasks are to be combined and written in one catch-all paragraph at the end of the job description.

PARTS II THROUGH V (Back side) - Complete each of these sections as directed and as they relate to your job.

SIGNATURES - After completing the job description, sign it and give it to your supervisor for his approval.

I. DESCRIPTION OF DUTIES:

II. List business machines and equipment used and show approximate % of time devoted to each.

    Name   % of Time

III. If supervisory duties are performed, list job titles of those supervised and the number of employees in each job.

IV. What contacts with other people are you required to make, other than your immediate superior and those under your supervision? Indicate title, frequency and method (in person, telephone, correspondence) of contact.

V. Enter below any explanatory comments which will help to clarify the duties of this position.

EMPLOYEE SIGNATURE

APPROVING SIGNATURE

PPG Industries, Inc.

Fig. 22-1
Prose-Type Questionnaire

interview may be undertaken at the employee's work station so that at the same time the job may be observed. Of all methods of obtaining job information for the purpose of evaluating jobs, interviews with the supervisor and with the employee performing the job are very commonly used.[1] The effectiveness of the interview method depends greatly upon the skill of the analyst, who must be trained in dealing with people in order to receive full cooperation from the workers and the supervisors being interviewed. At the beginning of the interview rapport with the worker must be obtained, and he or she must be put at ease so that there will be little hesitancy in replying to the questions asked. As the worker responds to the questions asked, the analyst may record the findings on a job information sheet such as that illustrated in Figure 22-2. In acquiring the information, the analyst must maintain objectivity so that personal bias does not influence the data being recorded. All information recorded should be read to the employee to confirm the correctness of the data. Following the interview the employee's supervisor should be consulted to verify the accuracy of the information obtained.

Another approach to analyzing jobs is to hold conferences with the workers and their supervisors. During the conference the analyst records the findings while the workers and their supervisors participate in clarifying the job requirements and in answering detailed questions about the jobs.

Observation Method

In addition to gathering job information by the questionnaire and the interview methods, the analyst may visually observe the workers while they are performing their tasks. This method permits the analyst to obtain job information firsthand and enables him or her to become acquainted with the working conditions, requirements for special skills such as finger dexterity, and equipment used. For jobs that are relatively simple and repetitive, such as keypunching, the observation method may be effectively used. For other types of jobs, the analyst may select one of the other methods or a combination of methods. In using the observation method, the analyst must establish rapport with each jobholder in order to remove any suspicions the worker may have and to put the worker at ease.

In some companies the analyst may be able to obtain job data from the time-study department. The time-study engineer is concerned with observing and studying all aspects of the job, including skill requirements, physical and mental effort required, job environment needs, and information flows — to name several factors — which may not be precisely included in job descriptions. These factors are necessary, however, for the preparation of performance standards, as explained in the following chapter.

Combination of Methods

Two or more of the methods described above may be combined when

---

[1]*Job Evaluation Policies and Procedures*, Personnel Policies Forum Survey No. 113 (Washington: The Bureau of National Affairs, Inc., June, 1976), p. 5. In this survey of the job evaluation plans for office workers used by 63 personnel executives, interviews with the supervisor were used in 60 percent of the plans; interviews with the employee performing the job in 48 percent; observation by the job analyst in 48 percent; questionnaire completed by the jobholder in 41 percent; and questionnaire completed by the supervisor in 30 percent.

JOB INFORMATION SHEET

(Questionnaire for Nonsupervisory Employees)

Date issued _____

Job Title _____ Dept. # _____ Date due _____

Name of your Supervisor _____

Describe your job fully _____

_____

_____

_____

_____

_____

1. EDUCATION REQUIRED. Indicate schooling required for your JOB by check mark.
   No schooling required_____ 2 yrs. high school_____ 4 yrs. high school_____
   Technical high school_____ Special schooling_____ College_____
   Do you make any reports? No_____ Yes_____ If yes, what are they? _____
   _____
   _____
   _____
   _____

2. EXPERIENCE AND TRAINING. Experience and training required for your JOB.
   Months: 1__ 2__ 3__ 4__ 5__ 6__ 7__ 8__ 9__ 10__ 11__ 12__
   Years: 1__ 2__ 3__ 4__ 5__ 6__ 7__ 8__
   Does your job require many skills? No__ Yes__ If yes, enumerate and describe briefly. _____
   _____
   _____

3. INITIATIVE AND INGENUITY. Do you make your own decisions? No__ Yes__
   Do you inspect someone else's job? No__ Yes__ Who inspects your job?
   _____ How often does your job repeat itself? Per Hour _____
   Per Day _____ Per Week _____ Per Month _____

4. PHYSICAL DEMAND. What kind of equipment do you use? _____
   What is the maximum weight of your work in pounds? Lifting _____
   Pulling_____ Pushing_____ The heaviest work is done___% of working
   time. Your work position is Sitting___ Standing___ Walking___ Shoveling___
   Holding steadily___ Lifting overhead___ Bending___

5. MENTAL OR VISUAL DEMAND. What accuracy is required on the job? _____
   Are the hands and eyes constantly coordinated? _____
   Are operations automatic? No___ Partly___ Yes___

6. RESPONSIBILITY FOR EQUIPMENT. What is the cost of possible damage to equipment? No damage___ Minimum $___ Maximum $___ Do you repair equipment? No___ Yes___ If yes, what kind? _____

7. **RESPONSIBILITY FOR MATERIAL OR PRODUCT.** Are you responsible for any materials? No___ Yes___ If yes, what are they? _____
How much spoilage may occur? Loss in dollars $___ What is required to avoid spoilage? _____
Can the spoiled work be repaired? No_____ Partly_____ Completely_____
Enumerate and briefly describe various materials you have to recognize.

_____
_____
_____
_____

8. **RESPONSIBILITY FOR SAFETY OF OTHERS.** How many people may be injured if carelessness would occur?___ Are there hazards which may cause injury? No___Yes___ If yes, what are they? _____

_____
_____
_____

9. **RESPONSIBILITY FOR WORK OF OTHERS.** Are you responsible for work of others? No___ Yes___ How many?___ For new employees only _____

10. **WORKING CONDITIONS.** Are the surrounding conditions Agreeable? _____
Disagreeable?___ In what ways do disagreeable conditions affect your job?
Noise___ Fumes___ Cold___ Hot___ Changes in temperature___ Dirt___ Dust___
Oil___ Steam___ Too wet___ Glare___ Somewhat dark___ Drafty___

11. **UNAVOIDABLE HAZARDS.** Is your health affected? No___ Yes___
If yes, in what way? _____
Which accidents may occur? Burns___ Shock___ Cuts___ Crushed Fingers___
Injury to _____ Feet___ Eyes___ Ears___ Lungs___

12. **SUPERVISION.** Received from _____
Occasionally___ Daily___ Hourly___
Do you supervise? No___ Yes___ If yes, how many?___ Occasionally___ Daily___
Hourly___

13. Would you prefer to be transferred to another job? No___ Yes___ If yes, which job could you perform? _____

14. **REMARKS.** Give additional information which has not been covered, and which may assist in a better description of your job. _____

_____
_____
_____
_____
_____

Fig. 22-2
Job Information Sheet

undertaking a job analysis. For example, employees may be sent a brief questionnaire with instructions to return it to their supervisors. At the same time a more elaborate questionnaire is sent to the supervisors, who are requested to return it to the analyst about the same time as the employees are returning theirs to the supervisors. The supervisor looks over the employees' forms, makes the necessary corrections and additions, and returns the forms to the analyst. The analyst then interviews employees in order to verify their answers. Later, at a conference of the supervisor and a group of employees' representatives, the job contents are further clarified for final adoption in the form of job descriptions.

JOB DESCRIPTIONS

The results of the job analysis are expressed in the job description, or the position description as it is often called. From the job description a job specification may be developed separately or it may be combined with the job description. The analysis of jobs and the preparation of job descriptions may entail a period of one year or more before the descriptions are refined to the point where they become a valuable tool to be used by managers and supervisors in all departments. Once developed, the job descriptions must be updated as needed, in order to reflect the dynamic environment in which most office personnel operate. Thus, as a result of changes in factors such as methods and procedures for processing information, personnel needs, budgetary control techniques, and equipment obsolescence, the job descriptions should be periodically reviewed and revised, possibly annually. Office workers should have easy access

to the company's file of job descriptions so that they can improve their performance, be fully aware of the dimensions of their jobs, know who in the firm can aid them in their work, see how their performance will be evaluated, and realize what are their opportunities for advancement.

Writing the Job Description

In preparing the job description, clarity and simplicity of expression are prerequisites. The terms used should have universal acceptance or be carefully defined since the descriptions will be used by several persons for many purposes, including wage surveys. Job titles and descriptions should compare as closely as possible with those listed in the two-volume *Dictionary of Occupational Titles (DOT)*, as revised, with the objective of eliminating job stereotyping by sex and age.[2] The *DOT* contains standardized descriptions for almost 22,000 jobs known by about 36,000 titles. Other valuable sources of job information are the *Occupational Outlook Handbook*[3] and the survey of office salaries conducted each year by the

---

[2]U.S. Department of Labor, *Dictionary of Occupational Titles*; Vol. I, *Definitions of Titles*; Vol. II, *Occupational Classifications*, (3d ed.; Washington: U.S. Government Printing Office, 1965). For the revised job titles, see U.S. Department of Labor, *Job Title Revisions to Eliminate Sex- and Age-Referent Language from the Dictionary of Occupational Titles*, (3d ed; Washington: U.S. Government Printing Office, 1975).

[3]U.S. Department of Labor, *Occupational Outlook Handbook* (Washington: U.S. Government Printing Office). Copies of the *Handbook* may be ordered from regional offices of the Bureau of Labor Statistics. Along with information on demand and supply factors, the *Handbook* contains sections dealing with short-run effects of business cycles on job opportunities for a number of occupations; high school courses useful in preparing for each occupation; and a guide to the current potentiality of occupations.

Administrative Management Society. The 20 job titles and descriptions used by the Administrative Management Society in its survey of office salaries are shown in Figure 22-3.

Job descriptions, when combined with job specifications, may include the following information:

> Name of job.
>
> Résumé or summary of job.
>
> Description of duties performed.
>
> Equipment, materials, and forms used on job.
>
> Special environmental conditions that facilitate performing the job, such as proper lighting, elimination of noise, and proper air conditioning.
>
> Relation to other jobs:
> > Transfer of work.
> > Checking of work of other departments, or vice versa.
> > Promotional opportunities of this job.
>
> Special qualifications for job:
> > Mental.
> > Physical.
> > Experience.
>
> Prerequisite knowledge for job.

Although there is no prescribed amount of detailed information that should be included in a job description, it should contain enough information to assure that the job can be accurately evaluated. The job — *not* the person holding the job — is to be described *as it is;* no modifications should be incorporated into the descriptions for what the job *ought to be*.

Typical Job Descriptions

Figure 22-4 shows a job description for a nonexempt office position, Computer Operator. Note that the latter part of the job description presents the employee specifications for that job. Sometimes positions are grouped and described concisely, as shown in Figure 22-5, which presents an accounting-finance grouping of five position titles and descriptions for middle managers.

JOB SPECIFICATIONS

A *job specification* describes the minimum requirements of the job in relation to the job factors of skill, effort, responsibility, and working conditions. The job specification is used primarily as the basis for rating the job in the process of job evaluation. Job specifications are the natural outcome of job analyses and, as indicated previously, may be combined with job or position descriptions. For example, in Figure 22-4 the specifications for the job of computer operator are combined with the position description.

Job specifications are often used in the employment, selection, training, and counseling of workers because the education and experience specifications imply what qualifications a person should possess in order to be hired. However, more effective use can be made of the *employee specification*, which states specifically the minimum qualifications a prospective employee must possess in order to be considered for employment. When the job specification and the employee specification are brought together, the interviewer has accurate data for matching the job applicant to the job opening.

The interviewer or job counselor has job specifications available, which are an aid in recommending courses of action to inexperienced or handicapped workers. Much information can be obtained from job specifications for rating

JOB TITLES AND DESCRIPTIONS

A   MAIL CLERK-FILE CLERK

Circulates office mail, delivers messages and supplies. May process incoming or outgoing mail and operate related machines and perform other routine duties. Performs routine filing and sorting operations according to an established system. Locates and removes material upon requests and keeps records of its disposition. May perform related clerical duties.

B   GENERAL CLERK B

Performs clerical duties in accordance with established procedures. Maintains records and may prepare reports from basic data which does not require the development of secondary data. Job requires considerable supervision.

C   GENERAL CLERK A

Performs complex and responsible clerical duties requiring independent analysis, exercise of judgment and a detailed knowledge of department or company policies and procedures. Minimum supervision required.

D   ACCOUNTING CLERK B

Checks, verifies and posts journal vouchers, accounts payable vouchers or other simple accounting data of a recurring or standard nature.

E   ACCOUNTING CLERK A

Keeps a complete set of accounting records in a small office, or handles one phase of accounting in a larger unit which requires the accounting training needed to determine proper accounting entries, prepare accounting reports, analyze accounting records to determine causes of results shown, etc. May direct work of junior clerks or bookkeepers. (Excludes supervisors)

F   BOOKKEEPING MACHINE OPERATOR

Operates a bookkeeping machine to record business transactions of a recurring and standardized nature, where proper posting has been indicated or is readily identifiable. May balance to control figures.

G   OFFSET DUPLICATING MACHINE OPERATOR

Sets up and operates offset duplicating machines. Cleans and adjusts equipment but does not make repairs. May prepare own plates and operate auxiliary equipment, and may keep records of kind and amount of work done.

H   TELEPHONE SWITCHBOARD OPERATOR

Operates a single or multiple position PBX telephone switchboard. May keep records of calls and toll charges, and may operate a paging system and perform duties of receptionist.

I   TYPIST-CLERK

Types letters, reports, tabulations, and other material in which setups and terms are generally clear and follow a standard pattern. May prepare stencils or offset masters. Performs clerical duties of moderate difficulty.

J   STENOGRAPHER

Transcribes from dictating equipment, or records and transcribes shorthand dictation involving a normal range of business vocabulary. May perform copy typing or clerical work of moderate difficulty incidental to primary stenographic duties. May operate as a member of a centralized stenographic area. May perform the secretarial function for a small group.

K   SECRETARY B

Performs secretarial duties for a member of middle management. General requirements are the same as Secretary A (listed in opposite column), but limited to the area of responsibility of the principal.

L   SECRETARY A

Performs secretarial duties for a top-level executive or a person responsible for a major function or geographic operation. Does work of a confidential nature and relieves principal of designated administrative details. Requires initiative, judgment, knowledge of company practices, policy and organization.

M   CORRESPONDENCE SECRETARY

Operates all types of automated equipment in a Word Processing Center. Is responsible for transcribing and copy typing the many types of work handled in the Center.

N   KEYPUNCH OPERATOR B

Operates an alphabetic or numerical keypunch machine to record pre-coded or readily usable data following generally standardized procedures. May verify the work of others, using a verifying machine.

O   KEYPUNCH OPERATOR A

Operates an alphabetic or numerical keypunch or verifier to record or verify complex or uncoded data working from source material which may not be arranged for keypunching. Selects appropriate number and kinds of cards. Follows a pattern of operations generally standardized but frequently including rules, exceptions, and special instructions which demand operator's close attention.

P   TABULATING MACHINE OPERATOR

Sets up, operates and wires a variety of punched card equipment, including tabulators and multipliers. Wires boards from diagrams prepared by others for routine jobs, uses prewired boards on complex or repetitive jobs. May locate and correct job difficulties and assist in training less experienced operators.

Q   COMPUTER OPERATOR B

Operates computers utilizing established programs or programs under development. Loads computer and manipulates control switch on console in accordance with programmed instructions. Observes functioning of equipment. Detects nature of errors or equipment failure and makes normal console adjustments. Maintains necessary operating records.

R   COMPUTER OPERATOR A

Operates computer utilizing established programs or programs under development. Oversees loading of computer and manipulation of controls. Detects nature of errors or equipment failure. May instruct or give limited directions to less experienced operators.

S   PROGRAMMER

With general supervision, analyzes and defines programs for electronic data processing equipment. Is generally competent in most phases of programming to work on his or her own, and only requires general guidance for the balance of the activities. Conducts analyses of sufficient detail of all defined systems specifications and develops block diagrams and machine logic flowcharts, codes, prepares test data, tests and debugs programs. Revises and refines programs as required and documents all procedures used throughout the computer program when it is formally established. Evaluates and modifies existing programs to take into account changes in systems requirements. May give technical assistance to lower level classifications. Normally progresses from this classification to a Lead programmer.

T   SYSTEMS ANALYST

Under close supervision, assists in devising computer system specifications and record layouts. Is qualified to work on several phases of systems analysis but requires guidance and direction for other phases. Conducts studies and analyses of existing and proposed operations. Prepares all levels of computer block diagrams and may assist in the preparation of machine logic flowcharting.

Fig. 22-3
Job Titles and Descriptions Used by the Administrative Management Society

EXHIBIT 6: JOB DESCRIPTION OF A NONEXEMPT POSITION

Computer Operator	Nonexempt	213.382
Job Title	**Status**	**Job Code**
July 1, 1975		Olympia, Inc. — Main Office
Date		**Plant/Division**
Arthur Allen		Data Processing — Information Systems
Written by		**Department/Section**
Juanita Montgomery		7 406
Approved by		**Grade/Level Points**
Senior Computer Operator		$7,800 — $9,360 — $11,232
Title of Immediate Supervisor		**Pay Range**

SUMMARY

Operates digital computer and peripheral equipment under general supervision. Performs other assignments as required.

JOB DUTIES

1. Follows specific technical and scheduling directives.
   .1 Follows technical directives and assigned schedules under spot-check supervision.
   .2 Processes data according to defined procedures and schedules.
2. Operates digital computer and associated peripheral equipment.
   .1 Monitors equipment; maximizes operating time; minimizes program errors.
   .2 Analyzes error messages; identifies possible causes.
   .3 Notifies proper authorities of machine malfunctions and program errors.
   .4 Corrects errors within specified areas of authority and responsibility.
   .5 Stores outputs and completed inputs in proper location.
   .6 Performs preventive maintenance as specified.
3. Reviews and analyzes data inputs.
   .1 Recommends changes in scheduling and application to maximize efficient use of equipment.
   .2 Assists in testing new applications.
4. Maintains logs and records.
   .1 Details individual running time of each program.
   .2 Records all equipment malfunctions and program errors.
5. Receives, stores, and maintains D.P.C. inventory.
   .1 Unloads delivery truck.
   .2 Maintains stockroom in orderly manner.
   .3 Maintains stock records.
   .4 Notifies appropriate authorities of inventory requirements.

Fig. 22-4
Job Description for a Computer Operator (page 1)

EMPLOYMENT STANDARDS

1. Knowledge and ability:
   - .1 Must know basic principles of operating a digital computer and associated peripheral equipment.
   - .2 Must be able to read and understand technical computer operation manuals.
   - .3 Must be able to follow prescribed standards and procedures.
   - .4 Must be able to follow computer scheduling instructions.
2. Physical requirements:
   - .1 Must be able to lift and store 60-lb. boxes.
   - .2 Must be able to load and off-load 20-lb. disk packages.
   - .3 Must be able to stand for ten hours a day.
3. Emotional demands:
   - .1 Must be able to withstand relatively high pitch and levels of noise.

ACCOUNTABILITIES

Timely completion of assigned schedules.
Prompt recognition of machine malfunctions.

JOB SPECIFICATION

Factor	Subfactor	Degree	Substantiating Data	Points
Knowledge	Education	4	Requires completion of vocational-technical program or equivalent on-the-job training.	64
Knowledge	Experience	4	Equivalent on-the-job training may be up to one year.	64
Knowledge	Skill	5	Requires ability to operate medium-size computer and peripheral equipment.	63
Problem-Solving	Interpretation	4 −	Analyzes error messages and takes corrective action in accord with procedures manuals and operating practices.	38
Problem-Solving	Compliance	4 −	Requires ability to read and understand technical computer operations manual.	37
Problem-Solving	Communication	4	Must maintain records of operation and communicate results.	53
Decision-Making	Interpersonal	2 +	Notifies authorities of machine malfunctions and program errors.	28
Decision-Making	Managerial	3 −	Follows technical direction and assigned schedules under spot check supervision. Has no supervisory responsibilities.	35
Decision-Making	Assets	2 +	Has some opportunity for influencing the planning and control of work assignments.	24

Total Points: 406

Source: Reprinted by permission of the publisher from *Supervisory Management* (February, 1976), pp. 14–15, © 1976 by AMACOM, a division of American Management Associations.

Fig. 22-4
Job Description for a Computer Operator (page 2)

MIDDLE MANAGERS IN ACCOUNTING AND FINANCE

1. **ACCOUNTING MANAGER** — Supervises the maintenance of the general accounting records and operation of the accounting systems, including gathering and reporting of correct financial information to management. Establishes internal control procedures and is responsible for developing, adapting, or revising the accounting systems. Projects accounting data to show effects of proposed plans on capital investment, income cash position, and overall financial condition. Supervises the preparation of periodic tax returns and determines that government tax regulations are being adhered to. Follows up on special accounting assignments and coordinates accounting functions with data processing. Assures standard accounting procedures are adhered to and supervises the maintenance of the accounting and voucher file.

2. **AUDITOR** — Audits the financial records and practices to appraise and verify the accounting accuracy of records, financial statements, and reports. Determines that accepted accounting principles and policies are followed and evaluates the adequacy of the accounting systems and controls. Verifies existence of recorded assets and inclusiveness of recorded liabilities, assures that income has been properly accounted for and that expenses are proper and substantiated. Makes suggestions for improvements of records, procedures, and internal controls. Prepares audit reports and trains auditors at entering professional levels.

3. **COST ACCOUNTANT** — Devises cost-accounting records and processes and compiles information to determine and record costs by department, division, cost centers, product, and other groupings. Devises classifications for labor, material, expenses, and other items for computing costs of new products or services. Analyzes costs appearing out of line with previous records. From available cost information, prepares reports, including manufacturing budgets, plant financial statements, operating control reports, and variations from standard cost and reasons thereof. Develops and improves methods of calculating and controlling costs.

4. **PAYROLL SUPERVISOR** — Supervises payroll functions, including the computation of required and voluntary deductions; preparation and verification of payrolls; maintenance of payroll records and reports; preparation of various reports for federal, state, and local government agencies and processing of payments to employees. Determines that proper controls are followed to assure wages, salaries, and deductions are being paid in accordance with established policy and labor agreements. Responsible for preparation of other compensation payments, for constant surveillance of changing payroll, tax, and reporting procedures and planning work schedules.

5. **WAGE AND SALARY ADMINISTRATOR** — Administers wage and salary plans for exempt and non-exempt personnel. Follows company pay philosophy in establishing pay procedures and approving salary adjustments. Devises new plans of compensation. Observes impact of trends in cost of living, area differential, and wage negotiations on rate structures and ranges. Conducts wage and salary surveys to obtain data to support changes in policy, practice, and rates of pay. Approves salary changes within certain limits and submits others for manager approval. Indoctrinates managers in wage and salary policies and procedures. Provides computer center with specifications and data to computerize pay data. Prepares payroll reports and complies with government wage and hour regulations.

Source: "1974 Middle Management Salary Survey," Philadelphia Chapter of Administrative Management Society.

Fig. 22-5
Accounting-Finance Grouping of Five Middle-Management Positions

JOB SPECIFICATION

Job Title: Senior General Clerk

Qualifications:

Educational: High school graduate.

Experience: Two or more years with company as general clerk and typist-clerk.
Experience in office systems and procedures.

Personal: Speed and efficiency in handling volume of detail.
Ability to instruct others in clerical jobs.
Ability to supervise work of others.

Duties:
1. Handle mail and dictate correspondence.
2. Check, index, and file important records and correspondence.
3. Handle all payroll records and reports.
4. Summarize and tabulate cost information and records.
5. Receive, take care of, and account for petty cash and office funds.
6. Supervise work of general clerks in routine jobs.

Promotional Opportunities:
Advancement to Assistant Chief Clerk after two years

Salary Range:
$600–$920 a month.

Fig. 22-6
Job Specification for Position of Senior General Clerk

the job in relation to other jobs in the company, for the development of a training program, for the establishment of physical requirements for workers from the standpoint of safety, for the purpose of conducting salary surveys, and for establishing lines of promotion and demotion.

The job specifications illustrated in Figures 22-4 and 22-6 can be used not only for a promotional program for office workers, but also for an employee training program, as indicated in Chapter 16. Every phase of the job is brought to light in the specification after the results of the job analysis are known. An employee specification can be used to assist in the proper selection of office employees, as shown in Table 22-1. This table indicates the education,

experience, appearance, and other qualifications required for four selected clerical positions.

JOB EVALUATION

Job analyses and descriptions are prerequisite to management's determination of the relative value of each job. Job evaluation aims at an equitable payroll policy on the basis of the estimated or measured worth of each job in relation to other jobs.[4] The larger the organization, the more necessary it becomes to evaluate office jobs. When jobs

[4]For an exceptionally fine, detailed analysis of job evaluation, see Herbert G. Zollitsch and Adolph Langsner, *Wage and Salary Administration* (2d ed.; Cincinnati: South-Western Publishing Co., 1970), Chs. 6–12, pp. 147–313.

EMPLOYEE SPECIFICATIONS FOR CLERICAL POSITIONS					
Job Title	File Clerk	Typist-Clerk	General Clerk	Senior General Clerk	
Monthly salary range	$420–$550	$550–$725	$500–$800	$600–$920	
Section A — to be determined by interview					
1. Education...........	High school	High school	High school	High school	
2. Experience..........	None	6 months	1 year	2 years	
Section B — to be determined by test					
3. Intelligence.........	I.Q. — 90	I.Q. — 95	I.Q. — 100	I.Q. — 105	
4. Arithmetic...........	80% of test	80% of test	85% of test	90% of test	
5. Spelling..............	80% of test	80% of test	85% of test	90% of test	Table 22-1
6. Typing or electronic calculator ..	....	50 words or 80% of test	60 words or 90% of test	65 words or 90% of test	

Note: Titles and salary ranges are illustrative and for comparison purposes only.

are properly evaluated, employees doing similar work under similar working conditions are paid approximately the same salary. However, the cost of living, the supply and demand of office workers, federal and state government regulations, and competitive conditions also influence the salaries paid for office jobs.

There are two basic plans of evaluating jobs in order to group those with the same apparent requisites so that salary schedules may be made comparable: (1) *nonquantitative* grouping of jobs according to their relative or estimated difficulty; and (2) *quantitative* grouping of jobs according to mental, physical, skill, and experience requisites. The two plans may be subdivided into the following five methods of job evaluation:

A. *Nonquantitative evaluation plans*
    1. Ranking method.
    2. Job classification method.
B. *Quantitative evaluation plans*
    1. Factor-comparison method.
    2. Point method.
    3. Guideline method.

In this part of the chapter, each of the five methods of job evaluation is described. The pricing of the jobs and the determination of pay ranges are discussed in Chapter 24, "Office Salary Administration."

Ranking Method

The *ranking method*, also known as the "rank order," "order of merit," and "order of importance system," is the simplest and oldest method of determining the economic value of a job. Under the ranking method the individual jobs are analyzed and ranked according to the difficulty and the overall responsibility of each job. Jobs are ranked according to job titles from the most important to the least important in relation to their contribution to the business. It is assumed that the salary increases as the job becomes more difficult. This is not always true, however, because sometimes a salary is determined by the working conditions, responsibility, or experience involved. A simple ranking of office jobs is given in Table 22-2.

The ranking of jobs is often accomplished by an evaluating committee consisting of supervisors and department heads. The ranking may be done in terms of job titles alone or by combining titles, job content, and compensation rates. The number of ranks will vary with the number of jobs or positions and the type of business organization. In Table 22-2, for example, the 21 jobs making up one activity field — office and clerical jobs — are arranged in rank order from 1 through 14.

Two types of job ranking methods sometimes used are the *card-ranking method* and the *paired-comparison method*. In both methods the supervisors are asked to rank the jobs in the order of their importance from highest to lowest, or vice versa.

Card-Ranking Method. In the card-ranking method each job title is placed on a 3″ × 5″ index card. The job analyst arranges the cards in the order of the relative importance of the jobs to the company, ignoring the present salary of the jobs, the historic position or status of the job in the company, and the performance of any particular employee holding that job. This approach to job evaluation provides an effective analysis of the jobs without the influence of established, historical precedents and appears more like an independent survey based upon sound operations. If there are too many jobs to be thus ranked, it may be necessary to rank them first by

SIMPLE RANKING OF OFFICE AND CLERICAL JOBS		
Rank Order	**Job Title**	**Median Monthly Salary (Midpoint of Salary Range)**
1	Office Manager	$1,525
2	Systems Analyst	1,350
3	Programmer	1,245
4	Tabulating Machine Operator	920
4	Computer Operator A	920
5	Administrative Secretary	845
6	Computer Operator B	800
7	Accounting Clerk A	765
8	Stenographer	725
8	Secretary	725
9	Bookkeeping Machine Operator	700
9	Telephone Switchboard Operator	700
9	General Clerk A	700
10	Offset Duplicating Machine Operator	680
11	Correspondence Secretary	660
11	Keypunch Operator A	660
12	General Clerk B	635
12	Keypunch Operator B	635
13	Accounting Clerk B	515
13	Typist-Clerk	515
14	Mail Clerk-File Clerk	465

Table 22-2

Note: Titles and median salaries are illustrative and for comparison purposes only.

groups of jobs and then to rank the jobs within each group.

Paired-Comparison Method. In the paired-comparison method each job is ranked against another job of comparable ranking on the basis of the total difficulty of the job. The more times a job is ranked as more difficult, the more important the job becomes. One type of form used in the paired-comparison method is shown in Figure 22-7.

In very small offices where comparatively few jobs (less than 25) are to be evaluated and where the employees respect the employer's integrity in ranking the jobs, the ranking method may be used satisfactorily. One advantage of the method is its simplicity; it is easily understood by all parties concerned. However, the rating is extremely subjective and is often incorrectly based on the employee performing the job rather than on the job itself. Also, the relative ranking of jobs depends greatly on current salary and wage rates which fluctuate upward or downward with economic conditions. The method can be installed without undue expense, but much grievance and loss of time may be caused by the inability to explain why one job is slotted above or below another when there are no objective studies to back up the established salary or wage rates. The evaluation process often becomes unwieldly when there is a large number of jobs, and it is unlikely that there is any one person who knows all the jobs and is thus qualified to evaluate them.

Job Classification Method

The *job classification method*, also known as the *grading method*, is an outgrowth of the ranking method. This method has long been used by civil service authorities in employing office and clerical workers and in granting periodic salary increments. Prior to the actual classification of jobs, a number of predetermined classes or grades are selected on the basis of common denominators

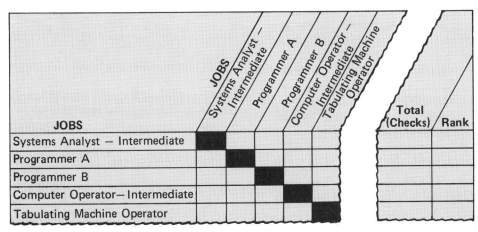

Directions: Compare the first job in the first column with each job in the slant columns. If the job in the first column is considered to have greater value to the firm than the job in the slant column, place a check mark (✓) in the box below the job in the slant column. Repeat process until all jobs have been compared. Tally check marks to find rank of jobs.

Fig. 22-7

Form Used in Paired-Comparison Method

such as levels of responsibilities, abilities or skills, knowledge, and duties that run through the jobs. The jobs or positions are then analyzed and grouped into specific classes or grades. The grades are arranged in order of importance according to the job and the work performed. Thus, it is assumed that each job or position involves duties and responsibilities that fit into the respective graded classification.

One method of grouping jobs in a classification chart is shown in Table 22-3. The nature of the work is combined with the salary range to show that there is a direct relationship between the rating of the importance of the job and the salary paid. In Table 22-3, the four family groupings are: clerical, stenographic, accounting, and data processing. Under each of these family groupings, the jobs are ranked according to their importance, which in turn is influenced by the salary range.

The most common example of the job classification method is the *General Schedule* used by the federal government, which covers all its jobs and positions (professional, scientific, clerical, administrative, and custodial). The General Schedule is composed of 18 job classes (GS-1 through GS-18) with the job classes differing in the levels of job difficulty, responsibilities, and qualification requirements of the work performed. The less difficult the job, the lower the job class number; the greater the responsibilities and qualifications needed to fill the job, the higher the job class number.

Like the ranking method the job classification method possesses the advantage of economy in installation. Also, like the ranking method the job classification method may be applied in small business firms or offices; only a

small amount of time and little or no trained personnel are needed to implement this method. Since there is usually a hierarchy already present in the office, this method of informally ranking employees may be easily accepted by the workers and serve as a good starting point for the introduction of a quantitative method of evaluating jobs, as discussed in the next section. The job classification method has the disadvantage of a subjective grading and rating of jobs by total content, which may create distrust among employees. In the same way, the very purpose of this method of job evaluation is defeated if outside influences, such as the existing wage rates or the present job holders, create a biased effect on the job classification rating.

Factor-Comparison Method

The *factor-comparison method*, a quantitative evaluation plan, is also known as the "key-job system," the "job-comparison system," and the "job-to-money method." This method refers to rating the jobs in terms of money. Each job is evaluated in terms of the following five critical factors, based on selected key jobs that are related to a money value, the "going rate":

1. Mental requirements (education, judgment, initiative, ingenuity, versatility).
2. Skill requirements (use of equipment and materials, dexterity, precision).
3. Physical requirements (strength, endurance).
4. Responsibility (for safety of others; for equipment, materials, and processes; cost of error; extent of supervision exercised).
5. Working conditions (accident hazard, environment).

BREAKDOWN OF JOB CLASSIFICATIONS BY JOB LEVELS AND MONTHLY SALARY RANGES

Job Level	Monthly Salary Range	Midpoint	Family Groupings			
			Clerical	Stenographic	Accounting	Data Processing
1	$ 500–$ 650	$ 575	General Clerk B	.....	Payroll Clerk	.....
2	550– 700	625	.....	.....	Accounting Clerk B	Keypunch Operator B
3	600– 750	675	Typist-Clerk	Correspondence Secretary	Bookkeeping Machine Operator	Keypunch Operator A
4	650– 800	725	General Clerk A	Stenographer	.....	.....
5	700– 850	775	.....	Secretary B	.....	.....
6	725– 925	825	.....	.....	Accounting Clerk A	Computer Operator B
7	775– 975	875	.....	Secretary A	.....	Tabulating Machine Operator
8	850– 1,000	975	.....	.....	Payroll Supervisor	Computer Operator A
9	950– 1,250	1,100	.....	.....	Cost Accountant	.....
10	1,075– 1,375	1,225	.....	.....	Auditor	Programmer
11	1,200– 1,600	1,400	.....	.....	Accounting Manager	Systems Analyst

Table 22-3

Note: Job titles and monthly salary ranges are illustrative and for comparison purposes only.

Installing the Factor-Comparison Method. The first step in using the factor-comparison method is to select 10 to 20 key jobs that represent a cross section of all the jobs that will be evaluated. In selecting the key jobs, the committee representing the workers and management should select jobs that range from the lowest to the highest paid jobs. The key jobs are next analyzed by each member of the committee. At this time the committee must also agree on the definition of each of the five basic factors so that each person will be interpreting each factor alike.

The key jobs are next ranked according to the five basic factors, one factor at a time, in the order of their relative importance. The ranking should first be arranged numerically, as shown in Table 22-4. Note that in the factor column "Mental Requirements," the highest rank (1) is given to the job of Senior Accounting Clerk while the lowest rank (10) is assigned to the Messenger. In the factor column "Physical Requirements," the job of Senior Accounting Clerk is assigned the next to lowest rank (9) while the job of Messenger is assigned the next to the highest rank (2). The jobs of Senior Accounting Clerk and Messenger are ranked in the same relative position in the factor column "Working Conditions."

The average salary is next established for all ranked key jobs and the

SIMPLE RANKING OF KEY JOBS IN FACTOR-COMPARISON METHOD

Rank	Mental Requirements	Skill Requirements	Physical Requirements	Responsibility	Working Conditions
1	Sr. Accounting Clerk	Private Secretary	Tabulating Machine Oper.	Sr. Accounting Clerk	Keypunch Operator
2	Private Secretary	Tabulating Machine Oper.	Messenger	Private Secretary	Messenger
3	Tabulating Machine Oper.	Sr. Accounting Clerk	File Clerk	Tabulating Machine Oper.	Tabulating Machine Oper.
4	Senior Stenographer	Senior Stenographer	Private Secretary	Telephone Operator	File Clerk
5	Senior Typist	Keypunch Operator	Keypunch Operator	Keypunch Operator	Telephone Operator
6	Telephone Operator	Senior Typist	Senior Stenographer	Jr. General Clerk	Senior Typist
7	Keypunch Operator	Telephone Operator	Telephone Operator	Senior Stenographer	Jr. General Clerk
8	Jr. General Clerk	Jr. General Clerk	Senior Typist	Senior Typist	Senior Stenographer
9	File Clerk	File Clerk	Sr. Accounting Clerk	Messenger	Sr. Accounting Clerk
10	Messenger	Messenger	Jr. General Clerk	File Clerk	Private Secretary

Table 22-4

money value for each job is divided among the five factors according to the importance of the respective factor to the key job. Table 22-5 shows the average monthly salary apportioned to the five basic factors for three of the key jobs ranked in Table 22-4. The assumed monthly salaries are distributed for each factor of the three jobs.

After the monthly salaries have been distributed to the key jobs according to the ranked and evaluated factors, the rankings are pooled in a master reference table such as Table 22-6. The titles of the key jobs are listed in the first column from the highest to the lowest paid job. The average monthly salaries are entered in the next column. The monetary rates, representing the factor rankings for each key job as well as the rank numbers, are recorded under the five major factors. The total distributed money values for each factor are then added horizontally to determine the established average monthly salary. The final step in the installation of the factor-comparison method is to study all jobs that can be compared with the key jobs listed in Table 22-6.

Advantages and Disadvantages of the Factor-Comparison Method. The major advantage of the factor-comparison method in relation to the ranking and the job classification methods is that each job is evaluated on the basis of five factors basic to the job. Since each job is compared against a key job, and factor against factor, it is possible to obtain a fair degree of accuracy and determine not only which job is worth more but also how much more. Thus, the method provides each firm with a tailor-made plan of job evaluation that meets the firm's own needs as a result of properly selecting and weighting the factors. Further, once the method has been installed, it is relatively easy to train union members and managers in its use. On the other hand, the method is difficult to explain and to communicate to workers. Although the method provides for the establishment of relationships within the firm, it is inflexible in dealing with salary rates outside the firm. Thus, if a salary level change for a particular job is brought about by a change in the outside labor market rate, changes must be made throughout the

---

AVERAGE MONTHLY SALARY APPORTIONED TO FIVE FACTORS FOR THREE KEY JOBS

Factor	Key Jobs and Graded Salaries		
	Private Secretary	Keypunch Operator	Messenger
Mental requirements........	$225	$ 85	$ 40
Skill requirements............	270	135	40
Physical requirements......	135	130	180
Responsibility..................	225	135	90
Working conditions...........	45	190	150
Total monthly salary......	$900	$675	$500

Table 22-5

Note: Job titles and monthly salaries are illustrative and for comparison purposes only.

JOB RANKINGS AND SALARY RATES IN THE FACTOR-COMPARISON METHOD

Key Job	Average Monthly Salary	Factor Rankings and Rates								
		Mental Requirements		Skill Requirements		Physical Requirements		Responsibility		Working Conditions	
		Rank	Rate	Rank	Rate	Rank	Rate	Rank	Rate	Rank	Rate
Sr. Accounting Clerk...........	$960	1	$270	3	$225	9	$105	1	$255	9	$105
Private Secretary...............	900	2	225	1	270	4	135	2	225	10	45
Tabulating Machine Operator...............	870	3	180	2	225	1	190	3	135	3	140
Senior Stenographer............	800	4	180	4	225	6	130	7	130	8	135
Keypunch Operator	675	7	85	5	135	5	130	5	135	1	190
Telephone Operator............	640	6	130	7	120	7	115	4	135	5	140
Senior Typist	640	5	175	6	135	8	105	8	90	6	135
Jr. General Clerk	570	8	80	8	120	10	105	6	130	7	135
File Clerk.....................	545	9	75	9	90	3	180	10	60	4	140
Messenger.....................	500	10	40	10	40	2	180	9	90	2	150

Note: Job titles and monthly salaries are illustrative and for comparison purposes only.

Table 22-6

entire salary structure in order to maintain internal equity if the relationships established by the factor-comparison method are to be maintained.[5]

Point Method

In the point method of job evaluation, each of the basic factors is divided into degrees, and points are assigned to each factor and its degrees. No wage or salary rates are taken into consideration. In evaluating most jobs, the four widely accepted factors used in the point method are: skill, effort, responsibility, and job conditions. Since these factors are broad and may be interpreted differently in different situations, each factor is divided into subfactors such as the following:

Skill:
1. Education and Job Knowledge
2. Experience and Training
3. Initiative and Ingenuity

Effort:
4. Physical Demand
5. Mental and/or Visual Demand

Responsibility:
6. For Equipment or Tools
7. For Material or Product
8. For Safety of Others
9. For Work of Others

Job Conditions:
10. Working Conditions
11. Unavoidable Hazards

Each of the subfactors is divided into a number of *degrees* which serve as a scale for measuring the distinct levels of each factor. The degrees, in turn, are evaluated separately by a number of *points*. The sum of all the points for all subfactors represents the total score for the job. In the job specification sheet for a computer operator, shown in Figure 22-4 on page 634, the total number of points is 406. Thus, in a firm using this point method, jobs with similar point values would be paid the same salary even though the points are related to different factors.

The point method is probably less subjective in its approach and provides more consistency of results than any of the other job evaluation methods since each subfactor is clearly defined in terms of degrees. With each subfactor divided into five to eight degrees, the rater can judge quickly and at the same time minimize discriminations and inequities. Since the job is analyzed and rated in its entirety, independently of wage and salary rates, the rater is not influenced by pressure from unions, workers, or management. The number of points assigned to a job as the result of an equitable rating remains the same until the job is changed. Thus, bargaining for wage and salary rates can be easily accomplished since the job evaluation continues to serve its purpose as a measuring stick.

Some critics of the point method feel that it is inflexible because of the limited number of degrees and the fact that the largest number of points depends on, and is assigned to, the highest factor degree. Also, some feel that the point system, with its elements of factors, degrees, and weighting, requires a great deal of time to develop, and personnel trained to administer the plan. Although the method is relatively uncomplicated, the rater must educate employees about the nature of the job evaluation program, perhaps by means of preparing an employee information sheet that describes the method. In one company the job evaluation supervisor

---

[5]Arthur H. Dick, "Job Evaluation's Role in Employee Relations," *Personnel Journal* (March, 1974), p. 178.

visits each plant at the request of the union or of management and conducts discussion sessions with the employees wherein the evaluation method is fully explained. Thus, a great deal of time is needed to install the method, and a large amount of clerical detail is required.

A company that uses the point method in evaluating its jobs must make sure that the plan complies with the Equal Pay Act of 1963, which amended the Fair Labor Standards Act of 1938. For example, the application of the equal pay standard is not dependent on job classifications or titles but on actual job requirements and performance. The fact that jobs performed by male and female employees may have the same total point value under an evaluation system in use by the employer does not in itself mean that the jobs concerned are equal according to the terms of the statute. Conversely, although the point values allocated to jobs may add up to unequal totals, it does not necessarily follow that the work being performed in such jobs is unequal when the statutory tests of the equal pay standard are applied.[6]

Guideline Method

In the guideline method of job evaluation, the techniques of direct market pricing, ranking, and grading are employed.[7] In contrast to the four methods of job evaluation described previously, the guideline method is little concerned with the relative values of jobs within

the firm. Instead, the method concentrates upon an interpretation of the relative value of jobs in the marketplace. Thus, in the final analysis the ruling factor in establishing internal salary grades is the market price of the job.

The guideline method uses a standard scale of salary ranges or grades that serves as a common scale for all jobs to be evaluated. Each salary grade consists of a minimum, a midpoint, and a maximum salary, as shown in Table 22-7. Typically the grade spread starts at 30 percent in the lower grades and gradually increases to 60 percent in the higher grades, following the fact that there is progressively less room open for promotion as employees move up the scalar chain. Thus, the salary ranges for higher levels must be wider in order to provide room for recognition of meritorious performance on the same job over considerable lengths of time.

Table 22-7 indicates that the midpoint of each preceding salary grade provides a definite overlapping of the successive ranges. Thus, it is possible to move jobs up or down one or even two grades in order to adjust internal relationships without fear of creating gross inequities.

To evaluate jobs using the guideline method, the following steps are taken:

1. A substantial number of key jobs, or benchmark jobs, are selected. The key jobs are those that are easily identified in the marketplace by other firms through salary surveys — the direct pricing feature of the plan. The greater the number of key jobs, the more effective the evaluation process.
2. Each job is evaluated by matching the average salary for the job with the nearest midpoint on the wage scale. At this point the manager in charge of the department being evaluated can

---

[6]See "Equal Pay for Equal Work" under the Fair Labor Standards Act Interpretative Bulletin, Title 29, Part 800 (Washington; United States Department of Labor, undated).

[7]Reprinted by permission of the publisher from *Management Bulletin No. 128*, "A New Dimension to Job Evaluation," by Anthony M. Pasquale © 1969 by the American Management Association, Inc.

THE GUIDELINE WAGE SCALE

Grade	Minimum	Midpoint	Maximum
1	$ 4,900	$ 5,775	$ 6,650
2	5,150	6,075	7,000
3	5,400	6,400	7,400
4	5,650	6,725	7,800
5	5,900	7,050	8,200
6	6,200	7,400	8,600
7	6,500	7,750	9,000
70	118,300	153,600	188,900
71	124,100	161,300	198,500
72	130,300	169,300	208,300
73	136,800	177,800	218,800
74	143,700	186,700	229,700
75	150,900	196,000	241,100
76	158,500	205,800	253,100

Table 22-7

change any relationships that appear to be inequitable from the standpoint of the inside labor market. Disparities between the company's present rate of pay and the outside labor market prices are then adjusted.

3. All key jobs are reviewed in relation to one another and necessary changes made as desired. The remaining jobs in the company for which no outside comparability can be established are now evaluated. This process is nothing more than the ranking method and is based solely on the evaluator's judgment by comparing each job with the key jobs already assigned grades. Thus, the key jobs have been evaluated on the basis of factual salary data and now become the guidelines for the remainder of the evaluation.

4. The complex array of jobs listed in each evaluated grade are now reviewed within each department and among the various other departments. The evaluators can correct any inequities existing as a result of this inspection.

The success of the guideline method of job evaluation, performed without the use of a job evaluation committee, is dependent upon the availability of factual salary survey data for all the key jobs selected. The method is simple to use, for no lengthy, time-consuming evaluations are necessary. The evaluation of 40 to 50 jobs can be done in less than one hour. The method is objective since bias and errors in human judgment are significantly reduced. The cost of the method is less than that of other methods, for savings arise in reduced staff requirements, fewer record-keeping procedures, and elimination of consulting fees. An experienced wage and salary administrator should be able to analyze, install, and keep the method current. Finally, there is no need to develop two or more salary structures to satisfy different geographic areas, for the guideline covers all employees and all locations in one integrated salary structure.

Relative Use of the Job Evaluation Methods

Although many trade and professional associations have developed job evaluation plans to meet the needs of their own members, as pointed out earlier in this chapter, most job evaluation experts recommend that a company not adopt in its entirety the method currently used by another firm. Any plan established and installed by another company or association should be modified to meet the individual peculiarities of the firm involved. Some companies have installed the ranking, job classification, and factor-comparison methods but have discarded them in favor of the point system, especially when the method is used as the basis for compensating the rank-and-file workers. In other companies two methods of job evaluation may be used concurrently, with each method keyed to different types of jobs.

Regardless of the method or methods used to evaluate jobs, the firm should be willing to discuss with its workers the basis for its job evaluation method. Therefore, the workers can see they are being treated equitably. The method or methods used in evaluating office jobs should be clearly set forth in written manuals, and special programs to communicate and explain the information on job evaluation plans should be provided for supervisors and workers. In addition, a formal procedure should be established whereby the results of any job evaluation plan may be appealed. For example, in one large manufacturing company the office supervisor may appeal a job evaluation to the person in charge of compensation and ask for a review of the evaluation based upon additional data or interpretation supplied by the supervisor; final authority on the evaluation lies with the compensation officer.[8]

The trend in job evaluation is toward a decline in use of the ranking and the job classification methods and an increased use of other plans, such as the point method or a combination of methods. In a 1972 study of the several job evaluation methods used by AFL-CIO and independent unions, it was found that for office-type jobs, the most popularly used method is the point method, followed by a combination of plans and the job classification method. The ranking of office-type job evaluation plans currently being used in the respective union contracts remains relatively unchanged from a similar survey conducted several years earlier.[9] The 1972 member survey of nonexempt salaried compensation practices, undertaken by the Administrative Management Society, showed that the point evaluation plan is favored by 60 percent of the administrators who conduct formal job evaluation plans. Other systems include factor comparison and overall job comparison (ranking), with each used by about 30 percent of the surveyed participants.[10] According to a 1975 survey conducted by the American Compensation Association, the most frequently used method of job evaluation for hourly and nonexempt employees is simple ranking; the most common method used for exempt and executive positions is the Hay Plan, a point system developed by Hay Associates.[11] In its 1976 survey of job evaluation policies and procedures, the Bureau of National Affairs found the point method the most popularly

---

[8]"Job Evaluation Policies and Procedures," Personnel Policies Forum Survey No. 113 (Washington: The Bureau of National Affairs, Inc., June, 1976), p. 7.

---

[9]Harold D. Janes, "Issues in Job Evaluation: The Union View," *Personnel Journal* (September, 1972), pp. 676–678.
[10]"Sounder Salary Guidelines," *Administrative Management* (November, 1972), p. 50.
[11]"Job Evaluation Techniques Surveyed," *Bulletin to Management* (Washington: The Bureau of National Affairs, Inc., August 28, 1975), p. 2.

used job evaluation method for office jobs, followed by the factor-comparison, job classification, market pricing, and simple ranking methods.[12]

The guideline method, designed to meet contemporary business challenges and to bring together job pricing and job evaluation, has gained increasing acceptance over the past few years among corporate wage and salary administrators.[13] One of the contemporary business challenges to the evaluation of jobs is the increasing application of automated systems and procedures, which makes necessary a thorough reexamination of the firm's present job evaluation method. With physical effort being practically eliminated on a particular job, it would no longer be valid in evaluating that job to employ a method that places great weight on the factor of physical effort. With the advent of many new office jobs that require different skills and abilities and increased responsibilities to work under different processes, the evaluator will need more technical knowledge in order to evaluate the jobs accurately.

---

[12]"Job Evaluation Policies and Procedures," *op. cit.*, p. 6.

[13]*Management Bulletin No. 128*, "A New Dimension to Job Evaluation," by Anthony M. Pasquale © 1969 by the American Management Association, Inc., p. 10.

QUESTIONS FOR REVIEW

1. Enumerate the benefits to be gained by a business firm from an ongoing program of job analysis.

2. What are the major advantages and disadvantages of using the questionnaire method of gathering job information?

3. Compare the interview method and the observation method of gathering job information.

4. For what reasons should office workers have easy access to their company's file of job descriptions?

5. What kinds of information are contained in job descriptions that are combined with job specifications?

6. Distinguish between a job description and a job specification, indicating the purpose of each.

7. Indicate some of the principal uses of job specifications.

8. Explain the procedure to be followed in using the ranking method to evaluate jobs.

9. Why is the job classification method of evaluating jobs looked upon as an outgrowth of the ranking method?

10. Why is the selection of key jobs essential in the use of the factor-comparison method of job evaluation?

11. What are the main advantages in using the point method of job evaluation which probably account for its relative popularity?

12. How does the guideline method of job evaluation differ significantly from other methods of evaluating jobs?

QUESTIONS FOR DISCUSSION

1. Norman Koller, manager of office services for Rex Cereals, and several supervisors and department heads feel that their firm is operating very smoothly without any formal job evaluation program. What benefits do you believe the company might obtain by establishing a formal job evaluation program? Do you foresee any potential disadvantages for the company as a result of having installed a job evaluation program? Explain your answers.

2. It is claimed that an efficient job study program improves the working conditions between workers and management. Evaluate the validity of this statement.

3. Carol D'Ambrosio, a payroll clerk, feels that her job should be ranked higher than it is under the company's ranking method. How would you, as D'Ambrosio's supervisor, justify to her your ranking of the job she holds?

4. Some firms "glamorize" or "dress up" their job titles, such as changing the job title Janitor to Building Maintenance Engineer. Why is this done? Do you favor this practice? Defend your answer.

5. To eliminate some of the disadvantages of each method of job evaluation, job analysts use the methods in various combinations and supplement them with new technical "twists" in order to formulate more scientific job evaluation schemes. Do you believe that job evaluation is scientific? Explain.

6. Who should have responsibility for determining which jobs are key jobs? How should the key jobs be determined?

7. Since most office employees have at least a high school education and, in many instances, some college education, they are qualified to write a satisfactory description of their jobs. Discuss the relevancy of this statement.

8. What are the advantages and disadvantages to both management and the union of having the union participate in job evaluation?

9. What qualifications should a job analyst possess? Why?

10. When interviewing Bernice Klingaman, supervisor of accounts payable, to determine the content of her job, you find that she does not remember many of the things that she does daily, weekly, and monthly. What steps should you take to complete your analysis of Klingaman's job?

PRACTICAL OFFICE MANAGEMENT CASES

Case 22-1   **Reanalyzing Office Jobs**

Harlow Exercise Equipment, manufacturers of a wide line of sporting goods, athletic supplies, and recreational games, employs 270 office workers. Although a job evaluation point plan has been in operation for more than a year, there is some discontent among the office workers arising from so-called salary inequities.

A job analysis was performed on each office job, and job descriptions and specifications were prepared on the basis of the data gathered in the analyses. In preparing each analysis, the office manager, Mary Reynolds, interviewed a typical worker in each department, chosen by the supervisor in whose department the work was performed. The analysis was verified by interviewing the worker's immediate supervisor. Later, the job descriptions and specifications for each job were verified by the appropriate supervisor.

Three or four of the supervisors have been with the company for many years and have received their promotions for performing outstanding work as accountants. The remaining supervisors have been promoted directly from clerical positions or have been recruited from outside the company.

Although the work performed in several of the departments tends to fall in similar labor grades (mostly skilled machine operators), the wages in those departments tend to be dissimilar. The wages in the departments headed by the former accountants tend to be higher than those in the other departments.

Prepare a concisely written report in which you answer the following questions:

1. What are some possible explanations for the differences in wages among departments?
2. Should the company require another analysis of the jobs? If not, why not? If yes, should the analysis be undertaken for all jobs, for those paying the lowest salaries, or for those paying the highest salaries? Why?
3. What can the office manager do to increase the accuracy of the job analyses?

Case 22-2 Recommending the Installation of a Job Evaluation Method

The Keynes Oil Company, a distributor of fuel oil for a major oil producer, is located in eastern Pennsylvania. Cyrus Keynes, the president of the company, is fourth in the line of family presidents that the company has had. His great grandfather founded the business, and most of his policies have been perpetuated over the years. The company employs 42 workers in its distributor operations (drivers and maintenance personnel). All of these workers are unionized, and their hourly wages are determined through union-management collective bargaining. In the office there are 11 employees, an office manager, and an assistant. The office staff, nonunionized, is paid on a monthly salary basis.

Harriette Beeman, the assistant office manager, graduated two years ago from a nearby community college. When employed by the company last year, Beeman was assigned the handling of all personnel functions. Last week she received a complaint from Peggy Trevor, the switchboard operator, who is dissatisfied with her salary. Trevor has heard that Dwayne Clark, a filing clerk, is earning more than she and thinks this is unfair since she has more seniority than Clark. Art Brogan, supervisor of the drivers, has remarked to Beeman about a similar dissatisfaction among the drivers. Two of the drivers are being paid less than the maintenance personnel, and the drivers feel that this is unfair since their jobs require more skills and responsibilities than those of the maintenance personnel.

Beeman believes that a job evaluation system should be installed in the office and in the yard in order to minimize the complaints about inequitable wages and salaries. Beeman has spoken to Bill Keller, the office manager, who agrees with her but believes that Keynes would never agree to such an evaluation system. Keller feels that any job evaluation method should be limited to the office workers since the drivers and the maintenance personnel are unionized.

Beeman has been instructed by Keller to write a report to Keynes on the situation in the office and in the yard. Assuming that you are the assistant office manager, write the report in which you make recommendations for a course of action to be taken in the Keynes Oil Company.

Chapter 23

WORK MEASUREMENT AND WORK STANDARDS

One of the greatest challenges facing office managers lies in their ability to control mounting administrative costs, especially salaries and employee benefits, which may represent as much as 60 to 75 percent of the total costs of office operations. Managers can control the bulk of salary costs only to a limited extent, for their firms must remain competitive with regard to the salary structure prevailing in the community. But one way that managers can control the use made of the office force and bring about increased productivity is by measuring the work done during working hours.

The pressing need for establishing formal controls over clerical personnel becomes evident when managers of small as well as of large offices, presently without any formal controls, realize that the office personnel are being utilized only some 50 to 60 percent of the time.[1] Thus, in offices where employees are paid for a 40-hour workweek, the company is obtaining perhaps only 55 percent productivity, or possibly 22 useful hours of work each week. If this same rate of return were related to the return on capital investment or to the productivity of workers in the plant, the situation would not be tolerated!

This chapter discusses the measurement of work and the development of work standards, one very effective approach that should be investigated by office managers who are searching for ways to achieve additional control over ever-rising office costs and to ensure that their firms are receiving a reasonable value in return for the office salaries expenditure.

NATURE OF WORK MEASUREMENT AND WORK STANDARDS

Work measurement is a tool of cost control used to determine how much work is completed and how effectively it is completed. Usually this suggests a measurement of the volume of work and the amount of time required (quantitative measurements) as well as the accuracy and appearance of the work (qualitative measurements). A *work standard* is a yardstick of performance, or "par," which indicates what is expected of office workers and by which their output can be evaluated. Work standards are tools of managerial control that are best applied to routine and repetitive operations such as typing, keypunching, transcribing, calculating, filing, billing, and posting. Although nonroutine, semicreative jobs are usually excluded from a formal work measurement program, some types of nonroutine work may be measured in the aggregate to provide useful results. By means of work standards administrative managers can determine what should be the quantity and quality of work produced and can compare this with the actual quantity and

---

[1]Harold W. Nance and Robert E. Nolan, *Office Work Measurement* (New York: McGraw-Hill Book Co., 1971), p. 8.

quality of work produced, thus providing a basis for managerial control. All work standards are aimed at obtaining 100 percent efficiency, which is defined as the rate of production at which the average, well-trained employee can work all day without undue fatigue, or simply stated, "a fair day's work."

To be most effective, standards must be set up in such a way that they are reliable. They must be realistic and capable of achievement under normal, reasonable working conditions. They should not have to be changed too often or confusion will result. They must be understood both by employees and by management. Standards must also be flexible in order to meet the variations in working conditions. For example, a standard for typing a one-page, 100-word letter of straight-copy matter is not the same as a standard for typing a one-page, 100-word letter involving technical material and tabular data. Similarly, setting standards for the number of invoices to be filed under an alphabetic filing system and those under a numeric filing system will not result in the same quantitative figure.

Benefits to Be Realized from Work Standards

By providing data on the elements of *volume, time,* and *quality,* a program of work measurement and work standards offers the administrative office manager many benefits. Standards aid in:

1. Determining the cost of the work performed, a hitherto unanswered question in many offices. Thus, management is aided in establishing realistic work targets, planning human resources needs, preparing budgets, and measuring the effectiveness of forecasts.

2. Exercising better control over the scheduling and routing of office work, which should result in improved service to customers by reducing the elapsed time for processing office work.

3. Evaluating employee performance. Employees know the performance goals expected of them in terms of volume, quality, and time; and, further, they know that these are objective figures based upon reasonable working conditions. The superior worker receives recognition for a job well-done, and the poorer worker is rated accordingly.

4. Installing wage-incentive systems whereby employees' earnings are based upon their productivity. (The development of wage-incentive systems is discussed in Chapter 24).

5. Evaluating the need for improving office systems and procedures and determining the feasibility of installing new machines and equipment. Knowing what volume of production should be maintained and the cost of salaries necessary to maintain this volume, the office manager is able to study and to lower the costs of systems, such as those involving automated operations. The manager is better able to answer questions pertaining to the installation of new equipment and utilization of facilities, since proposed costs and output can be realistically compared with present clerical costs and volume of production to ascertain whether a gain or a loss will be realized.

6. Measuring the effectiveness of departmental operations by comparing departmental achievements with the standards. Consistently lower performance by a department or a wide disparity of performance levels among several departments indicates that something is wrong, and thus the supervisor is prompted to learn the causes and to correct them.

7. Enabling the immediate supervisor to measure the effectiveness of a new

employee and the rate of learning that has taken place. At what point should a trainee on a specific job be able to handle a normal work load? This is the type of question that supervisors must be able to answer so that they may follow up on employees and determine if necessary training has been provided to ensure a high level of work performance.

In spite of the benefits to be realized from work standards, formal programs of clerical work measurement are not commonly found in offices, as noted in the following section. In fact, less than eight percent of the total clerical work force in the United States are under measurement control, as contrasted to over 80 percent of blue-collar workers who are working under some form of work measurement system.[2]

Reasons for Failure to Apply Work Measurement

In view of the rapid rate with which the size and cost of office staffs have grown during the past six decades, it would be expected that the measurement of clerical work would be utilized to a much greater extent. Several reasons are commonly advanced, however, to explain the failure to apply the principles of work measurement to office operations.

Perhaps the major reason for the lack of interest in measuring office work is the opinion that office work is either impossible to measure or the measurement is too difficult and costly to prove practicable. Proponents of this point of view feel that clerical work is so varied, so complex, and so nebulous that it does not lend itself to measurement. Repeti-

tiveness does not exist in many phases of office work to the same extent as it does in manufacturing operations. Often an office employee may process several kinds of work units — orders, invoices, vouchers — in a single day. Even though the work may be repetitive, there are phases of the job, such as answering and placing telephone calls and looking up information, that prove difficult, if not impossible, to measure. Others advance the argument that since in many offices the number of employees is small, there is no need for measurement. In other instances there is a lack of desire on the part of top management to engage in any work measurement program, for it is felt that the office work is going along well enough and there is no need to disturb the tranquility of the workers by attempting to measure their work load. Also, managers and first-line supervisors are often suspicious of and have misconceptions about the nature and intent of work measurement.

Many management consultants contend that most of the reasons offered for the failure to establish a work measurement program in the office are more imaginary than real. It is claimed, as discussed in the following section, that most routine and semiroutine office activities can be effectively measured quantitatively and qualitatively.

Office Operations That Can Be Measured

Estimates of the amount of office work lending itself to measurement range from two thirds to three fourths of all work done in the office. If this major portion of work were measured and work standards prepared, office managers would possess a tool of clerical cost control that would improve their office

---

[2]*Ibid.*, p. 15.

operations and enable them to gain a competitive edge. For measurement and the setting of standards, office activities should meet certain criteria:

1. The work must be done in a repetitive, reasonably uniform manner.
2. The content of the work must be consistently the same from one period to another.
3. The units of work must be countable (that is, discernible in precise quantitative terms, such as a punch card, a form, or a letter).
4. The volume of work must be sufficient to justify the costs of counting and recording.[3]

Office activities that meet the criteria described above are commonly found in those cost centers or groups that have the largest number of employees performing routine clerical tasks. Some of the office tasks that can be measured include: filing, typing, transcribing, addresser-printing, opening mail, stuffing and sealing envelopes, posting, billing, keypunching, and calculating. Each of these tasks is characterized as highly routine and repetitive. For jobs such as drafting, editing, proofreading, and writing specifications, where the work is semicreative, the task of measurement becomes more difficult, but not impossible, as explained later in this chapter.

When acceptable work standards are applied to certain types of office operations, experience shows that efficiency and output have increased. According to the management consulting firm, Serge A. Birn Company, the performance level in offices using clerical work measurement, with good standards and sound

control, may be increased from 55 percent to at least 80 to 90 percent.[4] Then, with the introduction of incentives or bonuses based on a work measurement program, a performance level of 100 percent may be approached.

PREPARING FOR THE WORK MEASUREMENT PROGRAM

For a work measurement program to be effective, top management must fully support the program and its objectives and make active use of the information obtained. The nature of the program and its aims must be communicated to employees so that they fully understand the program. A supervisor must administer the program at each level of office operations. Analysts who have some college training or equivalent work experience and a "feel" for paperwork should be properly selected. Finally, there must be a realization and acceptance of the fact that the clerical work standards developed are feasible and accurate.

Gaining Top Management's Support

Work measurement as a managerial tool of cost control must receive complete and unqualified endorsement by those for whose use the tool has been designed; otherwise there is little point in installing the program. Top management must understand the objectives of the program and how it will work, take an active interest in the program, be willing to make the decisions needed to implement the program, and demonstrate in a tangible way that all managers stand behind the program. Involved in management's support is an effective

---

[3]Lionel J. Deschamps, Systems Engineer, Albany Felt Company, Albany, New York, (In a paper given before the Charleston Chapter of AMS).

[4]Nance and Nolan, *op. cit.*, p. 18.

control over the replacement of personnel who have left the firm so that an adequate work load is assured each employee. Top management must convey to middle and first-line management the idea that the program is permanent and that its acceptance is mandatory.[5]

Communicating the Program to Employees

Since the work measurement program affects employees, they are naturally interested in the program; and consideration must be given to their feelings. Before the installation of the program the administrative office manager must provide the worker with a complete, honest, and satisfactory answer to the question: "How is this program going to affect me?" Although a satisfactory answer to the question may not be liked by all the workers, the answer is usually welcomed by the more capable, conscientious employee. What is important is that the workers understand the techniques to be used in the program and how the results of the program will be applied to them. Thus, employee fears and natural resistance to change will be lessened.

Employees must be convinced that in no way will they lose their jobs as a result of work measurement. In developing work measurement programs one group of specialists states that no one ever need lose his or her job as a result of the program, for turnover is invariably more than adequate to adjust the staff and to absorb expected increases in productivity.[6]

When informing the workers of the program, the timing and the nature of the communication medium are very important. Rather than have knowledge about the program circulate via the grapevine, it is recommended that a letter announcing and fully explaining the program be sent to all employees at the same time and from the same source. Thus, any suspicions and questions on the part of employees may be anticipated before the first phase of the program gets underway.

Administering the Program

The backbone of a work measurement program is the first-line supervisor, of whom much is required, for ultimately it is the supervisor who determines the success of the program. If the workers are given adequate supervision and leadership, most of them can meet the performance standards and will do so willingly. Supervisors must be able and willing to review their operations and to weed out inefficiencies which can cause the failure of their departments or cost centers to meet standards. The work of their units must be planned and scheduled, and work loads shifted in order to maintain a balance of work among employees. To coordinate the work flow and keep peak loads at tolerable minimums, a supervisor has to plan and consult with other supervisors. Adequate records must be kept to provide a sound basis for performance reports. Importantly, there is the need to evaluate individual productivity and to use the results of the program to determine training needs, to ready people for promotion, and to justify salary increases. Thus, the program takes on meaning in the eyes of the workers, and management is enabled to identify and to reward outstanding workers.

---

[5]David V. Swett, Executive Vice-President, Bruce Payne & Associates, Inc., "Work Measurement v. Unionization," *The Office* (November, 1970), p. 28.
[6]*Ibid.*

Through the effective accomplishment of these activities, the supervisor at each level is discharging his or her responsibilities for processing the work in the most economical manner.

In training sessions where first-line supervisors are introduced to the program and to the roles they will play, it must be made clear that the results of the program will not dictate how the supervisors' departments are to be operated, nor will their ability to operate the departments be restricted. The program should be introduced to supervisors as a managerial tool that will aid them in doing a better job.

Selection of Analysts

Often as a means of reducing employee fears about the work measurement program and to prevent any undue resentment, employees from within the firm are selected and trained as work analysts. Acceptability of the program as a whole is better assured when the work analysts are known to their fellow employees. In addition, analysts who have been recruited from within the ranks, such as from the systems and procedures division, are familiar with company routines, methods, and procedures. This knowledge is a valuable contribution when defining methods and setting standards. Although an analyst selected from within the firm must be trained in work measurement, an outsider must also be retrained in the special techniques used by the company. One important qualification needed by the employees selected from within the firm is the ability to sell their ideas to others. The TTC (Total Training Concept) approach to training used by the Serge A. Birn Company, a leading consulting firm, consists of three-week classroom sessions in which analysts learn how to

interview employees, analyze and improve the procedures, and measure the work.[7]

The Serge A. Birn Company recommends for the actual installation that a team of three to five people, including the team leader, be used in a medium-size office (200 employees). In very large organizations with as many as 10,000 clerical workers, 30 or more analysts may be involved. However, once the program is underway, no more than one third of the original team is needed to maintain lower office costs.[8]

Feasibility and Accuracy of the Standards

Regardless of the office task, some mental and physical effort is required to complete a unit of work, and the amount of the productive activity to accomplish the job can be measured. As noted earlier, there is a natural reluctance by many firms to establish clerical work standards, a fact that must be accepted at the outset when installing a work measurement program. Thus, the administrative manager should be resigned to obtaining something less than perfection in the program. When the development of a work measurement program is approached from this point of view, the office manager will be pleasantly surprised at how much can actually be accomplished through work measurement.

To encourage employee confidence in the standards, the workers must

---

[7]Robert E. Nolan, Manager, Office Services Division, Serge A. Birn Company, Louisville, Kentucky, "How to Prepare Clerical Employees for a Cost Improvement Program," *The Office* (October, 1970). See pages 20 and 22 for a detailed presentation of the program used for training work analysts.

[8]*Ibid.*, p. 15.

understand how the standards have been developed, what is included in each standard, and how they are to proceed if unforeseen conditions, such as machine breakdowns, occur. Standards must be accurate and consistent, for approximate standards will not gain the confidence of employees. It is recommended that management take the time and effort to insure that the standards are accurate to a minimum of ± 5 percent over the period for which performances will be calculated.[9]

METHODS OF MEASURING ROUTINE WORK AND SETTING STANDARDS

The earliest methods of measuring office work and setting standards were the same as those used in the factory by industrial engineers to measure the output of blue-collar workers. Many of the first attempts to measure office work were clumsy in their application of techniques that were designed to measure the output of workers in machine shops and foundries. With managers utilizing work measurement techniques that paid little attention to the feelings of the individuals being measured, many of the programs failed and in some cases the discontent among office workers paved the way for unionization activities. Later, however, techniques centering around a consideration for human values have been utilized.

Several of the various methods that are used chiefly to measure routine, repetitive office work and to set performance standards are described below. Then, in the last section of this chapter, some of the methods for establishing job performance standards for nonrepetitive,

semicreative office jobs will be briefly presented.

Historical Data

Under the *historical data* or *past performance* method, past production records of various office activities such as transcribing, typing, filing, and billing are studied to measure what was produced in the past. For example, the output of workers in a typing center may be measured by using one or more of the following bases:

1. *By the page, letter, belt, disk, or cassette.* Measurement according to this base is probably the simplest plan to use. However, simply counting the number of pages, letters, belts, cassettes, etc., is too inaccurate to be of much value, for letters vary in length, and belts, disks, and cassettes hold varying amounts of dictated matter.
2. *By standard lines.* Some companies count the number of standard typewritten lines produced. A standard line is usually 60 spaces — 15.24 cm (6 inches) for pica type and 12.7 cm (5 inches) for elite type. The number of lines may be counted either by hand or by use of a line counter, which is a cardboard or plastic scale graduated for pica and elite type. Such a base cannot easily be used for tabulated or statistical matter. The standard-line basis is particularly useful, however, where workers are compensated on a piece-rate basis.
3. *By square centimeters (cm²) or square inches.* Some companies use the square-centimeter or square-inch base in place of the standard-line base. In these firms the production of typists is measured by use of transparent celluloid sheets blocked off in square centimeters or inches. When a sheet is placed over a letter or a report, the number of square centimeters or inches of typewritten material may be

---

[9]Swett, *loc. cit.*

read at a glance. This base is especially satisfactory in the measurement of tabulated material.

4. *By key strokes.* A commonly used base is the number of key strokes made on the typewriter. By means of one type of electronic counter attached to typewriters, up to 5,000 key strokes can be accurately and automatically recorded each minute.

The past production of the group of typists, measured by one or more of the bases described above, is then used as a means of measuring what employees can do in the future. The *best performance* may be selected as standard on the theory that "we did it before; we should be able to do it again." Or an average output of the *best* worker and of the *poorest* worker may be used as a standard. Although the average output may be more reasonable than the best performance, the historical data method is little better than having no standards at all. By means of historical data, management is informed of simply how long a certain job took in the past rather than the amount of time the job should take at the present or in the future. Built into the performance reporting system are all the inefficiencies present during the period from which the data are drawn. Although the historical data method is a

very frequently used method for measuring office work, its use may cause difficulty if management becomes too accustomed to it and a decision is later made to install a more precise method of measurement. On the other hand, the historical data method can be easily installed at a very low cost, and there is no need for highly trained personnel to administer the program.

Time Log

Another simple method of measuring office work and establishing work standards is the *time log* or *time ladder* method. First, it is necessary to identify the work activity being performed during the day. For each of the various office activities, a simple code number is established. On a special time analysis recording sheet, such as the activity log shown in Figure 23-1, the employee participates in the measurement of his or her output by recording the actual time spent and the units of work produced for a period of a week or a month. At the end of the time period, the forms prepared by the various employees are summarized, reviewed, and edited to isolate any unusual patterns. A time log for the entire department is prepared, upon which each activity is summarized by

ACTIVITY LOG					
Date *April 15, 19--*				Employee *Betty Barnett*	
Activity Code	Units Produced	Time			Remarks
		Start	Finish	Elapsed	
43	10	8:20	9:10	50 min.	
38	176	9:15	12:30	3 hrs.	15 min. break
33	52	1:30	2:45	1 hr. 15 min.	
38	91	2:50	4:30	1 hr. 25 min.	15 min. break

Fig. 23-1
Time Log Recording Sheet

code number. This report provides the total time spent on each activity in a particular department. Dividing the total hours into the quantity produced converts the data into a rate-per-hour figure and places all the performances on a comparable basis. From these figures it is possible to establish a standard time for each item being processed.

The major advantage of the time log method is that it can be used with little additional cost. Permanent control over activities can be maintained by continuing to record work assignments on the activity log. The time log method becomes unreliable, however, to the extent that personal time allowances and absences from the work station are not recorded by the individual employees. Also, the selection of a standard time from the array of data involves a great deal of subjectivity.

Work Sampling

The *work sampling* method of measuring work is based on the fundamental laws of probability. If a sufficient number of valid random samples of the work are taken, the findings can be relied upon to represent the results that would have been obtained if the whole universe had been observed in a continuous 100 percent time study.

Using Work Sampling. In a work sampling study a trained observer makes a number of observations of the work being performed. The time of each observation and the person to be observed have been statistically predetermined for the observer. When the sample has been completed, the percentage of total observations recorded for each activity observed is determined. Next, the total employee time available for work during the study is calculated. This time, expressed in employee minutes and mul-

tiplied by each of the observation percentages developed above, equals the time spent on each activity observed. This activity time, divided by the corresponding volume count, produces the unit time or standard.

For example, suppose the observer wants to find out how much time a team of clerks spends on the various tasks that make up their day. Assume also that it is necessary to determine how long it takes to accomplish one unit of each of these tasks. Using work sampling, the observer would make a number of quick observations of one or another of the clerks. After each observation, the observer would immediately record what the clerk was doing when observed. When the sample has been completed and the observations tallied, the results might look like this:

Activity	Observations	Ratio	Percent of Total
Filing	100	100/1,000	10
Typing	300	300/1,000	30
Sorting	150	150/1,000	15
Merging	200	200/1,000	20
Personal	250	250/1,000	25
Total Observations	1,000		100

During the study the observer maintained the following record of the time that each clerk involved in the study was available for work:

Name	Minutes
Lucas	429
McTavish	429
Van Horn	324 (part-time employee, 9:30–3:30)
Doerr	Absent
Wiegand	254 (training ——— session 8:45–11:55)
Total available minutes	1,436

Having the total number of clerk minutes available for work, the observer can readily determine the time consumed by each activity:

Activity	Percent of Total Observations	× Minutes Available for Work	= Minutes Spent on Each Activity
Filing	10	1,436	143.6
Typing	30	1,436	430.8
Sorting	15	1,436	215.4
Merging	20	1,436	287.2
Personal	25	1,436	359.0
Total	100		1,436.0

In addition to maintaining a record of the work time available, the production counts for each activity were recorded. With this information the unit time or standard for each activity can be determined as follows:

Activity	Minutes Spent	÷ Work Counts	= Unit Time or Standard
Filing	143.6	450 cards	.32 min.
Typing	430.8	110 policies	3.92 min.
Sorting	215.4	600 pieces of mail	.36 min.
Merging	287.2	150 applications	1.91 min.
Personal	359.0		
Total	1,436.0		

These unit times have been based on the premise that the percentage distribution of the various activities as they occurred during the random observation period tends to equal the exact percentage distribution that would be found by continuous observation. The accuracy and validity of the study depend upon the care with which each step is performed.

Determining Proper Sample Size. The number of observations to be made in any work sampling study depends upon the following three factors: (1) how much tolerance will be accepted, (2) what portion of time is expected to be consumed by the smallest activity to be measured, and (3) how reliable the results have to be.

Tolerance refers to the degree of accuracy. Suppose it is specified that a tolerance of 10 percent will be acceptable. If the study results show that an activity consumed 5 percent of the available time, the analyst can be certain that the actual time consumed was within 10 percent of that 5 percent; that is, it was not less than 4.5 percent nor more than 5.5 percent. The larger the tolerance one is willing to accept, the smaller the number of observations that must be made.

Besides specifying an acceptable tolerance, an estimate must be made of the percentage of time consumed by the least time-consuming activity for which reliable results are required. This is an educated guess made after the observer has become familiar with the operations of the unit to be studied. The smaller this estimated critical percentage becomes, the larger the sample must be. For this reason, observation codes are often set up so that the smallest activity will account for at least 5 percent of the total number of observations. Whenever possible, separate observation codes are eliminated for those activities that are estimated to consume less than 5 percent of the available time. These activities can be combined with related work codes or grouped under a miscellaneous observation code.

As the size of a sample is increased, the reliability of the results also increases. However, nearly every sampling application reaches a point of diminishing returns — a point beyond which the increased reliability achieved does not

SAMPLE SIZES COMPUTED FOR 80 PERCENT RELIABILITY

Net Number of Observations When:

P is	T is ± 5% (of P)	T is ± 10% (of P)	T is ± 15% (of P)	T is ± 20% (of P)
1%	66,920	16,730	7,440	4,180
2	33,120	8,280	3,680	2,070
3	21,860	5,460	2,430	1,370
4	16,220	4,060	1,800	1,010
5	12,840	3,210	1,430	800
6	10,590	2,650	1,180	660
7	8,980	2,250	1,000	560
8	7,770	1,940	860	490
9	6,840	1,710	760	430
10	6,080	1,520	680	380
15	3,830	960	430	240
20	2,700	680	300	170
25	2,030	510	230	130
30	1,580	390	180	100
35	1,260	315	140	80
40	1,020	260	110	60
45	830	210	90	50
50	680	170	80	40

Table 23-1

P = Estimated Critical Percentage
T = Tolerance Factor

justify the additional time, effort, and expense required. A sample size that produces a reliability of 80 percent is generally considered to be sufficient for work sampling purposes.

Suppose a work sampling study is planned and:

1. An acceptable tolerance of 10 percent is specified.
2. The critical percentage is estimated to be 5 percent.
3. 80 percent reliability has been determined to be adequate.

Given these conditions, the table of sample sizes shown in Table 23-1 indicates that 3,210 observations must be made.[10]

---

[10]For those interested in learning how the sample size is derived by statistical formula, consult any basic textbook in statistics.

Suppose it had been decided that greater reliability, say 90 percent, were needed. In that case the number of observations for 80 percent reliability shown in Table 23-1 would be multiplied by the appropriate factor given in Table 23-2.

To find the net number of observations (N) required for $P = .05$, $T = .10$, with a reliability of 90 percent:

From Table 23-1:

When $P = .05$ and $T = .10$, $N = 3,210$

Using Table 23-2 for reliability of 90 percent:

$N = 3,210 \times 1.601$
$N = 5,139$

Pros and Cons of Work Sampling. If there are enough random samples taken over a long enough period of

RELIABILITY FACTORS*

Reliability	Factor	Reliability	Factor
50%	.269	85%	1.227
55	.337	90	1.601
60	.420	95	2.273
65	.517	96	2.496
70	.637	97	2.786
75	.783	98	3.204
80	1.000	99	3.926

Table 23-2

*Factors to be applied to sample sizes in Figure 23-1 to provide indicated degrees of reliability.

time to make the samples representative and valid, the data obtained under work sampling are considerably more reliable than those secured from the time analysis method. The major disadvantage of work sampling is the need for trained analysts to set up the study and to perform the required observations. In some cases the sampling method may prove to be uneconomical if the sample size required to produce valid results is too great. Also, some employees may not fully understand the sampling technique employed and may be wary of statistical arguments to the extent that they will alter their performance, such as slowing down, so that the sample being taken will produce a performance standard on the low side. Of course, such a sample would not be a valid one, nor would the performance standard derived from it. Thus, when introducing the work sampling method, employees must be thoroughly informed about the nature and objectives of the measurement program.

Using Probability Sampling to Reduce the Costs of Quality Control. Under a *quality control program*, an attempt is made to recognize and to remove the identifiable costs of defects

and variations from the standards that have been developed for the particular process or operation. Through the use of probability sampling, the costs of some types of quality control may be reduced. For example, rather than check the output of all billing clerks and record all errors made, a randomly selected sample can be taken of the work produced by each clerk. The sample size required to give valid and reliable findings can be statistically determined so that the costly checking of all records can be avoided. In one company a 60-day test was made using 100 percent checking and a 20 percent sample. The results were practically identical, and the firm is now using a 20 percent sample for its quality control.[11]

Motion Study and Time Study

In most office systems and procedures, there is usually one best way in which to perform each operation. By observing and timing workers at their jobs,

---

[11]For an excellent application of probability sampling as a technique for reducing office costs, see "Sampling Improves Forms Control 6 Ways," *Office Systems in Action: Case Study Profiles*, Manual 2S-106, *Administrative Management* (1968), pp. 1–3.

much waste motion and effort can be eliminated. The purposes of motion study and time study are not synonymous, for *motion study* is used primarily to improve work methods, while *time study* is used to determine time standards. However, in relation to measuring work performance and setting standards, motion study and time study are inseparable. To improve an old work method or to introduce a new job, it would be difficult to determine the most desirable procedure without utilizing *motion economy*. Similarly, the gains brought through the new method could not be measured without *time values* for comparison.

Motion Study. Detailed motion studies were originated by Frank and Lillian Gilbreth, as mentioned in Chapter 1. Motion study is a recognized fundamental of obtaining "the one best way to do work," a phrase used by the Gilbreths, who considered motion study a scientific method of waste elimination. According to their definition: "Motion study consists of dividing work into the most fundamental elements possible; studying these elements separately and in relation to one another; and from these studied elements, when timed, building methods of least waste."[12]

In a simple motion study, a single operation or a series of operations is studied visually by means of a stopwatch. However, if management can justify the cost of installation and the time required for analysis, the precise micromotion study is preferred. The Gilbreths originated the term *micromotion study* when they began to use motion pictures for studying the compo-

nent parts of an operation. In a micromotion study, the human and mechanical movements are observed and analyzed in order to reduce a given operation to the fewest component parts in their logical sequence. Instead of relying upon the uncertain eye of an observer, a motion picture camera is used. On each picture frame appears the face of a specially prepared clock called a *microchronometer*, which is divided into 100 sections. Since the clock revolves 20 times each minute, it is possible to obtain 2,000 pictures per minute. The 1/2,000 of the minute time division, shown on each picture frame, is the unit of measurement in a micromotion study.

Micromotion studies are especially useful in studying office work of a repetitive nature and of long-range duration. Although the micromotion technique involves time-consuming methods, expensive motion pictures, and detailed records, the study is worth the expenditure since the entire office operation is being analyzed and recorded simultaneously. As a result, ineffective work motions are eliminated or reduced, and thus overall management efficiency is increased.

Following either a motion study or a micromotion study, a standard time can be determined, which, in turn, becomes the basis for determining a fair day's work for a fair day's pay. The standard time becomes the basis for the most efficient method of doing a particular type of office work. It must be remembered, however, that the standard time must be adjusted, as explained below, for the fatigue and personal needs of the worker as well as for delays due to machine difficulties.

Time Study. The main purpose of time study in measuring job performance is to establish the time required

---

[12]Frank B. Gilbreth and L. M. Gilbreth, *Applied Motion Study* (New York: Sturgis & Walton Company, now the Macmillan Company, 1917), p. 43.

for performing each operation at an average pace. Another aim of time study is to develop standard time data that can be used as synthetic times for performance rating of similar operations without making further time studies. (The development of synthetic or predetermined times is explained later in this chapter.) Time studies are also helpful in comparing relative wage rates, as well as aiding in the control of production.

Generally workers accept standard operation times if they are assured that the time studies have been made under the best standardized conditions. Management, in turn, expects the operator to perform the job in the established time. Of course, adherence to a time standard requires that all standardized conditions and job specifications be described in detail, as discussed in Chapter 22.

Unless the time-study analyst has gained the confidence of the office personnel, the efforts expended in the study will be ineffective and morale problems will follow. The analyst must be capable of dealing with people honestly, tactfully, and sympathetically. A reputation must be established for making fair and accurate studies by using a systematic and exacting procedure when analyzing operations.

One limitation of the time study method is that a degree of subjectivity is involved in the initial selection of people who will be studied to determine a standard time value. The employee selected to be observed should be average and fully qualified, because such a person is respected by his or her coworkers. The worker should be chosen for his or her consistency in using the most efficient movements in working at a normal work pace. Of course, the time taken by the observed worker must be adjusted, as explained below, in order to obtain a standard of comparison.

On a time study sheet the analyst describes each element in the operation according to the sequence in which it occurs. Extreme care must be exercised to see that all operations are covered and that none are overlooked. The analyst must also decide on the number of work cycles to be studied. It is generally recognized that the more observations made and the more accurate the basic time, the greater the assurance that unnecessary delays and inconsistencies will be eliminated.

The stopwatch studies cover only the actual time that it takes the observed employee to perform the operational element. Thus, adjustments must be made in the actual time required in order to determine a realistic time standard for all employees. The technique of adjusting individual differences is called *performance rating* or *leveling*. The goal of performance rating is to obtain a theoretical "normal" time — neither slow nor fast — that average workers require to complete the job under standardized conditions.

Since workers cannot produce steadily and uninterruptedly throughout the day, allowances must be made for the extra time that may not be consumed in actual job performance. Therefore, in addition to the normal working time, proper time allowances must be determined for delays, fatigue, and personal needs such as walking to the drinking fountain and washing the face and hands. For most office situations the time allowances are expressed as percentages and vary from 10 to 20 percent of the normal work day.[13] Thus, if the elemental times of a particular work cycle add up to a total standard time of 2 minutes, a minimum allowance of 10

---

[13]Donald L. Caruth, *Planning for Clerical Work Measurement* (New York: American Management Association, Inc., 1970), p. 77.

percent for delays would increase the standard to 2 minutes and 12 seconds.

After all the allowances have been determined, the time study is complete. The necessary entries are made on a time study observation sheet for a permanent record and a list of the work standards, such as that shown in Figure 23-2, is prepared for everyone interested in the standard time.

Predetermined Times

The development of *predetermined times* or *synthetic basic motion times* is based on the assumption that if the same motions are used in all work activities and under the same conditions, the time values are constant and may be used to reduce subjective judgment. In all predetermined motion time methods, the elements of an operation are de-

scribed according to various physical or mental factors. Thus, by analyzing a job and dividing its elements into basic motions, each motion receives a time value which is obtained from a table. The total time for all motions involved in performing the element plus the addition of a time allowance for conditions such as delay, fatigue, and personal needs becomes the time standard for the job. The standard time values are usually developed from engineered stopwatch studies, micromotion studies, or laboratory studies of work motions. Many of the tables of standard time values have been developed and copyrighted by management consulting firms and professional associations and may be obtained for a fee.

In a survey of work measurement techniques being used in 106 establishments, it was found that predetermined

---

TRANSCRIBING

To transcribe dictation, 8-1/2 × 11 sheets, single spacing:		To hand transcribe letters consisting of 11 five-inch lines	7 letters an hour
Elite type —			
technical matter	4.3 pages an hour	To type salutation and address on form letters	100 an hour
non-technical matter	5.5 pages an hour		
proofreading	20.0 pages an hour		
Pica type —		To duplicate letters, 20 lines in body, with envelopes, using typewriter	10 an hour
technical matter	5.5 pages an hour		
non-technical matter	6.6 pages an hour		
proofreading	25.0 pages an hour	To cut stencils on 8-1/2 × 11 paper, single spaced	4 an hour
To type copy work, single spacing, 8-1/2 × 11 sheets		To type purchase orders from typed and handwritten requisitions, using continuous folded form equipment, each order averaging approximately 370 characters and spaces	21 an hour
technical matter	4.6 pages an hour		
non-technical matter	6.0 pages an hour		
proofreading	16.0 pages an hour		
To type from fairly legible long-hand text	175 lines an hour		
To type from printed copy	200 lines an hour		
To type from stenographic notes	125 lines an hour		

Fig. 23-2
Office Work Standards

(continued)

ADDRESSING

Average production for embossing plates of the chain metal method	5,400 characters an hour	Average production of addressing envelopes on loose filed metal plate machine:
		  Hand feed machines —
		    foot power
		    motor power
		  Automatic, high speed
			1,250 an hour
			1,875 an hour
			6,000 an hour

To address dick strips (mailing strips for addressing magazines) using the chain metal plate method	15,000 an hour		
Average production for embossing individual loose filed plates	2,200 characters an hour	To wet tissue stencils, insert in machine, to place list of names in holder and prepare stencils on the typewriter, three-line address	110 stencils an hour

To proof list new plates on card inserts and sight-verify the impression; manually inserted card inserts	125 an hour	Average production of addressing envelopes on stencil machines:
		  Hand feed machines —
		    foot power
		    motor power
		  Automatic, high speed
			1,250 an hour
			1,888 an hour
			6,000 an hour

To address regular size tabulating cards using machine for loose filed metal plates	3,000 an hour		
To address dick strips using machine for loose filed metal plates	6,000 an hour		

FILING

The usual number of filing guides are: For cards	1 guide for 30 cards	To file data by subject	147 pieces an hour
For correspondence	24 guides per drawer	Filing and re-filing of card records under average conditions in numeric file	375 cards an hour
To file cards in an alphabetic file	295 pieces an hour	To file IBM interpreted heading cards	225 sets an hour
To mark 8-1/2 × 11 letters for name file and make first a–z sort	290 pieces an hour	To file correspondence alphabetically, including inspection for file authorization stamp, arrangement in alphabetical sequence, punch and place in security type folders which must be removed from and returned to cabinet	100 pieces an hour
To sort and file letters in an alphabetic file	175 pieces an hour		
To file papers in an alphabetic file	285 pieces an hour		
To file papers in a geographic file; state, town and name	308 pieces an hour		

MAIL HANDLING

To three-fold letters and enclose in the envelopes	400 an hour	Average production for typing three-line addresses on envelopes	100 an hour
To manually stuff outlook envelopes with open windows, no glacene	975 enclosures an hour	To hand address envelopes or cards from a typewritten list	205 pieces an hour
To open envelopes and remove enclosed papers	525 an hour	To hand address envelopes or cards from a handwritten list	165 pieces an hour
To sort and open mail (top of envelope slit by machine at 250 per minute)	200 an hour	To hand address envelopes or cards from typewritten cards	136 pieces an hour

To fold 1,000 letters and circulars, two-fold:
  By hand
  By machine
	
	1.0 hour
	.25 hour
		To hand address envelopes or cards from handwritten cards	109 pieces an hour

MANUAL SORTING

To sort invoices into 3-digit numerical departmental sequence	1,500 an hour	To sort toll tickets into 4-digit numerical sequence using the rack method, 100 compartments	378 an hour

To sort checks (or documents of a similar size):
  Up to 30 classifications
  30–50 classifications
	
	2,000 an hour
	1,750 an hour
		To sort blocks of 5,000 checks into 6-digit numerical sequence, using a table sort to sort to the left-hand digit, then one handling for second and third digits	1,460 an hour

To sort time tickets to 3-digit sequence	850 an hour		

To sort 5-1/4 × 8-5/16 tickets into 4-digit sequence:
  Table top layout
  Depressed bin layout
	
	780 an hour
	1,070 an hour
		To needle sort to 10 groups (digits 0–9) using notched edge cards	12,000–22,000 cards an hour

To sort to 500, 750 or 1,000 divisions if media are clearly legible, using leaf type sort	1,500–2,000 an hour	Selection speed of needle sorting using notched cards	60,000 cards an hour
To sort vouchers in a numeric file	512 an hour		
To sort toll tickets into 4-digit numerical sequence using the desk method	318 an hour		

Source: Reproduced with permission of the Administrative Management Society, as appearing in *Management World* (April, 1974), pp. 6–7.

Fig. 23-2

Office Work Standards (concluded)

times were used by more establishments than any other measurement technique, followed by self-logging, work sampling, and stopwatch time study.[14] Similar results were found in a later survey of 55 firms with over 70,000 office employees. This study showed that most firms use some form of predetermined times to develop standards, followed by the methods of logging, historical data, and stopwatch.[15]

The advantages ascribed to the use of predetermined times include:

1. Micromotion or stopwatch time study can be eliminated on many job studies, thus conserving time in establishing time values and wage rates.
2. The time standards are more precise, consistent, and objective than those obtained under time study because the standards do not vary as does the daily efficiency of time-study personnel.
3. Use of synthetic time values may settle labor disputes more effectively. Predetermined time data are more realistic in settling grievances since the standard time values for each motion have been empirically established and are not based upon a small sample or a possibly faulty time study.
4. Workers are usually convinced that wage rates based upon the use of standard data are equitable.

On the other hand, there are several disadvantages in establishing time standards through the use of predetermined times:

1. There is less personal contact with employees. Standards set from actual observation, where the workers who

have to live with the standards can actually see the measurement of their work, tend to create greater confidence.
2. Only those tasks that are highly routine and repetitive lend themselves to measurement by predetermined times. Thus, the method is unacceptable for use in studying many office clerical activities.
3. A higher caliber of staff, requiring fairly high initial training costs, is usually needed more when standards are being synthesized than under other methods where the staff can be quickly taught the measurement techniques.

There are more than a dozen methods available for determining standard time data, but the basic techniques of each method are essentially the same. Among these methods are: Motion Time Analysis (MTA), Universal Maintenance Standards (UMS), Work-Factor (W-F), Methods Time Measurement (MTM), and Master Clerical Data (MCD). The latter two methods are briefly described in the following paragraphs to indicate the basic techniques common to each method.

Methods Time Measurement (MTM). The Methods Time Measurement system is built around basic motions developed from motion picture analysis in shops and offices as well as from laboratory experiments covering a variety of work. The motions required to complete a given activity are analyzed, and by applying standard time values for each motion, a theoretical standard is derived for each element of the operation. Thus, the emphasis is placed on the method and the job content rather than on the time the operator actually takes to do the job. Standard times are expressed as *time measurement units* (TMUs), each of which represents .01 of an hour, or .0006 of a minute.

[14]Donald L. Caruth, *Guidelines for Organizing a Work Measurement Program* (Cleveland: Association for Systems Management, 1971), p. 16.

[15]Harold W. Nance, President, Serge A. Birn Co., Inc., reported in "New Trends in Office Productivity," *Modern Office Procedures* (March, 1975), p. 67.

According to the MTM table of standard times, a "reach" to an object in a fixed location about nine inches way should take 8.3 TMUs.[16]

Master Clerical Data (MCD). Master Clerical Data consists of a catalog of standard elements (not body motions) that cover 95 percent of all clerical activities found in the office. This method uses an alphabetic coding that is clearly related to the words that describe the basic elements of each task. After the general actions that are involved in each task have been identified, the appropriate MCD time value for each action is worked out. The time values are then added to obtain the total time required for performing the entire task. By means of an MCD time value card, the analyst obtains method descriptions and standard values that are consistent and compatible with clerical activities and does so in a fraction of the time required under the detailed MTM method.[17]

JOB PERFORMANCE STANDARDS FOR NONROUTINE OFFICE JOBS

In the preceding section several methods were described for measuring routine, repetitive office work and for setting realistic standards. Although most measurement of office work focuses upon those jobs that are routine and repetitive, consideration should be given to the development of standards for those office activities that are classified as nonroutine, varied, or creative. Some examples of such office jobs are drafting, designing, editing, proofreading, and processing investment trust portfolios. Many nonroutine office jobs are complex and consist of ever-changing mental activities which affect job performance. Thus, such jobs are accomplished in a variety of ways, which means that it is extremely difficult, if not impracticable, to measure the work and to develop sound performance standards. However, job performance standards can be developed for some nonroutine jobs, as explained below, although the methods are not the same as those for routine jobs.

In answering the question, "How would you go about measuring semi-creative work?" Joseph H. Quick, originator of the Work-Factor Elemental Time System for measuring manual and mental productivity functions, states:

> . . . we observe the operation and discuss it with the person performing the function, enlisting his help to be sure we understand everything he does. As we go along, we inform him of things he might be able to simplify, eliminate, or combine. If he agrees, we work out a pattern that is beneficial to the employee and the company. At this point we establish an operation target time by referring to the data we have collected over the years. We then apply it to the elements of work that he must perform.[18]

Certain kinds of nonroutine work may be measured in the aggregate in order to provide useful results. For example, in the typing center of one large insurance company, no one operator is

---

[16]The MTM application data, expressed in TMUs, are copyrighted by the MTM Association for Standards and Research, 9–10 Saddle River Road, Fair Lawn, NJ 07410.

[17]Harold W. Nance and Robert E. Nolan, *Office Work Measurement* (New York: McGraw-Hill Book Co., 1971), p. 171. See Appendix A, "How MTM Led to MCD," pp. 162–176, for an illustration of the MCD card, which is copyrighted by the Serge A. Birn Company, Inc., of Louisville, Kentucky. Appendix B, pages 177–178, presents the "Detailed MCD Index."

[18]Joseph H. Quick, "Measuring Office Productivity," *The Office* (December, 1972), p. 16.

assigned to any particular typing task on a daily basis. Thus, the work load of the center is cyclically repetitive. The work load of the center is probably measurable in terms of total production for the cycle. Such a type of measurement can be used to determine optimum staffing needs or to compare the production of one cycle against another.

In establishing performance standards a company may utilize *Program Evaluation and Review Technique (PERT)*, which is designed to plan, schedule, and control complex projects that involve a long series of steps and that have to be completed in the shortest possible time. In using PERT, first a target date is set for the completion of a major task. Every event, large or small, that will occur in the completion of the job is defined. The events are linked together and plotted as a flowchart type of diagram. On the chart all the activities needed to achieve the events are shown as connecting arrows that form paths through what may be considered a network. The time required to complete each activity (the standard) is estimated through a simple statistical technique by those responsible for the work. The establishment of the completion time for each activity is, in reality, the establishment of a time performance standard that can be used to evaluate the worker or group of workers responsible for the activity. The time required to complete each activity along every possible path

through the network is then totaled. The longest path is labeled the *critical path* because no matter how quickly the events along the other paths are completed, the events along the longest path must be finished before the project can be terminated. The overall starting and completion dates are pinpointed, and target dates are established for each task. Unlike the Gantt chart discussed in Chapter 4, the PERT network is divided into the three aspects of time, cost, and performance to show the sequence, interrelationships, and dependencies of individual tasks in the project. The PERT technique lends itself to use in computerized projects, and most computer manufacturers offer a PERT software program along with their equipment.

At about the same time the PERT technique was being devised, a similar network control system, the *Critical Path Method (CPM)*, was being developed. In the critical path method the activities in a program are arranged in sequence, the time allowance (standard) to complete each activity is estimated, and all factors are plotted on a network diagram. The objective is to determine the minimum elapsed time for completing the entire project. The time required to complete each activity is related to its cost and it is determined whether the time could be shortened by spending additional funds.

QUESTIONS FOR REVIEW

1. What are the quantitative and the qualitative measurements provided by a program of work measurement?

2. What is a work standard? For what kinds of office activities are standards most commonly established?

3. Enumerate the benefits that are made available to the firm that establishes a program of work measurement and work standards.

4. Why are formal programs of work measurement not commonly found in today's offices?

5. To be capable of measurement, office activities should meet certain criteria. What are these criteria?

6. What are the major points to be kept in mind by the office manager when communicating to employees the nature of the planned work measurement program?

7. Describe the role played by first-line supervisors in administering a work measurement program.

8. What are the limitations of the historical data method when used to measure work and to set standards?

9. Explain how office employees participate in the measurement of their work when the time log method is used.

10. Upon what underlying premise is work sampling based? In determining the proper sample size to be used in work sampling, what factors should be taken into consideration?

11. What are the disadvantages of using work sampling to set standards?

12. What is the purpose of a quality control program? How may probability sampling be used to reduce the costs of quality control?

13. What is the essential difference between motion study and time study?

14. What are the characteristics that should be possessed by the office worker selected for observation in a time study?

15. Why must the actual times required by workers to complete operational elements be leveled?

16. Compare the advantages and disadvantages of using predetermined times in setting standards for office work.

17. Explain how performance standards may be established for nonroutine office jobs through the use of PERT.

QUESTIONS FOR DISCUSSION

1. Explain how the 72-stroke par for an 18-hole golf course serves as an excellent example of a standard.

2. According to a management consultant, clerical efficiency today is about 50 to 60 percent. In view of this level of productivity, what are the implications for the administrative office manager who is contemplating a work measurement and standards program?

3. Explain why you agree or disagree with this statement: "Once job performance standards have been determined, they should never be changed."

4. For your work measurement and standards program, you have adopted the following definition of a fair day's work: "A fair day's work is that amount of work that can be produced by a qualified employee when working at a normal pace and effectively utilizing the employer's time." One of your coworkers has asked what you mean by "normal pace." How will you answer the worker?

5. A unionized company uses micromotion study in measuring work and setting standards. Should the union be given access to the files of micromotion films for which the company has paid? Why or why not?

6. It is said that a time study is used to establish a time standard for performing a specific task by an average, qualified worker. How does one recognize a worker as being "average" and "qualified"?

7. Do not time allowances for fatigue and personal reasons defeat the very purpose of time study? Cite an example to justify your answer.

8. How precisely can standards be set for indirect labor, such as office and clerical workers, through motion and time study? Do you think that standards for indirect labor will become as widespread as those for direct labor? Why?

9. A work sampling study is planned for which a 15 percent tolerance factor is specified; the critical percentage is estimated at 6 percent; and 95 percent reliability has been determined. Determine the net number of observations to be made in the proposed study.

10. Valerie Jester, who manages a small office consisting of 28 employees, has been reading for the past six months about office work measurement. In a discussion with several other office managers at a recent chapter meeting of AMS, Jester remarks: "All of these work measurement programs sound good, but my office is too small to think about bringing in any direct controls. Besides, I know we are performing better than the average rate of 55 percent." How do you react to Jester's comments? Are her remarks valid, or is Jester "way off base" in her thinking?

11. Jay Comyn, accounting manager for Cornwells, Inc., was recently asked how many errors he will accept from the accountants he supervises. Right to the point Comyn stated, "We don't permit *any* errors." Do you conclude from Comyn's reply that the performance standard for the error rate of accounts is zero? Explain.

12. Malek Manufacturing's time-study analyst has completed the measurement of the posting work in the accounts receivable department and has arrived at the standard of 100 postings per hour. This standard has just been announced to the supervisor of the accounts receivable department and then in a separate memo to the posting

clerks. A confused and panicky situation has arisen, which is resulting in more errors, morale problems, and less work than before.

Assuming that the output of 100 postings per hour is feasible and accurate, discuss the use of this standard and the analyst's method of presenting it to the supervisor and employees.

PRACTICAL OFFICE MANAGEMENT CASES

Case 23-1   Using Work Sampling to Determine Standard Times

In using work sampling to measure the output and to set standards for four typist-clerks in the purchasing department of his company, Mort Tanenbaum obtained the summary data shown in Table A.

SUMMARY DATA FOR WORK SAMPLING

Activity	No. of Observations	Work Counts for Each Activity
Typing purchase orders from typed and handwritten requisitions, using continuous forms, with each order averaging 350 characters and spaces	900	400 purchase orders
Researching vendors' catalogs to locate sources of supply, current prices, etc.	250	120 references
Sorting requisitions into 6-digit sequence	350	1,600 requisitions
Collating copies of purchase orders and requisitions....................	500,	1,450 purchase orders and requisitions
Indexing copies of purchase orders and requisitions....................	450	1,510 purchase orders and requisitions
Filing purchase orders and requisitions..........	300	1,500 purchase orders and requisitions
Personal	750	
Total observations	3,500	**Table A**

During the period of the study Tanenbaum found that each of the four clerks was available for work as is shown in Table B.

WORK AVAILABILITY OF CLERKS	
Employee	**Minutes Available for Work**
Carbonari.......................	1,350
Scheele	1,125
Doyal............................	900
Huggins........................	1,350
Total available minutes	4,725 **Table B**

Based upon the data given above, prepare a report in which you:

1. Determine the unit time or standard for each activity studied.
2. Calculate whether a large enough sample was taken to provide for Tanenbaum's planned sample size, when $T = .10$, $P = .05$, and reliability is 95 percent.
   (a) If the number of observations made ($N = 3,500$) was not great enough to meet Tanenbaum's specifications, how many more observations will be needed?
   (b) What percent of reliability was obtained with $N = 3,500$? Is this percent of reliability usually sufficient for most work sampling purposes?

Case 23-2   Overcoming Resistance to Time and Motion Study

In the unionized computer center of Saunders, Inc., the workers have just learned via the grapevine that the company is planning to undertake a time and motion study to aid in developing an equitable clerical salary plan. The union business agent, Paul Overell, respects your abilities as Manager of Office Services and has asked you for information on what effect the proposed time and motion study will have on salaries. In talking with Overell, you sense that he is firmly opposed to any time study being made.

Several of the key-to-disk terminal operators have told you that they are not in accord with the firm's plan to conduct a time and motion study in their department. They claim that by establishing standards in the department, a number of workers will lose their jobs or employment will be shortened throughout the year. In the billing department you have overheard a heated discussion among several workers who feel that the time study is nothing more than a management trick to "speed up" the workers.

Prepare a report in which you:

1. Outline the approach you would follow in working with Overell, the union business agent.
2. Include all possible points and factors that will convince your workers that the time and motion study will bring favorable results not only to the company but also to them.

Case 23-3 Measuring Typewritten Work and Setting Standards

The Avery Insurance Company, which employs about 800 clerical workers, has for the past several years been considering the use of work standards in the centralized typing center. The objectives of the proposed program of work measurement are to reduce what appear to be excessive costs and to provide additional control over the scheduling and routing of work. In the typing center, there are 60 employees who perform a wide variety of work. Many of the typists transcribe from plastic belts, using transcribing machine equipment. Some do straight-copy typing and filling-in of insurance forms. A few typists specialize in preparing statistical copy and tabulated reports.

As supervisor of the typing center, prepare a report to the office services manager in which you discuss:

1. The appropriate method or combination of methods to be used in measuring each different kind of work.
2. What use the company may make of the results of the work measurement program.

Chapter 24   OFFICE SALARY ADMINISTRATION

Despite the high unemployment and inflation experienced during the economic recession of the 1970s, most employees consider job satisfaction, responsibility, and recognition more important than salary, according to surveys undertaken by the Personnel Services Center over the last several years.[1] This attitude toward salaries has been partly explained by the rapidly increasing level of education of employees, their affluence, their independence, their permissive home and school environment, and their acceptance of the concept of industrial democracy. Today's young workers are searching for more satisfying jobs, greater participation in decisions that affect their working lives, and an end to authoritarianism on the job. According to the head of the Work in America Institute Inc., "The society is changing faster than our institutions. . . . Unfortunately, the work place has been relatively immutable to these changes. What these young people are saying is that their expectations have gone up, and the response hasn't."[2]

THE GOALS OF OFFICE SALARY ADMINISTRATION

Today's goals for administering office salaries must respond to the expectations of office workers between 20 and 25 years of age, those who are generally less satisfied with their jobs than both younger and older workers. These are the men and women who within a few years will make up a majority of the nation's work force. Likewise, the program must be designed to relate to the needs of those office workers over 35 years of age, those who are the most satisfied with their jobs. An effective office salary administration program will attempt to attain the following goals:

1. To promote and attain salary equity, which in turn will minimize dissatisfaction and grievances among workers. Employees experience dissatisfaction and lose confidence in the salary program when a perceived salary inequity exists. Thus, salary differentials should be supported by objective appraisals concerning performance.
2. To establish and maintain sufficiently adequate salaries so that qualified, competent workers are attracted to and retained by the firm.
3. To stimulate and reward high-level performance, determined as objectively as possible by periodic employee evaluation. Periodic appraisal enables employees to know how well they are performing and insures communication between supervisor and subordinate. Employees thus become aware that their extra efforts and achievements will be recognized and rewarded by means of extra compensation. Of course, this objective of the salary administration program must be communicated to the workers before they expend their efforts, not after they have taken the action.

---

[1]"Editor to Reader," *Personnel Journal* (June, 1976), p. 266.
[2]"Worker Unrest: Not Dead, but Playing Possum," *Business Week* (May 10, 1976), p. 133.

4. To maintain competitiveness with other companies in the same geographical area while at the same time controlling labor costs with respect to gains in productivity.

To achieve these goals, a company must build its salary program upon a foundation of job analysis and job evaluation, which were discussed at length in Chapter 22. The importance of job analysis is indicated by its use in establishing levels or grades for office positions. Establishing these grades or levels is a form of job evaluation. For each grade or group of jobs, there must be a maximum and a minimum salary range, with periodic pay increments based upon successful performance of work as determined by some form of employee evaluation.

In designing its office salary program, the company should consider the placement of office workers on an incentive pay basis. Previous to installing an incentive pay system, the work must be measured and standards set, as explained in Chapter 23. In measuring work and setting standards, office managers have seemed interested but have taken little action. In order to set standards, the work must be carefully analyzed, all unnecessary motions and wasted time must be eliminated, and studies of output must be made in order to obtain an average performance figure. This average figure can then be used as the basis for setting wage-incentive payments.

Finally, an increasingly important aspect of the total compensation package for office employees relates to employee benefits, or the indirect compensation received by workers, which, as indicated in Chapter 14, amounts to about 33 percent of every payroll dollar. Since most employee benefits are concerned with security, they tend to meet a set of employee needs different from those met by direct compensation. The more security that is provided those to whom security is of primary importance, the more the workers may be demotivated, for it is the *need* that is the motivator of performance, not the *fulfillment* of that need. Thus, in considering the following factors that determine office salaries and in designing employee benefits programs, firms should recognize that highly attractive benefits packages appeal primarily to employees who are very security-oriented; thus, the greatest turnover will tend to take place among those to whom security, at least at that stage of their careers, is relatively less important.[3]

FACTORS TO CONSIDER IN DETERMINING OFFICE SALARIES

Once the office jobs have been evaluated by one of the methods described in Chapter 22, the next step is to answer the question: How much should each office worker be paid? However, in order to establish pay grades and salary ranges, several factors must first be examined. A basic factor to consider in determining salaries for office workers is that the salaries must not exceed the ability of the firm to pay and still earn a profit. There are other factors, too, such as the firm's philosophy toward office salary administration, the expectations of employees, the salaries paid by other companies in the same geographical area, government regulations, and collective bargaining agreements. These factors must be carefully analyzed and taken into consideration.

---

[3]O. Gene Dalaba, "Misuses of Compensation As a Motivator," *Personnel* (September–October, 1973), p. 34.

Company Philosophy Toward Office Salary Administration

Companies, influenced by the quality of workers they hope to attract, may adopt a policy of paying office salaries that match, exceed, or are less than the average salaries paid by other firms in the community. Some companies build their salary structure around the competition in their area for employees who perform similar types of work. For example, in an Administrative Management Society survey of nonexempt, salaried compensation practices, 85 percent of the firms place their clerical and data processing employees on the same salary structure as that prevailing in the community, if all the workers are situated in one given location.[4] Other companies prefer to relate their salary levels more closely to salaries paid employees within the same industry. A few firms follow a policy of paying higher-than-average salaries for better-than-average work and thus pay salaries that are higher than those paid by other companies. In firms that provide a wide program of employee benefits, the decision may be to pay a smaller base salary than that paid by other firms in the general labor market.

If a company is to realize the full benefit from its office compensation plan, the company must communicate to its employees the nature and the goals of the plan, that the basis for the plan is an objective evaluation of each job and an analysis of salaries paid by other firms, and that each worker has an opportunity to earn more as the result of good job performance. As a result, office employees can be expected to attain those goals more easily. With office em-

ployees working together toward a set of common goals, there should be less confusion, dissatisfaction, and turnover among workers. Finally, when office workers are aware of the goals and the gains to be realized, and when they perceive the importance that management places upon them in the organization, they are more easily motivated to produce their best. Thus, in developing its philosophy toward office salary administration, management must be aware of the differences in employees, their beliefs, and their motivations. Management must study its employees in order to understand their aspirations, abilities, and satisfactions so that the workers can obtain adequate enjoyment out of doing their work, which in turn should accomplish the goals of the firm.

Expectations of Office Employees

Like all other employees at every level in the firm, office workers bring to their jobs their own expectations and ideas on how they hope to fulfill them. To be reasonably satisfied with their work and motivated to perform, employees need a work climate wherein they can further develop their philosophy of life within which their jobs "make sense." They need a sense of purpose, the will to achieve, and the feeling of being wanted and accepted. Office workers expect to get satisfaction out of meeting their job challenges successfully and seeing that their efforts actually result in high performance. In turn, they expect their high performance to result in the receipt of desired rewards.

Office workers expect their salaries to provide them with enough money to support their families and to be able to continue improving their standard of living. They realize that if their salaries do not increase at least as fast as the

---

[4]"Sounder Salary Guidelines," *Administrative Management* (November, 1972), p. 50.

cost of living, their level of living standards will decline. They expect their salaries and periodic pay increases to give them financial security not only during their working careers but also later in their retirements.

Employees expect their pay to be fair and reasonable in comparison with that of other workers. They feel they should make "good" money when they work hard and have the opportunity to earn extra money when they work harder. They want a fair day's pay for a fair day's work, but they expect in turn, as discussed in Chapter 23, that a fair day's work will be accurately measured in order to determine a fair day's pay. Further, employees want some voice in the determination of their salaries or at least have an avenue of appeal in the event they are dissatisfied with their earnings.

Employees desire recognition for work well done through employee evaluation, by which the company takes note of the quality and quantity of work, and in some instances through the use of incentive pay systems in which additional rewards are given for an expectional quantity of work produced. Finally, employees expect promotion from within the business firm, not on the basis of seniority alone but also on the basis of merit.

Office Salaries
Paid by Other Companies

The most significant factor in establishing a salary structure for nonexempt office personnel (workers who must be paid overtime under the Fair Labor Standards Act of 1938, commonly called the Federal Wage and Hour Law) is the local going rate, according to the AMS survey of compensation for nonexempt, salaried personnel cited earlier. In 90

percent of the companies surveyed, the salary structures for nonexempt employees are set after serious consideration of local community rates.[5] To obtain data on office salaries paid for comparable jobs in similar industries within the community or in surrounding areas, the company may undertake a salary survey. A *salary survey* is a statistical picture of what the salary is for a particular geographic area, occupation, or industry at a given time.

The individual or committee in charge of preparing the office salary survey questionnaire should make sure that information is asked about a number of stable key jobs, such as those described in Figure 22-3, page 632. A standard job title should be listed on the survey form for each key job. Since the terminology of job content and level of responsibility may differ from company to company, a brief description of each job should accompany the questionnaire form so that all respondents are provided data about like jobs.

Since most companies provide indirect compensation in the form of employee benefits, the questionnaire should be designed to obtain data on the status of such benefits as paid vacations, group life insurance, and pension plans. Data pertaining to the nature and extent of wage-incentive payments may also be obtained from firms in the community by including questions about the incentive system used and the amount of average incentive earnings expressed as a percentage of base salary.

Rather than conduct their own salary surveys, companies may obtain comparative salary data from the Bureau of Labor Statistics, which conducts annual surveys of the salaries paid professional, administrative, technical, and clerical

---

[5]*Ibid.*

employees. Other sources of data on salaries paid office workers include The Bureau of National Affairs, employer associations, banks, consulting firms, chambers of commerce, and professional organizations such as the Administrative Management Society and the American Management Associations.

Government Regulations

The two federal statutes that are of most significance to the office salary administrator are the Fair Labor Standards Act and the Walsh-Healey Public Contract Act. The Fair Labor Standards Act (FLSA) pertains to the employment of workers in private and public industry, while the Walsh-Healey Public Contract Act imposes additional restrictions upon employers who are government contractors. In addition to federal legislation, regulations exist in most states whereby minimum wage rates are fixed for specific industries.

Fair Labor Standards Act of 1938. Workers are covered by the requirements of the FLSA if they are engaged either in interstate commerce or in the production of goods for such commerce. A firm is automatically covered by the law if it has at least two employees engaged in interstate commerce, or in the production of goods for interstate commerce, or in the handling, selling, or working on goods or materials that have been moved in or produced for such commerce by anyone else. If the employees of a firm are covered by the FLSA, they must be paid a certain minimum wage, equal pay for equal work, and an overtime premium for all hours worked beyond a certain number. The FLSA also places restrictions upon the employment of children, as explained below.

Minimum Wages. Unless specifically exempted from the provisions of the FLSA, all covered employees must be paid at least the applicable minimum wage, whether the employees are paid a salary or by the hour, piece work, or any other method. Under certain conditions wages lower than the minimum wage standard may be paid some employees. For example, full-time students may be employed by retail or service establishments and farms at 85 percent of the minimum wage.[6]

Equal Pay for Equal Work. The Equal Pay Act of 1963, an amendment to the FLSA, prohibits covered employers from setting wage differentials that are based solely on the sex of workers who are doing "equal work on jobs the performance of which requires equal skill, effort, and responsibility, and which are performed under similar working conditions." Wage differentials between sexes are allowable if the differences are based on a seniority system, a merit system, a payment plan that measures earnings by quantity or quality of production, or any factor other than sex. If there is an unlawful pay differential between men and women, the employer is required to raise the lower rate to equal the higher rate.

Overtime Hours and Overtime Pay. The FLSA requires that overtime be paid at the rate of at least one and one-half times the regular rate of pay for a workweek greater than 40 hours. The law does not require extra pay for Saturday, Sunday, or holiday work; nor does the law require vacation pay, holiday

---

[6]For current minimum wage rates, exemption categories, etc., of the FLSA and for details of other legislation affecting office salaries, see B. Lewis Keeling and Bernard J. Bieg, *Payroll Records and Accounting* (Cincinnati: South-Western Publishing Co., current annual edition).

pay, or severance pay. If, however, such types of pay and working conditions are agreed upon in union contracts, the employer cannot use the FLSA as an excuse for their nonpayment or nonfulfillment. Under the FLSA employers are not required to give rest periods to their employees. If, however, rest periods are given, either voluntarily by the employer or in keeping with the terms of a union contract or a state regulation, the rest periods must be counted as hours worked if they last 20 minutes or less. Likewise, coffee and snack breaks are compensable rest periods and cannot be excluded from hours worked.

Child-Labor Restrictions.

The FLSA restricts the employment of children by stipulating that children below certain ages may not be employed in interstate activities. A business is prohibited from the interstate shipment of its goods if the manufacture of those goods involves unlawful child labor. Generally, the regulations restrict the employment of children under 18 years of age. Within certain limits in retail, food service, and gasoline service establishments, children 14 and 15 years old may be employed. To be employed in manufacturing, mining, and certain other businesses and occupations, however, children must be at least 16 years old. Children below the age of 18 may not be employed in any occupation that is classified as hazardous by the Secretary of Labor.

In agricultural employment different rules apply, for generally children of any age may be employed outside their school hours. However, children under 16 years of age may not be employed in hazardous jobs.

Exempt Employees.

Certain types of employees such as executives, administrators, and professionals are fully exempt from the minimum wage and overtime pay requirements of the FLSA.

Executives. For purposes of the executive exemption, executives must possess discretionary powers and exercise managerial functions. Their primary duty must be to manage the enterprise in which they are employed, or at least to manage some customarily recognized department or subdivision of the firm. Generally, "primary duty" is defined to mean that executives must spend the major part or over 50 percent of their time in managerial duties. However, employees who may spend less than 50 percent of their time in managerial duties may be classed as exempt if they customarily and regularly direct the work of two or more other employees; if they can hire or fire employees or make suggestions and recommendations that will be given weight in deciding upon hiring, firing, or promoting the workers; or if they customarily and regularly exercise discretionary powers. In addition, the employee must be paid on a salary basis at a rate of not less than $155 a week.

For highly paid executives there is a short test to determine exemption. If the employees are compensated on a salary basis of at least $250 a week, they usually qualify as exempt executives, provided their primary duty consists of the management of an enterprise or of a recognized department or subdivision thereof, and if they regularly direct the work of two or more employees.

Administrators. Administrative employees are exempt from the minimum wage and overtime pay requirements of the FLSA if:

1. The employee assists an executive or administrative official in the routine

performance of duties; e.g., an executive secretary.

2. The employee acts in a staff or functional capacity; e.g., an advisory tax expert or a personnel director.
3. The employee performs special assignments, often away from the employer's place of business; e.g., a traveling auditor or a buyer.
4. The person is employed in the capacity of academic administrative personnel or is a teacher in elementary or secondary schools.

The primary duty of employees such as those described above is to perform office or nonmanual work directly related to the management's policies for a major part, or over 50 percent, of their time. In addition, the work customarily requires the exercising of discretion and independent judgment. Administrative workers, like executive employees, may perform a limited amount of work that is not directly and closely related to the employee's administrative work. Generally a 20 percent limitation is placed on the performance of such nonexempt work. The administrative employee is generally compensated on a salary or fee basis at a rate of not less than $155 a week. As for executive employees, there is a short exemption test for higher salaried administrative employees. If administrative employees are paid $250 or more a week and if their primary duty requires the exercise of discretion and independent judgment in the performance of their office or nonmanual work, they fall within the definition of administrative employee.

Professionals. Professional employees who are exempt from the minimum wage and overtime pay requirements of the FLSA include those (a) in learned professions such as lawyers, physicians, accountants, and engineers, who have acquired their professional knowledge through a prolonged course of instruction and study; (b) in the artistic professions such as actors, journalists, and writers; and (c) in the teaching professions. The work of the professional must require the consistent exercise of discretion and judgment in its performance, and the work must be predominantly intellectual and varied in character. The professional employee can spend no more than 20 percent of the workweek on nonexempt work without losing the exempt status. Under the general salary test, the professional must be paid at least $170 a week on a salary or a fee basis. Under the shorter exemption test, professionals who are paid $250 or more a week are generally exempt from coverage if their primary duties lie in one of the three areas listed above.

Other Exemptions from FLSA Requirements. Some workers are fully exempt from the minimum wage, equal pay, and overtime pay requirements of the FLSA. Among these workers are: employees of amusement or recreational establishments having seasonal peaks; employees of weekly, semiweekly, or daily newspapers with a circulation of less than 4,000 copies, the major part of which is in the county of publication or contiguous counties; and agricultural workers who did not use more than 500 man-days of agricultural labor in any quarter of the preceding calendar year.

For some workers, the FLSA exempts them from only the overtime pay requirement. This full overtime pay exemption pertains to: employees of railroads, express companies, and water carriers who are subject to the Interstate Commerce Act; salespersons employed by automobile, truck, or farm implement dealers; taxicab drivers; and agricultural employees.

Walsh-Healey Public Contract Act. Under the Walsh-Healey Public Contract Act, employers must pay the minimum wage and overtime to employees who are working on government contracts for the manufacture or furnishing of materials, supplies, articles, and equipment in an amount exceeding $10,000, unless the employees are otherwise exempt. The minimum hourly rates are fixed by the Secretary of Labor on an industry basis, and an overtime payment of one and one-half times those rates must be paid for hours worked in excess of eight each day or 40 during the workweek.

Other Federal Regulations. The Davis-Bacon Act of 1931 requires the payment of minimum wages to laborers and mechanics who are employed by either contractors or subcontractors on federal contracts that exceed $2,000 for the construction, alteration, or repair of public buildings. The minimum wage rates are determined by the Secretary of Labor after a study has been made of those rates that prevail in the area for similar work. Laborers and mechanics covered by the Davis-Bacon Act must be paid time and one half for hours worked in excess of eight daily or 40 weekly.

The Service Contract Act covers contracts entered into by the United States in excess of $2,500, the main purpose of which is to furnish services through the use of service employees. For example, the act covers contracts for the transportation of mail by common carriers such as railroads, airlines, and ocean vessels. As in the case of the Walsh-Healey Act, the prevailing minimum wage to be paid service employees is determined by the Secretary of Labor.

State Regulations. In most states minimum wage rates have been estab-lished for covered employees in specific industries. Where both the federal and state regulations cover the same employee, the higher of the two rates prevails. State wage orders not only set minimum wages but also contain provisions affecting pay for call-in time and waiting time, rest and meal periods, absences, split shifts, meals and lodging, and tips.

Collective Bargaining Agreements

If office employees are represented by a union, the collective bargaining agreement must be considered in developing the salary administration program. For organized workers, the agreement represents a policy guide that office supervisors must follow not only in determining pay rates but also in implementing procedures that affect employee earnings.

Of major importance at the bargaining table is the provision for general salary increases during the life of the contract, for a cost-of-living escalator clause is increasingly common in almost all industries. Other employee compensation items usually treated in contracts include supplementary pay (shift differentials, temporary transfer pay, and bonuses) and practices such as establishing incentive pay, time study, and job classification. Also, many contracts specify hiring rates and progression rates.[7]

Office salary administrators must thoroughly understand the provisions of the collective bargaining agreement. For example, they must know whether a new office position must be discussed with union representatives before it is established. If a worker's job assignment should change, the administrator

---

[7]For the major types of provisions and their frequency in collective bargaining contracts, see *Basic Patterns in Union Contracts* (Washington: The Bureau of National Affairs, May, 1975).

must know the procedure to be followed in reevaluating the position. All workers must be assigned their proper pay classifications, and pay progression practices set forth in the contract must be strictly followed.

PRICING THE OFFICE JOB

After having carefully studied and analyzed the several factors that influence the determination of office salaries, the office manager is ready to undertake the all-important task of pricing the individual jobs. In illustrating how pay grades and salary ranges are determined and office jobs are priced, the following example utilizes the point method of job evaluation. As described in Chapter 22, the point method is a relatively popular plan used in evaluating office jobs and probably provides more consistency of results than any of the other job evaluation schemes. (The techniques of pricing office jobs under the point method may be adapted to the determination of compensation under other methods of job evaluation, as briefly discussed at the end of this section.)

It was explained in Chapter 22 that in the point method, each factor common to a job is divided into subfactors and degrees, which are assigned point values. The job evaluator examines the factors and subfactors that are characteristic of each job independently of wage and salary rates. The total number of points is determined for each job and they may be listed as shown in Column 1 of Table 24-1, where the point values for 19 office jobs, coded A through S, have been arranged from the lowest to the highest. This arrangement makes it possible to add new pay grade numbers, if new jobs that exceed the highest point value come into existence or if the high-value jobs are reevaluated and assigned

a greater number of points. Also, it appears more logical to have the highest pay represented by the highest pay grade number.[8]

Next, as shown in Column 2, the jobs having about the same number of point values are grouped together and natural, logical cutoff points are selected. The number of job groupings is determined by the number of pay grades to be used and how the jobs naturally group themselves according to pay relationships surveyed in the labor market. After the job groupings have been established, it is understood that all jobs falling within a particular grouping have the same basic value. Thus, jobs F through K, which have point values of 282 through 300, are placed in one pay grade, No. 4.

In Column 3 the seven pay grades are established, using a constant progression of 40 points for each grade. There is no acceptable, definite number of pay grades to be used, for the number will vary according to the existing number of jobs in the office and the employee job groupings.

The findings from the salary survey are next entered in Column 4. In this illustration one key job for each of the seven pay grades matched the job description used in the survey, and the average weekly salary for each key job was recorded. Thus, since jobs A, B, and C are grouped into the same pay grade No. 1, all three jobs will receive the same pay, an amount to be determined when job B is priced.

---

[8]For exceptionally fine, more detailed presentations of the steps involved in pricing jobs, see Robert E. Sibson, *Compensation* (3d ed., New York: AMACOM, a Division of American Management Associations, 1974), Ch. 5, pp. 53–65; and Herbert G. Zollitsch and Adolph Langsner, *Wage and Salary Administration* (2d ed., Cincinnati: South-Western Publishing Co., 1970), Ch. 13, pp. 314–353.

STEPS IN PRICING THE OFFICE JOB*

(1) Point Values for Each Job Evaluated *Job Points*	(2) Job Groupings	(3) Pay Grades *Grade Points*	(4) Average Weekly Salary of Key Jobs Determined by Survey	(5) Weekly Base Salary	(6) Pay Range
A 180 ⎫ B 189 ⎬ C 195 ⎭	180–195	1 Under 200	B $120	$117	$100–$135
D 225	225	2 201–240	D $132	$132	$110–$155
E 260	260	3 241–280	E $146	$147	$125–$170
F 282 ⎫ G 282 ⎪ H 286 ⎬ I 289 ⎪ J 293 ⎪ K 300 ⎭	282–300	4 281–320	I $162	$157	$135–$185
L 342 ⎫ M 349 ⎬ N 358 ⎭	342–358	5 321–360	M $179	$185	$155–$210
O 365 ⎫ P 370 ⎬ Q 384 ⎭	365–384	6 361–400	O $191	$212	$180–$245
R 410 ⎫ S 430 ⎭	410–430	7 401–440	R $211	$225	$195–$260 **Table 24-1**

*Adapted by permission of the publisher from *Compensation*, Robert E. Sibson, pp. 53–65, © 1974 by AMACOM, a division of American Management Associations.

The salary survey data are used to determine the "best fit" for the weekly base salaries, which are listed in Column 5. In this illustration the company's salary administration policy is to set a weekly base salary that approximates the average salary paid by all firms and which is economically feasible in relation to the anticipated sales revenue.

The final step in pricing the 19 office jobs is to establish a pay range for each of the 7 base salaries. Here it was decided to use the base salary as the midpoint of each range. The company proceeded on the theory that the midpoint represents the "going rate" for each job and decided that any new workers would be hired at a salary between the minimum and the midpoint of the range. This point would not be exceeded unless the job applicant had unusual qualifications.

A company may set a flat percentage spread around the midpoint of each range, such as the 15 percent spread shown in Table 24-1. Or it may be decided to apply a percentage increase that becomes progressively greater, such as 10 percent for the lowest job level up through 40 to 50 percent for the highest level. If the salary ranges have been accurately developed and kept current, the minimum salary at each level should be sufficient to attract new employees to the company.

Charting the Salary Rates

A scatter chart, such as that shown in Figure 24-1, may be used to show the salary rates and salary distribution at a glance. By examining the chart, one can see to what extent any discrepancies in the present salaries being paid need to be adjusted in relation to the recommended pay ranges established as a result of the salary survey.

The 19 office jobs, labeled A through S, have been plotted on the vertical scale in relation to the current salary being paid each jobholder and on the horizontal scale according to the pay-grade point values for the jobs. The midpoints of the lowest and the highest pay ranges serve as anchor points to establish a trend line. The straight line drawn through the center of both anchor points is also known as the basic salary curve or the salary trend line.

The upper and lower limits of each pay range may be determined by drawing two more straight lines at a fixed percentage distance from the salary trend line. In Figure 24-1, two additional anchor points were established on a perpendicular 15 percent above and 15 percent below the midpoint for the lowest pay range. Similarly, two more anchor points were plotted 15 percent above and 15 percent below the midpoint of the highest pay range. By drawing straight lines through the anchor points above and below the salary trend line, the minimum and maximum salary rates for each pay grade were established.[9]

---

[9]The anchor point method is an accepted practice in establishing salary curves, as pointed

Adjusting the Salary Rates

Discrepancies in the amounts currently paid employees will often be found after the scatter chart has been prepared and is studied. Some workers may be receiving more than, while others are earning less than, the recommended averages. Any such inequities should be adjusted as soon as practical after the pricing of the jobs has been completed.

Rates of fully qualified workers that fall below the minimum line, such as those holding jobs F and G in Figure 24-1, are known as *green-circle rates*. These rates should be adjusted upward within the pay grade in accordance with the company's salary progression policy. To determine exactly where a worker should fit into the range, each worker should be examined individually in relation to the salary progression policy and availability of funds.

Sometimes the plotted salary dots appear above the maximum line, as in the case of job S in Figure 24-1. This *red-circle rate* is a case of overpayment and should be noted for special attention and adjustment. Consideration should be given to training and upgrading the red-circle worker to another job commensurate with the present salary, or the employee may be left on the job until a promotion occurs on the basis of employee evaluation and rating. For a worker with many years of seniority, he or she may be left on the job but given additional responsibilities commensurate with the red-circle rate.

---

out by Zollitsch and Langsner, *op. cit.*, p. 342. However, some authorities claim that the method does not produce a perfect curve. From a purely statistical point of view, the claim may be justified, since calculations and plottings established by the method of least squares, as explained in basic statistics textbooks, reflect a somewhat truer curve.

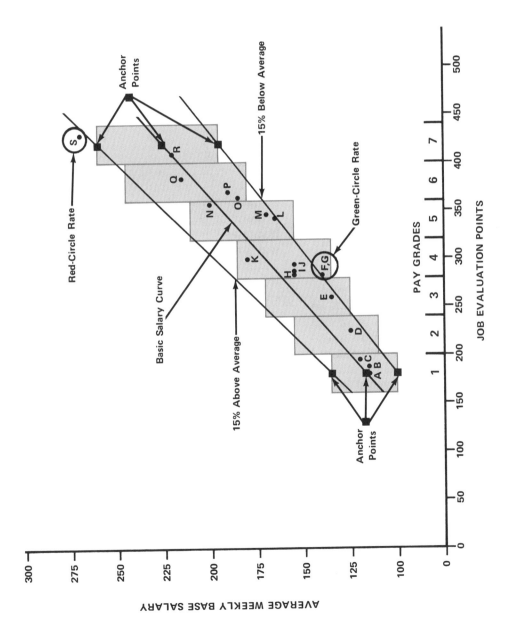

Fig. 24-1
Scatter Chart Showing Relationship Between Weekly Base Salaries and Job Evaluation Points

Establishing the Salary Progression Schedule

In a sound office salary administration program employees are provided the opportunity to receive periodic salary increases so that they may advance from the minimum to the maximum salary level in their pay grade. The progression system also provides for promotion from one pay grade to another. The spread within a pay grade appears to be an individual company matter that is dependent upon the employees' needs and desires and the firm's financial condition. Most authorities believe that to motivate employees, a pay grade spread should be at least 20 percent. That is, the minimum (or starting) rate is 10 percent below the average salary trend line and the maximum rate is 10 percent above this line. Most companies are more likely to have a spread of somewhere between 30 and 40 percent.[10] In Figure 24-1 the spread within each salary range is 30 percent.

Some companies grant their periodic salary increases according to a predetermined time period. Under such an *automatic progression* plan, a company might increase an office worker's salary $25 a month for a limited or unlimited number of years. So long as the workers are attaining a standard level of performance, they are entitled to receive automatically the set salary increase over a previously determined period of time. The policy of automatically providing salary increases should take into consideration the maintenance of employee purchasing power and the company's economic condition. If costs are rising each year at a rate of 10 to 15 percent, the firm must develop specific standards for its overall wage and salary increases

in order to determine the combined size of its automatic salary adjustments and its budgeted merit increases, which are discussed in the following paragraphs.[11]

Companies may also grant salary increases on the basis of the employee's performance or merit. Under a *merit progression* plan the employee's performance evaluation by his or her supervisor, which is discussed later in this chapter, is used as the justification for granting or rejecting a merit salary increase. Office workers must see a definite relationship between their performance and their compensation, or the salary increase will be forced into a hygienic role, as was noted by Frederick Herzberg.[12]

In a survey of compensation practices, The Executive Compensation Services of the American Management Associations found that more than 97 percent of the participating firms had budgeted for merit increase programs, with the majority allocating between 7 and 10 percent of their annual payrolls for merit increases; the average merit increase for nonexempt employees ranged between 1 and 22 percent. It was also noted that only about one fourth of the companies planned for general or cost-of-living increases and these ranged from 2 to 15 percent of the annual salary; for companies that had merit increase programs, the general or cost-of-living increase for nonexempt employees was about 5 percent.[13] Granting increases of less than 5 percent may keep employees "whole," as far as living costs are concerned, but such increases will have no real motivational value and

---

[10]Zollitsch and Langsner, *op. cit.*, p. 349.

[11]Richard J. Bronstein, "The Cost of Living and Salary Administration," *Personnel* (March–April, 1975), p. 17.

[12]See Chapter 1, page 17.

[13]"What's New in Compensation," *Personnel* (May–June, 1975), pp. 4–5.

may, in fact, have a negative effect on morale.[14]

Establishing Salaries under Other Methods of Job Evaluation

In the preceding discussion the techniques used in pricing office jobs were described for a company that had adopted the point method of job evaluation. A similar approach may be followed in applying these techniques to the other methods of job evaluation that were presented in Chapter 22.

Ranking Method. In the discussion of the ranking method of job evaluation it was pointed out that the jobs are ranked according to title from the most important to the least important, in relation to their contribution to the objectives of the organization. In determining salaries under the ranking method, salaries are set for the highest rated and the lowest rated jobs and all other jobs are assigned salaries that bear a direct or a relative ratio to the two extremes. (See Table 22-2, page 638.)

Job Classification Method. In the job classification method a number of predetermined classes or grades of jobs are selected on the basis of varying levels and responsibilities, and all other jobs or positions are analyzed and grouped into specific classes or grades in relation to the predetermined categories. For each job classification or family grouping of jobs, a salary range is established that bears a relationship between the importance of jobs in that group to all other groups of jobs. (See Table 22-3, page 641.)

Factor-Comparison Method. In the factor-comparison method each job is evaluated in terms of five critical factors, based on selected key jobs that are related to a money rate. (See Tables 22-4, 22-5, and 22-6, pages 642–644.) In each of these three methods of job evaluation, provision must be made for annual salary increments so that employees can progress from the lowest to the highest level of their salary range and then be promoted to the next grade of work.

Guideline Method. In the guideline method of job evaluation all jobs are evaluated against a standard scale of salary ranges or grades that is developed in relation to the market price of the jobs. As shown in Table 22-7, page 647, the higher salary ranges are wider, for at these levels there is progressively less room for promotion and the wider ranges permit the recognition of meritorious performance on the same job over a considerable period of time.

WAGE-INCENTIVE SYSTEMS

Under *wage-incentive systems* workers are able to increase their earnings by maintaining or exceeding an established standard of performance. Some office managers feel that the reward for increased production and outstanding work should be given in the nature of promotions when opportunities arise. For many employees, however, the time of promotion is too far away, especially if they lack some of the necessary qualifications. For these workers, an immediate financial reward is a

---

[14]Richard P. Rooney, "The Right Way to Pay," *Administrative Management* (October 1972), p. 76. In this article the writer advances several arguments for treating inflationary pressures within the merit increase program rather than through separate cost-of-living increases as supplements to salaries.

much more effective motivator. Evidence to date suggests that wage-incentive systems have a positive impact on employee motivation and productivity but a negative impact on employee satisfaction; on the other hand, the highest satisfaction with pay is obtained among the hourly paid groups.[15]

Wage-incentive systems may be used in the office where the work has been measured and standards developed. As noted in Chapter 23, the measurement of work and the development of standards are not commonly found in the office, although it is estimated that two thirds to three fourths of all the work done in offices lends itself to measurement. The office manager should consider the development of standards, if not for the purpose of installing a wage-incentive system, at least for establishing a more effective program of quality control. Many firms maintain production records that are used when employee performance is evaluated and recommendations for promotions and transfers are made. Thus, these companies achieve partially the effects of an incentive system of wage payment.

Wage-incentive systems for office workers fall into two major categories: (1) individual incentives and (2) group incentives.

Individual Incentives

In an *individual incentive plan*, the office worker is paid according to his or her own production or effort. An example of an individual incentive plan is the *piece-rate system*. For a piece-rate system to be successful, the following principles should be recognized in its development:

1. The incentive pay system should be characterized by a base pay that is given to all workers doing a certain kind of work. The base pay takes care of holidays when the workers would not be paid if they were on a straight incentive or piece-rate pay basis.
2. The incentive rates should be set so that 5 to 10 percent of the workers will earn more than the usual pay, 80 percent will just about make the standard set, and 5 to 10 percent will not quite make the grade. This last group should be given every opportunity to make the grade, but sooner or later these workers should be transferred to other positions or discharged.
3. The incentive rates must be fairly set and carried out in the spirit of fairness.

Underlying the installation of an individual wage-incentive system is the problem of measuring the employee's work. The more routine the work and the smaller the number of different kinds of work, the easier the job of measuring the work. An example of office work that lends itself to measurement under the individual incentive system is that of transcribing on a typewriter. (The various methods of measuring the work produced by typists were described in Chapter 23.) For example, in the transcription department of the Aetna Life & Casualty Co., transcription is made from magnetic disks and cassettes. Input is from a central dictating system with more than 53 recorders, and media are mailed to the center or delivered by a messenger. A typical transcription operator is expected to produce 2,600 lines (180,000 keystrokes) a week and average 30 words per minute. In this company wage incentives for an output of 70 percent or better are based on 180,000

[15]Donald P. Schwab, "Conflicting Impacts of Pay on Employee Motivation and Satisfaction," *Personnel Journal* (March, 1974), pp. 196–200.

keystrokes a week, with a projected efficiency of 100 percent.[16]

In a large department store, an incentive plan was established for the opening of incoming mail, a job consisting of removing the contents of envelopes and sorting the material. The proper time for completing the task and the bonus percentage were determined after a careful time study. In the incentive wage payment plan used, the bonus is calculated on the percentage of efficiency that is attained each week. The standard time allowance for opening each letter and placing the material in classified stacks was established at 0.17 minutes per letter. For a clerk who has an efficiency rating of 89 percent for the week, the bonus is calculated as follows:

$$\frac{\text{Standard minutes allowed}}{\text{Actual minutes on operation}} =$$

% of Efficiency

a. Number of letters opened during the week 11,280
b. Standard minute allowance per letter .... 0.17 Min.
c. Actual minutes on operation 2,160

$11,280 \times 0.17 =$ .. 1,918 Std. Min.

$1,918 \div 2,160 =$ ... 89% Efficiency Rating

Bonus rate paid at 89 percent efficiency is $7.17. (In this system a bonus payment commences at 66⅔ percent of efficiency.)[17]

Group Incentives

In a *group incentive plan*, the office worker shares in the achievement of a group of employees who are working as a unit to produce more than their expected efficiency. Group incentive plans may cover small groups or large groups such as an entire department. Included in group incentives are cash profit sharing, deferred profit sharing, and employee stock ownership plans, which were discussed in Chapter 14, pages 380–381. In theory, since all employees reap the benefits of reduced costs of production through the payment of cash bonuses, employees will become more cost-conscious and search for new cost-cutting methods.

EMPLOYEE PERFORMANCE EVALUATION AS PART OF THE OFFICE SALARY ADMINISTRATION PROGRAM

The larger the organization, the greater the tendency for an impersonal relationship to develop among workers and management. This is discouraging to employees, especially if a company implies that salary increments and promotions are the result of satisfactory or exceptional work. When an impersonal relationship exists, employees feel like small, inconsequential units in a large organization and experience feelings of insecurity and lack of recognition of their efforts and achievements. In many cases, such situations have encouraged workers to seek greater security through some form of employee organization, such as a labor union. Many large offices have tried to overcome this failing in human relations by instituting some form of merit rating, or employee performance evaluation.

[16]"Incentive Pay for Word Processors," *The Office* (March, 1976), p. 84.

[17]Zollitsch and Langsner, *op. cit.*, p. 544.

In an *employee performance evaluation plan*, the relative value of an employee's traits, personal qualifications, attitudes, and behavior is appraised. Performance evaluation is an overall study and analysis of the services and characteristics of the *employee*, not the job that is held. Such a study aids in developing an equitable compensation plan that rewards employees according to their true worth.

Information obtained from employee evaluation may be used in office administration for one or more of the following purposes:

1. To determine salary increases and to make decisions regarding promotion, transfer, and demotion.
2. To enhance the worker's morale, to contribute directly and indirectly to self-improvement, and to stimulate confidence in management's fairness.
3. To stimulate employees to improve their work.
4. To discover workers' needs for retraining and promotional training programs.
5. To uncover exceptional skills among employees.
6. To furnish a tangible basis for the discharge of unqualified or unfit employees.
7. To help in assigning work in accordance with the worker's ability by furnishing information for the proper placement, counseling, and guidance of the worker.
8. To aid in validating the selection process, especially in the areas of interviewing and testing.
9. To aid in settling disputes in arbitration cases.

From this list it becomes apparent that employee evaluation should provide a fair treatment of all employees, an objective rating, and a feeling by employees that they are not ignored or overlooked. A regular and consistent evaluation of employee performance factors will make each worker feel that his or her performance will be taken into consideration when salary increases are due and promotions are available.

Factors to Consider in Performance Evaluation

In the Bureau of National Affairs survey of large and small companies, it was found that the factors considered in the performance evaluation of office employees, arranged in rank order, are: quality of work, quantity of work, initiative, cooperation and ability to get along with others, dependability, job knowledge, attendance, and need for supervision. Other factors mentioned by respondents to the survey included: safety record; achievement of goals or objectives; housekeeping record; potential for promotion; and personal characteristics such as versatility, judgment, maturity, loyalty, and personal appearance.[18]

Methods of Evaluating Employee Performance

Several commonly used methods of evaluating employee performance are briefly described as follows:

1. *Discussion* or *essay*, in which the rater provides a written paragraph or more covering such topics as an employee's strengths, weaknesses, and potential. According to the Bureau of National Affairs survey cited earlier, this method is used most frequently in evaluating office workers.[19] In the American

---

[18]*Employee Performance: Evaluation & Control*, Personnel Policies Forum Survey No. 108 (Washington: The Bureau of National Affairs, February, 1975), p. 4.

[19]*Ibid.*, p. 3.

Management Society's survey of non-exempt salaried compensation practices, also cited earlier, 70 percent of those surveyed use written performance appraisals, often prepared in conjunction with written job descriptions.[20]

A big drawback in using the essay method is the variability in the length and content of the essays. Also, since the essays touch on different aspects of performance and personal characteristics, they are difficult to combine for comparison purposes.

2. *Rating scales*, in which factors dealing with quantity and quality of work are listed and rated. A numeric value may be assigned each factor and an effort made to weight the factors in the order of their relative importance. The rating scale is a widely used method of evaluating performance, for it is economical to develop and easily understood by the worker and the evaluator. In evaluating office workers at many levels, there is no need to use anything more complicated than a graphic scale supplemented by a few essay questions.[21]

3. *Simple ranking* or *grading*, wherein all employees are classified by rank as best, second-best, third-best, and so on throughout the entire employee group. Employees are evaluated on their overall usefulness and value to the firm and no attempt is made to describe and evaluate their performances, traits, qualifications, or characteristics. The simple ranking method is useful only in very small companies with fewer than 25 employees where a suitable criterion has been established as the basis for the rating.

4. *Rank order* or *order of merit*, in which the evaluator ranks all employees in order, from the best to the poorest, on the merits of performance and specific

factors such as quantity and quality of work. This method, which takes considerable time and is very subjective, is successful to the extent that employees accept the criteria used for the rankings and respect their rater's honesty.

5. *Forced distribution*, in which employees are rated on only two characteristics — job performance and promotability. A five-point job performance scale is used, and the supervisor is asked to allocate 10 percent of the workers to the best rating, 20 percent to the next best, 40 percent to the middle group, 20 percent to the group next to the lowest, and 10 percent to the lowest group. The method forces the supervisor or rater not to rank too many workers on the highest or the middle scale. Also, the rater will not appraise the poorest workers as medium or fair since they must be placed among the lowest 10 percent.

6. *Paired comparison*, in which each employee is paired with every other employee in the group. By means of comparing each pair of workers, the supervisor or rater decides which of the two workers is more valuable. When making each comparison, the supervisor underlines the name of the preferred worker on a specially prepared form. The employee's score is obtained by counting the number of times his or her name is underlined. After all workers in the group have been thus compared, a list is prepared to show the rank of each employee in order of merit, according to the number of times his or her name was underlined. The paired comparison method is workable only in very small groups of 10 to 12 employees, for in larger groups the job of rating becomes overly burdensome and time-consuming.

7. *Checklist* or *factor-comparison*, in which numerous phrases or questions referring to a specific factor are listed, as shown in Figure 24-2. The rater checks the statement or answers the

---

[20]"Sounder Salary Guidelines," *Administrative Management* (November, 1972), p. 50.

[21]Winston Oberg, "Make Performance Appraisal Relevant," *Harvard Business Review* (January–February, 1972), p. 63.

Factor	Question	Check Answer	
		Yes	No
A. Dependability	1. When you give the employee a job to do, are you confident that you will get what you want when you want it?	___	___
	2. Does the worker follow instructions on routine jobs with a minimum of supervision and follow-up?	___	___
	3. Does the worker frequently need follow-up on the most routine duties?	___	___
	4. Can you depend on the worker to try out new ideas?	___	___
B. Attitude	1. Is the employee a good team worker?	___	___
	2. Is the worker receptive to change and new duties?	___	___
	3. Does the worker go out of the way to cooperate with coworkers?	___	___
	4. Does the worker have a constructive attitude toward the company?	___	___
	5. Does the worker have a constructive attitude toward coworkers?	___	___

Fig. 24-2
A Partial Form Illustrating the Checklist Method of Employee Appraisal

questions "yes" or "no" to describe the appropriate characteristic of the worker being appraised. A numeric value is provided for each statement or question, and the complete rating is obtained by totaling all statement values. Using this method, the rater thinks critically about the employee's performance in terms of each important factor and is able to make a study of the worker's specific strengths and weaknesses. The specific statements provide a concrete basis for follow-up discussion with the subordinate and give useful data to check the employee's progress.

8. *Management by objectives* or *goal-setting*, in which a number of short-range goals or objectives are established that appear to be within the capabilities of the worker. (Management by objectives is discussed in more detail in Chapter 12, page 328.) The goals, agreed upon by the employee and the supervisor, become the job performance standards

upon which the employee is evaluated for the period of time for which the goals are established. The method rests on the premise that the only real measure of how an individual performs is whether he or she achieves specific results. Thus, the management by objectives method is results-oriented rather than trait-oriented. Although not practical for use at all levels and for all kinds of office work, the method provides for systematic goal-setting and performance reviews that concentrate upon the work accomplished rather than upon problems related to personality traits and characteristics.

Companies that have installed a program of work measurement and work standards, as discussed in Chapter 23, may use their work standards in conjunction with most of the evaluation methods discussed above. Since work targets aimed at improving productivity have been established, their use should make possible a more objective and accurate appraisal of the office worker's performance.

Illustrative Performance Evaluation Forms

An evaluation form commonly used by small companies that do not have elaborate merit increase policies is a single sheet for each employee covering all the factors to be rated. One such type of merit rating form is illustrated in Figure 24-3. This is a good form because it provides for an appraisal of six performance and personality factors, each of which may be marked by the rater along a qualitative scale of six degrees.

The two-page periodic employee appraisal form shown in Figure 24-4 is designed to be used in evaluating white-collar workers. Note that space is provided for recording the employee's attendance over a six-month period. This form is especially well-designed, for five degrees are contained in the range of each of the seven factors to be evaluated. The rater is further aided by a brief but clear definition of each of the degrees. On the second page space is provided for the rater to write a paragraph or two about the employee's potential leadership ability and to record any other information that may aid in appraising the employee's performance. The form also provides space for the rater to indicate an overall opinion of the employee and to record what improvement, if any, has taken place since the last appraisal. Any unfavorable factors discovered during the appraisal are discussed with the employee and his or her reactions are noted, along with the rater's comments.

The evaluation form shown in Figure 24-5 was designed for use in rating nonexempt and supervisory employees.

Note that the rater is asked to use the reverse side of the form to explain any rating that is abnormally low or exceptionally high. In evaluating office workers, the rater uses only factors Nos. 1 through 11, for factor No. 12 is reserved for the evaluation of supervisors. A combined numeric score may be obtained for each employee evaluated, since each of the factors, to be analyzed along a scale of five degrees, has been weighted.

Weaknesses of Employee Evaluation Forms

In the use of any appraisal instrument the rater should be concerned that the form selected will generate information that can help in important judgmental decisions and that can aid an individual in changing his or her behavior for future improvements.[22] However, an examination of employee evaluation forms indicates that some contain certain weaknesses that should be avoided. Some of the common weaknesses are:

1. Too many questions or characteristics to answer, check, or rate. Only enough factors and degrees should be given to provide a fair and reasonable picture of the work that is being done and of the employee who is doing it. Too many questions take too much time and may cause careless or routine and superficial rating. Probably six or eight factors, each with five or six degrees, are sufficient in most instances.
2. Poor phraseology of the questions. Using detailed and descriptive phrases motivates the rater to use more careful judgment than if he or she has only to check general terms. Instead of using such words as "very good," "good," "fair," or "poor" to describe a factor,

[22]William J. Kearney, "The Value of Behaviorally Based Performance Appraisals," *Business Horizons* (June, 1976), p. 77.

Merit Rating Form

Name _Doris Carver_   Clock No. _192_ Date Employed _6/15/78_ Score _81_

Job Title _Programmer_   Dept. _Computer Center_ Date Assigned This Job _6/15/78_

INSTRUCTIONS

Ratings can be reasonably accurate and uniform if the rating form is used properly and the worker rated on actual performance. The rater must be thoroughly familiar with the use of the form. The rating must be done on the basis of careful analysis instead of snap judgment. Please follow instructions carefully.

1. Use your own *independent* judgment.
2. Study the definitions of the factors to be considered.
3. Consider *typical* day-to-day performance. Do not be unduly influenced by some unusual instance.
4. Make your rating fair and square. Try to avoid any personal feelings.
5. Under "Remarks" give any facts which might have a bearing on making a fair rating.
6. Indicate your judgement on each factor by placing a mark (X) in the block which most nearly expresses your opinion. Marks may be placed between blocks.
7. Add any other details under "Remarks" or on the reverse side.

QUALITY according to operation and standards	Very poor	Poor	Slightly below standard	Acceptable quality	Very good [X]	Exceptional Quality
QUANTITY according to machine, tools, operation and material	Very low	Low	Slightly under average	Slightly over average [X]	Well over average	Unusually high
JOB KNOWLEDGE all phases	Practically none	Very limited	Somewhat lacking	Fairly good	[X] Very good practically all phases	Exceptional knowledge all phases
COOPERATION shop rules, workers, foreman	Antagonistic	Frequently in trouble	Always holds back	Usually cooperates	Never holds back	Active cooperation [X]
ATTENDANCE except for excusable absences or tardiness	Very irregular	Poor	Slightly under group average	Slightly over group average [X]	Well over group average	Practically perfect
INITIATIVE supervision received, resourcefulness	Very low	Requires constant supervision	Requires frequent supervision	Somewhat resourceful	Very resourceful [X]	Extremely resourceful, self-reliant

REMARKS _Carver's problems at home have been solved and her attendance will improve. She has enrolled in a management course at night to improve skills. Well satisfied with work._

Date _9/15/78_ Rated by _J.A. Embers_   Discussed with above employee—Date _9/15/78_ Signed _Doris Carver_

Man & Manager, Inc.

Fig. 24-3
One-Page Merit Rating Form

EMPLOYEE'S POSITION Designate concisely such as senior clerk, unit teller, stenographer, etc. _Unit Teller_	EMPLOYEE APPRAISAL Date _11/10/78_	EMPLOYEE'S NAME _John Markham_	PERIODIC APPRAISAL Return to Personnel Dept. not later than _Nov. 13, 1978_

Briefly Describe Nature of Specific Duties: _Receives funds for deposit, disburses funds, proof of cash daily, completes fill-in for savings bonds purchased_

ATTENDANCE RECORD

MO.	LATE	ABSENT
May	1	1
Jun	3	0
July	2	3
Aug	2	2
Sept	4	1
Oct.	0	3
TOTAL	12	10

QUANTITY OF WORK
Consider volume of work produced consistently

Unsatisfactory output	Limited. Does just enough to get by	Average output	Above average producer	Exceptional output
☐	☐	☒	☐	☐

QUALITY OF WORK
Consider accuracy and neatness

Very poor	Not entirely acceptable	Acceptable accuracy and neatness	Very neat and accurate	Exceptionally neat and accurate
☐	☐	☐	☒	☐

COOPERATION
Consider cooperation with associates and supervisors

Entirely uncooperative	Reluctant to cooperate	Adequately cooperative	Very cooperative	Unusually cooperative
☐	☒	☐	☐	☐

DEPENDABILITY
Consider amount of supervision required and application to work

Unreliable and inattentive	Needs frequent supervision	Generally reliable and attentive to work. Follows instructions carefully	Very reliable and conscientious, needs little supervision	Extremely reliable and industrious
☐	☐	☒	☐	☐

ABILITY TO LEARN
Consider ability to understand and retain

Very limited	Requires repeated instructions	Learns reasonably well	Readily understands and retains	Unusual capacity
☐	☒	☐	☐	☐

INITIATIVE
Consider originality and resourcefulness

Lacking	Routine worker	Occasionally shows initiative	Better than average	Outstanding
☐	☒	☐	☐	☐

JUDGMENT
Consider ability to evaluate situations and make sound decisions

Poor	Not always reliable	Good in most matters	Reliable	Decisions most logical and well founded
☐	☐	☒	☐	☐

Recommended Increase: _$75.00_ B.W.

By _Inez Hammond_
         Supervising Officer

Approved by Personnel Committee effective: _____

OVER   Next Review _May, 1979_

OK to FILE

Man & Manager, Inc.

Fig. 24-4
Appraisal Form Designed for Evaluating White-Collar Workers (page 1)

LEADERSHIP   (Does employee presently do supervisory work? Yes___ No _X_)
Consider ability to gain   Indicate your opinion of employee's ability:
cooperation inspire   _Markham needs to "open up" and try_
confidence and direct   _to help his coworkers more. He seems to_
       people   _shut himself off from everyone, except the_
customers at the window.

REMARKS: Furnish any additional information which you believe may be helpful in more fully evaluating this employee
None.

WHAT IS YOUR OVER-ALL OPINION OF THIS EMPLOYEE: Unsatisfactory ☐
                                                    Poor   ☐
                                                    Fair   ☐
                                                    Good   ☒
                                                    Very good   ☐
                                                    Outstanding   ☐

SINCE EMPLOYEE'S LAST APPRAISAL EMPLOYEE HAS   Improved   ☒
                                                 Made little or no change   ☐
                                                 Has slipped back   ☐

This employee has been informed regarding any unfavorable factors reflected in this report by _Inez Hammond_
Date _11/10/78_
Employee's reactions: _He agrees with evaluation of his being "up_
tight" around coworkers. Blames his "coldness" on
bad situation at last place of employment.

Your Comments: _Will purposefully try to "cultivate" more_
during next few months. Will add duties that bring
him more directly into contact with coworkers.

Inez Hammond   _Charles O. Rollins_
DEPARTMENT HEAD OR SUPERVISOR   OFFICER

FOR PERSONNEL DEPARTMENT USE ONLY:

Fig. 24-4   *Man & Manager, Inc.*
Appraisal Form Designed for Evaluating White-Collar Workers (page 2)

EMPLOYEE EVALUATION FORM   RATING FOR *Michelle Du Bois*

DEPT.   CLOCK NO. *17*

Word Processing

INSTRUCTIONS

1. Disregard your personal feelings. Judge this employee on the qualities listed below.
2. Study the definitions of each factor, and the various phases of each before rating.
3. Call to mind instances that are typical of employee's work and actions.
4. Using your own careful judgment — check the phrase in each factor that is typical.
5. If employee performs no supervision — do not rate additional factor for supervisory ability.
6. Explain on reverse side any unusual characteristic not covered in regular factors.

	FACTOR	RANGE					RATING
1	**QUALITY** Performance in meeting quality standards	Careless (4)	Just gets by (8)	Does a good job (12)	Rejects and errors rare ✓ (16)	Exceptionally high quality (20)	16
2	**JOB KNOWLEDGE** Understanding in all phases of work	Expert in own job and several others ✓ (25)	Expert but limited to own job (20)	Knows job fairly well (15)	Improvement necessary — just gets by (10)	Inadequate knowledge (5)	25
3	**QUANTITY** Output of satisfactory work	Turns out required amount but seldom more ✓ (8)	Frequently turns out more than required amount (12)	Slow — output is seldom required amount (4)	Exceptionally fast; output high (20)	Usually does more than expected (16)	8
4	**DEPENDABILITY** Works conscientiously according to instructions	Dependable; no checking necessary (20)	Very little checking (16)	Follows instructions ✓ (12)	Frequent checking (8)	Continuous checking and follow-up (4)	12
5	**INITIATIVE** Thinks constructively and originates action	Good decisions and actions but requires some supervision (9)	Minimum of supervision ✓ (12)	Thinks and acts constructively; no supervision required (15)	Requires constant supervision (3)	Fair decisions — routine worker (6)	12
6	**ADAPTABILITY** Ability to learn and meet changed conditions	Prefers old methods; does not remember instructions (3)	Learns slowly; reluctant to change (6)	Normal ability; routine worker ✓ (9)	Short period for mental adjustment; willing to change (12)	Learns rapidly — adjusts and grasps changes quickly (15)	9
7	**ATTITUDE** Willingness to cooperate and carry out demands	Good team worker ✓ (10)	Cooperative (8)	Limited cooperation (6)	Passive resistance (4)	Poor cooperation; argumentative (2)	10
8	**ATTENDANCE** Amount of excessive absenteeism	2 to 3 days normal or 2 days own accord (6)	1 to 2 days normal or 1 day own accord (8)	No days lost (10)	3 to 4 days normal or 3 days own accord (4)	More than 4 days absence (2)	8
9	**SAFETY AND HOUSEKEEPING** Compliance with safety and housekeeping rules	Safe and orderly worker; equipment well cared for (10)	Workplace clean and safe (8)	Occasional warning about safety and orderliness ✓ (6)	Warned repeatedly about safety and cleanliness (4)	Area dirty; safety rules ignored (2)	6
10	**POTENTIALITY** Potential ability to lead and teach others	Has no more growth (2)	Future growth doubtful (4)	Slow development ahead (6)	Bright future growth ✓ (8)	Exceptional possibilities (10)	8
11	**PERSONALITY** Ability to get along with associates	Disagreeable (2)	Difficult to get along with (4)	Average or reasonable (6)	Well liked and respected (8)	Winning personality ✓ (10)	10
12	**SUPERVISORY ABILITY** Additional rating for supervisors only	Poor organization and planning (7)	Inadequate supervision (14)	Nothing outstanding ✓ (21)	Good planning and effective organization (28)	Outstanding leadership (35)	21

Date rated *Aug. 3, 1978* Signed *Amy Ramosa*   TOTAL **145**

USE SPACE ON REVERSE SIDE FOR REMARKS. EXPLAIN ANY RATING THAT IS ABNORMALLY LOW OR EXCEPTIONALLY HIGH

Fig. 24-5

Factory Management and Maintenance

Employee Evaluation Form Used for Rating Nonexempt and Supervisory Employees

phrases such as the following may be used: (1) Shows extreme intelligence in doing work; (2) Shows some intelligence and initiative in performing work; (3) Understands simple routines and follows instructions; and (4) Little comprehension of work, needs constant instruction.

3. A pattern in the arrangement of the descriptive phrases for each factor. To provide for a less biased evaluation by the rater it is suggested that the form be arranged so that, for some factors, the highest rating degree appears first, and, for others, the highest rating degree appears last. Alternating, or otherwise differentiating, the order of the degrees requires the evaluator to make an individual appraisal of each employee.

The reversal of the descriptive phrases on the merit rating form may also minimize or possibly avoid evaluation errors such as the halo effect, the horns effect, and the central tendency. The *halo effect* is the tendency of the rater to evaluate an employee too high either because of a general impression or because of some outstanding characteristic that influences the rater's judgment. The *horns effect* is the tendency for the rater to evaluate the worker lower than the circumstances justify possibly because the rater lacks training in rating or because of bias. In the *central tendency* type of error, the rater tends to rate or classify all subordinates in the same category, which is usually average. When the descriptive phrases are presented in a mixed order, as shown in Figure 24-5, the evaluator is alerted and must proceed cautiously.

Frequency of Performance Evaluation

In most companies the performance of office workers is evaluated annually, although provisions may be made for more frequent reviews in the event of promotional openings, poor performance, or outstanding performance. Often during a new worker's probationary period or during the first year on a new job, the evaluations are made fairly frequently. Thus, a firm with a probationary period of six months may evaluate the new office workers at the end of one month, three months, and six months; thereafter, the employee is placed on permanent status and reviews are scheduled annually on the anniversary of the employee's hiring date. Anniversary-date reviews are very important to employees; therefore, supervisors should not procrastinate in reviewing employee performance, even if the reviews contain a great deal of negative criticism.

Who Should Evaluate Employees?

In answering the question, who should appraise employees, it seems logical that the evaluation should be made by those who come in direct supervisory contact with the workers. Thus, in many companies the appraisal is made by the employee's immediate supervisor and is reviewed by both the next higher level manager and the personnel department.

Generally the evaluation is discussed with the employee, who, in many companies, must sign the evaluation form to indicate that it has been discussed with him or her. The evaluation then becomes part of the employee's permanent personnel record. Sometimes the office worker may be given a copy of the evaluation. In many instances the office worker has the right to appeal or to protest the performance evaluation. If the employee is represented by a union, the appeal may be made through the regular grievance procedure. In nonunion offices the appeal procedure is informal and may consist of the employee's noting his or her disagreement with the evaluation, either in discussion with the supervisor or a representative from the personnel department or in writing on the review form.

QUESTIONS FOR REVIEW

1. Identify the goals of an office salary administration program.

2. In what respect does company philosophy affect the firm's office salary administration program?

3. What kinds of information should be solicited on an office salary survey questionnaire?

4. In addition to conducting its own office salary survey, what sources of comparative salary data are available to a company?

5. What are the major provisions of the Fair Labor Standards Act that are of significance to the office salary administrator?

6. Under what conditions are wage differentials between sexes allowable?

7. Describe the conditions under which administrative employees may be exempted from the minimum wage and overtime pay requirements of the Fair Labor Standards Act.

8. What are the implications of the collective bargaining agreement for the person who is developing a salary administration program in a union office?

9. How does the charting of salary rates and salary distributions aid in the pricing of office jobs?

10. What kinds of adjustments may be made in the case of red-circle rates that emerge when salary rates are plotted on a scatter chart?

11. Contrast the granting of salary increases under the automatic progression and the merit progression plans.

12. What are the three principles underlying the development of a piece-rate system?

13. Enumerate several of the ways in which information obtained from employee evaluation may be used in office administration.

14. Indicate how the discussion or essay method is used in evaluating employee performance. What are the disadvantages of using this method of evaluation?

15. Briefly describe the procedure followed in using the management by objectives (goal-setting) method to evaluate office employees.

16. How may performance evaluation forms be designed to minimize errors of bias such as the halo effect, the horns effect, and central tendency?

1. Despite studies which show the significant potential increase in pro-ductivity that accompanies the use of wage-incentive systems, very few white-collar workers are paid on an incentive basis. What are the major obstacles present in most offices that hinder the use of wage-incentive systems?

2. Regarding the use of money as a motivator, the following statements have been made: "Money isn't everything in life," "The meaning of money is conditioned by its value and importance to each worker," and "Money functions only as a symbol that represents more impor-tant psychological factors in the work situation." In view of these statements, why do many managers see money as a prime motivator?

3. What drawbacks do you see in the automatic progression plan of providing salary increases to office workers?

4. Al Fumero, who supervises three workers in the data processing de-partment, earns $270 a week. Very little of Fumero's time is re-quired for supervising the workers, most of his time being spent operating the data processing equipment along with the rest of the workers. Under the FLSA, would Fumero be classified as an exempt employee? Why?

5. Do you feel that data-entry terminal operators should work under an efficiency system of wage payment? As such an operator, would you be content to work for a firm that uses a wage-incentive system?

6. As office manager of the Fidelity Insurance Company, along with the other exempt employees at the supervisory and middle-management levels, you receive your annual salary increase "up front"; that is, the entire annual amount of the raise is given you right away on your anniversary date instead of in equal payments throughout the year. As the office manager, what advantages do you gain under this plan of providing salary increases? What advantages and disadvantages may your company experience as it grants "up front" salary increases?

7. It has been stated that, theoretically, management and the workers are always in conflict with each other's interests. Management aims to get as much work as possible accomplished efficiently at the lowest possible unit cost, while the workers strive to obtain as much income and security as possible from their employment. Do you agree that there is such a conflict of interests? How can the theoret-ical conflict of interests of management and office workers be over-come in part, if not entirely? Explain.

8. Several common weaknesses of employee evaluation forms are list-ed on pages 697 and 702. Using this list, evaluate the merit rating form illustrated in Figure 24-3.

9. Some companies grant separate cost-of-living increases in an at-tempt to keep their workers' salaries in line with living costs and to avoid having to equate economic increases with merit increases. Other companies prefer to recognize economic fluctuations through

the use of merit increases, whereby cost-of-living increases are treated within the merit increase system. What advantages do you see in combining cost-of-living increases with merit increases?

10. According to a report in the *Executives' Digest*, "Women's liberation notwithstanding, the earnings gap between working men and working women is wider today than it was 20 years ago. Today, women holding full-time jobs earn 43 percent less than the average for men; two decades ago, the disparity was only 36 percent. Among university graduates last year (1975), average earnings for men were $17,200; for women, $10,400."[22] What reasons can you advance to explain this "earnings gap?"

PRACTICAL OFFICE MANAGEMENT CASES

Case 24-1 **Pricing Office Jobs**

During the past two years a thorough analysis of office and clerical jobs has been undertaken at the Northern Insurance Company, which is located in Bangor, Maine. Three months ago it was decided to use the point method in evaluating the jobs. After all the jobs had been evaluated, the office manager, Rose Terhune, prepared Table A, which shows for eight nonexempt job grades the job titles, points assigned each job, and pay grades. From the payroll department Terhune obtained the amount of weekly salary currently being paid each of the jobholders. This information is also presented in Table A.

JOBS BY GRADE			
Job Code	Points	Job Title	Current Weekly Salary
		Grade I --------------203–230 Points	
A	203	Messenger	$105
B	218	Filing and Bursting	110
		Grade II --------------231–265 Points	
C	231	Mail Clerk-File Clerk	110
		Grade III -------------266–310 Points	
D	261	Policy Selector	115
E	278	Storage File	120
F	286	Clerk Junior, General	120
G	286	Typist	125

Table A

(continued)

---

[22]Quoted in "Editor to Reader," *Personnel Journal* (June, 1976), p. 268.

Job Code	Points	Job Title	Current Weekly Salary
		Grade IV ------------ **311–360 Points**	
H	315	Policy Typist	$125
I	319	Clerk Senior, General	130
J	331	Typist-Clerk, General	125
K	331	Application Clerk	110
L	341	Keypunch Operator, Junior	130
M	343	Checkwriter	125
N	345	Ordinary Policy Issue Clerk	130
O	347	Offset Press Operator	140
		Grade V ------------- **361–415 Points**	
P	367	Typist-Clerk, Senior	140
Q	372	Rewrite Clerk	135
R	379	License Clerk	135
S	381	Renewal Clerk	140
T	382	Disbursement Clerk	140
U	392	Stenographer Clerk	135
V	393	Switchboard-Receptionist	140
W	398	Keypunch Operator, Senior	145
X	408	Audit Clerk-Typist	160
Y	408	Contracts Clerk-Typist	155
		Grade VI ------------ **416–480 Points**	
Z	416	Computer Operator	160
AA	417	Accounting Clerk-Typist	150
BB	418	Group Billing Clerk	155
CC	420	Tabulating Machine Operator	160
DD	431	Photostat and Photographer	180
EE	440	Actuarial Clerk, Junior	160
FF	446	Secretary	165
GG	458	Group Premium and Commission Clerk	160
HH	458	Payroll Clerk	170
II	468	Deposit Clerk	175
JJ	474	Stenographer Clerk, Senior	170
		Grade VII ------------ **481–555 Points**	
KK	509	Actuarial Clerk, Senior	175
LL	510	Lay Underwriter	180
MM	518	Secretary, Legal	185
NN	520	Accounting Clerk Stenographer	180
OO	527	Purchasing Clerk	200
		Grade VIII ------------ **556–640 Points**	
PP	564	Bookkeeper, Affiliated Companies	180
QQ	575	Publications Editor	195
RR	592	Specialist, Health Claims	190
SS	600	Accounting Clerk, Senior	190
TT	613	Secretary, Senior	190
UU	627	Tab and Computer Operator	195

Table A

Last week Terhune received a copy of the annual office salary survey from the management association of which the company is a member. After studying the job titles and job descriptions contained in the salary survey for banking, insurance, and financial institutions in the eastern United States, Terhune found that 14 of the jobs surveyed match very well the content of 14 corresponding jobs at Northern. Therefore, Terhune has decided to look upon these 14 jobs as key jobs and from the survey she has listed in Table B the average weekly salaries for the key jobs.

SURVEY FINDINGS FOR KEY JOBS

Job Title	Average Weekly Salary
Mail Clerk-File Clerk...............................	$107
Clerk Junior, General	114
Clerk Senior, General	134
Typist-Clerk, General	118
Keypunch Operator, Junior....................	126
Offset Press Operator	137
Stenographer Clerk................................	131
Switchboard-Receptionist	133
Keypunch Operator, Senior	141
Computer Operator................................	159
Tabulating Machine Operator.................	150
Secretary	155
Secretary, Senior	185
Tab and Computer Operator	184

Table B

Terhune has given you copies of Tables A and B and has asked you, after studying and analyzing the information, to:

1. Determine a weekly base salary for each of the office and clerical jobs. The weekly base salary should approximate the average weekly salary paid by all firms surveyed.
2. Establish a pay range for each of the eight job grades, using the weekly base salary as the midpoint of each range and a 30 percent spread within each range.
3. Prepare a scatter chart showing:
   a. The basic salary curve.
   b. The upper and lower limits of each pay range.
   c. The plotting of each job in relation to its current weekly salary and the point value. To aid in identifying the plotted jobs, use the job codes given in Table A.
4. Evaluate the current salaries paid in relation to the trend lines drawn on the scatter chart. Are there any red-circle or green-circle rates? If so, what adjustments in salary rates do you recommend be made?

Case 24-2   Granting a Merit Raise Based upon Tenure

Ken Morneau, a clerk-typist in the Traffic Control department of Acme Trucks, has been with the firm six years and is now one step away from the top of his pay range. During his tenure with the firm, Morneau feels that he has been doing as well on the job as anyone else. He has violated no company practices, with the exception of one occasion upon which he received a warning for lateness in reporting to work. One morning Morneau approached his supervisor and asked for a raise, for he felt that after six years' tenure, he should be at the top of his pay scale. The supervisor indicated that he would discuss the matter with the manager. About a week later Morneau was told that no raise would be forthcoming. Morneau next filed a grievance on the grounds that he was entitled to the raise in view of his tenure and clean work record. During the grievance procedure, the manager stated that to get a merit raise at Acme, a person must do more than an ordinary job — it must be extraordinary.

Discuss these questions:

1. Do you agree with the manager's point of view that the mere length of service is insufficient grounds for awarding a merit increase?
2. What factors should be considered by Acme in determining the granting of merit increases?
3. As a member of the board of arbitration before whom the grievance is being presented, how would you rule in this case?

Chapter 25 **BUDGETARY CONTROL AND REPORT PREPARATION**

Time and wealth are scarce resources for all business organizations. To exercise safeguards over the use and conservation of these two resources, business firms establish programs of budgetary control. In every phase of business operations, top executives must look ahead and plan how the resources will be acquired and used and how their acquisition and use will be controlled in the forthcoming time period. On the basis of their estimates they plan the policies and procedures to be installed and carried out, either on a short-term basis of a few months or a year, or on a long-term basis of, say, three to five years. The activities planned may relate to many areas such as new products, sales revenue, expansion plans, and operating costs. The success of operating a business often depends upon the reliability of future plans that show the estimated income and operating costs.

To control costs and to obtain accurate financial information quickly, management relies upon budgets and reports received from various department heads. The *budget* is a carefully planned program of estimated operating conditions for a given period in the future. The important phase of budgetary control is not merely the preparation of the plan. It is the periodic comparison of the actual operating data with the planned or budgeted data so that the causes of any *variances* or differences between the two kinds of data can be identified and,

where possible, rectified. Through the use of budgets and periodic reports, top management strives to attain the following objectives:

1. To provide an organized procedure for the future planning of earnings whereby the organization's plan may be reviewed and changed where needed.
2. To offer a means of coordinating the activities of the various components of the company as the individual managers become more aware of the problems of other members of management.
3. To build a basis for managerial control by providing supervisory personnel with factual measures of achievement that they have participated in developing and for which they are held responsible.
4. To motivate individuals by creating a climate of cost consciousness in which they will be stimulated to strive to reach the stated goals.

BUDGETARY CONTROL OF OFFICE COSTS

Budgetary control refers to the use of a budget in regulating and guiding those business activities concerned with the acquisition and use of resources. Just where the office manager fits into the program of budgetary control is not the same in each firm. In some organizations he or she is a service department head, while in others, a controller or a vice-president.

Office managers who are primarily heads of service departments are responsible for coordinating the major information-processing activities required by accounting, administrative services, finance, production, and sales. Such a service function runs vertically through an organization and consists of rendering specific services that are needed to carry on the work of all the major divisions of the firm. Examples of service functions are word processing, telecommunications, records management, and data processing. The reports to be prepared by or for the office manager who is a service department head may include:

1. Estimated (budgeted) expenses for the various office services. This annual expense report is supported by schedules or data prepared by first-line supervisors.

2. Operating reports showing in detail the actual costs incurred compared with the budgeted figures, the amount or percentage of variance, and explanations of any variance.

3. Analytical reports showing the breakdown of costs in each department. For example, the supervisor of the filing department may prepare a report showing the cost of filing every one thousand documents; the supervisor of the word processing center may prepare reports showing the average cost of each letter produced.

4. Special reports, most of which are studies prepared at the request of a company official or initiated by the office manager in an attempt to improve some phase of the information-management function. For example, a report may be prepared comparing the cost of machine and stenographic transcription, or a feasibility study may be

undertaken to determine the practicability of converting from keypunch machines to data terminals for the processing of accounts receivable.

In larger offices where the office manager may be a controller or a vice-president of administrative services, he or she will receive detailed reports from various department heads, such as the supervisors in charge of records management, correspondence, transcription, mailing, and accounting. The office manager must examine these reports, consolidate and condense them into a report covering all the information-management activities, and then submit the final report to the budget director or the budget committee to whom he or she is held accountable. These reports will be further summarized and consolidated by the budget director or the budget committee, who may have the responsibility for developing the following reports and financial statements:

1. Master budget for the fiscal accounting period.

2. Summaries of the actual versus budgeted figures.

3. Interim or annual balance sheets and income statements. These financial reports may be prepared monthly for the company directors, and quarterly, semiannually, or annually for the stockholders. The financial reports are usually prepared for the stockholders after the accounting report has been received from the public accounting firm that has audited the books.

PRINCIPLES OF PREPARING A BUDGET OF ADMINISTRATIVE OFFICE EXPENSES

A well-prepared administrative office expense budget helps the office manager and his or her superiors plan their operations and gives them the financial data needed for decision making. The budget aids the office manager in heading off crises, directs attention to the less profitable office activities, and provides a yardstick for measuring progress in all areas under the office manager's jurisdiction. But the office manager must remember that the office expense budget will get results only in direct proportion to the skill, understanding, and effort that have been invested in its preparation. In the preparation of an office expense budget, the office manager should pay close attention to each of the following principles.

Principle of Responsibility

The initial phases of preparing the budget should be assigned to key personnel at the operational level so that budgets flow upward from the departmental supervisors to the office manager.

By beginning the budget-making process at the operational level, cost consciousness is developed among all employees and a mutuality of understanding about the budgetary process is provided. In one study it was found that if supervisors had almost complete or a significant say in setting budget allowances and spending the money budgeted to them, 78 percent were very much concerned with costs.[1] Having those who are close to the work participate in the budgeting process also aids in gaining acceptance of the plan of action, improves morale among employees and toward management, and may bring

about increased productivity. Participation in the preparation of a budget is a form of job enrichment and thus serves as a potential positive reinforcer for improving the job performance of most individuals.[2] If, on the other hand, the budget originates at the top-management level and is imposed from above, the effects of the budget may be punitive in many instances.

Principle of Objectivity

The budget should be realistic and show as objectively as possible what each department is capable of doing.

A sound budget can be neither unduly optimistic nor pessimistic, but must measure in an absolutely objective fashion what the office is capable of producing. Records of previous accounting periods may be used as guides, but the budget maker should not be bound to the past, for cost factors do not remain static.

To insure the development of objective, realistic budgets, the firm may wish to consider the use of *zero-base budgeting.* Under this relatively new concept, the budget maker examines every expenditure afresh each budget period and must rejustify the expenditure in light of current needs and developments. Thus, instead of basing the budget figures on an increase or decrease from the previous period or automatically carrying over into the new fiscal period the expenditures approved in the prior period, the budget maker starts from the base line (zero) each time, justifying the first as well as the last dollar to be spent.

---

[1]John H. Loew, "The Selling of the Budget," *Administrative Management* (April, 1972), p. 71.

[2]David J. Cherrington and J. Owen Cherrington, "Participation, Performance, and Appraisal," *Business Horizons* (December, 1974), pp. 41–42.

Principle of Target Setting

The budget prepared for each department, or for the office as a whole, should reflect the establishment of a specific target.

After a company target, such as a five percent increase in its share of the market, has been established and translated into sales dollars and number of units to be produced, a specific target should be set for each service department, or for the entire office, in order to achieve the overall company goal. At the operational level, standards of past performance for each employee should be reviewed and adjusted accordingly so that the overall performance of the department is geared to the newly established company target.

Principle of Flexibility

The budget should be sufficiently flexible and contain a "safety valve."

A flexible budget provides measures for emergency action that can be taken in case the company experiences a sharp reduction in income, a major strike, or a sudden move by competitors. The budget must not become so rigid that it stifles progress and prevents timely decisions. If, after a budget has been prepared, it is discovered that some objectives cannot be realized or that they are impractical, the conflicts must be resolved, or budget directives may have to be changed to agree with the reality of the situation. Although budget directives serve as standards, they should never become straitjackets.

One of the most common approaches to budgeting, known as the "tight but attainable" philosophy, is based on better than average performance. Any unfavorable variances are critically reviewed since this approach usually includes allowances for less than ideal performance. The "ideal performance" approach to budgeting, on the other hand, presumes that nothing will go wrong in the company's operations; it allows for no alterations or "slides" in schedules and contains no provisions for contingencies. Another budgeting method, termed the "suicide" approach, is characterized by managers who set a budget that is practically impossible to meet and who push hard enough so that unfavorable variances are kept to a minimum. Often the impossible is accomplished and the budget is met. The disadvantage of this method is its pessimistic attitude, for managers soon learn that such a budget is an impossible goal and stop trying to achieve it.[3]

Principle of Adherence

The completed office expense budget, as adjusted by the master budget, must be accepted and adhered to by supervisors and their subordinates at the operational level.

How the budget is accepted and adhered to at each level depends upon the tone set by top management. If top management is neutral about budget making and "budget following," they cannot expect that supervisors and their subordinates will be much concerned about adhering to the planned goals.

Principle of Review

The budget should be reviewed frequently in order to determine variances that can be overcome before the budget has lost its effectiveness.

---

[3]William R. King, C.P.A., "How Cost Management Is Used by Business Today," *The Office* (February, 1971), p. 43.

Delay in relating actual costs to estimated costs can be extremely costly. To overcome such delay, a program of reliable measurement and reporting of actual performance must be established. In some firms, computers are used on a daily basis to spot favorable and unfavorable variances from the budget. Since budgets are prepared on a theoretical or ideal basis and the numbers are often rounded to the nearest thousand (or other large multiple), actual results will rarely match the budgeted amounts. Depending on the individual company, variances of plus or minus one to three percent are normal.[4] At the departmental level, written reports should be required to explain significant deviations from the budget; at the operational level, oral explanations may be given by the employee to the supervisor.

PREPARING THE BUDGET OF ADMINISTRATIVE OFFICE EXPENSES

The budget of administrative office expenses must be coordinated with the thinking and the assumptions of those who are preparing budgets for other departments or cost centers of the firm. For example, the office expense budget has a direct relationship to the expected revenue to be realized by the firm according to the plans of the sales department. As indicated in the following paragraphs, some of the office costs incurred to earn the revenue are controllable, while other costs are not. The na-

ture and behavior of office costs must be analyzed in the preparation of an office expense budget.

Nature and Behavior of Office Costs

In the planning and control of administrative office expenses, one of the most important considerations is an analysis of office costs. This analysis is especially useful in planning the levels of office production, in budgeting costs, in estimating costs for special projects, and in determining break-even points. In an analysis of their behavior patterns, office costs are usually classified as fixed, variable, and semivariable.

Fixed Costs. *Fixed costs*, as described in Chapter 10, are those that are usually related to a time period and those that tend to remain unchanged when the volume of activity changes. As shown on the cost-volume graph in Figure 25-1, the fixed costs of $3,000 do not respond to changes in the volume level and are therefore represented by a horizontal line. Examples of fixed costs are: rent of office space and equipment, real estate taxes, property insurance, depreciation expense on building and equipment, and supervisory salaries. Over a period of time the office manager has little or no control over fixed costs.

Variable Costs. The more important and more controllable costs are known as *variable costs*, those that change in response to changes in the volume of activity. In the cost-volume graph shown in Figure 25-2, the variable cost pattern passes through the origin since there is zero cost associated with zero volume. In this illustration the variable costs respond in direct proportion to changes in volume; therefore, the variable cost line slopes upward to the right. The steepness of the slope

---

[4]Allen Sweeny and John N. Wisner, Jr., "Budgeting Basics: Hitting Budget Targets and Protecting Profits," Part 8 of "A How-To Guide for Managers," *Supervisory Management* (August, 1975), p. 15. This eight-part monthly series of budgeting guidelines, commencing in January, 1975, is especially recommended to those who wish to explore in more detail the "how-to-do-it" of budgetary control.

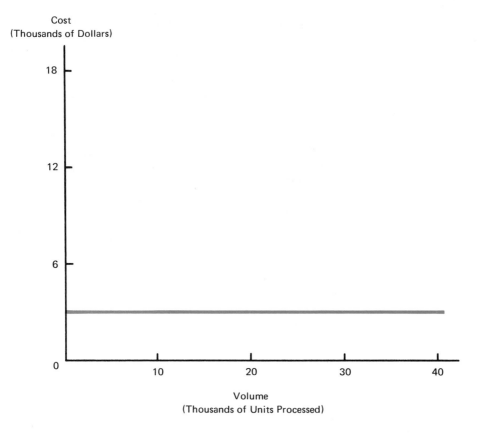

Cost
(Thousands of Dollars)

18 ⊢

12 ⊢

6 ⊢

0

10   20   30   40

Volume
(Thousands of Units Processed)

Fig. 25-1
The Pattern of Fixed Costs

depends on the amount of cost associated with each unit of volume; the greater the unit cost, the steeper the slope. In Figure 25-2, where volume is measured in thousands of units processed, the total variable dollar cost is twice as great for 20,000 units as for 10,000 units.

Examples of variable office costs include: stationery and supplies, equipment repair and maintenance expenses, and mailing expenses. In controlling the variable costs, office managers continually strive to implement new methods and procedures designed to reduce costs.

Semivariable Costs. Another important group of controllable costs is the *semivariable*, or *mixed*, *costs* — those that contain both fixed and variable components. A semivariable cost increases or decreases linearly with changes in activity, but at the zero level of activity the semivariable cost is some positive amount, as shown in Figure 25-3. Changes in total semivariable costs are not proportional to changes in operating volume. The electric power expense for the computer center may be considered an example of a semivariable cost. If the center were to be closed for a

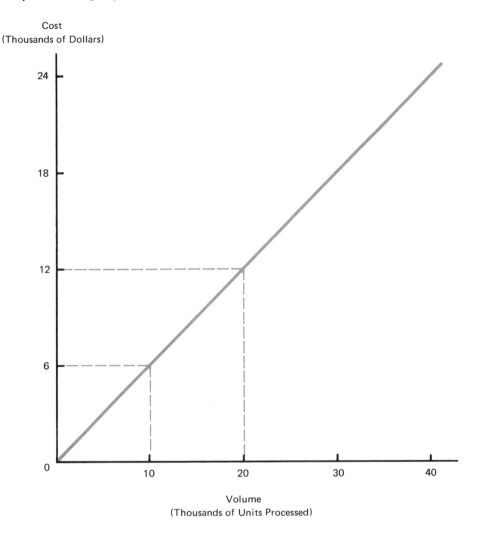

Cost
(Thousands of Dollars)

Volume
(Thousands of Units Processed)

Fig. 25-2
The Pattern of Variable Costs

period of time, the company would still be required to pay a minimum base charge for the power. Then, when the center reopens, the cost of the electric power would increase as the processing of data increased. Other examples of semivariable costs include telephone expense and the wages and salaries paid clerical workers.

Allocating Office Expenses

For most effective control, the office expenses should be studied and classified under the headings of fixed, variable, and semivariable, as described above. For example, rent or real estate taxes may be considered as fixed; supervision as fixed or semivariable; and

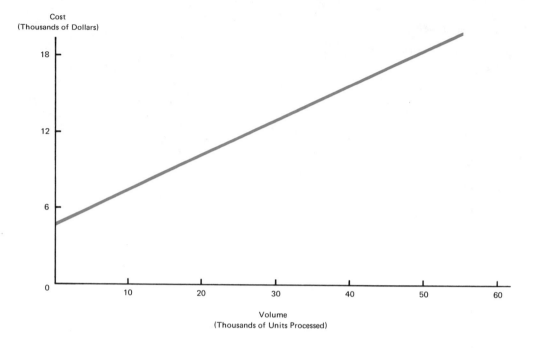

Fig. 25-3
The Pattern of Semivariable Costs

filing costs, as variable. With a grouping of this kind, the office manager can analyze the variable and semivariable expenses and can decide which offers the best opportunities for control.

To analyze office expenses from a budgetary viewpoint, it is necessary to prepare departmental budgets of operating expenses. Some expenses originate in and are chargeable directly to one department. For example, *direct* departmental expenses would include the depreciation expense of machines and equipment and the salaries of the workers in a given department. Other expenses are general in nature and may benefit several departments or the entire company. Such *indirect* expenses must be allocated on some logical basis among the departments. Some of the indirect expenses that must be allocated and their common bases of allocation are:

1. Telephone service and equipment, on the basis of the number of telephones in each department.
2. Long-distance telephone service, for which itemized charges billed by the telephone company may be allocated directly to each department.
3. Cost of the word processing center, either according to the number of word originators in each department or on the basis of time spent in transcription.
4. Rent or property taxes, on the basis of the square feet of floor space used by each department.

5. Printing and stationery expense, on the basis of requisitions filled.
6. Filing department expense, on the basis of the number of papers and microforms filed and retrieved.
7. Computer center costs, on the basis of terminal hours used by each department.
8. Postage and mailing services, on the same basis as the word processing center for first-class mail; otherwise, on the basis of direct charge.
9. Utilities, on the basis of kilowatt-hours of electricity or cubic feet of gas consumed by each department.

Comparing Budgeted Costs with Actual Costs

As indicated earlier, the purpose of a budget is to make a comparison of estimated costs with actual figures and to analyze any variances so that the controllable causes of the increasing expenses may be eliminated. Table 25-1 shows one type of form prepared monthly by each department for this purpose.

The year-to-date cumulative figure may indicate more accurately than a monthly figure the nature of the comparison of the budgeted and the actual figures. Some concerns therefore expand the comparison form to show the year-to-date budget figures and the actual year-to-date figures. Such a cumulative form is illustrated in Table 25-2.

The Master Budget

The preparation of the overall company budget, or the *master budget* as it is called, is usually placed under the supervision of the budget director (who may be the controller) or the budget committee. The responsibility for summarizing, combining, and consolidating the departmental budgets into a master budget should be assigned executives who have breadth of vision, versatility, a background in finance, an understanding of the corporate structure, and the ability to see the overall financial picture with all its components.

In addition to the office or administrative expenses commonly classified under the heading "General Expenses," the master budget includes estimates of

BUDGETED VERSUS ACTUAL EXPENSES
Sales Department: For Month of June, 19‒‒

Expenses	Budget	Actual	Gain (+) or Loss (−)
Salaries	$4,000	$4,000	$ 0
Rent (or taxes)	200	200	0
Insurance	75	75	0
Depreciation of equipment	300	300	0
Printing and stationery	210	187	−23
Transcribing costs	180	160	−20
Data processing costs	400	425	+25
Filing costs	40	60	+20
Telephone	92	100	+ 8
Postage and mailing	60	68	+ 8
Totals	$5,557	$5,575	$ +18

Table 25-1

BUDGETED VERSUS ACTUAL EXPENSES
Sales Department: For Month of June, 19--

Expenses	Budget Month	Actual Month	Monthly Variance + or −	Budget Year to Date	Actual Year to Date	Year-to-Date Variance + or −
Salaries..............................	$4,000	$4,000	$ 0	$24,000	$24,000	$ 0
Rent (or taxes)...................	200	200	0	1,200	1,200	0
Insurance..........................	75	75	0	450	450	0
Depreciation of equipment..	300	300	0	1,800	1,800	0
Printing and stationery........	210	187	−23	1,260	1,115	−145
Transcribing costs..............	180	160	−20	1,110	1,125	+ 15
Data processing costs.........	400	425	+25	2,500	2,450	− 50
Filing costs.......................	40	60	+20	240	360	+120
Telephone	92	100	+ 8	600	540	− 60
Postage and mailing	60	68	+ 8	360	420	+ 60
Totals	$5,557	$5,575	$+18	$33,520	$33,460	$− 60

Table 25-2

sales, cost of goods sold, and selling expenses. The budget may be prepared on a yearly basis and then subdivided into monthly, quarterly, or semiannual figures for better analysis and control. Whenever a master budget is used, there must be provision for a periodic comparison of the actual with the estimated figures so that variations may be noted and proper managerial control may be exercised.

The master budget, of which the office expense budget has come to play an increasingly important part, may be prepared as indicated by the seven steps listed in Figure 25-4. On the basis of these steps, an estimated (*pro forma*) income statement, similar to the one shown in Figure 25-5, may be prepared for comparison with actual operating results.

Problems of Cost Analysis Arising Through Budgetary Control

Among the various problems arising in cost analysis through the use of a budget, two stand out: (1) the need for standards, and (2) handling fluctuations in the volume of office work as a result of periodic or seasonal factors.

Need for Standards. Work measurement and the development of work standards have been discussed in Chapter 23. By having work standards and knowing the estimated volume of sales and the office activities required to attain that volume, it is possible to prepare a more reliable office expense budget. For example, as a result of having work measurement standards, the volume of each kind of work that has been measured can be obtained for the current year. With this information the volume of work for the next year may be projected in relation to the trends that have been forecast, and estimated requirements for personnel, space, equipment, and supplies may be determined.

Handling Fluctuations in the Volume of Office Work. Most firms attempt to operate with a minimum number of employees who are able to perform the usual volume of work without too much idleness, with little or no overtime, and still without too much

PLAN FOR PREPARING A MASTER BUDGET

Step 1. Preparation of sales budget:
   a. By products.
   b. By territories, districts, departments, or sales personnel if necessary.
   c. By months.

Step 2. Preparation of cost of goods sold or cost of production budget, depending upon whether the firm is classified as merchandising or manufacturing. To be most practical, the preparation of this budget should follow the pattern of the sales budget.

   If a merchandising company, this pattern will be:
   a. By products.
   b. By months.

   If a manufacturing company, the cost of production budget will show the data subdivided into cost of material, labor, and manufacturing overhead.

Step 3. Preparation of selling expense budget. Later, the sales budget may have to be revised to conform with the manufacturing budget.

Step 4. Preparation of general expense budget, which includes administrative office expenses.

Step 5. Preparation of consolidated budget and estimated income statement based upon Steps 1 to 4.

Step 6. Periodic compilation of actual figures in order to make a comparison with budgeted figures.

Step 7. Changes in business organization and administration or revision of budgeted figures to reduce the variation between budgeted and actual figures.

Fig. 25-4
Steps in Preparing a Master Budget

pressure being placed on the average employee. But many firms are characterized by periods during which there are peak loads that must be considered in preparing and using an office expense budget. For example, during certain periods of the month the payroll must be prepared and this increases the work load. Statements must be prepared and sent to customers. Quarterly or annual financial reports and statements must be prepared; inventories must be taken periodically. Although occurring with a certain amount of regularity, these activities complicate the planning, scheduling, and estimating of office costs, especially when the tasks must be completed by a definite date.

Recognition of the problem of peak-load fluctuations must be made by management, and the most efficient manner of controlling their cost must be followed. Office managers have used some or all of the following means to control the costs of peak-load fluctuations in office work:

1. *Overtime work.* This is an expensive method that increases costs 50 percent or more. Overtime work is best used where the overload is unexpected, or of short duration, and not expected to recur with any degree of regularity.

ESTIMATED INCOME STATEMENT
For the Year Ended December 31, 19—

		Percent of Sales
Estimated net sales..	$1,000,000	100.00
Product A	630,000	63.00
Product B	120,000	12.00
Product C	250,000	25.00
	$1,000,000	100.00
Cost of goods sold:		
Product A	$ 420,000	42.00
Product B	84,000	8.40
Product C	150,000	15.00
	$ 654,000	65.40
Gross profit..	$ 346,000	34.60
Operating expenses:		
Selling expenses:		
Sales salaries and commissions.............................	$ 60,000	6.00
Advertising expense	43,000	4.30
Shipping expense	28,000	2.80
Traveling expense...	16,700	1.67
Miscellaneous selling expense..............................	2,800	0.28
Total selling expenses	$ 150,500	15.05
General expenses:		
Administrative and office salaries...........................	$ 50,000	5.00
Office supplies	8,900	0.89
Depreciation — office equipment	7,200	0.72
Uncollectible accounts expense	6,400	0.64
Miscellaneous general expense..............................	4,300	0.43
Total general expenses.......................................	$ 76,800	7.68
Total operating expenses......................................	$ 227,300	22.73
Net income before income tax...................................	$ 118,700	11.87
Income tax..	50,476	5.05
Net income after income tax	$ 68,224	6.82
Dividends..	$ 50,000	5.00
Estimated increase in retained earnings.......................	$ 18,224	1.82

Fig. 25-5
Estimated Income Statement

2. *Cycle billing.* By means of cycle billing, it is possible to average out the volume of accounts receivable work that must be completed. Cycle billing was discussed in Chapter 19.

3. *Split-payroll dates.* By having different payroll dates for different departments, peak-load fluctuations in the preparation of the payroll occurring once or twice a month may be minimized. For example, in one firm it was decided to pay the clerical force and workers in the shipping and packing departments every two weeks; the exempt personnel continued to be paid twice a month on the 15th and the 30th. Thus, the peak load that formerly occurred on the 15th and the 30th was smoothed out and the services of the personnel in the payroll department were more effectively utilized throughout the entire month.

4. *Part-time help.* Part-timers make up about 15 percent of the working population and represent a significant growth that has stemmed partly from the rising number of wives who want to work — but not all day — and from an increasing number of young part-timers.[5] There are instances where the employment of part-time workers is very satisfactory. For example, some small employers find a surprising number of jobs ranging from the supervision of office activities to editing and legal work that can be handled by people, especially women, working on a part-time basis. In banks part-timers aid in meeting peak-hour demands because they often prefer to work during the midday hours when bank lines are longest. One big advantage to the employer is that the company may not have to pay for employee benefits since the part-timers may be willing to forfeit the employee benefits in order to obtain part-time work. There are other occasions when, because of the special nature and continuity of the work, the employment of part-time help may be disruptive to work routines and may result in excessive errors, confusion, and higher costs.

5. *Temporary office help.* As indicated in Chapter 11, a company that uses the services of temporary office personnel for varying periods of time realizes significant savings since a lower labor budget can be maintained without a decrease in the pay rates of full-time workers. For example, at the Chemical Bank of New York the use of temporary office workers in its "Chem Temps" pilot project enabled an executive to reduce office labor costs 50 cents to $1 per hour.[6]

Often during a recessionary period a company will lower its operating expenses by reducing the size of its full-time office work force. Shortly thereafter the firm may find that there is still more work than the reduced work force can handle. The company may then turn to the use of temporary office help until the return of a stable economy is signalled. Thus, the firm can fill in with temporary workers as needed without adding to its overhead.[7]

6. *Floating or traveling units.* Under this method, office workers "float" from one peak-load area to the other as the need arises. This method can be employed only where there are many departments affected, and the peak loads occur with a certain amount of regularity, but not on the same date.

7. *Outside service bureaus and data processing centers.* The increase in the number of "peak-load" service bureaus and data processing centers indicates that many business firms find these sources to be an answer to the periodic overloads of office work. The high degree of skill, the confidential nature of their work, and the comparatively low

---

[5]"Temporary Duty: Employees, Employers Both Discover the Joys of Part-Time Positions," *The Wall Street Journal*, March 7, 1973, p. 1.

[6]*Ibid.*

[7]"Temporary Help in Business Today," *The Office* (August, 1975), pp. 18–19.

cost have much to recommend this method for establishing cost control over the peak-load problems.

THE ROLE OF MANAGEMENT SCIENCE IN BUDGETARY CONTROL

In the budgetary control of office costs office managers strive to develop cost-conscious attitudes on the part of their employees. To lay the foundation for cost reduction as a continuing objective of budgetary control, the office manager should bear in mind the basic concepts of management science, as explained in Chapter 1, pages 18 and 19. In applying these concepts to problems of budgetary control, the office manager is aided by several tools of cost control, such as the Gantt chart, decision simulation, the Zero Defects plan, probability sampling, quality control programs, Program Evaluation and Review Technique (PERT), Critical Path Movement (CPM), and operations research. Each of these tools of cost control, with the exception of operations research, has been described in an earlier chapter as an approach that may be used by the office manager in solving specific problems.[8] Operations research and two of its techniques — linear programming and waiting-line analysis — are briefly discussed in the following paragraphs to show how this quantitative approach may be applied to decision-making aspects of budgetary control.

In *operations research* scientific methods of analysis are used to obtain optimum solutions to decision-making problems that involve the operation of complex systems. Involved in the techniques of operations research is the prediction of various courses of action that will provide a basis that a manager can use in making a choice between alternative courses of action that will maximize profits or minimize costs. The principles of operations research may be applied to the solution of business problems concerned with determining the optimum procedure to follow with respect to inventory control, capital budgeting, forecasting human resource needs, scheduling production for minimum costs, and establishing equitable bonus systems. In conducting operations research, which often makes use of an interdisciplinary team approach drawing upon persons from the fields of mathematics, statistics, physics, economics, accounting, and engineering, a model is usually formulated. The model, representing a simplified conceptual picture of the system or operation and containing all the factors of primary importance to the problem, is often set up in terms of mathematical equations.[9] A model is used for drawing conclusions or making predictions about the future since it is more convenient to manipulate the model rather than work with the actual system or operation.

Linear Programming

One of the most effective techniques of operations research is *linear program-*

---

[8]The Gantt chart is described in Chapter 4, page 74; decision simulation in Chapter 16, page 435; Zero Defects plan in Chapter 12, page 330; probability sampling in Chapter 23, page 664; quality control programs in Chapter 23, page 664; and PERT and CPM in Chapter 23, pages 671-672.

---

[9]Much literature is available on the many and varied types of models that have been developed. Since the scope of this presentation does not permit an exhaustive treatment of mathematical models, the reader is referred to standard textbooks in statistics and operations research.

ming, wherein a number of interdependent factors are mathematically related to one another in order to get the best results. Some objective function, such as the total cost incurred in a process is minimized or maximized, subject to those constraints that exist within the framework of the problem. For example, by means of linear programming, it is possible to schedule job orders on several machines in such a fashion so as to obtain the minimum overall processing time, subject to constraints such as the number of machines or workers available. By means of high-speed computing equipment, it is possible to solve business problems containing hundreds or thousands of linear equations.

Waiting-Line Analysis

Waiting-line, or *queuing, analysis* is another technique of operations research that can help the office administrator make decisions regarding staff needs as part of budgetary control. Several office activities such as filing, bank-teller operations, telephone switchboard work, typing center services, or mail sorting and delivery usually must be performed promptly. People or customers do not like to wait in a long line (queue) to receive answers to their questions, to receive file folders requested, to have their reports and letters typed, or to have entries recorded in their passbooks. It is not possible at all times to provide immediate service for each person in line unless extra workers are employed. If additional help were provided, then when the waiting line grows short as a result of completing the work, there would be some workers sitting idle. The problem facing the office administrator is to find the right balance — to have enough workers available to meet the needs of the queue but not to provide so many workers that at times some of them are idle.

In one application of waiting-line analysis to the file section of a medium-size utility company, it was found that several workers were idle at various times during the day. The type of service rendered by the seven women and their supervisor in this department consisted of answering calls from customers who wanted their power turned on, or a gas meter read, or an explanation of the last utility bill, or information about some other type of service. The number of incoming calls was charted by the supervisor and the length of each call was recorded in order to identify the patterns that emerged in calls from customers requiring service. Once these patterns were identified, the mathematical formulas of waiting-line analysis provided the information that the supervisor needed to render good service at minimal cost. As a result of this analysis, it was decided to reduce the staff from seven to five and to make use of any idle time by assigning the workers the task of stuffing envelopes.[10]

In the preceding example of reducing office costs as well as in all the other cost-reduction illustrations in this textbook, it must be remembered that the force that initiates, carries out, and measures cost reduction is the office manager and his or her superiors. In order to reduce and control the costs of performing their work, these executives prepare and utilize reports. These reports, which are discussed in the closing sections of this book, focus attention on what has been done, what is inefficient, what is good, and what is planned for the future.

---

[10]"The Use of Waiting-Line Analysis in Office Service Departments," prepared by AMS's National Operations Research Committee, F. B. Gardner, Chairman, *AMS Management Bulletin*, December, 1962, p. 2.

PRINCIPLES OF REPORT PREPARATION

Reports, usually considered as part of the information-management function and as the output phase of the information system, are prepared to reflect past, present, and future financial positions or operating results; to evaluate employees and their performance; and to serve as tools in controlling future operations. Reports are used by managers as an aid in making decisions and as a source of information for placing responsibility, for modifying policies, or merely as a matter of history. Reports deal with facts. For example, the sales manager may want a report on the sales volume of the various sales districts for the past six months; or in the area of administrative office expenses, the manager may want a report of what each department is presently doing, or what it is planning to do in the coming year.

The size and organizational structure of a firm determine the nature and frequency of reports. In a small company monthly financial reports prepared from the accounting records usually suffice. As the company grows, however, the work becomes functionalized, departments are provided with supervisors, and it becomes necessary to keep managers and supervisors informed by reports that are prepared more frequently. Since there is wide variation not only in the nature but also in the content of reports, the following principles for the preparation of reports are of a general nature.

Principle of Purpose

The report must have a sound and specific purpose which may be translated into more effective business management.

The main reason for writing a report is to tell someone something in the hope that action will be taken as a result of the conclusions reached in the report. Those who will read the report should be kept in mind when the report is written. Reports, as a rule, serve management in two ways: (1) they form the basis for a discussion of the facts and for recommendations, and (2) they serve as a historical record of that phase of the business activity.

Those charged with the preparation of reports to management must determine the minimum information requirements of each manager in relation to his or her needs to make particular decisions. Often managers may not know their needs exactly and may request more information in order "to play it safe." Thus, those charged with the responsibility of report preparation must make sure that they are meeting the needs, as opposed to the wants, of management.

Principle of Organization

The report should be well planned and well organized.

Since business reports differ widely in content, the organization of reports also varies. The report of operations is usually an accounting report supported by financial statements and schedules. Other reports are statistical, and still others are surveys or investigations that present answers to specific questions. The organizational plan of most reports includes:

1. *Purpose:* The introduction, which states the reason for the report, the information it contains, and the method employed in collecting the data.
2. *Summary:* A summary of the conclusions reached in the report. Many

managers prefer the summary at the beginning of the report since placing it first saves their time by not having to read the entire report. If they believe it necessary, they can examine the supporting details.

3. *Problems and Solution:* The body of the report, consisting of a logical development of the subject matter, treated either historically, chronologically, or as the status quo. A report dealing with present and proposed transcription methods, for example, might show the present methods and costs of transcription by use of shorthand, the average cost of each letter under this method, a description of the proposed machine method of dictation and transcription, the expected costs under this method, the advantages and disadvantages of each method, case studies of firms using each method, and recommendations. The logical sequence of such a report is apparent to the reader. This type of report deals with present conditions or the status quo and is based upon research. Solving the problem deals with analyzing and interpreting the data that are presented in order to substantiate the assumptions.

The content should be developed as objectively as possible. The report writer should avoid extravagant statements such as saying "many" when "only two" is meant.

4. *Recommendations:* Whenever a report results in recommendations for action, these should be stated positively, clearly, and completely. The recommendations may be stated in the form of a summary at the end of each section, or they may be part of the summary at the beginning of the report.

5. *Appendix:* Exhibits should be included whenever the textual narrative of the report needs amplification. Appendix items may be in the form of supporting letters, memorandums, charts, layouts, tabulations, or statistics. The supporting data should be carefully chosen and must be relevant.

A very long, formal report may include additional elements such as preliminary pages consisting of the flyleaf, a title page, the copyright page, the foreword, acknowledgments, contents, and a list of tables and charts; a bibliography; and an index.

Principle of Brevity

The report should be kept short.

The old adage, "If I had more time, I would have written less," applies to report writing. A verbose report creates a bad impression and raises the question of its necessity. Quick attention can be captured by reducing or eliminating a lot of the introductory material.

Reports should be reasonably brief because: (1) they are expensive to prepare; (2) long reports are complicated, are difficult to analyze, and usually indicate poor planning; (3) verbosity is usually an indication of too much emphasis on minor details or irrelevant matters; and (4) undue length evokes the criticism of inefficiency.

Principle of Clarity

Simple language should be used for fast and easy understanding.

The report writer should avoid long, involved sentences. Words should be carefully selected so that the meaning intended by the writer can be clearly communicated to the reader. New, technical terms that may create misunderstanding should be defined in order to eliminate communications "static," which may detract from the purpose of the message.

Principle of Scheduling

Reports should be scheduled so that they can be prepared without undue burden on the staff and with sufficient time to do the work well.

The interval between the compilation of data and the finished report should not be so long, however, that the material will have become obsolete by the time it is presented. With the availability of "real-time" information through the use of "on-line" terminals connected to a computer (see Chapter 2), management is greatly aided in scheduling and preparing business reports. Modern management information systems provide the facility of answering a user's question immediately with up-to-the-minute information so that much educated guesswork is eliminated in the decision-making process. For example, managers cannot control those unusually high costs that have already been incurred; but by means of timely reports a manager is able to detect cost deviations before they reach excessive proportions.

Principle of Cost

The preparation and the use of a report should be worth its cost.

With today's high-speed computer printers, undoubtedly many managers are flooded with useless reports that go under the guise of useful information. Therefore, some executive should be assigned the responsibility for evaluating the reporting needs of the firm to determine whether the cost of preparing and using the reports justifies their continuance. Such a study is aimed at determining the essential information needs of all managers, discontinuing any unneeded and questionable copies of reports, and revising reports to omit information not sufficiently useful to warrant the costs of collection and reporting.[11]

Definite procedures should be established and maintained for a cost-control study throughout the year so that any new reports are properly authorized.

PRESENTING DATA IN TABULAR AND GRAPHIC FORM

To aid the reader of business reports, many of the facts explained in quantitative form should be presented in some organized manner if their significance is to be understood. When a small number of items is being presented, the tabular form is the most common method of presenting the statistical data. Although all types of data can be depicted graphically, a chart is inferior to a table as a means of presenting data, since the reader can obtain only approximate values from a chart. The advantage of the chart, however, is that it emphasizes certain facts or relationships more dramatically than a table of figures.

Presenting Data in Tabular Form

The major parts of a table are the title, main body, footnotes, and source. In the main body of the table, the data are arranged in columns and rows. The heading of a column is referred to as a *caption;* the explanation of the material in a row is called a *stub*.

The *title* of the table should be brief, yet clearly indicative of the contents of the table. Information of secondary importance is often placed in a subtitle, as shown in Table 25-3.

The central point in the construction of a table is the arrangement of the data in columns and rows, which make up the *main body*. In most instances the classifications of data should be put in

---

[11]For guidelines on how to reduce the costs of reporting useless or marginally useful information, see William McNairn, "How to Clean Up Information Pollution," *Modern Office Procedures* (May, 1974), pp. 43–45.

CONSIGNMENT SALES OF STOCK NO. BT-4: 1968 TO 1978
Home Office and Branch Offices

Year	Sales				
	Total	Home Office	Tacoma	San Jose	Tucson
1968	3,780,000	2,206,000	705,000[1]	500,000	369,000
1969	4,162,000	2,475,000	772,000	506,000	409,000
1970	4,034,000	2,380,000	765,000	498,000	391,000
1971	4,218,000	2,533,000	763,000	487,000	435,000
1972	4,569,000	2,969,000	692,000	493,000	415,000
1973	4,551,000	2,994,000	701,000	502,000	354,000
1974	4,903,000	3,306,000	713,000	513,000	371,000
1975	4,988,000	3,401,000	719,000	525,000	343,000
1976	4,642,000	3,185,000	604,000	478,000	375,000
1977	4,820,000	3,268,000	623,000	540,000	389,000
1978	4,994,000	3,410,000	638,000	547,000	399,000

Table 25-3

[1]Data for last nine months of year only.

rows rather than in columns, for a column requires more space than a row. However, it is easier to make comparisons between figures when they are arranged in columns. It seems more natural for the eye to read down a column of figures than to read across a row. For example, in Table 25-3, it is somewhat easier to compare sales for 1978 with those for 1977 than to compare Home Office and Tacoma Branch Office sales for any year.

Footnotes are used to explain in more detail or to qualify the information and data contained in the title, stubs, captions, or in the main body. In Table 25-3 the footnote indicates that the 1968 data for the Tacoma Branch Office cover only the last nine months of that year. Both numbered and lettered footnotes are commonly found in business tables. Certain letters, however, have come to take on a fairly standard meaning in tabular construction. Thus "*e*" is used to indicate estimated amounts; "*p*," preliminary data; and "*r*," revised figures.

In the preparation of some reports, data may be obtained from a source outside the firm. The *source line* indicates the organization or individual that originally collected the information shown in the table. In the preparation of a table, such as Table 25-3, for which the data are obtained from within the firm itself, a source line is rarely used. In some instances when the information used has been copyrighted by the original collector or publisher, the source line is used to acknowledge permission to reproduce the tabular material. Information contained in the source line also enables the reader to turn to the source if further detailed facts are desired or if the accuracy of the information presented is to be verified.

Whenever possible, the tabular information should be laid out so that it is unnecessary for the reader to turn the report sideways in order to read the data. White space should be generously used so that the table may be more easily read and so that certain parts of the table will stand out in relation to one another.

The amount and type of ruling used in tables varies with the person designing the layout. In some tables no rulings are used; instead, white space is generously provided to set off totals or to emphasize certain sections of data. The important point is that whether or not rulings are used, the relationships depicted in the table should be clear and easy to see.

Presenting Data in Graphic Form

Several types of charts are used to analyze data and to emphasize facts and relationships much more vividly than tabular presentations. For added emphasis and dramatic effect, many charts make use of color.

Bar Chart. Vertical and horizontal *bar charts* are very commonly found in business reports, especially when growth or decline is being shown over a period of time. The scale that marks off the quantity should be so constructed and identified that the reader is able to interpret easily and quickly the significance of the length of the bars, as shown in Figure 25-6.

Pictogram. In a *pictogram*, each picture symbol represents a given magnitude. Although pictorial charts offer additional attractiveness in data presentation, accuracy in showing the information should not be sacrificed merely in order to gain attention. In Figure 25-7, the firm, as part of its first annual report to employees, symbolically depicts the growth that has occurred in five years.

Line Chart. A *line chart* is commonly used to indicate a trend or a cumulative effect of business information. Both scales on the line chart are quantitative, and the data plotted in relation to points of these scales are connected by straight lines. When time series data are plotted, the time classification is always laid out on the horizontal scale as shown in Figure 25-8. The data pertaining to each time period are plotted on the vertical scale.

Component Parts Chart. When the parts of a distribution of data are being compared with the total of that distribution, a *component parts chart* is

CURRENT EQUIPMENT PRODUCT GROUPINGS

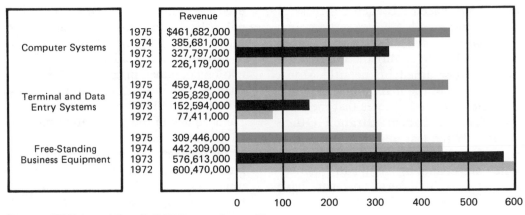

		Revenue						
Computer Systems	1975	$461,682,000						
	1974	385,681,000						
	1973	327,797,000						
	1972	226,179,000						
Terminal and Data Entry Systems	1975	459,748,000						
	1974	295,829,000						
	1973	152,594,000						
	1972	77,411,000						
Free-Standing Business Equipment	1975	309,446,000						
	1974	442,309,000						
	1973	576,613,000						
	1972	600,470,000						

0   100   200   300   400   500   600

Source: *1975 Annual Report*, NCR Corporation, p. 20.

Fig. 25-6

A Bar Chart

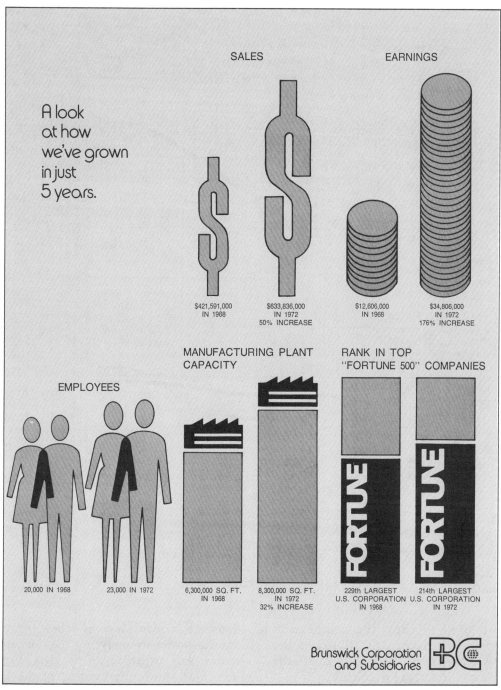

Source: *Annual Report to Employees, 1972–73*, Brunswick Corporation and Subsidiaries, p. 3.

Fig. 25-7
A Pictogram

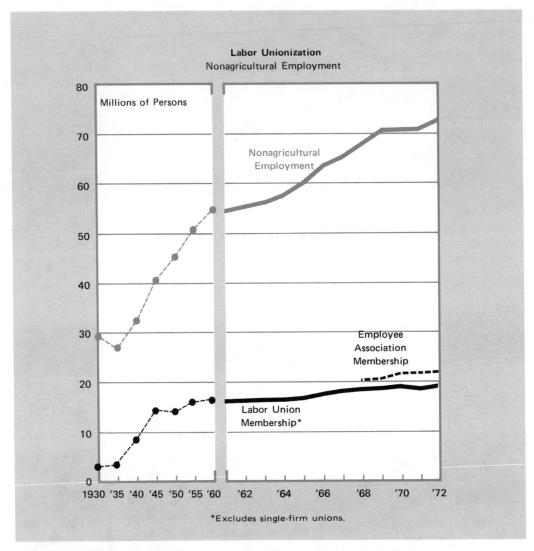

Source: *Road Maps of Industry No. 1757*, The Conference Board, March, 1975.

Fig. 25-8
A Line Chart

often used to show the comparison graphically. Figure 25-9 illustrates the *divided bar chart*, and Figure 25-10, the *circle and sector*, or *pie, chart*.

Map Chart. In the presentation of information for different geographical divisions, a *map chart* may be used to aid the reader in analyzing the concentration and dispersion of the data. Figure 25-11 shows the location of the 12 facilities, the sales offices, and the warehouses of a firm that manufactures and distributes electric transformers, springs, and metal parts.

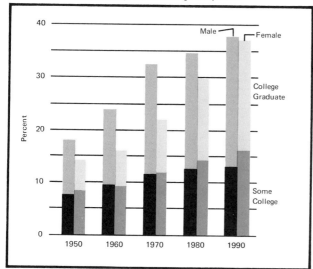

Source: *A Look at Business in 1990* (Washington: U.S. Government Printing Office, 1972), p. 73.

Fig. 25-9

A Divided Bar Chart

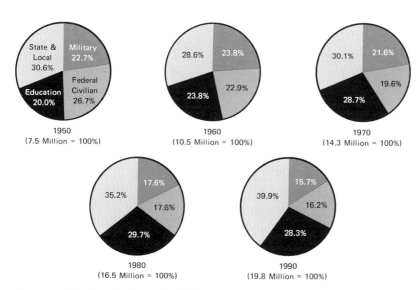

Source: *A Look at Business in 1990* (Washington: U.S. Government Printing Office, 1972), p. 61. Data obtained from Department of Commerce and The Conference Board.

Fig. 25-10

Circle and Sector Charts

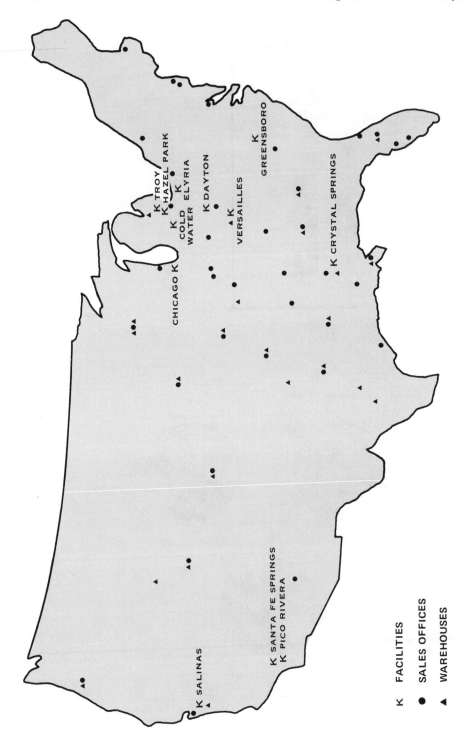

K   FACILITIES

●   SALES OFFICES

▲   WAREHOUSES

Source: *1975 Annual Report*, Kuhlman Corporation, p. 9.

Fig. 25-11
A Map Chart

QUESTIONS
FOR
REVIEW

1. What are the objectives that management is trying to attain in the use of budgets and periodic reports?

2. What kinds of reports are commonly prepared by or for the office manager who is the head of a service department?

3. How does a well-prepared budget of administrative office expenses aid the office manager in his or her daily work?

4. For what reasons should the budget-making process begin at the operational level?

5. Why should a budget contain a "safety valve"?

6. Why are variable and semivariable costs more controllable than fixed costs?

7. Distinguish between *direct* and *indirect* departmental expenses by giving an example of each kind of expense.

8. What is a commonly used basis for allocating each of the following indirect expenses: (a) monthly rent, (b) cost of operating the computer center, and (c) utilities?

9. What is a master budget? What is the relationship between the administrative office expense budget and the master budget?

10. How does the use of part-time and temporary office help aid the office manager who is faced with the problem of controlling costs during fluctuating peak-load and seasonal time periods?

11. Describe how waiting-line analysis may be used by the office manager as part of the budgetary control program.

12. Describe the organizational plan of many business reports.

13. What is communications "static"? Which principle of report preparation is concerned with the elimination of communications "static"?

14. Compare the presentation of data in tabular form with the portrayal of the same data in graphic form. What are the advantages and limitations of each form? Which form has the most dramatic impact upon the average reader? Which form generally presents the data most accurately?

QUESTIONS
FOR
DISCUSSION

1. A budget requires that a business firm use it for a long period of time before it actually becomes an effective tool of management. Explain the meaning of this statement.

2. A budgetary program has certain limitations. If this were not so, business executives who were positive and correct in their prognostications could make a great financial success on Wall Street. Explain the limitations of this statement.

3. The effectiveness of a budgetary program is measured by making each department head responsible for his or her departmental figures. Explain.

4. In discussing his budgetary needs for the forthcoming fiscal year, Len Policoff remarked to his supervisor of accounting operations, "I really need only eight workers, but those up above always cut my budget by 20 percent. So this year I'll ask for 10." How do you explain this type of attitude on the part of Policoff? What is your reaction to Policoff's philosophy of budgeting?

5. Most conscientious office managers want to know from time to time how they are doing. By means of monthly operating reports the office manager is informed of how well he or she is doing. Likewise, all others who receive copies of the monthly reports are informed of the office manager's progress (or lack of progress). As an office manager who has been receiving such monthly operating reports, how can you use the information in analyzing your own performance and in impressing upon others the progress that you have made in "holding the line" on costs?

6. Even though reports are necessary, there is a tendency for many managers to request more reports than necessary in their decision-making processes. Some of the reports are marginal in value and constitute a wasteful burden on business operations. Discuss how the office manager can improve the reporting phase of his or her firm's operations.

7. Should reports be prepared from the viewpoint of the writer or the recipient of the report? Why?

8. The number of copies of a report that must be made often has an influence on the form of presentation or reproduction of copies. Explain what this statement means.

9. Pam DeVenuto, a manager of office services, was recently overheard commenting about how many of her workers had a complete lack of knowledge about company operations. She indicated that although her workers received a copy of the firm's annual report each year, they still did not know how much business the company was doing, where the branch offices are located, how many persons are employed, the dollar value of their benefits, etc. What steps would you recommend that DeVenuto take to orient her workers more thoroughly on company operations, profitability, employment picture, etc.?

10. In most offices the types of reports and their purposes often determine the nature of the preparation. Some reports are made for an immediate superior or the top echelon in management. Others are directed at a group on lower managerial levels. Furthermore, it must be determined *why* the report is wanted. It is also necessary to determine before the preparation of a report what the reader will expect to get from the report and in what way the information will be

used. Your analysis of report writing indicates that there are two methods of preparation:

Methods of Report Writing

The Deductive Method	**The Inductive Method**
1. Purpose — why undertaken	1. Purpose
2. Scope — subject matter	2. Scope
3. Conclusions or recommendations	3. Facts
4. Facts	4. Fact analysis
5. Fact analysis	5. Conclusions or recommendations

Discuss the conditions under which you would use each of these methods in report preparation.

PRACTICAL OFFICE MANAGEMENT CASES

Case 25-1 **Preparing a Budget for the Word Processing Center**

In the Leinsdorf Company the budget of administrative office expenses is prepared by the office manager, Jane Sills, at the end of each year for the following fiscal year. This budget is a composite of all the functional departments under her supervision. Each department head is asked to prepare on a standard form the budget figures for the next fiscal year. These figures are analyzed on a monthly basis. Some of the costs submitted are fixed and thus are not affected by the volume of work to be done; other costs vary either directly or proportionately with the volume of work.

The budget of the fixed, variable, and allocated costs for the word processing center for the three months ending March 31, 19— is shown in Table A. The actual costs for the three months are shown in Table B.

Prepare a three-month comparison of the budgeted and the actual figures, completing the following:

1. On each month's statement show the budget year-to-date and the actual year-to-date figures.
2. On each month's statement show the dollar amount of and the percentage of variance between the actual and the budgeted figures.
3. Indicate the possible causes of any variance of plus or minus five percent.
4. After making allowances for form letters, fill-in letters, and interdepartmental communications, the volume of outgoing letters produced was: January, 13,000; February, 13,500; and March, 14,000. Compute the cost of each letter for each month.

BUDGETED COSTS FOR THREE MONTHS

	January	February	March
Salaries of principals and supervisor	$15,000	$15,000	$15,000
Salaries of correspondence secretaries	6,500	6,600	6,600
Postage............................	3,000	3,200	3,500
Telecommunications...........	3,000	3,000	3,300
Supplies...........................	2,000	2,000	2,100
Maintenance and repairs.....	100	100	100
Miscellaneous expense	150	160	165
Share of administrative expense.............................	1,500	1,500	1,500
Share of personnel department costs	800	800	800
Rent	900	900	900
Utilities.............................	400	390	380
Depreciation expense — equipment.......................	250	250	250
Insurance...........................	200	200	200
Payroll taxes	1,935	1,944	1,944

Table A

ACTUAL COSTS FOR THREE MONTHS

	January	February	March
Salaries of principals and supervisor	$14,800	$15,000	$15,200
Salaries of correspondence secretaries	6,300	6,500	6,600
Postage............................	3,300	3,350	3,800
Telecommunications...........	2,800	3,000	3,100
Supplies...........................	2,200	2,100	2,200
Maintenance and repairs.....	110	80	85
Miscellaneous expense	165	140	175
Share of administrative expense.............................	1,500	1,500	1,500
Share of personnel department costs	800	800	800
Rent	900	900	900
Utilities.............................	388	278	268
Depreciation expense — equipment.......................	250	250	250
Insurance...........................	200	200	200
Payroll taxes	1,899	1,935	1,962

Table B

Case 25-2 Preparing a Report of the "Real Costs" of Office Operations

You have just read an article wherein you learn that in a survey by a management consultant team it was found that a group of office employees studied were only 55 percent productive. During their usual 37½-hour week, they spend about 20 hours at work. In this same article you note that the average cost of employee benefits is about 33 percent of the employee's hourly pay.

Although you have not yet undertaken any detailed studies of productivity in your office, you feel that the following factors are at work to account for less than 75 percent productivity: time spent in getting underway on the job each morning; prolonged coffee breaks; unnecessary socializing on the job; extended lunch hours; boredom with the repetitive, unchallenging work; declining output at the end of the day; and early preparation for leaving at the end of the day.

You have brought together the following data that cover the hourly salary rates for workers in your office, the cost of employee benefits, and the "real costs" of your workers, assuming three different levels of productivity:

Hourly Rate	Employee Benefits at 33%	25% Nonproductive	35% Nonproductive	50% Nonproductive
$2.50	$3.33	$4.44	$ 5.12	$ 6.66
2.75	3.66	4.88	5.63	7.32
3.00	3.99	5.32	6.14	7.98
3.25	4.32	5.76	6.65	8.64
3.50	4.66	6.21	7.17	9.32
3.75	4.99	6.65	7.68	9.98
4.00	5.32	7.09	8.18	10.64
4.25	5.65	7.53	8.69	11.30
4.50	5.99	7.99	9.22	11.98
5.00	6.65	8.87	10.23	13.30

Prepare a report for the controller of your firm in which you show clearly and vividly what the nonproductive costs in your office may amount to, assuming the three levels of nonproductivity given above. The purpose of your report is to convince top management that funds should be expended to bring in a group of consultants to study the hidden costs of your office operations, with the aim of realizing significant savings. In your report present the tabular data in a graphic format so that the reader will be immediately impressed by the "real costs" of office operations.

INDEX